I0809453

CORNERSTONE BIBLICAL COMMENTARY

1-2 Samuel

J. Robert Vannoy

GENERAL EDITOR
Philip W. Comfort

featuring the text of the
NEW LIVING TRANSLATION

TYNDALE HOUSE PUBLISHERS, INC. CAROL STREAM, ILLINOIS

Cornerstone Biblical Commentary, Volume 4a

Visit Tyndale's exciting Web site at www.tyndale.com

Designed by Luke Daab and Timothy R. Botts.

Library of Congress Cataloging-in-Publication Data

Cornerstone biblical commentary.
p. cm.
Includes bibliographical references and index.
ISBN 978-0-8423-3430-3 (hc : alk. paper)
1. Bible—Commentaries. I. Vannoy, J. Robert
BS491.3.C67 2006
220.7′7—dc22 2005026928

Printed in the United States of America

29 28 27 26 25 24 23
8 7 6 5 4 3 2

CONTENTS

VOLUME 4a: 1–2 Samuel

J. Robert Vannoy
BA, Shelton College;
MDiv, STM, Faith Theological Seminary;
ThD, Free University of Amsterdam;
Professor Emeritus and Allan A. MacRae Chair of Biblical Studies at Biblical Theological Seminary.

SERIES EDITORS

General Editor
Philip W. Comfort
D. Litt. et Phil., University of South Africa;
Tyndale House Publishers;
Coastal Carolina University.

Consulting Editor, Old Testament
Tremper Longman III
PhD, Yale University;
Robert H. Gundry Professor of Biblical Studies, Westmont College.

Consulting Editor, New Testament
Grant R. Osborne
PhD, University of Aberdeen;
Professor of New Testament, Trinity Evangelical Divinity School.

Associate Editors
Jason Driesbach
MA, Biblical Exegesis and Linguistics, Dallas Theological Seminary;
Tyndale House Publishers.

Mark R. Norton
MA, Theological Studies, Wheaton Graduate School;
Tyndale House Publishers.

James A. Swanson
MSM, Multnomah Biblical Seminary;
MTh, University of South Africa;
Tyndale House Publishers.

GENERAL EDITOR'S PREFACE

The *Cornerstone Biblical Commentary* is based on the second edition of the New Living Translation (2007). Nearly 100 scholars from various church backgrounds and from several countries (United States, Canada, England, and Australia) participated in the creation of the NLT. Many of these same scholars are contributors to this commentary series. All the commentators, whether participants in the NLT or not, believe that the Bible is God's inspired word and have a desire to make God's word clear and accessible to his people.

This Bible commentary is the natural extension of our vision for the New Living Translation, which we believe is both exegetically accurate and idiomatically powerful. The NLT attempts to communicate God's inspired word in a lucid English translation of the original languages so that English readers can understand and appreciate the thought of the original writers. In the same way, the *Cornerstone Biblical Commentary* aims at helping teachers, pastors, students, and laypeople understand every thought contained in the Bible. As such, the commentary focuses first on the words of Scripture, then on the theological truths of Scripture—inasmuch as the words express the truths.

The commentary itself has been structured in such a way as to help readers get at the meaning of Scripture, passage by passage, through the entire Bible. Each Bible book is prefaced by a substantial book introduction that gives general historical background important for understanding. Then the reader is taken through the Bible text, passage by passage, starting with the New Living Translation text printed in full. This is followed by a section called "Notes," wherein the commentator helps the reader understand the Hebrew or Greek behind the English of the NLT, interacts with other scholars on important interpretive issues, and points the reader to significant textual and contextual matters. The "Notes" are followed by the "Commentary," wherein each scholar presents a lucid interpretation of the passage, giving special attention to context and major theological themes.

The commentators represent a wide spectrum of theological positions within the evangelical community. We believe this is good because it reflects the rich variety in Christ's church. All the commentators uphold the authority of God's word and believe it is essential to heed the old adage: "Wholly apply yourself to the Scriptures and apply them wholly to you." May this commentary help you know the truths of Scripture, and may this knowledge help you "grow in your knowledge of God and Jesus our Lord" (2 Pet 1:2, NLT).

PHILIP W. COMFORT
GENERAL EDITOR

ABBREVIATIONS

GENERAL ABBREVIATIONS

b. Babylonian Gemara
bar. baraita
c. *circa*, around, approximately
cf. *confer*, compare
ch, chs chapter, chapters
contra in contrast to
DSS Dead Sea Scrolls
ed. edition, editor
e.g. *exempli gratia*, for example
et al. *et alli*, and others
fem. feminine
ff following (verses, pages)
fl. flourished
Gr. Greek
Heb. Hebrew
ibid. *ibidem*, in the same place
i.e. *id est*, the same
in loc. *in loco*, in the place cited
lit. literally
LXX Septuagint
M Majority Text
m. Mishnah
masc. masculine
mg margin
ms manuscript
mss manuscripts
MT Masoretic Text
n.d. no date
neut. neuter
no. number
NT New Testament
OL Old Latin
OS Old Syriac
OT Old Testament
p., pp. page, pages
pl. plural
Q Quelle ("Sayings" as Gospel source)
rev. revision
sg. singular
t. Tosefta
TR Textus Receptus
v., vv. verse, verses
vid. *videtur*, it seems
viz. *videlicet*, namely
vol. volume
y. Jerusalem Gemara

ABBREVIATIONS FOR BIBLE TRANSLATIONS

ASV American Standard Version
CEV Contemporary English Version
ESV English Standard Version
GW God's Word
HCSB Holman Christian Standard Bible
JB Jerusalem Bible
KJV King James Version
NAB New American Bible
NASB New American Standard Bible
NCV New Century Version
NEB New English Bible
NET The NET Bible
NIV New International Version
NIrV New International Reader's Version
NJB New Jerusalem Bible
NJPS The New Jewish Publication Society Translation (*Tanakh*)
NKJV New King James Version
NRSV New Revised Standard Version
NLT New Living Translation
REB Revised English Bible
RSV Revised Standard Version
TEV Today's English Version
TLB The Living Bible

ABBREVIATIONS FOR DICTIONARIES, LEXICONS, COLLECTIONS OF TEXTS, ORIGINAL LANGUAGE EDITIONS

ABD *Anchor Bible Dictionary* (6 vols., Freedman) [1992]

ANEP *The Ancient Near East in Pictures* (Pritchard) [1965]

ANET *Ancient Near Eastern Texts Relating to the Old Testament* (Pritchard) [1969]

BAGD *Greek-English Lexicon of the New Testament and Other Early Christian Literature*, 2nd ed. (Bauer, Arndt, Gingrich, Danker) [1979]

BDAG *Greek-English Lexicon of the New Testament and Other Early Christian Literature*, 3rd ed. (Bauer, Danker, Arndt, Gingrich) [2000]

BDB *A Hebrew and English Lexicon of the Old Testament* (Brown, Driver, Briggs) [1907]

BDF *A Greek Grammar of the New Testament and Other Early Christian Literature* (Blass, Debrunner, Funk) [1961]

BHS *Biblia Hebraica Stuttgartensia* (Elliger and Rudolph) [1983]

CAD *Assyrian Dictionary of the Oriental Institute of the University of Chicago* [1956]

COS *The Context of Scripture* (3 vols., Hallo and Younger) [1997–2002]

DBI *Dictionary of Biblical Imagery* (Ryken, Wilhoit, Longman) [1998]

DBT *Dictionary of Biblical Theology* (2nd ed., Leon-Dufour) [1972]

DCH *Dictionary of Classical Hebrew* (5 vols., D. Clines) [2000]

DLNTD *Dictionary of the Later New Testament and Its Development* (R. Martin, P. Davids) [1997]

DJD *Discoveries in the Judean Desert* [1955–]

DJG *Dictionary of Jesus and the Gospels* (Green, McKnight, Marshall) [1992]

DOTP *Dictionary of the Old Testament: Pentateuch* (T. Alexander, D.W. Baker) [2003]

DPL *Dictionary of Paul and His Letters* (Hawthorne, Martin, Reid) [1993]

DTIB *Dictionary of Theological Interpretation of the Bible* (Vanhoozer) [2005]

EDNT *Exegetical Dictionary of the New Testament* (3 vols., H. Balz, G. Schneider. ET) [1990–1993]

GKC *Gesenius' Hebrew Grammar* (Gesenius, Kautzsch, trans. Cowley) [1910]

HALOT *The Hebrew and Aramaic Lexicon of the Old Testament* (L. Koehler, W. Baumgartner, J. Stamm; trans. M. Richardson) [1994–1999]

IBD *Illustrated Bible Dictionary* (3 vols., Douglas, Wiseman) [1980]

IDB *The Interpreter's Dictionary of the Bible* (4 vols., Buttrick) [1962]

ISBE *International Standard Bible Encyclopedia* (4 vols., Bromiley) [1979–1988]

KBL *Lexicon in Veteris Testamenti libros* (Koehler, Baumgartner) [1958]

LCL Loeb Classical Library

L&N *Greek-English Lexicon of the New Testament: Based on Semantic Domains* (Louw and Nida) [1989]

LSJ *A Greek-English Lexicon* (9th ed., Liddell, Scott, Jones) [1996]

MM *The Vocabulary of the Greek New Testament* (Moulton and Milligan) [1930; 1997]

NA^{26} *Novum Testamentum Graece* (26th ed., Nestle-Aland) [1979]

NA^{27} *Novum Testamentum Graece* (27th ed., Nestle-Aland) [1993]

NBD *New Bible Dictionary* (2nd ed., Douglas, Hillyer) [1982]

NIDB *New International Dictionary of the Bible* (Douglas, Tenney) [1987]

NIDBA *New International Dictionary of Biblical Archaeology* (Blaiklock and Harrison) [1983]

NIDNTT *New International Dictionary of New Testament Theology* (4 vols., C. Brown) [1975–1985]

NIDOTTE *New International Dictionary of Old Testament Theology and Exegesis* (5 vols., W. A. VanGemeren) [1997]

PGM *Papyri graecae magicae: Die griechischen Zauberpapyri.* (Preisendanz) [1928]

PG *Patrologia Graecae* (J. P. Migne) [1857–1886]

TBD *Tyndale Bible Dictionary* (Elwell, Comfort) [2001]

TDNT *Theological Dictionary of the New Testament* (10 vols., Kittel, Friedrich; trans. Bromiley) [1964–1976]

TDOT *Theological Dictionary of the Old Testament* (8 vols., Botterweck, Ringgren; trans. Willis, Bromiley, Green) [1974–]

TLNT *Theological Lexicon of the New Testament* (3 vols., C. Spicq) [1994]

TLOT *Theological Lexicon of the Old Testament* (3 vols., E. Jenni) [1997]

TWOT *Theological Wordbook of the Old Testament* (2 vols., Harris, Archer) [1980]

UBS^3 *United Bible Societies' Greek New Testament* (3rd ed., Metzger et al.) [1975]

UBS^4 *United Bible Societies' Greek New Testament* (4th corrected ed., Metzger et al.) [1993]

WH *The New Testament in the Original Greek* (Westcott and Hort) [1882]

ABBREVIATIONS FOR BOOKS OF THE BIBLE

Old Testament

Gen	Genesis	Deut	Deuteronomy	1 Sam	1 Samuel
Exod	Exodus	Josh	Joshua	2 Sam	2 Samuel
Lev	Leviticus	Judg	Judges	1 Kgs	1 Kings
Num	Numbers	Ruth	Ruth	2 Kgs	2 Kings

1 Chr	1 Chronicles
2 Chr	2 Chronicles
Ezra	Ezra
Neh	Nehemiah
Esth	Esther
Job	Job
Ps, Pss	Psalm, Psalms
Prov	Proverbs
Eccl	Ecclesiastes
Song	Song of Songs
Isa	Isaiah
Jer	Jeremiah
Lam	Lamentations
Ezek	Ezekiel
Dan	Daniel
Hos	Hosea
Joel	Joel
Amos	Amos
Obad	Obadiah
Jonah	Jonah
Mic	Micah
Nah	Nahum
Hab	Habakkuk
Zeph	Zephaniah
Hag	Haggai
Zech	Zechariah
Mal	Malachi

New Testament

Matt	Matthew
Mark	Mark
Luke	Luke
John	John
Acts	Acts
Rom	Romans
1 Cor	1 Corinthians
2 Cor	2 Corinthians
Gal	Galatians
Eph	Ephesians
Phil	Philippians
Col	Colossians
1 Thess	1 Thessalonians
2 Thess	2 Thessalonians
1 Tim	1 Timothy
2 Tim	2 Timothy
Titus	Titus
Phlm	Philemon
Heb	Hebrews
Jas	James
1 Pet	1 Peter
2 Pet	2 Peter
1 John	1 John
2 John	2 John
3 John	3 John
Jude	Jude
Rev	Revelation

Deuterocanonical

Bar	Baruch
Add Dan	Additions to Daniel
Pr Azar	Prayer of Azariah
Bel	Bel and the Dragon
Sg Three	Song of the Three Children
Sus	Susanna
1–2 Esdr	1–2 Esdras
Add Esth	Additions to Esther
Ep Jer	Epistle of Jeremiah
Jdt	Judith
1–2 Macc	1–2 Maccabees
3–4 Macc	3–4 Maccabees
Pr Man	Prayer of Manasseh
Ps 151	Psalm 151
Sir	Sirach
Tob	Tobit
Wis	Wisdom of Solomon

MANUSCRIPTS AND LITERATURE FROM QUMRAN

Initial numerals followed by "Q" indicate particular caves at Qumran. For example, the notation 4Q267 indicates text 267 from cave 4 at Qumran. Further, 1QS 4:9-10 indicates column 4, lines 9-10 of the *Rule of the Community*; and 4Q166 1 ii 2 indicates fragment 1, column ii, line 2 of text 166 from cave 4. More examples of common abbreviations are listed below.

CD	Cairo Geniza copy of the *Damascus Document*
1QH	*Thanksgiving Hymns*
1QIsa^a	Isaiah copy ^{a}
1QIsa^b	Isaiah copy ^{b}
1QM	*War Scroll*
1QpHab	*Pesher Habakkuk*
1QS	*Rule of the Community*
4QLam^a	Lamentations
11QPs^a	Psalms
11QTemple^{a,b}	*Temple Scroll*
11QtgJob	*Targum of Job*

IMPORTANT NEW TESTAMENT MANUSCRIPTS

(all dates given are AD; ordinal numbers refer to centuries)

Significant Papyri (𝔓 = Papyrus)

𝔓1 Matt 1; early 3rd
𝔓4+𝔓64+𝔓67 Matt 3, 5, 26; Luke 1–6; late 2nd
𝔓5 John 1, 16, 20; early 3rd
𝔓13 Heb 2–5, 10–12; early 3rd
𝔓15+𝔓16 (probably part of same codex) 1 Cor 7–8, Phil 3–4; late 3rd
𝔓20 Jas 2–3; 3rd
𝔓22 John 15–16; mid 3rd
𝔓23 Jas 1; c. 200
𝔓27 Rom 8–9; 3rd
𝔓30 1 Thess 4–5; 2 Thess 1; early 3rd
𝔓32 Titus 1–2; late 2nd
𝔓37 Matt 26; late 3rd
𝔓39 John 8; first half of 3rd
𝔓40 Rom 1–4, 6, 9; 3rd

𝔓45 Gospels and Acts; early 3rd
𝔓46 Paul's Major Epistles (less Pastorals); late 2nd
𝔓47 Rev 9–17; 3rd
𝔓49+𝔓65 Eph 4–5; 1 Thess 1–2; 3rd
𝔓52 John 18; c. 125
𝔓53 Matt 26, Acts 9–10; middle 3rd
𝔓66 John; late 2nd
𝔓70 Matt 2–3, 11–12, 24; 3rd
𝔓72 1–2 Peter, Jude; c. 300
𝔓74 Acts, General Epistles; 7th
𝔓75 Luke and John; c. 200
𝔓77+𝔓103 (probably part of same codex) Matt 13–14, 23; late 2nd
𝔓87 Philemon; late 2nd
𝔓90 John 18–19; late 2nd
𝔓91 Acts 2–3; 3rd
𝔓92 Eph 1, 2 Thess 1; c. 300
𝔓98 Rev 1:13-20; late 2nd
𝔓100 Jas 3–5; c. 300
𝔓101 Matt 3–4; 3rd
𝔓104 Matt 21; 2nd
𝔓106 John 1; 3rd
𝔓115 Rev 2–3, 5–6, 8–15; 3rd

Significant Uncials

א (Sinaiticus) most of NT; 4th
A (Alexandrinus) most of NT; 5th
B (Vaticanus) most of NT; 4th
C (Ephraemi Rescriptus) most of NT with many lacunae; 5th
D (Bezae) Gospels, Acts; 5th
D (Claromontanus), Paul's Epistles; 6th (different MS than Bezae)
E (Laudianus 35) Acts; 6th
F (Augensis) Paul's Epistles; 9th
G (Boernerianus) Paul's Epistles; 9th
H (Coislinianus) Paul's Epistles; 6th
I (Freerianus or Washington) Paul's Epistles; 5th
L (Regius) Gospels; 8th
P (Porphyrianus) Acts—Revelation; 9th
Q (Guelferbytanus B) Luke, John; 5th
T (Borgianus) Luke, John; 5th
W (Washingtonianus or the Freer Gospels) Gospels; 5th
Z (Dublinensis) Matthew; 6th
037 (Δ; Sangallensis) Gospels; 9th
038 (Θ; Koridethi) Gospels; 9th
040 (Ξ; Zacynthius) Luke; 6th
043 (Φ; Beratinus) Matthew, Mark; 6th
044 (Ψ; Athous Laurae) Gospels, Acts, Paul's Epistles; 9th
048 Acts, Paul's Epistles, General Epistles; 5th
0171 Matt 10, Luke 22; c. 300
0189 Acts 5; c. 200

Significant Minuscules

1 Gospels, Acts, Paul's Epistles; 12th
33 All NT except Revelation; 9th
81 Acts, Paul's Epistles, General Epistles; 1044
565 Gospels; 9th
700 Gospels; 11th
1424 (or Family 1424—a group of 29 manuscripts sharing nearly the same text) most of NT; 9th-10th
1739 Acts, Paul's Epistles; 10th
2053 Rev; 13th
2344 Rev; 11th
f^{1} (a family of manuscripts including 1, 118, 131, 209) Gospels; 12th-14th
f^{13} (a family of manuscripts including 13, 69, 124, 174, 230, 346, 543, 788, 826, 828, 983, 1689, 1709—known as the Ferrar group) Gospels; 11th-15th

Significant Ancient Versions

SYRIAC (SYR)

syr^{c} (Syriac Curetonian) Gospels; 5th
syr^{s} (Syriac Sinaiticus) Gospels; 4th
syr^{h} (Syriac Harklensis) Entire NT; 616

OLD LATIN (IT)

it^{a} (Vercellenis) Gospels; 4th
it^{b} (Veronensis) Gospels; 5th
it^{d} (Cantabrigiensis—the Latin text of Bezae) Gospels, Acts, 3 John; 5th
it^{e} (Palantinus) Gospels; 5th
it^{k} (Bobiensis) Matthew, Mark; c. 400

COPTIC (COP)

cop^{bo} (Boharic—north Egypt)
cop^{fay} (Fayyumic—central Egypt)
cop^{sa} (Sahidic—southern Egypt)

OTHER VERSIONS

arm (Armenian)
eth (Ethiopic)
geo (Georgian)

TRANSLITERATION AND NUMBERING SYSTEM

Note: For words and roots from nonbiblical languages (e.g., Arabic, Ugaritic), only approximate transliterations are given.

HEBREW/ARAMAIC

Consonants

א	*aleph*	= ʼ	מ, ם	*mem*	= *m*
בּ, ב	*beth*	= *b*	נ, ן	*nun*	= *n*
גּ, ג	*gimel*	= *g*	ס	*samekh*	= *s*
דּ, ד	*daleth*	= *d*	ע	*ayin*	= ʻ
ה	*he*	= *h*	פּ, פ, ף	*pe*	= *p*
ו	*waw*	= *w*	צ, ץ	*tsadhe*	= *ts*
ז	*zayin*	= *z*	ק	*qoph*	= *q*
ח	*heth*	= *kh*	ר	*resh*	= *r*
ט	*teth*	= *t*	שׁ	*shin*	= *sh*
י	*yodh*	= *y*	שׂ	*sin*	= *s*
כּ, כ, ך	*kaph*	= *k*	תּ, ת	*taw*	= *t, th* (spirant)
ל	*lamedh*	= *l*			

Vowels

ַ	*patakh*	= *a*	ָ	*qamets khatuf*	= *o*
חַ	*furtive patakh*	= *a*	ֹ	*holem*	= *o*
ָ	*qamets*	= *a*	וֹ	*full holem*	= *o*
ָה	*final qamets he*	= *ah*	ֻ	*short qibbuts*	= *u*
ֶ	*segol*	= *e*	ֻ	*long qibbuts*	= *u*
ֵ	*tsere*	= *e*	וּ	*shureq*	= *u*
ֵי	*tsere yod*	= *e*	ֲ	*khatef patakh*	= *a*
ִ	*short hireq*	= *i*	ֳ	*khatef qamets*	= *o*
ִ	*long hireq*	= *i*	ְ	*vocalic shewa*	= *e*
ִי	*hireq yod*	= *i*	ַי	*patakh yodh*	= *a*

GREEK

α	*alpha*	= *a*	ι	*iota*	= *i*
β	*beta*	= *b*	κ	*kappa*	= *k*
γ	*gamma*	= *g, n (before* γ, κ, ξ, χ)	λ	*lamda*	= *l*
			μ	*mu*	= *m*
δ	*delta*	= *d*	ν	*nu*	= *n*
ε	*epsilon*	= *e*	ξ	*ksi*	= *x*
ζ	*zeta*	= *z*	ο	*omicron*	= *o*
η	*eta*	= *ē*	π	*pi*	= *p*
θ	*theta*	= *th*	ρ	*rho*	= *r* (ῥ = *rh)*

σ, ς	*sigma*	= *s*	ψ	*psi*	= *ps*
τ	*tau*	= *t*	ω	*omega*	= *ō*
υ	*upsilon*	= *u*	῾	*rough breathing mark*	= *h (with vowel or diphthong)*
φ	*phi*	= *ph*			
χ	*chi*	= *ch*			

THE TYNDALE-STRONG'S NUMBERING SYSTEM

The Cornerstone Biblical Commentary series uses a word-study numbering system to give both newer and more advanced Bible students alike quicker, more convenient access to helpful original-language tools (e.g., concordances, lexicons, and theological dictionaries). Those who are unfamiliar with the ancient Hebrew, Aramaic, and Greek alphabets can quickly find information on a given word by looking up the appropriate index number. Advanced students will find the system helpful because it allows them to quickly find the lexical form of obscure conjugations and inflections.

There are two main numbering systems used for biblical words today. The one familiar to most people is the Strong's numbering system (made popular by the *Strong's Exhaustive Concordance to the Bible*). Although the original Strong's system is still quite useful, the most up-to-date research has shed new light on the biblical languages and allows for more precision than is found in the original Strong's system. The Cornerstone Biblical Commentary series, therefore, features a newly revised version of the Strong's system, the Tyndale-Strong's numbering system. The Tyndale-Strong's system brings together the familiarity of the Strong's system and the best of modern scholarship. In most cases, the original Strong's numbers are preserved. In places where new research dictates, new or related numbers have been added.[1]

The second major numbering system today is the Goodrick-Kohlenberger system used in a number of study tools published by Zondervan. In order to give students broad access to a number of helpful tools, the Commentary provides index numbers for the Zondervan system as well.

The different index systems are designated as follows:

TG	Tyndale-Strong's Greek number	ZH	Zondervan Hebrew number
ZG	Zondervan Greek number	TA/ZA	Tyndale/Zondervan Aramaic number
TH	Tyndale-Strong's Hebrew number	S	Strong's Aramaic number

So in the example, "love" *agapē* [[TG]26, [ZG]27], the first number is the one to use with Greek tools keyed to the Tyndale-Strong's system, and the second applies to tools that use the Zondervan system.

The indexing of Aramaic terms differs slightly from that of Greek and Hebrew. Strong's original system mixed the Aramaic terms in with the Hebrew, but the Tyndale-Strong's system indexes Aramaic with a new set of numbers starting at 10,000. Since Tyndale's system for Aramaic diverges completely from original Strong's, the original Strong's number is listed separately so that those using tools keyed to Strong's can locate the information. This number is designated with an S, as in the example, "son" *bar* [[TA/ZA]10120, [S]1247].

1. Generally, one may simply use the original four-digit Strong's number to identify words in tools using Strong's system. If a Tyndale-Strong's number is followed by a capital letter (e.g., [TG]1692A), it generally indicates an added subdivision of meaning for the given term. Whenever a Tyndale-Strong's number has a number following a decimal point (e.g., [TG]2013.1), it reflects an instance where new research has yielded a separate, new classification of use for a biblical word. Forthcoming tools from Tyndale House Publishers will include these entries, which were not part of the original Strong's system.

1–2 Samuel

J. ROBERT VANNOY

INTRODUCTION TO
1–2 Samuel

FIRST AND SECOND SAMUEL bear the name of the prophet whom God used to establish kingship in Israel. It was Samuel who guided Israel through the important transition from the period of the judges to that of the monarchy. In a nutshell, this reorganization of the theocracy is the most important thing that happens in 1 and 2 Samuel. The account of the events surrounding this transition is interlaced with themes emphasizing divine sovereignty over all of human history and the reversal of human fortunes. As we follow the lives of Samuel, Saul, and David, we see that God is indeed the King of kings and that it is his prerogative to exalt the humble and bring down the proud.

AUTHOR

Although this book—for 1 and 2 Samuel are in fact one literary work—bears Samuel's name because of his prominent role in bringing about the transition to a monarchy, he was not its author. We know this because Samuel's death occurred during the lifetime of Saul and is reported in 1 Samuel 25:1. Many of the narratives of the book, and particularly those concerning the time of David's reign, describe events that clearly took place subsequent to Samuel's death. This, however, is not necessarily to say that the book contains no material from Samuel's hand. We know, for example, that Samuel, along with other prophets of his time, wrote about the events of his day (1 Chr 29:29 speaks of *The Record of Samuel the Seer, The Record of Nathan the Prophet,* and *The Record of Gad the Seer*). Certainly the anonymous author of 1–2 Samuel either incorporated or consulted sources from earlier times in order to narrate events from the more-than-130-year period in Israel's history that the book portrays. One such source is explicitly mentioned (2 Sam 1:18, *The Book of Jashar*) and others (1 Chr 27:24 refers to "King David's official records") were certainly used. But because the book of Samuel is anonymous and because there is not adequate information either from within the book itself or from external sources concerning the circumstances surrounding the time of its composition, it is not possible to speak with certainty about who its author may have been. Moreover, the authorship of 1–2 Samuel is something that cannot be considered in isolation. The reason for this is that one's conclusion about the date of authorship is inseparably tied to a host of other complex questions concerning the literary character of the book as well as the purpose of its composition.

DATE AND OCCASION OF WRITING

The date for the composition of 1–2 Samuel is a matter on which there is little agreement among biblical scholars. Until recent times, most evangelical scholars opted for a date sometime shortly after the death of Solomon "perhaps about 920 or 900 BC" (Harrison 1969:709; cf. Young 1964:178). Among nonevangelical scholars there have been two broad categories of approach to the questions of date and authorship: In the first half of the twentieth century many attempted to apply the sort of documentary source analysis characteristic of Pentateuch studies to the books of Samuel. (In short, the idea was that four sometimes-parallel accounts, or literary sources, commonly cited as J, E, P, and D, were merged together into one larger work to form the Pentateuch.) The conclusion of many of these scholars was that the J and E documents of the Pentateuch could be traced on into Joshua, Judges, Samuel, and Kings (Budde 1890; Wellhausen 1899; Eissfeldt 1965). During the second half of the twentieth century, the majority of nonevangelical scholars shifted their viewpoint to some version of the Deuteronomistic History theory developed by Martin Noth in 1943. It was Noth's hypothesis that the entire corpus of Deuteronomy—2 Kings was for the most part the work of a single author (the "Deuteronomistic Historian") who wrote during the exilic period. Noth denied that the Pentateuchal sources of J, E, D, and P continued beyond the end of Deuteronomy. He argued that Deuteronomy itself consisted of old traditions recovered in 621 BC (the "law book" found in the Temple during the reign of Josiah; 2 Kgs 22) and originally consisted of only Deuteronomy 5–28. It was his view that the Deuteronomistic Historian of the exilic period added Deuteronomy 1–4 as an introduction to his entire history and then compiled Joshua, Judges, Samuel, and Kings as his complete theological presentation of Israel's history—one governed by the ideals of the older materials of Deuteronomy. Noth built on the work of a number of scholars who had questioned the validity of the documentary theory of the composition of Judges, Samuel, and Kings, and preferred to speak of self-contained tradition units rather than two or three parallel and continuous literary documents. Among the most important of these tradition units were the Ark Narrative (1 Sam 4:1–7:1; 2 Sam 6–7),[1] the Narrative of Saul's Rise and End (1 Sam 9:1–10:16; chs 11; 13–14; 31); the Narrative of the Rise of David (1 Sam 16:14—2 Sam 5); and the Succession Narrative (sometimes also termed the Court History of David; 2 Sam 9–20; 1 Kgs 1–2).

Of particular significance for the question of the time of 1–2 Samuel's composition is the so-called Succession Narrative, which spans the books of Samuel and Kings and terminates with David's death and the succession of Solomon to the throne. It was Rost (1926) who first argued that 2 Samuel 9–20 and 1 Kings 1–2 are two parts of an originally independent literary unit that was the product of a single author living in the time of Solomon and, most importantly, that its climax and conclusion are found in the report of Solomon's accession to the throne in 1 Kings 2.[2] If, as Rost's theory requires, there is no clear-cut division between the books of Samuel and Kings, because the "Succession Narrative" flows across the divide between the two books, then it would seem to suggest that the author or compiler of Kings was the author or compiler of Samuel as well. As Longman and Dillard

(2006:155) note, "The materials in 2 Samuel 21–24 are widely viewed as an intrusion to the Succession Narrative, separating the accession of Solomon (1 Kings 1–2) from the earlier narratives leading to that event." The Succession Narrative theory, then, fits nicely with Noth's Deuteronomistic History theory, which maintains that none of the historical books from Joshua to 2 Kings were written (at least in their present form) until the time of the Exile.

When one looks more closely at both the documentary source theory and the Deuteronomistic History theory as explanations of the origin and the nature of the composition of 1–2 Samuel, things quickly become much more complex. Within the documentary source theory, scholars are divided over whether the books of Samuel were the product of continuous sources or independent fragments. But whatever differences have surfaced in delineating the documents (and there are many), there is general agreement that in its final form the book reflects either a Deuteronomistic redaction, or else one of its later sources exhibits strong Deuteronomic influence. This in itself, however, brings along with it the inevitable conclusion that the book is to be dated comparatively late, that is, either during or after the Exile. The reason for this is the nearly axiomatic belief among mainstream biblical scholars that Deuteronomy is linked with the reform of Josiah and is to be dated to about 622 BC.[3] This dating for Deuteronomy was integral to Wellhausen's documentary source theory for the origin of the Pentateuch, and also to his reconstruction of the history of Israel's religious development.[4] It has remained a fundamental assumption of biblical scholars ever since. Moving the date of Deuteronomy away from the Mosaic era and placing it at the end of the kingdom period in the Old Testament inevitably has far-reaching implications for the literature of the Old Testament because theological ideas and linguistic expressions similar to those of Deuteronomy can be found in all of the historical books from Joshua to 2 Kings, as well as in many of the prophetic books. So the late dating of Deuteronomy has led to the conclusion that many other Old Testament books including 1–2 Samuel should be dated late as well.

It is of particular interest to me that some cracks are beginning to appear in the two most important theories that have influenced mainstream biblical scholars to adopt an exilic date for the final form of 1–2 Samuel. First of all, questions are increasingly being raised about Noth's Deuteronomistic History theory. Even though von Rad accepted Noth's literary thesis of a Deuteronomistic Historian and a Deuteronomistic History work, he disagreed from the very beginning with Noth's view of the aim or purpose of the work. Von Rad had misgivings concerning Noth's negative idea that the basic purpose of the Deuteronomistic History was to provide a theological explanation for the Exile as a necessary act of Yahweh's justice. Von Rad suggested that the Deuteronomistic Historian worked with a wide variety of traditional material that often did not readily accommodate itself to his basic theological attitude. For example, von Rad claimed that the material pertaining to the Davidic covenant is wholly un-Deuteronomic, and yet the Deuteronomistic Historian did not exclude it. Von Rad saw a basic conflict between the Mosaic and Davidic covenants, each reflecting different traditions and different interests. He said, "In taking up this strongly established tradition [David as the prototype of a theocratic monarch, and a model of obedience] the Deuteronomist has moved right away from his native climate of the book of *Deuteronomy*, whence his theological viewpoint originates. The wide extent to which the Deuteronomist employs this tradition in his work shows that the Deuteronomic tradition in its purest form could not hold its ground here. The obviously very powerful messianic conception has broken in upon it and demanded a hearing" (von Rad 1947:218). Certainly von Rad was correct in seeing a significant emphasis on the Davidic covenant in both Samuel and Kings, as well as the implications that this carries for an eschatological or messianic dimension for Israel's future history (cf. Provan 1995b; Satterthwaite 1995). This sharply contrasts with Noth's idea of a finished history with no vision for the future.

This tension, reflected in the themes of curse and blessing, and more broadly in the concepts of law and grace, has continued to fuel discussion around the character and purpose of the Deuteronomistic History. The general trend among nonevangelical scholars has been to attempt to resolve the tension by means of diachronic literary analysis and by the suggestion that the present form of the Deuteronomistic History is the result of multiple redactions or layers. According to F. M. Cross, the Deuteronomistic History was composed in two phases (1973:274-289). In its first phase, which Cross links with Josiah's reform, it expressed a positive or favorable outlook on the house of David and the kings of Judah. But according to Cross, this version of the national history was revised subsequent to the Exile, and material fundamentally opposed to the monarchy, as well as sections anticipating the Exile, were inserted. This twofold redaction theory to explain the origin of what are viewed as conflicting trajectories in the Deuteronomistic History presently receives broad support, particularly among American nonevangelical scholars.[5]

The present state of Deuteronomistic History studies, however, reflects widening differences on many issues, including the date of its origin, its limits, its purpose and manner of construction, as well as the identity of the Deuteronomist(s) (Klement 2000:44-51). Coggins (1999:26) comments that "there is no external evidence of any kind [for this] wide-ranging and influential" movement and "the whole history of tradition has to be worked out by inference. Deuteronomistic influence may be traced, but there is still no agreement as to who the Deuteronomists were." Westermann (1994) has questioned the existence of a unified Deuteronomistic History and argues that each of the books from Joshua to Kings had its own development and was separately edited after the fall of Jerusalem in 586 BC. Römer (2003:240) expresses frustration related to "the so-called Deuteronomistic History, which I believed to be one of the most reliable constructs in Old Testament research but which is now more and more disputed." He goes on to suggest (2003:251) that some of the books of Deuteronomy—2 Kings are more likely a collection of diverse texts that "were already available *before* the creation of an encompassing historical work covering the time from Moses to the fall of Judah." McConville (1993) has pointed out that even though one may speak of the "deuteronomic" character of the books from Joshua to 2 Kings, there are also significant differences of perspective and theological concern in each of these books that also need to be recognized and accounted for. These differences argue against a single final author, and close examination of the theology and content of each book shows adaptation to the concerns and needs of the people of God during a time much closer to the occurrence of the events described than to that of the exilic period. Auld (1999:116) has said, "Not only do I become less and less sure that I know *what* the Deuteronomists did in respect of the composition of the Former Prophets, I also wonder more and more with my British colleague Richard Coggins *whether* whoever-did-what should be called 'Deuteronomists.'" His inclination (1999:123) is to see the flow of influence as running backwards from Kings through Samuel to Deuteronomy, rather than the reverse. He says (1999:125), for example, that the "transition from Moses to Joshua is adapted from the transition from David to Solomon; as David did not built [sic] the holy 'place,' so Moses did not enter the land. The troubled period of Israel under the Judges follows on the Moses-Joshua story as the troubled story of Northern Israel follows on David-Solomon. An earlier story was built by redeveloping the classic story of Jerusalem's kings." Preuss (1993:394-395) suggests, in the conclusion to his summary of studies on the Deuteronomistic History from 1984–1991, that because of the different schools and models it seems that "every Old Testament scholar has fashioned not only his own theory of the composition of the Pentateuch, but also his own view of the Deuteronomistic History" (my translation).[6] R. R. Wilson (1999) goes so far as to say that recent research "may in fact have demonstrated, unwittingly, that the concept of Deuteronomism has become so amorphous that it no longer has any analytical precision and so ought to be abandoned. . . . Current trends in Deuteronomistic research may thus force scholars to take seriously the possibility that if everybody is the Deuteronomist, then there may be no Deuteronomist at all." Because of this unsettled nature of the contemporary scene in Deuteronomistic History studies, it is my view that one should be very cautious about drawing conclusions concerning the late date of the writing of 1–2 Samuel on the basis of its "Deuteronomistic" character.

Although in mainstream Old Testament studies, the late dating of Deuteronomy requires a late date for the historical books that carry a Deuteronomic imprint, a more nuanced approach is taken by some evangelical scholars who maintain that Deuteronomy is fundamentally a Mosaic book but nevertheless remain open to the idea that Samuel—Kings was edited during the exilic period by redactors who were looking at Israel's history from a Deuteronomic perspective. Longman and Dillard (2006:153) say that since "Samuel is part of the Deuteronomic History, most scholars view the final stages of its composition as the work of editors/authors during the period of the Exile; however, it is all but impossible to recover the compositional history of the book, and it may well have been produced in essentially its present form at a much earlier date." Because of the considerable uncertainties involved in the reconstruction of the compositional history of the book, as noted by Longman and Dillard, it is my view that it is preferable to regard the Deuteronomic character of the book as part and parcel of its original composition rather than as a secondary augmentation.[7] While the Deuteronomistic History hypothesis is not likely to disappear any time soon from the horizon of Old Testament studies, it is my view that evangelical scholars should be cautious about embracing it as a framework for their own studies.[8]

A second theory that has exerted considerable influence on moving biblical scholars to posit an exilic date for 1–2 Samuel is the Rostian Succession Narrative hypothesis, which has worked hand in glove with the Deuteronomistic History theory.[9] As noted above, Rost argued that 2 Samuel 9–20 and 1 Kings 1–2 were originally a single narrative unit and that "succession to the throne" was its central theme. In Rost's view, the original unity of this narrative is presently obscured by the "appendices in 2 Sam 21–24 which belong to various different sources" (1982:80). Recent studies have disputed this conclusion from a number of directions. Most importantly, Keys (1996) has thoroughly and convincingly challenged the idea that 2 Samuel 10–20 should be linked with 1 Kings 1–2. In her view, 2 Samuel 10–20 is not so much concerned with the succession of Solomon but rather with a theological evaluation of David.[10] The opening chapters of Kings are not the conclusion to the David account, but rather the introduction to the reign of Solomon.[11] At the same time, Klement (2000) has convincingly demonstrated that 2 Samuel 21–24 are not simply extraneous miscellaneous appendages to 1–2 Samuel, but rather are an appropriate conclusion for the entire book, as well as a key for discerning its structural framework (see "Literary Style," below). Rosenberg (1987:123-124) suggests that the "two widely accepted results of source-criticism—Leonhard Rost's notion of a tenth-century BCE 'Succession History' (2 Sam 11—1 Kings 2) and Martin Noth's notion of a sixth- or fifth-century 'Deuteronomic History' (Deut—2 Kings) have tended to obscure the literary character of the Samuel books by depriving them both of their autonomy as books and of the commonality of texture and perspective that unites them with most other books of the Hebrew Bible."

In view of the strong defense that has been made by a number of evangelical scholars for continuing to regard the book of Deuteronomy as belonging to the Mosaic era, or at least very close to it,[12] and in view of the host of questions being raised concerning the validity of both the Deuteronomistic History and the Succession Narrative theories, it is somewhat puzzling that a number of evangelical scholars have moved toward acceptance of an exilic date for 1–2 Samuel.[13] There seems to be good reason to retain the earlier consensus that the composition of 1–2 Samuel is best placed either during or shortly after the time of Solomon. This not only avoids enmeshment in many of the questionable assumptions concerning the date of Deuteronomy and the validity of the Deuteronomistic History and the Succession Narrative theories, but it also provides a better foundation for recognition of the uniqueness not only of 1–2 Samuel, but of each of the historical books from Joshua to Kings. As McConville (1993:77) has suggested, we should be careful not to prejudge "whether the different books that compose DtH [the Deuteronomistic History] might have distinctive theological concerns of their own, distinguishing them from each other."[14] Walters (2002:66) has called attention to several linguistic peculiarities[15] in 1–2 Samuel that suggest "that Samuel as a book had circulation and use independently of the books around it." Webb (1987:211) comes to a similar conclusion in connection with his study of the book of Judges, which he views as a distinct literary unit. In his opinion differences between the various historical books are "perhaps better accounted for in terms of an edited series of books than in terms of a series of more-or-less arbitrary units concealing an originally unified work."

On this basis Webb calls for a reopening of the question of how the Deuteronomic History came into existence.

Moving the origin of the present form of 1–2 Samuel away from the exilic period and placing it closer to the historical period about which it speaks does not, however, eliminate its anonymity. The book itself gives no indication of the author's identity. The realism of the description of David's reign in 2 Samuel 10–20 has led some scholars to suggest that the author was a contemporary, or near contemporary, to the events described, and that he wrote during the reign of Solomon. References, however, to "Israel and Judah" (1 Sam 11:8; 17:52; 18:16; 2 Sam 5:5; 24:1-9), as well as the expression "kings of Judah" in 1 Samuel 27:6 suggest that the author must have lived after Solomon's death and the division of the kingdom in 931 BC. Keys (1996:88) argues that 2 Samuel 10–20 "never had an independent existence, but was transmitted with the rest of the book from its initial composition." This conclusion, which seems to merit serious consideration, suggests that the author of 2 Samuel 10–20 was the author or compiler of the entire book. Although we do not know who this person was, and there is no need to give the writer a name as some have attempted to do,[16] it is certainly reasonable to conclude that the author was someone who stood in the prophetic tradition, and who lived in the early days of the divided kingdom period that began in 931 BC.[17]

AUDIENCE

The uncertainties associated with the compositional history of 1–2 Samuel complicate precise specification of the original audience for the book. The references to "Israel and Judah" and the "kings of Judah" mentioned in the previous paragraph do suggest that the book was written after the division of the kingdom in 931 BC. When an early date for Deuteronomy (Mosaic era, or close to it) is accepted, then the Deuteronomic language and concepts embedded in the narratives of 1–2 Samuel need not require a date subsequent to the reformation of Josiah (c. 622 BC) as is often assumed. While the realism of the narrative material, particularly in the description of David's reign, is a possible indicator of temporal proximity to David's reign, this quality is certainly not decisive in dating the book.

Perhaps the most important general indicator for suggesting an original audience early in the divided kingdom period is the book's focus on the themes of kingship and covenant. Israel's request for a king was a denial of the covenant and a rejection of the Lord, who was Israel's king. The Lord nevertheless told Samuel to give Israel a king, but in so doing, to define the role of the human king in terms consistent with Israel's covenant with the Lord. Israel's first king, Saul, failed to live up to this covenantal ideal and was therefore rejected. His successor, David, is presented as a true, although imperfect, representative of the ideal of covenantal kingship. In the books of 1 and 2 Kings, David is regularly presented as the standard by which subsequent kings are appraised, and the theme of kingship and covenant, introduced in 1–2 Samuel, is carried through until the time of the Exile. Throughout the entire kingdom period, the interface of the concepts of kingship and covenant was fundamental for Israel's self-understanding as a people who were simultaneously ruled by their divine sovereign, while being organized under the political structure of the monarchy. The covenantal concept of kingship in Israel not only defined the role of the king, but it also empowered the prophets of the Lord to hold Israel's kings accountable to their covenantal responsibilities. These are issues that Israel needed to understand from the earliest days of the kingdom period. It is only in 1–2 Samuel that they are introduced and addressed.

While it seems reasonable to conclude that the original audience for which 1–2 Samuel was written is to be located in the early days of the divided kingdom, this does not mean that a contemporary understanding of the meaning and significance of the narratives of Samuel should be limited by the interpretive horizon of its original audience. The Bible informs us quite clearly that its human authors wrote as they were inspired by the Holy Spirit (2 Tim 3:16; 2 Pet 1:20-21). This means that the writers of biblical materials were the secondary rather than primary authors of what they wrote. This understanding of the character of Scripture carries interpretive implications because it is possible that God's intended meaning for any specific scriptural passage may not correspond at every point with the limited horizon of the original human author and his audience.[18] The divine author knows the end from the beginning, which the human author does not. Every individual literary unit of Scripture contributes in some way to the unfolding drama of revelation and redemption that is designed and controlled by the divine author of both Scripture and history. This means that there may be levels of meaning intended in earlier Scriptures that only become apparent in the light of further revelation. This also means that while Christian interpreters should take their point of departure, as much as is possible, from the perspective of the original author and his audience, they must also read every narrative of Scripture in the ever-widening context of the growth of revelation and redemption as it is disclosed in the entirety of the Christian canon. Ultimately a proper reading and understanding of the narratives of 1–2 Samuel must be informed by an awareness that all of redemptive history finds its goal and focus in the person and work of Christ, in whom all of history receives its ultimate significance and meaning, including the history of early Israel. For this reason, the following commentary, where it is appropriate, will call attention to some of the theological and historical patterns, analogies, and trajectories by means of which the narratives of 1–2 Samuel can be viewed in their larger canonical context, and thus be seen to point beyond themselves to later biblical revelation, particularly in their connection with the person and work of Christ.[19] Of course, discernment of these things is only possible in light of the fuller revelation contained in the New Testament scriptures.

CANONICITY AND TEXTUAL HISTORY

The canonicity of 1–2 Samuel has never been questioned. It was included in the Septuagint (LXX) and numbered among the traditional 24 books making up the Jewish canon in all of the earliest listings (2 Esdr 14:44-47; Josephus *Against Apion* 1.8; *b. Baba Batra* 14b).

The Hebrew text of 1–2 Samuel is, perhaps, the least well preserved of any book in the Old Testament. While this gives the student of 1–2 Samuel numerous challenges in attempting to determine how the original text may have read, it should be understood that, for the most part, the textual problems are not of a nature that affects in any substantial way our understanding of the ideas or events about which the Samuel narratives speak.

The text-critical study of the Old Testament in general, and of the books of Samuel, in particular, has received a great deal of attention since the initial discovery of the Dead Sea Scrolls in 1947. The finding of these ancient texts was particularly significant because it provided the scholarly community with Hebrew manuscripts dated approximately a millennium earlier than the Ben Asher Manuscripts that were the basis for modern editions of the Hebrew Bible. One of the more significant results of the study of the Dead Sea Scrolls and their comparison with the Septuagint (LXX) and Masoretic Text (MT) has been that many scholars have concluded that in certain sections of the Old Testament the Septuagint represents a different Hebrew textual tradition than that found in the Masoretic Text, and that, consequently, the Septuagint readings should be given more weight in textual criticism than previously was thought to be warranted. This general conclusion is particularly widespread with respect to the text of the books of Samuel.

Evaluation of this general conclusion for the textual analysis of 1–2 Samuel is an extremely complex matter that cannot be thoroughly examined here. Any attempt to establish a history of the development of the text of the Old Testament is a difficult and tedious undertaking. As Talmon (1970:161) says, "There is probably no other extant text, ancient or modern, which is witnessed to by so many diverse types of sources, and the history of which is so difficult to elucidate as that of the text of the Old Testament." From the outset it should be recognized that proposals that attempt to account for the interrelationships of the various textual traditions must inevitably be viewed as tentative and recognized as working hypotheses, rather than as established fact. As Talmon (1970:159) points out, "Any account of the development of the text prior to c. 300 BC, (i.e., in the Persian period), not to mention the periods of the Babylonian Exile or of the First Temple, must perforce rely upon conjecture and, at best, upon deductions and analogies derived from later literature and later manuscripts."

Probably the most influential and comprehensive theory of the development of the text of the Old Testament is that proposed by what may be termed the Albright school. This approach was initiated by W. F. Albright, and developed and promoted, chiefly, by Frank Moore Cross, David Noel Freedman, and Ralph W. Klein. One of the major tenets of this approach is the postulation of what are termed "local texts." Cross (1985:20) has suggested that "three forms of the text appear to have developed slowly between the fifth century BC and the first century BC, in the Jewish communities in Palestine, in Egypt and in Babylon, respectively."[20]

Building on this theory of local texts, Cross, McCarter, and Klein have proposed an analysis of the text of Samuel—Kings in which, as Gooding (1975:122) points out, "three, if not four, types of Hebrew text can be discerned." These are as follows:

1. A Hebrew text, developed in Egypt and witnessed to by the parts of the Septuagint of Samuel—Kings that still contain the unrevised Old Greek translation.
2. A Hebrew text, developed in Palestine and witnessed to by certain Qumran Scrolls (especially 4QSam^a) and by the proto-Lucianic recension of the Septuagint.[21]
3. A proto-Masoretic Hebrew text, developed in Babylon and thence introduced into Palestine and witnessed to by certain scrolls from the Judean Desert (especially those from Masada) and by the *kaige* recension of the Septuagint.[22]
4. The Masoretic Text, witnessed to by later revisions of the Septuagint. Both Masoretic and proto-Masoretic texts are defective through much accidental omission.

In highly condensed form, this is the theory of textual history advocated in most of the recent major studies of the text of Samuel (see Cross 1966, 1975, 1985; Klein 1983:xxv-xxviii; Martin 1984; McCarter 1980b:5-11). While it may be difficult, if not impossible, to prove the theory wrong, it nevertheless builds on a number of assumptions that at least may be said to be questionable, and its advocates sometimes marshal evidence in ways that seem to be designed to produce results supportive of the theory rather than to objectively address the bewildering complexity of the textual problems.[23] As Gooding (1975:123) points out, "All these theories Klein illustrates with copious material; but to come to a balanced assessment of them, the beginner ought to be told in addition that other scholars are not equally convinced about all the elements in them, and why they are not convinced. Professor S. Talmon, for instance, rejects the theory of three local texts completely. Pere D. Barthélemy, who identified the *kaige* recension, thinks that F. M. Cross should give up his 'Egyptian Hebrew text' of Samuel—Kings. And E. Tov questions whether there ever was a proto-Lucianic recension."

There remain many questions that need to be answered before concluding that Cross's theories are sufficiently established to warrant the conclusions advocated by McCarter, Klein, and Martin in their treatments of the text of Samuel. The studies by Archer (1981), Eybers (1960), and Gooding (1975) provide an analysis of the same data addressed by Cross et al. with quite different ways of construing the data, and with quite different conclusions drawn. Archer (1981:236-237) concludes that there are a small number of cases where 4QSam^a and the Septuagint agree in a reading that seems definitely superior to that of a problematic reading of the Masoretic Text, and in these cases a careful use of these manuscripts may lead to a valid correction of the Masoretic Text reading, but there is no reason to prefer, prima facie, the Septuagint where it differs from the Masoretic Text, even when supported by a Qumran scroll. This is especially true because these texts are not early enough to supply improved readings for textual issues that arose before the third century BC. (He offers their lack of a good reading in 1 Sam 13:1 as one example of this.)

In my view, Archer's conclusion yields a working hypothesis for the present stage of research that is preferable to that of the Albright-Cross school. Archer's analysis and conclusion generally supports the analysis of Goslinga (1968:11-17). Goslinga considers Eyber's (1960) conclusions (which are similar to those of Archer) to be more balanced than those of Cross et al., although he cautions against any final judgments until the study of the Qumran material is complete. Fragments of the Qumran Scroll of 1–2 Samuel known as 4QSam[a] were published in 2001 (see Fincke), followed by the DJD publication in 2005 (see Cross). These materials from Qumran still require the long and tedious process of evaluation and analysis. In the meantime, it seems best to approach each textual problem in an unprejudiced way, evaluating any differing readings in the Qumran materials or the Septuagint on their own merits and on a case-by-case basis.

Goslinga (1968:15) has suggested the following helpful guidelines for handling the text of Samuel:

1. The Hebrew text of Samuel as it has been transmitted to us by the Masoretes is the object of our scholarly study (although the Masoretic pointing and annotations do not have the same authority as the consonants), and it is the task of exegesis to find its correct meaning.
2. In every place where the Masoretic Text yields a good and (in the context) acceptable meaning, exegesis must stick with that text.
3. Only where the Masoretic Text does not give a reasonable or acceptable sense is it necessary to attempt to restore a corrected, original text, with as little deviation as possible from the Masoretic Text and with the use of the ancient versions (especially the LXX), as the basis for exegetical work.
4. Only in very rare exceptions is it responsible to emend the transmitted text by means of conjecture. Precisely because it rests on a guess, one must be very cautious with conjectural criticism. It should be used only when all other means of establishment of the text have failed—yet it is not to be totally excluded.

More recently R. P. Gordon has advocated a similar approach as a working hypothesis for dealing with the text of Samuel. He says (1986:61), "The evidence as we have observed it encourages neither an attitude of Masoretic fundamentalism nor the wholesale adoption of every Qumran neologism. The practical implications for text critic and commentator alike are aptly summed up by Gooding: 'If the Masoretic text is not automatically to be regarded in any disputed case as representing the original, neither is the Septuagint, not even when it happens to be supported by some non-Masoretic Hebrew manuscript. One must judge each case on its merits.'"

On occasion the textual notes of this commentary will support the Masoretic Text even though the NLT has adopted the reading of the Septuagint, particularly when it is supported by materials from Qumran. In other cases, the NLT has given preference to "pluses" in the Septuagint when it appears that the "minuses" in the Masoretic Text are due to homoeoteleuton (a scribal error). Because analysis of the text of 1–2 Samuel is plagued by what someone has called the "head-breaking complexity of the textual data,"[24] it goes without saying that one must be extremely cautious in drawing conclusions on which reading is preferred. My own conclusions, as will be noticed in the notes on the text, have been heavily influenced by the analysis of the text of 1–2 Samuel by S. Pisano (1984). It is Pisano's contention that the vast majority of "pluses" in the Septuagint, the appearance of homoeoteleuton in the Masoretic Text notwithstanding, are nevertheless more properly assessed as additions to the original wording of the passage, which he finds retained in the Masoretic Text. In other words, in many cases, Pisano rejects the idea that the pluses in the Septuagint are to be judged as original because they have accidentally fallen out of the Masoretic Text. Pisano argues that this is also generally true of the pluses and minuses of 4QSam[a] in relation to the Masoretic Text. R. P. Gordon (1987:384) says that "Pisano has presented what is both a coherent case and a robust challenge to those in particular who have made so much of the LXX + 4QSam[a] coalition."

LITERARY STYLE

Structure. Recent decades have seen an important shift in the focus of the academic study of the literature of the Old Testament. Alongside the "source" and "form" criticism of the early part of the twentieth century that tended to fragment the text into either documentary strands or independent literary units there has developed a much greater interest in the unity and coherence of the final form of the text. This new focus centers on a type of literary analysis that in the broader field of the study of literature has generally been termed "literary criticism." J. Barton (1996:52) describes this sort of literary criticism (distinct from the source and form criticism characteristic of biblical studies) as "the attempt to give what is sometimes called a 'close reading' of the text, analyzing how the author/editor achieves his effects, why he arranges his material as he does, and above all what devices he uses to give unity and coherence to his work." In this type of analysis of Old Testament literature much attention is paid to matters of style, structure, and the aesthetic skill of the writer. Here the writer is taken seriously as the producer of a sophisticated work of literary art in which a wide variety of techniques are employed.[25]

This development is important because its main purpose is to focus on how the biblical text conveys ideas, and it is not intended as a "literary" study in the sense of merely formal analysis (Barton 1996:205). M. Sternberg (1985) and others have delineated some of the more prominent techniques and strategies employed by the authors of biblical narrative. Several stand out as rather common occurrences, including narrative structuring (including *inclusio* and chiasm), repetitions, narrative analogy, key words, wordplay, and irony.[26] As more and more interest has grown in giving attention to the use of these conventions in the composition of biblical narratives, the book of Samuel has drawn an enormous amount of attention. The reason for this is that 1–2 Samuel, both as a whole and in its parts, is widely recognized as a superb example of Hebrew prose.[27] A number of its individual narratives (e.g., David and Goliath; David and Bathsheba) are nearly universally known and have long been recognized as belonging to some of the best narrative writing in all of human literature. But these celebrated individual narratives are set in the larger narrative context of David's life and then beyond that in the still larger story of the rise of kingship in Israel; they can only be properly understood when they are not isolated from that larger context. Thus, recognition of narrative structure, both on a micro and macro level, becomes especially significant for competent reading of biblical narratives, including those of the book of Samuel.

Because of the enormous space requirements for a close reading of biblical narrative in commentary form, and because this type of analysis properly requires acquaintance with the Hebrew text, this commentary will not focus on the details of the literary analysis of 1–2 Samuel but rather on the book's major theological themes. Only in the most significant cases where the literary structures are pointers to the proper understanding of the text and its literary themes will this commentary draw attention to them.

One of the places where literary structure becomes quite important for understanding the larger coherence of the narrative flow in the books of Samuel was discussed briefly in the section on "Date and Occasion of Writing" above. I have made reference above to what has generally been considered the disruption of the Succession Narrative (2 Sam 9–20; 1 Kgs 1–2) by the collection of so-called miscellaneous appendices attached to the end of 2 Samuel (chs 21–24), which are more appropriately called the Samuel Conclusion. A six-part chiastic structure (*a-b-c-c-b-a*) in this section of 2 Samuel has long been recognized. In the first and last units (2 Sam 21:1-14; 24:1-25) God's judgment (famine and plague) falls on the people of Israel because of the sins of Saul (he put Gibeonites to death) and David (he took a census). The second and fifth units (2 Sam 21:15-22; 23:8-39) are two lists of David's warriors. At the center are two poetic units (2 Sam 22:1-51; 23:1-7): David's Song in Praise of God's Reign, and David's Last Words about His Reign. What has not been recognized until recently is how this structural arrangement may relate to structural arrangements found in other parts of the book. Klement's (2000) thorough examination of this question has produced some significant insights, not only into the structure of Samuel, but also into how the author has used structure to call attention to important theological themes.

Building on the work of Flanagan (1983) and Brueggemann (1988), Klement calls attention to a six-part chiastic structure in 2 Samuel 5:13–8:18 that is similar to that of what has usually been called "the Samuel Appendix." Here, too, the six literary units are arranged in an *a-b-c-c-b-a* structure. The first and last units (2 Sam 5:13-16; 8:15-18) contain two lists. The first is a list of the sons born to David in Jerusalem, and the second is a list of David's officials. The second and fifth units (2 Sam 5:17-25; 8:1-14) describe David's victories over the Philistines, and then over numerous neighboring nations. At the center are the two highly important narratives (2 Sam 6:1-23; 7:1-29) that tell of David's bringing the Ark of the Covenant to Jerusalem and of the Lord's promise of an eternal dynasty for David.

Klement then observes that the double lists of 2 Samuel 5–8 and the Appendix are not the only lists to be found in 2 Samuel. There is also a list of sons born to David in Hebron (2 Sam 3:1-5) as well as a second list of David's officials (2 Sam 20:23-26). This means that there are three double lists in 2 Samuel. These lists are of sons, of officials, and of warriors, all of whom would have been beneficiaries of a new order of society associated with David's royal court. When these lists are given a structuring function for 2 Samuel 3–20, a larger three-part structure appears (see chart on facing page).

In the first part of this larger structure, the *a-b-c-c-b-a* pattern is again found. The first and last units (2 Sam 3:1-5; 5:13-16) are formed by the lists of David's sons born in Hebron and Jerusalem. Between these two lists are four narrative units. The second and fifth units (2 Sam 3:6-21; 5:1-12) concern David's becoming king over all Israel, first in connection with a covenant made with Abner, and then later, after Ishbosheth's death, in connection with a covenant made with the elders of all Israel. At the center (2 Sam 3:22-39; 4:1-12) are the accounts of the murders of Abner and Ishbosheth, the two most important representatives of the remnant of Saul's kingdom. Here there seems to be an apologetic emphasis absolving David of any guilt or complicity in their deaths.

Just as the two lists of David's sons appear to serve a structuring function, so also do the two lists of David's officials. These lists frame material often associated with the so-called Succession Narrative. Here again an *a-b-c-c-b-a* pattern can be discerned. This is the third part of the larger structure of 2 Samuel 3–20. The first and last units (2 Sam 8:15-18; 20:23-26) are the lists of David's officials. The second and fifth units (2 Sam 9:1-13; 20:1-22) concern David's relationship with two members of the tribe of Benjamin (Saul's tribe): 2 Samuel 9:1-13 describes David's *khesed* toward Saul's son Mephibosheth, while 2 Samuel 20:1-22 describes the abortive coup of Sheba son of Bicri, a Benjamite. At the center are two larger blocks of material (2 Sam 10:1–12:31; 13:1–19:43 [44, MT]). The first of these deals with the Ammonite wars, and then the Bathsheba, Uriah, and Nathan incidents. The second deals with Absalom's rebellion and then the Tamar, Amnon, and Ahithophel incidents.

When all of this is put together, it suggests that the "Appendix" is not to be viewed as extraneous material improperly set in its present position, as has often been suggested,[28] nor is the structure of the Appendix to be viewed merely as a matter of aesthetics,[29] but rather as something that serves a structural function for the material preceding it in 2 Samuel 3–20. Thus it may rightly be called the "Samuel Conclusion." In this larger structure there are three chiastic centers: In the two outer centers, the murder of four important persons plays a dominant role. In the first of these there is the murder of Abner and Ishbosheth, and the loss of all official power by Saul's family. David is shown to be innocent of any involvement with these murders. In the second, we are told of the murder of Uriah and the subsequent chain of rape, fratricide, and murder involving Amnon and Absalom, and ultimately Abner and Amasa. David is directly involved only with the murder of Uriah, for which he receives divine forgiveness through repentance. But because of this sin, a series of dreadful consequences are brought upon David and his family. The middle chiastic center, standing at the most important place in the larger narrative complex, describes the bringing of the Ark to Jerusalem, and the promise of an eternal dynasty for David.

What emerges from this attention to literary structure is the following arrangement of literary units in which the six lists not only frame blocks of material but, in addition, display relationships between the individual units of the Appendix and the centers of each preceding chiasm.[30]

CENTRAL POINTS FROM 2 SAMUEL 3–20	UNITS IN THE APPENDIX (2 SAM 21–24)
3:2-5 List of sons	
3:6-21 David's kingship (covenant with Abner)	
3:22-39 Death of Abner	21:1-14 Death of Saul's sons
4:1-12 Death of Ishbosheth	
5:1-12 David's kingship (covenant with elders)	
5:13-16 List of sons	21:15-22 List of warriors (victors over the Philistines)
5:17-25 Victories over the Philistines	
6:1-23 Ark in Jerusalem	***22:1-51 Song of David: Yahweh's Kingdom***
7:1-29 Promise of the dynasty	***23:1-7 David's last words: David's kingdom***
8:1-14 Victories over all	
8:15-18 List of officials	23:8-39 List of warriors (all David's victors)
9:1-13 David's treatment of Mephibosheth	
10:1-12:31 Order to murder, adultery	24:1-25 Census as abuse of power, pestilence
13:1-19:43 Murder of Amnon, flight from Absalom	
20:1-22 David's treatment of Sheba	
20:23-26 List of officials	

The correspondence between the two poems of the Appendix (2 Sam 22:1-51; 23:1-7) and the central units of the central chiasm (2 Sam 6–7) is particularly striking. When 2 Samuel 22 is read "in conjunction with the account of the erection of the Ark sanctuary in Jerusalem, one notices that the psalm after the introduction of the Ark describes Yahweh's epiphany as he brings support to David. . . . In the same way the poetical text 2 Sam 23:1-7, in the centre of which is sung forth the eternal covenant of God with the house of David to reign in the justice and prosperity of God, has its corresponding narrative text in Nathan's prophecy in 2 Sam 7" (Klement 2000:84). Klement goes on to point out that the analogy between the two psalms in the Appendix and the two narratives in 2 Samuel 6–7 is heightened by the fact that they are both "flanked respectively by announcements of victory and the lists of victorious warriors" (2000:85). These findings suggest an intentional literary structuring of this material according to chiastic principles with the intent of accentuating the significance of the central units, particularly those of 2 Samuel 6–7 and 2 Samuel 22; 23:1-7.[31]

Working from the Appendix back toward the earlier sections of the book, Klement develops numerous additional structural insights that cannot be discussed here.[32] There is, however, one further structural feature of 1–2 Samuel that is important, and has long been noted. It is the clear correlation between the two poetic units at the end of the book (David's Song in Praise of God's Reign in 2 Sam 22, and David's

Last Words about His Reign in 2 Sam 23:1-7) and the poetic Song of Hannah (1 Sam 2:1-10) at the book's beginning.[33] These poetic units frame the entire book. In them are found a number of the major themes that flow through the various narratives of the book (see below under "Major Themes" and "Theological Concerns"). The reversal of fortune and the exaltation of the lowly as experienced by Hannah anticipates both the fall of Eli and the elevation of Samuel, Saul, and David from humble beginnings to positions of power and influence (1 Sam 2:4-8a). Hannah praises the Lord not only as creator (1 Sam 2:8b), but also as one who delivers from enemies (1 Sam 2:9-10a) and as one who will raise up his anointed king (1 Sam 2:10b). It is not by human strength that one prevails (1 Sam 2:9b), it is the Lord who exalts (1 Sam 2:1, 8, 10) and raises up (1 Sam 2:6, 8). David's Song in Praise of God's Reign (2 Sam 22) echoes similar themes. The Lord has delivered him from all his enemies (2 Sam 22:41, 44). It is the Lord who delivers the humble (2 Sam 22:28), and who has made David his anointed king (2 Sam 22:51). Radday (1974:31) concludes, "There is no need to stress that the basic ideas of Hanna's Prayer and David's Psalm are the same: Unshakable confidence in God, reward and punishment in this world, and the futility of power are the common denominator of both poems. Their difference in length is sufficiently warranted by the difference in social status of the speakers and in function: One is meant to be an anticipatory prologue, the other a recapitulative epilogue."

Historicity. One additional matter that demands our attention is the question of whether or not 1–2 Samuel should be considered historical writing, and if so, whether it is a reliable source of historical information. The historical value of 1–2 Samuel has long been a disputed issue. The older documentary source critics saw numerous doublets—for example, two, or even three, different stories of how Saul became king (1 Sam 9:1–10:16; 10:17-27; 11:14-15); two accounts of Samuel's rejection of Saul (1 Sam 13:8-14; 15:10-31); two stories about how David was introduced to Saul (1 Sam 16; 17); David twice escapes from the court of Saul (1 Sam 19:12; 21:1); Jonathan is twice convinced that David will become king (1 Sam 20:12-17; 23:16-18); two versions of how David spared Saul's life (1 Sam 24; 26); and David twice goes to Achish of Gath (1 Sam 21:10-15 [21:11-16, MT]; 27:2). These doublets were regarded as variant versions of the same events by the source critics. If this is a correct conclusion, then each of these multiple accounts of specific historical occurrences could not possibly contain a reliable report of what happened. Closely associated with the multiple source idea for the story of how Saul became king in 1 Samuel 8–12 was that idea that these sources reflected two different attitudes toward kingship. One source was said to be favorable toward the monarchy (1 Sam 9:1–10:16; 11), and another was said to be antagonistic toward the monarchy (1 Sam 8; 10:17-27; 12). The pro-monarchy source was considered early and more historically reliable than the anti-monarchy source, which was considered late and historically unreliable.[34] This approach to the literary analysis of 1–2 Samuel undermined its value as a source of reliable historical information.

Another characteristic of traditional source criticism was its close association with philosophical ideas growing out of Enlightenment thought in nineteenth-century Europe, including (1) the rejection of supernaturalism; (2) the idea that reason, not revelation, is the source of all truth; (3) the principle of the analogy of history (only what can be experientially or experimentally verified can be affirmed as having happened); and (4) an evolutionary worldview. These were powerful ideas, and when they were combined with a source-critical analysis of the historical narratives of the Old Testament, the result was an extreme skepticism concerning their historical worth. The sort of literary analysis governed by these principles automatically denied historicity to accounts that spoke of interventions of the Deity in human history, including God's providential direction of historical events, theophanies, and miracles. All occurrences for which one could not find analogous occurrences within one's own experience or horizon were denied historical worth.[35] It was said that narratives that tell about such things must of necessity be folktales or legends, rather than history writing, because these kinds of things simply do not happen.

Even when many scholars moved away from the documentary source view of the composition of Samuel to the idea that it was composed by the linkage of a number of large blocks of tradition units, the same rationalistic ideas concerning its historical value continued to be applied. Von Rad (1944:176) argued that the Succession Narrative identified by Rost (see above, "Date and Occasion of Writing") was the "oldest specimen of ancient Israelite historical writing." Quoting Schwartz, von Rad claimed that "genuinely historical writing which *faithfully represents its own era* always and invariably grows out of the political life of the day, whatever shape or form that may take" (my italics). He concluded (1944:192, 203) that the Succession Narrative had been composed during what he termed the "Solomonic Enlightenment" because in his view only "a political state which *makes* history can *write* history." He contrasted the literary character of the Succession Narrative, which he designated as "history writing" with the "sagas of heroes" that he found in Joshua, Judges, and sporadically in other parts of Samuel. While discussing the "hero saga" of Gideon and the divine intervention that brought him victory over the Midianites, von Rad (1944:174) says we need to recognize "that *this does not happen in historical writing,* where no sensational miracles are produced at the culmination of events, dropping as it were from heaven into a vacuum exhausted of all human activity" (my italics). Then he says (1944:201), "How different things look in this historical work [i.e., the Succession Narrative]! There is no miracle, and no charismatic leader appears. Events unwind themselves according to the laws of their own nature."[36]

Elsewhere in his writings, von Rad speaks of two kinds of history of Israel. There is *Historie* and there is *Heilsgeschichte. Historie* is what happened. *Heilsgeschichte* is what was confessed or believed. It is his view that the historical material of the Old Testament is, for the most part, *Heilsgeschichte,* rather than *Historie.* How much of Israel's history, in the sense of what actually happened, can be reconstructed from the source materials at our disposal is for von Rad a very dubious matter. This, however, does not unduly concern him, because in his view the real value of the Old Testament is not to be found in what happened, but rather in our identification with the kind of faith that comes to expression in Israel's "historical" writings. This, of course, raises serious questions about the nature of Israel's faith, as well as our own.

Before addressing the larger question of the relationship of faith and history from a biblical perspective, there is one further matter that deserves our attention. When the focus of literary analysis shifted from a diachronic form (how the text achieved its present shape, using source and form criticism) to a synchronic form (what literary strategies can be discerned in the final form of the text, using rhetorical criticism and close-reading techniques), the question of the historical reliability of biblical narratives did not disappear. One of the more prominent advocates of the literary approach to the analysis of Old Testament narrative is R. Alter. Unfortunately Alter does not regard the narrative material of the Old Testament as divine revelation, and he characterizes it as "historicized prose fiction."[37] He claims, "What the Bible offers us is an uneven continuum and a constant interweaving of actual historical detail (especially, but by no means exclusively, for the later periods) with purely legendary 'history'; occasional enigmatic vestiges of mythological lore; etiological stories; archetypal fictions of the founding fathers of the nation; folktales of heroes and wonder-working men of God; verisimilar inventions of wholly fictional personages attached to the progress of national history; and fictionalized versions of known historical figures. All of these narratives are presented as history, that is, as things that really happened and that have some significant consequence for human or Israelite destiny" (Alter 1981:24). Nevertheless, he says that the ancient Hebrew writers sought to utilize narrative to speak of "the enactment of God's purposes in historical events" (1981:33). Fiction is the principle means of doing this. With respect to 1–2 Samuel, he is of the opinion that the David stories may have a historical basis, but, "These stories are not, strictly speaking, historiography, but rather the imaginative reenactment of history by a gifted writer who organizes his materials along certain thematic biases and according to his own remarkable intuition of the psychology of the characters. . . . The author of the David stories stands in basically the same relation to Israelite history as Shakespeare stands to English history in his history plays" (1981:33). This sort of conclusion demonstrates that the move in Old Testament literary studies from a diachronic to a synchronic focus, which has sometimes been termed a paradigm shift, is more a reactive paradigm shift than a prime paradigm shift (Lee 1996). This is clearly the case because many of the practitioners of the new approach still start with some of the same ideas of the older approach that made it impossible to deal with the totality of the Old Testament as divine revelation in a holistic way.

So to return to our question concerning whether or not 1–2 Samuel should be considered historical writing, it becomes clear that this question cannot be answered simply by looking at the literary form of the narrative material. While the many references to chronological sequences, geographical locations, historical causation of various sorts, and historical personalities (both Israelite and non-Israelite) that are embedded in the narrative would seem to suggest a historiographical intent, it might be argued that fictional stories can mimic historical discourse by including these same features. The reasons normally advanced for denying historicity to the narratives of 1–2 Samuel, however, are not literary but philosophical in nature. The Bible presents itself as a written communication of God to people, mediated through human authors, and inspired by God's Holy Spirit. In this communication God tells his people how he has intervened in human history to implement his great plan of redemption for fallen humanity. That plan of redemption climaxed with the coming of Jesus Christ, the Son of David, into the world. The narratives of 1–2 Samuel inform us about some of the important steps along the way in the realization of this great plan of redemption. Neither the artful literary style in which these narratives are cast,[38] nor the theological perspectives that shape their outlook on human history negates their character as narratives that tell us about *things that happened.* When the events recorded in 1–2 Samuel are dehistoricized, by whatever means, they lose the significance that the Bible itself attributes to them by virtue of their presence and function in the onward movement of redemptive history.[39]

Before leaving the topic of the historical character of the narratives of 1–2 Samuel, one additional matter requires some comment. In the 1990s two important debates arose in the general field of Old Testament studies, both of which have significant implications for the assessment of the historical trustworthiness of the narratives of 1–2 Samuel.[40] These two debates have come to be known as the "minimalist-maximalist" debate, and the "tenth-century" debate. Davies, whose book *In Search of Ancient Israel* (1992) sparked the ongoing "minimalist-maximalist" controversy, considered what he termed "biblical Israel" (i.e., the Israel depicted in the narratives of the Old Testament) to be an "ideological construct" of Persian and Hellenistic times.[41] This would mean that the narratives of 1–2 Samuel, along with all the other narrative material of the Old Testament, should be regarded as fictitious inventions of a much later time, and not as a credible source of historical information. In the view of the "minimalists," the "interpretation of biblical texts should be 'liberated from historical considerations.' It should proceed strictly on the basis of literary analysis of the Bible's 'stories,' which reveal mainly the 'self-perception' of the narrators" (Dever 1998:41). For this reason, Davies, along with others who generally share his perspective (see Lemche 1998; T. L. Thompson 1999; Whitelam 1996), maintains that the biblical narrative should be set aside when attempting to create an authentic history of Israel.[42]

The result has been that scholars of this persuasion have replaced the literary testimony of the Bible with the testimony of various sorts of sociological, anthropological, and archaeological models in their search for "historical Israel" (see Long 1999:157). According to Davies (1992:65), the united kingdom of David and Solomon as described in the Old Testament "exists exclusively in the biblical literature and the biblical scholarship dependent on it" and therefore it is a "theoretical" kingdom rather than an actual kingdom. This conclusion is based on a number of things, including philosophical ideas about the nature of historiography, a postmodern, deconstructionist approach to the reading and interpretation of historical texts,[43] the absence of corroborating extrabiblical references or archaeological findings directly connected with the time of David, and the late dating of the entirety of the Old Testament. Davies (1992:64) says, "The biblical 'empire' of David and Solomon has not the faintest echo in the archaeological record—as yet . . . the elaborate administration ascribed to David in the biblical literature is impossible at that stage . . . the failure as yet to establish archaeologically the history of Jerusalem in the Iron Age is troublesome."

It is here that the "tenth-century debate" intersects with the "minimalist-maximalist" debate in questioning the existence of a united kingdom in Israel under David and Solomon. The "tenth-century" debate was sparked by Israel Finkelstein's claim (1996, 1998, 2001) that the monumental architecture (city waterworks, walls, palaces, and temples) found at such Iron Age sites as Beersheba, Dan, Hazor, Jerusalem and Megiddo are to be dated in the middle of the ninth century BC (the time of Ahab) rather than in the tenth century BC (the time of David and Solomon). Finkelstein's argument rests on his conclusion that a certain type of pottery (hand-burnished red slipware) that is associated with monumental architecture is to be dated exclusively to the ninth century. Finkelstein's position means that "construction projects assigned to David, Solomon, Rehoboam, and Jeroboam in the tenth century on the basis of the established chronology and on the strength of Biblical accounts of their building activities, projects that infer the presence of significant economic resources, a labor pool supportable by an economy greater than subsistence level, and an organized, central administration, are dated incorrectly. The projects could only have been undertaken by kings living no less than 50 years after the death of Solomon" (Zevit 2002:22). Finkelstein's revisionist chronology, however, has not gone unchallenged (see A. Mazar 1997; Mazar and Camp 2000), and it seems unlikely that in the long term his conclusions will survive the careful scrutiny of the archaeological community as a whole. Detailed discussion of the issues raised in these two debates cannot be addressed in the confines of this introduction. These issues are, however, thoroughly discussed in a competent manner by Kitchen in his book *On the Reliability of the Old Testament* (2003) and by Provan, Long, and Longman in their book *A Biblical History of Israel* (2003). These two books provide ample justification for continuing to regard the narratives of the Old Testament, including the narratives of 1–2 Samuel, as reliable sources of historical information.[44]

MAJOR THEMES

As was noted in the previous section ("Literary Style"), the major themes of 1–2 Samuel are highlighted in the three poetic accounts that frame the book (The Song of Hannah, 1 Sam 2:1-10; David's Song in Praise of God's Reign, 2 Sam 22; and David's Last Words about His Reign, 2 Sam 23:1-7). The most basic of these themes is *divine sovereignty* over all of human history. These three poems affirm that the Lord governs all the affairs of every individual life as well as those of the nation. It is the Lord who exalts, and it is the Lord who brings low. Closely linked with the theme of divine sovereignty is the theme of *the rise of kingship* in Israel. This is also the Lord's doing. Kingship is anticipated in the Song of Hannah (1 Sam 2:10) and celebrated in David's Song in Praise of God's Reign (2 Sam 22:51) and David's Last Words about His Reign (2 Sam 23:1, 5). David himself is presented as the "man anointed by the God of Jacob" (2 Sam 23:1). He is the one who says, "Is it not my family God has chosen? Yes, he has made an everlasting covenant with me. His agreement is arranged and guaranteed in every detail. He will ensure my safety and success" (2 Sam 23:5). These two themes are complemented by a third, related theme, that of *the reversal of fortunes*. It is customary for the Lord to bless the humble and raise them up, and to judge the proud and bring them down (1 Sam 2:5-10; 2 Sam 22:28; 23:1, 6).

These three major themes are fleshed out in the lives and events that make up the plotline of 1–2 Samuel. That plotline begins with a reversal of fortune for the barren Hannah, who prayed for a son whom she would devote to the Lord. The Lord granted her request and exalted her above Peninnah (1 Sam 1). Her son Samuel was called by the Lord to be a prophet (1 Sam 3), and it was he who became the human instrument the Lord used to establish kingship in Israel (1 Sam 8–12). Samuel defined kingship in covenantal terms (1 Sam 10:25) and then inaugurated Saul at a ceremony in which the people simultaneously renewed their allegiance to the Lord, who was their divine king—thus incorporating human kingship into the structure of the theocracy (1 Sam 11:14–12:25). When Saul, the first king, demonstrated that he was unwilling to exercise his kingship in subordination to the word of the prophet and law of the Lord, he was rejected as king (1 Sam 13, 15). The Lord then instructed Samuel to anoint David as a replacement for Saul (1 Sam 16). After David went through a long period of testing in which he showed himself to be faithful to the Lord (1 Sam 17–31), he was crowned as king, first of Judah (2 Sam 2), and then of the entire nation (2 Sam 5). David established Jerusalem as his capital city and brought the Ark there as a clear sign that he continued to recognize the Lord as the true sovereign of the nation (2 Sam 5–6). God promised David that his dynasty would endure forever, and that his dynasty would not be terminated as Saul's was (2 Sam 7). In his long reign David showed himself to be a true, although flawed, representative of the ideal of the true covenantal king. Although he sinned grievously in the matter of Bathsheba and Uriah, he also repented when he was confronted by Nathan the prophet (2 Sam 11–12). As a result, he was punished but not rejected as king.

Along the way, there are other reversals, including the rejection of Eli's sons as priests (1 Sam 2:12-36), and the Israelite defeat by the Philistines combined with the loss of the Ark (1 Sam 4–5). In all these events, God moved his program of redemption forward. The linkage of the kingship in Israel to the line of David lays the groundwork for the messianic expectation of subsequent revelation. It is only when the greater son of David sits on David's throne that the covenantal ideal of kingship will be realized in all of its fullness.

THEOLOGICAL CONCERNS

The theological concerns that come to expression in 1–2 Samuel are closely associated with the dominant themes discussed in the previous section. These theological concerns can be summarized under three headings: (1) the Deuteronomic outlook; (2) a lofty concept of God that acclaims divine sovereignty; (3) kingship and covenant (see Vannoy 1996).

The Deuteronomic Outlook. The theological outlook of Deuteronomy provides a "point of view" for the historiography of all the books from Joshua to 2 Kings, including 1–2 Samuel. Because these books, in varying degrees, reflect this particular theological outlook, which some scholars regard as having been secondarily imposed on older materials, their historical credibility has often been questioned. It should be understood, however, that a narrative's theological orientation is not in itself an adequate reason for questioning its historical reliability, because all worthwhile history writing must be governed by some well-defined point of view. If this were not the case, the author/historian would have no basis for selecting, organizing, and disclosing the significance of the events about which he speaks. For this reason, there is no such thing as purely objective or neutral historical writing. Historical writing is inherently interpretive. There may be reliable and unreliable historiography, but in the final analysis, all history writing must be based in some "point of view." The theological perspectives that both structurally and conceptually come to expression in Deuteronomy are the governing "point of view" for 1–2 Samuel. Deuteronomy has aptly been called the "Treaty of the Great King" with its form and content reflecting the international treaties of the Hittite empire (Kline 1963). These treaties describe the benevolent actions of the Great King on behalf of his vassal, and then place certain specified obligations on that vassal, which are accompanied by blessing and curse sanctions. In Israel the Great King is Yahweh, who has delivered his people from Egyptian bondage and called them to a life of obedience to the clearly specified demands of the Sinai covenant.

A Lofty Concept of God That Acclaims Divine Sovereignty. Here, again, the three poetic units that frame the book (The Song of Hannah, 1 Sam 2:1-10; David's Song in Praise of God's Reign, 2 Sam 22; David's Last Words about His Reign, 2 Sam 23:1-7) are particularly important. The reason for this is that the poems are more naturally given to explicit theological assertions than are the narrative sections of the book. Among the significant affirmations made about God in these three poetic units are the following: (1) *There is only one God, namely the LORD God of Israel* (1 Sam 2:2, "There is no one besides you"; 2 Sam 22:32, "For who is God except the LORD?"); (2) *This God has spoken, and his word is true* (2 Sam 22:31, "God's way is perfect. All the LORD's promises prove true"; 2 Sam 23:2-3a, "The Spirit of the LORD speaks through me; his words are upon my tongue. The God of Israel spoke, The Rock of Israel said to me"); (3) *The LORD God of Israel is sovereign over all things* (1 Sam 2:6-10, "The LORD gives both death and life. . . . The LORD makes some poor and others rich; he brings some down and lifts others up"; 2 Sam 22:33-46, "God is my strong fortress, and he makes my way perfect. . . . He trains my hands for battle; he strengthens my arm. . . . You have subdued my enemies under my feet. . . . You gave me victory over my accusers"); (4) *The LORD is a Rock, a place of refuge and security for those who trust in him* (1 Sam 2:2, "There is no Rock like our God"; 2 Sam 22:2-3, 32, 47, "The LORD is my rock, my fortress, and my savior; my God is my rock, in whom I find protection. . . . Who but our God is a solid rock? . . . The LORD lives! Praise to my Rock! May God, the Rock of my salvation, be exalted!"; 2 Sam 23:3, "The Rock of Israel").

These statements, when combined with scattered comments of either the narrator or participants in the dialogues of the book, clearly convey the idea that everything that happens in individual lives, as well as in the life of the nation, is under the sovereign control of Israel's God.[45] In addition to explicit assertions of this premise, there are also implicit examples of its reality embedded in the narratives themselves. One example is the incident in which Saul's forces were just about to discover David's hiding place when "an urgent message reached Saul that the Philistines were raiding Israel again. So Saul quit chasing David and returned to fight the Philistines"

(1 Sam 23:26-28). In context, the timing of this diversion of Saul can hardly be viewed as coincidence. God was sovereignly ordering events to protect David from capture by his enemy.

Although God is characterized as sovereign over all of history, he is not portrayed as an impersonal, fatelike force. The narratives of 1–2 Samuel depict a God who repeatedly responds to the needs and concerns of his people. He is forgiving and gracious toward those who truly seek him with all their heart and are repentant for their sins. But he also disciplines and punishes those who rebel against his commands and show no true repentance. In 2 Samuel 24, when the prophet Gad gives David three options for punishment after his sin in the matter of the census taking, David says, "Let us fall into the hands of the LORD, for his mercy is great. Do not let me fall into human hands" (2 Sam 24:14). Later, in this same chapter, we are told, "As the angel was preparing to destroy Jerusalem, the LORD relented and said to the death angel, 'Stop! That is enough!'" (2 Sam 24:16). So God is merciful, even in judgment. He is a personal God, not an unmoved mover, although this does not mean he is permissive or lax. When Saul refused to obey the Lord's command to completely destroy the Amalekites along with all their cattle and then attempted to justify his behavior by shifting the blame to his soldiers, saying that his troops had kept some of the better cattle for sacrifices, the Lord spoke through Samuel: "Because you have rejected the command of the LORD, he has rejected you as king" (1 Sam 15:23).

The narratives of 1–2 Samuel also tell us, although not in the neat formulations of systematic theology, that while God's sovereignty extends to all human actions (both good and evil), this neither annuls human responsibility nor invalidates God's justice or holiness. It seems clear that the narrator understands that in whatever way the notions of divine sovereignty and human responsibility may be defined and correlated, ultimately they are not inconsistent. God is the sovereign ruler of the universe, including all that comes to pass in human history, yet human beings are consistently held accountable for their actions (cf. e.g., Eli, who was held responsible for the evils practiced at the Tabernacle during the time of his priesthood [1 Sam 2:12-36; 3:11-14]; Saul, who was held responsible for his rejection of the word of the Lord [1 Sam 13:13-14; 15:11-26]; David, who was held responsible for his actions in the incident with Bathsheba [2 Sam 12:7-11]).[46]

Kingship and Covenant. Subservient to the overarching perspective of God's sovereignty and the human responsibility of responding in faith and obedience to his revealed will, the interface of the themes of kingship and covenant is also woven into 1–2 Samuel's account of Israel's history. The interrelationship of these two concepts provides the conceptual framework for understanding the significance of the many events described in the book. A number of subthemes are integrated into the design of 1–2 Samuel by virtue of their connection to these major themes of kingship and covenant. Among the most important of these subthemes are the role of the prophet in relation to the king, the significance of the Ark, and the Davidic covenant and its messianic implications.

When the narrative flow of 1–2 Samuel is viewed from the perspective of the concepts of kingship and covenant, the book can be divided into four distinct blocks of material:

1. Kingship as requested by the people was a denial of the covenant (1 Sam 1–8). The first seven chapters of 1 Samuel provide the background and context for Israel's request for a king in 1 Samuel 8. Chapters 1–3 tell of the birth of Samuel and his call to be a prophet and leader of Israel. Israel's loss of the Ark of the Covenant and its subsequent return (1 Sam 4–6) demonstrate that while God could not be manipulated by his own unfaithful people carrying the Ark into battle, neither would he permit the Philistines to think that Dagon was more powerful than the God of Israel. After the return of the Ark to Israel, Samuel led the people in a confession of their sin that, in turn, resulted in the Lord giving them a great victory over the Philistines (1 Sam 7). So when the elders of Israel asked for a king shortly thereafter (1 Sam 8), to "judge us and lead us into battle" (1 Sam 8:20), Samuel was very displeased (1 Sam 8:6). But the Lord told Samuel that even though their request effectively rejected God's kingship (1 Sam 8:7), Samuel was to give them a king (1 Sam 8:9, 22). Although Samuel warned the people (1 Sam 8:9-18) about what a king like those of "the nations around us" (1 Sam 8:20) would be like, they persisted in their demand to be given a king. First Samuel 8, then, makes it very clear that the people of Israel wanted the wrong kind of king for the wrong reasons. The Lord was their Great King. He had promised his people security and victory over their enemies if they were faithful to their covenant obligations (Exod 23:22; 34:11; Deut 20:1-4). He had demonstrated his steadfast covenant faithfulness in giving them a recent victory over the Philistines (1 Sam 7) just as he had throughout the period of the judges (Judg 2:11-19; cf. 1 Sam 12:6-12). But evidently the repeated demonstration of Yahweh's faithfulness to his promises was not sufficient for the Israelites. They wanted a human ruler. They wanted to be like the neighboring nations with an earthly king to fight their battles and to provide them with a visible symbol of national unity and security. Unfortunately this desire was, at the same time, a rejection of the Lord, who was their king.

2. Kingship as given by Samuel was consistent with the covenant (1 Sam 9–12). The people had sinned in requesting a king (1 Sam 10:19; 12:17, 19), but God said a monarchy would be established in Israel nevertheless (1 Sam 8:9, 22; 9:16; 10:1). Certainly kingship in itself was not wrong for Israel, and, in fact, had been anticipated in previous revelation (cf. Gen 17:6; 49:10; Num 24:17; and especially Deut 17:14-20). After Samuel, in accordance with the Lord's instructions, had anointed Saul privately (1 Sam 9:1–10:16), he called all Israel to an assembly at Mizpah (1 Sam 10:17-27), where Saul was selected publicly by lot. Samuel then clearly defined the role and responsibilities for an Israelite king (1 Sam 10:25). After Saul's choice as king was confirmed by his leading Israel to victory over the Ammonites (1 Sam 11:1-13), Samuel called for an assembly at Gilgal where he presided over the inauguration of Saul's reign at a public ceremony that at the same time renewed Israel's covenant with the Lord (1 Sam 11:14–12:25). At the occasion, Samuel made it clear that even though human kingship was now being incorporated into the structure of the theocracy, in accordance with the Lord's command (1 Sam 12:12-15), this in no way annulled the responsibility of either the people or the newly installed king to continue to recognize the Lord as their ultimate sovereign (1 Sam 12:20, 24, 25). Kingship in Israel was to function in a way that was consistent with the Mosaic covenant, in which the Lord was Israel's Great King.

3. The kingship of Saul failed to correspond to the covenantal ideal (1 Sam 13–31). Saul quickly demonstrated that he was not prepared to submit to the requirements of covenantal kingship. When the Philistines gathered to attack Israel, Saul did not wait for Samuel, as he had been instructed, but instead offered a sacrifice himself (1 Sam 13:8; cf. 1 Sam 10:8). Because of this disobedience to the word of a prophet, Samuel confronted him, saying, "How foolish! . . . You have not kept the command the LORD your God gave you" (1 Sam 13:13). Later, after Samuel had instructed Saul to completely destroy the Amalekites and everything that belonged to them, Saul spared their king, Agag, along with the best of the plunder from the battle (1 Sam 15:9, 18). Samuel, thereupon, again confronted Saul: "Because you have rejected the command of the LORD, he has rejected you as king" (1 Sam 15:23). So Saul rebelled against the Lord (1 Sam 15:23) and failed to rule in a way consistent with the requirements of a covenantal king.

4. The kingship of David was an imperfect but true representation of the covenantal ideal (1 Sam 16–2 Sam 24). David's reign is described in great detail in 2 Samuel 2–24. The climax of these narratives comes in 2 Samuel 7 where Nathan the prophet tells David, "Your house and your kingdom will continue before [God] for all time, and your throne will be secure forever" (2 Sam 7:16). This promise of an enduring dynasty for David carried forward the promise made centuries earlier to Abraham, and confirmed to Isaac and Jacob, that through his offspring "all the nations of the earth will be blessed" (Gen 12:3; 18:18; 22:18; 26:4; 28:14). Ultimately, these promises find their roots in the statement of Genesis 3:15 that the offspring of the woman would crush the head of the serpent. In 2 Samuel 7 it becomes clear that this promised offspring will arise from among the descendants of David and sit on the royal throne.

In view of this promise, it is surprising that David is not presented in the narratives of 2 Samuel as a king whose reign perfectly conformed to the covenantal ideal. David sinned in treacherous ways with Bathsheba and Uriah (2 Sam 11). He betrayed his reliance on military might rather than trust in the Lord when he took a census of his army later in his reign (2 Sam 24). David is clearly not a perfect example of the covenantal king. But in contrast to Saul's case, the Lord was merciful to David and promised him an eternal dynasty. The question arises, "Why did God treat these two sinful men so differently?" The answer lies in the general pattern of covenant consistency or inconsistency reflected in their lives, as well as in the character of their attitudes after they had sinned. When Saul sinned he made excuses and tried to justify his actions (1 Sam 13:12; 15:15, 21, 24). When David sinned he confessed the error of his ways and repented ("I have sinned against the LORD," 2 Sam 12:13; cf. 2 Sam 24:10, 17). It is for this reason that David is termed a "man after [God's] own heart" (1 Sam 13:14; Acts 13:22). It was David's desire to serve the Lord faithfully, even though his obedience was far from perfect.[47]

David himself described the covenantal ideal for kingship in words given to him by God: "The Rock of Israel said to me: 'The one who rules righteously, who rules in the fear of God, is like the light of morning at sunrise, like a morning without clouds, like the gleaming of the sun on new grass after rain'" (2 Sam 23:3-4). And in spite of his flaws, the narrator tells us, "David . . . did what was just and right for all his people" (2 Sam 8:15). His reign became the standard by which all the subsequent kings of Israel were measured (cf. e.g., 1 Kgs 9:4; 11:33, 38; 15:11; 2 Kgs 14:3; 16:2).

Perhaps the key to best understanding the difference between David and Saul is found in 2 Samuel 22:21-23 where David says "I have kept the ways of the LORD" and "I have not turned from my God to follow evil. I have followed all his regulations." One might wonder how David could make these statements when it is clear that David's obedience was not perfect, and that he "despised the word of the LORD" by doing a "horrible deed"—nothing less than murder and adultery (2 Sam 12:9). It would thus appear that David's claim in 2 Samuel 22 is not that his life was completely perfect, but rather that his life, in general, was characterized by a fervent desire to serve the Lord and be faithful to the covenant. His "innocence" (2 Sam 22:21, 25) and his "[keeping] the ways of the LORD" (2 Sam 22:22) were not exhaustive or absolute in scope, but they were appreciable. The general pattern of his life reflected covenant faithfulness rather than unfaithfulness. When he sinned, he was quick to repent. David affirmed that "to the faithful you [the LORD] show yourself faithful" (2 Sam 22:26), and that "you [the LORD] rescue the humble" (2 Sam 22:28). He clearly viewed himself as included among the "faithful" and the "humble." It is in these traits that David truly, although imperfectly, exemplifies the ideal of the covenantal king (see commentary on 2 Sam 22).

As mentioned above, the broader theme of kingship and covenant provides a context wherein a number of subthemes come into view. These are the role of the prophet in relation to the king, the significance of the Ark, and the Davidic covenant and its messianic implications.

The Role of the Prophet. The narratives of 1–2 Samuel contribute in a significant way to our understanding of the role of the prophet in ancient Israel. The early chapters of 1–2 Samuel tell of Samuel's birth (1 Sam 1–2) and his call to be a prophet (1 Sam 3). These narratives prepare the way for Samuel's role in the establishment of the monarchy. In the account of Samuel's childhood, we are told that "in those days messages from the LORD were very rare" (1 Sam 3:1). As Samuel becomes a young man, we are told that "all Israel . . . knew that Samuel was confirmed as a prophet of the LORD" (1 Sam 3:20). Samuel's prophetic credentials were used by the Lord in anointing Saul as Israel's first king (1 Sam 9:1–10:16). This meant that kingship was never autonomous in Israel. Israel's kingship was established by the word of a prophet, and from its inception onward was strictly limited in its authority. The king in Israel was required to submit to the laws of the Sinai covenant as well as to the Lord's word through his prophet. This requirement of submission to the word of the prophet was clearly stated at the time of Saul's inauguration, when Samuel told the king and the assembled people that he would continue to teach them "what is good and right" (1 Sam 12:23). When Saul subsequently and repeatedly disobeyed the word of the Lord given by Samuel, he was confronted by Samuel and rejected as king (1 Sam 13, 15). The Lord then sent Samuel to anoint David as his replacement (1 Sam 16).

From the early narratives in 1–2 Samuel we find that at the time of the establishment of kingship in Israel, a foundation was laid upon which the work of Israel's ensuing prophets would rest. During all of Israel's history, there were always prophets who were not fearful of calling the kings of Israel and Judah to account when they went astray from the covenant. The reason for this was that the Lord had used a prophet to establish kingship.[48] So from the very beginning of the monarchy the prophets were invested with divine authority to hold Israel's kings accountable to the covenant. To a large degree the prophets functioned as messengers of the covenant. They constantly called both the king and people to covenant faithfulness, even though for many of the prophets, their specific focus was primarily on the king. The reason for the prophet's special attention to the kings was that the prophets were the guardians of the theocracy, and they often, although not always, functioned at its center—that is, at the royal court.

The Significance of the Ark. In addition to the narratives describing the lives of Samuel, Saul, and David, there are a group of narratives in 1–2 Samuel that focus on the Ark of the Covenant (1 Sam 4–6; 2 Sam 6). Instructions for the building of the Ark are recorded in Exodus 25:10-22. It had a lid of solid gold, and at each end was a golden cherub. The Lord told Moses that he would meet with him from the space above the lid of the Ark between the two cherubim, and from this place he would give Moses commandments for Israel (Exod 25:22). Subsequently, the Ark held the two tablets of the Decalogue (Exod 25:16, 21; 40:20; Deut 10:5), the law of the divine king. Because of the close identification of the Ark with the presence of God among his people, he was said to be "enthroned between the cherubim" (1 Sam 4:4; 2 Sam 6:2). This phrase suggests that the Lord reigned over his people as divine king from the throne seat provided by the Ark (see note on 4:4 and the commentary on 1 Sam 4, endnote 2).

Because of the close identification of the Ark with God's presence (cf. e.g., the role it played at the crossing of the Jordan [Josh 3–4] and the fall of Jericho [Josh 6]), it is not surprising that the elders requested that the Ark be brought to the battlefield after the Israelites had been defeated by the Philistines (1 Sam 4). It was their thought that the presence of the Ark would ensure God's presence and would therefore ensure victory in battle. To their great surprise and dismay, they were again defeated by the Philistines, and, worst of all, the Ark was captured. When the Philistines placed the Ark in the temple of their god, Dagon, at Ashdod, they found on the next day that the image of their deity had fallen to the floor and was broken in pieces before the Ark of the Lord (1 Sam 5). In addition, a plague of tumors broke out among the people of the city. When the Ark was moved to other cities, the same tumors appeared among their inhabitants. Eventually the Philistines were forced to send the Ark back to Israel, where it remained for 20 years in the house of Abinadab (1 Sam 6:1–7:2). In these narratives it becomes clear that while the Lord would not permit his people to manipulate the symbol of his presence to gain victory over the Philistines, neither would he permit the Philistines to conclude that because they had defeated the Israelites, their god, Dagon, was more powerful than the God of Israel.

The Ark remained in obscurity during the reign of Saul. It was not until David was made king that the Ark was returned to its rightful place at the political and religious center of the nation. David brought the Ark to his capital city, Jerusalem

(2 Sam 6). In so doing he was recognizing, in a very public way, that the nation's ultimate sovereign was the Lord, who sat "enthroned between the cherubim," and that his own kingship was subordinate to that of the Lord. This is the perspective of a true covenantal king.

When, in his later years, David was driven from Jerusalem by the revolution led by his son, Absalom, the priests brought the Ark along when they fled from the city. But David instructed Zadok the priest to "take the Ark of God back into the city. 'If the LORD sees fit . . . he will bring me back to see the Ark and the Tabernacle again. But if he is through with me, then let him do what seems best to him'" (2 Sam 15:25-26). David recognized the true significance of the Ark as a symbol of the presence and power of the Great King of Israel. He knew that possession of the Ark was not an automatic guarantee of the Lord's blessing. He also understood that it was fitting for the Ark to remain in Jerusalem, because, in the final analysis, the Lord was the true sovereign of the land.

The Davidic Covenant and Its Messianic Implications. Perhaps the most significant theological feature of 1–2 Samuel is its contribution to the development of the messianic idea in Scripture.[49] Early in the book, "anointing" is associated with kingship for the first time in the Old Testament (1 Sam 2:10b, 35; 9:16; 10:1; 12:3; 16:3, 6; 24:6, 10; 26:9, 11, 16, 23; 2 Sam 1:14, 16, 21; 19:21; 22:51; 23:1).[50] In order to understand the connection between "anointing" and the "messianic idea" it is necessary to know that the English term "Messiah" is simply a transliteration of the Hebrew noun *mashiakh* [TH4899, ZH5431] meaning "anointed one."[51] When the use of this terminology is traced into the New Testament, we find that the term *christos* [TG5547, ZG5986] (Christ), also meaning "anointed one," is the Greek equivalent for the Hebrew "Messiah." The expression "the LORD's anointed" is used so frequently in 1–2 Samuel that it nearly becomes synonymous with the word "king." Although the technical sense of "Messiah" as an "ideal king of the future" did not emerge until later in Israel's history, the foundation for its usage lies in the association of anointing with kingship that is first introduced in 1 Samuel.

Along with the introduction of "messianic" terminology, 1–2 Samuel also contains the announcement of the Davidic covenant (2 Sam 7; 23:5). This covenant was the promise that the Lord gave to David through Nathan the prophet that his dynasty would endure forever (2 Sam 7:16). David designated this promise "an *everlasting covenant*" (2 Sam 23:5, my italics), and it is termed a "covenant" in Psalm 89 as well: "I will love him and be kind to him forever; my *covenant* with him will never end. I will preserve an heir for him; his throne will be as endless as the days of heaven. . . . No, I will not break my *covenant;* . . . I have sworn an oath to David, and in my holiness I cannot lie: His dynasty will go on forever" (Ps 89:28-29, 34-37, my italics).

It is the Davidic covenant that provides the framework for the flow of redemptive history from the old covenant (the Sinai covenant) to the new covenant. The Davidic covenant is often termed a "promissory covenant" and placed in sequence with the Abrahamic covenant, which was also promissory in its basic thrust. The center of the Abrahamic promise was the pledge that Abraham would have a descendant through whom "all the families on earth will be blessed" (Gen 12:3; 18:18; 22:18; 26:4; 28:14; cf. Gal 3:8). The Abrahamic and Davidic covenants have also sometimes been termed "unconditional" covenants because of their promissory nature, and then contrasted with the Sinai covenant, which is viewed as a "law covenant" and considered "conditional" in nature. The terms "promissory" and "unconditional" as applied to the Abrahamic and Davidic covenants and the terms "law" and "conditional" as applied to the Sinai covenant certainly have some validity as indicators of the primary emphasis found in each of these covenants. Yet it must be noticed that the Sinai or "law" covenant is not completely without a promissory element (cf. Judg 2:1; 1 Sam 12:22), and the promissory nature of the Abrahamic and Davidic covenants does not mean that they entail no law or obligation (cf. Gen 12:1; 17:1; 2 Sam 7:14-15; 1 Kgs 2:4; 8:25; 9:4, 5; Ps 89:30-33). From these texts it is clear that both the Abrahamic and Davidic covenants brought obligations on those to whom the promise was given. In the Davidic covenant it seems clear that the conditionality referred to in the above texts pertains to individual participation in the promised blessings, but not to the certainty of the fulfillment of the promise itself. Here it becomes clear that the Davidic covenant is not only an extension of the Abrahamic promise, but it is also entwined with the Sinai covenant in connection with individual participation in its benefits. Failure to live up to these obligations would invalidate the benefits of the covenant to the person involved (cf. Jer 22:30), but it would not jeopardize the ultimate fulfillment of the promise through the line of Abraham and David.

A survey of Israel's subsequent history reveals that David's descendants (not to mention the line of kings in the northern kingdom) failed more miserably than David had in living up to the ideal of the covenantal king. As it became increasingly apparent that the Davidic kings were unworthy of the high office to which they were called, the prophets and psalmists of Israel began to speak of a future king who would come in the line of David—one who would be a worthy occupant of his throne. The surprising thing about this future king is that he is not only spoken of as a descendant of David, but he is also spoken of in terms of deity (see, e.g., Pss 2; 45; 72; 110; Isa 7:14; 9:6-7; Jer 23:5, 6; 33:15, 16; Mic 5:2). Unblemished covenantal kingship would only be completely realized when God himself entered human history in the person of Jesus, to sit on the throne of his father David (humanly speaking) and to rule in righteousness and justice forever (Matt 1; Luke 1:32-33, 67-80; Rev 22:16).

OUTLINE

I. The Historical Setting for the Establishment of Kingship in Israel (1 Sam 1:1–7:17)
- A. Samuel's Birth; Judgment Pronounced on the Elides; Samuel Becomes a Prophet (1 Sam 1:1–4:1a)
  1. Samuel's birth (1 Sam 1:1-28)
     - a. Elkanah's family (1 Sam 1:1-3)
     - b. Hannah's sorrow (1 Sam 1:4-8)
     - c. Hannah's vow (1 Sam 1:9-11)
     - d. Hannah and Eli (1 Sam 1:12-18)
     - e. Samuel's birth (1 Sam 1:19-23)
     - f. Hannah presents Samuel to the Lord at Shiloh (1 Sam 1:24-28)

   2. The Song of Hannah (1 Sam 2:1-10)
   3. Samuel serves the Lord in Shiloh; judgment pronounced on the house of Eli (1 Sam 2:11-36)
   4. Samuel called to be a prophet (1 Sam 3:1–4:1a)
  B. Judgment on the Elides; the Ark of the Covenant Captured and Returned by the Philistines (1 Sam 4:1b–7:1)
   1. The Ark captured; the deaths of Eli and his sons (1 Sam 4:1b-22)
   2. The Ark in the land of the Philistines (1 Sam 5:1-12)
   3. The Ark returned to Israel (1 Sam 6:1–7:1)
  C. Samuel the Judge (1 Sam 7:2-17)

II. Kingship Established in Israel under the Guidance of Samuel the Prophet (1 Sam 8:1–12:25)
  A. Israel's Sinful Desire for a King (1 Sam 8:1-22)
  B. Saul Privately Anointed by Samuel to Be King (1 Sam 9:1–10:16)
  C. Saul Publicly Chosen to Be King (1 Sam 10:17-27)
  D. Saul's Kingship Confirmed by His Victory over the Ammonites (1 Sam 11:1-13)
  E. Saul's Reign Inaugurated in a Covenant Renewal Ceremony (1 Sam 11:14–12:25)

III. The Beginning of Saul's Reign (1 Sam 13:1–15:35)
  A. Samuel's Rebuke of Saul (1 Sam 13:1-15)
  B. Israel's Struggle against the Philistines (1 Sam 13:16–14:52)
  C. God's Rejection of Saul as King (1 Sam 15:1-35)

IV. David's Rise and Saul's Decline (1 Sam 16:1–28:2)
  A. Samuel Anoints David to Be King (1 Sam 16:1-13)
  B. An Evil Spirit Torments Saul; David Enters Saul's Service (1 Sam 16:14-23)
  C. David's Victory over Goliath; Jonathan's Covenant with David (1 Sam 17:1–18:4)
  D. David as a Military Leader and Son-in-law (1 Sam 18:5-30)
  E. Jonathan Defends David (1 Sam 19:1-7)
  F. Saul Tries to Kill David (1 Sam 19:8-17)
  G. Samuel Protects David (1 Sam 19:18-24)
  H. The Covenant between Jonathan and David (1 Sam 20:1-42)
  I. David and Ahimelech the Priest (1 Sam 21:1-9)
  J. David as a Fugitive (1 Sam 21:10–22:5)
  K. Ahimelech and the Priests at Nob Are Murdered (1 Sam 22:6-23)
  L. Saul Pursues David (1 Sam 23:1-29)
  M. David Spares Saul's Life a First Time (1 Sam 24:1-22)
  N. Samuel's Death; David, Nabal, and Abigail (1 Sam 25:1-44)
  O. David Spares Saul's Life a Second Time (1 Sam 26:1-25)
  P. David with Achish, King of Gath (1 Sam 27:1–28:2)

V. The End of Saul's Reign (1 Sam 28:3–31:13)
  A. Saul and the Medium at Endor (1 Sam 28:3-25)
  B. David Is Delivered from Fighting against Saul (1 Sam 29:1-11)
  C. David Defeats the Amalekites (1 Sam 30:1-31)
  D. The Deaths of Saul and Jonathan (1 Sam 31:1-13)
VI. David Becomes King over Judah (2 Sam 1:1–3:1)
  A. The Deaths of Saul and Jonathan Reported to David (2 Sam 1:1-16)
  B. David's Lament for Saul and Jonathan (2 Sam 1:17-27)
  C. David Becomes King over Judah (2 Sam 2:1-7)
  D. War between the House of Saul and the House of David (2 Sam 2:8–3:1)
VII. David's Reign (2 Sam 3:2–20:26)
  A. David's Sons Born in Hebron (2 Sam 3:2-5)
  B. Abner Defects to David's Kingship (2 Sam 3:6-21)
  C. The Murder of Abner; David's Lament (2 Sam 3:22-39)
  D. The Murder of Ishbosheth (2 Sam 4:1-12)
  E. David Becomes King of All Israel and Captures Jerusalem (2 Sam 5:1-12)
  F. David's Sons Born in Jerusalem (2 Sam 5:13-16)
  G. David Defeats the Philistines (2 Sam 5:17-25)
  H. David Brings the Ark to Jerusalem (2 Sam 6:1-23)
  I. The Lord Makes a Covenant with David (2 Sam 7:1-29)
  J. All David's Enemies Defeated with the Lord's Help (2 Sam 8:1-14)
  K. List of David's Officials (2 Sam 8:15-18)
  L. David Befriends Mephibosheth (2 Sam 9:1-13)
  M. The Ammonite War; David, Bathsheba, Uriah, and Nathan (2 Sam 10:1–12:31)
    1. The Ammonites defeated (2 Sam 10:1–11:1; 12:26-31)
    2. David, Bathsheba, Uriah, and Nathan (2 Sam 11:2–12:25)
  N. Civil War; Tamar, Amnon, Absalom, and Ahithophel (2 Sam 13:1–19:43)
    1. Amnon's sin against Tamar (2 Sam 13:1-22)
    2. Absalom murders Amnon (2 Sam 13:23-39)
    3. The wise woman of Tekoa (2 Sam 14:1-24)
    4. Absalom's reconciliation with David (2 Sam 14:25-33)
    5. Absalom conspires against David (2 Sam 15:1-12)
    6. David flees Jerusalem and sends the Ark back (2 Sam 15:13-37)
    7. David's kindness to Ziba (2 Sam 16:1-4)
    8. Shimei curses David (2 Sam 16:5-14)
    9. Ahithophel's advice to Absalom (2 Sam 16:15–17:29)
    10. Absalom's death (2 Sam 18:1-18)
    11. David mourns for Absalom (2 Sam 18:19–19:8)
    12. David's return to Jerusalem (2 Sam 19:9-43)

- O. Sheba's Rebellion against David; the Murder of Amasa (2 Sam 20:1-22)
- P. List of David's Officials (2 Sam 20:23-26)

VIII. The Samuel Conclusion (2 Sam 21:1–24:25)
- A. The Lord's Anger against Israel; Saul's Offense (2 Sam 21:1-14)
- B. List of Warriors (2 Sam 21:15-22)
- C. David's Song in Praise of God's Reign (2 Sam 22:1-51)
- D. David's Last Words about His Reign (2 Sam 23:1-7)
- E. List of Warriors (2 Sam 23:8-39)
- F. The Lord's Anger against Israel for David's Sin (2 Sam 24:1-25)

ENDNOTES

1. For more discussion about the existence of an independent Ark Narrative, see endnote 1 in the commentary on 1 Sam 4. In short, there is insufficient evidence to conclude that the so-called Ark Narratives ever existed as an independent tradition; see the arguments in Smelik 1989.
2. Prior to Rost this material was generally designated the Family History of David (Thenius 1864:192), the Court History of David (Smith 1912:xxvi) or some other similar title. The unit was normally limited to material within 2 Samuel (although Wellhausen [1899:259] had very early on linked 1 Kgs 1–2 with 2 Sam 9–20 as part of the same source document). It was usually viewed as beginning with either 2 Sam 10 or 11 and running through ch 20. Rost's "discovery" of the idea of succession to the throne within this material quickly gained widespread acceptance. This led to the displacement of the earlier designations for this block of material among most mainstream biblical scholars, and it brought about the nearly unanimous consensus that it crossed the boundary between the books of Samuel and Kings. See further Keys (1996:14-15).
3. Wenham (1985:15) notes that "in the whirlpool of conflicting modern theories, one point in the critical consensus has escaped serious challenge: namely, the date of Deuteronomy. It is well-nigh universally assumed by mainstream scholarship that Deuteronomy was written in the late seventh century and should be associated with Josiah's reform c. 622 BC." Weinfeld (1996:38) comments, "King Josiah of Judah instituted a religious reform in 622 BCE that scholars refer to simply as Josiah's Reform. It might well be called the Deuteronomic Reform. Israelite religion would never be the same."
4. G. W. Anderson (1951:283), in discussing the approach to the religion of Israel referred to as Wellhausenism, says, "At no point has the conflict been keener than in connection with the date and nature of Deuteronomy, the *keystone* in the Wellhausen system of chronology. If there is serious uncertainty here, the entire structure of the theory is weakened and may collapse" (my italics). Eissfeldt (1965:71) speaks of the dating of Deuteronomy as a "point of Archimedes" by means of which Pentateuchal criticism can deliver itself from the bonds of church and synagogue tradition and provide an alternate dating for the Pentateuch and its various parts. Other similar expressions have been used to highlight the crucial significance of the late date of Deuteronomy for the critical analysis of the OT and its literature for nonevangelical scholars. Dahl (1928:360) calls the date of Deuteronomy the "keystone of the arch of OT research." Other designations include "a fixed point," and a "sort of Meridian of Greenwich" (ibid). For a thorough discussion of this entire issue see M. J. Paul (1988).
5. As McConville (1997:4) notes, "The advantage of Cross's work is that it accommodates the positive material on the monarchy rather better than Noth's theory could do. Against it is the sudden change of direction that has to be assumed when Dtr2 revises Dtr1."

6. As Klement (2000:47) points out, in reviewing O'Brien's (1989) reassessment of the Deuteronomistic History hypothesis, Gerstenberger (1995:114-115) summarizes the present mood in this area of study with an amusing comment: "Can the Deuteronomistic History Work still be rescued? After so many ingenious and contradictory literary analyses, many experts think, 'Rest in peace—1943 to 1993—a fulfilled life for a hypothesis!'" (my translation).
7. In assessing the date of the composition of the book of Joshua, Longman and Dillard (2006:127) comment that "Conservative scholars have commonly assigned a time not long after the events (Woudstra 1981) or early in the monarchy (Harrison 1969, 673). Making such determination is very difficult. While one may reject the negative skepticism of the more critical approaches, a distinction is still necessary between the date of sources and the later editor(s) who produced the book in its present form. The book does share the viewpoint of the Deuteronomistic History (Joshua–Kings) and could reflect some compositional or editorial work as late as the exilic editor of Kings (2 Kings 25:27-30)." With respect to 1–2 Kings, Longman and Dillard (2006:171) say that "the book of Kings is marked by the same theological themes and vocabulary that characterized Joshua–Samuel, and these books together with Kings should be thought of as a single literary work."
8. There is a widespread consensus among contemporary mainstream biblical scholars, and to some degree among evangelical scholars as well, that the final form of the text of the OT has come to us as the result of a long process of reminting in which editors added new material to existing traditions. In doing so, it is normally alleged that these editors not only modified previously existing material in order to smooth over, as much as possible, the conflicting ideas and content of the various traditions with which they worked, but also that they gave the resultant "new edition" of the text a revised theological orientation reflecting their own historical circumstance, which was, in many cases, much later than the time of the events described in the new edition of the text. For evangelical scholars the acceptance of at least some features of this sort of analysis of the text of Scripture raises important questions concerning how one is to define the concept of the divine inspiration of Scripture. If one suggests that biblical literature was produced by a long process of text modification, how does one understand this concept in light of biblical statements such as 2 Pet 1:20-21 ("Above all, you must realize that no prophecy in Scripture ever came from the prophet's own understanding, or from human initiative. No, those prophets were moved by the Holy Spirit, and they spoke from God."). Is it legitimate to understand biblical statements about the divine inspiration of Scripture in the sense that God providentially directed the forging of the final form of the text by a process in which biblical texts were reshaped over long periods of time? This question is made particularly acute when it is alleged that during this process, the theological perspective of the text was adapted to new times and circumstances. Does the Bible's teaching on the inspiration of Scripture place any boundaries on the application of the historical-critical method to the analysis of the compositional history of the text? Can the acknowledgement of God's providential direction of a long process of text formation make any and every historical-critical theory of the origin of biblical literature evangelically acceptable? (Cf. R. Schultz [2004:158,159] for a discussion of this question in connection with the compositional history of the book of Isaiah.) These are questions that merit further reflection and discussion.
9. Fokkelman (1981:418) says that the Succession Narrative theory "has crippled OT science for almost 50 years."
10. McCarter (1984:308) also disputes the idea that the birth of Solomon is the primary focus of 2 Sam 10–12, because from "beginning to end it is a story about David, not Solomon." He notes that while Solomon's birth is extraneous to the major thematic concerns of the story of David and Bathsheba, when seen in a larger perspective it is still a momentous event. So he warns against overlooking its significance on the one hand, but on the other hand, he cautions against letting "the tail wag the dog."

11. McConville (1993:117) has also said that "it can no longer be assumed that 1 Kings 1–2 is the true ending of SN [the succession narrative]. It may be a natural sequel, but to see it as the true end of SN seems to me to narrow the concerns of the latter too much. On the contrary, the so-called Appendix to 1, 2 Samuel (2 Sam 21–24) is almost certainly misrepresented by that name; rather than being an afterthought, these chapters are the true conclusion of 1, 2 Samuel. When this is recognized, the story of David from 2 Samuel 9 on need not be seen only through the lens of 'succession,' but rather as a reflection on the Davidic kingship."
12. See the extended discussions of this issue in Kitchen 1970; 1989; and 2003; Kline 1963 and 1972; Manley 1957; McConville 1984 and 1993; Merrill 1994; M. J. Paul 1988; Wenham 1985.
13. House (1995:36) expresses acceptance of the idea of a Deuteronomistic historian who was "an anonymous individual who carefully collected source data and shaped this material into a great history that, despite the objection of Keil, Driver, and others, spans Joshua—Kings. This author wrote about 550 BC and was influenced by covenant theology such as that found in Deuteronomy and the prophets." R. Pratt (1990) and T. Longman and R. Dillard (2006) are other evangelicals who seem open to some form of a Deuteronomistic History theory. Howard (1993:182) concludes that the author of 1 and 2 Kings "was indeed a single person, writing during the Exile." But he then goes on to say, "This author's relationship with the earlier materials is more difficult to judge, but his work certainly is of a piece with the books of Joshua, Judges and 1 & 2 Samuel (and Deuteronomy), both in terms of style and outlook, and it is perhaps possible to speak of him as the 'author' of Joshua, Judges, and 1 & 2 Samuel as well, in the sense spoken of above" (that is, as the person responsible for the final form of the text). Although this conclusion appears compatible with some version of the Deuteronomistic History theory, Howard seems less inclined toward this approach in his commentary on Joshua (1998:30) when he says that "portions of the book [Joshua] were written in Joshua's day and . . . it was substantially complete by the time of David at the latest."
14. Although McConville (1997:10) does not argue that 1–2 Samuel was written in the Solomonic period, he has suggested that the various books of the Deuteronomistic History may have constituted separately transmitted blocks. He goes on to comment, however, that "This is not to say that the books must have achieved their present form all at once. It is likely, rather, that they constitute distinctive units of tradition, which have grown into their present shape in the context of their own particular history. They may also, however, have been adjusted in relation to each other, as part of a process of transmission. How this 'horizontal' adjustment related to the 'vertical' development is probably impossible to trace in detail. I agree with Provan, however, when he says: 'I am persuaded . . . that the books of the Old Testament generally grew gradually into their present form in dialogue with each other, each shaping the developing tradition and being shaped by it.'" McConville suggests that this sort of proposal would explain "why the individual historical books are found to have their own concerns, which cannot successfully be reduced to those of the Exile."
15. An example that Walters (2002:65) gives concerns usage of one of the customary titles for a military general ("commander of the army," *sar tsava'* [TH8269/6635, ZH8569/7372]). The man who performed this function for David, namely Joab, is never designated by this term in 1 and 2 Samuel, even though the designation is used for Abner, Joab's predecessor, and for Amasa, whom David appointed to replace Joab. Yet in 1 and 2 Kings the designation does appear in connection with Joab (1 Kgs 1:19; 11:15, 21).
16. Various names have been suggested, including Abiathar, Ahimaaz, and Hushai. Vriezen (1961:32, 141), however, suggests that the author may have been Zabud, the son of Nathan the prophet, who is mentioned in 1 Kgs 4:5 as being both a priest and a trusted adviser to Solomon.
17. Harris (1971:177) argues that the historical books "were written over the years by prominent prophets, largely in the style of court historians." The rabbis (*b. Bava Batra* 15a) suggested that Gad and Nathan finished the book after Samuel died (1 Sam 25:1).

the leadership in Israel. It deals with the institutions of priesthood (Eli and his sons), of prophetism (Samuel and his sons) and kingship (Saul or David). Also David is moving toward destruction, but because of the intervention of Jhwh, the fifth main part ends with David again. This is confirmed in the last main part, the conclusion. Through the chiastic structure of the book it appears that the vision of the messianic kingship in the introduction reaches its goal in the person of David and his dynasty in the conclusion." Koorevaar is familiar with Klement's work and says that in his proposal the "study of the structure and theology of the Book of Samuel has reached a new height." He goes on to comment (1997:57) that "Klement works with the approach of literary content and I work with formal criteria. As Klement shows that a six part chiastic structure is an important approach by the author, a six part chiastic macrostructure [Koorevaar's proposal suggests a six-part macrostructure while Klement suggests a five-part macrostructure] could be in accordance with such a structure. A possible synthesis is a challenge. This task remains open."

33. Radday (1974:29) comments, "There is hardly one single word in 1 Sam 2:1-10 which is not repeated at least once in 2 Sam 22.. . . I shall try to prove that in every single respect it is an expansion of and counterpart to Hannah's prayer." In a similar vein, Polzin (1989:31) says, "In fact, the song of Hannah could easily serve as an abbreviated version of 2 Samuel 22, so that when the reader of the exploits of Saul and David comes upon David's hymn at the end of 2 Samuel, it will be no accident to hear within it echoes of that shorter hymn with which the story of Israel's move to kingship is inaugurated. Hannah's initial song and David's final hymn of praise form a poetic *inclusio* for the history contained within the books of Samuel."
34. Wellhausen (1957:249), for example, said of 1 Sam 12 (the "late, anti-monarchy" source) that there "cannot be a word of truth in the whole narrative." He considered it to be a product of exilic or postexilic Judaism that had lost all knowledge of the real conditions behind the rise of kingship in Israel.
35. Gunkel (1964:7-8), working on the principle of "the analogy of history," says, "The clearest criterion of legend is that it frequently reports things which are quite incredible. . . . However cautious the modern historian may be in declaring anything impossible, he may declare with all confidence that animals—serpents and she-asses, for instance—do not speak and never have spoken, that there is no tree whose fruit confers immortality or knowledge, that angels and men do not have carnal connexion, and that a world-conquering army cannot be defeated—as Genesis xiv. declares—with three hundred and eighteen men."
36. Von Rad's willingness to classify the Succession Narrative as "history writing" has found both supporters (see, e.g., Tucker 1973:36) and detractors (e.g., Whybray 1968).
37. Alter (1981:20) asserts that traditional exegesis had "far-reaching assumptions about the text as literal revelation which most of us no longer accept." He makes this comment after having noted that there "is no point, to be sure, in pretending that all the contradictions among different sources in the biblical texts can be happily harmonized by the perception of some artful design."
38. Blocher (1988:117) comments, "As to the great number of history-like narratives in Scripture, however, we are not aware of any hints that we should read them as nonhistorical. Artistic concerns are definitely subordinate to other intentions. . . . Complex compositions, intricate adornment, elaborate symmetries, may point away from an overly literal or crude interpretation (e.g., in Genesis 1), but they are not likely to suppress generally the basic reference to space-time events 'out there'." See further Long (1994:58-87).
39. Blocher (1988:119-120) rightly says, "The knot of the matter . . . is the *essential* part which historical reference plays in Biblical religion. Because it is the very soul of Biblical faith, it cannot be laid aside as a secondary concern. . . . [Otherwise,] faith becomes worthless, we are the most miserable among all men. It is an either–or, an all-or-nothing debate: either true history, or the most perverse of all illusions; there is no intermediate category." Yet there have long been attempts to separate "theological

truth" from "historical truth" in the OT narratives. Vriezen (1962:89), for example, says that the historical accuracy of a piece of historical writing is not decisive with regard to its truth value because such narratives were not included primarily because of their historical content but because of their message. He says (1962:93) that to admit that "the OT contains historical errors and uses sources which are legends rather than true history . . . detracts in no way from the truth proclaimed by the OT with respect to the relation between God and man, man and the world, and man and his fellow-man." Such attempts to separate the theological truth of the Bible from its historical truth are ultimately destructive of genuine biblical faith because the message of the Bible is inseparably connected with the history it describes—the history of God's redemptive work. If the events of this history have not happened, or happened in ways different from what the Bible describes, then faith becomes an irrational leap and is vain (cf. 1 Cor 15:14).

40. These debates have generated a vast amount of literature. For brief summaries of the major issues involved, along with documentation of pertinent literature, see Zevit 2002.

41. Davies's book was complemented in the same year by a similar work by T. L. Thompson in which he argued (1992:110) that the "character of the [biblical] narratives themselves is not historical, and historicity—even historical relevance—cannot be assumed of them. . . . 'External evidence' is no longer a luxury but a necessity, and without it we simply cannot write a history of Israel." In his book, T. L. Thompson expresses the same skeptical attitude toward the Old Testament portrayal of later periods of Israel's history that he had previously expressed in his 1974 work with respect to the patriarchal narratives.

42. Davies (1992:13) says, "All story is fiction, and that must include historiography. The historian may like to invest trust in these stories, but should never avoid the question 'why is this story being told?' The answer can never be 'because what it describes happened,' for not only is that untrue, since stories do not neatly reproduce 'what happened,' but the fact of something happening does not of itself provide an adequate reason for telling it." Davies is correct that it is important to ask why a particular story is being told and that just because something has happened is not in itself an adequate reason for reporting that it has happened; however, these considerations hardly justify Davies' extreme skepticism about the possibility of historical writing being capable of producing a description of "things that happened" in a responsible and trustworthy manner.

The conclusion that biblical narratives are of little value as sources for historical information is commonplace today among biblical scholars, and not just among those who have aligned themselves with the "minimalist" side of the "minimalist-maximalist" debate. W. Brueggemann is one such example. In his study of the David narratives, entitled *David's Truth* (2000a), he asserts that "David's truth" has little or no connection with the "historical truth" of the biblical narratives since the David of history cannot be found in the biblical texts; instead we find self-serving portraits of David derived from the special interests of the social, economic, political, or religious agendas of those who produced the texts. Thus, regarding David, he finds four different truths: "The Trustful Truth of the Tribe" (1 Sam 16:1—2 Sam 5:5); "The Painful Truth of the Man" (2 Sam 9–20 and 1 Kgs 1–2); "The Sure Truth of the State" (2 Sam 5:6–8:18); and "The Hopeful Truth of the Assembly" (1 Chr 10–29; Pss 89; 132; Isa 55:3; Lam 3:21-27). He likewise comments (2000a:9-10) that "the *story* is the *truth*. It is not the whole truth, nor objective truth, but it is, for this community, *our* truth. . . . No matter how much of it is imaginative reconstruction, . . . the tellers and the listeners must in this moment take the narrative at face value."

43. For responses to the postmodern strand in the minimalist initiative, see Provan, Long, and Longman 2003:43-44; Dever 2000; and Windschuttle 1997.

44. For additional surveys and analysis of the historiographical issues connected with the interpretation of biblical narrative, see Provan 1995a; 1997; Yamauchi 1994; and Long 1994.

45. For examples of the narrator's comments in this regard, see 1 Sam 1:5; 2:25; 10:9; 26:12; 2 Sam 8:6; 17:14.For the comments of various characters, see 1 Sam 12:22 [Samuel]; 24:10 [David]; 25:26 [Abigail]; 2 Sam 12:7-8 [Nathan]; 15:25-26 [David].
46. During the last century, the legitimacy of the affirmation that God providentially directs everything that comes to pass has been seriously challenged. This is a topic that generates a host of complex philosophical and theological issues. Unfortunately, they cannot be addressed within the confines of this commentary. For a good survey of the questions involved, along with the presentation of 11 different models of divine providence, see Tiessen 2000.
47. In a volume that was yet unpublished during the writing of this commentary, Borgman (2008) draws a number of conclusions similar to my own, calling attention to some of the same structural features of the narratives depicting Saul and David that are highlighted in this volume. Borgman (2008:5, 7) says, "To the extent that the story is concerned with uncovering the character of this man after God's own heart—including how it is that David is 'better' than Saul—to that extent the audience will come to understand God's heart. . . . But it takes a long narrative . . . to discover the reason for God's choice of David. . . . He seems infinitely worse than Saul, not a 'better man,' . . . Just why or how David is superior to Saul is what the story promises to disclose—which is to afford a glimpse into the divine way of seeing, knowing, deciding. . . . As the story brings to light what has remained hidden about David, so, too, the story brings to light what has been kept hidden about God's choosing of the mystery man. The greatness of this story is its pressing toward the resolution of the double-ended mystery of character, God's and David's."
48. Walters (2002:68) argues that 1–2 Samuel teaches us that kingship is to be viewed from a prophetic perspective. He points out that the book bears the name of Samuel rather than David, and says that Samuel is the one who "presided (if sometimes reluctantly) over the introduction of the kingship and who sought to ensure that Israel's kingship should be faithful and true to the Lord (1 Sam 10:25)."
49. Discussion of messianic expectation in the OT is a complex undertaking, but one that carries enormous significance. McConville (1995:17) has argued that "the validity of a Christian understanding of the Old Testament must depend in the last analysis on the cogency of the argument that the Old Testament is messianic." This statement suggests how important the messianic concept is for understanding the OT in its relationship with the NT. For evangelical views on the messianic idea in the OT, see Van Groningen 1990; Kaiser 1995; Satterthwaite, Hess, and Wenham 1995 (cf. Kaiser 1999:99-102); and Porter 2007. For a broad collection of articles on various aspects of kingship and messianic expectation in the OT, mostly by mainstream biblical scholars, see Day 1998. For a focused discussion of David's role in messianic expectation, see Satterthwaite 1995.
50. For a discussion of anointing in the OT see Hamilton (TWOT 1.530), who comments that when *mashakh* is used in connection with religious ritual it "involved a ceremonial application of oil to items such as the tabernacle, altar or laver (Exod 40:9-11), or even the sin offering (Exod 29:36). More frequently *mashakh* is used for the ceremonial induction into leadership offices, an action which involved the pouring of oil from a horn upon the head of an individual. Easily the most frequent mention of *mashakh* is with kings such as Saul and David of Israel (2 Sam 12:7; but note Hazael, an Aramaean, 1 Kgs 19:15). The high priest was anointed (Exod 29:7; Num 35:25) and so were other priests (Exod 30:30). Twice there is mention of anointing a prophet (1 Kgs 19:16; Isa 61:1)."
51. For a good discussion of the Hebrew terms *mashakh* [TH4886, ZH5417] and *mashiakh* [TH4899, ZH5431], see Van Groningen (1990:23-28).

COMMENTARY ON

1–2 Samuel

◆ I. The Historical Setting for the Establishment of Kingship in Israel (1 Sam 1:1–7:17)

A. Samuel's Birth; Judgment Pronounced on the Elides; Samuel Becomes a Prophet (1 Sam 1:1–4:1a)

1. Samuel's birth (1 Sam 1:1-28)

a. Elkanah's family (1 Sam 1:1-3)

There was a man named Elkanah who lived in Ramah in the region of Zuph* in the hill country of Ephraim. He was the son of Jeroham, son of Elihu, son of Tohu, son of Zuph, of Ephraim. [2]Elkanah had two wives, Hannah and Peninnah. Peninnah had children, but Hannah did not. [3]Each year Elkanah would travel to Shiloh to worship and sacrifice to the LORD of Heaven's Armies at the Tabernacle. The priests of the LORD at that time were the two sons of Eli—Hophni and Phinehas.

1:1 As in Greek version; Hebrew reads *in Ramathaim-zophim;* compare 1:19.

NOTES

1:1 *Ramah in the region of Zuph.* The KJV and NASB translate the Hebrew *haramathayim tsopim* as "Ramathaim-zophim," which is a geographical designation. The NIV and NEB translate the phrase as "Ramathaim, a Zuphite" which takes *haramathayim* [TH7436A, ZH8259] as the name of the place of Elkanah's residence, and *tsopim* [TH6690.3, ZH7435] as a designation of the clan to which Elkanah belonged. This is supported by the statement in 1:1b that Elkanah was a descendant of Zuph, and by the reference to the land of Zuph in 9:5. In 1:19 and 2:11 Elkanah is said to reside in Ramah (*haramah*). It seems likely that *haramathayim* is an alternate form, used only here, for the name Ramah. The *-ayim* sufformative is probably locative rather than dual (compare Gath/Gittaim; see note on 2 Sam 21:9; B. Mazar 1954:230). This is likely the same Ramah where Samuel later established his headquarters (7:15-17) after the destruction of Shiloh.

1:2 *Elkanah had two wives.* Although the creation narrative (Gen 2:24), as well as certain sections of the Wisdom Literature (cf. Prov 5:15-20; 18:22; 31:10-31), clearly imply monogamous marriage as God's standard for the marital relationship, bigamy and polygamy came to be tolerated in ancient Israel as socially acceptable (e.g., Esau, Jacob, Gideon, Saul, David, Solomon, Rehoboam, Abijah, Ahab, Jehoram). The words Jesus spoke about regulations for divorce in the Mosaic law ("Moses permitted divorce only as a concession to your hard hearts, but it was not what God had originally intended," Matt 19:8) apply equally well to polygamy. Just as with divorce, polygamy is not explicitly prohibited in the Mosaic law but instead regulated in order to ameliorate its destructive effects (Deut 21:15-17). As Wright (1983:177) observes, "The story of Elkanah and his rival wives (ch 1) was hardly written for the primary purpose of criticizing bigamy, but it is a vivid illustration of the potential agonies it can produce." See further ISBE 3.901-902; Kaiser 1983:182-190.

1:3 ***the* L*ORD* *of Heaven's Armies.*** Lit., "the LORD of Hosts" (*yhwh tseba'oth* [TH3068/6635, ZH3378/7372]). This is the first occurrence in the OT of what becomes a common title for the God of Israel (there are 260 occurrences of it in the OT, mostly in Samuel, Kings, Isaiah, Jeremiah, Haggai, Zechariah, and Malachi). It appears to be a shortened form of "the LORD God of Hosts" (*yhwh 'elohe tseba'oth;* cf. 2 Sam 5:10; Hos 12:5 [6]; Amos 3:13; 4:13). The precise significance of *tseba'oth* in the title has long been discussed with no consensus achieved. By itself it is used to designate the armies of Israel (17:45; cf. Deut 20:4), celestial bodies (Deut 4:19; 17:3; 2 Kgs 17:16; 21:3-5; 23:4-5; Isa 40:26), or heavenly creatures such as angels (1 Kgs 22:19; Pss 103:21; 148:2). Vos (1975:243) comments, "Jehovah of Hosts is His royal name. It designates Him as the almighty King both in nature and history [Ps 103:19-22; Isa 6:5; 24:23; Jer 46:18; 48:15; 51:57]." Whatever its specific meaning in the title, which may in fact vary in different contexts, it clearly seems to be intended to depict Israel's God as supreme over all powers in heaven and earth. The LXX either transliterates the term (*sabaōth* [TG4519, ZG4877]), or renders it by *kurios pantokratōr* [TG2962/3841, ZG3261/4120] (Lord Almighty) or *kurios tōn dunameōn* [TG1411, ZG1539] (Lord of the Powers). Because Rom 9:29 and Jas 5:4 also transliterate the term, as was sometimes done in the LXX, "Sabaoth" is often transliterated in modern languages, producing phrases such as "the Lord Sabaoth" and "the Lord of Sabaoth."

COMMENTARY

The narratives of 1 Samuel 1–7 do three important things: (1) They present Samuel as a faithful leader who serves in the multiple roles of prophet, priest, and judge; (2) they depict the disastrous situation into which Israel had fallen by turning away from covenant faithfulness during the period of the judges; and (3) they clearly show that Israel had no legitimate reason for desiring to have a king like the nations around them. All of these things are important for understanding the conditions attending the establishment of the monarchy under Samuel's direction in 1 Samuel 8–12.

First and Second Samuel depict Israel's momentous transition from the period of the judges to that of the monarchy. These books do not provide us with a detailed political history of this time, but are rather, for the most part, a collection of biographical stories pertaining to the leading personas in this period of Israel's history, namely, Samuel (chs 1–12), Saul (chs 13–31), and David (2 Sam 1–24). The narrative reaches its climax with the kingship of David, and particularly with God's promise to him that his dynasty would endure forever (2 Sam 7).

Even though the central focus of the narratives of 1–2 Samuel is the rise and reign of David, the story begins with the birth of Samuel rather than with the birth of David. When David appears on the scene in later chapters, there is still no description of his birth but only the story of his being chosen and anointed by Samuel when he was a young man. By this rhetorical means, the narrator, from the very beginning of his account, subordinates David's position as king to the word and work of the prophet Samuel.

Samuel was born during a dark period of Israel's history. The religious and moral deterioration characteristic of this time is clearly portrayed in the two stories appended to the book of Judges: A private sanctuary is robbed of its idols and priest

(Judg 17–18); and a civil war is fought against Benjamin because of the rape and murder of a woman traveler (Judg 19–21). Yet contrary to outward appearances, God was still at work among his people. The book of Ruth shows us that in the private sphere of family life the Lord was even then preparing the line from which David would be born (Ruth 4:18-22).

First Samuel 1 reveals that the Lord was also at work in another family, even though this family also had a dark side: In the household of Elkanah there was internal strife. Elkanah had two wives, Hannah and Peninnah. Hannah was barren but Peninnah was not. Peninnah used her own fecundity to torment Hannah. In this situation, the Lord intervened on the side of Hannah. As de Jong (1978:51) suggests, Samuel was born not by might nor by power, not by the will of man nor by the will of the flesh, but according to the Lord's will. In fact, it is the Lord who is at the center of the entire narrative.[1] It was the Lord who had closed Hannah's womb (1:5-6); and the Lord who remembered her (1:19); and Hannah confesses at the end of the chapter that it was the Lord who had granted her request (1:27). It is clear that the Lord is faithful to his people when they are ready and willing to submit to him in faith, obedience, and worship. It is Hannah who personifies these qualities.

As a prelude of things to come, this chapter also introduces the reader to the high priest, Eli, and his two sons, Hophni and Phinehas. Eli is presented as a priest who is deficient in spiritual discernment but dutiful in his priestly tasks. No hint is given about the personal qualities of Hophni and Phinehas.

The first chapter begins with an introductory formula ("There was a man," 1:1) that is also found at the beginning of the Samson narratives (Judg 13:2). The formula suggests that what follows is to be read as the beginning of a new sequence of narratives in the context of the preceding stories of the judges. The man about whom the narrative speaks is Elkanah, who lived in the hill country of Ephraim. Hannah, one of Elkanah's two wives, remained barren. The familiar biblical theme of the barren wife (e.g., Sarah, Rebekah, Rachel, Samson's mother) raises the prospect, if not the expectation, of divine intervention on Hannah's behalf. This potentiality is heightened when the reader learns in 1:5 that "the LORD had given her no children."

Every year Elkanah and his family went to Shiloh to worship at the Tabernacle. Elkanah was evidently a godly man and consistent in his performance of ritual observances. Whether the yearly trip to Shiloh was occasioned by one of the three annual festivals (Passover, Festival of Harvest, Festival of Shelters; see Exod 23:14-19; 34:23; Deut 16:16-17) or was a special family observance is not made explicit in the text.[2] Perhaps it was the Festival of Shelters, the most exuberant of Israel's feasts and the one at which the participants celebrated God's care for his people during the wilderness wandering (Lev 23:43), as well as his blessing in the recent harvest (Deut 16:13-15).[3] In any case, at Shiloh Elkanah brought his sacrifices and worshiped "the LORD of Heaven's Armies" (see note on 1:3). It is particularly significant that this designation for Yahweh appears for the first time in the Old Testament in these narratives, which prepare the way for the establishment of kingship in Israel. At this time in history, Israel was extraordinarily in need of a reminder of the power and sovereignty of Yahweh, its Great King.

ENDNOTES

1. Brueggemann (1990b:47) notes that while the focus of 1 Samuel is on David, behind David is Saul and behind Saul is Samuel. But then we are still required to ask, "Whence comes Samuel?" Brueggemann responds, "The answer of course is that behind Samuel stands Hannah, frail, distressed, weeping, not eating. It is Hannah who finally dares to pray and to vow, to receive, to yield, and to worship. Israel's monarchy, we are told, begins in this voiceless voice of hopeless hope. . . . And behind Hannah? There is only Yahweh who closes wombs, who remembers, who answers prayers, and gives sons. There is only Yahweh and Yahweh has initiated the sequence of Hannah, Samuel, Saul and David *ex nihilo*, out of nothing but hurt brought to voice, hope dared, uttered fidelity, petitions risked, and vows kept."
2. Haran (1969:22) has argued that this is a "unique family custom not mentioned in any of the Pentateuchal law-codes which was observed once a year, independent of any definite date."
3. Judges 21:19 refers to an "annual festival of the LORD held in Shiloh." Since this festival is spoken of in connection with "vineyards" (Judg 21:20) and may have been held at the time of the grape harvest, it is often taken as a reference to the Festival of Shelters (Wolf 1992:505). Perhaps the same festival is in view here.

b. Hannah's sorrow (1 Sam 1:4-8)

[4]On the days Elkanah presented his sacri-
fice, he would give portions of the meat
to Peninnah and each of her children.
[5]And though he loved Hannah, he would
give her only one choice portion* because
the LORD had given her no children. [6]So
Peninnah would taunt Hannah and make
fun of her because the LORD had kept her
from having children. [7]Year after year it
was the same—Peninnah would taunt
Hannah as they went to the Tabernacle.*
Each time, Hannah would be reduced to
tears and would not even eat.
[8]"Why are you crying, Hannah?" Elka-
nah would ask. "Why aren't you eating?
Why be downhearted just because you
have no children? You have me—isn't that
better than having ten sons?"

1:5 Or *And because he loved Hannah, he would give her a choice portion.* The meaning of the Hebrew is uncertain. 1:7 Hebrew *the house of the LORD;* also in 1:24.

NOTES

1:4 *he would give portions of the meat.* From Lev 3; 7:11-21, 28-34, we learn that the ritual for the fellowship offering (sometimes called the peace offering) included a sacrificial meal. Both the priest and those who offered the sacrifice ate a part of the sacrificed animal. The fat was burned, and the blood was sprinkled on the altar.

1:5 *only one choice portion because the LORD had given her no children.* Or, "And because he loved Hannah, he would give her a choice portion because the LORD had given her no children." The Hebrew of this phrase is difficult. The difficulty centers in the word *'appayim* (NLT, "choice") which normally means "both nostrils," "anger," or "face." The NIV and NASB, following Keil and others, understand the expression *manah* [TH4490, ZH4950] *'akhath 'appayim* to mean "one portion for two persons (i.e., faces)" or a "double portion." The KJV (much like NLT), following the Targum, renders the expression "a worthy portion" (i.e., "a portion of the face" in the sense of a portion of honor). Both of these suggestions, however, seem somewhat contrived in their attempt to produce an acceptable meaning. It has been widely recognized that the LXX (Vaticanus) provides a sensible and, given the alternatives, probably the preferable reading (*plēn hoti* [TG4133/3754, ZG4440/4022], "except that") that presupposes a minor modification of the MT to *'epes ki* [TH657A/3588, ZH700/3954] (nevertheless), in place of *'appayim ki* [TH639/3588, ZH678/3954] (cf. Num 13:28; Deut 15:4; Judg 4:9). The idea of the statement, then, is that even though Hannah received only one portion, this was not because Elkanah did not love her, but simply because she was barren. In addition, he recognized that her condition was not simply misfortune, but was due to an intervention of the Lord.

1:6 *Peninnah would taunt Hannah.* Lit., "Her rival, however, provoked her intensely to aggravate her." Peninnah is designated *tsarathah* [TH6869A, ZH7651] (her rival), which is a technical term for a rival wife in Syriac and Arabic (S. R. Driver 1913:9) but is used only here in the Hebrew OT. The term suggests that Peninnah had become a second wife to Elkanah subsequent to his marriage to Hannah, perhaps even because of Hannah's barrenness. The verbal form of the same root occurs in this sense in Lev 18:18. McCarter (1980b:60) notes that the "Hebrew *tsarah* became virtually a technical, legal designation for a man's second wife in the Talmudic period, when bigamy was permitted (though not encouraged) until its general prohibition in the tenth century CE."

COMMENTARY

When the time came for distribution of portions of the sacrificial meal to the family members, Hannah received only one portion. This was not because Elkanah did not love her, but simply because Hannah had no children. Hannah's barrenness is rhetorically emphasized by a repetition (1:5) of the statement that the Lord had closed her womb (1:2). Her sterility, however, provides the occasion for Peninnah (her rival, see note on 1:6) to taunt her and cause her great emotional distress. This unjust treatment of Hannah by Peninnah highlights the contrast between the two women, one of whom is cruel and arrogant and the other afflicted and crushed. Similar contrasts are drawn between other individuals throughout 1–2 Samuel (e.g., Eli's sons and Samuel; Saul and David; Saul and Jonathan; Michal and Abigail). So here, even before his birth, Samuel is aligned with the side of honor and godliness through his oppressed but pious mother (cf. Eslinger 1985:73).

◆ c. Hannah's vow (1 Sam 1:9-11)

**9 Once after a sacrificial meal at Shiloh,
Hannah got up and went to pray. Eli
the priest was sitting at his customary
place beside the entrance of the Taber-
nacle.* 10 Hannah was in deep anguish,
crying bitterly as she prayed to the LORD.
11 And she made this vow: "O LORD of
Heaven's Armies, if you will look upon
my sorrow and answer my prayer and
give me a son, then I will give him back
to you. He will be yours for his entire
lifetime, and as a sign that he has been
dedicated to the LORD, his hair will never
be cut.*"**

1:9 Hebrew *the Temple of the LORD.* 1:11 Some manuscripts add *He will drink neither wine nor intoxicants.*

NOTES

1:9 *Eli the priest.* Previously Eli's two sons were introduced as priests at Shiloh (1:3). It is to be understood that Eli was the high priest (see 2:28), although no specific term is used. Prior to this point in Scripture, the term for "high priest" (*hakkohen haggadol* [TH3548/1419,

ZH3913/1524]) occurs only three times in the Pentateuch (Num 35:25, 28 [twice]) and once in Josh 20:6. In other places the high priest is called "the priest who is highest among his brothers" (Lev 21:10) or the "anointed priest" (Lev 4:3, 5, 16; 6:22 [MT 15]). The expression "chief priest" (*kohen haro'sh* [TH7218, ZH8031]; NLT, "high priest") occurs in 2 Kgs 25:18; 2 Chr 19:11; 24:11; 26:20; 31:10; Ezra 7:5; Jer 52:24.

1:11 *his hair will never be cut.* The LXX (Vaticanus), and perhaps 4QSam[a] (which is fragmentary but requires a text longer than MT), has a fuller text that reads, "Then I shall set him before you as a Nazirite until the day of his death, and wine and strong drink he will not drink, and a razor will not touch his head." McCarter (1980b:53-54) and Klein (1983:3), however, think that the appearance of "Nazirite" in this verse, although appropriate, is probably secondary, perhaps under the influence of v. 22 (see 1:22, NLT mg). Pisano (1984:19-24) argues that the less explicit MT is to be preferred as the earliest text and that the pluses in LXX and 4QSam[a] represent an insertion inspired by Num 6:3 or by the similar promise of Samson's birth in Judg 13:4.

COMMENTARY

Even though Hannah did not participate in the eating and drinking, she was present at the meal. Out of her "deep anguish" (1:10, lit., "bitterness of soul," cf. Job 3:20; Prov 31:6), Hannah turned to the Lord in prayer. Apparently she prayed for a long time, but only her request for a son and her vow to dedicate him to the Lord are included in the narrative. Her vow was a lifelong commitment of her son to the Lord's service, marked by abstinence from cutting his hair. Vows were serious obligations, not to be made lightly (Num 30:2; Deut 23:22-23). Regulations in the Pentateuch, however, allow for a husband to nullify a vow of his wife's with which he disagrees (Num 30:6-8). In this case, it is clear that Elkanah honored Hannah's commitment and supported her in carrying out her vow (1:21-23).

Parallels have long been drawn between Hannah's vow and the Nazirite vow (cf. Num 6:1-21), even though the term Nazirite is not used here or elsewhere in the MT to designate Samuel. (The ms 4QSam[a], however, uses the word Nazirite of Samuel later on; cf. 1:22, NLT mg.) The Nazirite vow, which was voluntary, enabled persons who were not of the priesthood, whether male or female, to consecrate themselves to the Lord in a special way for a limited period of time. The requirements of the Nazirite vow included: (1) separation from everything that comes from the vine; (2) abstinence from cutting one's hair; and (3) keeping oneself from contact with a dead body. Hannah's vow of consecration for the son whom she requested from the Lord differed from the Nazirite vow in that it was not for a limited period of time, and it made no reference to two of the three requirements for the Nazirite vow. Nevertheless, it is likely that Hannah's intent was for her son to be a Nazirite for life, as was the case with Samson. The Samson narrative also does not mention all the requirements of the Nazirite vow, but Samson is specifically termed a Nazirite from birth to the day of his death (Judg 13:5-7). Even though Samson's Nazirite status differs from Samuel's, in that he was so designated prior to his birth, and this was on the Lord's initiative rather than his mother's, it is possible that Hannah's vow reflects her acquaintance with lifelong Nazirite vows, and the desire for her son to fulfill such a calling.

d. Hannah and Eli (1 Sam 1:12-18)

[12]As she was praying to the LORD, Eli watched her. [13] Seeing her lips moving but hearing no sound, he thought she had been drinking. [14]"Must you come here drunk?" he demanded. "Throw away your wine!"

[15]"Oh no, sir!" she replied. "I haven't been drinking wine or anything stronger. But I am very discouraged, and I was pouring out my heart to the LORD. [16] Don't think I am a wicked woman! For I have been praying out of great anguish and sorrow."

[17]"In that case," Eli said, "go in peace! May the God of Israel grant the request you have asked of him."

[18]"Oh, thank you, sir!" she exclaimed. Then she went back and began to eat again, and she was no longer sad.

NOTES

1:15 *I am very discouraged.* Hannah describes herself as *'ishah qeshath-ruakh* [TH7186/7307, ZH7997/8120] (a woman troubled of spirit). This expression occurs only here in the OT and is difficult to translate. The root *qashah* [TH7185, ZH7996] comes from an agricultural milieu emphasizing (1) the effect of bearing a heavy yoke and (2) the resistance of oxen to accepting such a yoke (TWOT 2.818). Here the adjectival form of the root is perhaps best understood as emphasizing the weight of the troubles with which Hannah was burdened. The context does not favor translating the phrase "a persistent woman" as suggested by Ahlström (1979:254) and followed by Klein (1983:9).

1:16 *a wicked woman.* Heb., *bath beliya'al* [TH1323/1100, ZH1426/1175] (daughter of Belial); *beliya'al* occurs 27 times in the OT. Its etymology is disputed (TDOT 2:131-136), but usage in numerous places suggests linkage with various types of wrongdoing. In Judg 19:22; 20:13 it is used to describe the homosexuals at Gibeah, and in 1 Kgs 21:10-13 it describes the false witnesses against Naboth. Proverbs 6:12 equates "the man of Belial" ("worthless," NLT) with the "wicked man." In 2:12 it is used for the wicked sons of Eli, and in 2 Sam 20:1 for Sheba, who stirred up a rebellion against David. In later Judaism, the term Belial was used as a proper name for Satan himself (2 Cor 6:15).

COMMENTARY

Because Hannah was greatly distressed and prayed for so long, Eli concluded she was intoxicated. Drunkenness may not have been unusual at the Tabernacle, thus explaining, though not excusing, Eli's mistaken inference (see Judg 9:27 for similar behavior among the Canaanites, and Isa 28:7 for condemnation of drunkenness at Israelite religious observances). Hannah, however, respectfully but categorically denied Eli's allegation and described herself as deeply troubled (see note on 1:15). She then begged Eli not to regard her as a wicked woman (see note on 1:16) and explained that she had been pouring her heart out to the Lord (1:15) and praying because of her "great anguish and sorrow" (1:16). The noun "sorrow" is from the same Hebrew root (*ka'as* [TH3707, ZH4087]) used earlier in the narrative to describe Peninnah's tormenting and taunting Hannah (1:6). It is not clear whether Hannah told Eli exactly what her request had been, although their subsequent conversation at the time she brought Samuel to the Tabernacle to begin his service there (1:26-27) suggests this possibility. In any case, Eli pronounced a priestly blessing on her (1:17; cf. Num 6:22-27; Deut 10:8) with the result that she went away encouraged that God had heard her prayer.

e. Samuel's birth (1 Sam 1:19-23)

**19 The entire family got up early the next
morning and went to worship the LORD
once more. Then they returned home to
Ramah. When Elkanah slept with Hannah,
the LORD remembered her plea, 20 and in
due time she gave birth to a son. She
named him Samuel,* for she said, "I asked
the LORD for him."**

**21 The next year Elkanah and his family
went on their annual trip to offer a sacri-
fice to the LORD. 22 But Hannah did not go.
She told her husband, "Wait until the boy
is weaned. Then I will take him to the
Tabernacle and leave him there with the
LORD permanently.*"**

**23 "Whatever you think is best," Elkanah
agreed. "Stay here for now, and may the
LORD help you keep your promise." So she
stayed home and nursed the boy until he
was weaned.**

1:20 *Samuel* sounds like the Hebrew term for "asked of God" or "heard by God." 1:22 Some manuscripts add *I will offer him as a Nazirite for all time.*

NOTES

1:20 ***She named him Samuel.*** Various attempts have been made to explain the etymology of the name Samuel (see Keil 1956:25; McCarter 1980b:62; van Zijl 1969:39). While some of these suggestions are possible, the name is likely to be explained via a popular, rather than a scientific, etymology. In this case, the name is a reflection of *sha'ul me'el* [TH7592/410A, ZH8626/446] (asked of God), something recognized as far back as the Hebrew grammarian and Rabbi David Kimchi (AD 1160–1235). Tsevat (1987:251) notes that the symbolic significance of names in OT narratives often does not lie in strict etymology or phonetic congruence, but in the ability to elicit association, with as much or as little phonetic similarity as necessary. Here the association would lie in assonance, and the last phrase of the verse ("I asked the LORD for him") would be understood as an explanation of the name. There is no convincing basis here for the theory that ch 1 was originally the birth story of Saul rather than Samuel. Advocates of this view have appealed to the wordplay on *sha'al* [TH7592, ZH8626] (ask) in ch 1 (especially 1:20, 27), which is alleged to be more easily applied to Saul than to Samuel (cf. Hylander 1932; J. Blenkinsopp 1983:65; McCarter 1980b:64-66; and the opposing view in Klein 1983:9; Willis 1972:33-61). As Tsevat points out, a mistaken idea of the manner in which the OT deals with names lies at the base of this theory, and it rests more on a commitment to certain hypotheses of composition than on any requirements of the text.

1:23 ***may the LORD help you keep your promise.*** The NLT here follows the LXX and 4QSam[a] rather than MT ("may the LORD establish his word"). In the context, there is no reference to a divine promise given to Elkanah and Hannah at the time they made their vow, although as Campbell (2003:380) notes, Walters (1988:410-412) "reads the MT as 'his word' understood as YHWH's word to raise up a prophet like Moses (Deut 18:18)." Walters supports this interpretation by saying that Elkanah's statement alludes to Deut 18:18; "the people asked (*sha'al* [TH7592, ZH8626]) for this at Horeb, God says, to which the abundant use of the root *sha'al* 'ask' in 1 Samuel provides a telling pointer: the request for a prophet remains unfulfilled, and so Hannah (=God's people) will ask again. This time, Elkanah believes, the faithful God will fulfill his word. The story is therefore about God's faithfulness to promise, and by extension in the present context, God's faithfulness to the prophetic word" (2002:71).

COMMENTARY

The succinct wording of 1:19 moves the narrative forward swiftly and significantly. Elkanah and his family worshiped the Lord and returned to their home in Ramah.

Then Elkanah had relations with Hannah, and we are told, "the LORD remembered her plea." This is a response to her supplication when she had pleaded with the Lord to "remember" her (1:11; NLT, "answer my prayer") and give her a son. "Remember" (*zakar* [TH2142, ZH2349]) in Hebrew usage is not limited to intellectual recall but often includes the idea of resultant action (cf. TDOT 4.66). Here it refers to God's gracious intervention in Hannah's life by answering her prayer (see Gen 8:1; 30:22 for similar usages). It was the Lord who had closed her womb (1:6), and it was the Lord who enabled her to conceive.

The birth of Samuel is the climax of chapter 1. It is clear that his name expresses Hannah's conviction that it was the Lord who gave her a son in response to her prayer, even though it is not clear how the etymology of the name Samuel is to be explained (see note on 1:20).

When the time came for the yearly journey to Jerusalem (1:21-23), Hannah remained at Ramah with her infant son because the trip was too difficult for a nursing mother. She pledged to Elkanah, however, that as soon as Samuel was weaned, she would bring him to Shiloh so that he might remain there indefinitely in the service of the Lord (1:11). Elkanah responded by expressing his desire that the Lord would enable her to fulfill her vow.

◆ f. Hannah presents Samuel to the Lord at Shiloh (1 Sam 1:24-28)

24When the child was weaned, Hannah took him to the Tabernacle in Shiloh. They brought along a three-year-old bull* for the sacrifice and a basket* of flour and some wine. 25After sacrificing the bull, they brought the boy to Eli. 26"Sir, do you remember me?" Hannah asked. "I am the woman who stood here several years ago praying to the LORD. 27I asked the LORD to give me this boy, and he has granted my request. 28Now I am giving him to the LORD, and he will belong to the LORD his whole life." And they* worshiped the LORD there.

1:24a As in Dead Sea Scrolls, Greek and Syriac versions; Masoretic Text reads *three bulls.* **1:24b** Hebrew *and an ephah* [20 quarts or 22 liters]. **1:28** Hebrew *he.*

NOTES

1:24 *a three-year-old bull.* There has been nearly universal agreement that the MT should be emended here from the plural *beparim sheloshah* [TH7969, ZH8993] (three bulls) to the singular *bepar meshullash* [TH8027, ZH8992] ("a three-year-old bull"; cf. Gen 15:9) as is found in the LXX and the Syriac (S. R. Driver 1913:20; Klein 1983:2, 10; McCarter 1980b:56-57; Smith 1912:14; Thenius 1864:8; Wellhausen 1871:41; NLT, NEB, NIV, NRSV, RSV). Ratner (1987), however, has argued convincingly for the "three bulls" reading of the MT on both contextual and syntactic grounds. He concludes, "There is no reason internal to the text, be it contextual or grammatical, that calls the MT into question. The MT no longer needs to be explained. Perhaps the versions do."

1:25 *the bull.* The MT reads *happar* [TH6499, ZH7228]. It is usually argued that this singular reading supports the emendation from "three bulls" to "a three-year-old bull" in 1:24 (see above). Ratner (1987:101), however, has argued that *happar* here is collective in signification, although morphologically definite and singular, and accordingly should be translated as "the bulls." He appeals to similar usages in Gen 15:10 and 2 Sam 6:18 for support.

COMMENTARY

In the ancient world, children were nursed much longer than in most of the world today. In 2 Maccabees 7:27, we read of a nursing period of three years. It is likely that Samuel was at least three years old before Hannah took him to Shiloh.

Even though an offering of three bulls (see note on 1:25) may seem extravagant, it is probably best understood as reflecting Hannah's great thankfulness as well as Elkanah's relative affluence. Wenham (1979:79) has suggested that one bull was for the burnt offering, one for the purification offering expected after childbirth (Lev 12), and one for the peace offering made in payment of Hannah's vow. He notes that an ephah of flour (about half a bushel) is approximately three times the quantity of flour normally offered with a single bull (Num 15:9), supporting the idea that three bulls were offered.

After offering their sacrifices they brought Samuel to Eli (1:25-28). Hannah reminded Eli of their encounter some years earlier and said that since the Lord had answered her prayer, she was now prepared to fulfill her vow to the Lord. Then either Samuel, or more likely Elkanah as the head of the household, placed a seal on Hannah's action by bowing to the ground before the Lord (reading "he" in the last phrase of 1:28 with the MT; cf. NLT mg).

◆ 2. The Song of Hannah (1 Sam 2:1-10)

Then Hannah prayed:

"My heart rejoices in the LORD!
The LORD has made me strong.*
Now I have an answer for my enemies;
I rejoice because you rescued me.
2 No one is holy like the LORD!
There is no one besides you;
there is no Rock like our God.

3 "Stop acting so proud and haughty!
Don't speak with such arrogance!
For the LORD is a God who knows what you have done;
he will judge your actions.
4 The bow of the mighty is now broken,
and those who stumbled are now strong.
5 Those who were well fed are now starving,
and those who were starving are now full.
The childless woman now has seven children,
and the woman with many children wastes away.
6 The LORD gives both death and life;
he brings some down to the grave*
but raises others up.
7 The LORD makes some poor and others rich;
he brings some down and lifts others up.
8 He lifts the poor from the dust
and the needy from the garbage dump.
He sets them among princes,
placing them in seats of honor.
For all the earth is the LORD's,
and he has set the world in order.

9 "He will protect his faithful ones,
but the wicked will disappear in darkness.
No one will succeed by strength alone.
10 Those who fight against the LORD will be shattered.
He thunders against them from heaven;
the LORD judges throughout the earth.
He gives power to his king;
he increases the strength* of his anointed one."

2:1 Hebrew *has exalted my horn.* **2:6** Hebrew *to Sheol.* **2:10** Hebrew *he exalts the horn.*

NOTES

2:1 ***Lord.*** This is the reading in the MT (and in 4QSam[a]); the LXX reads "my God."

2:2 The MT and LXX each have three cola for this verse, but each differs in wording and order. Particularly significant is the LXX's "there is none holy beside you" (third cola) in place of MT's "for there is no one besides you" (second cola). The four cola that 4QSam[a] has in this verse seem to be a conflation of MT and LXX.

2:3 ***he will judge your actions.*** Lit., "by him deeds are measured." The idea is effectively captured in the NLT rendering.

2:5 ***those who were starving are now full.*** Lit., "the hungry *khadal.*" Historically this phrase has been understood as saying that those who were hungry cease (*khadal*), the implication being that they cease to hunger. But the existence of a second *khadal* [TH2308A, ZH2532] root, meaning "be fat" or "become fat" instead of "cease," has been demonstrated by Thomas (1957) and Calderone (1961, 1962).

2:8-9 Verses 8b and 9 differ from MT in both LXX and 4QSam[a]. Both the latter include the phrase "he gives to the vower his vow." The words appear to be an addition intended to link the song more closely to Hannah's personal experience.

2:10 ***Those who fight.*** The Kethiv of MT is singular: "he who fights." The NLT follows the plural, "those," found in the Qere reading of MT and in many Hebrew mss.

will be shattered. The LXX has a longer text here with strong similarities to the LXX of Jer 9:22-23 (Klein 1983:13). 4QSam[a] also has a longer text here, which, although it is too fragmentary for complete reconstruction, does show a few words that indicate differences with text of the LXX, and probably at least one line reminiscent of the Jeremiah passage. McCarter (1980b:68-71) adopts the very fragmentary 4QSam[a] plus as original. Klein (1983:13) suggests the longer text was a gloss already present in the Hebrew copy of Samuel used by the LXX translator. The longer texts of LXX and 4QSam[a] are probably best understood as products of literary expansion.

against them. Corresponding to "those who fight," above. The MT Kethiv is singular: "against him." The Qere and many Hebrew mss are plural. S. R. Driver (1913:27) suggests the singular particularizes individual members of the class of those who contend with the Lord. McCarter (1980b:70-73) and Klein (1983:13, 19), followed by NRSV, propose a correction of *'alayw* [TH5921/2050.2, ZH6584/2257] (against him) to a form of the divine name *'eli* [TH5920A, ZH6604] (the Most High). This results in the reading, "The Most High thunders in heaven." This, however, is conjecture and not preferable to MT.

COMMENTARY

Hannah's experience of God's grace in her life provided the occasion for this remarkable song of praise and thanks to the Lord. In her song, Hannah speaks with deep insight into God's sovereign dominion over nature and history and into the ways in which he accomplishes his purposes in surprising and transforming ways. Her words embrace, but at the same time transcend, the experience of divine faithfulness and blessing in her own life, because with prophetic insight, only to be accounted for by the inspiration of the Holy Spirit, she anticipated the rise of kingship in Israel (2:10).

Contrary to this assessment of Hannah's song, it has been the consensus of many mainstream biblical scholars that the psalm is not original in its present setting and that its words have been placed in Hannah's mouth by a late redactor.[1]

This conclusion rests on a variety of considerations, including the text critical,[2] the literary critical,[3] and the exegetical.[4] The most significant of these, however, is the reference to kingship in 2:10, the authenticity of which is regarded as highly dubious prior to the time of the establishment of the monarchy in Israel.[5]

There is little agreement among advocates of the secondary nature of the song on either the date of its origin or the date of its insertion into its present context. McCarter (1980b:75-76) dates it in the monarchical period as early as "the ninth or late tenth century"[6] but says its "insertion may have taken place quite late in the literary history of the Samuel corpus." In spite of the uncertainty about its origin and date, most scholars agree that the psalm does have at least some connection with Hannah's situation and, more importantly, that it serves to introduce themes that are significant for the rest of 1–2 Samuel.[7] Gutbrod (1956:22) says it introduces the central concerns of the subsequent narratives. Childs (1979:273) goes so far as to say that it provides an "interpretive key" for the entire history. But, as Eslinger (1985:100) points out, this sort of recognition of thematic continuity with the rest of 1–2 Samuel "undermines [the critic's] reason for calling the song redactional."

Acceptance of the song as authentic to Hannah still leaves open the question of whether she composed it herself, or adopted an already existent psalm that was fitting for her situation.[8] This question cannot be answered with certainty. Perhaps some of both are involved. Hannah may have drawn on expressions and terminology familiar to worshipers at the Tabernacle along with added insights given to her directly by the Holy Spirit. In the final analysis, the method by which the psalm was composed is not important. Its authenticity as an inspired word from God given through Hannah is.

Hannah's song is one of the greatest prayers of praise and thanksgiving to God found in the entire Bible. Comparisons have often been drawn between the basic themes of Hannah's song and those of Mary's Magnificat (Luke 1:46-55; for example, cf. 2:4, 7-8 with Luke 1:52; 2:5 with Luke 1:53), and also with the hymn of praise to the Lord found in Psalm 113 (cf. 2:8 and Ps 113:7-8a). (For a fuller discussion of the parallels, see Willis 1973.) The song begins with Hannah's joyful affirmation of how greatly the Lord has blessed her (2:1). God has done a wonderful and mighty act on her behalf in giving her a son. Yet the real source for her joy is not her personal gain, but rather God himself. Hannah views her own deliverance as something that both exalts the Lord and enables her to exult in God for his grace as a response to her enemies. In the three poetic lines of 2:2, Hannah addresses God with a remarkably profound description of his excellencies: He is one who is absolutely holy, completely unique (there is no God but the Lord), and supremely strong. Hannah understands that God is separate from his creation; he alone is God, and in him, his people can find refuge and protection. In view of God's exalted character, all people should bow before him because he will hold them accountable with righteous judgment for all that they say and do (2:3).

Hannah saw her own experience of God's deliverance (2:1-3) as an example of how God works in the larger world of people and nations (2:4-9). In both realms God's justice is often visible in his lifting up the weak and humble and in his bringing down the strong and arrogant. Hannah used a series of seven contrasts (mighty and weak [2:4], well fed and starving [2:5a], barren and fertile [2:5b], death and life [2:6a], sickness and health [2:6b], poor and rich [2:7], common and noble [2:8]) to depict the reversals of status that God sovereignly brings about in the affairs of individuals and nations. God can do this because "all the earth is the LORD's" (2:8). It is all the work of his hands.

The dual themes of contrast and reversal introduced in these verses anticipate much of what will be described in the remainder of 1–2 Samuel. Even later in this chapter (2:12-26) one cannot but be struck by the contrast between Hannah and the sons of Eli. Hannah is a humble and godly woman, while the sons of Eli are priestly officials who are dishonest and immoral. Hannah and her house are elevated, but the house of Eli is ultimately removed from priestly responsibility. Other major contrasts and reversals in 1–2 Samuel include the loss of the Ark to the Philistines and its eventual return to Israel, Samuel's anointing of David instead of the more likely candidates among his older brothers, the relationship between Saul and David and between David and Goliath, and the relationship between the Philistines and Israel. In addition, Hannah's song lays the groundwork for understanding why Israel's request for a king (cf. chs 8 and 12) was a denial of the Lord's kingship. Hannah's song clearly acknowledges God's sovereignty and his providential guidance of the destinies of peoples and nations. It affirms that deliverance from oppression and humiliation comes only from the Lord. But as the narratives of 1 Samuel unfold, we learn that Israel was not willing to find their national security in God's faithful, providential care for them as a people. Rather, they wanted to seek it in a human king, whom they thought would be able to lead them to victory over their enemies in battle, as did the kings of the other nations around them. This refusal to trust in the protection of the Lord, their covenantal king, was a denial of the same covenant faithfulness and sovereign power of God that Hannah's song acclaims.

In 2:9-10 Hannah looks forward with prophetic insight to a time when God will cause justice to triumph in all the earth. This will be accomplished by a messianic (anointed) king. As such its reference is ultimately to Christ at his second advent, but at the same time it reflects Hannah's anticipation of the realization of the promise of kingship for the nation of Israel (cf. Num 23:21; Deut 17:14-15).

ENDNOTES

1. See, for example, Brueggemann 1990a; Hertzberg 1964; Klein 1983; Mauchline 1971; McCarter 1980b; Smith 1912; Stoebe 1973; van Zijl 1989.
2. Klein (1983:14) says the "slightly divergent positions of the poem in MT, 4Q, and LXX imply its secondary character even from a text-critical perspective."
3. Carlson (1964:45) says, "It is perfectly evident that Hannah's song of praise is a Deuteronomic insertion into the web of tradition, intended to deepen the ideological interpretation of the events described in 1–2 Sam." A view such as this is rooted in the theory of a Deuteronomistic redaction of the entire corpus of historical material from Joshua to 2 Kings (see comments in Introduction).
4. Klein (1983:14) comments, "While 1 Samuel speaks of Hannah as mother of six children (Samuel, plus the five children mentioned in 2:21), the song itself speaks of a barren woman who has seven children (2:5). The tone of the poem is national, alluding to male enemies and military metaphors (e.g., 2:4), neither of which are appropriate to

Hannah. The final prayer for the king is impossible for Hannah: her son Samuel, as an old man, held earthly kingship to be a rejection of Yahweh's kingship." Brueggemann (1990a:16) says, "The song has public, national dimensions in speaking of enemies (v. 1), war (v. 4), and eventually even of a king (v. 10). It is likely that the song was originally used by the royal establishment to celebrate monarchial victories in war."

5. Commentaries and introductions are nearly unanimous in their agreement that the song cannot predate the monarchy. See Willis (1973:139-140) for an extensive list. Eissfeldt (1965:281) says, "The possibility of genuineness can hardly be seriously considered with reference to the Song of Hannah." Klein (1970:675) says that the strongest argument against the song having originated with Hannah is the reference to the king in 2:10. He comments, "How, scholars ask, could Hannah pray for blessings on the king long before the time when aged Samuel anointed Saul as first king?" McCarter (1980b:75) says, "The lyrics presuppose the monarchy . . . and the song cannot have been contemporary with the events to which the composers of the present narrative relate it."
6. Albright (1968:20-22) and Willis (1973:139-154) argue for an eleventh-century BC date. Particularly significant in the argument of Willis is his demonstration of similarities between the Song of Hannah and other early Hebrew poems in poetic style, language, and thought. These other early poems include the Song of the Sea (Exod 15:1-18), the Balaam oracles (Num 23:7-10, 18-24; 24:3-9, 15-19, 20-24), the Song of Moses (Deut 32:1-43), the Blessing of Moses (Deut 33:1-29), and the Song of Deborah (Judg 5).
7. Stoebe (1973:106-107) says that with this psalm "the entire subsequent course of history is exposed as an outflow and manifestation of the wisdom of God (2:2-3). . . . And as with the narratives of Samuel's youth, so also this Song presupposes the contents of the books of Samuel." See additional discussion in the Introduction under the headings "Literary Style," "Major Themes," and "Theological Concerns."
8. Ridderbos (1939:311) suggests that Hannah utilized an already existing psalm. Ridderbos argues that it cannot be denied that expectation of the "endtime" (*Endzeit*) possibly already existed in Israel during the time of Hannah. In his view the statement in 2:10 that the Lord will judge the ends of the earth, along with the references to the "king" and "his anointed," are to be understood in the context of that expected end-time.

◆ 3. Samuel serves the Lord in Shiloh; judgment pronounced on the house of Eli (1 Sam 2:11-36)

11 Then Elkanah returned home to Ramah without Samuel. And the boy served the LORD by assisting Eli the priest.

12 Now the sons of Eli were scoundrels who had no respect for the LORD 13 or for their duties as priests. Whenever anyone offered a sacrifice, Eli's sons would send over a servant with a three-pronged fork. While the meat of the sacrificed animal was still boiling, 14 the servant would stick the fork into the pot and demand that whatever it brought up be given to Eli's sons. All the Israelites who came to worship at Shiloh were treated this way. 15 Sometimes the servant would come even before the animal's fat had been burned on the altar. He would demand raw meat before it had been boiled so that it could be used for roasting.

16 The man offering the sacrifice might reply, "Take as much as you want, but the fat must be burned first." Then the servant would demand, "No, give it to me now, or I'll take it by force." 17 So the sin of these young men was very serious in the LORD's sight, for they treated the LORD's offerings with contempt.

18But Samuel, though he was only a
boy, served the LORD. He wore a linen gar-
ment like that of a priest.* 19Each year his
mother made a small coat for him and
brought it to him when she came with her
husband for the sacrifice. 20Before they
returned home, Eli would bless Elkanah
and his wife and say, "May the LORD give
you other children to take the place of
this one she gave to the LORD.*" 21And the
LORD gave Hannah three sons and two
daughters. Meanwhile, Samuel grew up in
the presence of the LORD.

22Now Eli was very old, but he was aware
of what his sons were doing to the people
of Israel. He knew, for instance, that his
sons were seducing the young women who
assisted at the entrance of the Tabernacle.*
23Eli said to them, "I have been hearing re-
ports from all the people about the wicked
things you are doing. Why do you keep sin-
ning? 24You must stop, my sons! The reports
I hear among the LORD's people are not
good. 25If someone sins against another
person, God* can mediate for the guilty
party. But if someone sins against the LORD,
who can intercede?" But Eli's sons wouldn't
listen to their father, for the LORD was al-
ready planning to put them to death.

26Meanwhile, the boy Samuel grew
taller and grew in favor with the LORD and
with the people.

27One day a man of God came to Eli and
gave him this message from the LORD: "I
revealed myself* to your ancestors when
the people of Israel were slaves in Egypt.
28I chose your ancestor Aaron* from
among all the tribes of Israel to be my
priest, to offer sacrifices on my altar, to
burn incense, and to wear the priestly
vest* as he served me. And I assigned the
sacrificial offerings to you priests. 29So
why do you scorn my sacrifices and offer-
ings? Why do you give your sons more
honor than you give me—for you and they
have become fat from the best offerings
of my people Israel!

30"Therefore, the LORD, the God of Is-
rael, says: I promised that your branch of
the tribe of Levi* would always be my
priests. But I will honor those who honor
me, and I will despise those who think
lightly of me. 31The time is coming when
I will put an end to your family, so it will
no longer serve as my priests. All the
members of your family will die before
their time. None will reach old age. 32You
will watch with envy as I pour out pros-
perity on the people of Israel. But no
members of your family will ever live out
their days. 33Those who survive will live in
sadness and grief, and their children will
die a violent death.* 34And to prove that
what I have said will come true, I will
cause your two sons, Hophni and Phine-
has, to die on the same day!

35"Then I will raise up a faithful priest
who will serve me and do what I desire. I
will establish his family, and they will be
priests to my anointed kings forever. 36Then
all of your surviving family will bow before
him, begging for money and food. 'Please,'
they will say, 'give us jobs among the
priests so we will have enough to eat.'"

2:18 Hebrew *He wore a linen ephod.* **2:20** As in Dead Sea Scrolls and Greek version; Masoretic Text reads *this one he requested of the LORD.* **2:22** Hebrew *Tent of Meeting.* Some manuscripts lack this entire sentence. **2:25** Or *the judges.* **2:27** As in Greek and Syriac versions; Hebrew reads *Did I reveal myself.* **2:28a** Hebrew *your father.* **2:28b** Hebrew *an ephod.* **2:30** Hebrew *that your house and your father's house.* **2:33** As in Dead Sea Scrolls, which read *die by the sword;* Masoretic Text reads *die like mortals.*

NOTES

2:12 ***scoundrels.*** Lit., "sons of Belial" (*bene beliya'al* [TH1121/1100, ZH1201/1175]). See note on 1:16.

who had no respect for the LORD. Lit., "who did not know the LORD." "Know" (*yad'u* [TH3045, ZH3359]) is to be understood here in the covenantal sense of recognizing the authority of Yahweh, and viewing his covenantal stipulations as binding.

2:25 ***was already planning.*** Heb., *khapets* [TH2654, ZH2911]. In this context it expresses God's purpose or plan to do something. It is used in a way similar to Isa 53:10: "It was the LORD's good plan [*khapets*] to crush him and cause him grief." In Isa 55:11, God says his word always accomplishes "all I want it to" (*khapatsti*).

COMMENTARY

This section is clearly designed to highlight the contrast between two homes, and the ways in which the Lord was working out his purposes in and through each of them. There is the home of Elkanah, Hannah, and Samuel on the one hand, and that of Eli, Hophni, and Phinehas on the other. The contrast between these families is brought into focus by four positive comments made by the narrator concerning young Samuel (cf. 2:11, 18, 21, 26) that are distributed among detailed descriptions of the wickedness of Eli's sons and the judgment that God was to bring on Eli's house. This contrast, disclosed by narrative structure, is heightened in the Hebrew text by a linguistic parallel in which Samuel is depicted as growing (*gadal* [TH1431, ZH1540]) in stature and favor before the Lord (2:21, 26), while the iniquity of Eli's sons is characterized as great (2:17; *gadol* [TH1419, ZH1524]; NLT, "very serious"). So the outworking of the reversal of fortune theme of Hannah's Song (2:1-10), in which God lifts up the weak and humble and brings judgment on the arrogant and proud, again begins to take on human form.

The section begins with the announcement (2:11) that Samuel remained at the Tabernacle in Shiloh to serve as an assistant to Eli the priest when his parents returned to their home in Ramah. This is immediately followed by a description of the unscrupulous behavior of Eli's sons (2:12-17), who enriched themselves unjustly by taking, with force if necessary, inappropriate amounts of uncooked meat from the sacrificial offerings, in violation of Mosaic law (Lev 7:29-34; 10:14, 15; Deut 18:1-5). They are characterized as "scoundrels who had no respect for the LORD or for their duties as priests" (2:12-13; see note), and their sin is described as "very serious in the LORD's sight, for they treated the LORD's offerings with contempt" (2:17). These are strong statements, and they arouse the expectation that judgment is just around the corner.

Things were quite different, however, in the home of Elkanah and Hannah (2:18-21). They continued to make their yearly pilgrimage to Shiloh for worship as before, but now each year Hannah took along a new linen tunic for their son Samuel to wear. Eli respected Hannah's faithfulness to her vow (1:11), and he blessed her and her husband when they came (2:20), asking that the Lord would give them additional children. In due time, by the Lord's mercy, this came to pass. So the parents, who had willingly given their son to the service of the Lord at the Tabernacle, were blessed with three more sons and two daughters (2:21). From this point forward, we hear no more of Elkanah and Hannah in the narratives of 1–2 Samuel. They had fulfilled their role in the Lord's plan, not only by bringing Samuel into the world, but also by committing him to the service of the Lord at Shiloh. After this passage, the narrative focus shifts to Samuel and his role in the Lord's plans for his people.

After describing God's blessing on the family of Elkanah and Hannah, the author returns to the household of Eli. In 2:22-25 we learn that Eli's sons not only had contempt for their priestly duties, but that they also engaged in sexual misconduct at the very place where Moses had consecrated Aaron and his sons to serve the Lord as priests (that is, at the entrance to the house of the Lord; cf. Exod 29:1-9). These were men uncommonly corrupt in both their religious and moral behavior. Their scandalous actions were public knowledge throughout the land. An old man, Eli rebuked them for their conduct, but took no action to remove them from their official duties. Because Eli, the high priest, the one who wore the gold plate on his turban inscribed with the words "HOLY TO THE LORD" (Exod 28:36-38), could do no better than offer a weak protest against the outrageous conduct of his sons, he in effect condoned their activities, and the name of the Lord continued to be profaned.

A sobering statement is contained in 2:25b. The wording should be carefully noticed (see note on 2:25). It does not say that Eli's sons had become so hardened in their sinful ways that the Lord decided to put them to death, but rather that Eli's sons did not listen to him *because* the Lord was *already planning to put them to death.* In other words, the resistance of Hophni and Phinehas to Eli's call to repentance was not the *reason* for God's judgment but was the *result* of his prior judgment. Here, as elsewhere in the Bible, we find that God sometimes punishes sin by giving those who persist in disobedience over to the sinful desires of their hearts (e.g., Pharaoh, Exod 4:21; 7:3; 9:12; and even Saul, as will be suggested later; cf. Ps 81:11-12; Rom 1:24; Heb 3:13). When this happens, the time for repentance is past. This sort of judgment had already fallen on Hophni and Phinehas.[1] This statement, of course, raises difficult theological questions, particularly those centering around the Bible's teaching on divine sovereignty and human responsibility in connection with the evil actions of human beings. How is it possible for God's providence to embrace everything that comes to pass (Ps 103:19) and for God to still not be the author of sin? See the discussion in the Introduction under Theological Concerns: "A Lofty Concept of God That Acclaims Divine Sovereignty" (cf. also Article 13 of the Belgic Confession, "The Providence of God and His Government of All Things").

In this particular case, interpreters have taken two quite different directions in their analysis of God's action, depending largely on prior theological assumptions. Those who find multiple theologies embedded in Old Testament traditions tend to view this incident as an example of a situation in which human beings have become pawns in the hands of a scheming deity who leads them toward a fate beyond their control because of sins that were really not their own fault. Eslinger (1985:153) says that "Yahweh has engineered the unnecessary destruction of the Elides. . . . If he had not desired to kill Eli's sons, perhaps they would have listened to their father." This sort of interpretation, however, is unacceptable because it reflects a theological concept that is in direct conflict with numerous Old Testament statements that declare God to be holy, righteous, and good (Lev 19:2; Pss 92:15; 119:68; Isa 6:3; Hab 1:13). Throughout 1–2 Samuel God is seen as trustworthy, not as capricious and arbitrary in his actions. He is presented as a gracious and merciful God who cares for his people, but at the same time as a holy God who brings judgment on sin and disobedience. This theme of protection for the godly and destruction for the wicked is central to the poetic sections that frame the book ("He will protect his faithful ones, but the wicked will disappear in darkness. . . . Those who fight against the LORD will be shattered" 2:9-10; "To the faithful you show yourself faithful; . . . but to the wicked you show yourself hostile," 2 Sam 22:26-27) and is exhibited repeatedly throughout the narratives that these poems enfold. While God's judgments, as Calvin has said, are a "great deep" that should be regarded with admiration rather than complaint, he shows himself to be trustworthy and gracious to those who humbly seek to worship him in sincerity and truth. Here, as in other cases of hardening in the Old Testament, we encounter something that is not "arbitrarily imposed on a righteous or even morally neutral object. Rather, his [Yahweh's] hardening was an element of his righteous judgment on recalcitrant sinners."[2]

After a brief comment that Samuel was growing in favor with the Lord and the people (2:26), the narrator gives a detailed description of a message of judgment against Eli and his sons, delivered by an unnamed prophet of the Lord (2:27-36). Eli is first reminded how the Lord had given his ancestor Aaron important tasks in connection with Israel's deliverance from Egypt (cf. Exod 4:13-17, 27-31; 7:1) and then how he had chosen the descendants of Aaron to assume the priestly office with the responsibilities of serving at the altar (Lev 1–7), burning incense (Exod 30:1-10), and wearing the ephod (a means of receiving divine revelation; cf. Exod 28:4-13; 39:2-7). In connection with these duties, the priests were allotted, for their own use, specific portions of the sacrifices that the people brought to the altar (Lev 6:14-18; 7:28-36). In view of these things, Eli is charged with both scorning the Lord's sacrifices and offerings and honoring his sons more than the Lord by his toleration of their abuse of priestly authority and by their and his profiteering from the offerings brought to the Lord (2:29). Eli's actions spoke louder than his words. On the basis of a principle that is prominent throughout the books of Samuel (blessing for obedience, and judgment for disobedience; see 2:30), Eli is told that his progeny will be excluded from full participation in the privileges and responsibilities of the priestly office that had been given to Aaron and his descendants. As a sign that this judgment will certainly come to pass, he is told that his sons, Hophni and Phinehas, will die on the same day (2:34).

Lest there be any misunderstanding, it should be noted that 2:30 is not telling us that God is hereby revoking a promise formerly made to the house of Aaron. It is not fitting to conclude along with Brueggemann (1990a:23) that in this action "Yahweh nullifies the eternal promise." What happens here is that Eli is informed that his descendants will suffer greatly and they will ultimately be replaced by "a faithful priest who will serve me and do what I desire" (2:35). Interpreters are divided on the identification of this "faithful priest" of the future. Some have argued that it is a reference to Samuel who is to displace Eli as the religious authority in the land. But it should be noted that in the very next chapter Samuel is called to be a prophet rather than a priest, and that while he did perform priestly functions in connection with the offering of sacrifices, it seems better to understand the reference in 2:35 to a priest in the more distant future, who would be a descendant of Aaron through the line of Eleazar rather than through the line of Ithamar to which Eli belonged. During the reign of David, both Abiathar, from the line of Ithamar, and Zadok, from the line of Eleazar, served in the role of high priest. But in the time of Solomon, Abiathar was removed from the priesthood as a fulfillment of this prediction (cf. 1 Kgs 2:26-27). From that point forward, the line of Zadok continued to hold the high priestly office until the rule of Antiochus Epiphanes (175–164 BC) when the priesthood was sold to Menelaus (cf. 1 Chr 6:8-15; Ezra 3:2; 2 Macc 4:23-50). In a typological sense, the "faithful priest" of 2:35 ultimately looks beyond the Old Testament period and points forward to Christ, who combines in one person all that the Old Testament offices of prophet, priest, and king prefigure.

ENDNOTES

1. The predicament of Hophni and Phinehas is much like that of those described in the Woman Wisdom's speech of Prov 1:20-33; they are rejected when they call upon her because they had refused her prior call to them. As Longman (2006:111, 113-114) comments, "[The Woman Wisdom] shows no mercy to those who come to their senses in the midst of the punishment that their foolish action brings on them. . . . They rejected her advice, so now they must experience the results of their own counsels."
2. Chisholm (1996:432). Chisholm continues (1996:434), "Divine hardening, whether accomplished directly or indirectly, is an element of divine judgment whereby God exhibits His justice and sovereignty. The objects of such judgment are never morally righteous or neutral, but are rebels against God's authority. Divine hardening is never arbitrarily implemented, but comes in response to rejection of God's authoritative word or standards."

◆ 4. Samuel called to be a prophet (1 Sam 3:1–4:1a)

Meanwhile, the boy Samuel served the
LORD by assisting Eli. Now in those days
messages from the LORD were very rare,
and visions were quite uncommon.

2One night Eli, who was almost blind by
now, had gone to bed. 3The lamp of God
had not yet gone out, and Samuel was
sleeping in the Tabernacle* near the Ark
of God. 4Suddenly the LORD called out,
"Samuel!"

"Yes?" Samuel replied. "What is it?"
5He got up and ran to Eli. "Here I am. Did
you call me?"

"I didn't call you," Eli replied. "Go back
to bed." So he did.

6Then the LORD called out again,
"Samuel!"

Again Samuel got up and went to Eli.
"Here I am. Did you call me?"

"I didn't call you, my son," Eli said. "Go
back to bed."

7Samuel did not yet know the LORD be-
cause he had never had a message from
the LORD before. 8So the LORD called a third
time, and once more Samuel got up and
went to Eli. "Here I am. Did you call me?"

Then Eli realized it was the LORD who
was calling the boy. 9So he said to Samu-
el, "Go and lie down again, and if some-
one calls again, say, 'Speak, LORD, your
servant is listening.'" So Samuel went back
to bed.

10And the LORD came and called as be-
fore, "Samuel! Samuel!"

And Samuel replied, "Speak, your ser-
vant is listening."

11Then the LORD said to Samuel, "I am
about to do a shocking thing in Israel. 12I
am going to carry out all my threats against
Eli and his family, from beginning to end.
13I have warned him that judgment is com-
ing upon his family forever, because his
sons are blaspheming God* and he hasn't
disciplined them. 14So I have vowed that
the sins of Eli and his sons will never be
forgiven by sacrifices or offerings."

15Samuel stayed in bed until morning,
then got up and opened the doors of the
Tabernacle* as usual. He was afraid to tell
Eli what the LORD had said to him. 16But
Eli called out to him, "Samuel, my son."

"Here I am," Samuel replied.
17"What did the LORD say to you? Tell
me everything. And may God strike you
and even kill you if you hide anything
from me!" 18So Samuel told Eli everything;
he didn't hold anything back. "It is the
LORD's will," Eli replied. "Let him do what
he thinks best."
19As Samuel grew up, the LORD was with
him, and everything Samuel said proved
to be reliable. 20And all Israel, from Dan in
the north to Beersheba in the south, knew
that Samuel was confirmed as a prophet
of the LORD. 21The LORD continued to ap-
pear at Shiloh and gave messages to Sam-
uel there at the Tabernacle. 4:1And
Samuel's words went out to all the people
of Israel.

3:3 Hebrew *the Temple of the LORD.* 3:13 As in Greek version; Hebrew reads *his sons have made themselves contemptible.* 3:15 Hebrew *the house of the LORD.*

NOTES

3:13 ***sons are blaspheming God.*** This is the reading of the LXX, and this is one of 18 so-called *tiqqune sopherim* (scribal corrections). The Masoretes proposed that the MT reading, "made themselves contemptible" (so NLT mg), was an early change in the text in order to avoid disrespect to the Deity (in this case by not even speaking of someone blaspheming).

3:17 ***may God strike you and even kill you if you hide anything from me!*** Lit., "May God do so to you, and more also." This is a curse formula, and was perhaps accompanied by a gesture signifying the means of punishment.

COMMENTARY

The narrator clearly links this new literary unit with the preceding narrative by introducing it with another commendatory comment on Samuel, "Meanwhile, the boy Samuel served the LORD by assisting Eli" (3:1). The comment is much like the ones distributed throughout 2:11-26 (2:11, 18, 21, 26). From this point forward, the chapter displays a chiastic structure (or ring composition) that places the focus of the report on a repetition of the judgment pronounced on the Elides, but this time with a significant difference: The word of the Lord now comes to the young lad Samuel.[1]

- A. The absence of the prophetic word (3:1)
  - B. Eli's decline (3:2)
    - C. The Lord calls Samuel (3:3-9)
      - D. A prophecy of judgment on the Elides given to Samuel (3:10-15)
    - C'. Eli calls Samuel and requests a report (3:16-18)
  - B'. Samuel grows as a man of God (3:19a)
- A'. The presence of the prophetic word (3:19b–4:1a)

This concentric structure that highlights the prophecy of judgment on the Elides is combined with a clear progression from the absence of the divine word at the beginning of the chapter (3:1) to its presence at the end, with Samuel becoming the person who would bring God's word to all Israel (3:19–4:1a). Because Samuel is given such an important role as the bearer of God's word in this chapter (initially to Eli, but then beyond Eli to all Israel), many have viewed the chapter as an example of a "prophetic call narrative" (cf. Exod 3 [Moses]; Judg 6:11-24 [Gideon]; Isa 6;

Jer 1). This assessment, however, may be questioned because the narrative lacks a number of the characteristic elements of other call narratives.[2] More recently, it has been argued that the genre classification should be that of an ancient Near Eastern "dream theophany" rather than call narrative (Gnuse 1982, 1984).[3] It should be noted, though, that the description of Samuel's condition in this passage has no resemblance to a dream, and it is highly questionable whether the message he received should be classified as an example of "dream revelation." It does appear that Samuel encountered some sort of manifestation of the Lord's presence in which he both heard and saw the Lord (cf. 3:10, lit., "The LORD came and stood and called"). Accordingly, the description seems to be that of a visionary experience (cf. 3:15b, lit., "He was afraid to tell Eli *the vision*"), much like those of many of Israel's classical prophets.

While the genre of this chapter may be disputed, it is clear that the chapter is telling us about some very important things: (1) An inescapable judgment is pronounced on the house of Eli for the behavior described in 2:12-15, 22; (2) the situation in Israel changes from one in which a message from the Lord was highly unusual (3:1) to one in which this was normal (3:21); (3) Samuel is recognized by the people of Israel as a prophet of the Lord (3:20). It is this latter occurrence that assumes enormous significance in the ensuing narratives. It is by the word of the prophet Samuel that kingship is established in Israel. Because kingship is inaugurated by the word of a prophet, all the kings of Israel are accountable to the prophetic word. The foundation for the important relationship between kings and prophets in Israel's later history begins to emerge in this chapter.

After describing the scarcity of the prophetic word in the time of the judges (3:1) and the failing eyesight of the elderly Eli (3:2; cf. 2:22 where we are told "Eli was very old"), we are given a description of how the Lord spoke directly to Samuel for the first time (3:3-9). Eli and Samuel slept within the Tabernacle precincts, with Samuel's place being close to the Ark of God (3:3; note that it is the Ark that becomes the focus of events described in chs 4–6). It was there above the atonement cover (or "mercy seat," cf. Exod 25:17, KJV) that the Lord had come to dwell among his people, and it was from this place that he had spoken in the time of Moses (cf. Exod 25:21-22; 29:43-46). The Ark symbolized the Lord's presence and had enormous importance in the life of the nation as the throne seat of Israel's divine King. However, in spite of the presence of this symbol, the word of the Lord had been absent in Shiloh.

When the Lord did again speak at Shiloh (3:4, 6), the narrator tells us that Samuel did not discern that it was the Lord who was calling him because he "did not yet know the LORD because he had never had a message from the LORD before" (3:7). This is not to say that Samuel had no knowledge of who the Lord was or of what he desired from his people, but rather that he had not yet experienced God speaking to him in such a direct manner. When the Lord called a third time, it was Eli who realized that the Lord was speaking, and he told Samuel that if he heard the call again to respond "Speak, LORD, your servant is listening" (3:9). At the Lord's next calling, Samuel did so, seeing a manifestation of the divine presence (3:10 literally says "the LORD came and stood there and called"). This was a visionary experience for Samuel (3:15b) in spite of the fact that, as 3:1 says, visions were "quite uncommon" in that time. There is no information given concerning the form of God's appearance, nor about Samuel receiving a specific call to be a prophet. But Samuel did as Eli instructed him, and as a result he received a direct revelation from the Lord.

Ironically enough, the message that Samuel received (3:10-15) was one of judgment on Eli and his family, in agreement with the prophecy of 2:27-36. On this occasion, the judgment focused on Eli for not disciplining his sons (3:13); its time was imminent (3:11), and its terrifying character is described as something that would "make the ears of everyone who hears of it tingle" (3:11, lit.; NLT, "I am about to do a shocking thing in Israel"), an expression used later in Israel's history when God's judgment of the Exile had become inevitable (2 Kgs 21:12; Jer 19:3). This judgment was now also inevitable because the Lord said that the sacrifices that the house of Eli held in contempt (cf. 2:17, 29) would no longer serve to bring atonement (3:14; see note on 2:25).

Not surprisingly, Samuel was afraid to tell Eli what the Lord had said to him (3:15), but the next morning Eli called Samuel and insisted upon a full report (3:16-18). Using a curse formula, Eli put Samuel under oath (see note on 3:17), and Samuel told him all that the Lord had said. Eli's reaction was striking. He accepted the punishment as from the Lord's hand and bowed in humble submission to the Lord's will (3:18b; cf. David's similar reaction after being forced to flee Jerusalem by his son Absalom [2 Sam 15:26; 16:11-12]; and Job's reaction to the disasters that struck him and his family [Job 1:21; 2:10]).[4] Even though Eli accepted the divine verdict, and recognized the justice of his sentence, this was insufficient to remove the guilt and punishment of his previous behavior.

In the last of a long series of commendatory comments (3:19; cf. 2:11, 18, 21, 26; 3:1) that enable us to follow Samuel's development from childhood to the assumption of the prophetic function, we are told that the Lord was "with him" so that whatever he said in the name of the Lord came to pass (lit., "[the Lord] let none of [Samuel's] words fall to the ground," 3:19). In this way, all the people of Israel became aware that there was a prophet in their midst (cf. Deut 18:21-22). Even though his first assignment as a prophet was a difficult one, he was faithful in the performance of his duty and did not shrink from an unpleasant task. Such would be his calling many more times in the future. In the meantime, the situation in Israel had changed radically from that described in 3:1 ("messages from the LORD were very rare, and visions were quite uncommon") to that of 3:20-21 ("And all Israel . . . knew that Samuel was confirmed as a prophet of the LORD. The LORD continued to appear at Shiloh and gave messages to Samuel there"). The word of God had now broken into the darkness of the time of the judges. In response to the religious and moral decay that had spread through the land, the Lord had become silent. But then God took a new initiative and sent his word to his people, not through the discredited religious officials of the land but rather through a young lad who had been born as an answer to prayer and had been dedicated to the Lord from before his birth. God's word through this faithful servant was about to cause enormous changes in Israel's national life.

ENDNOTES

1. See Fishbane (1982:193-194) and Youngblood (1992:592).
2. See Habel (1965) who isolated six characteristic elements in the call narratives of Gideon and Moses, including: (1) divine confrontation; (2) introductory word; (3) commission; (4) objection; (5) reassurance; and (6) sign.
3. See the helpful reviews in Gordon 1985 and Long 1985.
4. Eslinger's rather cynical suggestions (1985:154-155)—that Eli's response to the words of Samuel (lit., "He is the Lord; let him do what is good in his eyes") is ambiguous and that hidden behind this seemingly pious statement is anger and frustration—are unfounded. Eslinger suggests Eli knew that Yahweh's claim that he did not try to stop his sons was untrue and for this reason he said "He is Yahweh, he does as he pleases." Eslinger understands Eli's statement to mean that he realizes that "Yahweh is answerable to no one. Fearing a fate worse than death, Eli hides his cynicism about Yahweh beneath the guise of piety and submission to the Almighty."

◆ B. Judgment on the Elides; the Ark of the Covenant Captured and Returned by the Philistines (1 Sam 4:1b–7:1)

1. The Ark captured; the deaths of Eli and his sons (1 Sam 4:1b-22)

At that time Israel was at war with the Philistines. The Israelite army was camped near
Ebenezer, and the Philistines were at Aphek.
2The Philistines attacked and defeated the
army of Israel, killing 4,000 men. 3After the
battle was over, the troops retreated to their camp, and the elders of Israel asked, "Why did the LORD allow us to be defeated by the Philistines?" Then they said, "Let's bring the Ark of the Covenant of the LORD from Shiloh. If we carry it into battle with us, it* will save us from our enemies."

4So they sent men to Shiloh to bring the Ark of the Covenant of the LORD of Heaven's Armies, who is enthroned between the cherubim. Hophni and Phinehas, the sons of Eli, were also there with
the Ark of the Covenant of God. 5When all
the Israelites saw the Ark of the Covenant of the LORD coming into the camp, their shout of joy was so loud it made the ground shake!

6"What's going on?" the Philistines asked. "What's all the shouting about in the Hebrew camp?" When they were told it was because the Ark of the LORD had
arrived, 7they panicked. "The gods have*
come into their camp!" they cried. "This is a disaster! We have never had to face
anything like this before! 8Help! Who can
save us from these mighty gods of Israel? They are the same gods who destroyed the Egyptians with plagues when Israel was in
the wilderness. 9Fight as never before,
Philistines! If you don't, we will become the Hebrews' slaves just as they have been ours! Stand up like men and fight!"

10So the Philistines fought desperately, and Israel was defeated again. The slaughter was great; 30,000 Israelite soldiers died that day. The survivors turned and
fled to their tents. 11The Ark of God was
captured, and Hophni and Phinehas, the two sons of Eli, were killed.

12A man from the tribe of Benjamin ran from the battlefield and arrived at Shiloh later that same day. He had torn his clothes and put dust on his head to show
his grief. 13Eli was waiting beside the road
to hear the news of the battle, for his heart trembled for the safety of the Ark of God. When the messenger arrived and told what had happened, an outcry resounded throughout the town.

14"What is all the noise about?" Eli asked.

The messenger rushed over to Eli, [15]who
was ninety-eight years old and blind. [16]He
said to Eli, "I have just come from the
battlefield—I was there this very day."

"What happened, my son?" Eli demanded.

[17]"Israel has been defeated by the Philistines," the messenger replied. "The people have been slaughtered, and your two sons, Hophni and Phinehas, were also killed. And the Ark of God has been captured."

[18]When the messenger mentioned what had happened to the Ark of God, Eli fell backward from his seat beside the gate. He broke his neck and died, for he was old and overweight. He had been Israel's judge for forty years.

[19]Eli's daughter-in-law, the wife of Phinehas, was pregnant and near her time of delivery. When she heard that the Ark of God had been captured and that her father-in-law and husband were dead,
she went into labor and gave birth. [20]She
died in childbirth, but before she passed away the midwives tried to encourage her. "Don't be afraid," they said. "You have a baby boy!" But she did not answer or pay attention to them.

[21]She named the child Ichabod (which means "Where is the glory?"), for she said, "Israel's glory is gone." She named him this because the Ark of God had been captured and because her father-in-law and
husband were dead. [22]Then she said, "The
glory has departed from Israel, for the Ark of God has been captured."

4:3 Or *he.* **4:7** Or *A god has.*

NOTES

4:1b ***At that time Israel was at war with the Philistines.*** This phrase, beginning 4:1b, introduces a new scene in the narrative. Before 1b, the LXX has a lengthy addition: "Eli grew very old, and his sons continued to act more and more wickedly in the presence of Yahweh." The addition adds to the scene set by the opening words of 1b.

4:4 ***enthroned between the cherubim.*** *Yosheb* [TH3427, ZH3782], translated here "enthroned," means "to sit" on either a chair or a throne (cf. 2 Kgs 11:19; Jer 33:17 for its use in connection with sitting on a throne). Because no preposition is included in the Hebrew for this phrase it could be translated "enthroned" or "seated" either "on," "between," or "above" the cherubim. In G. H. Wilson's discussion of *yosheb* (NIDOTTE 2.550-551) he says, "A special use of the vb. describes Yahweh as sitting enthroned 'between the cherubim' above the Ark of the Covenant (1 Sam 4:4; 2 Sam 6:2; 2 Kgs 19:15; 1 Chr 13:6; Ps 99:1; Isa 37:16) or in Zion (Ps 9:11)."

4:11 ***The Ark of God was captured.*** This expression occurs five times in the remainder of the chapter and is the dominant theme of the entire passage (4:11, 17, 19, 21, 22).

4:21 ***Ichabod (which means "Where is the glory?").*** Heb., *'i-kabod* [TH350, ZH376]. Interpreters are divided over whether the particle *'i* is to be taken as a negative particle ("*no*-glory") or as an interrogative particle ("*where* [TH335, ZH361] is the glory?"). The NLT opts for the latter understanding. In either case, the name signifies that the glory has gone.

COMMENTARY

First Samuel 4 is a chapter of fulfillment (de Jong 1978:25). God's judgment on the Elides, which had been prophesied on two separate occasions (2:27-36; 3:11-14), was not an idle threat. Its administration through the instrumentality of the Philistines demonstrated that God's word is trustworthy and reliable. God will fulfill all that he promises, whether blessing or cursing. Although chapters 4–6 are closely connected with the prophecy of judgment on the Elides, this section of 1 Samuel does interrupt the story of Samuel's life, which is one of the primary concerns of chapters 1–3. Samuel is never mentioned in chapters 4–6, but he reappears in chapter 7 where, in contrast to chapter 4, the Lord comes to the rescue of the Israelites when they are once again threatened by the Philistines. It seems that the purpose of the author is to highlight the contrast between Israel's vulnerability to defeat by enemy attacks when they had turned away from covenant faithfulness as compared to their invulnerability to the same threats when they confessed their sins and committed themselves wholly to the Lord (7:3, 6). In these chapters it is clear that Israel's security as a nation is closely linked with faithfulness to her covenant obligations.

The Ark plays a central role in chapter 4.[1] It is mentioned by name 12 times in the short span of 22 verses, and it is described as the throne seat of the Lord of Heaven's Armies (4:4). Israel's God, of whom no image was to be made (Exod 20:4-5), is portrayed as ruling over his people from a throne located between the cherubim at each end of the Ark's cover (Exod 25:17-22).[2] Yahweh was Israel's divine king, and the Ark was his throne. Inside the Ark were the stone tablets, on which were written the terms of the covenant by the finger of God himself (Exod 25:21; 31:18; 34:1). While the designation given to the Ark varies ("Ark of God," 4:11, 13, 17, 18, 19, 21, 22; "Ark of the LORD," 4:6; "Ark of Covenant of the LORD," 4:3, 5; "Ark of the Covenant of God," 4:4; "Ark of the Covenant of the LORD of Heaven's Armies," 4:4), the linkage of the Ark with Israel's covenant relation to the Lord in three of these five designations is of particular significance. At its most basic level a covenant is a sworn agreement to certain commitments under specified sanctions. In Israel's covenant relationship with the Lord, honoring the covenant stipulations was essential for the realization of the covenant blessings. That the Ark of God is designated the "Ark of the Covenant" four times in this chapter calls attention to the extreme importance of Israel's responsibility to live out her covenant obligations before the Lord. Israel must always remember that the promise of the Lord's presence and the assurance of his protective assistance for his people were given in the context of covenant. When Israel failed to fulfill her covenant obligations, she could not count on either the Lord's presence or his help (van den Berg 1996a:40).

The narrative begins with the report that the Philistines had defeated Israel in battle and had killed 4,000 Israelite soldiers (4:2). This surprising turn of events caused Israel's leaders to ask why the Lord had allowed them to be defeated by the Philistines (4:3). Were they not the Lord's covenant people? If this was so, how could the Lord allow his people to be defeated by a heathen nation? Was it not the Lord's sworn obligation to protect and deliver the nation he had chosen for himself? It appears that Israel had gone into battle with the assumption that God would be with them and give them victory. But to their surprise and dismay, they were defeated. Although this was a shocking experience, it would have proven beneficial if it had caused the people of Israel to recognize that something must be wrong in their relationship with God. But that did not happen. For some reason it did not occur to the leaders of the nation that the lack of covenant faithfulness was the essential issue in their failure to experience God's blessing and presence. Instead of seeking an explanation for the disaster by looking within themselves, they concluded (4:3) that if they carried the Ark of the Covenant of the Lord into battle, then victory over the Philistines would surely be guaranteed. They reasoned that since the Ark is the throne seat of the Lord (4:4), to carry it into battle would of necessity compel the Lord to grant them victory. Their reasoning, however, was pagan rather than covenantal. It reflected acceptance of the heathen idea that the Ark possessed an inherent magical power they could manipulate in a mechanical way. What Israel's leaders forgot was that the Ark was the symbol of divine presence in the context of the covenant (van den Berg 1996a:43). When the covenant was scorned, the Ark was of no significance, and on this occasion, as always, God's presence could not be coerced.[3] So the response of the leaders of the nation was not one of repentance and faith but rather one of superstition (Davis 1994a:52).

When the leaders sent to Shiloh for the Ark, it was Hophni and Phinehas, the sons of Eli, who helped to carry the Ark to the scene of the battle (4:4). The reference to Hophni and Phinehas is an ominous sign. The reader has already been told about the death warrant resting on their heads (2:34). But when the Ark arrived in the Israelite camp, the shout of joy was so loud that the Philistines asked what had happened. And when they learned that Israel's celebration was due to the arrival of the Ark in their camp, they were gripped by fear. The Philistines had the same magical idea about the Ark that the Israelites did. The Philistines knew about the power of the God of Israel, who had defeated the Egyptians by bringing plagues on their land (4:7-8). But then, contrary to what might be expected, the Philistines became energized to fight for their lives instead of becoming paralyzed by fear (4:9-10). This was a reverse reaction to that of the Canaanites who "lost heart and were paralyzed with fear" after Israel had crossed the Jordan at the time of their entrance into Canaan (Josh 5:1). At that time Rahab, from the Canaanite city of Jericho, told the Israelite spies, "We are all afraid of you. Everyone in the land is living in terror. For we have heard how the LORD made a dry path for you through the Red Sea when you left Egypt. . . . No wonder our hearts have melted in fear! No one has the courage to fight after hearing such things" (Josh 2:9b-11). Indeed, at Mount Sinai the Lord had promised his people, "I will send my terror ahead of you and create panic among all the people whose lands you invade. I will make all your enemies turn and run" (Exod 23:27). One question this passage raises is, why had the Canaanites been paralyzed by fear of the Israelites and their God, but on this occasion the Philistines were not? The only answer is that God's sovereignty extends even to the psychological mind-set of Israel's enemies, and on this occasion it was God's purpose for the Philistines to defeat the Israelites. God, therefore, caused the coming of the Ark into the Israelite camp to result in a rallying of the Philistine forces, even though their initial response had been one of fear.

When the battle began again, Israel was soundly defeated, and 30,000 Israelites were killed (4:10). Furthermore, "The Ark of God was captured, and Hophni and Phinehas, the two sons of Eli, were killed" (4:11). For Israel, the unthinkable had happened. It seemed that not only had Israel been defeated, but that Israel's God had been defeated at the same time. When a messenger ran from the battlefield with news of the defeat, we are told that Eli, who was now 98 years old and blind, expected the worst ("his heart trembled for the safety of the Ark of God," 4:13). Eli knew all too well that the Lord could not be coerced to give victory to Israel. When the news reached him that not only had Israel been defeated and Hophni and Phinehas been killed, but also that the Ark of God had been captured (4:17), he fell from his chair, broke his neck, and died (4:18). The judgment of God pronounced by the unnamed prophet (2:27-36) had been fulfilled down to its last detail. But that was not all. When Eli's pregnant daughter-in-law, the wife of Phinehas, heard the news about the Ark, she went into labor and died in childbirth. Before she died, she named her newborn son Ichabod, saying "Israel's glory is gone" (see note on 4:21). The phrase "Israel's glory is gone" is used twice in 4:21-22, emphasizing the great significance of what had happened. The departure of the "glory of Israel" is to be understood as a reference to Israel's God, not to the Ark (cf. 15:29; Ps 106:19-22). The wife of Phinehas recognized that the loss of the Ark signified that God himself had withdrawn his presence from his people. God's presence was Israel's glory. It was God's presence among his people that set Israel apart from all other nations on earth.

This was not the first time that God had withdrawn his presence from his people, nor would it be the last. In the aftermath of the golden calf incident, shortly after the establishment of the covenant on Mount Sinai, God told his people that he would send an angel with them, but that he would no longer go with them on their journey to Canaan (Exod 33:2-3). In response to this statement, Moses begged the Lord to return to their midst, saying, "If your Presence does not go with us, do not send us up from here. . . . What else will distinguish me and your people from all the other people on the face of the earth?" (Exod 33:15-16, NIV). Later in Israel's history, during the time of the Exile, Ezekiel saw a vision of the glory of the Lord departing from the Temple in Jerusalem (Ezek 10). And again, the loss of the Ark in Samuel's day was a sign that God's presence was no longer in the midst of his people. This, however, is not to be understood as implying that God had abandoned the covenant. To the contrary, it confirmed that the covenant remained in effect and that Israel was experiencing the reality of the covenant curse. As Amos was to say in a later period of Israel's history (Amos 3:2), "From among all the families on the earth, I have been intimate with you alone. That is why I must punish you for all your sins." Judgment and defeat when Israel fails to live up to her covenantal obligations are just as much a part of the covenant as blessing and victory are when she is faithful to the covenant. Nevertheless, the loss of the Ark was a clear sign of God's displeasure with his people and signified the withdrawal of his presence from their midst (cf. Ps 78:56-65).

As bad as all this was, things were not as dark as they might seem because the groundwork for reformation and restoration had already been laid in God's call of Samuel to be a prophet (ch 3). In due time, the word of God would again come to his people through Samuel (ch 7).

ENDNOTES

1. As was noted in the Introduction, chs 4–6 along with 2 Sam 6–7 have commonly been designated "the Ark Narrative" and are viewed as an independent block of tradition originally written to inform visitors to the Ark sanctuary in Jerusalem of how the Ark had come to be located there. In 1926, Rost (1982:6-34) gave this view its classic formulation and argued that the purpose of the Ark Narrative was to "depict the fate

of the Ark from its removal from Shiloh until its installation in Jerusalem" (1982:9). He claimed (1982:34) that its author was "a member of the community of priests who took care of the Ark during the latter part of David's reign or at the beginning of Solomon's reign." Although Rost's analysis was challenged in a variety of ways in the 1970s, particularly with respect to its purpose (Campbell 1975; Schicklberger 1973), as McCarter (1980b:23) says, "This hypothesis has been among the most durable of modern scholarship." This is not to say, however, that there have not been legitimate questions raised about the existence of an independent self-contained Ark Narrative. Smelik (1989:133), for example, has argued that there are "no compelling reasons to assume the pre-existence of an Ark narrative before the composition of the book of Samuel." And Polzin (1989:6) says, "Lacking the discovery of an ancient manuscript containing an approximation of Miller and Roberts's original ark narrative, I find their analyses, like those of the scholars I will shortly discuss, highly speculative and ultimately disappointing."

2. Some interpreters have disputed the idea that the Lord is invisibly "enthroned" above the Ark between the cherubim. Hague (NIDOTTE 1.506) comments that, "There is no warrant, linguistic or otherwise, for construing the atonement cover as an earthly throne. There also is no example in which the word *kisse'* [throne] is linked with the ark itself, its cover, or the cherubim." It should be noted, however, that there are numerous references in the Old Testament to Yahweh "enthroned" or "sitting" above or between the cherubim, or to the Ark as his "footstool" (1 Sam 4:4; 2 Sam 6:2; 2 Kgs 19:15[//Isa 37:16]; 1 Chr 28:2; Pss 99:5; 132:7-8; Lam 2:1). Part of Hague's opposition to the idea that the Ark can be understood as the throne seat of Yahweh is connected with his opposition to rather complex theories (as that of von Rad 1931) concerning the transcendence and immanence of Yahweh's presence in Israel. Regarding these qualities, Waltke's (2007:458) synthesis provides a reasonable alternative to a rejection of the idea of the Ark of the Covenant as the throne seat of Yahweh: "As God's presence is paradoxically both spatially ubiquitous and immanent, it is also paradoxically both temporally permanent and intermittent. When he withdraws his presence from his sinful people, he abandons them temporarily to their own devices (2 Chron. 12:5; Ezek. 29:5). The ark, symbolizing the throne of the invisible God, expresses his abiding presence, while the tent reflects God's intermittent presence."

   Additionally, variations in the description of the Ark as a throne seat have caused some to question whether the Ark is to be understood as the throne seat (4:4; 2 Sam 6:2) of Yahweh or specifically as the "footstool" of God's throne (1 Chr 28:2; Ps 132:7). As de Vaux (1961a:300) has argued, it "is pointless to ask how the Cherubim and the Ark could be both a throne and a foot-stool; it is like asking how Yahweh could actually sit down there, and the question would have seemed as absurd to the Israelites as it does to us." In keeping with the NLT translation that Yahweh was "enthroned between the cherubim" (4:4; 2 Sam 6:2) this commentary will speak of the Ark as the "throne seat of [Yahweh]."

3. Jeremiah 3:16-17 demonstrates that God was not inseparably bound to the Ark.

◆ 2. The Ark in the land of the Philistines (1 Sam 5:1-12)

After the Philistines captured the Ark of God, they took it from the battleground at Ebenezer to the town of Ashdod. [2]They carried the Ark of God into the temple of Dagon and placed it beside an idol of Dagon. [3]But when the citizens of Ashdod went to see it the next morning, Dagon had fallen with his face to the ground in front

of the Ark of the LORD! So they took Dagon
and put him in his place again. 4But the
next morning the same thing happened—
Dagon had fallen face down before the Ark
of the LORD again. This time his head and
hands had broken off and were lying in the
doorway. Only the trunk of his body was
left intact. 5That is why to this day neither
the priests of Dagon nor anyone who en-
ters the temple of Dagon in Ashdod will
step on its threshold.

6Then the LORD's heavy hand struck the
people of Ashdod and the nearby villages
with a plague of tumors.* 7When the peo-
ple realized what was happening, they
cried out, "We can't keep the Ark of the
God of Israel here any longer! He is against
us! We will all be destroyed along with
Dagon, our god." 8So they called together
the rulers of the Philistine towns and
asked, "What should we do with the Ark
of the God of Israel?"

The rulers discussed it and replied,
"Move it to the town of Gath." So they
moved the Ark of the God of Israel to
Gath. 9But when the Ark arrived at Gath,
the LORD's heavy hand fell on its men,
young and old; he struck them with a
plague of tumors, and there was a great
panic.

10So they sent the Ark of God to the
town of Ekron, but when the people of
Ekron saw it coming they cried out, "They
are bringing the Ark of the God of Israel
here to kill us, too!" 11The people sum-
moned the Philistine rulers again and
begged them, "Please send the Ark of the
God of Israel back to its own country, or
it* will kill us all." For the deadly plague
from God had already begun, and great
fear was sweeping across the town.
12Those who didn't die were afflicted with
tumors; and the cry from the town rose
to heaven.

5:6 Greek version and Latin Vulgate read *tumors; and rats appeared in their land, and death and destruction were throughout the city.* 5:11 Or *he.*

NOTES

5:4 *Only the trunk of his body was left intact.* The MT reads, "Only Dagon was left to him" suggesting a textual defect. The LXX reads, "Only the stump of Dagon was left." S. R. Driver (1913), Klein (1983), McCarter (1980b), and others suggest the insertion of *gew* ("back," i.e., "torso") before Dagon.

5:6 *Then the LORD's heavy hand struck the people of Ashdod and the nearby villages with a plague of tumors.* This verse is loaded with wordplay. It reads literally, "The hand of the LORD was heavy on the people of Ashdod. He devastated them and smote them with tumors." Notice it is the *hand* of Yahweh that is heavy against Ashdod. While the hand of Dagon lies broken and useless, the hand of Yahweh is powerful and active. It is described as being "heavy" (*kabed* [TH3513, ZH3877]) against Ashdod. In English this is a somewhat peculiar expression, but in Hebrew the word "heavy" is the same word root as the "glory" (*kabod* [TH3519, ZH3883])—that which had departed from Israel according to the daughter-in-law of Eli (4:21-22). In fact, this phrase ("the hand of the LORD was heavy") becomes the most important theme in the remainder of the chapter, occurring twice in the space of a few verses (5:6, 11), along with two additional references to the "hand" of the Lord in 5:7, 9.

5:8 *The rulers discussed it and replied.* NLT represents the MT's, "And they said." The LXX reads, "And the men of Gath said, 'Let the Ark of God be brought to us.'"

they moved the Ark . . . to Gath. This follows the reading in 4QSam^a and LXX; "to Gath" is not included in MT.

5:9 *men, young and old.* For the Hebrew construction, see Williams 1976:§313.

with a plague of tumors. The LXX adds *eis tas hedras autōn* (in their seats) based on mistakenly reading *sathar* [TH5641, ZH6259] (be hidden) rather than the similar-sounding *sathar*

[TH8368, ZH8609] (break out), which is in the text. The Latin Vulgate rendering (*in secretiori parte natium*, 5:6) has been preserved in the KJV by the expression "in their secret parts."

COMMENTARY

The Philistines brought the Ark of the Lord to the city of Ashdod where they placed it in the temple of their principal deity, Dagon. Dagon was a fertility deity associated with vegetation or grain (McCarter 1980b:121-122, contra the suggestion that Dagon was a fish-god—so Holter 1989), and was worshiped not only by the Philistines but also by other peoples of the ancient Near East from as early as 2500 BC. The Hebrew wording of 5:1-2 says that the Philistines "took and brought" the Ark from the battlefield to Ashdod, and then they "took and brought" the Ark into the temple of Dagon. Repetition is one of the subtle means by which Hebrew narrative calls attention to important emphases in the text. The suggestion of this repetition pertains to the mentality of the Philistines who thought that the Ark was now completely under their control, and they could do with it as they pleased (de Jong 1978:34). The Philistines—just as the Israelites in the previous chapter—made the mistake of identifying the Ark with Yahweh. Because they controlled the chest, they thought they controlled Israel's God. So in a disposition of surprised and elated triumph, they celebrated the capture of the deity who had earlier given Israel victory over the Egyptian pharaoh (cf. 4:8) and over the inhabitants of the land of Canaan. In their view, the capture of the Ark demonstrated that Dagon was more powerful than Yahweh.

But Yahweh will not be mocked. Early the next morning when the citizens of Ashdod went to the temple of Dagon, they discovered that the statue of Dagon had fallen on its face to the ground in front of the Ark of the Lord. The stance of Dagon before the Ark was that of a defeated ruler before a conquering king. Not fully understanding how or why this had happened, and perhaps concluding that the whole ordeal was some sort of strange coincidence, the Philistines picked up the image of Dagon and put it back in its place. Note the irony! Dagon is a deity who must be propped up by his own devotees (cf. Isa 40:20). But there is more to the story. On the next morning Dagon had not only again fallen with his face to the ground before the Ark, but this time his head and his hands were broken off and lay on the threshold of the temple. Dagon had lost both his head and his hands! Without a head Dagon could not think, and without hands he could not act (van den Berg 1996a:55). Symbolically, Dagon was not only humiliated before Yahweh, he was totally disabled.[1]

But this is only the beginning of Dagon's belittlement. As the "hand" of Dagon lay broken on the threshold of the temple, powerless to act, the "hand" of the Lord rose up against the inhabitants of Ashdod (see note on 5:6). Appearances to the contrary, Yahweh was demonstrating in a clear and tangible way that he was far from being defeated and impotent. He still retained his power and glory, even though he allowed the defeat of Israel. And he will display that power forcefully to those who think they have placed him under their control. The precise medical nature of the plague of tumors is uncertain,[2] but on the basis of the reference to a plague of rats in 6:4, 11, 15, and 18 (as well as in the addition of the LXX in 5:6, see NLT mg), many commentators have concluded that it was a form of bubonic plague.[3] Whatever it was, the people of Ashdod were severely afflicted and greatly disturbed by it. They perceived quite clearly that the things that had happened to them and to Dagon had been caused by the God of Israel (5:7). Realizing that Dagon had been unable to protect them from the scourge that plagued them, they called the Philistine rulers together and demanded the removal of the Ark from their city (5:7-8). As with many people who become disappointed with religion (the people of Ashdod were no doubt frustrated by Dagon's impotence), the Philistines of Ashdod turned to a political solution (van den Berg 1996a:55-56). The political solution arrived at by their leaders was to move the Ark from Ashdod to Gath. But as is often the case with political solutions, no real answer was provided, and the problem was merely shifted from one place to another. So when the Ark arrived at Gath and the plague broke out there as well, the people of Gath were thrown into panic (5:9). It was then decided to send the Ark on to Ekron (5:10), but the inhabitants of Ekron regarded the Ark of the God of Israel as a threat to their lives and vehemently protested against its coming into their city. The Philistine rulers were called again and urged to send the Ark back to Israel where it belonged, in order to prevent a slaughter of the Philistine people (5:11).

This entire episode is a clear demonstration of the sovereignty and power of the God of Israel, contrasted with the foolishness and futility of Philistine idol worship. The focus of the chapter is not so much on the punishment of the Philistines connected with the movement of the Ark among them, as it is on the inability of Dagon to protect Philistia against the sovereign power of Yahweh. Although God refused to be manipulated by his own people (ch 4), he would not permit the Philistines to conclude that their victory over Israel demonstrated Dagon's superiority over himself. The Philistines were brought to their knees and forced to recognize that the God of Israel was more powerful than Dagon, and he was at work in their midst. With his "heavy (*kabed* [TH3513, ZH3877]) hand," Yahweh gained glory (*kabod* [TH3519, ZH3883]) for himself, much as he had done at the Exodus, when he plagued the Egyptians and forced them to recognize his existence and power (Exod 14:4, 17-18); the Lord would act similarly in the future when Israel's security was threatened by heathen nations, as in the days of Hezekiah, when the Lord miraculously delivered his people (cf. Isa 36:14–37:36). Hezekiah's prayer when faced with Sennacherib's attack uses language found in 1 Samuel (see notes on 1:3 and 4:4; cf. Isa 37:16) and reflects awareness, many centuries later, that Israel's divine king is the ruler over all the earth. The Lord alone is God, and no one can insult him with impunity (Isa 37:17, 20).

ENDNOTES

1. Cutting off the head and hands demonstrated the total defeat of an enemy. Miller and Roberts (1977:44) comment, "The cut-off hands and head of Dagon suggest a fatal fall in combat—like that of Goliath." In Maccabean times the Syrian general Nicanor was defeated by the Jews, who then cut off his head and right hand and displayed them in Jerusalem as proof of his defeat (1 Macc 7:47; 2 Macc 15:28-37). For other illustrations of the loss of head and hand as proof of the complete conquest of an adversary, see Zwickel 1994.

improper way (6:19). The exact nature of their offense is not clear, and the text simply says that they looked at the Ark of the Lord (see note on 6:19). Read in this literal way, the text suggests that the offense was not the violation of some protocol, as was the case later with Uzzah, who reached out and touched the Ark when David was bringing it to Jerusalem (2 Sam 6), but was rather an attitudinal offense inherent in the manner in which they looked at the Ark (de Jong 1978:45). Yes, the men of Beth-shemesh rejoiced to see the Ark, but perhaps this text is telling us that their rejoicing was not sanctified but profane. Perhaps they looked at the Ark with the proprietary sense of finally having gotten back what they thought really belonged to them. If so, this attitude was an offense to God and was severely punished. Others have suggested that the offense involved a violation of the regulations of Numbers 4 requiring that the Ark be wrapped in coverings when it was taken out of the Holy of Holies in order to prevent anyone from looking directly at it. Still others see the infraction as one of looking *into* the Ark, or as refusing to join in the celebration over its return (cf. the LXX rendering in the note on 6:19). Whatever the precise nature of the offense, God reminded the Israelites that he was a holy God who was to be treated with obedience, reverence, and awe. So the inhabitants of Beth-shemesh learned very quickly that when the glory (*kabod* [TH3519, ZH3883]) came back, life was dangerous (cf. Josh 24:19-20). They asked, "Who is able to stand in the presence of the LORD, this holy God?" (6:20), and then they mimicked the behavior of the Philistines by sending the Ark to another place (Kiriath-jearim, 6:21). It seems as if nothing had been learned by the experiences of the previous seven months. There is no word about confession of sin or violation of regulations concerning the handling of the Ark. Thus, even though Israel as a nation had not repented (this does not happen until ch 7), God graciously returned the symbol of his presence to his own people. It does, however, appear that the inhabitants of Kiriath-jearim better understood the reverent treatment due the Ark as the symbol of the holy Lord of hosts. We are told that the Ark remained in their town for 20 years, apparently without further incident (7:2).

This chapter concludes the first two sections of 1 Samuel (chs 1–3 and 4–6). In chapters 1–3, God pronounced judgment on the priestly line of Eli and raised up Samuel as a spokesman (prophet) for himself. In chapters 4–6 God carried out judgment on the house of Eli and also demonstrated forcefully that Israel could not assume the guarantee of divine protection while ignoring her obligation to covenant fidelity. At the same time, God showed the Philistines that their victory over Israel was not a defeat of Yahweh but an act of discipline toward his own people Israel. In each of these sections the theme of divine sovereignty is prominent. The question asked by the Philistines, "Who can save us from these mighty gods of Israel?" (4:8) and the question asked by the Israelite inhabitants of Beth-shemesh, "Who is able to stand in the presence of the LORD, this holy God?" (6:20), are in essence the same question. The answer is also the same: No one can. The response of Eli (3:18) to the Lord's pronouncement of judgment is the only proper response: "It is the LORD's will. . . . Let him do what he thinks best." This mighty God is the Lord of Heaven's Armies (1:3), he is the holy God (6:20), he is the only God (2:2), and he is the creator and sustainer of the universe (2:8b). He rules over all peoples and nations and delights in doing things in surprising ways. In these chapters the divine reversal of fortunes anticipated by Hannah's song of praise (2:1-10) is prominently displayed (e.g., Hannah's barrenness and the birth of Samuel [ch 1]; judgment on the Elides and the call of Samuel to be a prophet [chs 2–3]; the loss and return of the Ark to Israel [chs 4 and 6]; and the victory and defeat of the Philistines [chs 4–6]).

ENDNOTE

1. Phillip Johnson (1991, 1995) exposes the fallacies of the banishment of God from law, science, and education by the naturalistic philosophy of the American cultural elite.

◆ C. Samuel the Judge (1 Sam 7:2-17)

The Ark remained in Kiriath-jearim for a
long time—twenty years in all. During that
time all Israel mourned because it seemed
the LORD had abandoned them.

3Then Samuel said to all the people of
Israel, "If you are really serious about
wanting to return to the LORD, get rid of
your foreign gods and your images of
Ashtoreth. Determine to obey only the
LORD; then he will rescue you from the
Philistines." 4So the Israelites got rid of
their images of Baal and Ashtoreth and
worshiped only the LORD.
5Then Samuel told them, "Gather all of
Israel to Mizpah, and I will pray to the
LORD for you." 6So they gathered at Miz-
pah and, in a great ceremony, drew water
from a well and poured it out before the
LORD. They also went without food all day
and confessed that they had sinned
against the LORD. (It was at Mizpah that
Samuel became Israel's judge.)
7When the Philistine rulers heard that
Israel had gathered at Mizpah, they mobi-
lized their army and advanced. The Israel-
ites were badly frightened when they
learned that the Philistines were ap-
proaching. 8"Don't stop pleading with the
LORD our God to save us from the Philis-
tines!" they begged Samuel. 9So Samuel
took a young lamb and offered it to the
LORD as a whole burnt offering. He plead-
ed with the LORD to help Israel, and the
LORD answered him.
10Just as Samuel was sacrificing the
burnt offering, the Philistines arrived to
attack Israel. But the LORD spoke with a
mighty voice of thunder from heaven that
day, and the Philistines were thrown into
such confusion that the Israelites defeat-
ed them. 11The men of Israel chased them
from Mizpah to a place below Beth-car,
slaughtering them all along the way.
12 Samuel then took a large stone and
placed it between the towns of Mizpah
and Jeshanah.* He named it Ebenezer
(which means "the stone of help"), for he
said, "Up to this point the LORD has
helped us!"
13So the Philistines were subdued and
didn't invade Israel again for some time.
And throughout Samuel's lifetime, the
LORD's powerful hand was raised against
the Philistines. 14The Israelite villages
near Ekron and Gath that the Philistines
had captured were restored to Israel,
along with the rest of the territory that
the Philistines had taken. And there was
peace between Israel and the Amorites in
those days.
15Samuel continued as Israel's judge for
the rest of his life. 16Each year he traveled
around, setting up his court first at Beth-
el, then at Gilgal, and then at Mizpah. He
judged the people of Israel at each of
these places. 17Then he would return to
his home at Ramah, and he would hear
cases there, too. And Samuel built an altar
to the LORD at Ramah.

7:12 As in Greek and Syriac versions; Hebrew reads *Shen.*

NOTES

7:2 ***all Israel mourned.*** The meaning of *wayyinnahu* [TH5091, ZH5629] is uncertain (this is the only occurrence of the root in the Niphal stem). S. R. Driver (1913:61) says, "*nahah* in Heb. means *to mourn* or *lament* (Ezek 32,18): so, if the reading be correct, it will be most safely explained as a pregnant construction, *mourned* or *sighed after Yahweh* = went after him mourning or sighing."

COMMENTARY

Although the Ark had returned to Israel, it was not returned to its home at the Tabernacle in Shiloh. Whether this was because the Philistines had destroyed Shiloh and the Tabernacle when they defeated Israel and captured the Ark, or for some other unexplained reason is not clear.[1] What is clear is that when David brought the Ark to Jerusalem many years later at the beginning of his reign (2 Sam 6), it was brought from the house of Abinadab (2 Sam 6:3) where it had been placed soon after it was returned to Israel by the Philistines (1 Sam 7:1-2).

After 20 years of discontent stemming from the experience of the Lord's displeasure, Samuel told the people that the Lord would rescue them from Philistine oppression if they returned to the Lord with all their hearts, got rid of their heathen idols, and lived in obedience to their covenant obligations (7:3). The first commandment given at Sinai was, "You must not have any other god but me" (Exod 20:3; cf. Deut 6:13-15). Yahweh required exclusive devotion to himself. No compromise was possible. The choice was a radical one. The challenge of Samuel was like that of Joshua before him ("Put away forever the idols your ancestors worshiped. . . . Choose today whom you will serve"; Josh 24:14-15) and Elijah after him ("How much longer will you waver, hobbling between two opinions? If the LORD is God, follow him! But if Baal is God, then follow him!"; 1 Kgs 18:21). The Israelites accepted Samuel's challenge and destroyed the images of Baal and Ashtoreth, the chief god and goddess of the Canaanite pantheon (7:4). Their mourning and sorrow (7:2) showed itself not to be merely an expression of resentment or self-pity (cf. Rev 16:10-11), but rather a true remorse that led to genuine repentance (cf. 2 Cor 7:10).

But Samuel knew additional steps were necessary, so he called for an assembly at Mizpah where the people poured out water before the Lord and engaged in fasting and public confession of sin. Samuel prayed to God on their behalf (7:5-6). The otherwise unknown ritual of drawing water and pouring it out before the Lord seems to be intended as an expression of the giving of themselves completely to the Lord (Lam 2:19).[2] True fasting, as opposed to an empty ritual, represents a heart that is broken before the Lord (Isa 58:1-7), and confession of sin is inseparable from true repentance. On this occasion, Samuel, as Moses before him (Exod 32:11-14; 33:12-17), showed himself to be a true mediator between God and his people (Ps 99:6; Jer 15:1). His prayers were graciously used by God as one of the important means by which the relationship between himself and his wayward people was restored. So here, as elsewhere in the Bible, ritual is viewed as important for the people of God, but only when it is performed by those whose hearts are sincerely expressing repentance for sin and true devotion to God. Ritual without obedience and repentance is an abomination to the Lord (cf. 15:22-23; Isa 1:11-17; Amos

5:21-24), and repentance without public ritual privatizes religious faith and gives insufficient recognition to the corporate nature of the people of God. The ritual of sacrifice offered upon the return of the Ark to Beth-shemesh in the previous chapter (6:14-15) appears to have been an empty form and was quickly followed by a radical expression of the Lord's anger (6:19); conversely, the ritual of this gathering at Mizpah resulted in an amazing demonstration of the Lord's blessing (7:10). By these actions Samuel placed himself among the judges: those leaders and deliverers of Israel who operated between the time of Joshua and the establishment of kingship in Israel (7:6).[3]

The Lord's gracious response, however, was not immediately apparent. The Philistines learned of the Israelite gathering at Mizpah, and assuming that it had military implications, they mobilized their army for an attack. Israel's fearful reaction (7:7) was similar to the reaction of the Philistines when Israel brought the Ark into their camp at Ebenezer[4] (4:7) many years earlier. Being faced with the prospect of a sudden battle against a far-superior military force was hardly what the Israelites had expected as a result of their repentance. Although Israel's fear in one sense reflected insufficient trust in the covenantal promises that God had given them,[5] it was nevertheless a healthy fear rather than a paralyzing fear. It was a fear that drove the people to beg Samuel to pray to the Lord for deliverance from the imminent threat (de Jong 1978:52-53). Samuel not only prayed, but he also offered a burnt offering to the Lord. The Lord responded with such a violent thunderstorm that the Philistines were confused[6] and the Israelites were enabled to defeat[7] them in battle. The thunder was a clear and definite answer to Samuel's prayer. It was a literal fulfillment of Hannah's words: "Those who fight against the LORD will be shattered. He thunders against them from heaven" (2:10).

Samuel placed a large stone between Mizpah and Jeshanah and called it Ebenezer, "the stone of help." The stone was to be a reminder that the victory just achieved was attributable to the Lord and not to Israel's military strategy or supremacy over the Philistines. The Ebenezer of this chapter contrasts sharply with the Ebenezer of 4:1 (see endnote 4), the place where Israel had suffered a disastrous defeat at the hands of the same Philistines. This most recent battle marked a turning point in the relationship between Israel and the Philistines. For as long as Samuel lived, the hand of the Lord continued to restrain Philistine designs on the territory of Israel (7:13-14).[8] From this time forward, Samuel was known not just as a prophet (3:20), but also as a judge (7:15). He provided religious and civil leadership to the nation, much like Moses and Joshua before him, traveling annually on a circuit to Bethel, Gilgal, and Mizpah from his home in Ramah (7:16-17).

The issues in this chapter are covenantal: After silence about Samuel in chapters 4–6, he reappears in this chapter as the individual whom the Lord used to call Israel back to covenant faithfulness. The result was that the Lord again showed his power, this time in blessing rather than judgment. Israel's victory over the Philistines was facilitated by the confusion caused by the severe thunderstorm sent by Yahweh. The inescapable conclusion is that Israel's national security was closely correlated with Israel's faithfulness to covenantal obligations.[9] As Brueggemann

(1990a:50) comments, "The claims and assumptions of the covenantal order are shown to be reliable and effective." Although the defeat of chapter 4 was never explicitly explained, its context shows that it was a manifestation of covenant cursing because Eli's sons and their followers among the people had abandoned their covenantal obligations. This notion of covenant blessing and cursing, connected with the matter of national security, is extremely important for understanding why Samuel rebuked Israel so severely in the following chapters (8–12) for requesting a king "like the nations around us" who could "lead" them into battle (8:20). Their request betrayed their profound lack of trust in Yahweh and rejection of his kingship over them as it was an attempt to find security in something other than Yahweh.

ENDNOTES

1. References to the destruction of Shiloh in Ps 78:60-61; Jer 7:12; and 26:9 have often been understood as references to the time that the Philistines defeated Israel and captured the Ark (1 Sam 4). In connection with these references Bright (1981:186) comments that after the Ark was captured, the "Philistines then proceeded to occupy the land. Shiloh was taken and the shrine of the tribal league destroyed." This scenario, however, does not explain scattered references to the existence of the Tabernacle and the bronze altar between the time of Samuel and the building of the Temple during the reign of Solomon (1 Chr 6:32; 16:39; 21:29; 2 Chr 1:3,13; 5:5) at which time the Tabernacle is said to be located at Gibeon. These references suggest that the Tabernacle and the bronze altar somehow survived the destruction of Shiloh. Perhaps the Tabernacle was dismantled and quickly moved along with the bronze altar before the city was destroyed. Although there is no reference to the Tabernacle in 1 Sam 21, we are told that Ahimelech the high priest served the Lord at Nob along with 85 other priests at what appears to be a central sanctuary, because of references to the ephod (v. 9) and the Bread of the Presence (v. 6). When the Tabernacle was relocated to Gibeon is unclear (cf. 1 Kgs 3:4; 1 Chr 21:29; 2 Chr 1:2-6).
2. Various other suggestions have been made. Keil (1956:73) views it as a "symbolical representation of the temporal and spiritual distress in which they were at the time." Gordon (1986:107) suggests it "formed part of the self-denial of the occasion as the participants solemnly proclaimed their abstention from even this necessity of life." Baldwin (1988:79) suggests it is "a symbol of the washing away of communal guilt, for which Samuel prayed . . . the visible sign reinforcing the divine response to the confession of sin." The association of a ritual "water pouring" with the Feast of Shelters in the NT era (perhaps the background for Jesus' statements about living water in John 7:37-39) is a later development within Judaism and is not prescribed in the Mosaic law, nor is there evidence it was practiced in the OT period.
3. The term "to judge" (*shapat* [TH8199, ZH9149]) in the books of Judges and 1 Samuel clearly represents a broader function than that of deciding legal disputes, although the range of duties of the "judges" is much disputed. Here, Samuel's "judging" is associated with providing religious leadership for spiritual renewal. Often (particularly in Judges) the term is associated with military leadership and the deliverance of Israel from political oppression (cf. Judg 2:16-18). It would appear that the function of the charismatic leaders known as judges in early Israel involved spiritual (7:6; Judg 4:4; 6:25-27), judicial (Judg 4:5), and military responsibilities. However, NIDOTTE 4.213-220 questions whether it is justified to read Samuel's religious activities as judge back into the use of *shapat* in the book of Judges.

4. This site (identified with Izbet Sartah, about two miles east of Aphek) is to be distinguished from the site that Samuel named Ebenezer in 7:12.
5. The Sinai covenant contained "protection clauses" in which the Lord promised to guarantee the security of his people if they remained faithful to their covenantal obligations (cf. Exod 23:22 and 34:11-14, where Israel's security is explicitly linked with their cutting down Asherah poles and not worshiping any other God). Because of these promises, Israel was exhorted to never fear her enemies but to always trust confidently in Yahweh (Exod 14:13; Num 14:9; Deut 20:1-4; Josh 10:8; 2 Sam 10:12; 2 Chr 20:17).
6. This is the same word (*hamam* [TH2000, ZH2169], "confuse" or "cause panic") as is used in Josh 10:10a on the occasion of Israel's great victory over a coalition of five Canaanite kings.
7. This is the same word (*nagap* [TH5062, ZH5597], Niphal, "be smitten") used in 4:3 of the Israelite defeat by the Philistines. In fact, ch 7 shows a number of contrasting parallels with ch 4 (cf. Davis 1994a:73). Note, for example: 4:3 // 7:3-8 (manipulation contrasted with repentance); 4:6-8 // 7:7-8 (the Philistines' fear contrasted with Israel's fear on account of the Philistines); 4:21 // 7:12 (Ichabod contrasted with Ebenezer).
8. As Davis (1994a:77, note 12) says, chs 13–14 "do not contradict but explicate 7:13."
9. It should, of course, be understood that Israel's obedience did not merit Yahweh's divine favor. Vos (1975:127) has pointed out that the association of blessing with obedience within the context of the Sinai covenant is to be understood as belonging to the symbolico-typical sphere of *appropriateness of expression* rather than to the legal sphere of *merit* (see Vos in loc. for a fuller explanation of this distinction). This is supported by numerous passages in the Old Testament in which God's blessings are portrayed as undeserved favors, rather than as merited rewards (Deut 9:4-6; 2 Kgs 13:22-23; 14:26-27; Neh 9:19-35; Jer 2:6-7; Amos 2:9-11; see further, NIDOTTE 4.1142-1143). So the relationship between Israel's obedience and God's blessing on (and protection of) his people is not a mechanical one in which God can be manipulated (cf. Ps 44, in which Israel pleads for God's favor after suffering defeat by an enemy, even though "we have not forgotten you. We have not violated your covenant" [Ps 44:17]). God always remains completely sovereign, but at the same time, he is faithful to his covenant. As Davis (1994a:72) points out, "Genuine repentance is the proper preparation for God's mercy. Not that repentance coerces such mercy. There is no merit in such repentance, but there is no saving help without such repentance. Repentance is not the cause but only the condition of Yahweh's deliverance."

◆ II. Kingship Established in Israel under the Guidance of Samuel the Prophet (1 Sam 8:1–12:25)

A. Israel's Sinful Desire for a King (1 Sam 8:1-22)

As Samuel grew old, he appointed his sons to be judges over Israel. 2Joel and Abijah, his oldest sons, held court in Beersheba. 3But they were not like their father, for they were greedy for money. They accepted bribes and perverted justice.

4Finally, all the elders of Israel met at Ramah to discuss the matter with Samuel. 5"Look," they told him, "you are now old, and your sons are not like you. Give us a king to judge us like all the other nations have."

6Samuel was displeased with their request and went to the LORD for guidance. 7"Do everything they say to you," the LORD replied, "for it is me they are rejecting, not you. They don't want me to be their king any longer. 8Ever since I brought them

from Egypt they have continually aban-
doned me and followed other gods. And
now they are giving you the same treat-
ment. 9Do as they ask, but solemnly warn
them about the way a king will reign over
them."

10So Samuel passed on the LORD's warn-
ing to the people who were asking him for
a king. 11"This is how a king will reign over
you," Samuel said. "The king will draft your
sons and assign them to his chariots and
his charioteers, making them run before
his chariots. 12Some will be generals and
captains in his army,* some will be forced
to plow in his fields and harvest his crops,
and some will make his weapons and char-
iot equipment. 13The king will take your
daughters from you and force them to
cook and bake and make perfumes for him.
14He will take away the best of your fields
and vineyards and olive groves and give
them to his own officials. 15He will take a
tenth of your grain and your grape harvest
and distribute it among his officers and
attendants. 16He will take your male and
female slaves and demand the finest of
your cattle* and donkeys for his own use.
17He will demand a tenth of your flocks,
and you will be his slaves. 18When that day
comes, you will beg for relief from this king
you are demanding, but then the LORD will
not help you."

19But the people refused to listen to
Samuel's warning. "Even so, we still want
a king," they said. 20"We want to be like
the nations around us. Our king will judge
us and lead us into battle."

21So Samuel repeated to the LORD what
the people had said, 22and the LORD re-
plied, "Do as they say, and give them a
king." Then Samuel agreed and sent the
people home.

8:12 Hebrew *commanders of thousands and commanders of fifties.* 8:16 As in Greek version; Hebrew reads *young men.*

NOTES

8:11 *This is how a king will reign over you.* Lit., "This will be the manner of the king who will reign over you." The expression "manner of the king" (*mishpat hammelek* [TH4428/4941, ZH4889/5477]) is not to be understood as a description of what an Israelite king *should do,* but rather what a king like those of the nations around Israel *would* in fact *do.* What follows is a description of the kind of king that Israel was asking for (8:11-18). It was not until Saul was publicly chosen by lot at Mizpah (10:20-24) that Samuel described (10:25; see note there) what a king in Israel *should do:* "Samuel told the people what the rights and duties of the king were" (*mishpat hammelukah* [TH4410, ZH4867]). This view is contra Talmon (1986:61, note 27), who argues that there is "no distinction" between the *mishpat hammelek* and the *mishpat hammelukah,* and that "they are not to be set up as separate concepts." He regards the practices enumerated by Samuel (although admittedly in a somewhat sarcastic way) as things permitted and expected of any king at that time. These were then presented in more complete form in 10:25 according to Talmon.

COMMENTARY

First Samuel 8 begins a new section of 1 Samuel. Chapters 1–7 have set the stage for the establishment of kingship in Israel. Chapters 8–12 describe the events associated with the inauguration of Israel's first king and the fundamental changes in the organization of the theocracy that it would entail.[1] Chapters 1–7 have a dual emphasis. Initially the focus is on the birth of Samuel (ch 1) and his maturation into the position of prophet and judge (chs 2–3, 7). This is followed by clear depictions of how the security of the nation was inseparably tied to covenant fidelity (chs 4–7). Samuel is thus positioned as the person whom God prepared in advance to lead

Israel through the transition from the era of the judges to that of the monarchy by anointing Saul and David as Israel's first two kings and by providing for covenant continuity through this important restructuring of the theocracy.

It is indisputable that kingship had always been part of God's purpose for his people. Many centuries earlier, God had told Abraham that there would be kings among his descendants (Gen 17:6, 16). Jacob predicted that a king would spring from the tribe of Judah (Gen 49:10). Balaam prophesied that there would be a king in Israel (Num 24:7, 17, 19), and Moses included the "law of the king" in his renewal of the Sinai covenant on the plains of Moab (Deut 17:14-20). And at the beginning of 1 Samuel, Hannah anticipated the day when God would give "power to his king" and increase the "strength of his anointed one" (2:10). When kingship finally came, it did not arrive without prior expectation. It was clearly God's will for Israel to have a line of kings who would anticipate and point forward to the great messianic king of the house of David.

But even though kingship was within God's purpose for his people, it did not materialize in the way that one might have expected. When the elders of Israel came to Samuel and requested that he give them a king, he responded by telling them that they had been wicked and had sinned in asking for a king (12:17, 19). Nevertheless, God instructed Samuel to give them what they wanted (8:7, 9, 22). But the reign of Israel's first king, Saul, proved to be a disaster. After assuming the royal office, Saul quickly demonstrated his unwillingness to live up to the responsibilities and duties of a true covenantal king. His life was eventually lost in a battle with the Philistines, and Israel's national security was more threatened at the end of his life than it had been at the beginning (ch 31). Subsequent to Saul's rebellion against the word of the Lord spoken to him by Samuel on two different occasions (chs 13, 15), God told Samuel to anoint David as Saul's replacement (ch 16). History would show that David also had serious flaws, but, unlike Saul, he would show himself to be a man after God's own heart (13:14).

Chapter 8 commences a long time after the miraculous deliverance described in chapter 7. In chapter 7 Samuel is first recognized as a judge (7:6, 15), but in chapter 8 he is already in his old age (8:1). Because of his advanced age, Samuel appointed his sons Joel and Abijah to assist him in rendering decisions in legal disputes,[2] but unlike their father they perverted justice for monetary gain (8:2-3). This gave the national leaders an opportunity to ask Samuel to give the people "a king to judge us like all the other nations have" (8:5).[3] It seems likely that the corruption of Samuel's sons was merely a convenient excuse to justify their desire for a king. These leaders wanted something much more far-reaching than just the discipline of Samuel's sons. They wanted to create a new social order, that is, a new structure for the theocracy. The role they describe for the king reveals that their deepest motivation arose more out of a lack of confidence in Yahweh than it did out of concern over the corruption of Samuel's sons.

The request was upsetting to Samuel (8:6), not only because he took it personally, as an insinuation that he was no longer sufficiently competent to provide human leadership for the nation, but also because it suggested that a direct theocracy (that is, one in which Yahweh alone ruled the nation as the divine king) was no longer good enough for Israel. The request implied that Israel was inferior to neighboring countries simply because Israel had no human king to go out before her and lead her into battle (8:20), particularly in the face of Philistine (9:16) and Ammonite (12:12) threats. At its core, this attitude was a rejection of the kingship of Yahweh (8:7; 10:19; 12:12, 17, 19) and a denial of the covenant. This was a rejection of the very thing that set Israel apart from all other nations.[4] It was a denial of the confession of Psalm 44:2-8:

> You drove out the pagan nations by your power
> and gave all the land to our ancestors.
> You crushed their enemies
> and set our ancestors free.
> They did not conquer the land with their swords;
> it was not their own strong arm that gave them victory.
> It was your right hand and strong arm
> and the blinding light from your face that helped them,
> for you loved them.
>
> You are my King and my God.
> You command victories for Israel.
> Only by your power can we push back our enemies;
> only in your name can we trample our foes.
> I do not trust in my bow;
> I do not count on my sword to save me.
> You are the one who gives us victory over our enemies;
> you disgrace those who hate us.
> O God, we give glory to you all day long
> and constantly praise your name.

The people's request was an attempt to replace the rule of Yahweh with a human institution that was viewed as more visible, more trustworthy, and better able to guarantee the security of the nation.[5]

In spite of this, the Lord instructed Samuel to grant the request of the Israelite leaders. He told Samuel that the central issue was not so much that they had rejected him, but rather that they had rejected Yahweh and did not want him "to be their king any longer" (8:7). So while Samuel was instructed to give them what they wanted, he was at the same time told to warn them about what having a "king . . . like all the other nations have" (8:5) would entail (8:9). Verses 11-18 are best understood as a description of the routine practices of a typical king of a Canaanite city-state of that time.[6] The word that most clearly characterizes these kings is "take" (*laqakh* [TH3947, ZH4374]), used four times (8:11, 13, 14, 16) and implied several more times. Samuel told the leaders of Israel that a king like those of the surrounding nations would be a king who would *take* their sons (8:11), *take* their daughters (8:13), *take* the best of their fields and vineyards (8:14), *take* a tenth of their grain (8:15), *take* male and female servants (8:16), *take* the best of their cattle and donkeys (8:16), and *take* a tenth of their flocks (8:17). The result would be that the people of Israel would be reduced to slavery, much like what they had experienced in Egypt (8:17).

But Samuel's warning fell on deaf ears. After listening to Samuel, the leaders insisted even more strongly than they had before (cf. 8:5 and 8:20) that they wanted a king "to judge us" and "lead us into battle" (8:20). They wanted the wrong kind of king for the wrong reasons. Yet God tells Samuel three times in this chapter to "do as they say" (8:7, 9, 22). Here is a situation in which the Lord consented to the people's wicked request but then turned their evil aspiration into something that would ultimately work for the good of the nation (Gen 50:20). When kingship was finally introduced by Samuel to the people at Mizpah (10:17-27) and Gilgal (11:14–12:25), it was of a different kind than that for which the people had asked. Kingship in Israel, as defined by Samuel, was to be a covenantal kingship—the duties and responsibilities of a king in Israel were to be radically different than those of the kings of the surrounding nations (see comments on 10:25 and 11:14–12:25). Kingship in Israel would be designed in a way that integrated human kingship into administration of the covenant. So this chapter marks the beginning of a very important new initiative in God's plan of redemption. Kingship would now be incorporated into God's redemptive purposes for his people. As Israel's history further unfolded, it was the consistent failure of her human kings that eventually gave rise to the hope for a future messianic king in the line of David who would be both human and divine (cf. Isa 7:14; 9:6; Jer 23:6; 33:16). Ultimately it would be Jesus, the root and offspring of David (Rev 22:16), who would completely fulfill this ideal of the true covenantal king. And we are told by Paul that when all of history reaches its final consummation, Jesus "will turn the Kingdom over to God the Father, having destroyed every ruler and authority and power" (1 Cor 15:24).

ENDNOTES

1. It has long been alleged that chs 8–12 include narratives from two different traditions that reflect two different attitudes toward kingship in Israel. The one tradition (9:1–10:16 and ch 11) is said to be an early one that reflects a favorable attitude toward the monarchy. The other tradition (ch 8; 10:17-27; 12:1-25) is said to be a later one (probably as late as the exilic period) that reflects opposition to the monarchy, primarily because of the bad experience that Israel had with the majority of her kings. Those who advocate a view of this sort (there are many varieties of this basic approach) consider the present book of Samuel to be the composite result of the effort of a writer living in the time of the Exile to arrange these narratives in a way that preserves both of these two originally conflicting outlooks on kingship in Israel. This is, of course, a highly complex literary and theological issue that cannot be addressed here. For details and analysis of the theory, see Vannoy 1978.
2. It is not likely that Samuel's purpose was an attempt to modify the position of judge from that of a direct divine call to one of a family birthright. It is more likely that he merely sought his sons' assistance in settling legal disputes in a geographical area (Beersheba) to the south of his normal travels (cf. 7:16-17).
3. The "law of the king" in Deut 17:14-20 uses the expression "a king . . . like the other nations around us" in a way that suggests that it was appropriate for Israel to make a request for this kind of king, although when this actually occurred, as described in 1 Sam 8, it was regarded by the Lord as sinful (1 Sam 8:7). McConville (2002:293), however, points out that while the request in these terms was not necessarily wrong, "In 1 Sam 8:7, Yahweh points to a whole history of sin against him as the context of

the request; and the addition in 1 Sam 8:20 is significant: '. . . and go out before us and fight our battles,' a right that is not granted to the king in the deuteronomic law (cf. Boecker 1969:91-92)."

4. In view of the fact that all of the nations surrounding Israel were ruled by monarchs, it might be asked why Israel had not adopted this form of political organization much earlier in her history. Some have suggested that this delay in establishing kingship was a result of the need for a long period of time to make a transition from the nomadic way of life in the wilderness period to a sedentary way of life in the land of Canaan. Others have suggested that the tribal arrangements, along with the so-called Gibeonite wedge (cf. Josh 9) were a hindrance to the development of a central political authority. The OT, however, does not view the answer to this question as a historical issue, but rather as a principial one. Israel was chosen by Yahweh to be his "own special treasure" (Exod 19:5), over whom he was king, and in whose midst he dwelt, with the Ark as the symbol of his throne. The fact that Israel existed for so long with no human king is explained primarily by the fact that Israel was a theocracy and Yahweh was Israel's king (Koolhaas 1957:54).
5. The juxtaposition of ch 8 with ch 7 presents the reader with a very visible contrast. In ch 7 Israel is miraculously delivered from a Philistine attack after confessing its sin, getting rid of heathen idols, and asking Samuel to intercede. In ch 8 the leaders of Israel are looking for national security in the person of a human king rather than in the covenant promises of Yahweh. In this sense ch 8 is parallel to ch 4. As Davis notes (1994a:84), "Israel turns around and in chapter 8 makes the same error as in chapter 4; that is, trusting in some mechanical provision for her security. There it appeared as superstition ('the ark among us'), manipulating God; here it is political ('a king over us'), substituting for God. But it is the same idolatry."
6. See note on 8:11 above. It has sometimes been argued (Clements 1974) that 8:11-17 is really a description of the abuses of Israel's own kings, especially Solomon, and that it was written after Israel's long and unhappy experience with these rulers. This view is questioned by, among others, Ben-Barak (1972), Mendelsohn (1956), and Thornton (1967). Thornton (1967:418-419) comments, "The description of the behaviour of the king given in 8:10-18, as Mendelsohn has pointed out, reflects current Canaanite practice. But it is also important to note that this description does not reflect the situation that seems to have prevailed in the post-Davidic Israelite monarchies. . . . We need not suppose, then, that the picture described in 1 Samuel 8:10-18 is necessarily intended as a portrayal of conditions that existed under the later Davidic dynasty. Certainly there is evidence that later kings raised taxes and used forced labour, but it is questionable how far Israelite kingship in practice was as powerful and arbitrary as 1 Samuel 8:10-18 would suggest."

◆ B. Saul Privately Anointed by Samuel to Be King (1 Sam 9:1–10:16)

**There was a wealthy, influential man
named Kish from the tribe of Benjamin.
He was the son of Abiel, son of Zeror, son
of Becorath, son of Aphiah, of the tribe of
Benjamin. 2His son Saul was the most
handsome man in Israel—head and shoul-
ders taller than anyone else in the land.
3One day Kish's donkeys strayed away,
and he told Saul, "Take a servant with you,
and go look for the donkeys." 4So Saul
took one of the servants and traveled
through the hill country of Ephraim, the
land of Shalishah, the Shaalim area, and
the entire land of Benjamin, but they
couldn't find the donkeys anywhere.
5Finally, they entered the region of**

Zuph, and Saul said to his servant, "Let's go home. By now my father will be more worried about us than about the donkeys!"

6But the servant said, "I've just thought of something! There is a man of God who lives here in this town. He is held in high honor by all the people because everything he says comes true. Let's go find him. Perhaps he can tell us which way to go."

7"But we don't have anything to offer him," Saul replied. "Even our food is gone, and we don't have a thing to give him."

8"Well," the servant said, "I have one small silver piece.* We can at least offer it to the man of God and see what happens!" 9(In those days if people wanted a message from God, they would say, "Let's go and ask the seer," for prophets used to be called seers.)

10"All right," Saul agreed, "let's try it!" So they started into the town where the man of God lived.

11As they were climbing the hill to the town, they met some young women coming out to draw water. So Saul and his servant asked, "Is the seer here today?"

12"Yes," they replied. "Stay right on this road. He is at the town gates. He has just arrived to take part in a public sacrifice up at the place of worship. 13Hurry and catch him before he goes up there to eat. The guests won't begin eating until he arrives to bless the food."

14So they entered the town, and as they passed through the gates, Samuel was coming out toward them to go up to the place of worship.

15Now the LORD had told Samuel the previous day, 16"About this time tomorrow I will send you a man from the land of Benjamin. Anoint him to be the leader of my people, Israel. He will rescue them from the Philistines, for I have looked down on my people in mercy and have heard their cry."

17When Samuel saw Saul, the LORD said, "That's the man I told you about! He will rule my people."

18Just then Saul approached Samuel at the gateway and asked, "Can you please tell me where the seer's house is?"

19"I am the seer!" Samuel replied. "Go up to the place of worship ahead of me. We will eat there together, and in the morning I'll tell you what you want to know and send you on your way. 20And don't worry about those donkeys that were lost three days ago, for they have been found. And I am here to tell you that you and your family are the focus of all Israel's hopes."

21Saul replied, "But I'm only from the tribe of Benjamin, the smallest tribe in Israel, and my family is the least important of all the families of that tribe! Why are you talking like this to me?"

22Then Samuel brought Saul and his servant into the hall and placed them at the head of the table, honoring them above the thirty special guests. 23Samuel then instructed the cook to bring Saul the finest cut of meat, the piece that had been set aside for the guest of honor. 24So the cook brought in the meat and placed it before Saul. "Go ahead and eat it," Samuel said. "I was saving it for you even before I invited these others!" So Saul ate with Samuel that day.

25When they came down from the place of worship and returned to town, Samuel took Saul up to the roof of the house and prepared a bed for him there.* 26At daybreak the next morning, Samuel called to Saul, "Get up! It's time you were on your way." So Saul got ready, and he and Samuel left the house together. 27When they reached the edge of town, Samuel told Saul to send his servant on ahead. After the servant was gone, Samuel said, "Stay here, for I have received a special message for you from God."

CHAPTER 10

Then Samuel took a flask of olive oil and poured it over Saul's head. He kissed Saul and said, "I am doing this because the LORD has appointed you to be the ruler over Israel, his special possession.* 2When

you leave me today, you will see two men
beside Rachel's tomb at Zelzah, on the
border of Benjamin. They will tell you that
the donkeys have been found and that
your father has stopped worrying about
them and is now worried about you. He is
asking, 'Have you seen my son?'
3"When you get to the oak of Tabor, you
will see three men coming toward you
who are on their way to worship God at
Bethel. One will be bringing three young
goats, another will have three loaves of
bread, and the third will be carrying a
wineskin full of wine. 4They will greet you
and offer you two of the loaves, which
you are to accept.
5"When you arrive at Gibeah of God,*
where the garrison of the Philistines is
located, you will meet a band of prophets
coming down from the place of worship.
They will be playing a harp, a tambou-
rine, a flute, and a lyre, and they will be
prophesying. 6At that time the Spirit of
the LORD will come powerfully upon you,
and you will prophesy with them. You
will be changed into a different person.
7After these signs take place, do what
must be done, for God is with you. 8Then
go down to Gilgal ahead of me. I will join
you there to sacrifice burnt offerings and
peace offerings. You must wait for seven
days until I arrive and give you further
instructions."
9As Saul turned and started to leave,
God gave him a new heart, and all Samu-
el's signs were fulfilled that day. 10When
Saul and his servant arrived at Gibeah,
they saw a group of prophets coming to-
ward them. Then the Spirit of God came
powerfully upon Saul, and he, too, began
to prophesy. 11When those who knew Saul
heard about it, they exclaimed, "What? Is
even Saul a prophet? How did the son of
Kish become a prophet?"
12And one of those standing there said,
"Can anyone become a prophet, no matter
who his father is?"* So that is the origin
of the saying "Is even Saul a prophet?"
13When Saul had finished prophesying,
he went up to the place of worship.
14"Where have you been?" Saul's uncle
asked him and his servant.
"We were looking for the donkeys," Saul
replied, "but we couldn't find them. So we
went to Samuel to ask him where they
were."
15"Oh? And what did he say?" his uncle
asked.
16"He told us that the donkeys had al-
ready been found," Saul replied. But Saul
didn't tell his uncle what Samuel said
about the kingdom.

9:8 Hebrew *1/4 shekel of silver,* about 0.1 ounces or 3 grams in weight. **9:25** As in Greek version; Hebrew reads *and talked with him there.* **10:1** Greek version reads *over Israel. And you will rule over the LORD's people and save them from their enemies around them. This will be the sign to you that the LORD has appointed you to be leader over his special possession.* **10:5** Hebrew *Gibeath-elohim.* **10:12** Hebrew *said, "Who is their father?"*

NOTES

9:9 *"Let's go and ask the seer," for prophets used to be called seers.* This explanatory remark is probably a gloss, written to explain the term seer (*ro'eh* [TH7200A, ZH8014]) in 9:11b. If so, it is an editorial addition to the original text and more properly belongs between 9:11 and 9:12. In any case, as it now reads in MT, this remark raises some serious questions. A prophet (*nabi'* [TH5030, ZH5566]) was still called a seer (*ro'eh*) long after the time of Samuel (cf. e.g., Isa 30:10). And the word *nabi'* was in use long before the time of Samuel (cf. e.g., Gen 20:7, of Abraham; Num 12:6; Deut 13:2; 18:15; etc.). In fact, Samuel himself is called a *nabi'* in 1 Sam 3:20. If the word *nabi'* (prophet) was used before the time of Samuel, how can this parenthetical statement claim that what was later called a prophet was called a seer in the time of Samuel? Does this imply that all the texts in the OT in which *nabi'* occurs are to be dated after the time of Samuel? The wording of the LXX sheds some helpful light on these questions. The LXX reading, "for the people formerly called the 'prophet' the 'seer,'" suggests that the difference in terminology is primarily one of technical versus popular usage. This suggests that *ro'eh* (seer) was a more popular designation in Israel's early history, while *nabi'* (prophet) was a more technical or official term. The LXX reading makes the statement less absolute than the MT, and allows for the occurrence of *ro'eh* in later times as well as *nabi'* in earlier times.

9:14 ***as they passed through the gates, Samuel was coming out toward them.*** For the syntax indicative of simultaneous action, see Williams 1976:§236.

9:15 ***Now the LORD had told Samuel.*** For Hebrew indication of the pluperfect, see Williams 1976:§162; S. R. Driver 1913:73.

9:16 ***Anoint him to be the leader of my people, Israel.*** The precise meaning of the term *nagid* [TH5057, ZH5592] (leader) is disputed. Various suggestions include "leader" (NIV, NLT), "ruler" (NRSV, NJPS), "prince" (NASB and Klein 1983:81), and "commander" (NAB and Bright 1981:190). McCarter (1980b:178-179) argues that the term should be translated as "king delegate." BDB 617-618 suggests the meanings "leader (lit. probably *one in front*), ruler, or prince." Usage in the OT suggests that the term is an alternate word for a king much as sovereign or monarch would be in English. It is used with reference to Saul, David, Solomon, Jeroboam, Baasha, Hezekiah, and Abijah. In this particular context, it would appear that the Lord deliberately chose not to use the common term "king" (*melek* [TH4428, ZH4889]) because of its association with the sinful request of the people for a "king [*melek*] . . . like all the other nations have" (8:5, 20). By use of the word *nagid*, the Lord indicates that his idea of kingship differs significantly from that of the people's request (van den Berg 1996a:79). In Israel the king is not to use his position for personal advantage or to oppress the people over whom he rules, because the people do not belong to him but to the Lord. In Israel a king is not to be a person who owes his position to either political maneuvering or the voice of the people, but rather is to be a person whom the Lord himself designates for the position (Deut 17:14-15).

9:17 ***The LORD said.*** For use of *'anahu* [TH6030, ZH6699] (answer) in this sense, see S. R. Driver 1913:73-74.

9:24 ***even before I invited these others!*** Lit., "saying, 'I have invited the people.'" The Hebrew here is obscure. Neither the LXX nor 4QSam[a] offer any help. Various conjectural emendations have been suggested, the most common (Budde 1890) being, "that you may eat with the guests."

10:5 ***When you arrive at Gibeah of God.*** There are two questions connected with determining the location of the place in view in this phrase. The first is whether *gib'ath* [TH1390, ZH1497] should be understood as a proper name (Gibeah of God) or as a common feminine noun (hill [TH1389, ZH1496] of God). The proper name translation would link this spot with Gibeah, the hometown of Saul (10:10, 26; 11:4). The common feminine noun translation would open up numerous possibilities. The references to Gibeah in vv. 10 and 26 as well as to "Gibeah of Saul" in 11:4 suggest it is best taken as a proper name. The second question is how the Gibeah of this chapter is to be related to the Geba of chs 13 and 14 where both names occur intermittently. Some have argued that Gibeah and Geba are the same place (see J. M. Miller 1975), while others have viewed the reference in 13:3 to Geba as a textual error for Gibeah (involving the difference of a single letter in Hebrew) following the LXX and Targum. All things considered, this latter position is to be preferred. A related question is that of why Gibeah is designated "Gibeah of God." In the context, the name would seem to be suggesting that this place belongs to God rather than to the Philistines (cf. 10:5b), and that Saul is being gently reminded that the land of Canaan is God's land, and that as Israel's newly chosen leader he has the responsibility to rid the land of the heathen Philistine presence.

where the garrison of the Philistines is located. The best translation of *netsibe* [TH5333, ZH5907] (garrison) in this context is disputed (BDB 662d), with "pillar," "garrison," and "governor" all being valid options. When viewed in connection with Jonathan's attack on Gibeah/Geba in 13:3, either "governor" or "garrison" seems preferable to "pillar" here.

10:7 ***do what must be done.*** Lit., "Do what your hand finds [to do]." As Alter (1999:55) suggests, "The biblical idiom means do whatever is within your power."

COMMENTARY

At the end of chapter 8 Samuel sent the representatives of the people back to their homes while he awaited further instructions from the Lord concerning how he should proceed with the task of giving them a king (8:22). The present pericope is an excellent example of how the Lord often chooses to accomplish his purposes through the ordinary experiences of everyday life. The narrative tells of the lost donkeys of Kish, a wealthy man from the tribe of Benjamin, who had a handsome son named Saul. Kish sent Saul with an unnamed servant to search for the missing livestock. After looking for three days (9:20) with no success, Saul's servant suggested consulting with the "man of God" (i.e., Samuel; 9:6, 8, 10) who lived in a nearby town, in the hope that he could provide information about the lost donkeys. Unknown to Saul but announced to the reader (9:15-16) is the significant fact that the Lord had told Samuel that the person who would come to him on the next day was the person whom he had chosen "to be the leader of my people, Israel" (9:16).

Although Saul's search for the lost donkeys (9:1-14; 10:14-16) is the larger setting for the events narrated in this section, the focus of the narrative is found in 9:15–10:13, where Saul's interaction with Samuel is described in great detail. This section may be divided into four subsections: (1) 9:15-16, the Lord's instructions to Samuel; (2) 9:17-24, Samuel's first encounter with Saul and the Lord's designation of Saul as the one he had chosen to be king; (3) 9:25–10:8, Saul's anointing by Samuel, a description of the three signs that would authenticate his calling, and Samuel's instructions to Saul concerning his future responsibilities; (4) 10:9-13, Saul's empowerment by God's Spirit for his task.[1]

The Lord's Instructions to Samuel (9:15-16). These verses tell the reader something about which Saul himself was completely unaware: namely, that his impending meeting with the man of God to ask about the lost donkeys would have a much greater significance than he could ever imagine and that this meeting with Samuel was not a mere happenstance, but a divine appointment. The Lord had told Samuel on the previous day that he would send "a man from the land of Benjamin," and that this would be the person whom Samuel should anoint "to be leader" (see note on 9:16) of God's people, Israel. Notice that in all these events, it is the Lord who takes the initiative (emphasized by the Hebrew word order, in which the subject [Yahweh] rather than the verb begins the sentence). It is the Lord who sent Saul to Samuel, albeit by the circuitous route of a mundane search for lost donkeys. So in spite of the people's wrong motives in requesting a king, the Lord told Samuel that he would accede to their request because he had heard their cries of distress under the Philistine oppression (9:16).[2] What the people had wanted for the wrong reasons, God, in his mercy, would employ for their good.[3] It was the Lord's purpose for Saul to "rescue" the Israelites from their Philistine oppressors.

As subsequent narratives unfold, it becomes clear that these high expectations for Saul will not be realized. At the end of 1 Samuel we find that Saul and his sons were killed in a battle with the Philistines, and as a result, the Philistine threat to Israel remained just as great as it had been before, if not greater (ch 31). When we reflect on Saul's disappointing and unsuccessful reign, we may wonder about what happened to the lofty divine purpose for which God made him king (9:16). The conclusion seems inescapable that God's announced plans are not always carried out in precisely the way in which they are initially described (van den Berg 1996a:80). The narratives of biblical history clearly demonstrate that even though in some instances God's announced plans are consummated in spite of concerted and vehement human opposition, on other occasions this does not happen. God's announced plan for Saul is an example of the latter. This does not mean that Saul nullified God's merciful purpose to deliver his people from Philistine oppression, because ultimately they were delivered. This deliverance, however, was not accomplished by Saul but by his successor David. So in this instance, we find that the timing and manner of Israel's deliverance were modified because of Saul's failure to carry out the responsibilities that the Lord had placed upon him.[4]

Samuel's First Encounter with Saul and the Lord's Designation of Saul as Chosen King (9:17-24). When Samuel saw Saul in passing, the Lord told him that this was the person about whom he had spoken (9:17). Here was the one whom the Lord had chosen to "rule"[5] over God's people. This all took place before Saul had spoken a word to Samuel. When Saul approached Samuel to ask him where he could find the seer, Samuel identified himself as the seer, and then, after inviting Saul to dine with him, told him not to worry about the lost donkeys because they had been found. He concluded by telling Saul that he and his family were "the focus of all Israel's hopes" (9:20). Saul certainly must have been surprised to be told that the lost donkeys had been found before he had even asked about them, but he must have been even more surprised to hear that he and his family were "the focus of all Israel's hopes" (a veiled reference to Israel's desire for a king). It would seem unlikely that Saul fully understood the implications of Samuel's words, although he immediately protested that he came from an insignificant family and tribe, and that he could not understand why Samuel was speaking to him in such terms (9:21). When the time came for Saul and his servant to participate in the sacrificial meal with Samuel, they were given the seats of honor, and Saul was given the best piece of meat (9:22-24).

Samuel Anoints Saul and Instructs Him of His Responsibilities (9:25–10:8). After the sacrificial meal, Samuel talked with Saul on the roof of his house (9:25). There is no record of the topics discussed in this conversation, but under the circumstances it seems likely that Samuel attempted to prepare Saul for what would happen on the next day, including some discussion of the Lord's desire for him to deliver Israel from Philistine oppression (cf. 9:16). Early the next morning Samuel arranged to anoint[6] Saul in complete privacy and then told him "the LORD has appointed you to be the ruler over Israel, his special possession" (10:1). What an enormous privilege and responsibility was suddenly thrust upon Saul! The unanswered question is how well Saul would respond to this completely unexpected and very challenging task.

In this story of the anointing of Saul, we are introduced to the second of the three people (Samuel, Saul, and David) who will figure prominently in the remainder of 1 Samuel. As the narrative progresses, we find that Saul's life proved to be a tragic failure. After disobeying the Lord on two occasions (chs 13 and 15), Saul was rejected as king, and the Lord sent Samuel to Bethlehem to anoint David as his replacement. From this point forward, the contrast between the life and destiny of Saul and that of David becomes so pronounced that many readers have perceived Saul as a person who could do little that was right, while David has been celebrated as one who could do little wrong. Because of this contrast between Saul and David, Saul has generally been treated in Christian tradition with "a large measure of hostility" (Gunn 1980:23).[7] In more recent times a more sympathetic view of Saul has been advocated by a number of interpreters who view Saul more as a victim to be pitied than as an evil person to be censured. Saul is viewed more as a casualty of the machinations of a vindictive deity who for some inscrutable reason was predisposed to reject him as king, than as a willfully disobedient individual who not only repeatedly failed to fulfill the duties and requirements of a covenantal king, but who also refused to repent when he was confronted with his disobedience.[8] At its core, much of the current discussion surrounding the analysis of Saul's life centers on the question of whether his tragic life is to be seen as a "tragedy of fate" or a "tragedy of flaw." If it was a "tragedy of flaw," then Saul's disobedience was the cause of his downfall; if it was a "tragedy of fate," then Saul was the victim of forces beyond his own control.[9] In this context, Gunn suggests that "Yahweh functions as Fate itself, as the 'dark destiny' which holds sway over the king," so that Saul is really "the innocent victim of God" (1980:30, 123).

These are important issues. Recent trends suggesting that Saul was a victim (cf. 13:12; 15:20-21) tend to minimize Saul's own responsibility for the tragic downward spiral of his life.[10] This approach agrees not only with the opinion that Saul had of himself but also with the contemporary tendency to account for many human failures by appealing to victimization. While it is clear that Saul faced great difficulties in assuming the responsibilities of his office, it is not so clear that his behavior is properly understood as that of a pawn moved about on the chessboard of life by a malevolent deity. Although Saul could not bring himself to accept that his behavior warranted the punishment that he received, it should be remembered that Saul repeatedly refused to embrace the spiritual and moral requirements that his office entailed.

Subsequent to anointing Saul, Samuel told him in advance about three things that would happen to him on his way back home (10:2-6): (1) he would meet two men by Rachel's tomb at Zelzah who would tell him that the donkeys he had been looking for had been found and that now his father was more worried about him than about the donkeys (10:2); (2) at the great tree of Tabor he would meet three men who were on their way to sacrifice at Bethel, and they would offer him two loaves of bread (10:3-4); (3) at Gibeah, where there was a Philistine garrison, he would meet a company of prophets who were prophesying[11] to the accompaniment of musical instruments, and when the Spirit of the Lord came upon him, he would join with them in prophesying (10:5-6).

After telling Saul that these three things would happen to him on his journey homeward, Samuel instructed him to (1) do what was in his power to do (10:7); and (2) go to Gilgal and wait there for seven days until Samuel came to offer sacrifice and give him further instructions (10:8). Although the specific intention of the instruction of 10:7 is implied rather than explicit, in context it seems clear that Samuel was telling Saul to take an appropriate action against the Philistine garrison or governor (see note on 10:5) located in Gibeah (cf. 10:5; Long 1989:51-66). In other words, Samuel was telling Saul in veiled language that he now had the obligation to take the initiative in exercising his newly given responsibility of being a "ruler over Israel" (10:1) and delivering the Israelites from Philistine oppression (cf. 9:16). This instruction was followed up with a command to go to Gilgal and to await the arrival of Samuel, who would consecrate the battle as well as instruct Saul concerning what he should do further. Fulfillment of this twofold commission, however, was delayed until the occurrence of the events described in 13:3-15, and then was fulfilled in only a qualified sense (Long 1989:64-65).

Saul's Empowerment by God's Spirit for His Task (10:9–13). As Saul left Samuel, God produced a change in Saul's heart. Exactly what is meant by this expression is not further indicated. That it is not to be understood in soteriological terms of spiritual regeneration seems clear because of Saul's later persistence in willful disobedience to the Lord. In this context, it would appear to be a reference to the Lord's equipping Saul with the necessary disposition of mind and will to assume the responsibilities of kingship. As Saul went on his way, all three of the things described by Samuel happened exactly as Samuel said they would (10:9). In this remarkable way, God graciously confirmed to Saul that he was truly the one whom the Lord had chosen to lead Israel, and at the same time, Samuel's words were shown to be the very words of God.

The occurrence of the third of the three signs, which happened just as Saul approached his hometown of Gibeah, is described in some detail. Saul encountered a company of prophets, and when this happened the Spirit of God came powerfully upon Saul as well, so that he joined in with the company of prophets in prophesying (see endnote 11). The behavior of Saul on this occasion was such a surprise to the people of the town that they wondered what had happened to him. Apparently he was not known by his neighbors as a person who would easily be given to a public display of such unusual conduct. The people of the town were so struck by this noticeable change in the Saul whom they had known that they asked in some wonderment, "Is even Saul a prophet?" Yet unknown to the people was the fact that God was preparing Saul not for the function of prophet, but for the office of king.

Saul's Return Home (10:14–16). When Saul came to the altar at Gibeah he met his uncle (perhaps Ner, the father of Abner of subsequent narratives, cf. 14:50), who asked where he had been. When Saul told him that he had been looking for the lost donkeys of his father and had gone to ask Samuel for help, his uncle wanted to know what Samuel had told him. Saul said that Samuel told him that the donkeys had been found, but he did not tell his uncle anything about the kingship. One may wonder why Saul was so reluctant to share this momentous news with a member of his own family. Was it due to shyness or modesty? Was it due to fear of a negative reaction to a claim that might be viewed with a great deal of skepticism? Or is this a first hint that Saul has some personal reservations concerning his role in God's plan for his life (van den Berg 1996a:87)? Even though Saul had been given a new heart (10:9) and the Holy Spirit had come upon him (10:10), is this an indication that he was not entirely ready to fully embrace the task that he had been given? That such a conclusion might be justified is perhaps also supported by the fact that Saul failed to take any action against the Philistine outpost or governor (see note on 10:5) located in his hometown, even though Samuel had commissioned him to do so (10:5, 7).

ENDNOTES

1. See Brueggemann (1990a:71) for these subdivisions.
2. When the Lord sent Moses to Egypt to deliver his people from Egyptian bondage, the same reason was given (Exod 3:9).
3. Davis (1994a:92) comments, "Note that Yahweh's providence is in the service of his pity."
4. This is the truth contained in Jer 18:7-10: "If I announce that a certain nation or kingdom is to be uprooted, torn down, and destroyed, but then that nation renounces its evil ways, I will not destroy it as I had planned. And if I announce that I will plant and build up a certain nation or kingdom, but then that nation turns to evil and refuses to obey me, I will not bless it as I said I would." While God remains absolutely sovereign over all that comes to pass, this does not mean that human behavior is excluded from the ways in which divine sovereignty is worked out in the life experience of individuals and in the history of nations. The concept of God in biblical revelation is not that of an impersonal fatalistic force. The Bible teaches that God not only responds to the prayers of his people, but also to their obedience and disobedience to his commands. God's announced plans and promises for his people may include a conditional element that is sometimes unexpressed, but which is, nevertheless, an integral feature of the time and way in which these plans and promises are ultimately realized (e.g., cf. 1 Kgs 21:19 with 2 Kgs 9:26; see also Isa 38:1-5; Jonah 3:4-10). For a more complete discussion, see Oehler 1891:492-494 and Payne 1973:62-68.
5. Here an unusual verb (*'atsar* [TH6115, ZH6808]; 9:17) is used for "rule" rather than the more familiar *malak* [TH4427, ZH4887] (reign) or *mashal* [TH4910, ZH5440] (rule). This is probably for the same reason that the word *nagid* [TH5057, ZH5592] (leader) is used instead of *melek* [TH4428, ZH4889] (king); see note on 9:16.
6. To anoint an individual or object signified separation unto the service of God by divine authorization. Prior to this time priests had been anointed (cf. Exod 29:7; 40:12-15; Lev 4:3 [NLT mg]; 8:12), but from this point forward it is usually the king who is referred to as the "anointed of the Lord" (cf. 12:3; 24:6; 26:9-11; 2 Sam 1:14-16; 19:21; 22:51; 23:1; Ps 2:2-6). "Anointed" and "Messiah" are the translation and transliteration (respectively) of the word (*mashiakh* [TH4899, ZH5431]). The Greek translation of this Hebrew word is *christos* [TG5547, ZG5986], "Christ." See additional discussion in the Introduction, "The Davidic Covenant and Its Messianic Implications"; see also NIDOTTE 2.1123-1127.
7. Gunn (1980:23) comments, "Perhaps one of the roots of such hostility lies in the fact that for many early commentators David is seen as both the progenitor of Christ 'in

the flesh' and the 'type' of Christ in terms of his spiritual significance. In a sense, therefore, Saul who persecuted David, persecuted also Christ." Although Gunn is skeptical of this early Christian analysis of the Saul stories, there is, perhaps, more legitimacy to it than he is willing to accept.

8. Gunn (1980:129) comments, "If we are to condemn Saul for his jealous persecution of David, how much more is Yahweh to be condemned for his jealous persecution of Saul!"
9. Gunn (1980:123) suggests that the "moral/theological evaluation depends ultimately not on the text, for the text offers no independent evaluative judgments, but on the stance of the reader." While it may be true that the narratives of Samuel themselves contain little in the way of evaluative judgments, these narratives do not stand alone, but are placed in the context of the whole of the biblical canon, in which there is abundant material for making evaluative judgments about them. Gunn's own "stance" on "moral/theological" evaluation is such that it permits him to conclude that Saul may be viewed "as essentially an innocent victim of God, and thus of seeing God in negative as well as in positive terms" (1980:123). This raises profound theological issues that at their core are questions concerning the "goodness" and "justice" of God. Gunn's own view (1980:128) is that "Saul falls victim to Yahweh's resentment at an imagined insult (the 'sin') and becomes the pawn (or scapegoat) in a process (the 'expiation') whereby Yahweh vindicates his shift of attitude towards the monarchy and buttresses his shaken self-esteem." This, however, is certainly not the sort of concept about God that emerges from a careful look at the whole of biblical revelation.
10. Another defender of the victimization view of Saul is Brueggemann (1997). In speaking of God's dealings with David and Saul, he comments (1997:371), "While the text is pro-David in its outcomes, the witness of Israel presents for us the illicit nature of Yahweh's activity as pertains to Saul. In fact, Saul is treated unfairly by Yahweh, . . . he can only lose. Saul will lose partly because David is bold, lucky, attractive, and 'destined.' Saul will lose because 'forces' conspire against him. Israel, moreover, does not hesitate to assign those conspiring forces exactly to Yahweh." Brueggemann then cites a number of passages in 1–2 Samuel that, in his view, support this conclusion.
11. "Prophesy" (*naba'* [TH5012, ZH5547]) has a wider range of meaning in Hebrew than it does in contemporary English usage. In English "prophesy" has become nearly synonymous with "predict" or "foretell." In Hebrew usage the central idea of the word is to be an authorized spokesperson (cf. e.g., Exod 6:28–7:1). In the Old Testament a prophet is thus a person who speaks for God (cf. Deut 18:18; Jer 1:9). In some contexts, however, *naba'* [TH5030, ZH5566] (prophesy) takes on the connotation of engagement in some type of abnormal behavior (cf. 19:18-24; 1 Kgs 18:29). In this particular context the word seems to suggest an "enthusiastic praising of God." See further TWOT 2.544-545, MacRae 1975, and NIDOTTE 4.1067-1078.

◆ C. Saul Publicly Chosen to Be King (1 Sam 10:17-27)

**17 Later Samuel called all the people of
Israel to meet before the LORD at Mizpah.
18 And he said, "This is what the LORD, the
God of Israel, has declared: I brought you
from Egypt and rescued you from the
Egyptians and from all of the nations that
were oppressing you. 19 But though I have
rescued you from your misery and distress, you have rejected your God today
and have said, 'No, we want a king instead!' Now, therefore, present yourselves
before the LORD by tribes and clans."**

**20 So Samuel brought all the tribes of
Israel before the LORD, and the tribe of**

Benjamin was chosen by lot. 21 Then he
brought each family of the tribe of Ben-
jamin before the LORD, and the family of
the Matrites was chosen. And finally Saul
son of Kish was chosen from among them.
But when they looked for him, he had dis-
appeared! 22 So they asked the LORD,
"Where is he?"

And the LORD replied, "He is hiding
among the baggage." 23 So they found him
and brought him out, and he stood head
and shoulders above anyone else.

24 Then Samuel said to all the people,
"This is the man the LORD has chosen
as your king. No one in all Israel is like
him!"

And all the people shouted, "Long live
the king!"

25 Then Samuel told the people what the
rights and duties of a king were. He wrote
them down on a scroll and placed it be-
fore the LORD. Then Samuel sent the peo-
ple home again.

26 When Saul returned to his home at
Gibeah, a group of men whose hearts God
had touched went with him. 27 But there
were some scoundrels who complained,
"How can this man save us?" And they
scorned him and refused to bring him
gifts. But Saul ignored them.

[Nahash, king of the Ammonites, had been grievously oppressing the people of Gad and Reuben who lived east of the Jordan River. He gouged out the right eye of each of the Israelites living there, and he didn't allow anyone to come and rescue them. In fact, of all the Israelites east of the Jordan, there wasn't a single one whose right eye Nahash had not gouged out. But there were 7,000 men who had escaped from the Ammonites, and they had settled in Jabesh-gilead.]*

10:27 This paragraph, which is not included in the Masoretic Text, is found in Dead Sea Scroll 4QSam[a].

NOTES

10:25 ***rights and duties of a king.*** This is the *mishpat hammelukah,* the description of what a king should do, as opposed to the *mishpat hammelek* of 8:11-17, a description of what kings would do. For fuller discussion see note on 8:11.

on a scroll. For the use of the Hebrew definite article when the idea is indefinite in English translation, see GKC §126s; Joüon and Muraoka §137m; Williams 1976:§84.

10:27a ***scoundrels.*** Lit., "sons of Belial" (cf. 1:16; 2:12; 25:17, 25; 30:22; and note on 1:16).

10:27b–11:1 ***But Saul ignored them. [Nahash, king of the Ammonites, had been grievously oppressing the people of Gad . . . Jabesh-gilead.] About a month later.*** The bracketed portion of text comes from 4QSam[a] (cf. NLT mg). The NLT's "Saul ignored them" is an interpretive rendering of the MT's *wayehi kemakharish* [TH3509.1/2790A, ZH3869/3087] (lit., "He was as one who was silent"). In 4QSam[a] this phrase is not included in 10:27, but it seems to occur after the added material in a slightly different form as an introduction to 11:1. There, it reads "about a month later" (*wayehi kemo khodesh* [TH2320, ZH2544]), which, when written in Hebrew, looks very similar to the MT's phrase. The LXX also reads "about a month later" rather than "he was as one who is silent," but it does not include the plus found in 4QSam[a] (i.e., the bracketed material in the NLT). In Josephus's account (*Antiquities* 6.68-70), part of that addition is included, but the addition begins with "after a month" instead of ending with it.

While Klein (1983:102-103) and McCarter (1980b:198-200) adopt the 4QSam[a] reading as more likely to be original, this conclusion is challenged by Pisano (1984:91-98) and Barthélemy (1982). After a detailed discussion of particulars, Pisano (1984:98) concludes: "4QSam[a] seems clearly to witness to a textual tradition with expansionist tendencies and, considering the total absence of the plus of 10:27–11:1 in MT and LXX, plus the *lectio difficilior* which MT contains with *wayehi kemakharish,* it seems much more likely that 4Q has an expanded text here as well, part of whose tradition was shared by Josephus, and a smaller part of which was known to LXX, as far as the agreement on *kemo khodesh* is concerned. Thus the shorter and more difficult MT seems preferable here." Gordon (1986:64) suggests that the "wise course for the present, therefore, is to reserve judgment on the status of these additional lines in 4QSam[a]." Gordon's suggestion is still valid.

COMMENTARY

Subsequent to privately anointing Saul, probably at Ramah, Samuel called for a national assembly to be held at Mizpah.[1] Samuel's reason for calling this assembly was to give a public response to the request for a king (made at Ramah by the leaders of the nation, ch 8) by presenting them with the person whom the Lord had chosen for this office. At Ramah Samuel had listened to their request, he had warned them about the dangers of the type of kingship that they desired, and then he had sent them home (8:22). On that occasion, however, the Lord had already instructed Samuel to comply with their request and give the people a king (8:7, 9, 22).

Once the Lord had privately designated Saul as the one whom he had chosen to be king (9:1–10:16), the time had arrived for Samuel to take the next step in the process of establishing kingship in Israel. Samuel opened the assembly at Mizpah by reminding Israel of the Lord's covenant faithfulness and mighty deliverances in their past history (10:18). The Lord had brought a weak and powerless people out of Egypt by his mighty power. After entering into covenant with them at Mount Sinai, he had given them entrance into Canaan and ordained the capture of the city of Jericho without even a fight. He had granted Joshua a miraculous victory over a coalition of Canaanite kings (Josh 10), and he had given Gideon a remarkable victory over the Midianites (Judg 7–8). He had delivered Israel from all their many oppressors during the period of the judges, including their most recent victory over the Philistines at Mizpah, the very place where Israel was now assembled. The Lord had repeatedly shown himself to be Israel's great guardian and defender ever since the time of their deliverance out of Egypt. Israel's response, however, was ingratitude, if not downright contempt for the Lord's faithfulness (10:19). By their request for a human king they had said, in effect, that the protection afforded them by a divine king was insufficient to provide them with an adequate sense of national security. They wanted a more tangible sort of leadership, a leadership that, in their view, would provide a more reliable form of protection. In short they wanted a king "like the nations around us" to go out and lead them in battle (8:20).

After reminding the people of these things, Samuel was ready to carry out the Lord's mandate to give the people a king. The procedure used was that of casting lots, first for a particular tribe and then for a specific clan and family within the chosen tribe. The lot fell to the tribe of Benjamin, and eventually to the family of Kish and the person of Saul. But at the crucial moment, Saul was nowhere to be found; the Lord had to tell the people to look for him among the supplies brought along by those attending the assembly (10:22).

In view of Saul's private anointing in the immediately preceding narrative (9:1–10:16), Saul must have fully expected that Samuel would publicly present him to the people as their newly chosen king at the Mizpah assembly. Why, then, would he have gone into hiding during the process of public selection? Was this a reflex of modesty and humility as is usually suggested by several commentaries? (See Josephus *Antiquities* 6.63; Goslinga 1968:233; Kirkpatrick 1918:111; Smith 1912:73; Gordon [1986:121] notes that one of the Targums says that he had "slipped off for some quiet prayer and Bible study!") Or was this reticence on the part of Saul just one more example of his reluctance to take on the responsibilities of kingship, adding to those suggested by the previous narrative? Perhaps this was also an ominous hint of even worse things to come in the future?[2]

However one may view Saul's self-imposed seclusion, he was presented to the gathered assembly by Samuel as the one whom the Lord had chosen to be their king. Saul was an imposing figure of royal stature, standing taller than anyone else at the assembly (10:23); he was immediately hailed with enthusiasm by the people: "Long live the king!" (10:24). This was exactly the kind of king that they wanted! Samuel, however, did not want the people to think that now that they had been given a king, their king would rule in the same way as the kings did in the surrounding nations. So Samuel was careful to explain to the people the "rights and duties of a king" (lit., "the manner of the kingdom," 10:25).[3] By so doing, Samuel took a first step toward resolving the tension between the people's sinful desire for a king and the Lord's acquiescence to their request. Unfortunately, no copy of the written regulations that Samuel deposited in the sanctuary (perhaps at Mizpah, 10:25) has survived.[4] Whatever the precise content of these regulations may have been, it seems clear that they were a more complete description of the duties and responsibilities of Israelite kings than Moses had given in Deuteronomy 17:14-20, and that they were intended to establish kingship in Israel as what in more recent times might be described as a constitutional monarchy: Israel's kings would not have autonomous power. They would always be subject to the laws of the Sinai covenant and the words of the prophets. Kingship in Israel would be integrated into the covenantal structure of the theocracy, and it would be consistent with the continued sovereignty of the Lord over the nation because it was intended to serve as a vehicle for the Lord's rule over his people.

When Samuel dismissed the assembly, Saul went back to Gibeah escorted by a group of men who desired to express their acceptance of him as the new leader of the nation. There were some others, however, who questioned whether Saul would be able to deliver them from their enemies. Right at the outset there were two opposite reactions to this change in the structure of the theocracy, as well as to the choice of Saul as the first king. Those who objected to Saul's being chosen king are termed "scoundrels" (10:27), presumably because they refused to accept the Lord's selection of Saul. Because Saul was the Lord's anointed one, he deserved the respect and support of God's people.[5]

The last phrase of this section (in the NLT, "But Saul ignored them"; in the NIV, "But Saul kept silent") has often been taken as evidence of Saul's inner strength, born of the self-assurance given him by his certainty that God had called him to be king. This statement is then combined with understanding his disappearance at the time of his selection as evidence of personal humility and a self-effacing character (see discussion above). One must be cautious, however, of reading too much into this last phrase, since the Qumran fragment, supported by similar readings in LXX and Josephus, reads "about a month later" and introduces the next pericope rather than closing this one (see note on 10:27b–11:1).

ENDNOTES

1. Mizpah was located in the territory of the tribe of Benjamin about seven and a half miles north of Jerusalem. This is the same place in which Samuel had led the nation in an assembly of national repentance, and then interceded for them when the Philistines attacked the gathered people (ch 7). The result on that occasion was a remarkable victory for Israel. This was also one of the cities to which Samuel made regular annual visits (7:16).
2. Alter (1999:58) says, "Saul the diffident farm boy had expressed a sense of unworthiness for the high office Samuel conferred on him. Now, confronted by the assembled tribes and 'trapped' by the process of lot drawing, he tries to flee the onus of kingship, farcically hiding in the baggage."
3. The "manner of the kingdom" (*mishpat hammelukah* [TH4941/4410, ZH5477/4867]) of 10:25 is to be clearly distinguished from the "manner of the king" (*mishpat hammelek* [TH4428, ZH4889]) of 8:11. In 8:11 Samuel warned Israel about the dangers of kingship like the nations round about, but here in 10:25 he defines kingship in Israel as an instrument of the Lord's rule over his people. It was Samuel's intent to see that the *mishpat hammelukah* (10:25) would be normative in Israel rather than the *mishpat hammelek* (8:9-11). See the note at 8:11 and Vannoy 1978:231.
4. In addition to the Ten Commandments that were deposited in the Ark (Exod 25:16; 40:20), and the "Book of Instruction" (Deuteronomy) that was placed beside the Ark (Deut 31:26), two other written documents defining Israel's covenant relationship with the Lord are mentioned in Exod 24:7 and Josh 24:26. Of these all but Josh 24:26 are included in the biblical text.
5. Davis (1994a:108) comments, "The local scoundrels were rejecting Saul not merely as a person but also in his office as Yahweh's appointed king through whom he willed to save his people."

◆ D. Saul's Kingship Confirmed by His Victory over the Ammonites (1 Sam 11:1-13)

About a month later,* King Nahash of Ammon led his army against the Israelite town of Jabesh-gilead. But all the citizens of Jabesh asked for peace. "Make a treaty with us, and we will be your servants," they pleaded.

2"All right," Nahash said, "but only on one condition. I will gouge out the right eye of every one of you as a disgrace to all Israel!"

3"Give us seven days to send messengers throughout Israel!" replied the elders of Jabesh. "If no one comes to save us, we will agree to your terms."

4When the messengers came to Gibeah of Saul and told the people about their plight, everyone broke into tears. 5Saul had been plowing a field with his oxen, and when he returned to town, he asked, "What's the matter? Why is everyone crying?" So they told him about the message from Jabesh.

6Then the Spirit of God came powerfully upon Saul, and he became very angry. 7He took two oxen and cut them into pieces and sent the messengers to carry them throughout Israel with this message: "This is what will happen to the oxen of anyone who refuses to follow Saul and Samuel into battle!" And the LORD made the people afraid of Saul's anger, and all of them came out together as one. 8When Saul mobilized them at Bezek, he found that there were 300,000 men from Israel and 30,000* men from Judah.

9So Saul sent the messengers back to Jabesh-gilead to say, "We will rescue you by noontime tomorrow!" There was great

joy throughout the town when that message arrived!

[10]The men of Jabesh then told their enemies, "Tomorrow we will come out to you, and you can do to us whatever you wish." [11]But before dawn the next morning, Saul arrived, having divided his army into three detachments. He launched a surprise attack against the Ammonites and slaughtered them the whole morning. The remnant of their army was so badly scattered that no two of them were left together.

[12]Then the people exclaimed to Samuel, "Now where are those men who said, 'Why should Saul rule over us?' Bring them here, and we will kill them!"

[13]But Saul replied, "No one will be executed today, for today the LORD has rescued Israel!"

11:1 As in Greek version; Hebrew lacks *About a month later.* **11:8** Dead Sea Scrolls and Greek version read *70,000.*

NOTES

11:1 ***About a month later.*** See note on 10:27b–11:1 for the place of this phrase in the textual tradition. The phrase is not only supported by the LXX (cf. NLT mg), but also occurs in 4QSam[a].

COMMENTARY

After being publicly designated as the one whom the Lord had chosen to be king, Saul returned to his home in Gibeah (10:26) and continued to work in the fields as he had done before (11:5). The designation of Saul as "king-elect" (by private anointing, 9:1–10:16, and public selection by lot, 10:17-27) represented only the first stage in a three-stage process by which the monarchy was placed in operation in Israel.[1] The three-stage process involved designation, confirmation, and finally inauguration.[2] First Samuel 11 describes the second and third stages in this process. The victory over the Ammonites under Saul's leadership provided a clear confirmation of his appointment to the royal office (11:1-13), and this immediately led to his inauguration as king in a covenant renewal ceremony held at Gilgal that was convened by Samuel (11:14–12:25).

Nahash, king of the Ammonites, attacked Jabesh-gilead, a city located on the north side of the Wadi Yabis, about two miles east of the Jordan River and 40 miles north of the Dead Sea. The Ammonites were descendants of Lot (Gen 19:30-38) and occupied territory northeast of the Dead Sea in Transjordan. Their capital city was Rabbah, present-day Amman. During the period of the judges, they had been defeated by Jephthah (Judg 11) after having oppressed the Israelites living in Gilead and fighting with the tribes of Judah, Benjamin, and Ephraim (Judg 10:9). Because the inhabitants of Jabesh-gilead did not think that they had sufficient military strength to withstand the Ammonite attack, they offered to enter into a treaty with Nahash and become his vassals (11:1).[3] In a display of brutal and cruel arrogance, Nahash said that he would only enter into a treaty with them on the condition that he gouge out the right eye of all the men of the city. This was not only a humiliating and painful physical mutilation, but it also had military implications because it prevented the continued use of the bow and arrow. According to the additional information contained in the Dead Sea scroll text, Nahash had already performed this atrocity on many Gadites and Reubenites in Transjordan, who were the traditional enemies of Ammon because they occupied territory that formerly had belonged to the Ammonites. About 7,000 of the Gadites and Reubenites had fled to Jabesh-gilead to find refuge from Nahash, and Nahash now wanted to take revenge on Jabesh for providing shelter to his enemies. His real purpose, however, went beyond military and political control of the city of Jabesh-gilead. He wanted to bring disgrace on all of Israel (11:2b).

Being unwilling to immediately submit to Nahash's condition for a treaty, the elders of Jabesh requested a seven-day period of respite in which they would attempt to find some help. If help did not materialize in that time, then they would agree to Nahash's terms. Surprisingly, Nahash accepted their counterproposal. Apparently he was so certain of his military superiority that he thought it unlikely that anyone would dare to come to Jabesh's defense, and even if they did, he would then not only have the opportunity to take the city but also to defeat their collaborators as well.

So the elders of Jabesh-gilead sent messengers to Gibeah, the hometown of Saul.[4] There they told the story of their predicament and appealed for the needed assistance. When Saul heard about the crisis, the Spirit of God rushed (*tsalakh* [TH6743, ZH7502])[5] upon him, and he burned with anger (11:6). He summoned the fighting men of Israel and Judah to muster at Bezek (in northern Israel, about 17 miles directly west of Jabesh-gilead) by sending the dismembered pieces of two oxen throughout the land along with the message that the oxen of those who did not respond to the summons, sent by Samuel and himself, would be given the same treatment (11:7-8; cf. Judg 19:29). The result was that 330,000 fighting men quickly assembled at Bezek.[6] Saul's anger and his resulting action was prompted by God's Spirit that empowered him to rise to the occasion and defend the honor of the Lord and his people, Israel. This work of God's Spirit in Saul was accompanied by the Lord's causing "fear" to come on those to whom the summons was sent so that they regarded it as something that they dare not ignore (11:7b).

Saul sent the messengers back to Jabesh with the assurance that by the middle of the next day the city would be delivered from the Ammonite threat (11:9). Upon receiving this good news, the leaders of Jabesh cleverly told Nahash that on the next day they would "come out" to him, implying, but not literally saying, that they would surrender, and that he could then do with them as he pleased (11:10). During the night, Saul led his forces in a surprise attack against the Ammonite camp, and by noon of the next day, the Ammonite forces had either been killed or driven away. The Lord gave Saul a resounding victory.

When some of the people demanded that those who had questioned whether Saul was fit to be king and able to deliver Israel from her enemies should be rounded up and put to death, Saul firmly declared that no one would be put to death because it was not he but the Lord who had delivered Israel. Saul's response shows clear insight into the true nature of covenantal kingship. Israel's security did not rest upon the existence or performance of her human kings; it rested on the grace and promises of a covenant-keeping God. Saul rightly discerned that it was the Lord who had given Israel her victory over the Ammonites.

This victory that the Lord gave Israel under Saul's leadership served to confirm or ratify his selection as king designate. While this is the most important function of this story in the succession of events that led to Saul's royal inauguration, on another level the story may carry an additional significance. When an ancient Israelite heard or read this story of deliverance from a bitter foe, it is possible that an association would be made that is unlikely to occur to English readers. In Hebrew the name *nakhash* [TH5176, ZH5731] (i.e., Nahash, the king of Ammon) means "snake."[7] For the ancient Israelite, 11:1 would read "'Snake' the Ammonite went up and laid siege to Jabesh-gilead." Hearing this word could easily evoke associations with the story of Genesis 3.[8] There one reads, "*Nahash* (*nakhash* [TH5175, ZH5729]) was more crafty than any of the wild animals the LORD God had made" (Gen 3:1). In both 1 Samuel 11 and Genesis 3, "Nahash" is a powerful adversary. In Genesis 3 "Nahash" attacked Adam and Eve. They became his subjects. But God intervened and declared war on "Nahash." He set enmity between "Nahash" and the woman, between her seed and his seed. The story of 1 Samuel 11 echoes the story of Genesis 3. The attempt by Nahash the Ammonite to bring "disgrace to all Israel" (11:2) is nothing but another incident in the ongoing battle spoken of in Genesis 3:15 between the seed of the woman and the seed of Nahash. And in whom do we find the seed of the woman in the story of 1 Samuel 11? It is certainly in Israel, but more particularly in Saul, the Lord's anointed one. Saul is the "messiah" who will crush the head of "the serpent/ Nahash" and be the instrument of divine deliverance. Finding this sort of significance in the narrative of chapter 11 might seem to some to border on allegorization. But the story is not an allegory. It is a description of a historical event that embodies the same truth found in the narrative of Genesis 3, but at a later stage of redemptive history. The name Nahash serves to call attention to the redemptive historical correspondence. Here is one more incident in the long history of the clash between the kingdom of Satan and the Kingdom of God. On this occasion, God gave victory. Nevertheless, the battle continues and awaits a final victory when, as Paul says, "The God of peace will soon crush Satan under your feet" (Rom 16:20).

ENDNOTES

1. Advocates of source-critical and tradition history analyses of chs 8–12 have maintained that this section of 1 Samuel reflects the combination of several documentary sources, tradition complexes, or perhaps even independent story units that represent originally divergent versions of how kingship arose in Israel. It is alleged that these conflicting traditions have been combined by redactors into the composite narrative now before us in chs 8–12 (Bright 1981:188). These theories generally suggest variations on the idea that in one tradition Saul was chosen and anointed by Samuel at Ramah (9:1–10:16), in a second tradition he was chosen by lot at Mizpah (10:17-27), and in a third he was acclaimed by the people after his victory over the Ammonites at Gilgal (11:14-15). For analysis of the details of many of these theories, see Vannoy 1978.
2. Building on the work of Halpern (1981a), Edelman has suggested that the narratives in chs 9–11 are structured around a three-part process of designation, testing, and coronation, that she and Halpern (who uses slightly different terms) recognize as a pattern used in "the kingship ritual of Israel and Judah, and elsewhere in the ancient Near East" (1984:198). In Edelman's view the designated champion who is to become the king must prove his fitness for the office by success in battle. It is only then that the person is enthroned as king. This proposal does not mean that Edelman regards the

narratives of chs 9–11 as historically trustworthy reports of Saul's rise to the throne (because in her view the structuring principle of chs 9–11 is the three-part kingship *ritual* rather than *historical reality,* and for various reasons she regards ch 11 as a "literary fiction" rather than a historical report); nevertheless, her suggestion provides a good framework for analysis of the narrative flow in chs 9–11.

3. The readiness of the inhabitants of Jabesh-gilead to concede defeat to Nahash shows how far Israel had fallen from the standards of the covenant. God had told them that when they encountered an army greater than their own, they were not to fear because the God who brought them out of Egypt would be with them and fight for them (Exod 23:22; Deut 20:1-4). Israel was not to fear her enemies but believe in the Lord (Exod 14:13; Num 14:9; Josh 10:8; 2 Sam 10:12; 2 Chr 20:17) and trust in him for deliverance.
4. There were historical and familial ties between Jabesh-gilead and the tribe of Benjamin. When the Benjamites were decimated by civil war during the period of the judges, wives were brought from Jabesh-gilead to help in reestablishing the tribe (Judg 21:6-14).
5. The same word is used in 10:6-10 and also of Samson in Judg 14:6-19; 15:14. Davis (1994a:114-115) comments, "True, the Spirit had equipped other judges (e.g., Judg 3:10; 6:34; 11:29), but the verb *tsalakh* is used of him, and that three times. Now this verb is used for the third time in 1 Samuel in relation to the Spirit's equipping of Saul. He is Saul but there are shades of Samson about him."
6. Some interpreters consider this number to be much too high. As Youngblood (1992:638) notes, "We cannot be sure whether *'elep* [TH505, ZH547] means 'thousand' or is used in a more general sense to refer to a military 'unit' (as in 17:18; 29:2; 2 Sam 18:4)."
7. While *nakhash* used as a proper name may have a different etymology than *nakhash* used as a masculine noun meaning "snake," the words are pronounced and spelled the same way (Youngblood 1992:636).
8. Cf. van den Berg (1996a:96-99) for a more detailed development of the basic idea of this paragraph.

◆ E. Saul's Reign Inaugurated in a Covenant Renewal Ceremony (1 Sam 11:14–12:25)

[14]Then Samuel said to the people, "Come,
let us all go to Gilgal to renew the king-
dom." [15]So they all went to Gilgal, and in
a solemn ceremony before the LORD they
made Saul king. Then they offered peace
offerings to the LORD, and Saul and all the
Israelites were filled with joy.

CHAPTER 12

Then Samuel addressed all Israel: "I have
done as you asked and given you a king.
[2]Your king is now your leader. I stand here
before you—an old, gray-haired man—and
my sons serve you. I have served as your
leader from the time I was a boy to this
very day. [3]Now testify against me in the
presence of the LORD and before his
anointed one. Whose ox or donkey have I
stolen? Have I ever cheated any of you?
Have I ever oppressed you? Have I ever
taken a bribe and perverted justice? Tell
me and I will make right whatever I have
done wrong."

[4]"No," they replied, "you have never
cheated or oppressed us, and you have
never taken even a single bribe."

[5]"The LORD and his anointed one are my
witnesses today," Samuel declared, "that
my hands are clean."

"Yes, he is a witness," they replied.

[6]"It was the LORD who appointed Moses
and Aaron," Samuel continued. "He brought

your ancestors out of the land of Egypt. 7 Now stand here quietly before the LORD as I remind you of all the great things the LORD has done for you and your ancestors.

8 "When the Israelites were* in Egypt and cried out to the LORD, he sent Moses and Aaron to rescue them from Egypt and to bring them into this land. 9 But the people soon forgot about the LORD their God, so he handed them over to Sisera, the commander of Hazor's army, and also to the Philistines and to the king of Moab, who fought against them.

10 "Then they cried to the LORD again and confessed, 'We have sinned by turning away from the LORD and worshiping the images of Baal and Ashtoreth. But we will worship you and you alone if you will rescue us from our enemies.' 11 Then the LORD sent Gideon,* Bedan,* Jephthah, and Samuel* to save you, and you lived in safety.

12 "But when you were afraid of Nahash, the king of Ammon, you came to me and said that you wanted a king to reign over you, even though the LORD your God was already your king. 13 All right, here is the king you have chosen. You asked for him, and the LORD has granted your request.

14 "Now if you fear and worship the LORD and listen to his voice, and if you do not rebel against the LORD's commands, then both you and your king will show that you recognize the LORD as your God. 15 But if you rebel against the LORD's commands and refuse to listen to him, then his hand will be as heavy upon you as it was upon your ancestors.

16 "Now stand here and see the great thing the LORD is about to do. 17 You know that it does not rain at this time of the year during the wheat harvest. I will ask the LORD to send thunder and rain today. Then you will realize how wicked you have been in asking the LORD for a king!"

18 So Samuel called to the LORD, and the LORD sent thunder and rain that day. And all the people were terrified of the LORD and of Samuel. 19 "Pray to the LORD your God for us, or we will die!" they all said to Samuel. "For now we have added to our sins by asking for a king."

20 "Don't be afraid," Samuel reassured them. "You have certainly done wrong, but make sure now that you worship the LORD with all your heart, and don't turn your back on him. 21 Don't go back to worshiping worthless idols that cannot help or rescue you—they are totally useless! 22 The LORD will not abandon his people, because that would dishonor his great name. For it has pleased the LORD to make you his very own people.

23 "As for me, I will certainly not sin against the LORD by ending my prayers for you. And I will continue to teach you what is good and right. 24 But be sure to fear the LORD and faithfully serve him. Think of all the wonderful things he has done for you. 25 But if you continue to sin, you and your king will be swept away."

12:8 Hebrew *When Jacob was.* The names "Jacob" and "Israel" are often interchanged throughout the Old Testament, referring sometimes to the individual patriarch and sometimes to the nation. **12:11a** Hebrew *Jerub-baal,* another name for Gideon; see Judg 6:32. **12:11b** Greek and Syriac versions read *Barak.* **12:11c** Greek and Syriac versions read *Samson.*

NOTES

12:2 ***Your king is now your leader.*** The Hebrew wording ("The king is now walking before you") is idiomatic for his assuming the leadership of the people. S. R. Driver (1913:38) comments, "To *walk before* any one is to live and move openly before him; especially in such a way as (a) to *deserve,* and consequently (b) to *enjoy* his approval and favour."

12:3 ***and perverted justice?*** Lit., "that I might hide my eyes in it." The LXX reads, "Have I ever taken a bribe and a pair of shoes?" This rendering presupposes only a slight difference in the Hebrew *Vorlage.* Although the LXX version may seem to make little sense, on the basis of references to sandals in two Nuzi texts as "token payments to validate special transactions by lending them the appearance of normal business practice," Speiser (1940) understands the reference here to sandals as a legal symbol. He finds similar usages in the OT in Ruth 4:7; Amos 2:6; 8:6. On the basis that the more difficult reading deserves preference, Speiser, with this "outside support," favors the LXX reading. Without more decisive evidence it is difficult to give strong preference to either of these alternatives for the best reading of the text.

12:7 ***as I remind you of all the great things.*** The use of the Niphal of *shapat* [TH8199, ZH9149] (here translated as "remind you") expresses the idea of entering into legal proceedings (Williams 1976:§137; GKC §51d). S. R. Driver (1913:92-93) comments that the Niphal sometimes acquires "a *reciprocal* force as *nishpat to judge one another,* i.e., *to plead or dispute together in judgment.*" The sense in this verse is that of pleading a case as is done in a judicial procedure before a judge, who in this instance is Yahweh himself. This case would be argued by Samuel *on the basis of* (here indicated by the sign of the object) all the "great things" (*tsidqoth* [TH6666, ZH7407], lit., "righteous acts") which the Lord had done for the people and their ancestors. The construction in MT is admittedly somewhat awkward (*shapat* as a Niphal and *'eth kol-tsidqoth*), but it is not impossible (cf. Ezek 17:20).

12:8 ***When the Israelites were in Egypt.*** The LXX adds the phrase "and the Egyptians oppressed them." This reading is adopted by S. R. Driver (1913:93), Klein (1983:110-111), McCarter (1980b:208, 210), the NRSV, and others. S. R. Driver (1913:93) comments, "The words are needed on account of the following *wayyiz'aqu* [TH2199, ZH2410] (they cried out): a copyist's eye passed from the first *mitsrayim* [TH4714A, ZH5213] (Egypt) to the second." P. K. McCarter (1980b:210) adds, "Space considerations indicate that 4QSam[a] shared a longer reading like the LXX." While these proposals are possible, it seems preferable to leave the verse as it stands in the MT because adopting the LXX reading raises the additional problem of the singular "Jacob" and the plural suffix of the verb "oppressed them." This in turn necessitates another addition to the verse, that, in fact, is also included in the LXX ("and his sons") so that the verse reads, "When Jacob *and his sons* went to Egypt . . ." The absence of "and his sons" (*ubanayw* [TH1121, ZH1201]) is not as easily explained as the absence of the previous phrase.

12:11 ***Bedan.*** The name Bedan occurs elsewhere in the OT only in 1 Chr 7:17, where it designates a different person. For this reason most commentators give preference to the "Barak" reading of the LXX and Syriac. Keil (1956:118), after considering and rejecting several possibilities such as rendering Bedan as an appellative (i.e., the Danite, "ben-Dan"), and thus connecting the name to Samson, concludes, "There is no other course left, therefore, than to regard *Bedan* as an old copyist's error for Barak (Judg 4), as the LXX, Syriac, and Arabic have done—a conclusion which is favored by the circumstance that Barak was one of the most celebrated of the judges, and is placed by the side of Gideon and Jephthah in Heb 11:32." Goslinga (1968:247), with hesitation, also adopts this view, saying that the Barak reading is strongest because the army of Sisera was defeated by Barak. This represents a change in position from Goslinga's earlier commentary (1948:151), where he says it is hard to believe that a scribe would write "Bedan" if there were no judge by this name. But he also says that it is difficult to accept that Samuel would mention the oppression of Sisera and not the hero who defeated him. Thus he concludes that the best solution seems to be that Bedan is another name for Barak that was known just as well to Samuel's audience; there is a parallel in the use of Jerub-baal as another name for Gideon. This suggestion of Goslinga's seems more plausible than assuming a scribal error since the name of Barak was so well known that a scribal error here seems unlikely. This also seems preferable to concluding that this is the name of a judge not mentioned in the book of Judges at all as some commentators suggest (Goldman 1962:65; Stoebe 1973:233). Nevertheless,

Stoebe is probably correct in suggesting that the occurrence of this name is indicative of an independent tradition.

Samuel. The Lucianic mss of the LXX and the Syriac read "Samson" instead of Samuel. The "Samson" reading is adopted by, among others, McCarter (1980b:208) and the NRSV. Klein (1983:110-111), in my view correctly, prefers the MT "Samuel" as the "more difficult reading." The "Samson" reading is most likely a correction based on the assumption that Samuel would not include his own name with the list of judges of whom he speaks.

12:14 ***then both you and your king will show that you recognize the Lord as your God.*** This clause is often taken as part of the protasis (see NIV, NRSV, NJPS). Such translations then provide an implied apodosis (NIV, "good"; NRSV, "it will be well"; NJPS, "well and good" [placed in brackets]; Alter 1999:68, "He will rescue you" [based on Lucianic mss of the LXX]). The NIV and NRSV use neither italics nor brackets. This type of construction is termed aposiopesis (i.e., a suppressed apodosis, cf. GKC §167a). Understanding the verse in this way, however, does not give sufficient weight to the structural parallel with 12:15, where the apodosis clearly begins in the same way as in 12:14. In my view, it also misconstrues the meaning of what Samuel is saying. See the commentary below.

COMMENTARY

A Brief Summary of the Covenant Renewal Ceremony Held at Gilgal (11:14–15). Building upon Saul's confession that credit for the victory over the Ammonites was to be given to the Lord rather than to himself, Samuel called for an assembly to be held at Gilgal in order to "renew the kingdom" (11:14). It has often been argued that the "kingdom" that Samuel wanted to "renew" was the kingdom of Saul. This understanding, however, brings up a host of questions. Not the least is the question of how Saul's kingdom could be "renewed" if he had not yet begun to reign. After the assembly at Mizpah, Saul had gone back to his home in Gibeah and resumed working in the fields (11:5). He had clearly not begun his reign as king. In fact, "making Saul king" (i.e., inaugurating his reign) was one of the things that Samuel intended to do at the assembly in Gilgal (11:15).

Among source and tradition history analyses of the sequencing of the events in chapters 9–11, the most common conclusion has been to view the phrase "let us all go to Gilgal to renew the kingdom" as a redactional insertion that has attempted to transform the tradition of Saul becoming king by acclamation after his victory over the Ammonites (11:15) into a "renewal" of his kingship, in order to harmonize this Gilgal tradition with the allegedly conflicting tradition that he became king after being selected by lot at an assembly held at Mizpah (10:17-27). Birch (1976:101) gives a representative summary of this position when he says, "Most scholars have regarded this verse [11:14] as the clearest evidence of redactional activity in this chapter, and there would seem to be little reason for challenging this conclusion. . . . It would seem clear that an editor has . . . attempted to harmonize an apparent duplication. Saul has already become king in 10:24, so the instance in 11:15 has been transformed into a renewal."

If one understands the "kingdom" in 11:14 as a reference to Saul's kingdom, it is difficult, although perhaps not impossible, to explain how Saul's kingdom could be "renewed" if he had not yet "been made king" (11:15).[1] It is therefore preferable to understand "kingdom" in this phrase not as a reference to Saul's kingdom, but rather as a reference to the Kingdom of Yahweh.[2] In fact, Israel's disavowal of the kingship of Yahweh is the central issue that runs through the entirety of chapters 8–12. When Israel asked for a human king, they rejected the Lord, who was their king (8:7; 10:19; 12:12). This rejection of the kingship of the Lord subverted the covenant relationship established between the Lord and his people at Sinai. In spite of this wickedness on the part of Israel (12:17, 19), the Lord, in his grace and mercy, told Samuel to give the people a king (8:7, 9, 22). Now that the time had arrived for Saul's inauguration, Samuel chose to accomplish this in a ceremony that not only initiated the reign of Saul but also, and even more importantly, restored the broken covenant relationship. The significant thing that happens in 11:14–12:25 is that kingship in Israel is established *in the context of covenant renewal.* It was only in connection with Israel's affirmation of her continued recognition of the Lord as her divine king that human kingship could assume its proper place in the structure of the theocracy.

So 11:14-15 introduces and briefly summarizes the transactions of the assembly at Gilgal. A more detailed account of this same assembly is given in 12:1-25.[3] Comparison of these two (perhaps originally independent) literary units reveals that while they agree in their major emphases, they describe the Gilgal assembly from slightly different perspectives. There are two foci of attention in both 11:14-15 and 12:1-25. These are (1) transition in leadership and (2) restoration of covenant fellowship after covenant abrogation.

In 11:14-15 the theme of transition in leadership is seen in the reference to the inauguration of Saul ("they made Saul king," 11:15), while the theme of restoration of covenant fellowship after covenant abrogation is seen in the reference to the sacrificing of peace offerings (11:15)[4] and the rejoicing of the people.[5] In chapter 12, the theme of transition in leadership is seen primarily in the testimony to Samuel's covenant faithfulness during his past leadership of the nation (12:1-5), as well as his continuing prophetic function in the future (12:23) when human kingship assumes a legitimate place in the structure of the theocracy. The theme of restoration of covenant fellowship after covenant abrogation focuses on Samuel's legal demonstration of Israel's apostasy in requesting a king (12:6-12), and then on Israel's confession of the sinfulness of their wrongly motivated desire for a king (12:16-22).

In both passages the primary purpose of the assembly is the renewal of allegiance to Yahweh. This purpose is, in fact, far more prominent in the description of the Gilgal assembly in chapter 12 than is the inauguration of Saul. Yes, the inauguration of Saul as king at Gilgal is referred to in both 11:15 and 12:13, but this happens only in connection with reaffirmation of a continued recognition of Yahweh as Israel's true sovereign (11:14; 12:14-15). It is this perspective that explains how Samuel could say, "Let us all go to Gilgal to renew the kingdom" when, in fact, this is the same ceremony at which Saul would be "made king."

This understanding of 11:14–12:25 has been accepted by, among others, Kaiser[6] and Dumbrell[7], and is adopted at least in part by Long[8] and Fokkelman.[9] When 11:14-15 is taken in this way and directly linked with the covenantal focus of chapter 12, it becomes apparent that Samuel's primary concern at the Gilgal assembly was to provide for covenant continuity during this important restructuring of the theocracy, as well as transition in the civil leadership of the nation from himself to Saul. This is not the first time that covenant renewal was linked with transition in leadership. When Moses's death was imminent, he led Israel in covenant renewal on the plains of Moab to ensure covenant continuity through the transition from his leadership to that of Joshua (this, in fact, is the reason for the book of Deuteronomy).[10] When Joshua was old, he called for an assembly at Shechem (Josh 24) in which Israel was challenged to renew their commitment to Yahweh as they entered the period of the judges.[11] First Samuel 11:14–12:25 describes the next significant change in leadership for the nation because the action of the Gilgal assembly marks the end of the period of the judges and the beginning of an entirely new structure for the theocracy. And here, again, covenant continuity through a period of transition in leadership is of prime importance. Human kingship would become an instrument of the Lord's rule over his people. This ceremony marked the beginning of the kingdom period in ancient Israel, and right at its inception, kingship was integrated into covenant: Kingship and covenant would be inseparable. The covenant provided the norm for kingship, and kingship would function as an integral feature of covenantal administration.

A More Detailed Description of the Covenant Renewal Ceremony Held at Gilgal (12:1-25). First Samuel 12:1-25 describes Samuel's challenge to Israel to renew her allegiance to Yahweh on the occasion of the introduction of kingship into the structure of the theocracy. When Samuel presented Saul to the people as their newly inaugurated king (12:1-2), he at the same time secured from the people a judicial vindication of his own covenant faithfulness during the previous conduct of his office as the spiritual and civil leader of the nation (12:3-5). The implication of this vindication is not only that Samuel's leadership had been the kind of leadership that the newly installed king should seek to emulate, but also that Samuel's past integrity had provided a solid basis for future confidence in his continuing role as prophet and spiritual leader of the nation.[12] Samuel had not used his position of leadership for any personal advantage, or for the obstruction or perversion of justice. Most particularly, he had not "taken" from the people (cf. 8:11-17, Samuel's warning to Israel that a king like those of other nations would *take* from them), nor had he defrauded anyone (cf. Lev 19:13; Deut 24:14), oppressed anyone, or taken a bribe (cf. Exod 23:8; Deut 16:19). Samuel's leadership was one fully consistent with the requirements of covenantal law. He had performed his duties throughout his life as a true servant of the Lord and of the Lord's people.

In 12:6-12 Samuel turned from the matter of the character of his own previous leadership of the nation to the matter of the people's request for a king. Samuel viewed their request as a covenant-breaking act and serious apostasy. After asserting Yahweh's primacy in the establishment of the nation (12:6), Samuel initiated the second legal proceeding of the Gilgal assembly (12:7-12; see note on 12:7). Contrary to what one might expect, Samuel did not focus directly on the people's behavior in requesting a king. Instead, he used a judicial scrutiny of the "righteous acts of Yahweh" as a foil for illuminating the people's conduct and thus as an instrument for their indictment. The summary of the Lord's righteous acts in 12:8-11 is designed to emphasize the constancy of the Lord's covenant faithfulness toward his people in their past history in contrast to their own unfaithfulness. The Lord had delivered Israel out of Egypt and had given them the land of Canaan, but Israel repeatedly turned away from the Lord to idolatry. It is significant that Samuel placed his own name among the list of deliverers (see note on 12:11), and by so doing, he brought the historical overview up to the point in time that the people expressed their desire to have a king like the nations round about. It is clear that even in Israel's most recent history the Lord had continued to provide for their security (cf. 7:3, 8, 10, 12). The climax of Samuel's historical overview is found in 12:12 where the people's desire for a king to deliver them from Nahash the Ammonite[13] is explicitly represented as a rejection of the kingship of Yahweh, and thus as the last of a long series of apostasies.

According to 12:13, Samuel presented Saul to the people and emphasized that it was the Lord who had given them a king—in spite of their apostasy in asking for one. Samuel then confronted Israel with her continuing obligation of complete and total loyalty to Yahweh now that human kingship was being integrated into the structure of the theocracy (12:14-15).[14]

There has long been a general consensus of interpreters that 12:14 has a protasis (the subordinate clause expressing a condition in a conditional sentence) but lacks any apodosis (the "then" clause describing the consequence of the condition; see note on 12:14). The translation usually adopted for the verse is similar to the RSV and NIV: "If you will fear the LORD and serve him and hearken to his voice and not rebel against the commandment of the LORD, *and if* (*wihyithem* [TH2050.1/1961, ZH2256/2118]) both you and the king who reigns over you will follow the LORD your God, [it will be well]" (my italics). The last phrase, "It will be well," does not occur in the Masoretic Text and must be added in order to complete the sentence. But it may be that this is incorrect and that there is in fact an apodosis in the verse, for as Smith (1912:88) has argued, "to begin the apodosis with *wihyithem* is grammatically the correct thing to do." Yet Smith claims that to do so produces a redundancy because "it makes an identical proposition: *if you fear Yahweh . . . then you will follow Yahweh.*" When one compares the structure of 12:14 with that of 12:15, however, it is clear that the apodosis of 12:15 does begin with a structure parallel to *wihyithem.*

Smith's objection turns on his understanding of the phrase *wihyithem . . . 'akhar yhwh* [TH310, ZH339] (you will follow after Yahweh). This phrase "follow after" occurs in several other places in the Old Testament (including 2 Sam 2:10; 15:13; 1 Kgs 12:20; 16:21). In all of these instances the expression is used to indicate that the people of Israel, or a segment of the people, have chosen to follow one particular king in a situation where there was another alternative.[15] When one understands the expression in this way and applies it to the situation of Israel at the time of the Gilgal assembly, then one can say that with the introduction of kingship into the theocracy, the potential for divided loyalties between Yahweh and the human king became very real. Samuel was challenging the people and their newly installed king to renew their determination to obey Yahweh and not to rebel against his commandments, and asserting that by so doing they would *demonstrate that they continued to recognize Yahweh as their sovereign.* It is, then, not necessary to conclude that the expression "if you fear Yahweh . . . then you will follow Yahweh" is a redundancy or an identical proposition; rather, it is a sensible apodosis.

So at this assembly, the Sinai covenant's conditions (cf. Exod 19:5-6; Deut 11:13-15, 22-25, 26-28) are given a new dimension. Verses 14-15 express the conditions of the covenant in terms of the new era that Israel was entering: If Israel and her new king fear Yahweh, this will show that they continue to recognize Yahweh as their sovereign, even though human kingship has been introduced into the structure of the theocracy. In other words, these two verses are saying that Israel must not replace her loyalty to Yahweh with loyalty to a human ruler, should there ever be conflict between the two, because if Israel rebels against the Lord, then the hand of the Lord will be against her just as it was against her disobedient ancestors. These verses are also saying quite pointedly that Israel's human king must also recognize the supreme sovereignty of Yahweh.[16] In the final analysis, this means that Israel's expectation that a human king would guarantee national security was a fundamentally flawed idea. If Israel and her king do not submit themselves in trust and obedience to the Lord, the monarchy will be of no value. Everything was still dependent on Israel's relationship with the Lord.

In 12:16-22 Samuel tells the people that at his request the Lord will do a "great thing" in their midst that will cause them to realize how wicked they have been in asking for a king. The "great thing" was the coming of a thunderstorm in the time of the wheat harvest. When the Lord actually sent thunder and rain in response to Samuel's request, "all the people were terrified of the LORD and of Samuel." The question that naturally arises is why a thunderstorm in the time of the wheat harvest would provoke such a strong reaction among the people of the Gilgal assembly. It has usually been argued that the function of the thunderstorm was to demonstrate the power of the Lord and to authenticate the words of Samuel. Longman (1983:169) has questioned this reading of these verses, however, and argued that "the rainstorm theophany of 1 Sam 12:16-19 is not only a sign of Yahweh's omnipotence, but a manifestation of the covenant curse both to illustrate God's displeasure with the people's covenant-breaking request for a king and also to motivate the people to keep the covenant sanctions which Samuel had just delivered to them (vv 14-15)."

Longman argues that a severe rainstorm at the time when the wheat was still standing was not only something extremely rare (Prov 26:1), but also something that would jeopardize the crop and threaten famine (Prov 28:3). The people's request of Samuel, "Pray to the LORD your God for us, or we will die" (v. 19), was not unfounded because unless the storm ceased, the possibility of starvation would be very real. In a general way, the blessings and curses attached to the Sinai covenant entail rain and bountiful crops when God's people are faithful to the covenant as well as drought and famine when they fail to be faithful to their covenantal responsibilities (Lev 26; Deut 28). Longman (1983:171) argues that "a crop-damaging rainstorm can . . . be considered a curse. . . . As a matter of fact, the punishing rainstorm here is highly appropriate in the context. The people's sin was their rejection of Yahweh as divine warrior. They felt they needed a human war leader to accomplish what the Lord promised he would do for his obedient people—drive out the enemy. Yahweh as the divine warrior often appeared in the form of a driving rainstorm (Pss 18:7-25; 29). In the rainstorm in 1 Sam 12, Yahweh is manifesting himself as the divine warrior, but against his people due to their disobedience." So the sudden appearance of thunder and rain startled the people into a recognition and confession of their sin in asking for a king (12:19).[17]

Samuel gave words of assurance to the people and then admonished them to worship the Lord with all their hearts, and not turn away from following after him. This, in a nutshell, was the fundamental obligation of the covenant relationship (cf. Deut 6:5; 10:12; 11:13; Josh 22:5). Samuel thus brought into focus the central issue in the controversy surrounding the establishment of kingship in Israel: The evil was not in kingship itself, but rather in *turning away from following after the Lord.* In his admonition, Samuel again used the same terminology, *'akhare yhwh* [TH4480/3068, ZH4946/3378] ("following after the LORD"; 12:20) that he had used earlier to formulate the covenant conditional in 12:14 (*'akhar yhwh* = "follow after the LORD"). The supreme obligation of the children of Israel had not changed with the establishment of the monarchy. Their duty, as it always had been, was to follow after the Lord—to worship him with all their heart. The alternatives for Israel were clear (12:21). They could follow the Lord and find prosperity and security, or they could follow the "nothingness" (*tohu* [TH8414, ZH9332])[18] of anything that would exalt itself against the Lord. What Samuel was saying was that Israel should not follow anything that subverted or replaced their worship of the Lord, be that a person, a king, a nation, a god, or an idol. To follow anything or anyone to the detriment of following the Lord is to follow a "nothing," and a "nothing" could not deliver them. After this admonition, Samuel restated the wonderful promise that the Lord would never abandon his people (12:22; cf. Deut 31:6, 8; Josh 1:5; Ps 94:14).

In 12:23-25 Samuel describes his own continuing function in the new order of the theocracy (12:23), and then concludes his remarks with a repetition of Israel's central covenant obligation (12:24), reinforced by the threat of the covenant curse if Israel again apostatized (12:25). Samuel's statement in 12:23 is a clear indication that he did not intend to withdraw from his role as a national leader. He would continue not only to intercede for the people (a priestly function, cf. 7:8-9; 12:19), but he would also instruct them in their covenantal obligations (a prophetic role).[19] This continued activity of Samuel would prove to be of great significance for Saul. As Saul took up his responsibilities as king, his actions would always be subject to the scrutiny of Samuel, who would not hesitate to rebuke him should his conduct deviate from the regulations described in the law of the king (Deut 17:14-20), from the regulations of the kingship of 10:25, from covenantal law generally, or even from the word of the Lord given through himself or another prophet. But even more importantly, Samuel's continuing activity would set a pattern that would remain valid for all future occupants of the throne in Israel. Kings in Israel would never possess autonomous authority. They would always be accountable to the prophets from the time of Samuel until the end of the Old Testament period (cf. Acts 3:24).[20] In 12:24 Samuel described how the people could walk in the "good and right way." Much as Joshua had done before him (Josh 24:2-14a), Samuel framed the core of Israel's covenant obligation in words that demanded complete loyalty to the Lord, a loyalty born out of heartfelt gratitude for the great things that he had done for them. These great things included the Lord's provisions for his people (summarized in 12:8-11). But they also included the more recent victory over the Ammonites (11:13), the giving of a king in spite of the sinfulness of the people's request (12:13), and the sending of thunder and rain as a call to repentance (12:17-18). Certainly the Lord had been gracious and faithful to his people. Their obligation was complete and total loyalty to him in gratitude for all he had done for them. Samuel concluded the assembly by warning the people that persistence in turning away from the Lord would ultimately lead to the destruction of the nation and her king (12:25).

This chapter has been treated in more detail than some others in 1–2 Samuel because of its pivotal significance not only in the books of Samuel but in the whole of the Bible. The issues addressed in this chapter set the course for the flow of redemptive history throughout the remainder of the Old Testament, into the New Testament, and, for that matter, all the way into the eschaton. This chapter tells us about the inauguration of kingship in Israel. Kingship in Israel was distinctly different from kingship in any other nation because it was a covenantal kingship—that is, it was designed to be an instrument of the Lord's rule over his people. Kingship carries a central role in the ongoing flow of redemptive history because of its close linkage with messianic expectation and the promise given to David that his dynasty would endure forever (2 Sam 7). When Israel's kings failed to live up to the covenantal ideal, the prophets began to speak of a divine-human king, who at some future date would establish peace and justice on the earth (e.g., Isa 9:6-7; Jer 23:5-6; 30:9; 33:15-17). The New Testament records the initial coming of this king to his people in the person of Jesus, the prophet from Nazareth (Matt 21:11). At his birth (Luke 1:32, 69; 2:11) and during his teaching ministry (Matt 9:27; 12:23; 15:22; 20:30-31; 21:15; 22:42), Jesus was recognized and affirmed as the son of David. Just before his crucifixion he came into Jerusalem riding on a donkey (Matt 21:1-9; Mark 11:1-10; Luke 19:29-38; John 12:12-15; cf. 1 Kgs 1:33, 44) to publicly proclaim that he was the one whom the prophets had said would someday sit on the throne of David (2 Sam 7:11-14; Zech 9:9). Subsequently, he affirmed before the Sanhedrin that he was the Messiah (Matt 26:57-68; Mark 14:53-65; Luke 22:67-71; John 18:36-37), even though at his First Advent his primary mission was to be the suffering servant who would make atonement for the sins of his people (cf. Isa 53; 55:3).

The early church clearly understood that Jesus was, indeed, the Messiah prophesied in the Old Testament Scriptures, and the apostles were careful to explain why it was that Jesus was crucified, resurrected, and ascended to heaven (Acts 2:25-36; 3:20-26; 13:27-37; 18:28). Both Jesus and the apostles spoke of a future day when Jesus would return (John 14:3, 28) and restore all things (Rom 8:20-21). In the last book of the Bible, the coming of a royal figure of the house of David (Rev 22:7, 16) is pictured in all the fullness and glory of the messianic expectations of the Old Testament prophets (Rev 15:3; 17:14; 19:11-16).

ENDNOTES

1. The NIV has attempted to ameliorate this problem by translating *khadash* [TH2318, ZH2542] as "reaffirm" the kingship, instead of "renew" the kingship (11:14), and *wayyamliku* [TH4427, ZH4887] as "confirm" Saul as king, instead of "make" Saul king (11:15). Usage elsewhere (9 occurrences in the Piel), however, suggests that *khadash* speaks of the restoration or repair of something that already exists, whether it is a material or immaterial entity, that in some way is in a condition of deterioration. It means "renew," not "reaffirm." And in 11:15 *wayyamliku* means "inaugurate" the reign of a king (on the basis of 49 occurrences of the Hiphil of *malak*), not "confirm" the reign of a king.
2. For a defense of this position, see Vannoy 1978:61-91.
3. The absence of a time or place designation at the beginning of ch 12 is an indication that ch 12 is intended to be read as a continuation of the description of the Gilgal assembly introduced in 11:14-15.
4. The distinguishing feature of these offerings (the *zebakhim shelamim* [TH2077/8002, ZH2285/8968]; often translated as "peace offerings," "fellowship offerings," or "communion offerings") is the communal meal, symbolizing fellowship with God. In a thorough study, Schmid (1964) demonstrates the close relationship of these offerings to covenant making, restoration, and strengthening, although he perhaps goes too far by suggesting that they should be designated the "covenant offerings." Rowley (1967:123) describes the offering in a broader way by saying the *zebakhim shelamim* were "for the maintenance or restoration of good relations with God." These offerings were an important element in the covenant ratification at Sinai (Exod 24:5, 11), so it is certainly appropriate, if not to be expected, that the same sacrifices would be offered at Gilgal when this covenant was renewed.
5. Rejoicing (*samakh* [TH8055, ZH8523]) is associated with peace offerings in Deut 27:7; 2 Chr 29:35-36; and with "eating before Yahweh" in Deut 14:26; 27:7. Rejoicing appears as an activity associated with covenant renewal in the time of Joash (2 Kgs 11:20), in the time of Asa (2 Chr 15:15), and Hezekiah (2 Chr 29:36). Here in 11:15 the rejoicing is to be understood as the expression of a people who have renewed their commitment to Yahweh, have confessed their sin (cf. 12:19), and have been given a king.
6. Kaiser (1992:144-145) comments, "The most critical problem in connection with the sequencing of the events [of chs 8–12] is the relationship between 1 Sam 11:14-15 and 1 Sam 10:17-27, particularly in connection with the statement in 11:14, 'Come let us go to Gilgal and there *reaffirm* the kingship.' This phrase constitutes the most compelling evidence for the argument that several accounts have been put together in these chapters. The simplest, and best, explanation for the meaning of this debated phrase, however, is that the reference is not to Saul, but to a renewal of allegiance to Yahweh and his covenant. It is a call for the renewal ceremony that is described in greater detail in 1 Sam 12. This explanation makes the most sense and makes possible the best harmonization of the parallel accounts of Saul's accession to the throne in 1 Sam 10:17-27 and 11:15."
7. Dumbrell (1984:135) comments, "What may be meant by the 'renewal of the kingdom' may be not the renewal of Saul's mandate to reign so much as the renewal of the kingdom structure within Israel—i.e., the recognition at Gilgal again of divine kingship over Israel, since the word 'kingdom' at 1 Sam 10:16, 25, as well as at 11:14, seems to be used in the wider sense of the administration of Israel as the domain of Yahweh. . . . It is likely therefore that the renewal of the kingdom at Gilgal was in fact covenant renewal and logically the appointment of Saul formally as king, as Vannoy

has seen (only public recognition had so far been offered, cf. 1 Sam 10:24), took place within the reconstitution of the kingdom, and thus covenant, relationship. In these circumstances the farewell speech of Samuel in chapter 12 provides for the continuation of the covenant by the formal renewal of the kingdom to which 11:14 has obliquely referred."

8. Long (1989:224-228) interprets the phrase "renew the kingdom" in 11:14 as a reference to Saul's kingdom, even though he accepts the covenant renewal idea as an important feature of ch 12. He does this by viewing 11:14 as part of the designation, confirmation, and inauguration pattern mentioned in my discussion of ch 11. Long points out that "kingdom" terminology has been used in connection with Saul's reign in 10:16, 25, so it is "admissible to speak of Saul's 'kingship' from the very beginning of the accession process" (1989:227). While this may be so, it could also be said that these "kingdom" references have the fully functioning reality of Saul's reign in view rather than its preinaugural preliminary stage (king designate). In any case, if Saul's kingship is in view in 11:14 the question is in what sense had Saul's kingship deteriorated, since the time of his anointing, so that it was now in need of "renewal"? Long suggests that because Saul had not done "what his hand found to do" (10:7, an implied commission to attack the Philistine outpost at Gibeah, by means of which Saul's selection as king would be confirmed; see comments on 10:5-7), "The accession process was, temporarily at least, arrested" (1989:227). But the victory of Saul over the Ammonites in 11:1-13 was sufficient to "set the accession process back on track." So Long suggests that "the 'renewing of the kingdom' served as a public recognition of this change in the situation" (1989:228). While this understanding of the phrase is certainly possible and has the merit of viewing the narratives of chs 9–12 as describing stages in a process of establishing kingship, rather than as multiple accessions, as has so often been done, it does not provide as explicit a resolution to the overarching unresolved issue of chs 8–12 (Israel's sin in requesting a king, and Yahweh's decision to grant their request), nor does it connect directly with the clear covenantal character of both the form and content of ch 12. The "renewal of Yahweh's Kingdom" view does resolve these issues and fits well with the covenantal character of ch 12. In fact, Edelman (1984:199), who, like Long, is an advocate of the designation, confirmation, inauguration pattern in chs 9–11, says that the "use of the verb *khadash* [TH2318, ZH2542] to characterize the Gilgal coronation ceremony is problematic for my proposed sequence when the commonly accepted translation 'renew' is followed."

9. Fokkelmann (1993:491) comments, "The question as to whether 11:14 refers to the monarchy of Saul or that of God is so dangerous and misleading because it seems to insist on our making a choice, and that choice would carry an exclusive answer with it. Samuel is going to give an inclusive answer: both forms of monarchy come together in a kind of merger; and he wants to signal straightaway: the relationship is a hierarchical one, in the sense that the human king is not next to God or above the law, but under the law—i.e., the divine norm. That is what he means by the renewal of the kingship."

10. See Kline 1963 for a full exposition of this idea in connection with the book of Deuteronomy.

11. Both the book of Deuteronomy and Josh 24 exhibit many of the structural features of the Old Testament "covenant formulary," which has similarities to the literary form of the Hittite suzerain treaties. For discussions of the covenant formulary in the Old Testament see Baltzer 1971; Kitchen 1966:91-102; Kline 1963, 1968, 1972; McCarthy 1972, 1978; Rendtorff 1998. First Samuel 12 also exhibits some of the characteristic features of the covenant formulary. Baltzer (1971:67), for example, says, "In short,

the schema of the covenant renewal is preserved almost intact. All that is missing is explicit mention of a new ratification on the part of the people." Some of the clear characteristic elements of the formulary in ch 12 are an appeal to antecedent history (12:6-12); a challenge to the fundamental covenantal obligation of complete allegiance to the Lord introduced by the transitional "and now" (12:14a, 15a, 20-21, 24); blessing and curse sanctions (12:14b, 15b, 25); and a theophanic sign (12:16-18a).

12. First Samuel 12 has often been labeled "Samuel's farewell address." While it is true that Samuel was approaching the end of his life (12:2, he was an "old, gray-haired man") and was preparing the nation to carry on without him, he is not simply retiring, nor is he transferring all of his functions to the king. What Samuel does in this chapter is initiate a new order of administration of the theocracy in which there will be a new division of responsibility among Israel's leaders. While Saul would assume responsibility for the civil affairs of the nation, Samuel would continue to function in the role of prophet and spiritual adviser to the nation (12:23). In this new order, the relationship between prophet and king would be of great significance.
13. While it is true that the request for a king is not specifically linked with the Ammonite threat in chs 8, 10, or 11, there is nothing in these passages that contradicts this linkage, and in these passages the request for a king is linked with the desire for a deliverer. It would seem that the combination of Philistine pressure from the west (9:16) and Ammonite pressure from the east lay behind the desire for a human deliverer.
14. In terms of the "covenant formulary" these verses represent the "basic stipulation" (the fundamental obligation of loyalty on the part of the vassal to the Great King, cf. Deut 6:4-5) of the Sinai covenant, but cast in conditional terminology. Samuel's purpose in 12:14a, 15a is to confront the people with the alternatives now open to them as they enter the new era of the monarchy. Obedience or disobedience to this basic stipulation will determine whether Israel experiences God's blessing or curse in their future life as a nation.
15. In 2 Sam 2:10, the expression refers to the decision of Judah to follow David while Ishbosheth reigned over the remainder of the nation. In 2 Sam 15:13 it refers to the choice of the men of Israel to give allegiance to Absalom as king instead of to David at the time of Absalom's rebellion. In 1 Kgs 12:20, Judah followed the house of David at the time of the division of the kingdom rather than Jeroboam. In 1 Kgs 16:21 it has reference to the people's divided loyalties between Tibni and Omri after the death of Zimri.
16. Brueggemann (1990a:93) with good reason comments, "The king is deliberately subsumed under the conventional structure of blessing and curse. Indeed, the king has no individual role to play but is simply one more member of the covenant community, subject to the same summons, available for the same blessings and curses." Brueggemann overstates the case, however, when he goes on to say that "the rhetoric in fact denies kingship any theological significance. Theologically these verses nullify the institution of kingship!" These verses do not nullify the institution of kingship, they merely integrate it into covenant. The covenantal ideal for kingship has enormous theological significance as the history of redemption moves forward.
17. As was noted in the commentary on ch 8, the elders of the nation had demanded that Samuel give them a king like the surrounding nations had, a king who could go out before them and lead them in battle (8:19-20). At the heart of this request was the unspoken assumption that security for the nation could best be achieved through a human leader, rather than through trusting in the Lord's promise of protection. This constituted a serious breach of covenant. It displayed a disregard for previous deliverances and demonstrations of the Lord's faithfulness (12:6-11) and a serious lack of

confidence in Yahweh's covenant promises. A prominent feature of the Hittite suzerainty treaties (to which Israel's covenant has clear analogies, cf. note 11 above) was the Great King's promise to protect his vassals against their enemies. Yahweh had given a similar promise to Israel (Exod 23:22; cf. Exod 34:11). It was in this promise that Israel was to find her sense of national security. On the plains of Moab, Moses told Israel not to fear when their enemy was greater or more powerful than they were (Deut 20:1-4). Israel had forgotten these things when they asked for a king.

18. The root meaning of *tohu* [TH8414, ZH9332] is "emptiness" or "nothingness." The term is used here in a collective sense and has often been interpreted as a reference to heathen gods or idols, as is reflected in the NLT rendering.
19. That the "good and right" way is the way of covenantal obedience is clear from comparison of this expression with Deut 6:18; 12:28.
20. E. F. Campbell (1967:182) appropriately notes that the role of the prophet in Israel "is dramatic evidence that no man is king in Israel in an absolute sense, and that a vital office exists side by side with the office of kingship which will never let the king forget who is really sovereign in Israel."

◆ III. The Beginning of Saul's Reign (1 Sam 13:1–15:35)
A. Samuel's Rebuke of Saul (1 Sam 13:1-15)

Saul was thirty* years old when he be-
came king, and he reigned for forty-two
years.*
2Saul selected 3,000 special troops
from the army of Israel and sent the rest
of the men home. He took 2,000 of the
chosen men with him to Micmash and the
hill country of Bethel. The other 1,000
went with Saul's son Jonathan to Gibeah
in the land of Benjamin.
3Soon after this, Jonathan attacked and
defeated the garrison of Philistines at
Geba. The news spread quickly among the
Philistines. So Saul blew the ram's horn
throughout the land, saying, "Hebrews,
hear this! Rise up in revolt!" 4All Israel
heard the news that Saul had destroyed
the Philistine garrison at Geba and that the
Philistines now hated the Israelites more
than ever. So the entire Israelite army was
summoned to join Saul at Gilgal.
5The Philistines mustered a mighty
army of 3,000* chariots, 6,000 charioteers,
and as many warriors as the grains of
sand on the seashore! They camped at
Micmash east of Beth-aven. 6The men of
Israel saw what a tight spot they were in;
and because they were hard pressed by
the enemy, they tried to hide in caves,
thickets, rocks, holes, and cisterns. 7Some
of them crossed the Jordan River and es-
caped into the land of Gad and Gilead.

Meanwhile, Saul stayed at Gilgal, and his
men were trembling with fear. 8Saul wait-
ed there seven days for Samuel, as Samuel
had instructed him earlier, but Samuel still
didn't come. Saul realized that his troops
were rapidly slipping away. 9So he de-
manded, "Bring me the burnt offering and
the peace offerings!" And Saul sacrificed
the burnt offering himself.
10Just as Saul was finishing with the
burnt offering, Samuel arrived. Saul went
out to meet and welcome him, 11but Sam-
uel said, "What is this you have done?"
Saul replied, "I saw my men scattering
from me, and you didn't arrive when you
said you would, and the Philistines are at
Micmash ready for battle. 12So I said, 'The
Philistines are ready to march against us
at Gilgal, and I haven't even asked for the
LORD's help!' So I felt compelled to offer
the burnt offering myself before you
came."
13"How foolish!" Samuel exclaimed.
"You have not kept the command the LORD
your God gave you. Had you kept it, the

**LORD would have established your king-
dom over Israel forever. [14]But now your
kingdom must end, for the LORD has
sought out a man after his own heart. The
LORD has already appointed him to be the
leader of his people, because you have not
kept the LORD's command."**

**[15]Samuel then left Gilgal and went on
his way, but the rest of the troops went
with Saul to meet the army. They went
up from Gilgal to Gibeah in the land of
Benjamin.* When Saul counted the men
who were still with him, he found only
600 were left!**

13:1a As in a few Greek manuscripts; the number is missing in the Hebrew. **13:1b** Hebrew *reigned . . . and two;* the number is incomplete in the Hebrew. Compare Acts 13:21. **13:5** As in Greek and Syriac versions; Hebrew reads *30,000.* **13:15** As in Greek version; Hebrew reads *Samuel then left Gilgal and went to Gibeah in the land of Benjamin.*

NOTES

13:1 *Saul was thirty years old when he became king, and he reigned for forty-two years.* The Hebrew text reads, "Saul was [ ] year[s] old when he began to reign and he reigned two years over Israel." It seems clear that two numerals have either dropped out of the Hebrew text or were never included, perhaps due to uncertainty on the part of the original writer. LXX Vaticanus excludes the entire verse, most likely because of its obvious deficiency. A few late LXX mss read "Saul was 30 years old," but this seems too young in view of the age of Saul's son Jonathan (he was in charge of 1,000 troops, 13:2; 14:1-52) shortly after Saul's accession to the throne. Although some scholars have defended a two-year reign for Saul, this is extremely difficult to harmonize with all the events reported in chs 13–31 (cf. especially 14:47-52). Josephus (*Antiquities* 6.378) and Acts 13:21 describe the length of Saul's reign as 40 years, but elsewhere Josephus (*Antiquities* 10.143) says Saul reigned 20 years. Various attempts have been made to make sense of the verse as it stands in the MT; see the "poetic couplet theory" of Althann (1981:242-246), the interpretive suggestions of the medieval Jewish commentator Isaac Abrabanel (see summary by Long 1989:75), and a "symbolic view," in which the "two years" represents an implicit unfavorable judgment on the reign of Saul by the historian who inserted the numeral (Long 1989:75). None are compelling.

13:3-4 *garrison.* See note on 10:5.

Geba. As previously noted (10:5), Geba is perhaps best understood as an alternate name for Gibeah, as indicated by the LXX, and the similar statement about it in 10:5. Miller (1975:145-166) argues that Geba, Geba of Benjamin, Gibeath, Gibeah of Benjamin, Gibeah of Saul, and perhaps Gibeath-elohim all refer to the same place, namely, Geba.

13:12 *I felt compelled.* The expression *wa'eth'appaq* [TH2050.1/662, ZH2256/706] (lit., "I forced myself") may be taken in two ways: "'My conscience told me that I should wait for you, but I suppressed its voice' (Rashi); or 'I steeled myself to take this difficult decision' (R. Isaiah)" (Goldman 1962:71).

13:13 *the LORD would have.* The *ki 'attah* [TH3588/6258, ZH3954/6964] refers to an implied condition (see GKC §159dd).

13:13-14 There is a play on words in these two verses with the four occurrences of the verbal and noun forms of the Hebrew word "to command" (*tsawah* [TH6680, ZH7422]). A more literal translation would read, "Samuel said to Saul: You have acted foolishly. If you had kept the command (*mitswath* [TH4687, ZH5184]) of the LORD your God which he commanded you (*tsiwwak*), the LORD would have established your kingdom over Israel for all time. But now your kingdom will not endure. The LORD has sought out a man after his own heart, and the LORD has commanded (*waytsawwehu*, i.e., "appointed") him to be the leader of his people because you have not kept what the LORD commanded (*tsiwweka*) you."

13:15 ***Samuel then left Gilgal.*** The LXX gives a longer reading than the MT (see NLT mg). The longer reading has been generally accepted as in NLT (S. R. Driver 1913; Klein 1983; McCarter 1980b; Smith 1912; NRSV) on the basis of homoeoteleuton being the cause of the shorter reading in MT—the scribe's eye skipping from the first *min-haggilgal* [TH1537, ZH1652] (from Gilgal) to the second. This conclusion is contested, however, by Pisano (1984:175-183) and Stoebe (1973:245) largely on the basis of difficult "unhebraic" elements in the usual suggestions for retroversion, as well as on the apparent harmonistic function of the additional wording. Stoebe and Pisano find evidence for a seam between different sources in the unevenness found between 13:15 and 16 in the MT. The LXX, in their view, is a secondary harmonization. Because a firm conclusion is problematic, preference should probably be given to the MT.

COMMENTARY

Provocation of the Philistines (13:1-7a). The beginning of Saul's reign is marked by 13:1. The private anointing (9:1–10:16) and public selection of Saul to be king by lot (10:17-27), the confirmation of his selection by victory over the Ammonites (11:1-13), and his inauguration at a covenant-renewal ceremony at Gilgal (11:14–12:25), led to the formal beginning of Saul's reign as king. That Saul's official reign does not begin until after the covenant-renewal ceremony at Gilgal (11:14–12:25) is indicated by the placement of the typical regnal formula at the beginning of this chapter.[1] Verse 1, along with the summary of Saul's reign in 14:47-52, frames a narrative (chs 13–14) that draws a clear contrast between Saul and his son Jonathan[2] and demonstrates Saul's failure to live up to the ideal of the covenantal king.

First Samuel 13:2-7 provides background information for the encounter between Samuel and Saul found in 13:7b-15, which is the focal point of the chapter.[3] One of the first things Saul did as king was to assemble an army of 3,000 men that was divided into two groups under the command of himself and his son Jonathan respectively (13:2). The narrative takes a surprising turn when it tells us that Jonathan, rather than Saul, took the initiative to attack the Philistine garrison at Geba (see notes on 10:5 and 10:7). This act of Jonathan calls to mind the instructions that Samuel had given to Saul shortly after his private anointing (cf. 10:7-8). On that occasion he had been told to "do what must be done," implying that he was to attack the Philistine garrison at Gibeah of God when he returned home from his anointing (10:5). Subsequently he was to go to Gilgal and wait there for Samuel to come and offer sacrifices and give him further instructions (10:8). Saul, however, not only did not take any action against the Philistines when he returned to Gibeah, he did not even tell his uncle about the momentous task to which the Lord had called him (see commentary on 9:1–10:16). In any case, Jonathan's attack on the Philistine garrison aroused the Philistines to action. They assembled a large army of chariots and warriors and encamped at Micmash (13:5). In the meantime, word spread among the Israelites that the Philistine garrison had been attacked and that Saul had summoned additional troops to join him at Gilgal (13:4). There is something ominous, though, in the way the scene is depicted. As Brueggemann (1990a:98) notes, these verses "portray the Philistines as having superior numbers and superior technology. Conversely the Israelites are frightened and intimidated, and they behave in a cowardly way." In 13:6 we are told that the Israelites hid in caves and cisterns because they were in a "tight spot" and "hard pressed" by the Philistines. In 13:7 Saul's men at Gilgal are said to be "trembling with fear," while others deserted to the east of the Jordan River. The picture here is not like that of chapter 11, where Saul was energized by God's Spirit (11:6), rose to meet the arrogant challenge of Nahash, and then led Israel to a resounding victory. On this occasion, we see a people with little confidence in either Saul's leadership or the Lord's protection. The irony is that the people had asked for a king in order to find a sense of safety and security. Now that they had a king, they were just as fearful as they had been before kingship was established.

Saul's Disobedience and Samuel's Rebuke (13:7b-15). In the meantime, Saul went to Gilgal as he had been instructed (10:8). He waited for Samuel for seven days, but Samuel did not come as he had promised. With the military situation becoming more and more precarious by the hour, Saul gave an order for sacrifices to be offered without waiting for Samuel's assistance. But just as these offerings were being completed, Samuel did arrive (apparently late on the seventh day), and he confronted Saul by asking, "What is this you have done?" (13:11; the question implies strong disapproval). Saul's response was defensive, suggesting that he knew his actions were dubious and needed some justification. He explained to Samuel that because his own men were deserting and the Philistine attack appeared to be imminent, he felt "compelled" (see note on 13:12) to offer the sacrifices and to ask for the Lord's help even though Samuel had not arrived (13:11-12). Samuel did not discuss Saul's excuses; instead, he severely rebuked him. He told Saul that he had been "foolish" because he had disobeyed the command that the Lord had given him. And because of this, Samuel told Saul that his dynasty would not endure and that the Lord had already chosen another ruler who would be a "man after his own heart" (13:13-14).[4]

Both the harshness and the fairness of Samuel's rebuke of Saul have often been discussed. Some interpreters have seen the whole scenario in this chapter as a setup in which Samuel and God are "out to get" Saul.[5] In the view of these interpreters, Saul never had a chance. The die was cast before any of the events of the chapter took place. Brueggemann (1990a:99-101) comments that "Saul's [welcome of Samuel] appears to be properly and guilelessly deferential. Samuel's answer to Saul, by contrast, is harsh, unresponsive, and accusatory." Brueggemann says further that Samuel "does not wish to be disturbed either by facts or by Saul's deferential argument." He concludes that Saul "never had a chance—because the narrative has stacked the cards in favor of David; because Samuel is so partisan; because the literature is deeply committed to David, even before David explicitly appears in the literature; because Yahweh had committed to David before the literature was ever cast." These are serious charges with important literary[6] and theological[7] implications.

Even among those who would not concur with a "setup" interpretation, there are still legitimate questions to be asked concerning the severity of Samuel's rebuke to Saul. For example, David did things that were much worse than what Saul did on this occasion, and yet David is the one who is described in advance as a person who is "after [God's] own heart" (13:14). Of course, the most familiar misdeeds of David are his sins of adultery and murder in the Bathsheba story of 2 Samuel

11, and his census taking in 2 Samuel 24. But these incidents do not stand alone. The ethics of some of David's military tactics may also be questioned (see 27:9; 2 Sam 8:2). When these things are measured against Saul's actions in this chapter, is it not possible to say that Saul compares quite favorably with David? And if this is so, why then did the Lord refuse to give Saul an enduring dynasty and, instead, bestow this honor on David (2 Sam 7)? Is the God of Israel a God who is arbitrary in his judgments, a God who rejects one person for rather insignificant offenses while accepting another person in spite of much more serious transgressions? These are certainly legitimate questions, but as van den Berg (1996a:107) suggests, the problem with framing them in this way is that it betrays how much our thinking is influenced by moralistic reasoning. The fallacy of this way of assessing the contrast between Saul and David is the assumption that God behaves on the basis of the same moralistic standards that we do in ranking the relative seriousness of specific sins. When sins are categorized as serious, less serious, or insignificant, and then this sort of construct is projected on God, we find that God rejected Saul for what in our judgment might appear to be an insignificant offense, but he accepted David in spite of what we might consider to be much more serious sins. The inevitable conclusion, then, is that God is unjust. But, as van den Berg proposes, could it not be that this is an improper way to frame the problem? Does not the problem lie more with human moralistic thinking than with God's alleged injustice? The difference between God's judgment and ours is that while we tend to look at outward appearances, God looks on the heart (16:7). God's concern with any individual is primarily, although not exclusively, with the inner motives and disposition of the heart (cf. Isa 29:13). By God's standards, someone with impeccable behavior may be rejected if there is no place in that person's heart for God, while someone who miserably fails may be accepted because the desire of his heart is to love and serve the Lord (van den Berg 1996a:108).

The central question in chapter 13 is not what Saul did, but how what he did was related to the inner motives of his heart. Was what he did the manifestation of a weakness of the flesh that was contrary to the true desire of his heart,[8] or was it symptomatic of an inner unwillingness to submit himself without reserve to the will of God for his life? In the light of the whole corpus of the Saul narratives, it appears that the latter is more probable. All things considered, it would appear that what Saul did in this chapter reflected an underlying rebellious disposition toward the Lord, a disposition that was initially veiled but gradually came to dominate his life (van den Berg 1996a:198). Previous indications of Saul's personal reservations about God's plan for his life have been noted in his refusal to initiate action against the Philistine garrison upon his return to Gibeah, his reluctance to inform his uncle about being chosen to be king (10:14-16), and his hiding among the supplies at the Mizpah assembly (10:17-27). More incidents of this sort, pointing strongly in the same direction, are yet to appear.

What should not be diminished in this discussion is that Saul had "not kept the command the LORD . . . God gave [him]" (13:13). Exactly what command was disobeyed, or even whether or not he really did disobey a command, is something on which interpreters have disagreed.[9] Brueggemann (1990a:100) goes so far as to even question the existence of a command when he says, "This is a remarkable statement because Samuel cites no commandment that has been broken, *nor can we construe one* [my italics]. The commandment that seems to have been broken is, 'thou shalt not violate Samuel's authority.'"[10] Such a statement, however, can be made only if one is willing to deny the legitimacy of Samuel's prophetic function, a function that is central to his entire life and ministry (cf. 3:20) since Samuel, as the prophet of the Lord, had given Saul two commands (or charges) in 10:7-8. So the issue here is not, as Brueggemann suggests, the personal authority of Samuel. Rather, it is Samuel's function as a prophet of the Lord and the responsibility of Saul, as a king under the covenant, to be obedient to the words of the Lord's prophets.[11]

Yet there still remains the question of what specific commandment of the Lord Saul violated. Some have suggested that the violation was cultic in nature and consisted in Saul's offering sacrifices, which was something that could legitimately be done only by a priest.[12] It is not at all clear, however, that Saul offered sacrifices without the assistance of a priest (14:18 indicates that the priest Ahijah was among Saul's attendants), and even if he did, the specific commandment to which Samuel referred (13:13) seems clearly to be the charge he had given Saul in 10:8. It is a command that Samuel said the Lord gave directly to Saul (13:13). This appears to be more explicit than merely the general requirements for sacrifice as found in the ritual prescriptions of the Mosaic law. In fact, it seems that the writer wants to draw the reader's focus to the word "command" because he uses it in its verbal or noun form no less than four times in 13:13-14 (see note). Saul had violated the *command* he had been given, and because of this the Lord would *command* another person to assume the role that he had abdicated—that of being the leader of God's people (see note on 13:13-14). But to return to the question of what specific command to Saul is in view, and why such importance was attached to it, Long (1989:90) argues that the command is found in 1 Samuel 10:8 and that its purpose was to clarify the "division of labor between king and prophet" that was inherent in the newly restructured theocracy. The king had responsibility for the execution of military affairs, "but only as directed by the prophet whose responsibility it was to receive and communicate the divine initiative." Kingship in Israel, unlike that of the surrounding nations, was acceptable only "insofar as the king was willing to acknowledge his subordination to the Great King and his designated spokesman. The command of 10:8, that Saul should await Samuel's arrival in order to consecrate battle and receive instructions, was designed to safeguard this theocratic authority structure." It is for this reason that Saul's disobedience was treated as such a serious offense.

In confronting Saul, Samuel emphasized the foolishness of what he had done, and told him forthrightly that the consequence of his disobedience would be the loss of an enduring dynasty. It should be noted that Samuel held Saul accountable in spite of Saul's attempt to justify his behavior on the basis of the seriousness of the Philistine threat, the disintegration of his army, the imminent battle, and his pious motive in these circumstances (see note on 13:12). Saul's excuses betrayed his mistake of letting circumstances determine his actions rather than the commandment of the Lord. No doubt the circumstances he encountered were alarming and the test he underwent was a severe one, but at the same time it was an extremely important test. The issue at stake was whether Saul would be a king *under God,* or a king *in place of God* (de Jong 1978:97). Was he a person who was prepared to wait on the Lord in complete submission and trust, no matter what the circumstances might be, or was he someone who viewed himself as above the word and law of the Lord? This was the central issue of covenantal kingship. This issue was not erased by Saul's attempt to justify his disobedience by a pious motive (asking for the Lord's help) and a religious act (offering sacrifices prior to battle). It is easy to confuse genuine piety with religious words and acts, but it should be remembered that such things do not necessarily coincide with walking in the way of the Lord (cf. van den Berg 1996a:110). It is not religious words and acts in and of themselves that determine the integrity and honor of a person's behavior. The more important question is whether or not what a person does arises out of love for God and trust in his word, and whether or not one's behavior is consistent with God's commands. Saul used a religious argument, much as he would later (ch 15), but as Samuel told him on that occasion, "Obedience is better than sacrifice, and submission is better than offering the fat of rams" (15:22). Saul showed himself to be a person who, in the words of George MacDonald (1983:157), "had not much notion of obedience to God, but he had some idea of respect to religion."[13] In the final analysis, it was Saul's lack of confidence and trust in the Lord that led him to make a foolish decision.

ENDNOTES

1. The regnal formula gives the age of a king at the time of his accession and the duration of his reign (cf. 2 Sam 2:10; 5:4; 1 Kgs 14:21; 2 Kgs 8:17, 26; 12:1; 15:2, 33; 16:2; 18:2; 21:1, 19; 22:1; 23:31, 36; 24:8, 18). This particular example of the formula happens to be defective in that two of its numerals are missing (see note on 13:1).
2. Long (1989:40-41) comments, "By placing Saul and Jonathan side by side in this way, the narrator creates an atmosphere in which the actions of the one will quite naturally be judged in the light of how the other acts in similar situations." Among the contrasts between Saul and Jonathan that Long notes are: Saul's passivity (14:2; cf. 13:13b; 14:16-18) contrasted with Jonathan's activity (14:1, 6; cf. 13:3); Jonathan's discovery of the Lord's will (14:9-10) and Saul's failure to do so (13:8-9; 14:18-19; 14:36).
3. See Long (1989:43-66) for refutation of the view that 13:7b-15 and its anticipation in 10:8 are secondary insertions in their present contexts. This view is advocated in S. R. Driver 1956:176; McCarter 1980b:228; Smith 1912:93ff; and Wellhausen 1957:257. Birch (1976:126) comments, "The prevailing opinion among scholars that 13:7b-15a is a later insertion into the chapter seems well-founded." One of the reasons for this conclusion is the assumption that the two instructions given to Saul by Samuel in 10:7-8—(1) Do what your hand finds to do [10:7] and (2) Go to Gilgal and wait for me for seven days [10:8]—are contradictory instructions. It is alleged that the ability to do the first is negated by the second. In addition, because the second instruction is not carried out until ch 13, it is concluded that both 10:8 and its fulfillment in 13:7b-15 are secondary insertions. This construal of things has been challenged by Long who has pointed out that the instructions of 10:7-8 should not be viewed as contradictory, but rather as complementary, with the second (going to Gilgal) contingent on having fulfilled the first (which, in the context of 10:5, was an implicit instruction to attack the Philistine garrison at Gibeah of God). Since Saul never fulfilled the first instruction, it was not until Jonathan attacked the Philistine garrison that fulfillment of the second (going to Gilgal to await Samuel) was appropriate.

4. McCarter (1980b:229) has suggested that this expression (Heb., *kilbabo* [TH3824, ZH4222]) is better translated "a man of his own choosing" and asserts that 13:14b "has nothing to do with any great fondness of Yahweh's for David or any special quality of David, to whom it patently refers." Noting a similar expression in a Babylonian text, Long (1989:92) concludes that while "divine choice seems to be the major import of *kilbabo* in 13:14b, the more traditional understanding of the phrase as implying something about the character of the chosen one *vis-à-vis* the chooser is not ruled out entirely, for implicit in the selection of a vassal is an expectation that the new appointee will act in harmony with the suzerain's will and purpose, viz. 'in accord with his heart.'"
5. Gunn (1980:66-67) speaks of Saul in this chapter as "the plaything of fate" (cf. the discussion in the commentary on 9:25–10:8). He comments, "Can this extraordinary timing of Samuel's arrival be merely accidental, we wonder? . . . It is as though that condemnation, and the accompanying judgment, was the primary object of Samuel's visit. At the very least we might say that Samuel (which also must mean God) has seized this opportunity with both hands." Gunn goes on to say that the "ambiguity of the instruction" (10:8) "becomes the trap."
6. The literary assumption is that 1–2 Samuel reflect a bias toward David that is propagandistic in nature. Such a view is difficult to harmonize with trustworthy historical writing.
7. The idea that God is a scheming and manipulative deity is difficult to harmonize with God's attributes of holiness and justice, which are repeatedly emphasized in 1–2 Samuel and throughout the Bible.
8. Cf. Rom 7:18-19 (assuming that this passage is speaking of Paul's experience as a regenerated believer).
9. Smith (1912:97-98) comments: "It is difficult to discover anything in the text at which Samuel could justly take offence. The original command was to wait seven days, and this Saul did. In the circumstances he might well plead that he had been too scrupulous. It would not be impertinent to ask why Samuel had waited so long before appearing." Mauchline (1971:113-114) says, "Saul seems to come well out of the incident. Samuel's riposte sounds unconvincing to us (vss. 13-14). . . . The impression left on the reader unquestionably is that the sentence was unfair and against the evidence." Hertzberg (1964:105-106) says, "Saul . . . justifies his conduct in a modest and at all points irrefutable way. From the description of the affair we seem to have a vindication of Saul rather than a charge against him. Saul has done what was permissible for him to do according to Samuel's express instructions, indeed what he had to do as commander-in-chief, especially in view of the dwindling of his manpower. If anyone is in the wrong here it is Samuel, and not Saul."
10. Gunn (1980:39-40) suggests that the command was ambiguous in its time designation, and that on "Samuel's interpretation Saul has not waited as instructed, for he should have waited until the prophet came and issued further instructions; as Saul sees it he has waited precisely the required time, seven days, before being at liberty to take action himself." If this is the case, then the real question becomes why it is that the Lord through Samuel requires "of Saul 'this' rather than 'that' interpretation." Gunn concludes that the reason lies not in Saul's action, but rather in the Lord's attitude toward him (see discussion of Gunn's view of Saul in the commentary on 9:25–10:8). Polzin (1989:252) comments, "Samuel's presumed reference to 10:8 as God's command characterizes the prophet in ch 13 as stretching a point in order to condemn Saul and highlights the prophet's failure to come, rather than Saul's failure to obey."

11. Long (1994:218) suggests that the charge that Samuel gave to Saul in 10:8 "seems designed to create an authority structure whereby human kingship can be accommodated within what remains essentially theocratic rule. In the new order to be established by Samuel in his first charge to Saul, the king is to become the military agent, but the prophet is to remain the recipient and mediator of the divine initiative."
12. Bright (1981:192), for example, says, "In 1 Sam 13:4b-15 Saul is accused of usurping the function of the priesthood of the league, while in ch 15 he is said to have violated the *kherem* [TH2764, ZH3051], a feature of sacral law regarding the conduct of the Holy War."
13. This well-phrased statement occurs in MacDonald's novel *The Baronet's Song* and refers to a clergyman who plays a major role in the story about the orphan known as Wee Sir Gibbie.

◆ B. Israel's Struggle against the Philistines (1 Sam 13:16–14:52)

[16]Saul and Jonathan and the troops with them were staying at Geba in the land of Benjamin. The Philistines set up their camp at Micmash. [17]Three raiding parties soon left the camp of the Philistines. One went north toward Ophrah in the land of Shual, [18]another went west to Beth-horon, and the third moved toward the border above the valley of Zeboim near the wilderness.

[19]There were no blacksmiths in the land of Israel in those days. The Philistines wouldn't allow them for fear they would make swords and spears for the Hebrews. [20]So whenever the Israelites needed to sharpen their plowshares, picks, axes, or sickles,* they had to take them to a Philistine blacksmith. [21](The charges were as follows: a quarter of an ounce of silver* for sharpening a plowshare or a pick, and an eighth of an ounce* for sharpening an ax, a sickle, or an ox goad.) [22]So on the day of the battle none of the people of Israel had a sword or spear, except for Saul and Jonathan.

[23]The pass at Micmash had meanwhile been secured by a contingent of the Philistine army.

CHAPTER 14

One day Jonathan said to his armor bearer, "Come on, let's go over to where the Philistines have their outpost." But Jonathan did not tell his father what he was doing.

[2]Meanwhile, Saul and his 600 men were camped on the outskirts of Gibeah, around the pomegranate tree* at Migron. [3]Among Saul's men was Ahijah the priest, who was wearing the ephod, the priestly vest. Ahijah was the son of Ichabod's brother Ahitub, son of Phinehas, son of Eli, the priest of the LORD who had served at Shiloh.

No one realized that Jonathan had left the Israelite camp. [4]To reach the Philistine outpost, Jonathan had to go down between two rocky cliffs that were called Bozez and Seneh. [5]The cliff on the north was in front of Micmash, and the one on the south was in front of Geba. [6]"Let's go across to the outpost of those pagans," Jonathan said to his armor bearer. "Perhaps the LORD will help us, for nothing can hinder the LORD. He can win a battle whether he has many warriors or only a few!"

[7]"Do what you think is best," the armor bearer replied. "I'm with you completely, whatever you decide."

[8]"All right then," Jonathan told him. "We will cross over and let them see us. [9]If they say to us, 'Stay where you are or we'll kill you,' then we will stop and not go up to them. [10]But if they say, 'Come on up and fight,' then we will go up. That will be the LORD's sign that he will help us defeat them."

[11]When the Philistines saw them coming, they shouted, "Look! The Hebrews are crawling out of their holes!" [12]Then the men from the outpost shouted to Jona-

than, "Come on up here, and we'll teach
you a lesson!"

"Come on, climb right behind me," Jon-
athan said to his armor bearer, "for the
LORD will help us defeat them!"

13So they climbed up using both hands
and feet, and the Philistines fell before
Jonathan, and his armor bearer killed those
who came behind them. 14They killed some
twenty men in all, and their bodies were
scattered over about half an acre.*

15Suddenly, panic broke out in the Phi-
listine army, both in the camp and in the
field, including even the outposts and
raiding parties. And just then an earth-
quake struck, and everyone was terrified.

16Saul's lookouts in Gibeah of Benjamin
saw a strange sight—the vast army of Phi-
listines began to melt away in every direc-
tion. 17"Call the roll and find out who's
missing," Saul ordered. And when they
checked, they found that Jonathan and
his armor bearer were gone.

18Then Saul shouted to Ahijah, "Bring
the ephod here!" For at that time Ahijah
was wearing the ephod in front of the
Israelites.* 19But while Saul was talking
to the priest, the confusion in the Philis-
tine camp grew louder and louder. So
Saul said to the priest, "Never mind; let's
get going!"*

20Then Saul and all his men rushed out
to the battle and found the Philistines
killing each other. There was terrible con-
fusion everywhere. 21Even the Hebrews
who had previously gone over to the Phi-
listine army revolted and joined in with
Saul, Jonathan, and the rest of the Israel-
ites. 22Likewise, the men of Israel who
were hiding in the hill country of Ephraim
joined the chase when they saw the Phi-
listines running away. 23So the LORD saved
Israel that day, and the battle continued
to rage even beyond Beth-aven.

24Now the men of Israel were pressed to
exhaustion that day, because Saul had
placed them under an oath, saying, "Let a
curse fall on anyone who eats before eve-
ning—before I have full revenge on my
enemies." So no one ate anything all day,
25even though they had all found honey-
comb on the ground in the forest. 26They
didn't dare touch the honey because they
all feared the oath they had taken.

27But Jonathan had not heard his fa-
ther's command, and he dipped the end of
his stick into a piece of honeycomb and
ate the honey. After he had eaten it, he
felt refreshed.* 28But one of the men saw
him and said, "Your father made the army
take a strict oath that anyone who eats
food today will be cursed. That is why ev-
eryone is weary and faint."

29"My father has made trouble for us
all!" Jonathan exclaimed. "A command
like that only hurts us. See how refreshed
I am now that I have eaten this little bit
of honey. 30If the men had been allowed
to eat freely from the food they found
among our enemies, think how many
more Philistines we could have killed!"

31They chased and killed the Philistines
all day from Micmash to Aijalon, growing
more and more faint. 32That evening they
rushed for the battle plunder and butch-
ered the sheep, goats, cattle, and calves,
but they ate them without draining the
blood. 33Someone reported to Saul, "Look,
the men are sinning against the LORD by
eating meat that still has blood in it."

"That is very wrong," Saul said. "Find a
large stone and roll it over here. 34Then go
out among the troops and tell them,
'Bring the cattle, sheep, and goats here to
me. Kill them here, and drain the blood
before you eat them. Do not sin against
the LORD by eating meat with the blood
still in it.'"

So that night all the troops brought
their animals and slaughtered them there.
35Then Saul built an altar to the LORD; it
was the first of the altars he built to the
LORD.

36Then Saul said, "Let's chase the Philis-
tines all night and plunder them until sun-
rise. Let's destroy every last one of them."

His men replied, "We'll do whatever you
think is best."

But the priest said, "Let's ask God first."

37So Saul asked God, "Should we go
after the Philistines? Will you help us
defeat them?" But God made no reply
that day.
38Then Saul said to the leaders, "Some-
thing's wrong! I want all my army com-
manders to come here. We must find out
what sin was committed today. 39I vow by
the name of the LORD who rescued Israel
that the sinner will surely die, even if it is
my own son Jonathan!" But no one would
tell him what the trouble was.
40Then Saul said, "Jonathan and I will
stand over here, and all of you stand over
there."
And the people responded to Saul,
"Whatever you think is best."
41Then Saul prayed, "O LORD, God of Is-
rael, please show us who is guilty and who
is innocent.*" Then they cast sacred lots,
and Jonathan and Saul were chosen as
the guilty ones, and the people were de-
clared innocent.
42Then Saul said, "Now cast lots again
and choose between me and Jonathan."
And Jonathan was shown to be the guilty
one.
43"Tell me what you have done," Saul
demanded of Jonathan.
"I tasted a little honey," Jonathan ad-
mitted. "It was only a little bit on the end
of my stick. Does that deserve death?"
44"Yes, Jonathan," Saul said, "you must
die! May God strike me and even kill me
if you do not die for this."
45But the people broke in and said to
Saul, "Jonathan has won this great vic-
tory for Israel. Should he die? Far from it!
As surely as the LORD lives, not one hair on
his head will be touched, for God helped
him do a great deed today." So the people
rescued Jonathan, and he was not put to
death.
46Then Saul called back the army from
chasing the Philistines, and the Philistines
returned home.

47Now when Saul had secured his grasp
on Israel's throne, he fought against his
enemies in every direction—against Moab,
Ammon, Edom, the kings of Zobah, and
the Philistines. And wherever he turned,
he was victorious.* 48He performed great
deeds and conquered the Amalekites, sav-
ing Israel from all those who had plun-
dered them.
49Saul's sons included Jonathan, Ish-
bosheth,* and Malkishua. He also had two
daughters: Merab, who was older, and
Michal. 50Saul's wife was Ahinoam, the
daughter of Ahimaaz. The commander of
Saul's army was Abner, the son of Saul's
uncle Ner. 51Saul's father, Kish, and Ab-
ner's father, Ner, were both sons of
Abiel.
52The Israelites fought constantly with
the Philistines throughout Saul's lifetime.
So whenever Saul observed a young man
who was brave and strong, he drafted him
into his army.

13:20 As in Greek version; Hebrew reads *or plowshares.* **13:21a** Hebrew *1 pim* [8 grams]. **13:21b** Hebrew *1/3 of a shekel* [4 grams]. **14:2** Or *around the rock of Rimmon;* compare Judg 20:45, 47; 21:13. **14:14** Hebrew *half a yoke;* a "yoke" was the amount of land plowed by a pair of yoked oxen in one day. **14:18** As in some Greek manuscripts; Hebrew reads *"Bring the Ark of God." For at that time the Ark of God was with the Israelites.* **14:19** Hebrew *Withdraw your hand.* **14:27** Or *his eyes brightened;* similarly in 14:29. **14:41** Greek version adds *If the fault is with me or my son Jonathan, respond with Urim; but if the men of Israel are at fault, respond with Thummim.* **14:47** As in Greek version; Hebrew reads *he acted wickedly.* **14:49** Hebrew *Ishvi,* a variant name for Ishbosheth; also known as Esh-baal.

NOTES

13:21 ***a quarter of an ounce of silver.*** See NLT mg. The expression *wehaytah happetsirah pim* [TH6477/6310A, ZH7201/7088] (lit., "the charge was a pim") was not understood until it was discovered that *pim* was the name of a weight for measuring silver. Unaware of this, S. R. Driver (1913:104) regarded the text as "hopelessly corrupt." Polzin (1989:253, note 18) comments, "The statement in 13:21 ('the charge was a *pim* [*happetsirah pim*] for the plowshares and for the mattocks') is a good illustration of modern scholarship's growing awareness of the text's 'factuality.'"

14:2 ***the outskirts of Gibeah.*** McCarter (1980b:235) suggests emending Gibeah to Geba (cf. the note on 13:3-4) on the basis of the topographical considerations required by 14:16, which locates the site close enough to the Micmash pass for Saul's watchmen to observe the battle. Stoebe (1973:258), however, suggests that "outskirts of Gibeah" is to be understood as the border of Gibeah's area of influence.

Migron. Isaiah 10:28 indicates Migron was located to the north of Micmash. Exactly where is not known. Klein (1983:131), Long (1989:104), McCarter (1980b:235), and Stoebe (1973:258) suggest reading "under the pomegranate tree *by the threshing floor,*" on the assumption that *bemigron* [TH871.2/4051, ZH928/4491] reflects a corruption of *bemo goren* [TH1119/1637, ZH1198/1755].

14:4 ***rocky cliffs.*** Lit., "a tooth of rock on this side and a tooth of rock on that side."

14:5 ***Geba.*** See notes at 10:5; 13:3-4. In this instance, Geba may be identified with a site about two miles southwest of Micmash, on the south side of the Wadi Suweinit.

14:6 ***those pagans.*** Lit., "these uncircumcised."

14:7 ***I'm with you completely, whatever you decide.*** Lit., "I am with you according to your heart." The LXX reads, "My heart is as your heart." S. R. Driver (1913:107), Klein (1983:131), and McCarter (1980b:236) suggest the MT has lost *lebabi* [TH3807.1/3824/2967.1, ZH4200/4222/3276] (my heart) by haplography. This is far from certain. The somewhat unusual wordings in the MT of this verse may reflect a popular form of Hebrew expression.

14:13 ***and the Philistines fell.*** The LXX is fuller: "They turned before Jonathan and he smote them." Klein (1983:131) notes that the MT is more "difficult and therefore preferable."

14:15 ***everyone was terrified.*** Lit., "It became a trembling [panic] of God." The NRSV translates the phrase, "and it became a very great panic." Gordon (1986:137) has pointed out that *'elohim* [TH430, ZH466] is sometimes used as a superlative (as in Jonah 3:3, "Nineveh was a very great city"), but here the Hebrew is indicating the source of the Philistine discomfiture.

14:16 ***melt away in every direction.*** As it stands the MT is untranslatable: "and they went and hither" (*wayyelek wahalom* [TH1980/1988, ZH2143/2151]). With reference to LXX's *enthen kai enthen* [TG1759.1, ZG1925] (hence and thence), S. R. Driver (1913:109) suggests that *wayyelek* is a corruption of *halom.* The meaning is that the troops were disorganized and dispersed (melted away) in every direction (*halom wahalom* (hither and thither).

14:18 ***ephod.*** This is the reading of the LXX; the MT reads, "Bring the Ark here" (see NLT mg). As S. R. Driver (1913:110) and others have pointed out, the ephod, not the Ark, was the organ of divination, and as 23:9 and 30:7 demonstrate, *nagash* [TH5066, ZH5602] (NLT, "bring") is the word used for bringing the ephod, rather than the Ark, into use. For a well reasoned defense of the preference for the LXX reading, see Kio 1996. For defense of the idea that "ephod" is a harmonizing correction and that the MT should be maintained as the *lectio difficilior,* see van der Toorn and Houtman 1994. Van der Toorn and Houtman argue that the ephod references in 1–2 Samuel hide an original alternate Ark tradition, and that there has been a regular substitution of the word "ephod" for "Ark," with the exception of this text (14:18), which they argue has correctly preserved this editorially obscured alternate Ark tradition. All things considered, this theory raises many more questions than it answers.

For at that time Ahijah was wearing the ephod in front of the Israelites. This is the reading of the LXX; the MT reads, "for at that time the Ark of God was—and the Israelites." The Hebrew at the end of the MT phrase (*ubene yisra'el* [TH2050.1/1121, ZH2256/1201]) lacks any clear sense in the context. The suggested LXX retroversion would read *lipne yisra'el* [TH3807.1/6440, ZH4200/7156], a change of only two letters.

14:23 ***beyond Beth-aven.*** The LXX contains a longer reading at 23b-24a: "And the war passed through Bamoth; and all the people with Saul were about 10,000 men. And the battle extended itself to every city in Mount Ephraim. And Saul committed a great trespass of ignorance in that day." Pisano (1984:37-41) argues for MT priority and notes that "the possibility of a textual accident from which MT could have resulted from LXX does not seem plausible."

14:24 ***Now the men of Israel were pressed to exhaustion that day, because Saul had placed them under an oath.*** Long (1989:114) says that "14:24 suggests that the distress of the men of Israel may have *prompted* rather than resulted from Saul's oath." The statement of 14:24 is thus retrospective providing the necessary background for the account of Jonathan's inadvertent action that follows (14:25-30). In Long's view, the "distress" or "panic" (NLT, "exhaustion") is the same panic referred to in 13:6, where the same Hebrew word is used (NLT, "They were hard pressed"). Thus this "panic" was the cause of Saul's imposition of an oath rather than the result of it.

14:25 ***they had all found honeycomb.*** It seems clear that the text of 14:25a has undergone some sort of corruption. Proposed reconstructions are complex and speculative (see S. R. Driver 1913:113-114; McCarter 1980b:245). The NIV translates 14:25a, "The entire army entered the woods" with a text note suggesting an alternative, "Now all the people of the land entered the woods." The NASB reads, "Now all *the people of* the land entered the forest." It is likely that part of the present confusion in the text is due to the ambiguity of the root *ya'ar* [TH3293/3293A, ZH3623/3624], that can mean either "forest" or "honeycomb."

14:30 ***think how many more Philistines we could have killed!*** The MT reads, "for now the slaughter of the Philistines has not been great." 4QSam[a] and LXX read, "the slaughter among the Philistines would have been greater."

14:34 ***brought their animals.*** The MT reads, "brought the ox in his hand." The LXX reads "whatever he had at hand," which assumes the reading *'asher* [TH834, ZH889] (whatever) for *shoro* [TH7794/2050.2, ZH8802/2257] (his ox).

14:35 ***it was the first of the altars he built to the LORD.*** Although this is normally the way 14:35b has been translated (cf. NIV, NASB, NRSV) the wording of the Hebrew is far from clear. Literally, 14:35b reads, "[that is] he began to build an altar to the LORD." It is not clear whether *hekhel* [TH2490, ZH2725] conveys the idea of doing something for the "first time" or, as normally used, to indicate "commencing" a certain action. If the latter is the meaning, it is unclear whether Saul ever finished the project (for a more detailed discussion of this suggestion, see Long 1989:121-123).

14:41 ***show us who is guilty and who is innocent.*** Lit., "give a true decision." The LXX contains a lengthy addition in which the last two words (see italicized words below) are equivalent to *habah thamim* [TH3051/8549, ZH2035/9459] (give a true decision). The LXX reads, "Why have you not answered your servant today? If this guilt is on my account or on account of Jonathan, my son, then, O LORD God of Israel, give Urim! But if it is on account of your people Israel, *give Thummim!*" Numerous commentators (e.g., S. R. Driver, Smith, Klein, McCarter) as well as translations (e.g., RSV, NRSV, NEB, NAB, JB) accept the originality of the additional words. Pisano (1984:183-199) discusses the complex arguments for and against the originality of the LXX, including the difficulties of retroversion, and concludes (1984:199) that "it does not seem possible to arrive at a definite decision either in favor of MT or of LXX here." Since the MT makes good sense as it stands, particularly with the disputed phrase *habah thamim* (give a true decision), there is no convincing reason to adopt the LXX reading.

14:42 ***Jonathan.*** The MT adds, "my son." Once more the LXX has additional wording that various commentators (Klein 1983:131-132; McCarter 1980b:244, 248) have considered original because it looks like the MT has an omission on the basis of homoeoteleuton (i.e., the scribe's eyes moved from "Jonathan my son" to "Jonathan his son" and left out what was in between). Here, the LXX has the words, "The one the LORD takes shall die. Although the troops said it shouldn't be this way, Saul forced them and they cast between him and Jonathan his son." There is less of a consensus on these words among translations and commentators than there is regarding the additional wording in 14:41. S. R. Driver (1913:118), for example, following Wellhausen, says that although omission could be explained by homoeoteleuton, "its originality is very doubtful." Pisano (1984:199-204) concurs. The NRSV, while adopting the LXX addition of 14:41, does not adopt the addition of 14:42, and in fact, does not even footnote it.

14:44 ***Yes . . . you must die!*** "Yes" here represents the *ki* [TH3588, ZH3954] of asseveration with an oath formula; see GKC §149d.

14:47 ***he was victorious.*** This is the reading of the LXX, which presupposes *yiwwashea'* [TH3467, ZH3828] ("he was saved" or "delivered," BDB 957d) instead of MT's *yarshi'a* [TH7561, ZH8399] (make guilty, act wickedly) often translated here as "inflicted punishment" or "condemned." Alter (1999:85) comments, "The Hebrew *yarshi'a* usually means to condemn someone as guilty in a court of justice. But notice that a related idiom, 'to do justice' *'asot shephatim* [TH8201, ZH9150; cf. Num 33:4], also means to carry out punitive acts against an enemy. The Masoretic version is to be preferred to the Septuagint's *yoshi'a*, 'he would deliver,' because in this narrative, God, not Saul, is represented as the deliverer. Apparently, the implication is that he carried out punishing expeditions against Israel's enemies to the east of the Jordan without actually conquering them, as David was to do." Alter's suggestion, while not conclusive, certainly provides a good rationale for retaining the MT rendering.

14:51 ***Saul's father, Kish, and Abner's father, Ner, were both sons of Abiel.*** This reading (cf. NIV) makes sense on the basis of 9:1, but requires emendation of "son" from singular to plural. The MT, 4QSam[a], and the LXX all read singular "son": "Kish was the father of Saul, and Ner the father of Abner was the son of Abiel."

COMMENTARY

Israel's Military Predicament (13:16-23). First Samuel 13:16-23 describes the threatening maneuvers of the Philistine troops and the attrition of Saul's forces to a mere 600 men as he left Gilgal to join up with Jonathan at Gibeah. Three groups of Philistine marauders went plundering through the land to the north, west, and east (13:17-18). The Israelites found themselves at a great disadvantage because the Philistines controlled the iron technology that was important for the manufacture and repair of weapons (13:19-21, see note on 13:21). Only Saul and Jonathan were in possession of a sword and spear. The situation was desperate. So far, kingship had been of little help.

Jonathan's Confidence in the Lord (14:1-23). First Samuel 14 picks up the thread of the conflict between the Philistines and Israel with which chapter 13 ended. The Philistine forces were encamped at Micmash (13:16; 14:5) to the north of Wadi Suweinit (a wadi running from the hill country eastward toward Jericho and the Jordan), while Saul and his 600 men were encamped near Gibeah (14:2), southwest of the wadi.[1] At the end of chapter 13, Saul and Jonathan were singled out as the only two men in Israel who possessed a sword and spear (13:22). But as chapter 14 opens, the narrative contains overtones of contrast, and perhaps even tension between the father and the son, rather than those of similarity and closeness. It is Jonathan instead of Saul who decided to take initiative against the Philistines (just as he had done in 13:3; cf. Smelik 1977:124), but it is noted that Jonathan did not tell his father about his plans.[2] In the subsequent events it is Jonathan's deeds rather than Saul's that are cast in a favorable light. It is Jonathan who plays the primary role in what turns out to be a successful attack on the Philistines. When Saul finally takes a central role in the narrative, his actions cast a dark shadow over what should otherwise have been a joyous celebration. It is this contrast between Jonathan and Saul that brings focus to the chapter. As Long (1989:105) notes, "The simple juxtaposing and comparing of Saul and Jonathan in chapter 13 evolves in chapter 14 into a rivalry and progressive alienation between them."

In addition to this contrast between Jonathan and Saul, the opening description of the setting for the events that are to unfold in the remainder of the chapter includes information concerning Saul's entourage (in a parenthetical statement) that elicits some foreboding in the mind of the reader. The reader is told in 14:3 that Ahijah the priest, who wore the ephod, was among Saul's men. The genealogy of Ahijah, however, is highly unusual. He is said to be the son of Ichabod's brother Ahitub, the son of Phinehas, the son of Eli, the priest who had served at Shiloh. The disclosure that Ahijah was a nephew of Ichabod is not customary information for inclusion in an abbreviated genealogy. Normally, it would say that Ahijah was the son of Ahitub. It seems clear that the writer deliberately chose to call attention to Ahijah's association with Ichabod (meaning "the glory has departed"; 4:21-22), and by so doing he reminded the reader of the events surrounding the capture of the Ark many years earlier, intimating a connection between the situation at that time and the one described here (van den Berg 1996a:113-114). The exact nature of the connection is not explicit. But is it too much to suggest that the writer is subtly hinting that the Lord's presence had departed from Saul, much as it had departed from Israel at the time of the capture of the Ark?[3] Could it be that this linkage of Ahijah, Ichabod, and Saul is intended to be understood as a veiled indication of what will become explicit in 15:23 (the Lord rejects Saul as king) and 16:14 (the Spirit of the Lord departs from Saul)? In any case, the introduction to this chapter presents us with a king whose dynasty has been rejected being assisted by a priest whose priestly line has been rejected (Davis 1994a:136). Can anything positive emerge from this alliance?

Jonathan's proposal to his armor bearer was to cross the ravine that separated the Philistine and Israelite forces, and to raid a Philistine outpost (14:1, 6). He told his armor bearer, "Perhaps the LORD will help us, for nothing can hinder the LORD. He can win a battle whether he has many warriors or only a few!" (14:6). This bold proposal was an expression of Jonathan's faith and one that could only be made by someone with complete confidence in the power of the Lord.[4] He knew that if God were to intervene on behalf of his people, the number of soldiers needed to accomplish a victory was not of decisive importance (cf. Judg 7:7, 14). As Jonathan was well aware, there is a fine line between faith and presumption, and one must be careful not to do things that overstep that line, and that might be characterized as tempting or testing the Lord (cf. Deut 6:16).[5] So Jonathan said to his armor bearer, "Perhaps the LORD will help us."[6] In order to determine if his idea was truly in accord with the Lord's will, some further confirmation was needed. Therefore, Jonathan suggested that if the Philistines were to invite his armor bearer and himself to "come on up and fight" when they saw them crossing the ravine, then this would be "the LORD's sign" that he would help them defeat the Philistines.[7] And sure enough, when the Philistines saw them, they dared them to climb up the ravine, boasting, "We'll teach you a lesson!" (14:12). This was the assurance Jonathan needed in order to affirm with certainty, "the LORD will help us defeat them!"

To the surprise of the Philistines, Jonathan and his armor bearer climbed up the side of the ravine and engaged their outpost in combat, killing 20 of their men. At the same time a great panic broke out across the entire Philistine army, which was intensified by a sudden earthquake. Although the panic may have had some connection with the spread of rumors concerning a surprise Israelite attack, it seems clear that there was also a supernatural dimension to its occurrence (see note on 14:15). When Israel was at Sinai the Lord promised that he would send his "terror" (*'emah* [TH367, ZH399]) ahead of them and "create panic" (or "throw into confusion"; Heb., *hamam* [TH2000, ZH2169]) every nation they encountered during the time of the conquest (Exod 23:27). While the word for "panic" (*kharadah* [TH2731, ZH3010]) in 1 Samuel 14:15 is not the same word used for "terror" in Exodus 23:27, there is little if any difference in meaning between the two. Rahab confirmed that the Lord had sent "terror" on the Canaanites at the time of the conquest when she said, "I know the LORD has given you this land. . . . We are all *afraid of you* (*'emah*). Everyone in the land is *living in terror* (*mug* [TH4127, ZH4570])" (Josh 2:9). In Deuteronomy 7:23 Moses told the Israelites that God would deliver the Canaanites into their hands: "He will throw them into complete *confusion* (*mehumah* [TH4103, ZH4539]) until they are destroyed." This same Hebrew word is used in this chapter (14:20) when the Philistines began to kill each other, and we are told that "there was terrible *confusion* everywhere." So Israel's experience of divine intervention to bring about the defeat of the Philistines was consistent with what the Lord had promised and done at the time of the conquest.[8] The confusion that resulted in Philistines killing each other was a major factor in Israel's victory and is reminiscent of a similar incident at the time of Gideon's battle with the Midianites (Judg 7:22). On that occasion this improbable phenomenon is explicitly said to have been caused by the Lord.

In the meantime, as Saul's sentries reported that the Philistine forces were dissipating, Saul wanted to know if any of his own soldiers were missing. When the roll was called, it was determined that Jonathan and his armor bearer were not accounted for. This prompted Saul to order Ahijah to bring him the ephod (see note on 14:18). Saul seemed to sense that in these circumstances it was important for him to find out what the Lord might expect of him. But as the panic among the Philistines became more and more apparent, and as those who had previously deserted from Saul's army began to return, Saul decided not to wait for an answer from the Lord but rather to immediately engage the Philistines in battle. Apparently the circumstances convinced Saul that the time for action was now and that there was no time to wait for a word from the Lord. It is remarkable how similar Saul's behavior in this situation was to his behavior in the previous chapter at Gilgal, where the pressure of circumstances was also the cause of unacceptable behavior. Although on this occasion there was no indication that Saul had broken a command of the Lord, the similarity between the two incidents belies Saul's trust in and dependence on the Lord. In the final analysis, Saul concluded that it was more important for him to join in the battle immediately, than it was to wait for instruction from the Lord, suggesting an unhealthy confidence in his own ability to achieve success in the impending military encounter.

The conclusion to this first section of chapter 14, and in a very real sense the climax of the entire chapter, is given in the statement of 14:23 ("So the LORD saved Israel that day"), in which the author gives a divinely inspired interpretation of what he has just described. This conclusion is later confirmed by all the people when they say of Jonathan, "God helped him do a great deed today" (14:45). The victory was ultimately neither Jonathan's nor Saul's; rather, it was the Lord's. At the same time, it was Jonathan rather than Saul who was shown to be the one whom the Lord used to achieve the victory.

Saul's Foolish Curse (14:24-46). Saul not only decided to go into battle without waiting for any instruction from the Lord; he also decided to place a curse on anyone who ate anything before that evening, that is, "before I have full revenge on my enemies" (14:24, see note). The wording of Saul's malediction reflects a self-centered, imperious attitude that is inconsistent with true covenantal kingship. He speaks in the first person, saying that no one is to eat until "*I* have full revenge on *my* enemies." Saul's language personalizes the impending battle, draws attention to himself, and fails to acknowledge that ultimately the battle is the Lord's and not his own (14:6, 23, 45). This imprudent attempt to coerce his troops into all-out action precipitated serious, unintended consequences.

Jonathan, of course, was unaware of the prohibition against eating. When he saw some honey in the forest, he refreshed himself with its nourishment. Upon being told that his father had forbidden any soldier to eat on that day, his spontaneous response was, "My father has made trouble for us all! . . . A command like that only hurts us" (14:29).[9] Jonathan's initiative, born of faith, unleashed a chain reaction that led to panic and confusion among the Philistines (14:15), an earthquake (14:15), the return of Israel's deserters to Saul's army (14:21-22), and the flight of the Philistine army (14:22, 31). All of this was the Lord's doing (14:23). Saul's imprudent and self-centered malediction, however, served as a hindrance to Israel's success and as an impediment to the full realization of the Lord's deliverance. Jonathan said, "Think how many more Philistines we could have killed"—if the soldiers had been able to eat (see note on 14:30). By his blunder,[10] Saul became an opponent rather than an accomplice to the fulfillment of the Lord's purpose for his people.

What is more, when the day was over, Israel's troops had become so faint and hungry from the exertion of the battle and pursuit of the Philistines that they butchered the animals plundered from the Philistines and ate them without draining the blood (14:32). This naturally was a violation of covenantal law (Lev 17:14; Deut

12:23). Upon hearing the news, Saul, seemingly unconcerned that it was his own prohibition of eating that had occasioned their failure to follow the ritual law, ordered them not to eat meat with the blood still in it (14:34) and provided a stone on which they could kill the animals and drain the blood (14:33-34). In the meantime, Saul began to construct an altar, that was apparently never completed because of his desire to pursue the Philistines through the night (see note on 14:35).[11] This ambitious proposal, however, prompted Ahijah, the priest, to suggest that before going on such a venture, they should first ask for divine guidance (14:36-37; cf. 14:3).[12] But the Lord did not respond to Saul's inquiry.[13] Saul concluded that God's silence was caused by someone's violation of the oath against eating, and he suspected that his son was the guilty party.[14] After the casting of lots established this (14:41-42), and Jonathan confessed his guilt (14:43), Saul ordered Jonathan's death (14:44).[15] The people, however, would not hear of this. They asked Saul why the person who won such a great victory for Israel should die. They then challenged Saul's authority and declared that, "Not one hair on his head will be touched, for God helped him do a great deed today" (14:45).

There are a number of troubling things concerning Saul that surface upon a reading of this narrative. One of the most apparent is that way in which Saul repeatedly covered his self-centered and imprudent behavior with pious language and religious acts. In 14:34 he said, "Do not sin against the LORD by eating meat with the blood still in it." In 14:35 he began to build an altar to the Lord. In 14:39 he vowed by the name of the Lord. In 14:41 he prayed, and in 14:44 he used God's name in an oath. In 14:24-25 a reference is made to an oath that Saul imposed on the people, presumably taken in the name of the Lord. In 14:37 he sought divine counsel. In all of these statements and actions, Saul projects the appearance of a pious and spiritual person. But the reality is that Saul was not acting as a true servant of the Lord; rather, he sought to coerce the Lord into serving his own ambitions. In addition, it seems clear that in Saul's mind, his son Jonathan was a transgressor deserving of death rather than a man of faith whom the Lord used to give Israel a great victory. To the reader, however, the reality seems to be much closer to the reverse. Saul mistakenly regarded Jonathan as the one who had "troubled Israel" (i.e., the person whose sin had caused divine silence), while Jonathan, with much more justification, had the same view of his father (he was the person who hindered Israel's success in battle; see note on 14:30). Long (1989:128) sums up the chapter very well when he comments, "Thus, the day that began with Jonathan placing his life in jeopardy by his daring attack against the Philistine outpost ends with him narrowly escaping death at the hands of his own father. And the day which held promise of a crushing victory over the Philistines ends rather meekly with Saul giving up the pursuit and the Philistines simply returning 'to their own place' (14:46). Rebuked by Yahweh, forsaken by Samuel, at odds with Jonathan, Saul ultimately finds himself completely isolated, alienated by his own obduracy even from his own troops."

A Summary of Saul's Reign (14:47-52). Even though Saul reigned for many years after the battle with the Philistines described in the preceding verses, the summary of his reign is placed here, before any record of his death for two apparent reasons: First, in the following two chapters Saul is rejected as king (ch 15), and second,

David is anointed as the person who will replace him on the throne (ch 16). So there is a sense in which this point in time marked the conclusion of Saul's abortive reign, even though he continued to rule the nation during a long period of transition between himself and David. During this transition period there were two "anointed ones" in Israel. The comparison and contrast of David and Saul during the period of David's rise and Saul's demise is central to the narratives, running from David's anointing (ch 16) until Saul's death (ch 31).

This brief summary of Saul's accomplishments, given its context in the midst of narratives that do not place Saul in a very favorable light, is rather surprising in its positive tone. Notice is given of his battles with various surrounding nations, and it is said that "wherever he turned, he was victorious" (or "inflicted punishment," see note on 14:47), and he saved "Israel from all those who had plundered them" (14:48). While it is said that Saul "conquered the Amalekites" (anticipating the events of ch 15), this is not said of the Philistines who continued to be a threat ("the Israelites fought constantly with the Philistines throughout Saul's lifetime," 14:52). So while Saul had some success in securing Israel's borders, he did not rescue Israel from the Philistines, which was one of the primary purposes for which he had been made king (9:16; "he will rescue [Israel] from the Philistines"). In fact, he would eventually die in his unsuccessful struggle with the Philistines. Perhaps more significant than what this summary says about Saul, is what it does not say (Long 1989:130). There is no mention of either his own covenant faithfulness, nor of the Lord's blessing on his reign. This contrasts sharply with the summary of David's reign in 2 Samuel 8 where it is said, "So the LORD made David victorious wherever he went" (2 Sam 8:6). This is particularly significant with respect to Israel's victories over the Philistines. In every other case in which Israel defeats the Philistines in 1–2 Samuel, there is some reference to Israel's confidence in the Lord's sovereign power to deliver (see Klement 2000:133). This confidence in the Lord is sadly lacking in the Saul narratives, and victory over the Philistines was never accomplished. In addition, there is no statement about Saul that corresponds to the statement in the summary of David's reign that he did what was "just and right for all his people" (2 Sam 8:15).

The other information in this summary of Saul's reign concerns family relationships (14:49-51). Besides listing Saul's wife, sons, and daughters, reference is made to his cousin Abner, who became the commander of his army and who played a significant role in succeeding events in the lives of both Saul and David.

At the end of 1 Samuel 13–14, the high expectations that accompanied the establishment of the monarchy in 10:24 and 11:15 have largely dissipated. Saul did not live up to the expectations of the people or the requirements of a true covenantal king. He became increasingly alienated from Samuel (13:13-14), from his son Jonathan (14:29, 40-44), and from the people (14:45). The highly contrastive picture of Saul and Jonathan in chapter 14 does not place Saul in a favorable light.[16] It was Jonathan who took the initiative against the Philistines and expressed confidence in the Lord's deliverance, while Saul was passive and timid.[17] His behavior, while often outwardly religious, failed to reflect obedience to the Lord's commands and wholehearted confidence in the Lord's promises to protect and guide his people.

ENDNOTES

1. See the description and map of the Micmash pass in Y. Aharoni and M. Avi-Yonah 1993:89.
2. The reason why Jonathan did not share his plans with his father is not given. Could it be that Jonathan intuitively recognized that his father's lack of confidence and trust in the Lord (reflected in his disobedience to the Lord's command at Gilgal, described in the previous chapter), would mean that any proposal for an initiative of faith would be squelched with complaints of senseless and reckless behavior? This sort of anticipated objection might have been enhanced by Jonathan's awareness that his previous initiative (his attack on the Philistine outpost at Geba [13:3]) resulted in a more severe oppression by the Philistines (ch 13), and that his new idea might seem much too dangerous.
3. Jobling (1976:368) also makes note of the "odd and needless genealogical reference to Ichabod . . . reminding the reader that 'the glory has departed.'" But Jobling suggests that the significance of the allusion here is that if Saul's "own royal glory [is] gone, where else would we expect Saul to be than with a relative of 'Glory gone.'" In Jobling's construction the "glory" is associated with Saul rather than God. This, however, breaks the parallel with the significance of the name in ch 4.
4. As Davis (1994a:137) notes, "Faith arises in such a situation because it looks not to circumstances but to God." Here again we find a contrast between Jonathan and Saul. Saul's looking to circumstances was the very thing that led him to disobey God's command in ch 13.
5. Deuteronomy 6:16 ("You must not test the LORD your God") was quoted by Jesus during his temptation in the wilderness when Satan challenged him to throw himself down from the highest point of the Temple so that he could be delivered by the angels (Matt 4:6-7). Testing in the sense referred to in these texts is an attempt to force the Lord to give a demonstration of his power by providing the desired help.
6. Davis (1994a:138) comments, "Jonathan's 'perhaps' is part of his faith. He both confesses the power of Yahweh and retains the freedom of Yahweh. Faith does not dictate to God, as if the Lord of hosts is its errand boy. Faith recognizes its degree of ignorance and knows it has not read a transcript of the divine decrees for most situations. All this, however, does not cancel but enhances its excitement. Who knows what this omnipotent God may be delighted to do against these uncircumcised Philistines!"
7. On a few other occasions in the OT we encounter someone asking for a sign from the Lord (Abraham's servant, Gen 24:14; Gideon, Judg 6:17; Hezekiah, 2 Kgs 20:8; cf. Ahaz, Isa 7:10-11). These examples, however, are sporadic, and similar ones are not found in the NT (van den Berg 1996a:116). In fact, in the NT asking for signs seems to carry a more negative connotation (cf. Matt 12:38; 16:1; John 6:30). It appears that with the progress of revelation, the giving of the Holy Spirit, and the completion of the Canon, the function of signs as a means of divine revelation is greatly diminished, if not abandoned. This is not to say the Lord cannot or does not still use such signs, but today the normal means for determining the Lord's will is application of the teaching of Scripture to the decision that needs to be made, the exercising of prudence and sound judgment, the seeking of godly counsel, and prayer for divine guidance.
8. The fear and confusion experienced by the Philistines fit with the pattern of the Yahweh War (often termed the "Holy War") in which God operates not only on the level of military confrontations but also on the psychological plane by controlling the enemy's psyche (see Niehaus 1988).

9. Jobling (1976:370) comments, "Jonathan implicitly contrasts himself with his father as he compares his own refreshed condition—'see how my eyes have become bright, because I tasted a little of this honey'—with the troops' debilitation; he, not his father, has correctly interpreted Yhwh's will." Long (1989:120) calls attention to the "root-play involving alef and resh" which "takes on added significance when viewed in the context of 14:24-29." In the space of these six verses, "Verbal roots containing alef and resh appear six times (twice *'arar* [TH779, ZH826], "curse"; twice *'or* [TH215, ZH239], "shine, brighten"; once *yare'* [TH3372, ZH3707], "fear"; and once *ra'ah* [TH7200, ZH8011], "see"). Jonathan's root-play, converting curse to brightening, adds to the developing contrast between himself and his father."
10. The LXX addition between 14:23b and 14:24a includes the statement, "Saul committed a great trespass of ignorance in that day" (see note on 14:23). McCarter (1980b:243) accepts this longer reading and suggests a Hebrew *Vorlage* that would be translated as "Saul made a great blunder that day."
11. This is another example of circumstances rather than commitment to higher principles being the thing that determined Saul's course of action.
12. As various commentators have noted (Budde 1890:100-101; Hertzberg 1964:116; Long 1989:123), nowhere else in the OT does a priest remind someone to consult the oracle, and it should have been Saul who took the initiative on this occasion, not the priest. Long notes that this fits with "an overall pattern in chs 13–14 of Saul's declining commitment to discovering the divine will" (cf. 13:8, 9; 14:18, 19; 14:36).
13. Long (1989:123-124) points out that there is an "implication of judgment in the divine silence" and that this is a reminder of "Samuel's warning to the people in 1 Sam 8 that, as a result of their sinful request for a king, 'Yahweh will not answer you in that day' (8:18)."
14. Alter (1999:83), referencing Fokkelman, suggests Saul may have had Jonathan in mind and that "there seems to be some deep ambivalence between father and son well before the appearance of David at court."
15. As Long (1989:124) notes, there is not even "the slightest sign of regret or sorrow on Saul's part when the life of his son seems forfeit." This contrasts sharply with the grief of Jephthah in Judg 11 when his child must die as a result of a foolish vow.
16. Bergen (1996:161) summarizes 14:24-45 by saying it "is a stunningly effective critique of all monarchies. This passage showcases a spectrum of frailties and follies that beset monarchies. Using Saul, Israel's first monarch, as an example, the narrative demonstrates that kings could lead Israel into battle, but they could also diminish a nation's capacity to achieve victory. Kings could build altars for their subjects to sacrifice to God, but they could not guarantee an encounter with the divine. They could utter powerful words—curses and oaths—but lacked the power to bring about their fulfillment."
17. Davis (1994a:141) points out that "chapter 11 used the root *yasha'* [TH3467, ZH3828] (to save) three times in reference to Saul's activity (11:3, 9, 13) while chapter 14 uses the same root three times in connection with Jonathan's deeds (14:6, 23, 45; see also 14:39). Not Saul but Jonathan has, in human terms, become the savior of Israel."

◆ C. God's Rejection of Saul as King (1 Sam 15:1-35)

One day Samuel said to Saul, "It was the LORD who told me to anoint you as king of his people, Israel. Now listen to this message from the LORD! 2This is what the LORD of Heaven's Armies has declared: I have decided to settle accounts with the nation

of Amalek for opposing Israel when they
came from Egypt. 3Now go and complete-
ly destroy* the entire Amalekite nation—
men, women, children, babies, cattle,
sheep, goats, camels, and donkeys."
4So Saul mobilized his army at Telaim.
There were 200,000 soldiers from Israel
and 10,000 men from Judah. 5Then Saul
and his army went to a town of the Ama-
lekites and lay in wait in the valley. 6Saul
sent this warning to the Kenites: "Move
away from where the Amalekites live, or
you will die with them. For you showed
kindness to all the people of Israel when
they came up from Egypt." So the Kenites
packed up and left.
7Then Saul slaughtered the Amalekites
from Havilah all the way to Shur, east of
Egypt. 8He captured Agag, the Amalekite
king, but completely destroyed everyone
else. 9Saul and his men spared Agag's life
and kept the best of the sheep and goats,
the cattle, the fat calves, and the lambs—
everything, in fact, that appealed to them.
They destroyed only what was worthless
or of poor quality.

10Then the LORD said to Samuel, 11"I am
sorry that I ever made Saul king, for he
has not been loyal to me and has refused
to obey my command." Samuel was so
deeply moved when he heard this that he
cried out to the LORD all night.
12Early the next morning Samuel went
to find Saul. Someone told him, "Saul
went to the town of Carmel to set up a
monument to himself; then he went on to
Gilgal."
13When Samuel finally found him, Saul
greeted him cheerfully. "May the LORD
bless you," he said. "I have carried out the
LORD's command!"
14"Then what is all the bleating of sheep
and goats and the lowing of cattle I hear?"
Samuel demanded.
15"It's true that the army spared the
best of the sheep, goats, and cattle," Saul
admitted. "But they are going to sacrifice
them to the LORD your God. We have de-
stroyed everything else."
16Then Samuel said to Saul, "Stop! Lis-
ten to what the LORD told me last night!"
"What did he tell you?" Saul asked.
17And Samuel told him, "Although you
may think little of yourself, are you not
the leader of the tribes of Israel? The
LORD has anointed you king of Israel.
18And the LORD sent you on a mission and
told you, 'Go and completely destroy the
sinners, the Amalekites, until they are all
dead.' 19Why haven't you obeyed the
LORD? Why did you rush for the plunder
and do what was evil in the LORD's
sight?"
20"But I did obey the LORD," Saul in-
sisted. "I carried out the mission he gave
me. I brought back King Agag, but I de-
stroyed everyone else. 21Then my troops
brought in the best of the sheep, goats,
cattle, and plunder to sacrifice to the LORD
your God in Gilgal."
22But Samuel replied,

"What is more pleasing to the LORD:
  your burnt offerings and sacrifices
  or your obedience to his voice?
Listen! Obedience is better than
    sacrifice,
  and submission is better than
    offering the fat of rams.
23 Rebellion is as sinful as witchcraft,
  and stubbornness as bad as
    worshiping idols.
So because you have rejected the
    command of the LORD,
  he has rejected you as king."

24Then Saul admitted to Samuel, "Yes, I
have sinned. I have disobeyed your in-
structions and the LORD's command, for I
was afraid of the people and did what
they demanded. 25But now, please forgive
my sin and come back with me so that I
may worship the LORD."
26But Samuel replied, "I will not go back
with you! Since you have rejected the
LORD's command, he has rejected you as
king of Israel."
27As Samuel turned to go, Saul tried to
hold him back and tore the hem of his
robe. 28And Samuel said to him, "The LORD

has torn the kingdom of Israel from you today and has given it to someone else—one who is better than you. 29And he who is the Glory of Israel will not lie, nor will he change his mind, for he is not human that he should change his mind!"

30Then Saul pleaded again, "I know I have sinned. But please, at least honor me before the elders of my people and before Israel by coming back with me so that I may worship the LORD your God."
31So Samuel finally agreed and went back with him, and Saul worshiped the LORD.

32Then Samuel said, "Bring King Agag to me." Agag arrived full of hope, for he thought, "Surely the worst is over, and I have been spared!"* 33But Samuel said, "As your sword has killed the sons of many mothers, now your mother will be childless." And Samuel cut Agag to pieces before the LORD at Gilgal.

34Then Samuel went home to Ramah, and Saul returned to his house at Gibeah of Saul. 35Samuel never went to meet with Saul again, but he mourned constantly for him. And the LORD was sorry he had ever made Saul king of Israel.

15:3 The Hebrew term used here refers to the complete consecration of things or people to the LORD, either by destroying them or by giving them as an offering; also in 15:8, 9, 15, 18, 20, 21. 15:32 Dead Sea Scrolls and Greek version read *Agag arrived hesitantly, for he thought, "Surely this is the bitterness of death."*

NOTES

15:2 ***I have decided to settle accounts.*** The form of *paqad* [TH6485, ZH7212] here may be understood as a present perfect (GKC §106g) and translated as in NLT. But it also may refer to future action (GKC §106m) in the sense of "I will settle accounts," or as a normal past tense in the sense of "I have observed what Amalek did to Israel."

for opposing Israel. Lit., "that he set to [Israel]." This is best understood as a technical military use of *sim* [TH7760, ZH8492] (put, place, set); thus "when he set himself against [Israel]" (S. R. Driver 1913:122; BDB 964b.4.a).

15:5 ***and lay in wait.*** The word *wayyareb* is probably a defectively written Hiphil (*wayya'areb*) of the root *'arab* [TH693, ZH741] (lie in ambush) rather than *rib* [TH7378, ZH8189] (contend, plead a case). See GKC §68i; BDB 936d; 70c.

15:9 ***the fat calves.*** Lit., "the double portions." This is usually translated as "the fatlings" because of the likelihood that in *hammishnim* [TH4932, ZH5467] (the doubles?) the Shin and the Mem have been accidentally transposed from an original *hashemanim* [TH8081, ZH9043], which is a plural form of the adjective *shemen* (fat) and is to be taken as a substantive in apposition with what precedes, resulting in a rendering such as "the best of the sheep and cattle, that is, the fatlings."

worthless. Lit., "despised." The MT's anomalous *nemibzah* here is best read as *nibzeh* (Niphal participle of "despise," *bazah* [TH959, ZH1022]). Cf. S. R. Driver 1913:124.

poor quality. This translates an unusual use of the Niphal participle of *masas* [TH4549, ZH5022] meaning "dissolve" or "melt." Here the idea may be "wasted," "thin," or "diseased." Some suggest reading *nim'asah* or *nim'eseth,* also Niphal participles, but from *ma'as* [TH3988, ZH4415], meaning "reject," thus "worthless" (BDB 549).

15:11 ***I am sorry.*** A more literal rendering is "I *repent* that I made Saul king" (*nakham* [TH5162, ZH5714]). This is repeated in 15:35b: "The LORD *repented* that he had made Saul king over Israel." These two statements are to be contrasted with the statement of 15:29 (lit.): "Moreover, the Everlasting One of Israel does not lie nor *repent,* for he is not a man that he should *repent.*" It is not clear from the NLT rendering of these verses that the same Hebrew word is used in them in a way that might seem to be contradictory. See the commentary on 15:29 for further discussion.

15:13 ***When.*** LXX Vaticanus inserts a lengthy phrase at the beginning of this verse ("and behold he was offering up a whole burnt offering to the LORD, the chief of the spoils which he brought out of Amalek. And Samuel came to Saul . . ."). Pisano (1984:204-207) and Long (1989:143-144) provide good reasons for giving preference to the shorter reading of MT.

15:15 ***the army spared the best of the sheep.*** The Hebrew word translated "army" is *'am* [TH5971A, ZH6639] (see also vv. 21, 24), a word normally translated more broadly as "people." But as Hulst (TLOT 2.904) points out, in 1 Sam 15 and 2 Sam 10 "*'am* always refers to the fighting unit accompanying a person, belonging to him, and standing under his leadership."

15:19 ***Why haven't you obeyed the LORD?*** Lit., "Why, then, have you not obeyed (*shama'* [TH8085, ZH9048]) the voice (*qol* [TH6963, ZH7754]) of the LORD?" This wording is a clear reflection of the wording of Samuel's charge to Saul in 15:1: *shema leqol dibre yhwh* ("listen to the voice of the words of the LORD"; NLT, "listen to this message from the LORD").

15:22 ***Listen!*** For the use of *hinneh* [TH2009, ZH2180] as a reinforcement of an affirmation (often translated "surely"), see Joüon and Muraoka §164a.

15:23 ***stubbornness as bad as worshiping idols.*** The comparison of rebellion and stubbornness with witchcraft and worshiping idols suggests the extreme seriousness of such sins.

he has rejected you. Heb., *wayyim'aseka* [TH3988, ZH4415]. The Waw here (cf. *wa* in the transliteration) is not the coordinating conjunction "and" but a "waw of apodosis," frequent in causal clauses (cf. Joüon and Muraoka §176e).

15:26 ***as king.*** For the use of *min* [TH4480, ZH4946] (from) with a consecutive meaning before an infinitive (cf. 15:23 "so as to be far *from* being king"), see Joüon and Muraoka §133e.

15:32 ***full of hope.*** The derivation and meaning of *ma'adannoth* [TH4575A, ZH5051] is disputed. Some (as NLT), including the NIV ("confidently") and NASB ("cheerfully"), ascribe it to the root *'adan* [TH5727, ZH6357] ("luxuriate," cf. Neh 9:25). Others, including NRSV ("haltingly"), ascribe it to *ma'ad* [TH4571, ZH5048] ("totter," cf. Ps 26:1). Still others, including McCarter (1980b:260, 264), Stoebe (1973:289, 292), and Youngblood (1992:680), ascribe it by metathesis to *'anad* [TH6029, ZH6698] ("bind," cf. Prov 6:21)—"Agag arrived bound." Since the word occurs only here and in Job 38:31, where it is in parallelism with a word meaning "bands," this latter derivation is probably to be preferred.

15:33 ***cut . . . to pieces.*** The word *shasap* [TH8158, ZH9119] occurs only here in the OT. Its meaning is obscure. BDB suggests "hew in pieces," which has been followed by most translations. The LXX has the more general *esphaxen* [TG4969, ZG5377] ("he slaughtered").

COMMENTARY

Saul Continues to Fall Short of the Ideal of the Covenantal King (15:1-9). In the preceding chapters Saul has repeatedly fallen short of his responsibilities as a covenantal king. Upon his return to Gibeah after being anointed king, he took no action against the Philistine garrison located there, in spite of the implicit suggestion of Samuel that he do so (see comments on 10:7; 13:3). Moreover, when he was questioned by his uncle about what Samuel had said to him, he avoided telling him that he had been chosen to be king (cf. commentary on 10:14-16). At the Mizpah assembly, he hid among the supplies during his public selection by lot to be king (see commentary on 10:22), and then after his inauguration, he disobeyed the Lord's command through Samuel to wait for seven days for Samuel's arrival at Gilgal (see commentary on 13:7b-15). Samuel rebuked him for this offense and told him that because of his disobedience he would not have a continuing dynasty. In chapter 14 Saul compares unfavorably with his son Jonathan, and in Israel's battle with the Philistines, initiated by Jonathan, he is more of a hindrance to Israel's success than a help (see commentary on ch 14). All of this combines to raise serious questions about Saul's future as Israel's anointed king.

As chapter 15 opens, Samuel came to Saul with a new word from the Lord, and thus presented him with a new opportunity to demonstrate a willingness to assume the responsibilities that were his as king over God's covenant people. Samuel's opening words were reminders to Saul of his anointing and of his responsibility to be obedient to the words of the Lord's prophet (15:1). Saul was then given a clearly defined task that was presented to him as a "message from the LORD" (15:1-3). Saul and his army were to be the instrument of God's judgment on the Amalekites for their attack on Israel at the time of the Exodus (cf. Exod 17:8-15; Deut 25:17-19). Saul was told that he must completely destroy the Amalekites along with all their possessions. A faithful execution of this task would demonstrate that, in spite of past failures, Saul truly did desire to be a faithful servant of the Lord.

Although the task was clearly defined, it was not an easy one. This was a command to extend the practice of *kherem* [TH2764, ZH3051], which had been carried out against the inhabitants of the land of Canaan at the time of the conquest, to the Amalekites.[1] Israel's normal rules of engagement in warfare did not include *kherem*. Deuteronomy 20, in fact, limits its application to the inhabitants of Canaan. When Israel fought with nations beyond the borders of Canaan, they were to make offers of peace, they were not to kill the women and children, and they were permitted to take plunder for their own use (Deut 20:10-15). But because of the Amalekites' particularly egregious attack against Israel while they were on their journey from Egypt to Mt. Sinai, the Lord had vowed that he would "erase the memory of Amalek from under heaven" (Exod 17:14). On that occasion, the Amalekites had attempted to prevent Israel from reaching Sinai, where they were to enter into covenant with the Lord and be established as his covenant people. The Amalekites were not just another heathen people. They were a people bent on destroying Israel. This was an act that would challenge God's redemptive purposes. Much later in the Old Testament period, Haman the Agagite (likely a descendant of Agag, cf. Esth 3:1) again attempted to destroy all the Jewish people in the Persian kingdom of Xerxes. This was as Moses had said at the time of the Exodus—that the Lord would "be at war with Amalek generation after generation" (Exod 17:16). Saul had been called to participate in this war. This war was not merely a conflict between Israel and the Amalekites, nor between Saul and Agag, but rather a war between Yahweh and Amalek. Saul has been chosen as an instrument in the Lord's hands to bring his judgment on Amalek.

Saul responded promptly to Samuel's message and assembled a large army at Telaim in the southern part of Judah (15:4). Because the Kenites inhabited some of the same territory as the Amalekites, and because they, unlike the Amalekites, had been friendly to the Israelites at the time of the conquest, and even later,[2] Saul gave them advance warning about the impending attack, and they left the area (15:6). The war was clearly not designed for territorial expansion. If it were, the Kenites would not have been warned in advance. It was a war of Yahweh against a people that had set themselves up against Israel.

Saul's success in battle is described in 15:7. He swept through the area south of Judah and killed Amalekites all the way to the eastern frontier of Egypt (Shur). But 15:8-9 informs us that he spared the Amalekite king, Agag, and kept the best of the livestock, killing only what was "worthless or of poor quality" (see notes on 15:9). These were clear violations of the mandate of 15:3. It appears that Saul again failed to function as a true covenantal king.

Samuel Confronts Saul and Announces That the Lord Has Rejected Him as King (15:10-35). While Saul was returning from the battle, the Lord spoke to Samuel and informed him that Saul had not performed the task that he had been given. Two specific things are mentioned in the Lord's indictment of Saul (15:11). He turned aside from following the Lord (NLT, "has not been loyal to me"), and he did not carry out the Lord's commands (lit., "my words"). The language specifying this dual offence defines the essence of covenantal kingship. Following after the Lord (i.e., to be *'akhar yhwh* [TH310/3068, ZH339/3378]) means recognizing afresh the sovereignty of Yahweh over Israel and its human king. This was the fundamental requirement of the restructuring of the theocracy as it was defined by Samuel in 12:14b (see commentary on 12:14). Saul demonstrated his unwillingness to do this. The refusal to carry out the Lord's commands was a violation of the very words that the Lord had spoken to Saul through Samuel (15:2-3). Consequently, the Lord said he was sorry that he ever made Saul king (15:11a).

Samuel was deeply upset by what the Lord said (15:11). The Hebrew reads, "Samuel burned with anger" (*kharah* [TH2734, ZH3013]). Although the specific focus of Samuel's anger is not specified, it would not appear to be an anger directed at God, but rather at Saul for another failure to do his duty as covenantal king. In spite of this, Samuel interceded for Saul all through the night, apparently in an attempt to dissuade the Lord from his plan to reject Saul as king (15:11). Here we see a side of Samuel that is often overlooked in connection with the sternness of Samuel's treatment of Saul in the remainder of the chapter. This verse, along with the statement of 15:35 that Samuel "mourned constantly" for Saul, shows that he took no pleasure in confronting Saul with the Lord's words of rejection, but to the contrary, even though he was deeply disturbed by Saul's disappointing behavior, he pleaded for mercy on his behalf.

The next morning Samuel set out to find Saul. The seemingly incidental report in 15:12 that Saul had set up a monument to himself at Carmel, and that he had gone on to Gilgal, carries enormous significance for understanding the remainder of the chapter. The reference to a monument in Saul's honor speaks volumes concerning Saul's frame of mind subsequent to Israel's victory over the Amalekites. That Saul would set up a monument to himself suggests that in his own mind the battle against Amalek had ceased to be the Lord's battle. It had become his own battle.[3] He apparently viewed himself as the successful military leader whose accomplishment merited the sort of recognition that a victory monument would secure.[4] From this perspective, it is only a short step to the conclusion that as payment for such a great accomplishment Saul had a right to share in the plunder and participate in a victory celebration in which the defeated enemy king would be put on display and a monument to the victorious king would be unveiled (van den Berg 1996a:129). In this scenario, Saul was no longer subordinate to Yahweh as an instrument of Yahweh's judgment on Amalek, but rather he had become the autonomous absolute monarch. In effect, he had become the antitheocratic king. By telling the reader in advance about Saul's erection of a monument to himself, the narrator has given the reader good reason to question Saul's subsequent protestations of innocence and his effort to put a pious spin on his actions.

When Samuel found Saul, Saul greeted him warmly. Before Samuel could say a word, Saul told him "I have carried out the LORD's command!" (15:13). Saul's statement flatly contradicts the Lord's statement to Samuel in 15:11 ("he has not been loyal to me and has refused to obey my command"). Saul's claim of obedience, even before Samuel had asked him a question, seems a bit suspicious. It is as if Saul had something to hide and he was well aware of it. Samuel did not directly challenge Saul's statement, but simply inquired, "What is all the bleating of sheep and goats and the lowing of cattle I hear?" (15:14). Saul had a ready and quick response. He claimed that they had spared the best animals in order to offer them as sacrifices to the Lord (15:15). While the response may seem to be a perfectly reasonable justification for saving the best of the animals, a close look at the wording of Saul's response suggests that everything was not as it might appear to be.[5] It should be noted that Saul claimed that the animals were for a sacrifice to "the LORD *your* God." Does this not inadvertently let slip the truth? He did not say "the LORD *our* God," but "the LORD *your* God." By putting it in this way, it appears that Saul did not include himself among followers of Yahweh.[6] Although as things progress he may attempt to cover his disobedient behavior with pious talk, it becomes clearer and clearer that deep down Saul's heart is not right with the Lord.

Samuel responded by reminding Saul that he was the anointed king of Israel (15:17) and that the Lord had sent him on a specific mission, which included completely destroying the Amalekites and taking no plunder (15:18). He then told Saul that he had not obeyed the Lord, and he had done evil in the Lord's sight (15:19, see note). Saul, however, was still not prepared to admit his guilt, and he attempted to justify his actions by claiming that he had listened (*shama'* [TH8085, ZH9048]) to the voice (*qol* [TH6963, ZH7754]) of Yahweh (NLT, "but I did obey the LORD"), that he had killed all the Amalekites except Agag, and that it was his troops who had kept some of the best of the animals to offer as sacrifices "to the LORD your God in Gilgal" (15:20-21). Samuel, however, did not want to hear any more of Saul's excuses, and he responded in 15:22-23 with one of the most profound statements in the Old Testament concerning the distinction between true religion and religious or ritual acts.[7] This statement climaxed with Samuel's telling Saul that because he had rejected the command of the Lord, the Lord had rejected him as king.

Samuel's statement that "obedience is better than sacrifice" (15:22) was the same message that Israel's prophets repeatedly proclaimed to a people who "come near to me with their mouth and honor me with their lips, but their hearts are far from me" (Isa 29:13, NIV; cf. Matt 15:8; Mark 7:6). The prophets' denunciation of Israel for ritualism was so strong that sometimes their critiques of it almost seemed to suggest that they favored abolishing the cult and replacing it with ethics.[8] But this was not their point, nor was it Samuel's. What both Samuel and the prophets championed is consistent: God is not interested in displays of outward piety that are used as a cover for disobedience. Religious or ritual acts that are performed in the absence of a heart desire to live in obedience to the Lord's commands are not only unacceptable, they are an abomination (cf. Isa 66:2b-4). The tendency for religious people to move toward this sort of hypocrisy is a constant danger.

When Samuel says that "rebellion is as sinful as witchcraft" (15:23), his language echoes what he had said at the time of the inauguration of the monarchy at Gilgal (12:14-15, see commentary) when he told the people and Saul that "if you do not rebel against the LORD's commands, then both you and your king will show that you recognize the LORD as your God. But if you rebel against the LORD's commands . . . his hand will be . . . heavy upon you." Saul had violated a fundamental requirement of the terms governing the theocracy, terms that had been made clear to him at the time he assumed office. So Samuel concluded by telling him that because he had rejected the command of the Lord, the Lord had rejected him as king (15:23b).

Upon hearing that his disobedience would result in dismissal from the royal office, Saul appeared to reverse himself and confess his sin. Although Saul had said that he had carried out the Lord's command in 15:13, now he said, "I have disobeyed your instructions and the LORD's command" (15:24), and he prefaced this confession by admitting that he had sinned. He then asked for Samuel's forgiveness and requested Samuel to accompany him in the worship of the Lord (15:25). Saul's confession, however, fell on deaf ears, because Samuel refused the request to go with him, and he repeated almost verbatim what he had said before: "Since you have rejected the LORD's command, he has rejected you as king of Israel" (15:26). It is clear that in Samuel's mind Saul's confession was not acceptable. The question is why.

The first thing to notice is that Saul's confession was a sort of "yes, but" response (Frisch 1996:98). He said, "Yes, I have sinned," but then he qualified this acknowledgment by saying, "I was afraid of the people and did what they demanded" (15:24). He then added to his confession the double request to Samuel to not only forgive him but also to accompany him in the worship of the Lord (15:25). This "yes, but" sort of confession contrasts with David's unqualified confession in the aftermath of the Bathsheba affair (2 Sam 12:13) and his similar confession after his sin of numbering the people (2 Sam 24:10).[9] In addition, close attention to the wording of Saul's confession reveals a serious deficiency. The word obey (*shama'* [TH8085, ZH9048], see note on 15:19) has occurred several times earlier in the chapter (15:1, 19-20, 22 [x2]) in connection with obeying God's words (*debarim* [TH1697, ZH1821]) or God's voice (*qol* [TH6963, ZH7754]). But in Saul's confession he said he feared the people and "obeyed (*shama'*) their voice (*qol*)." As Frisch (1996:99) has pointed out, "In 15:24 a shift occurs, so that obedience to God's command becomes instead yielding to the voice of the people, as a reason for disobeying God's command."[10]

But it is not only the term "obey" (*shama'*) that appears in an inverted sense in Saul's confession; the same thing happens with his use of the term "fear" (*yare'* [TH3372, ZH3707]). When Samuel laid out the governing principles of the theocracy at the time of the inauguration of Saul as king, he said, "Now if you fear and worship the LORD and listen to his voice, and if you do not rebel against the LORD's commands, then both you and your king will show that you recognize the LORD as your God" (12:14). Saul's justification for not obeying the Lord's command but rather obeying the voice of the people was because "I was afraid of the people" (15:24). So in Saul's confession, fear of the people has been substituted for fear of God, but this in fact serves to intensify rather than justify his sin (Frisch 1996:100).

Added to Saul's inadvertently self-incriminating attempt to justify his disobedience and shift responsibility for it from himself to the people was his desire to avoid any public loss of face through an open break between himself and Samuel. Because of this he requested Samuel to accompany him in the worship of the Lord (15:25). The real purpose of his request becomes clear when, after Saul refused to accede to it (15:26), Saul repeated the request with the added explanation, "At least honor me before the elders of my people and before Israel" (15:30). When confession of sin becomes so closely linked with concern about public image and honor, the quality of the confession is suspect.[11] In this case, after Samuel denied his request and began to walk away, Saul tore the hem of his robe, either in an attempt to hold him back, or as a symbolic gesture of supplication (15:27).[12] This incident gave Samuel an additional opportunity to reaffirm Saul's rejection by the Lord, using the torn robe as a symbol of Saul's loss of the kingdom (15:28). The person to whom the kingdom had been given, of course, as yet unknown to both Samuel and Saul, was David, who is characterized in 15:28 as someone who is "better" than Saul.

Samuel then reinforced the finality of the Lord's rejection of Saul and his choice of a person "better" than he with the statement that "the Glory of Israel will not lie, nor will he change his mind, for he is not human that he should change his mind!" (15:29). Samuel's assertion that the Lord will not change his mind (*nakham* [TH5162, ZH5714]) is often said to contradict the statements in 15:11 and 35, where it is said that the Lord was "sorry" (*nakham*) he had made Saul king.[13] Long (1993b:52), however, has argued that this alleged "contradiction is more apparent than real" and that, in agreement with Numbers 23:19, the statement in 15:29 is intended "to combat the erroneous idea that it is easy to talk God round, and that his threats and promises need not be taken seriously" (Eichrodt 1961:1, 216, quoted by Long). With respect to the statements in 15:11 and 35, Long argues that in view of "the range of meaning of *nakham* in the Niphal (e.g., 'regret,' 'relent,' '[allow oneself to] be sorry')," it is not inconsistent to say that "God may *regret* having made Saul king, while still refusing to *change his mind* with respect to Saul's rejection." In other words, Long is suggesting that 15:11, 35 and 15:29 are to be understood in a complementary rather than contradictory sense.[14] Both speak the truth. God is a personal being, not an Unmoved Mover. He responds appropriately to the faithfulness or unfaithfulness of his people (cf. Jer 18:7-10; Joel 2:13-14), but at the same time he remains constant in his purposes.[15] In God's doing all things according to the counsel of his own will (Eph 1:11), he does not act arbitrarily or unjustly, as do human beings. The Lord's initial choosing of Saul and his subsequent rejection of him is, therefore, not in conflict with the constancy of who he is, but, rather, is consistent with it. While this interpretation provides a reasonable harmonization for the seeming discord between the two statements, Fretheim (1985) offers a different suggestion that merits serious consideration as well.

In Fretheim's view, the focus of the statement in 15:29 is on David rather than Saul (the previous verse reads, "The LORD has torn the kingdom from you today and has given it to someone else—one who is better than you" [15:28]). Fretheim suggests that the statement about God not changing his mind in 15:29 is forward looking rather than backward looking, and it does not address the matter of Saul's rejection, but instead speaks about the irrevocable nature of God's decision to give the kingdom to David. Given this understanding, Fretheim (1985:597-598) says, "God has made a decision with respect to David, and with respect to that decision God will not repent. This statement, therefore, does not have general reference to God as one who never repents with regard to anything. Rather, it has reference to God's decision to give the kingdom to David. That decision is irrevocable . . . the point is not that God's repentance is a divine action which is not to be repeated ever again in any situation; the point is that God's repentance regarding the promise to David is foreclosed. There may well be other persons and actions concerning which God will repent of a promised good (cf. Jer 18:9-10)." This understanding also addresses the seeming contradiction between 15:10, 35 on the one hand, and 15:29 on the other, and in addition it connects well with the anointing of David in the very next chapter. It is notable that Psalm 110:4 also speaks of the Lord "not repenting" (cf. KJV) with respect to the inviolability of the royal Davidic line.[16]

Saul's response was to admit for a second time that he had sinned (15:30; cf. 15:24), but his confession was again linked with a request that Samuel accompany him in worship (cf. 15:25), so that there would be no public evidence of a break between them. Saul appealed to Samuel to "at least honor me before the elders of my people and before Israel," and went on to say that he wanted Samuel to accompany him so that he could worship "the LORD *your* God" (15:30, my italics). Saul's use of pronouns indicates that he not only has a faulty view of his role as king (the people were not *his* people, but were the *Lord's* people, cf. 14:24), but also that he has distanced himself from inclusion among the Lord's people (he does not say the Lord *my* God, cf. 15:21). First Samuel 15:31 has usually been understood to say that Samuel changed his mind, and contrary to his previous denial of Saul's request (15:26), he now, for some unexplained reason, decided to accompany him. This understanding is reflected in the NLT rendering of 15:31—"Samuel finally agreed and went back with him, and Saul worshiped the LORD."[17]

Samuel's concern, however, was quite different from Saul's. Samuel's concern was for the honor of God's Kingdom, not for the personal honor of Saul. So Samuel set out to complete what Saul had left undone. He called for Agag, the king of the Amalekites, to be brought to him, and he executed him in fulfillment of the Lord's original command to Saul (15:32-33). Samuel and Saul then parted ways, Samuel going back to Ramah, and Saul to Gibeah (15:34). This was the last time they spoke to each other (15:35).[18] Their parting not only marked the end of a personal relationship, but it also terminated the continuing legitimacy of Saul's reign as a covenantal king.[19] His abortive kingship had proven to be a failure because he was unwilling to submit to the requirements of his office, which were explained to him by Samuel at the beginning of his reign (cf. 10:25; 12:14-15). The stage was now set for the introduction of the person "better than [Saul]" (15:28) to fulfill the role in which Saul had failed.

ENDNOTES

1. This is the word translated "*completely destroy* the entire Amalekite nation" (see 15:3, NLT mg). Translation of the word *kherem* [TH2764, ZH3051], which occurs in both verbal and noun forms, is difficult. The verbal form has been translated, among other ways, as "put under the ban" (Alter 1999:87; Klein 1983:144), "devote-to-destruction" (Fox 1999:69), "proscribe" (Josh 6:17, NJPS), "accurse" or "devote" (Josh 22:20; Num 18:14, KJV). The general idea is to set something apart from personal use to be completely devoted to the Lord, either by placing it in the Lord's service or by destroying it. NIDOTTE 2.276-277 defines the term as "a special act of consecration. It involves consecration of something or someone as a permanent and definitive offering for the sanctuary; or in war, the consecration of a city and its inhabitants to destruction and the carrying out of this destruction. The verb denotes also the total annihilation of a population in war." This latter feature of *kherem* is described by Alter as "one of the cruelest practices of ancient Near Eastern warfare" and as a "ferocious imperative" (Alter 1999:87). The practice has often been viewed as a primitive form of savage brutality that discredits the God concept of the OT. What should be understood, however, is that the conquest of Canaan is not viewed in the OT as simply an aggressive war of territorial expansion by Israel against the Canaanites, but rather as God's judgment on the Canaanites for their wickedness through the instrumentality of Israel's practice of *kherem* (cf. Gen 15:16; Deut 20:16-18). In this perspective, the destruction of the Canaanites is to be understood as a portrayal of divine wrath against ungodly people that anticipates the eschatological Day of the Lord (Isa 13; Joel 2–3; Amos 5:8-20; Zech 14:1-11; 1 Thess 5:1-10; 2 Pet 3:10). As Kline (1972:162-164) has said, the conquest of Canaan should not be viewed as an example of "arrested evolution" in the ethical sphere, but rather as an example of "anticipated eschatology." See further: Longman and Reid 1995; McConville 2002:322-323; NIDOTTE 4.816-817 and especially the contributions of Longman to the volume edited by Stanley N. Gundry (2003) on "Four Views of God and Canaanite Genocide." In this volume Longman (2003:184-185) argues that "there is both continuity and discontinuity between the Old and New Testaments on the issue of *kherem* warfare. The God of the Old Testament is not a different God from the God we encounter in the NT. Nor did God change his mind. The war against the Canaanites was simply an earlier phase of the battle that comes to its climax on the cross and its completion at the final judgment. The object of warfare moves from the Canaanites, who are the object of God's wrath for their sin, to the spiritual powers and principalities, and then finally to the utter destruction of all evil, human and spiritual."
2. The Kenites were a Midianite tribe. Moses had a Kenite wife (Exod 2:16, 21-22; Judg 1:16), and Jael, the wife of Heber the Kenite, killed Sisera, the commander of Jabin's army, in the victory of Deborah and Barak over the Canaanites (Judg 4–5).
3. This is the same attitude reflected in Saul's statement: "Let a curse fall on anyone who eats before evening—before I have full revenge on *my* enemies" (14:24, my italics; see commentary).

4. Long (1989:142-143) notes some of the different views on the nature of Saul's monument. While most interpreters agree that the monument was a victory stela of some sort, it is disputed whether or not it was inscribed, and if it was, whether it ascribed the victory to the Lord or to Saul. Long comments, "It is rather doubtful, however, that the import of Saul's monument, whether inscribed or not, can be understood as gratitude to Yahweh. . . . Saul's monument was erected 'to (or for) himself' (*lo* [TH3807.1/2050.2, ZH4200/2257])."
5. Gunn (1980:48-54), however, argues that Saul gives a "splendidly forthright reply" with no evasion of the "pertinent 'facts.'" For this reason Gunn suggests that it is not the "facts" that are in dispute, but rather "their interpretation vis-à-vis the instruction." He then argues that the problem is ambiguity in the original instruction, involving a confusion of *kherem* [TH2764, ZH3051] (the ban) and *zebakh* [TH2077, ZH2285] (sacrifice) in Saul's mind, so that he was unaware that it would be objectionable to bring the animals and Agag to Gilgal to be sacrificed and killed there instead of doing so on the battlefield. Gunn's conclusion (1980:56) is that "there is essentially no failure on Saul's part to be accounted for, no failure, that is to say, for which he can be held seriously culpable." This fits with Gunn's overall view that Saul is a victim of fate (see commentary on 9:25–10:8).
6. There is a similar statement by Hezekiah to Isaiah in Isa 37:4 (paralleled in 2 Kgs 19:4) in which Hezekiah seems to distance himself from Yahweh. Oswalt (1986:646-647) notes that some commentators, such as, for example, J. Calvin, understand Hezekiah's reference to "your God" in speaking to Isaiah to be a reference to "Isaiah's special calling as a prophet," but others, such as Delitzsch, understand it as expressing a "certain reticence on Hezekiah's part." Oswalt thinks the latter is the more likely, and says, "The king is aware that, from one perspective at least, had God been truly his, as he claimed, he would have been more careful of God's honor. So here in shame he testifies that if God is to help them it will not be because he, the king, has some special claim upon God."
7. First Samuel 15:22-23 is in the form of Hebrew poetry rather than in the characteristic prose of the surrounding narrative. The abrupt change to the poetic form (which Alter has called "heightened speech") signals the importance of these two verses. Long (1989:29) points out that "the elevated diction of the verses is an indication of their *significance* or *weight*." He cites Alter (1981:28) who says that the inset of formal verse is "a common convention in biblical narrative for direct speech that has some significantly summarizing or ceremonial function." A similar sudden intrusion of poetic speech into a prose narrative is found in Gen 2:23.
8. See for example: Isa 1:11-17; Jer 7:21-23; Hos 6:6; Amos 5:21-27; Mic 6:6-8.
9. Brueggemann (1990a:115) calls attention to the contrast between the Lord's acceptance of David's confession and his rejection of Saul's. He notes that, "In both accounts the king is indicted and guilty. In both the king admits guilt, repents, and seeks forgiveness. Then, however, the narratives present sharply contrasting outcomes. Saul is rejected; his confession is ignored and no forgiveness is offered. By contrast David has his confession accepted. He is forgiven and permitted to continue his rule (2 Sam. 12:13)." Brueggemann's conclusion is that "Either the God who forgives is arbitrary or we must acknowledge the bias of the tradition for David and against Saul." This conclusion, however, ignores the significant qualitative differences between the two confessions.

   In subsequent comments on this passage, Brueggemann (1997:370-371) puts the above argument in even more stark terms. He comments, "David can do anything he wants, because David is linked to Yahweh in modes of acceptance and affirmation heretofore unavailable in Israel and certainly with Saul. In 1 Samuel 15 we note another matter. Saul is presented as an honorable, straightforward man. He does not argue with Samuel about the savage indictment pronounced against him . . . Saul seeks forgiveness for a confessed sin . . . so that he may 'worship the Lord.' But Samuel will have no part of forgiveness. It is as though Samuel (and Yahweh) is in a hurry, prepared to use any theological, political occasion in order to displace Saul with 'a neighbor of yours.' . . . The contrast between Saul's fate at the hands of Yahweh and that of David is stunning. . . . after the Uriah-Bathsheba episode, David also responds directly, 'I have sinned' (2 Sam 12:13). That is all. David does not, like Saul, appeal for forgiveness. But forgiveness is in any case promptly granted by Nathan . . . the narrative evidences no curiosity about why penitent Saul cannot be forgiven while David can. . . . Nonetheless these contrasts . . . attest that Yahweh is not a consistent God of command and sanction or, alternatively, of deed and consequence. Conversely, they attest that Yahweh is not a God who consistently forgives. . . . Saul is treated unfairly by Yahweh." Brueggemann's argument fails by not taking into account either the legitimate questions about the sincerity of Saul's confession as compared to David's, nor the explicit statements that both Samuel and the Lord grieved over Saul's failures (15:11, 35).

10. Frisch (1996:99) cites Alter (1981:93), who comments, "Saul apologizes that he has transgressed the word of the Lord and instead listened to the voice of the people (*vox populi* being here the thematic opposite of *vox dei*)."
11. In the terms of 2 Cor 7:10, Saul's response to Samuel's rebuke seems to be a "sorrow without repentance." As Hughes (1962:272-273) notes, this sort of "sorrow of the world" is "not sorrow because of the heinousness of sin as rebellion against God, but sorrow because of the painful and unwelcome consequences of sin. Self is its central point. . . . Thus the sorrow of the world manifests itself in self-pity rather than in contrition and turning to God for mercy." In Saul's case, self-pity is clearly prominent in his subsequent outlook on life (cf. 22:8, "For not one of you has told me. . . . You're not even sorry for me," and 23:21 where Saul says to the Ziphites, "The LORD bless you. . . . At last someone is concerned about me!"
12. On the basis of comparative religious material from Mesopotamia and Ugarit, Kruger (1988) has argued that the symbolic gesture of "grasping the hem" is best understood as an "act of supplication."
13. Brueggemann (1990a:115) says, "This verse contradicts verse 10 [*sic*, 11] (and later 15:35), which asserts that Yahweh does repent and change heart, so that Yahweh could both choose and reject Saul at different times." McCarter (1980b:268) argues that "the contradiction to 15:11 ('I [Yahweh!] repent . . .') that this statement ('Israel's Everlasting One . . . does not repent . . .') contains is so blatant that we must question its originality. It may be a late addition to the text (derived from Num 23:19?), penned by a redactor to whom the suggestion of a divine change of mind was unacceptable."
14. Peels (1996:70) says, "The notion of God's 'repentance' in 1 Samuel 15 has two sides that both contain a truth. They do not correct each other but rather supplement each other. God has 'sorrow' or 'repentance' over Saul (15:11, 35), but this does not mean uncertainty or arbitrariness (15:29). It does mean, however, that God may react or change his manner of dealing with his creatures (15:11, 25). Summary: God's 'repentance' is a reality, it is a response to human guilt—but this 'repentance' is not the same as human 'repentance' that may be capricious or arbitrary" (translation mine). Of the similar statement in Num 23:19 ("God is not a man, so he does not lie. He is not human, so he *does not change his mind*" (*nakham* [TH5162, ZH5714]), Peels says

(1996:71) that this statement is also not saying that God cannot "repent" but rather it is saying that God does not repent in a human manner, just as is the case in 15:29.

15. Kaiser (1983:250) comments, "God can and does change in his actions and emotions towards men so as not to change in his basic character. God's repentance does not prove him to be fickle, mutable, and variable in his nature or purpose." Advocates of "open theism" have often appealed to texts like 15:11, 35 as support for their view that God was in some way taken by surprise by Saul's unexpected and disappointing behavior, and he was, therefore, forced to move to "plan B" and the choice of David to replace him. In assessing this viewpoint, B. Ware (2000:90-91) says that "when God is said to repent, it indicates (1) his awareness that the human situation has altered and (2) his desire to act in a way fitting to this changed situation. In Exodus 32:14, God was aware of and took into account the urgent prayer of Moses. In 1 Samuel 15:11 and 35, God was aware of and took into account the failure of Saul. In no cases of the divine repentance is it necessary to go further than this and say that God *learned* something new *by* this changed situation. Rather, these expressions of repentance may indicate more narrowly that God was aware of what had changed and chose to act in accordance with this new situation. His awareness and choice to act accordingly *may have been from eternity*, yet he interacted in the temporal and existential flow of developing and changing human situations."

16. Moberly (1998:120), in discussing the statement of 15:29 that God will "not change his mind," says that in the context of 15:28b (where it is stated that God will give the kingship to David as a replacement for Saul), what this statement denies is "not the responsive dynamics of divine 'repentance' as consistently presupposed and expounded elsewhere in the story [15:11, 35]. Nor is the concern as such to deny that God could 'repent of his repentance' in the particular case of Saul. Rather, the text specifies the positive commitment of God to make David king over Israel. It is this on which God will not go back, as though it were in any way an equivocal or deceptive undertaking such as humans commonly make."

17. Alter (1999:93), however, has questioned this conclusion. Alter translates 15:31, "And Samuel turned back from Saul, and Saul bowed to the LORD." He comments, "All English versions render this, erroneously, to indicate that Samuel nevertheless accompanied Saul to the sacrifice. But the expression 'turn back with' (*shub 'im* [TH7725/5973, ZH8740/6640]), as in verse 30, and 'turn back from [lit., after]' (*shub 'akhare*, [as in 15:31]) are antonyms, the latter meaning unambiguously 'to abandon.' (It is precisely the latter idiom that we see in God's condemnation of Saul in verse 11 [NLT, "for he has not been loyal to me," i.e., he has turned back from me, which uses *shub* and *'akhare*].) Samuel is completing his rejection of Saul here by refusing to accompany him in the cult, shaming him by forcing him to offer the sacrifice without the officiating of the man of God."

18. Although the text literally says this was the last time that Samuel and Saul "saw each other," the idea is that this was the last time Samuel spoke to Saul as a prophet would speak to a king. They did see each other at least one more time (cf. 19:24).

19. Long (1989:168) sees ch 15 as a transitional chapter in the overall structure of 1 Samuel that "marks the effective end of Saul's reign. *De facto* Saul will continue to occupy the throne for some time to come, but *de jure* his rejection is an accomplished fact. Having rejected Yahweh's word, he will no longer receive it (cf. 28:15). The vital link with Israel's Great King has been severed, and henceforth Yahweh's attention will fall upon another. In this sense, then, the chapter also serves as an introduction to the 'Rise of David.' After ch 15, David will be the protagonist and Saul the antagonist."

◆ IV. David's Rise and Saul's Decline (1 Sam 16:1–28:2)
A. Samuel Anoints David to Be King (1 Sam 16:1-13)

Now the LORD said to Samuel, "You have mourned long enough for Saul. I have rejected him as king of Israel, so fill your flask with olive oil and go to Bethlehem. Find a man named Jesse who lives there, for I have selected one of his sons to be my king."

[2]But Samuel asked, "How can I do that? If Saul hears about it, he will kill me."

"Take a heifer with you," the LORD replied, "and say that you have come to make a sacrifice to the LORD. [3]Invite Jesse to the sacrifice, and I will show you which of his sons to anoint for me."

[4]So Samuel did as the LORD instructed. When he arrived at Bethlehem, the elders of the town came trembling to meet him. "What's wrong?" they asked. "Do you come in peace?"

[5]"Yes," Samuel replied. "I have come to sacrifice to the LORD. Purify yourselves and come with me to the sacrifice." Then Samuel performed the purification rite for Jesse and his sons and invited them to the sacrifice, too.

[6]When they arrived, Samuel took one look at Eliab and thought, "Surely this is the LORD's anointed!"

[7]But the LORD said to Samuel, "Don't judge by his appearance or height, for I have rejected him. The LORD doesn't see things the way you see them. People judge by outward appearance, but the LORD looks at the heart."

[8]Then Jesse told his son Abinadab to step forward and walk in front of Samuel. But Samuel said, "This is not the one the LORD has chosen." [9]Next Jesse summoned Shimea,* but Samuel said, "Neither is this the one the LORD has chosen." [10]In the same way all seven of Jesse's sons were presented to Samuel. But Samuel said to Jesse, "The LORD has not chosen any of these." [11]Then Samuel asked, "Are these all the sons you have?"

"There is still the youngest," Jesse replied. "But he's out in the fields watching the sheep and goats."

"Send for him at once," Samuel said. "We will not sit down to eat until he arrives."

[12]So Jesse sent for him. He was dark and handsome, with beautiful eyes.

And the LORD said, "This is the one; anoint him."

[13]So as David stood there among his brothers, Samuel took the flask of olive oil he had brought and anointed David with the oil. And the Spirit of the LORD came powerfully upon David from that day on. Then Samuel returned to Ramah.

16:9 Hebrew *Shammah*, a variant spelling of Shimea; compare 1 Chr 2:13; 20:7.

NOTES

16:2 ***If Saul hears about it, he will kill me.*** This is an expression of "a condition and its consequence that is capable of fulfillment" by use of the perfect consecutive in the protasis and apodosis; on this grammatical construction, see GKC §159g.

16:4 ***they asked.*** Lit., "he said." Many Hebrew mss, Sebir, and the versions are plural. BHS (i.e., the Leningrad Codex B19A) has the singular.

Do you come in peace? The question is indicated by word order and perhaps intonation rather than the Hebrew interrogative particle (He). See Joüon and Muraoka §161a.

16:7 ***The LORD doesn't see things the way you see them.*** Lit., "for it is not [a matter of] what man sees." The Hebrew expression is elliptic. Many translations (NLT, KJV, NIV, NRSV) have supplied a fuller rendering much as the LXX does ("For God does not see as man sees"). Although possible, it is not necessary to conclude that *yir'eh 'elohim* [TH7200/430, ZH8011/466] (God sees) has mistakenly dropped out of the MT due to homoeoarchton.

16:12 ***He was dark and handsome, with beautiful eyes.*** Lit., "He was ruddy, attractive to the eyes, and of good appearance." It is possible to translate as NLT (and NRSV: "He was ruddy, and had beautiful eyes, and was handsome") although it seems preferable to take *'enayim* [TH5869, ZH6524] (eyes) in the sense of "appearance" as in 16:7 (cf. also 17:42 for a similar expression).

COMMENTARY

The Structure of 1 Samuel 16:1–19:24. As was noted in the Introduction (see "Date and Occasion of Writing"), at about the middle of the twentieth century, the majority of nonevangelical scholars moved away from the idea that 1–2 Samuel was a product of the combination of two or three parallel narrative strands (the predominant view of the nineteenth and early twentieth century).[1] The prevalent view came to be that the book was a product of the combination of a number of originally independent but unified blocks of tradition, among which the most important were the Ark Narrative (4:1–7:1; 2 Sam 6–7); the Narrative of Saul's Rise and End (9:1-16; 11; 13–14; 31); the History of David's Rise (16:14—2 Sam 5); and the Succession Narrative (sometimes also termed the Court History of David; 2 Sam 9–20; 1 Kgs 1–2). According to this approach, chapter 16 (or in the view of some, ch 15) marks the beginning of the narrative unit that tells the long story of how David became Saul's successor on the throne of Israel.

While there is general agreement that the narratives of this section of 1–2 Samuel are "pro-Davidic," there is not agreement on which specific pieces of the larger narrative may be original (as compared to later supplements or Deuteronomistic additions),[2] nor on the time and place of its origin (for details, see N. P. Lemche 1978; P. K. McCarter 1980a).[3] A. Weiser (1966) argued that the purpose of this larger narrative was to show that David's rise to the throne was lawful, and that he had a legitimate claim to the kingship of all Israel, including the northern tribes as well as Judah. The individual narrative units show that David had no responsibility for the deaths of Saul, Jonathan, Ishbosheth, or Abner, and in addition they show that he was a loyal member of Saul's court until he was forced to flee for his life. J. H. Grønbaek (1971) added a theological dimension to Weiser's emphasis on the legitimation idea, by noting that David's many successes are attributable to his having been blessed with divine favor and the Lord's presence (16:18), while the Spirit of the Lord had "left Saul" (16:14). H. A. Hoffner (1975) called attention to points of similarity between this section of 1–2 Samuel (that he calls the "Apology of David") and the late thirteenth-century BC "Apology of Hattusili III." Hattusili III was one of the great kings of the Hittite Empire. Hoffner (1975:50) argues that while it may not be possible to "prove any formal link between the Apology of Hattusili and the royal propaganda of David and Solomon, it is not impossible to speak of a tradition of royal apologies in the Hittite kingdom or even of a certain loose literary form which several of them seem to assume." In his view, the "Apology of David" may have had independent existence before being incorporated into the present book of Samuel, and the nature of its content suggests an origin in the time of either David or Solomon.[4]

While many of the observations of these studies are insightful, and while they have called attention to some of the major themes of the narratives and shown how carefully and extensively the various narratives have been interconnected by the writer or compiler, the advocates of this approach usually express reservations about the historicity of the events portrayed. The assumption is that the apologetic character of the narrative undermines its historical credibility, the reason being that the literature is propagandistic, and, therefore, must be viewed with a certain skepticism. N. P. Lemche (1978:3) says that when "we consider the obvious tendency of this narrative it is rather strange that nobody should have wanted to use the results of the analyses of 'David's Rise' to show that this narrative must be of dubious value as a historical source for the earlier history of David." While P. K. McCarter (1986:119) shows less skepticism, saying that "we can probably rely on the general accuracy of reports of events that were publicly known," he also notes that the purpose for which this document was produced "was not to record historical data but to defend and justify David's behavior." McCarter (1986:119) goes on to say that "we must be cautious in evaluating accounts of private events and doubly cautious in accepting the narrator's interpretation of events and comments about human motives." This, of course, raises fundamental questions about the general trustworthiness of biblical historiography, including that of 1–2 Samuel, and about what implications the Bible's claims that the Holy Spirit superintended its writing may have for its accuracy and reliability. It might be questioned, however, whether falsification of history would be as effective an apology for David (if that is truly what this section is) as would a straightforward recounting of events as they happened, in combination with the author's comments on their significance and meaning. It should also be recognized that the material in this section is not uniformly positive in its descriptions of David's actions and behavior. David, for example, was providentially rescued from a very serious mistake when he decided to take revenge on Nabal (ch 25). David's leaving Israel and going into the service of Achish, the Philistine ruler of Gath (ch 27) was also not something David could later be proud of (ch 29). So questions may be raised about the characterization of this material as an official "apology for David," as well as about whether or not this material existed for a time independently of the other parts of 1–2 Samuel. It may also be questioned whether the "apology model" fits the material as well as another approach does—namely, one that views the narratives as positive and negative portrayals of the reigns of David and Saul, framed by the theme of kingship and covenant. In this model, Saul is depicted as a king who turned away from his responsibilities as a covenantal king, while David is a person who imperfectly but substantively embraced them.

In our own discussion of this material we will not follow its generally accepted boundaries (i.e., 16:14—2 Sam 5), but will divide it into "David's Rise and Saul's Decline" (16:1–28:2); "The End of Saul's Reign" (28:3-25); and "David Becomes King over Judah" (2 Sam 1:1–3:1). Dividing it in this way accommodates some of the structural observations of Klement (2000), who finds here examples of ring structures similar to that found in 2 Samuel 21–24 (see the Introduction, "Literary Style"). The first of these ring structures, found in 16:1–19:24, is outlined as follows (adapted from Klement 2000:138):[5]

16:1-13 *Samuel* anoints David to be king
16:14-23 An *evil spirit* torments Saul; *David enters* Saul's service
17:1–18:4 David's victory over *Goliath; Jonathan's* covenant with David
18:5-30 David as a military leader and a son-in-law; Saul's fear of David
19:1-7 *Jonathan* defends David on the basis of his victory over *Goliath*
19:8-17 An *evil spirit* torments Saul; *David leaves* Saul
19:18-24 *Samuel* protects David; prophetic divesting of Saul's office

As Klement notes:

> *An evil spirit from Yahweh took possession of Saul following the anointing of David. This both provided the reason for David's entry into the royal court in 16.14-23 and became the cause of his flight in 19:8-17. On both occasions a rôle is played by David's ability to play the harp. The flight takes place because David is in danger of death at the hand of Saul. From then on the evil spirit dominates his actions, even against David's effective harp playing.*
>
> *The victory over Goliath (1 Sam 17) had brought liberty to Israel. It forms the basis for Jonathan's covenant with David. The parallel between Jonathan and David had already been brought to expression through the confidence of both in Yahweh's readiness to come to their aid in 1 Sam.14.6 and 17.45ff. The victory over Goliath provides Jonathan with an argument to pacify Saul, whose increasing fear of David was based, in the centre of 1 Sam. 16–19, on David's extraordinary successes.* (2000:137)

First Samuel 16 divides into two closely related but distinct parts: (1) 16:1-13 describes Samuel's anointing of David as the successor of Saul and (2) 16:14-23 describes how David was introduced to Saul's court and gained Saul's favor.[6] This chapter, therefore, marks a major transition point in 1–2 Samuel because from this point forward, until the death of Saul and the installation of David as the ruler over the entire nation (2 Sam 5:1-5), these two anointed kings are compared and contrasted as individuals who either conform with or depart from the covenantal standards for Israel's kings.[7] Samuel, whose birth and youth were the focus of the beginning chapters of the book (chs 1–3), is the person whom God chose to anoint both of these individuals as king (10:1; 16:13). Although Samuel was initially opposed to the establishment of kingship in Israel, because he regarded it as a rejection of the Lord who was Israel's king (8:6-7), he nevertheless obeyed the Lord's instruction (8:9, 22) and gave the nation a king (9:1–10:16; 10:17-27; 11:14–12:25). However, when he did so, he did not give them a king "like the nations around [them]," as they had requested (8:5, 20), but instead he defined Israel's kingship in a way that was consistent with the continued sovereignty of the Lord over the nation (10:25). He then inaugurated Saul's reign in the context of a covenant renewal ceremony in which Israel not only accepted their new king, but also renewed their allegiance to the Lord (11:14–12:25). In light of this background, Samuel undoubtedly had great expectations for Saul and for the future of the nation under his leadership. So when Saul repeatedly showed an unwillingness to live up to his responsibilities as a covenantal king, and when it became Samuel's responsibility to tell him that the Lord had rejected him as king

(15:23), it is understandable that Samuel became disillusioned and distressed (15:11, 35).

The Anointing of David. In the opening verse of chapter 16, the Lord told Samuel that in spite of Saul's failures, God's redemptive work with his people must go forward. Samuel was instructed to go to the family of Jesse at Bethlehem and to anoint one of his sons to be king in place of Saul. This time Israel's king would not come from the tribe of Benjamin. He would come from the tribe of Judah (cf. Gen 49:10).[8] The anointing of this new king would mark a fresh beginning for Israel in which God's work would move in a new direction, a direction that would ultimately lead to the messianic hope centered in the one who is both "the source of David and the heir to his throne" (Rev 22:16). So in the unfolding of events recorded in chapter 16 we are reminded that even in the dark and distressing situations of life, God calls his people to turn away from discouragement and disappointment because in spite of human failures, God is still at work. The God of biblical revelation is a God who, time and again, and in amazing ways, turns disappointments and human failures into the advancement of his Kingdom and the accomplishment of his purposes. It is this valuable and life-transforming perspective that is presented to us in the first verse of chapter 16.

Samuel, however, had serious reservations about going to Bethlehem to anoint a successor for Saul because he was convinced that Saul would not hesitate to kill him if he were to learn about what he was doing (16:2a).[9] The Lord responded to Samuel's concerns, however, by telling him that he should take a heifer along on the journey, so that if he were asked about his mission he could say that he had come to Bethlehem "to make a sacrifice to the LORD" (16:2b).[10] He was then to invite Jesse to the sacrifice, and the Lord would show him which of Jesse's sons he should anoint as king. When Samuel arrived at Bethlehem, the elders of the town met him in fear and trembling, and asked him if he came in peace (16:4). The cause of their fear is not indicated. Whether it was related to a reputation that had become attached to Samuel for bringing messages of rebuke and judgment (which was heightened by his recent killing of Agag and his split with Saul) is not clear. In any case, Samuel assured them that he came in peace and told them to prepare for the sacrifice.[11]

When the people had gathered for the sacrifice, Samuel saw Eliab, Jesse's eldest son, and concluded immediately that he was the one whom the Lord had chosen to be king. But the Lord issued a corrective: "Don't judge by his appearance or height, for I have rejected him." This was followed by the familiar statement that "people judge by outward appearance, but the LORD looks at the heart" (16:7). The use of the word reject (*ma'as* [TH3988, ZH4415]) might seem strong, but in the context it provides a verbal link between Eliab and Saul whom the Lord had rejected (*ma'as*) in the previous chapter (15:23). The implication is that Samuel was now looking at Eliab in the same way that he had earlier looked at Saul (de Jong 1978:119). Both Eliab and Saul were imposing figures with a royal stature. When Saul had been chosen by lot at Mizpah (10:17-27), he was described as standing "head and shoulders above anyone else" (10:23). Samuel said on that occasion, "This is the man the LORD has chosen as your king. *No one in all Israel is like him*" (10:24, my italics). Samuel was making the same mistake with Eliab that he had made in his initial evaluation of Saul, so he was warned not to be deceived by appearances because it is not outward qualities that ultimately count in finding a person suitable for the service of the Lord.

It is in this setting that 16:7 draws the contrast between man's looking on the outward appearance (lit., "Man sees what is before his eyes"), and the Lord's looking on the heart. This text (along with Jer 17:9-10) suggests that it is not possible for any human being to see the inner recesses of anyone else's heart (or for that matter, even that person's own heart), because that can only be done by God. Jeremiah 17:9 speaks of the pernicious character of the human heart, which seeks to camouflage its deepest desires and inclinations. It is by nature a source of deception and is dangerous to oneself and to others. Because it is out of the heart that both good and evil actions flow, it is of extreme importance that a person, above all else, guard his own heart (Prov 4:23). But in spite of the mysterious and devious qualities of the human heart, the Lord is able to search it and know it, and then reward a person not on the basis of appearances, but on the basis of what that person really is and does (Ps 139:23-24; Jer 17:10). In the context of the events of this chapter, this statement explains the fundamental difference between Saul and David. David was a person who was "better" than Saul (15:28), and David was a "man after [God's] own heart" (13:14). In the final analysis this observation of "hearts" is the explanation for God's judgment on and rejection of Saul, and his willingness to forgive and extend mercy to David.

The Lord's warning to Samuel, however, should not be misunderstood. Even though humans can only look at outward appearances, this does not mean that outward appearances are of no consequence. Certainly good appearance, competence at specific tasks, or any other outwardly attractive personal qualities may be of great importance in connection with a person's ability to accomplish what the Lord has called a person to do. Thus while on the one hand, if someone's heart is not right, attractive personal qualities in themselves do not qualify that person to serve the Lord, on the other hand, they do not disqualify that person either. This is clearly the case with David in this chapter. After Samuel had all the sons of Jesse brought before him and no one was found whom the Lord had chosen, he asked Jesse if he had any other sons (16:8-11). Jesse told him that his youngest son, David, was out in the fields with the sheep. When David was brought before Samuel, he is described as having a good appearance: "He was dark and handsome, with beautiful eyes" (see note on 16:12). Later in the chapter, he is described by one of Saul's servants as not only being a talented harp player, but also "a brave warrior, a man of war, and has good judgment. He is also a fine-looking young man, and the LORD is with him" (16:18; cf. also 18:12, 14, 28). So David was not disqualified as the Lord's chosen one because he was skilled and attractive.[12] The more important thing, however, was that he had a right heart, and "the LORD was with him" (18:14).

ENDNOTES

1. Advocated by, among others, K. Budde (1890), O. Eissfeldt (1965), J. Wellhausen (1899).
2. G. Fohrer (Sellin and Fohrer 1965:220-221), for example, suggests that some of what he terms "doublets" (e.g., different versions of David's flight [ch 20]; his joining the Philistines [21:11-15; 27]; his magnanimity toward Saul [chs 24 and 26]) within this section may be attributed to a "supplementary stratum."
3. P. K. McCarter (1980b:492-493), for example, lists a host of passages that he regards as secondary, "probably or certainly of deuteronomistic origin."
4. P. K. McCarter (1980a:502) argues for an original formulation in the time of David connected with such events as the Shimei incident (2 Sam 16:5-14) and Sheba's revolt (2 Sam 20:1-22), when David was being censured "for the blood of the house of Saul. It is to this censure that our document finally addresses itself."
5. H. Klement (2000:138) divides the center passage (18:5-30) into two units, presumably to maintain the parallel with the ring structure of the Appendix (2 Sam 21–24), which has two parallel units at its center. Because of the close similarity of emphasis in 18:5-16 and 18:17-30 we will treat both passages as a single unit for purposes of commentary.
6. Polzin (1989:152) puts it this way: "Chapter 16 is about the choosing of David first by God (16:1-13) and then by Saul (16:14-24)."
7. The transition between 16:13 and 16:14 speaks of the Spirit of the Lord coming on David at the time of his anointing (16:13) and the Spirit of the Lord departing from Saul (16:14), providing a hinge for the entire book of 1–2 Samuel. This marks the beginning of the end for Saul, and the beginning of a long and arduous road to the throne for David. See the helpful article by Howard (1989:477) in which he says, "The movements of the figures here—YHWH's Spirit, Samuel, the evil spirit—in relationship to each other effectively tell the story of the transfer of political and spiritual power from Saul to David."
8. As Youngblood (1992:683) notes, "Jesse of the tribe of Judah (cf. Ruth 4:12, 18-22) and his hometown, Bethlehem in Judah, would forever become associated with the Messiah (Isa 11:1-3, 10; Mic 5:2; Matt 1:1, 5, 6, 16-17; 2:4-6)."
9. Saul's killing of the priests at Nob (22:6-19) suggests that Samuel's concern was not imaginary or unfounded.
10. The subterfuge here authorized by the Lord has often been brought into discussions of whether or not there are ever situations in which it is ethically permissible, according to biblical standards, to lie to or deceive another person. Some have argued that this is never permissible, without exception (Kaiser 1983:224-227, 271-274). Others have said that in certain extreme situations a person is not required to speak the truth because there may be a higher obligation, usually that of protecting innocent life (Hodge 1952:440-443). In Hodge's view there are "circumstances in which a man is not bound to speak the truth, and therefore there are cases in which speaking or intimating what is not true is not a lie." This argument is based to a large extent on the ninth commandment, in which the prohibition against bearing false witness against one's neighbor is not formulated as an impersonal prohibition (not lying) but as a prohibition in which another person is involved. You may not damage your neighbor with your words. But this sometimes leads to a conflict: Are there cases in which one must consider his obligation to his neighbor as a higher obligation than his witness concerning reality (i.e., a formal statement of truth)? The answer would be yes, because to formally speak the truth in such situations would in reality violate the spirit and intent of the ninth commandment (i.e., to protect our neighbor with our words).

Those who say that deception or lying is never permissible usually deal with the Lord's instruction to Samuel in 16:2 by making a distinction between concealing and lying. Kaiser (1983:225), quoting Mahan (*Moral Philosophy*, 285), says, "Lying should be carefully distinguished from concealing. It is proper to conceal facts from individuals whom we have no right to deceive. Concealment is a sin when and only when, an obligation exists to reveal the fact which is concealed." According to Kaiser this was Samuel's position in 16:1-3. Kaiser (1983:226), quoting John Murray (*Principles of Conduct*, 139), says: "'Without question here is divine authorization for concealment by means of a statement other than that which would have disclosed the main purpose of Samuel's visit to Jesse.' But it is just as important to note that Samuel had no special prerogative to speak a falsehood either. The only point that may legitimately be made is that concealment, in some situations, is not lying. Only what was true was presented to Saul. As for Samuel's ultimate intentions, nothing is affirmed or denied, and nothing incited Saul's mind to probe concerning what may have been Samuel's ultimate motives for coming to Bethlehem at this time. Had such questions been raised, an altogether different problem would have confronted Samuel and he would have to avoid either affirming or denying what those purposes were or face the wrath of Saul in his disclosure." One may wonder, however, whether this line of argument really resolves the problem. Samuel was instructed not just to "conceal" his intentions from Saul, but to deceive Saul concerning the real purpose for his trip to Bethlehem, should that become necessary. It would seem to be difficult to defend the proposition that this is telling the truth in the sense that Scripture elsewhere requires. How much difference is there between deliberately misleading another person and lying to that person? Would it not be better in cases such as this to accept the fact that the Lord has told Samuel to deceive Saul, and therefore to conclude that here we find an example of a situation in which there is no obligation to tell the truth as is argued by Hodge (see above). In that case this situation is similar to that of the midwives in Exod 1:17-21, Rahab in Josh 2:1-14, and "the woman" in 2 Sam 17:18-21.

11. Ultimately the peace with which Samuel came to Bethlehem had implications that were much greater than either Samuel or the leaders of the town could ever imagine, because Samuel's coming to Bethlehem is the event that opened the door for the appearance of that great Prince of Peace, the Son of David (van den Berg 1996b:18-19).
12. In this respect David stood in sharp contrast to his greater son, who according to Isa 53:2-3, had no beauty or majesty to attract us to him. Outward appearances are not decisive in qualifying a person to serve the Lord.

◆ B. An Evil Spirit Torments Saul; David Enters Saul's Service (1 Sam 16:14-23)

14Now the Spirit of the LORD had left Saul, and the LORD sent a tormenting spirit* that filled him with depression and fear.

15Some of Saul's servants said to him, "A tormenting spirit from God is troubling you. 16Let us find a good musician to play the harp whenever the tormenting spirit troubles you. He will play soothing music, and you will soon be well again."

17"All right," Saul said. "Find me someone who plays well, and bring him here."

18One of the servants said to Saul, "One of Jesse's sons from Bethlehem is a talented harp player. Not only that—he is a brave warrior, a man of war, and has good judgment. He is also a fine-looking young man, and the LORD is with him."

19So Saul sent messengers to Jesse to say,

"Send me your son David, the shepherd."
20 Jesse responded by sending David to Saul,
along with a young goat, a donkey loaded
with bread, and a wineskin full of wine.
21 So David went to Saul and began
serving him. Saul loved David very much,
and David became his armor bearer.
22 Then Saul sent word to Jesse asking,
"Please let David remain in my service, for
I am very pleased with him."
23 And whenever the tormenting spirit
from God troubled Saul, David would play
the harp. Then Saul would feel better, and
the tormenting spirit would go away.

16:14 Or *an evil spirit;* also in 16:15, 16, 23.

NOTES

16:14 ***filled him with depression and fear.*** Lit., "was afflicting him" or "used to afflict him." For the perfect with Waw consecutive as a frequentative, for actions rooted in the past, see GKC §112h; Joüon and Muraoka §119v. This clause is the NLT's translation of the verbal root *ba'ath* [TH1204, ZH1286], which occurs 16 times in the OT, meaning to "frighten" or "terrify." NIDOTTE 1.692 says that a "predominant function of this word is to express the terror of a lesser individual who stands in the presence of a greater individual—often times a human being before a numinous being." Saul experiences this terror when tormented by the evil spirit sent from Yahweh (1 Sam 16:14-15). Hoftijzer (1995) suggests the word refers to an experience of extreme fear and incapacitation.

16:17 ***Find me.*** Lit., "Provide [see] for me." This is the rather unusual combination of the verb *ra'ah* [TH7200, ZH8011] (see) with the preposition *l* [TH3807.1, ZH4200] (to, for) and the first person singular pronoun *i* [TH2967.1, ZH3276] (me). This is a play on the identical phrase the Lord used in 16:1 to inform Samuel that he had selected a new king. See commentary.

16:18 ***he is a brave warrior.*** The expression *gibbor khayil* [TH1368A/2428, ZH1475/2657] is difficult to translate. The term *khayil* ranges in meaning from "strength" to "ability" to "wealth." The combination *gibbor khayil* seems to suggest different ideas in different contexts such as, among other uses, from "warrior," or "mighty man of valor" in a military context to a "wealthy man," or "a man from a respected family" in a social context. See further TDOT 2.367-382 and McCarter (1980b:173).

fine-looking young man. Lit., "a man of form." Cf. 1 Kgs 1:6 for a similar but fuller expression.

16:20 ***a donkey loaded with bread.*** Lit., "a donkey of bread" (*khamor lekhem* [TH2543/3899, ZH2789/4312]). Tsumura (1992) has suggested that "donkey" in this expression does not refer to an animal, but is a unit of measure called a "donkey." He finds evidence for this type of measure in Akkadian literature where "'the ass-measure' is widely attested in northern Mesopotamia from the early 2d mill. on as the most common large capacity measure." On the basis of this understanding "a donkey of bread" is a donkey-load of bread.

16:21 ***began serving him.*** Lit., "stood before him." It is not clear whether this expression (*wayya'amod lepanayw* [TH5975, ZH6641]) simply refers to David's initial appearance before Saul, or is to be taken in the more specific sense of "entering Saul's service" (cf. 16:22; 1 Kgs 1:2; 12:8 etc.).

16:23 ***tormenting spirit from God.*** Lit., "the spirit from God." The LXX adds *ponēron* [TG4190, ZG4505] (evil), and a few Hebrew mss add *ra'ah* [TH7451, ZH8273] (evil). The NRSV reads, "the evil spirit from God." As Stoebe (1973:308) comments, this is a pedantic clarifying addition to avoid misunderstanding (cf. the last phrase of the verse where "evil spirit" is used).

COMMENTARY

After Samuel anointed David, the Spirit of the Lord immediately came powerfully upon him (16:13). This event occasions an important scene transition in the narrative from the place of David's anointing at Bethlehem to that of the court of Saul at Gibeah. Immediately juxtaposed to the narrator's telling us that the Spirit powerfully came on David, he informs us that the Spirit "had left Saul," and that "the LORD sent a tormenting spirit that filled him with depression and fear" (16:14). Here the great contrast between Saul and David is accentuated. While being equipped by God's Spirit was indispensable for David to be able to fulfill the responsibilities of the covenantal king,[1] this does not mean that the coming of the Spirit in some mysterious way provided him with any greater intelligence or organizational skills. No, David was the same person he was before. However, the empowerment of God's Spirit mobilized his God-given talents in the execution of the task to which he was now called (van den Berg 1996b:26). At the same time that David was equipped by God's Spirit for performing his newly assigned task in the theocracy, this same operation of the Spirit was removed from Saul. But, more ominously, not only did God's Spirit depart from Saul—we are told that it was replaced by an "evil spirit from the LORD" (16:14, lit.; see NLT mg).

This reference to an "evil spirit from the LORD," and other similar references in this section of 1 Samuel (cf. 16:14-16; 18:10; 19:9) have often been troubling to the readers of these narratives. Some of the questions that surface are: How is this spirit to be identified; what function did it perform; and in what sense was it sent from God? From the context it seems clear that a true spirit being is in view, and that the designation "evil spirit" is not to be understood as a metaphor for something like a bad attitude or a guilty conscience.[2] The dramatic effects that this evil spirit had on Saul do not seem to be the sorts of things that could reasonably be said to be produced merely by a guilty conscience (cf. 18:10-11; 19:9).[3]

Wood (1976:127-128) suggests two possibilities for answering the question of what type of spirit being is in view. It is "either a good spirit, meaning an angel, or a bad spirit, meaning a demon sent by Satan. It, of course, could not have been God's Holy Spirit, for he had just been withdrawn from his place of empowerment in Saul's life. Of the two possibilities, it could not have been a good spirit either, for this spirit is specifically called an 'evil spirit.' It must, then, have been a demon sent by Satan." This conclusion, however, raises the question of how this spirit could be said to have been (lit.) "from the LORD" (16:14), "of God" (16:15, 23; 18:10), or "of the LORD" (19:9). Wood's response (1976:128) is that "the spirit was sent from God in the sense that God permitted it to begin to influence Saul when God's true Spirit had been removed. This sending was passive in nature, not active. Satan was the active agent. . . . No doubt, God saw fit to grant the permission [to Satan] as a punishment for Saul's disobedience." An examination of the language used[4] to describe the relation of this spirit to Saul suggests that this evil spirit did not work from within Saul's personality (as would be the case in demon possession) but rather brought influence on Saul while working from outside his personality (Wood 1976:131-133).

The first effect of the coming of the evil spirit on Saul was to fill him with "depression and fear" (16:14, see note). When this fearful and suspicious demeanor descended on Saul and was observed by his subordinates, the suggestion was made that perhaps soothing music would help him feel better. Saul agreed with this suggestion and ordered that a good harp player be brought to the court (16:17). That person turned out to be David because he was known to one of Saul's officials as a person well qualified for the task. The language that Saul used to give the order to bring such a person to the court heightens the irony of the chapter because it directly parallels the language of the Lord's statement in 16:1 that he had provided for himself one of Jesse's sons to be the new king (see note on 16:17). So the chapter opens with the Lord saying "I have *provided for me* a king from among Jesse's sons" and now Saul unwittingly gives the order to "provide for me" someone who plays the harp, who, in fact, turns out to be the very person whom the Lord had provided for himself to replace Saul as king.[5] Unknowingly Saul had invited into his court the very person who would ultimately replace him as king.[6]

In any case, David came to the court of Saul and entered into his service. Saul was very impressed with him and asked him not only to play the harp but also to be one of his armor bearers (16:21). David did this, and the chapter concludes with the statement that "whenever the tormenting spirit from God troubled Saul, David would play the harp. Then Saul would feel better, and the tormenting spirit would go away" (16:23). The statement that the evil spirit would "go away" (*sur* [TH5493, ZH6073]) when David played his stringed instrument suggests that this evil spirit "did not possess Saul, but only influenced him from without" (Wood 1976:136-137), and David's music, blessed in some mysterious way by God's Spirit, enabled Saul to overcome the deleterious effects of the evil spirit that had come upon him.

ENDNOTES

1. Even though being equipped by the Spirit was indispensable for performing the tasks of the true covenantal king, it should also be understood that this work of God's Spirit was not mechanical or automatic. That it was possible to quench the Spirit (cf. 1 Thess 5:19) was clearly demonstrated by Saul's life.
2. Caird (1953:969) suggests that the reference to this spirit is to be understood as "a bad conscience produced by his [Saul's] own disobedience to what he believed to be the will of God, and his consequent break with the man who had been instrumental in bringing him to the throne." McCarter (1980b:280-281) says "we may speak of mental illness if we want—Saul manifests some symptoms of paranoia, others of manic-depressive illness—but surely Hertzberg is correct to stress the fact that 'Saul's suffering is described theologically, not psycho-pathetically or psychologically.'"
3. Howard (1989:482) comments, "Concerning the nature of this spirit, it must be seen as more than a mere mental disturbance in Saul's case. It certainly introduced the effects of mental disturbance but, coming immediately after the departure of YHWH's Spirit, it must be seen as an active, external power. Some see a demon here, although it may have been more in the nature of a spirit of calamity or distress."
4. Wood (1976:129-132) compares the use of verbs and prepositions that describe the evil spirit's relation to Saul with the verbs and prepositions used to describe the work of God's Spirit, who worked "from within the personalities of those he empowered." His conclusion is that many of the verbs used "regarding God's Spirit connote the idea of taking control of a person, working from 'within'" (e.g., "fill, clothe, rest upon, come

in," and "move"). The verbs used in connection with the evil spirit, however, do not necessarily suggest inner control ("terrify," "overpower"). The same is true with the prepositions ("upon," *'al* [TH5921, ZH6584], is most often used with God's Spirit, while "unto," *'el* [TH413, ZH448], is most often used with the evil spirit).

5. Brueggemann (1990a:125) puts it nicely when he says "David is 'provided' by Yahweh and is 'provided' to Saul."
6. Polzin (1989:161) comments, "It may appear to Saul and his retinue that David is the answer to their problem; up to a point he is. Nevertheless, the heart of the matter, as the reader already knows, is that Saul is really helping to bring about his own downfall. God's 'having David brought' to Samuel marks its true purpose: to make a king; David's 'coming to comfort Saul' merely masks its true purpose: to unmake one."

◆ C. David's Victory over Goliath; Jonathan's Covenant with David (1 Sam 17:1–18:4)

The Philistines now mustered their army for battle and camped between Socoh in Judah and Azekah at Ephes-dammim. [2]Saul countered by gathering his Israelite troops near the valley of Elah. [3]So the Philistines and Israelites faced each other on opposite hills, with the valley between them.

[4]Then Goliath, a Philistine champion from Gath, came out of the Philistine ranks to face the forces of Israel. He was over nine feet* tall! [5]He wore a bronze helmet, and his bronze coat of mail weighed 125 pounds.* [6]He also wore bronze leg armor, and he carried a bronze javelin on his shoulder. [7]The shaft of his spear was as heavy and thick as a weaver's beam, tipped with an iron spearhead that weighed 15 pounds.* His armor bearer walked ahead of him carrying a shield.

[8]Goliath stood and shouted a taunt across to the Israelites. "Why are you all coming out to fight?" he called. "I am the Philistine champion, but you are only the servants of Saul. Choose one man to come down here and fight me! [9]If he kills me, then we will be your slaves. But if I kill him, you will be our slaves! [10]I defy the armies of Israel today! Send me a man who will fight me!" [11]When Saul and the Israelites heard this, they were terrified and deeply shaken.

[12]Now David was the son of a man named Jesse, an Ephrathite from Bethlehem in the land of Judah. Jesse was an old man at that time, and he had eight sons. [13]Jesse's three oldest sons—Eliab, Abinadab, and Shimea*—had already joined Saul's army to fight the Philistines. [14]David was the youngest son. David's three oldest brothers stayed with Saul's army, [15]but David went back and forth so he could help his father with the sheep in Bethlehem.

[16]For forty days, every morning and evening, the Philistine champion strutted in front of the Israelite army.

[17]One day Jesse said to David, "Take this basket* of roasted grain and these ten loaves of bread, and carry them quickly to your brothers. [18]And give these ten cuts of cheese to their captain. See how your brothers are getting along, and bring back a report on how they are doing.*" [19]David's brothers were with Saul and the Israelite army at the valley of Elah, fighting against the Philistines.

[20]So David left the sheep with another shepherd and set out early the next morning with the gifts, as Jesse had directed him. He arrived at the camp just as the Israelite army was leaving for the battlefield with shouts and battle cries. [21]Soon the Israelite and Philistine forces stood facing each other, army against army. [22]David left his things with the keeper of supplies and hurried out to the ranks to

greet his brothers. 23As he was talking
with them, Goliath, the Philistine cham-
pion from Gath, came out from the Philis-
tine ranks. Then David heard him shout
his usual taunt to the army of Israel.

24As soon as the Israelite army saw him,
they began to run away in fright. 25"Have
you seen the giant?" the men asked. "He
comes out each day to defy Israel. The
king has offered a huge reward to anyone
who kills him. He will give that man one
of his daughters for a wife, and the man's
entire family will be exempted from pay-
ing taxes!"

26David asked the soldiers standing
nearby, "What will a man get for killing
this Philistine and ending his defiance of
Israel? Who is this pagan Philistine any-
way, that he is allowed to defy the armies
of the living God?"

27And these men gave David the same
reply. They said, "Yes, that is the reward
for killing him."

28But when David's oldest brother, Eliab,
heard David talking to the men, he was
angry. "What are you doing around here
anyway?" he demanded. "What about
those few sheep you're supposed to be tak-
ing care of? I know about your pride and
deceit. You just want to see the battle!"

29"What have I done now?" David re-
plied. "I was only asking a question!" 30He
walked over to some others and asked
them the same thing and received the
same answer. 31Then David's question was
reported to King Saul, and the king sent
for him.

32"Don't worry about this Philistine,"
David told Saul. "I'll go fight him!"

33"Don't be ridiculous!" Saul replied.
"There's no way you can fight this Philis-
tine and possibly win! You're only a boy,
and he's been a man of war since his
youth."

34But David persisted. "I have been tak-
ing care of my father's sheep and goats,"
he said. "When a lion or a bear comes to
steal a lamb from the flock, 35I go after it
with a club and rescue the lamb from its
mouth. If the animal turns on me, I catch
it by the jaw and club it to death. 36I have
done this to both lions and bears, and I'll
do it to this pagan Philistine, too, for he
has defied the armies of the living God!
37The LORD who rescued me from the
claws of the lion and the bear will rescue
me from this Philistine!"

Saul finally consented. "All right, go
ahead," he said. "And may the LORD be
with you!"

38Then Saul gave David his own armor—
a bronze helmet and a coat of mail. 39Da-
vid put it on, strapped the sword over it,
and took a step or two to see what it was
like, for he had never worn such things
before.

"I can't go in these," he protested to
Saul. "I'm not used to them." So David
took them off again. 40He picked up five
smooth stones from a stream and put
them into his shepherd's bag. Then, armed
only with his shepherd's staff and sling,
he started across the valley to fight the
Philistine.

41Goliath walked out toward David with
his shield bearer ahead of him, 42sneering
in contempt at this ruddy-faced boy. 43"Am
I a dog," he roared at David, "that you come
at me with a stick?" And he cursed David
by the names of his gods. 44"Come over
here, and I'll give your flesh to the birds
and wild animals!" Goliath yelled.

45David replied to the Philistine, "You
come to me with sword, spear, and javelin,
but I come to you in the name of the LORD
of Heaven's Armies—the God of the armies
of Israel, whom you have defied. 46Today
the LORD will conquer you, and I will kill
you and cut off your head. And then I will
give the dead bodies of your men to the
birds and wild animals, and the whole
world will know that there is a God in Is-
rael! 47And everyone assembled here will
know that the LORD rescues his people,
but not with sword and spear. This is the
LORD's battle, and he will give you to us!"

48As Goliath moved closer to attack, Da-
vid quickly ran out to meet him. 49Reach-
ing into his shepherd's bag and taking out

a stone, he hurled it with his sling and hit the Philistine in the forehead. The stone sank in, and Goliath stumbled and fell face down on the ground.
50So David triumphed over the Philis-
tine with only a sling and a stone, for he
had no sword. 51Then David ran over and
pulled Goliath's sword from its sheath. David used it to kill him and cut off his head.

When the Philistines saw that their champion was dead, they turned and ran.
52Then the men of Israel and Judah gave
a great shout of triumph and rushed after the Philistines, chasing them as far as Gath* and the gates of Ekron. The bodies of the dead and wounded Philistines were strewn all along the road from Shaaraim,
as far as Gath and Ekron. 53Then the Isra-
elite army returned and plundered the
deserted Philistine camp. 54(David took
the Philistine's head to Jerusalem, but he stored the man's armor in his own tent.)
55As Saul watched David go out to fight
the Philistine, he asked Abner, the commander of his army, "Abner, whose son is this young man?"

"I really don't know," Abner declared.
56"Well, find out who he is!" the king
told him.
57As soon as David returned from killing
Goliath, Abner brought him to Saul with the Philistine's head still in his hand.
58"Tell me about your father, young man,"
Saul said.

And David replied, "His name is Jesse, and we live in Bethlehem."

CHAPTER 18

After David had finished talking with Saul, he met Jonathan, the king's son. There was an immediate bond between
them, for Jonathan loved David. 2From
that day on Saul kept David with him and
wouldn't let him return home. 3And Jona-
than made a solemn pact with David, because he loved him as he loved himself.
4Jonathan sealed the pact by taking off
his robe and giving it to David, together with his tunic, sword, bow, and belt.

17:4 Hebrew *6 cubits and 1 span* [which totals about 9.75 feet or 3 meters]; Dead Sea Scrolls and Greek version read *4 cubits and 1 span* [which totals about 6.75 feet or 2 meters]. **17:5** Hebrew *5,000 shekels* [57 kilograms]. **17:7** Hebrew *600 shekels* [6.8 kilograms]. **17:13** Hebrew *Shammah*, a variant spelling of Shimea; compare 1 Chr 2:13; 20:7. **17:17** Hebrew *ephah* [20 quarts or 22 liters]. **17:18** Hebrew *and take their pledge*. **17:52** As in some Greek manuscripts; Hebrew reads *a valley*.

NOTES

17:2 ***troops.*** Lit., "the man of Israel." See Joüon and Muraoka §135c for use of a singular noun as a noun of species or category.

17:4 ***champion.*** Heb., *'ish-habbenayim* [TH376/1143, ZH408/1227], lit., "a certain man-in-between." The expression occurs only here in the OT and is therefore difficult to translate with certainty. R. de Vaux (1971c) has argued that it designates a "champion"—that is, "a man who steps out to fight between the two battle lines" by engaging in single combat. McCarter (1980b:290-291) translates the phrase as "a certain infantryman" based on frequent usage of the expression (in a plural form) in the War Scroll from Qumran. De Vaux regards the Qumran usage as a weakening of the original force of the expression.

over nine feet tall. The NLT prudently retains the MT's reading of Goliath's height rather than the smaller height of LXX or 4QSam[a]. Hays (2005) argues that the smaller height is more likely the original reading. This is disputed by Bergen (1996:189, note 49) who views the smaller reading as "a pious emendation designed to increase the text's credibility."

17:8 ***Choose.*** This is a modification of the vowel pointing of the MT's *beru* (root *barah* [TH1262, ZH1356], "eat") to *boru* (root *barar* [TH1305, ZH1405], "choose"; cf. 1 Chr 7:40). An emendation to *bekharu* [TH977, ZH1047], (select), as suggested by S. R. Driver (1913:140) and others, is unnecessary.

17:12 ***Jesse was an old man.*** Lit., "He was old, coming among men." The expression is unusual; following the Lucianic mss of the LXX, Syriac, and Vulgate it has often been suggested (cf. NRSV, Klein, McCarter) that *zaqen ba' ba'anashim* [TH376, ZH408] be emended to *zaqen ba' bashanim* [TH8141, ZH9102] (an elder, advanced in years [lit., "coming into the years"]). The difficulty with this proposal is that the normal Hebrew expression for "advanced in years" would be *ba' bayyamim* [TH3117, ZH3427] (coming into the days). Barthélemy (1979:184) has made the more compelling suggestion that the phrase be translated, "He was an elder, distinguished among men." Youngblood (1992:704, note 12) comments that Barthélemy's suggestion is supported by comparison with the expression *habba'im beshemoth* [TH8034, ZH9005] (the ones coming with names) in 1 Chr 4:38 (NIV, "the men listed . . . by name"). This seems to speak of men "distinguished by name" since in the same verse they are also termed "leaders of their clans."

17:13 ***had already joined.*** Lit., "had gone" (*halak* [TH1980, ZH2143]). The verb "to go" is utilized twice in two different forms in the Hebrew text. Rather than assume a copyist's error for one of them (as S. R. Driver 1913:141), it is better with Stoebe (1973:322) to regard this simply as a stylistic peculiarity.

17:22 ***to greet his brothers.*** Lit., "He asked concerning their welfare" (*leshalom* [TH7965, ZH8934]). The expression is sometimes used simply as a greeting, much like the English expression, "How are you?" Because of this, some translations (e.g., NLT, NIV, NRSV, NASB) render the expression "He greeted his brothers." But the full context of 17:18—lit., "observe (*tipqod* [TH6485, ZH7212]) your brothers as to well being" (*leshalom*)—suggests that here it might be better to translate this phrase along the lines of "he asked how his brothers were doing."

17:25 ***Have you seen the giant?*** Perhaps the *ha* [TH1886.2, ZH2022] is better understood here as exclamatory instead of interrogative and translated, "You have indeed seen the giant!" (Joüon and Muraoka §161b).

17:31 ***sent for him.*** For a similar use of *laqakh* [TH3947, ZH4374] in the sense of "summon," see 16:11; Judg 11:5.

17:35 ***If the animal turns on me.*** The use of a *wayyiqtol* form for frequentative action in the past is unusual, but see Joüon and Muraoka §118n.

17:39 ***and took a step or two.*** Lit., "attempted to walk" (*wayyo'el laleketh* [TH1980, ZH2143]). It is unnecessary to modify *ya'al* [TH2974, ZH3283] (determine, begin to) to *la'ah* [TH3811, ZH4206] (be weary, strenuously exert oneself), following LXX, since MT gives an adequate sense as it stands.

17:41 ***walked out toward.*** Lit., "came on, approaching nearer." See Joüon and Muraoka §123s for the idea of continuity expressed by the infinitive absolute (Joüon suspects the consonants *hlk* [TH1980, ZH2143] represent the infinitive absolute *halok* rather than the participle *holek* found in MT).

17:48 ***As Goliath moved closer to attack.*** Lit., "When the Philistine rose up, he came and drew near to meet David."

17:51 ***champion.*** On the meaning of this word (*gibbor* [TH1368A, ZH1475]), see note on 16:18.

17:55-58 For a discussion of literary and text-critical questions that pertain to these verses, see the commentary.

18:1 ***for Jonathan loved David.*** Lit., "Jonathan loved [David] as his own soul."

18:3 ***And Jonathan made a solemn pact with David.*** Jonathan is the subject of both verbs in this verse. The translation, "Jonathan and David made a covenant" (Klein 1983:171;

McCarter 1980b:300) ignores the singular form of the verbs. Stoebe (1973:343) concludes that the Waw [TH2050.1, ZH2256] prefixed to *dawid* [TH1732, ZH1858] is softening in function and need not be emended to *le* [TH3807.1, ZH4200] or *'et* [TH853, ZH906] *dawid.*

COMMENTARY

The story of David and Goliath is one of the great pieces of narrative writing in all of human literature. It is a story that is nearly universally known, and one that still captures the imagination of those who read or hear it even though they may live in an entirely different time and cultural context. In spite of its enduring appeal, the reasons why this story is included among the narratives of 1–2 Samuel are usually not understood. For most people today the story has become little more than a parable for triumph against overwhelming odds. Its appeal is linked with the widespread perception that it incarnates the idea of "the victory of the underdog."

This sort of trivialization of the narrative does not do justice to either its biblical context or to its central theological affirmations. The first thing to note is that chapter 17 carries forward the contrast between David and Saul established in the preceding chapter. The Spirit of the Lord has come upon David (16:13) and abandoned Saul (16:14). Even though the Spirit is not mentioned in the chapter, his presence behind the scenes is very real (van den Berg 1996b:32). The contrast between the actions of David and Saul clearly reflects the difference between a person controlled by God's Spirit and one who is not. David was outraged by Goliath's ridicule of the God of Israel, and he rose to the challenge of defending the honor of both Israel and Israel's God. Saul was intimidated by Goliath's bluster and cowered in fear before his threats and his invitation to battle. David is portrayed as a person of great faith in sharp contrast to Saul, who was paralyzed by fear. David's primary concern was with God's honor. In his view, the battle with Goliath was "the LORD's battle" (17:47), and he not only wanted "the whole world [to] know that there is a God in Israel" (17:46b); he also wanted Israel to know that "the LORD rescues his people, but not with sword and spear" (17:47). So David's victory carries a significance far beyond any purely personal accomplishment, because it presents us with a paradigm for Israel's approach to the issue of national security. Israel was not to find her security in military weapons or clever strategies but in dependence on the God who had promised to defend his people, and who had time and again demonstrated his faithfulness to his promises.

But in its biblical context, this story not only carries forward the contrast between David and Saul, it also reveals something of the antagonism that exists toward God and his people among unbelievers and heathen nations, which is part of the warp and woof of the long history of fallen humanity. This story is one more episode in the ongoing drama of the unfolding of redemptive history. Although David and Goliath are real historical individuals, they play a representative role in their battle. Goliath is twice described as "the pagan Philistine" (17:26, 36).[1] He was the embodiment of an uncircumcised culture, which was diametrically opposed to the way of life of God's people, Israel.[2] David, on the other hand, represents the ideal of the true covenantal king, that is, a king who was to be the instrument of God's rule over his people. So the conflict between David and Goliath symbolically transcended the personal and the national to reflect the enmity between the seed of the serpent and the seed of the woman (Gen 3:15)—the enmity between the Kingdom of God and the kingdom of Satan. At certain points in the history of redemption, such as the confrontation of David and Goliath, the struggle between these two kingdoms becomes more sharply defined than it is at other times.

David's Victory over Goliath (17:1-58). The chapter opens with a description of the geography of the battle scene (17:1-3). Once again the Philistine army was threatening Israel. On this occasion they brought their army into the territory of Judah in the region of the valley of Elah, near Socoh, in the Shephelah (the foothills), about 15 miles west of Bethlehem. Saul responded by gathering his troops to defend the approaches into Israel's central highlands. Thus, the two armies were encamped facing each other across a broad valley. On this occasion, the Philistines had a particularly intimidating battle strategy. Among their soldiers was a giant named Goliath who challenged someone from the Israelite army to engage him in individual combat. Goliath pledged that if he was defeated the Philistines would become slaves to Israel, but if he were victorious then Israel would become slaves to the Philistines (17:9). Goliath is introduced in 17:4 and described in 17:5-7. He was over nine feet tall and was armored with equipment reflecting the most advanced technology of that time. He had an assistant who walked ahead of him carrying a heavy shield. The scornful taunt with which he had been harassing Israel on a daily basis for a period of 40 days (17:16) is described in 17:8-10. The taunt climaxed with a statement of defiance toward the armies of Israel (17:10, 25-26), which was at the same time a statement of defiance against the God of the armies of Israel (cf. 17:26, 36, 45). The response of Saul and the Israelite army to this humiliating invective (17:11) was only dismay (*khathath* [TH2865, ZH3169]) and fear (*yare'* [TH3372, ZH3707]). No one dared to take Goliath up on his challenge.

It is in this context that David is introduced to the narrative. The background for David's visit to the camp of the Israelite army is described in 17:12-18, and what happened upon David's arrival at the camp is described in 17:19-24. David's three older brothers (Eliab, Abinadab, and Shammah) were serving with the Israelite forces. Jesse told David to take some supplies to his brothers and bring back a report on how they were doing (this had apparently become a rather regular routine for David, cf. 17:15). David did as he had been instructed by his father, and while he was talking with his brothers (17:23), Goliath began to shout his usual invective against the army of Israel. The response of the Israelites was the same as it had been previously (17:11); they fled in fear (17:24). Unlike what Saul did when he heard about the Ammonite threat to the inhabitants of Jabesh-gilead (ch 11), he took no initiative and instead cowered in fear. The difference was that at the time of the Ammonite threat, the Spirit of God had come powerfully upon Saul (11:6), but now the Spirit has departed from him. This carried with it serious detrimental effects, not only for Saul, but for Israel as well.

In contrast to 17:1-24, which contains mostly narration, 17:25-47 contains mostly dialogue and centers around David's conversations with his brothers and the troops (17:25-30), then with Saul (17:31-39), and finally with Goliath (17:43-47; cf. Polzin 1989:167). In the first of these dialogues, soldiers in the camp inform

David of Saul's promise to reward the man who kills Goliath by giving him one of his daughters as a wife, and exempting his family from taxation (17:25). Saul's strategy shows that he had lost all pretense of being a true covenantal king. Instead of attempting to motivate his troops by urging them to put their confidence in the name of the Lord, he appealed to their desire for prestige and wealth. In effect, he turned the battle for the name of the Lord into a battle for self-interest (van den Berg 1996b:35). Upon hearing David talking with some of the soldiers about Goliath, David's oldest brother, Eliab, perhaps sensing that David was prepared to accept Goliath's challenge, lashed out at him in anger, questioning why he had come to the battlefield and charging him with pride and deceit (17:28-29). In Eliab's eyes David was not a man of faith but rather a self-serving, conceited individual in search of an opportunity for personal honor. Eliab's unprovoked attack on David, however, tells us more about Eliab's character than about David's. Because Eliab sensed that his brother would not look with approval on the fear of Saul and his soldiers, including himself, he directed this angry outburst against him. David did not respond in kind. He simply said, "What have I done now? . . . I was only asking a question!" (17:29). Eliab's words reveal the kind of scorn to which the faith of David, as well as the faith of all who walk in David's footsteps, is subject. The reason for this sort of reaction is that expressions of faith always include something of a condemnation of those who do not share that faith (de Jong 1978:125). David was not deterred by Eliab's remarks. His faith was a faith that could withstand the challenge of skeptical questioning.

This brings us to David's dialogue with Saul (17:31-39). When David's questions about Goliath were reported to Saul, he requested that David be brought to him (17:31). David's first words to Saul were, "Don't worry about this Philistine . . . I'll go fight him!" (17:32). But Saul found David's suggestion preposterous. Instead of rejoicing that someone had the courage and faith to stand up to Goliath's challenge, Saul attempted to dissuade David from exercising his faith in such a dramatic way. David responded by telling Saul how he had rescued lambs from the jaws of lions and bears and then clubbed the predators to death, and he said that because this "pagan Philistine . . . has defied the armies of the living God" he would do the same thing to him (17:36). This is the second time that David refers to Goliath in this way (cf. 17:26).[3] David's deep concern for the honor of the God of Israel was clearly the driving force behind his decision to accept the responsibility for meeting Goliath's challenge. He then added that just as the Lord had rescued him from the lions and bears, so he would rescue him from this Philistine (17:37).[4] David's decision to fight Goliath was born out of concern for the honor of God, and was grounded in his unshakable confidence that God would give him victory on this occasion just as he had in the past. David was not speaking merely out of youthful enthusiasm or unfounded self-confidence, but rather out of a deep-seated trust in the Lord, whom Goliath had scorned. So Saul and David, the two anointed ones, had two very different perceptions of the situation with which Israel was confronted. Saul, from whom the Spirit had departed, could see only the physical power of the Philistine giant, while David, upon whom the Spirit had come, had a vision for the power of the Lord, who was able to deliver him from the hand of the giant.

Confronted by this unshakable confidence, Saul relented and gave his permission for David to fight Goliath, and then even went so far as to say "may the LORD be with you" (17:37b).

Saul then gave David his own armor (17:38) but after trying it on, David concluded it would be more of a hindrance than a help and refused to use it (17:39). He advanced against Goliath with only five stones, his shepherd's staff, and his sling. Goliath had a javelin, a spear, and a sword (17:45). Since he could not carry all three of these weapons in his two hands, one was strapped to his back (17:6). In contrast to this, David was armed very lightly, although he carried an effective weapon—in those days the sling was an important weapon of war. Judges 20:16 speaks of 700 elite troops who were left-handed and "each of them could sling a rock and hit a target within a hairsbreadth without missing." Even in later times slingers were a regular part of Israel's army (cf. 2 Kgs 3:25; 1 Chr 12:2; 2 Chr 26:14). The sling was recognized as a very useful weapon, one whose effectiveness should not be minimized. The stones used in the slings of that time were two or three inches in diameter with a weight of a pound or more. They could be cast at 100–150 miles an hour and had a strategic advantage over a javelin or sword as a long-range weapon.[5]

So as we reflect on David's courageous act, born of his faith, we should not regard it as something reckless or foolhardy that was tantamount to tempting God. David was not irresponsible in what he undertook, but he did choose to arm himself in a way that left room for God's help (de Jong 1978:129). In doing so he countered the natural human desire for certainty of result before commitment to some endeavor in the work of God's Kingdom. This is the way a true follower of the Lord should live. Ecclesiastes 11:4 says, "Farmers who wait for perfect weather never plant. If they watch every cloud, they never harvest." If a farmer waits for 100 percent certainty in planting and reaping, he will never do either. Just as the farmer must take some risk in order to accomplish his task, so the work of the Lord's Kingdom often requires people to risk failure, with the result that they experience the Lord's power in their lives. That is precisely what David chose to do by going against Goliath armed only with five stones, his staff, and his sling.

First Samuel 17:43-47 contains David's third dialogue, this time with Goliath. As David advanced toward Goliath on the battlefield, Goliath mocked him: "Am I a dog . . . that you come at me with a stick?" Then he cursed David in the names of the Philistine deities (17:43). David responded by saying, for the third time in this chapter, "I come to you in the name of the LORD of Heaven's Armies—*the God of the armies of Israel, whom you have defied*" (17:45, my italics; cf. 17:26, 36). David announced that the Lord would deliver Goliath into his hands, and when he did, David would kill him, cut off his head, and then give the "dead bodies of your men to the birds and wild animals" (17:46).[6] All of this would occur so that "the whole world will know that there is a God in Israel" and that "everyone assembled here will know that the LORD rescues his people, but not with sword and spear" (17:46-47). In David's view, this battle was linked with things that far transcended the spectacle of a lightly armed shepherd boy fighting a huge and heavily armed warrior. Its purpose was twofold: to demonstrate the existence and power of the God of Israel, and to show the superiority of Israel's God over the deities of Goliath and the Philistines. Beyond this, it was intended to remind Israel that her security as a nation did not stand or fall with the sophistication of her military weaponry (cf. Pss 20:7; 33:16-19; 44:6-7; 147:10-11).[7] This perspective was central to Israel's identity as a nation and as God's covenant people. David's last words to Goliath sum it up: "This is the LORD's battle, and he will give you to us!" (17:47b).

David's battle with Goliath and its aftermath are described in 17:48-54. The narration is entirely descriptive with no interpretive comments inserted by the author. The battle description is given with an economy of words and characterized by a very high proportion of verbs (36 verbs in seven verses).[8] David quickly hurled a stone from his sling, which hit Goliath and apparently struck him unconscious. David ran to him, pulled his sword from its sheath, and cut off his head. This is all summarized in the succinct statement of 17:50, "David triumphed . . . with only a sling and a stone, for he had no sword," which, while being descriptive rather than interpretive, is pregnant with meaning in its context (cf. David's assertion in 17:47). The sudden and unexpected defeat of Goliath caused the Philistine army to flee, whereupon the Israelite army took up pursuit and chased them as far as the Philistine cities of Gath and Ekron (17:52). The parenthetical statement of 17:54 concerning the taking of Goliath's head to Jerusalem and the placing of Goliath's armor in David's tent took place at a later time, as 17:57 makes clear.[9]

After observing this remarkable victory, Saul and Abner, the commander of his army, had an interchange concerning David's identity (17:55-58) that resulted in David's being brought to Saul, still holding Goliath's head in his hand (17:57). Saul repeated the question he had asked Abner to David himself, asking about his family and lineage. Saul's apparent ignorance of David's identity has provoked long and complex discussions over the question of how these verses in 1 Samuel 17 can be harmonized with the statements in 1 Samuel 16 concerning David's prior introduction to the court of Saul. It has often been argued that the differences between the Masoretic Text and Septuagint in 1 Samuel 16–18 (among these differences is the absence of 17:55-58 from the LXX) provide the key for understanding this alleged inconsistency in the narrative. The Septuagint version of chapters 16–18 is about 44 percent shorter than the corresponding passage in the Masoretic Text.[10] Traditionally, scholars have explained the difference in one of two ways: (1) The Septuagint translators abridged the Hebrew text to eliminate the appearance of tensions or discrepancies in the narrative; or (2) the Septuagint translators utilized a shorter Hebrew text than the one preserved for us in the Masoretic Text.

More recently a third explanation for the difference has been proposed. This proposal adds a significant new twist to explanation (2) above: The Masoretic Text is a conflated account composed by utilizing two originally separate versions of the same episode.[11] A volume by Barthélemy, Gooding, Lust, and Tov (1986) contains the results of a study of the text-critical and literary-critical problems of 1 Samuel 16–18 by four scholars from four different countries, working over a period of about four years. The volume includes initial contributions, responses, and conclusions by each scholar. It is striking that in this extensive and careful study, no consensus was reached on either the proper method of approach to the issues in question or on the conclusions to be drawn.

While it is not possible here to enter into the details of the argumentation of each participant in this discussion, it is clear that issues of importance to both literary and textual criticism are addressed. It is also clear that each scholar's presuppositions play a formative role in his choice of methodology. Gooding says that his presupposition is "that a biblical (or classical) narrative should be presumed to be a unity unless indisputable evidence is adduced for considering it composite." He notes that Lust's presupposition "seems to be that a biblical narrative must be presumed to be composite unless it is in strict logic proved otherwise—and the proof will be difficult, if not impossible" (Barthélemy, Gooding, Lust, and Tov 1986:117). Gooding notes that when this latter assumption governs analysis, it is much too easy to find imaginary discrepancies that confirm the initial assumption, while missing the contribution that each part contributes to the thought flow of the whole (Barthélemy, Gooding, Lust, and Tov 1986:58). So while it may appear that Lust and Tov have a text-critical basis for their literary-critical conclusion, in reality they are using a literary-critical assumption as a basis for their text-critical conclusion.[12]

The alleged discrepancy within chapters 16–18 that is most often cited as evidence for internal inconsistency is that Saul seems to be unaware of David's identity in 17:55-56 (after his victory over Goliath), even though David had already been brought to the court prior to this time in order to play the lyre for him (16:17-23; cf. NLT, "harp"). Since 17:55-58 is one of the sections not included in the Septuagint version of the story, this difficulty does not arise in the shorter Septuagint narrative.

Gooding addresses this question head-on and shows that there is no need to find a discrepancy within the narrative on this issue unless one is predisposed to do so. He comments:

> *This discrepancy depends on the insistence that 16:18-22 must mean nothing less than that Saul informed himself fully on everything to do with David's father, and on a similar insistence that 17:55-58 must not mean anything more than that Saul was interested to know the name of David's father. Neither insistence is necessary, nor, in the light of the narrative thought-flow, reasonable. Having been supplied by his servants with an acceptable harpist, it was natural for Saul to "request" (i.e. command) his father to let the young man stay at the royal house. It is not true to life to imagine that means that Saul sent the message directly himself—he would have left that to one of the officers who had found and suggested David. It is not even true to life to imagine that Saul thereafter necessarily remembered the name of David's father, or cared twopence about him, let alone investigated his background, family and all about him. Similarly, it is not true to life to imagine that in 17:55-58 Saul is simply concerned to know the name of David's father. Saul has just promised to give his daughter in marriage to the man who kills Goliath, and to make his father's house free in Israel (17:25). Naturally, when Saul sees David actually going out to meet Goliath, and even more so when he sees him returning triumphant, Saul will be concerned to know not just the name of, but everything about, David's father and the family which, if he keeps his promise, is now to be allied by marriage with the royal family. And we as readers must at this point be made aware that David is of the house of Jesse, for it is the house of Jesse that has at this moment eclipsed the house of Saul in military prowess, and is destined eventually to supplant it as the reigning house. (Barthélemy, Gooding, Lust, and Tov 1986:19-20)*

Gooding concludes that even though this alleged "discrepancy" is adequately resolved in the manner he suggests, it is certainly possible that some ancient editor, just like many modern scholars, concluded that the discrepancy was irreconcilable and accordingly may have removed the whole section 17:55–18:5 as a corrective. On the basis of this reasoning, the shorter Septuagint text may be viewed as a harmonistic effort on the part of the translator, which in turn entails recognition of primacy for the fuller Masoretic Text.

In spite of many enigmas and obscurities, and in spite of the intricacy of the debate and the difficulty of reaching definitive conclusions, it is nevertheless apparent that the method used by some scholars to address the problem of the text of 1–2 Samuel has blurred the traditional distinction between text criticism and literary criticism.[13] It is important to be aware of this development since it introduces a significant degree of subjective judgment, based on literary-critical assumptions, into the formulation of text-critical conclusions. And awareness of the assumptions involved is important for assessing the validity of the conclusions drawn.

Jonathan's Covenant with David (18:1-4). Just as chapter 17 carried forward the contrast between Saul and David rooted in the coming of God's Spirit upon David and his departure from Saul as described in chapter 16, so chapter 18 draws a contrast between the reactions of Saul and his son Jonathan to David's stunning victory described in chapter 17. First Samuel 18:1-4 tells us that Jonathan's reaction was characterized by an open and unselfish friendship for David, while 18:5-30 tells us that Saul's reaction was characterized by a high degree of suspicion and a reluctant acknowledgment of David's triumph.

We might wonder why Saul's reaction was so different than Jonathan's. If anyone should have felt threatened by David's victory, it should have been Jonathan rather than Saul (cf. de Jong 1978:133). Jonathan was the crown prince. He was the one who would have every right to expect to succeed his father Saul on the throne. But this was of no importance to Jonathan. A few chapters later we find that Saul scolded Jonathan, saying, "As long as that son of Jesse is alive, you'll never be king. Now go and get him so I can kill him!" (20:31). But the thing to notice in chapter 18 is that Jonathan is more concerned with the welfare of God's people than he is with his own advancement or self-interest. It is this concern for the welfare of God's people that is at the root of his friendship and love for David (de Jong 1978:133). Jonathan recognized in David someone who lived out his faith in the work of God's Kingdom. For him David was a kindred spirit and a real "soul mate" in the struggle against the Philistines. Remember, Jonathan had also won a single-handed victory over the Philistines (ch 14), and on that occasion he had said to his armor bearer, "Nothing can hinder the LORD. He can win a battle whether he has many warriors or only a few!" (14:6). Jonathan's confession was born of the same sort of faith as was David's statement when he confronted Goliath and said, "The LORD rescues his people, but not with sword and spear. This is the LORD's battle, and he will give you to us!" (17:47). So Jonathan's friendship with David was rooted in a common faith. They quickly became close associates in the work of the Kingdom. The precise nature of the "solemn pact" (18:3, NLT; lit., "covenant") that was made at Jonathan's initiative on the occasion of their first recorded meeting is not entirely clear because the terms of the pact are not described.[14] At the very least it would appear to be a mutual pledge of loyalty and friendship. Saul's reaction, however, was quite different. Saul certainly did not "love David as his own soul" (see note on 18:1). As close as Saul was to his son Jonathan, the two went in opposite directions in their relationship with David.

ENDNOTES

1. NLT translates "*uncircumcised* Philistine" as "*pagan* Philistine."
2. Beamer (1992:611) notes that the "Philistines are always represented in the OT as ungodly, uncovenanted, and uncircumcised. They do not listen to God, are carnally obsessed, and worship false gods. Hence they persist as aliens and adversaries in exegetical tradition. In English literature the 'Philistine' appears most often as an enemy of the Jews, until the 17th century. Milton's blind hero Samson Agonistes is an example of one fighting the enemy who are outside God's covenant."
3. Davis (1994b:41), citing D. F. Payne (1970:296), notes that in 17:26, "David injects the first theological note into the narrative."
4. Davis (1994b:44) comments, "Looking back in faith enables him to look forward in faith. . . . Faith is sustained in the present and for the present as it remembers Yahweh's provision in the past."
5. See Hoffmeier 1991b and Reimer 1991. After describing a demonstration of the use of a sling by a modern Syrian youth, Reimer comments (1991:21), "My final conclusion was that Goliath never had a chance."
6. Brueggemann (1990a:132) comments, "David answers the Philistine's threats with a series of first-person verbs: I will strike, I will cut off, I will give."
7. This twofold purpose linked with David's defeat of Goliath is similar to the twofold purpose for which God sent the plagues on Egypt at the time of the Exodus. At that time God said that these things happened in order that "the Egyptians will know that I am the LORD" (Exod 7:5, 17; 9:14, 16, 29). But he also said that these things happened so that Israelites might "tell your children and grandchildren about how I made a mockery of the Egyptians and about the signs I displayed among them—and *so you will know that I am the LORD*" (Exod 10:2). This twofold purpose also is reminiscent of the reasons for which Joshua set up the stone memorial to the crossing of the Jordan River. These stones were to be "a memorial among the people of Israel forever" (Josh 4:7), and also so that "all the nations of the earth might know that the LORD's hand is powerful" (Josh 4:24).
8. This averages over five verbs per verse with eight verbs in 17:48 and nine in 17:51! Polzin (1989:171) notes that this "appears to be the main means of stylizing the account of the contest itself by having the narrative imitate the active, rapid movement of the military events described therein: the narrator narrates as quickly as David runs in verses 48 and 51, or as the ranks flee and pursue in verses 51 and 52."
9. A literal translation of 17:54 reads, "David took the head of the Philistine and brought it to Jerusalem, and he put his armor in his tent." There is some ambiguity concerning the meaning of "his tent." If it is a reference to David's own tent (as suggested by the NLT rendering and supported by Klein [1983:181] and McCarter [1980b:294]), the question might be asked why David would have a tent at the battleground, if he was only a visitor in the military camp. On the basis of parallels in Egyptian and Assyrian literature, Hoffmeier (1991a) suggests that the tent is Goliath's tent and that this statement reflects the practice of the taking of the tent of a defeated enemy to put it on display among the spoils of battle. Hoffmeier (1991a:22) also suggests that David

may have taken Goliath's head to Jerusalem long before his later capture of the city (2 Sam 5), as a way of "putting the Jebusites on notice that just as the Philistine had fallen victim to David, Jerusalem's demise was only a matter of time."

10. Large blocks of material (17:12-31; 17:55–18:5; 18:10-11, 17-19, 29b-30) as well as several smaller sections (17:41, 48, 50; 18:6, 12, 21) are missing in LXX Vaticanus. At the same time additions are found in the Greek text at 17:26, 43. LXX Alexandrinus contains the MT pluses as do the Old Latin, Syriac, Aquila, Symmachus, Theodotion, and Vulgate.
11. See the proposals of Tov and Lust in Barthélemy, Gooding, Lust, and Tov 1986. For a summary of Tov's argument, see Tov 1986.
12. Traditionally, textual criticism (sometimes referred to as "lower criticism") concerns itself with attempting to discern the original wording of a given text on the basis of available manuscript evidence. Among other things, textual criticism identifies differences in wording found in various manuscripts and versions, categorizes various types of scribal errors, determines the relative dates of the manuscripts involved, and then suggests the most likely explanation for the differences in manuscripts and versions based on a comparative study of all the factors involved. Various canons of textual criticism have been established in order to provide, as much as is possible, some objective criteria for textual analysis so that the conclusions drawn might avoid arbitrariness and subjectivity. For a discussion of these principles, see Würthwein (1979). Würthwein (1979:76) argues that there are some basic principles "which are generally recognized, if not always in practice at least in theory, and these help to place textual criticism on a firm basis and to avoid the excesses of arbitrariness and subjectivity. These basic points are not specifically theological, but have developed from the application of the normal methods of scientific textual criticism to the particular needs of the Old Testament." As distinguished from textual criticism, literary and historical criticism (sometimes referred to as "higher criticism") deals with such matters as the assessment of literary structure and rhetorical techniques, as well as with questions of a text's authorship, date, and method of composition. It is particularly in the area of the method of composition that subjectivity plays a significant role, especially in the development of speculative theories concerning the presence of hypothetical sources that are allegedly identified in the final form of the text.
13. An example of this may be found in McCarter (1980b:284-309). McCarter does not treat ch 17 as a unit but divides the material into two sections that he treats in two separate chapters (Chapter XXIV-A, David and the Philistine Champion [17:1-11, 32-40, 42-48a, 49, 51-54]; Chapter XXIV-B, David and the Philistine Champion: A Second Account [17:12-31, 48b, 50, 55-58; 18:1-5, 10-11, 17-19, 29b-30]). The material placed in the "second account" is the material that is missing in LXX Vaticanus (cf. note 12 above). It is McCarter's view that this material was "absent from the Hebrew tradition behind LXX and indeed from the primitive text of Samuel itself" (1980b:306). It is McCarter's opinion that "this alternative account of David's early days at court may have belonged to the idealized David traditions that had long circulated in Jerusalem" (1980b:309). It was not until the fourth century BC that it was appropriated by a redactor and fused with the material McCarter places in his "first account." McCarter identifies 17:14b-15 as "redactional" and "designed to harmonize the two stories, in one of which David is already in the service of Saul while in the other he is still at home with Jesse" (1980b:303). This is a form of source-critical analysis in which the conclusion is based on the assumption that the biblical text is a composite rather than an original unity.

14. Some have argued that there are distinct political overtones to the language in which the relationship between Jonathan and David is described in 18:1-4. J. A. Thompson has suggested that Jonathan's "love" (*'ahab* [TH157, ZH170]) for David, while certainly denoting genuine personal affection for him, may also have the political implication of acknowledging "David's sovereignty over himself and over the nation" (1974:336). Thompson bases this suggestion on the use of the word "love" in both biblical and extrabiblical texts to represent a conception of love that "may be defined in terms of loyalty, service and obedience" (cf. Moran 1963:82). This is the same language that is used to describe relationships between suzerains and vassals in biblical and extrabiblical treaties. That political overtones are intended by the language of "love" and "covenant" in 18:1-4 may also be supported by Jonathan's symbolic act of sealing the pact between himself and David by giving David his robe, tunic, sword, bow, and belt (18:4). Rummel (1976) has called attention to a tablet from Ugarit in which a crown prince gives up his claim to the throne by placing his clothes on the throne. In this text the garments of the crown prince symbolize his position. In view of this extrabiblical analogy, Rummel suggests (1976:7) that "when Jonathan gave his garment to David . . . he thereby irrevocably yielded his right to the throne to David. This is the content of the covenant." While these suggestions are inferential, and one must be careful not to read too much into either the language or the symbolic act of these verses, they nevertheless merit serious consideration. Alter (1999:112) notes that "Fokkelman [1986:198] has proposed that 'with his cloak Jonathan is conveying to David the crown prince's rights and claims to the throne.'" Alter's own comment is, "Perhaps one should say that he is conveying these subliminally or proleptically rather than as a fully conscious act." If, however, these suggestions are accepted, then David's victory over Goliath may take on the same significance as Saul's victory over the Ammonites, that is, a confirmation of his prior designation (anointing) to be king. It is success in battle that proves fitness for office (cf. commentary on ch 11). While it is true that there is no evidence that Jonathan knew that David had been anointed by Samuel to be king, there is nevertheless evidence that Jonathan had some serious reservations about the manner in which his father was fulfilling the responsibilities of his office (cf. 14:29-30). It is also not clear whether Jonathan knew that Samuel had informed Saul that he would have no continuing dynasty (ch 13) and that the Lord had rejected him as king (ch 15).

◆ D. David as a Military Leader and Son-in-law (1 Sam 18:5-30)

5Whatever Saul asked David to do, David did it successfully. So Saul made him a commander over the men of war, an appointment that was welcomed by the people and Saul's officers alike.

6When the victorious Israelite army was returning home after David had killed the Philistine, women from all the towns of Israel came out to meet King Saul. They sang and danced for joy with tambourines and cymbals.* 7This was their song:

"Saul has killed his thousands,
and David his ten thousands!"

8This made Saul very angry. "What's this?" he said. "They credit David with ten thousands and me with only thousands. Next they'll be making him their king!"
9So from that time on Saul kept a jealous eye on David.

10The very next day a tormenting spirit* from God overwhelmed Saul, and he began to rave in his house like a madman. David was playing the harp, as he did each day. But Saul had a spear in his hand,
11and he suddenly hurled it at David, intending to pin him to the wall. But David escaped him twice.

12 Saul was then afraid of David, for the
LORD was with David and had turned away
from Saul. 13 Finally, Saul sent him away
and appointed him commander over 1,000
men, and David faithfully led his troops
into battle.
14 David continued to succeed in every-
thing he did, for the LORD was with him.
15 When Saul recognized this, he became
even more afraid of him. 16 But all Israel and
Judah loved David because he was so suc-
cessful at leading his troops into battle.

17 One day Saul said to David, "I am
ready to give you my older daughter,
Merab, as your wife. But first you must
prove yourself to be a real warrior by
fighting the LORD's battles." For Saul
thought, "I'll send him out against the
Philistines and let them kill him rather
than doing it myself."
18 "Who am I, and what is my family in
Israel that I should be the king's son-in-
law?" David exclaimed. "My father's fam-
ily is nothing!" 19 So* when the time came
for Saul to give his daughter Merab in
marriage to David, he gave her instead to
Adriel, a man from Meholah.
20 In the meantime, Saul's daughter Mi-
chal had fallen in love with David, and
Saul was delighted when he heard about
it. 21 "Here's another chance to see him
killed by the Philistines!" Saul said to
himself. But to David he said, "Today you
have a second chance to become my son-
in-law!"
22 Then Saul told his men to say to David,
"The king really likes you, and so do we.
Why don't you accept the king's offer and
become his son-in-law?"
23 When Saul's men said these things to
David, he replied, "How can a poor man
from a humble family afford the bride
price for the daughter of a king?"
24 When Saul's men reported this back
to the king, 25 he told them, "Tell David
that all I want for the bride price is
100 Philistine foreskins! Vengeance on my
enemies is all I really want." But what
Saul had in mind was that David would be
killed in the fight.
26 David was delighted to accept the of-
fer. Before the time limit expired, 27 he and
his men went out and killed 200 Philis-
tines. Then David fulfilled the king's re-
quirement by presenting all their foreskins
to him. So Saul gave his daughter Michal
to David to be his wife.
28 When Saul realized that the LORD was
with David and how much his daughter
Michal loved him, 29 Saul became even
more afraid of him, and he remained Da-
vid's enemy for the rest of his life.
30 Every time the commanders of the
Philistines attacked, David was more suc-
cessful against them than all the rest of
Saul's officers. So David's name became
very famous.

18:6 The type of instrument represented by the word *cymbals* is uncertain. **18:10** Or *an evil spirit.* **18:19** Or *But.*

NOTES

18:6 ***They sang and danced.*** Lit., "to sing and the dances." As S. R. Driver (1913:151) notes, the "two words correspond in form so imperfectly that the text can scarcely be in its original form." Perhaps the MT is to be corrected to *bamekholoth* ("with dancing"; cf. Exod 15:20; Judg 11:34).

18:8 ***Next they'll be making him their king!*** Lit., "and there is still only the kingdom [to give] to him."

18:10 ***a tormenting spirit from God overwhelmed Saul, and he began to rave in his house like a madman.*** Lit., "An evil spirit from God rushed upon Saul and he prophesied in his house." For discussion of the meaning of "prophesy" in this context, see endnote 11 on 9:1–10:16 and the commentary below.

18:11 ***intending to pin him to the wall.*** Lit., "I will smite David and the wall," i.e., "I will smite them together."

COMMENTARY

This chapter's description of the initial manifestations of what progressively became an intense antagonism on the part of Saul toward David sets the stage for the remaining narratives of 1 Samuel. In these narratives it becomes clearer and clearer that the Lord is with David and has departed from Saul. The story of David's circuitous but inexorable rise to the throne is contrasted with Saul's debilitating mental and emotional instability and with his ever-increasing isolation from his family, the members of his court and, most importantly, from God himself.

Subsequent to David's victory over Goliath, Saul kept David at the court (18:2) and sent him on additional military missions. David's consistent success led to his appointment as a commander in Saul's army with the approval of both the military establishment and the people of the land (18:5). But David's rise in the court of Saul was not all that it appeared to be. Verses 6-11, which are a flashback to the time immediately after David's victory over Goliath, make this very clear. Saul, unlike Jonathan, was suspicious of David from the very beginning. Because of David's very public success in the Goliath episode, it was nearly impossible for Saul to avoid extending official recognition to him, but he did this only reluctantly and then with ulterior motives. In spite of outward signs of acceptance, Saul was inwardly hostile toward David. The spark that had originally ignited Saul's suspicion of David was the song of the women that placed David's accomplishments above those of himself immediately after Israel had routed the Philistines following the victory over Goliath (18:6-7).[1] It appears that when Saul heard the women sing this song, he became convinced that David was the one of whom Samuel had spoken when he said, "The LORD has torn the kingdom of Israel from you today and has given it to someone else—one who is better than you" (15:28). This immediately led him to the conclusion, "Next they'll be making him their king!" (18:8). We are thus informed that "from that time on Saul kept a jealous eye on David" (18:9). In other words, from the very first day that Saul retained David at the court after his victory over Goliath, he suspected that David was the person whom the Lord had chosen to replace him as king. Unknown to David, this was the beginning of a long period of severe testing. By the end of the chapter we are told explicitly that Saul was "David's enemy for the rest of his life" (18:29).

There is a sense in which it can be said that this chapter begins to describe for us how Saul became the "antimessiah" (i.e., the anti-anointed one, as argued by de Jong 1978:134-135). The prefix "anti-" has two meanings, both of which are relevant to what is happening here. One meaning is "against." In this chapter Saul clearly takes a position against David; he becomes David's sworn enemy. But "anti-" also has the meaning "in place of." And Saul is the "antimessiah" in that sense, as well, because he was unwilling to surrender his position as king to the person who had become the legitimate "anointed of the LORD." As the chapter opens, it is still not too late for Saul to submit to the Lord's direction. Had he humbly submitted himself to David's kingship, there surely would have been a place for him in David's service, just as there would be for Jonathan. But rather than relinquish his cherished position as king, Saul wanted to prevent David from becoming king. This attempt to retain his role of the anointed one (messiah) in the place of David, who was now God's true anointed one, turned Saul into an antimessiah.

This is the tragedy of this chapter and of the remainder of Saul's life. Here is a person who had received from the Lord a calling to a high position and who had been given great abilities, who then used that position and those abilities to oppose and persecute the Lord's anointed (de Jong 1978:135). The result was that the progress of the Kingdom of God was hindered for many years simply because the most highly placed individual in Israel sought his own interests rather than submitting them to God's revealed will. Viewed from the perspective of the forward movement of redemptive history, we find in this instance that opposition to God's redemptive program does not come from outside of God's covenant people (i.e., from the uncircumcised Philistines), as it does in chapter 17, but from within, from a person identified with the people of God. In fact, it comes from the highest place of leadership in the land.

From this point forward in 1 Samuel we have two "anointed ones." We have David, who is the true anointed one, and Saul, whom the Lord has rejected because of his disobedience. Saul represents the long line of those who set themselves in opposition to the work of God's Kingdom, often by masquerading as legitimate leaders of God's people. David, on the other hand, was an imperfect but true representative of the ideal of the covenantal king. What we see taking place in David's life anticipates in certain respects what we see later in the life of Christ (de Jong 1978:138). The Lord's true anointed ones will always encounter opposition. Psalm 2 speaks of those who conspire against the Lord and his anointed. Acts 4:27 says, "For Herod Antipas, Pontius Pilate the governor, the Gentiles, and the people of Israel were all united against Jesus, your holy servant, whom you anointed." While David's life in some respects anticipated that of Christ, at another level David represents all of God's believing people. We can learn much about our own struggles for the advancement of God's Kingdom by noticing how the Lord worked in the life of David, in spite of the strong opposition that he faced, in order to accomplish his purposes.

The day after the victory celebration over the defeat of the Philistines, Saul fell into one of his fits (described as "depression and fear" in 16:14), prompted by a "tormenting spirit from God" (18:10, cf. commentary on 16:14-16).[2] Two times Saul tried to kill David by throwing his spear at him while David was playing his harp in an attempt to soothe Saul's mind. Somehow David escaped both assaults. But the significant thing about this incident is the statement of 18:12: "Saul was then afraid of David, for the LORD was with David and had turned away from Saul." The first part of 18:12 is also revealing because after Saul had attempted to murder David, one might expect the verse to say that David was afraid of Saul. But surprisingly it says the reverse. The fear was on Saul's side, not David's. This is particularly surprising because, humanly speaking, Saul clearly had the upper hand. He was the ruling monarch. He had all the power of his office and his court to coerce David into doing his will (in 18:2 Saul would not permit David to return home; in 18:5 and 13 Saul placed David in high-ranking positions in his army). The chapter tells us of the cynical games Saul played with David and the multiple attempts he made to arrange for his death. In 18:17-19, Merab, Saul's daughter, who had been promised to David as a wife, and who rightly should have been given to him for the slaying of Goliath, was instead given to another man. On a number of occasions, Saul sent David into battle in the hope that he would be killed (18:17b, 21, 25b; it is ironic that David would later do the same to his officer Uriah; cf. 2 Sam 11:14-15). So humanly speaking, Saul had the power to make or break David. Yet, as de Jong points out (1978:137), in spite of Saul's position of superiority to David, 18:12, 15, and 29 tell us no less than three times that the great and powerful Saul was afraid of David. The reason for this fear, however, is also made very clear and is also repeated three times. It was because "the LORD was with David" (18:12, 14, 28). The theme of Saul's fear of David contrasted with David's success is the thought that is highlighted by its position at the center of the ring structure of 1 Samuel 16–19 (see commentary at 16:1).

This calls our attention to an important truth. When the Lord is with a person, he is secure no matter what forces may be arrayed against him. And when the Lord is with a person, then his enemy will fear him, even though, humanly speaking, that enemy may be in a position to do him great harm or even kill him (de Jong 1978:137). This is no less true today than it was in the time of David and Saul. Even today if God's people are faithful to their Lord, they can know that in spite of the hostility of the world, the Lord is with them and that often, contrary to what might appear to be the case, even their most powerful enemies are fearful of them. It is this abiding principle that, to a large extent, explains the extreme hostility of non-Christian political and social movements toward Christianity that is so prevalent even in our own time.

One other important feature of this chapter is the remarkable way in which, on the one hand, David achieved the love and respect of the people of the land as well as the members of Saul's family and court, while, on the other hand, Saul became increasingly isolated from those around him. David's popularity is attributable in large measure to his very visible success in all that he did. David's success is mentioned four times in the chapter (cf. 18:5, 14, 16, 30). The reason for his success was that "the LORD was with him" (18:14).[3] Because of his success, David was loved by Saul's son Jonathan (18:1, 3), by all Israel and Judah (18:16), and by Saul's daughter Michal (18:20, 28). In addition we are told that David's appointment as a commander in the army was "welcomed by the people and Saul's officers" (18:5). Clearly the alignment of the people in the chapter is toward David and away from Saul—David's entrance into the household of Saul brought division. This was so because God was "with David" and his Spirit rested upon him, and those who were around him were thereby inevitably confronted with a choice (cf. van den Berg 1996b:49-50). The same was true of David's greater son, Jesus, who said, "Don't imagine that I came to bring peace to the earth! I came not to bring peace, but a sword. 'I have come to set a man against his father, and a daughter against her mother, and a daughter-in-law against her mother-in-law. Your enemies will be right in your own household!'" (Matt 10:34-36).

Verses 28-30 sum up the entire chapter by using the four key words that have dominated the narrative: "success," the presence of the Lord "with David," "love," and "fear." It is these key word repetitions that call attention to the central themes of the chapter. Upon David's arrival at the court of Saul, he became *successful* in all he did (18:5, 14-15, 30); the reason for this is that the Lord was *with him* (18:12, 14, 28). The result was that he was *loved* by those around him (18:1, 3, 16, 20, 22, 28), but he was *feared* by Saul (18:12, 15, 29). The chapter presents us with a clear portrayal of the sort of reversal of fortune that was anticipated by Hannah's song at the beginning of the book (cf. 2:1-10). When David arrived at Saul's court and was offered one of his daughters as a wife, he said, "Who am I, and what is my family in Israel that I should be the king's son-in-law? . . . My father's family is nothing!" (18:18). When the chapter ends, its final words are, "David's name became very famous" (18:30b).[4]

ENDNOTES

1. Alter (1999:113) points out that in biblical poetry "when a number occurs in the first verset, it must be increased in the parallel verset." He then comments, "Saul shows himself a good reader of biblical poetry: he understands perfectly well that the convention is a vehicle of meaning and that the intensification or magnification characteristic of the second verset is used to set David's triumphs above his own. Saul, who earlier had made the mistake of listening to the voice of the people, now is enraged by the people's words."
2. On this occasion the MT says that Saul "prophesied" (*wayyithnabbe'* [TH5012, ZH5547]; see note on 18:10). This clearly does not mean that Saul gave a message from God, the most usual meaning of the verb "to prophesy" (*naba'*). This is one of several places in the OT where "prophesy" apparently has reference to some sort of frenzied behavioral activity (cf. 1 Kgs 18:29)—probably in this instance it was a display of an uncontrollable and raging anger.
3. In 18:28 (cf. also 18:12 and 14) we are told explicitly that even Saul knew that "the LORD was with David." Because of Saul's unwillingness to accept the consequences of this awareness, his guilt was compounded.
4. Brueggemann (1990a:140) notes that in this narrative, "David takes no initiatives. He does not assert himself or express any ambition. He only receives what is given. (In the language of Gunn [1975] it is all 'gift' without 'grasping.') David has received the submission of Jonathan, Saul's heir apparent. He is married to the king's daughter who loves him, which gives him legitimacy. He is the hero of the public . . . the only explanation is that it is the Lord's doing. . . . We are invited to watch while history works its relentless way toward God's intention. History is not a blind force or an act of sheer power. There is a purpose at work that regularly astonishes us."

◆ E. Jonathan Defends David (1 Sam 19:1-7)

**Saul now urged his servants and his son
Jonathan to assassinate David. But Jonathan, because of his strong affection for
David, 2 told him what his father was
planning. "Tomorrow morning," he
warned him, "you must find a hiding
place out in the fields. 3 I'll ask my father
to go out there with me, and I'll talk to
him about you. Then I'll tell you everything I can find out."**

**4 The next morning Jonathan spoke with
his father about David, saying many good
things about him. "The king must not sin
against his servant David," Jonathan said.
"He's never done anything to harm you.
He has always helped you in any way he
could. 5 Have you forgotten about the time
he risked his life to kill the Philistine giant
and how the LORD brought a great victory
to all Israel as a result? You were certainly happy about it then. Why should you
murder an innocent man like David? There
is no reason for it at all!"**

**6 So Saul listened to Jonathan and
vowed, "As surely as the LORD lives, David
will not be killed."**

**7 Afterward Jonathan called David and
told him what had happened. Then he
brought David to Saul, and David served
in the court as before.**

NOTES

19:3 ***everything I can find out.*** Lit., "And I will see what [is to be seen]."

COMMENTARY

Up to this point in the Samuel narratives, it might be possible, at least in some minor degree, to excuse Saul's actions against David. We noticed in the previous chapter (18:10-11) that Saul twice tried to kill David by throwing his spear at him, but he did this when he was under the influence of the tormenting or evil spirit. So perhaps it could be argued that this was something that he would not have done had he been in a more normal frame of mind (de Jong 1978:139). But at the opening of this chapter, Saul very soberly and deliberately spoke with his son Jonathan, and with some other members of his court, about arranging for David's murder (19:1). This time there is no evidence that Saul was in a frame of mind brought on by the tormenting spirit. In addition, the incident in this chapter does not seem to be the result of any specific provocation by David. Saul simply announced, without providing any reason or justification, that David must die. In the larger context, the only apparent motivation is the previously displayed enmity toward David that was born of Saul's jealousy (18:8-9) and fear (18:12, 15, 29). So the shocking thing at the opening of chapter 19 is that the reigning king of Israel—that is, the highest-ranking leader of God's covenant people—proposes aloud the murder of David, the person whom God had chosen to succeed him as king.

In chapter 18 it seems that Saul was ashamed of his feelings of hatred toward David, and as much as possible tried to hide his inward feelings toward him from his associates. In 18:17 the narrator tells us, "Saul thought, 'I'll send him out against the Philistines and let them kill him rather than doing it myself.'" On that occasion there is no indication that Saul shared his private thoughts with those around him. But now any lingering shame about his hatred toward David seems to have disappeared. We are not told what Saul's attendants thought of his radical proposal to murder David, but we are told that because of Jonathan's fondness for David, he warned him of his father's plot and then attempted to dissuade his father (19:1-5). Jonathan told Saul that he should not wrong a person who had not wronged him. But his strongest line of argument against his father's conspiracy was that the Lord had chosen to give Israel victory over the Philistines through David's leadership (19:5).[1] This was a profound warning for Saul. If he chose to continue to carry out his plan to kill David, he would place himself in opposition not only to David, but also to God's great works of deliverance for his people as well. And he would do this as the reigning monarch of Israel. Saul had observed the many victories that the Lord had given Israel under David's military leadership, and on occasion, he had even rejoiced in them (19:5). So Jonathan brought his argument to a conclusion by saying, "Why should you murder an innocent man like David? There is no reason for it at all!" (19:5).[2]

Surprisingly, Saul listened to his son Jonathan and made an oath, saying, "As surely as the LORD lives, David will not be killed" (19:6). What value, if any, was to be attached to Saul's oath became clear quickly enough. But at this point in the narrative it would seem that Saul was not yet so hardened in his rejection of God's will for himself and for David that he would no longer listen to good advice and appeals to conscience. At this point, Saul had a new opportunity to turn away from the direction that his life had been taking and to desist from his intent to take David's life. For the moment it seems hopeful that this might indeed happen, because Saul has listened to Jonathan's advice and sworn an oath in the name of the Lord recanting his intent to kill David. The result was that David felt safe enough to return to the palace (19:7).

ENDNOTES

1. Cf. de Jong 1978:141. As D. M. Gunn (1980:82) notes, "The phrase descriptive of David's defeat of the Philistine [19:5]—'and Yahweh wrought a great victory (*teshu'ah* [TH8668, ZH9591]) for all Israel'—takes us back to Saul's own initial triumph, at Jabesh-gilead, and to his own words to the people (11:13)—'today Yahweh has wrought a victory [deliverance] in Israel'—thus emphasizing that David is treading the road to kingship that Saul once trod."
2. When we read these words we may hear their echo in the words of Christ who applied to himself the similar words about David in Ps 69:4: "They hated me without cause" (John 15:25). In principle this is the same reaction that can be seen today in the world's rejection of Christ, as well as in its animosity toward and persecution of the church. Even though the church is not without sin, the world's antipathy toward the church is, for the most part, also a hatred without cause (de Jong 1978:141).

F. Saul Tries to Kill David (1 Sam 19:8-17)

**[8]War broke out again after that, and Da-
vid led his troops against the Philistines.
He attacked them with such fury that
they all ran away.**

**[9]But one day when Saul was sitting at
home, with spear in hand, the tormenting
spirit* from the LORD suddenly came upon
him again. As David played his harp,
[10]Saul hurled his spear at David. But David
dodged out of the way, and leaving the
spear stuck in the wall, he fled and es-
caped into the night.**

**[11]Then Saul sent troops to watch Da-
vid's house. They were told to kill David
when he came out the next morning. But
Michal, David's wife, warned him, "If you
don't escape tonight, you will be dead by
morning." [12]So she helped him climb out
through a window, and he fled and es-
caped. [13]Then she took an idol* and put it
in his bed, covered it with blankets, and
put a cushion of goat's hair at its head.**

**[14]When the troops came to arrest Da-
vid, she told them he was sick and couldn't
get out of bed.**

**[15]But Saul sent the troops back to get
David. He ordered, "Bring him to me in his
bed so I can kill him!" [16]But when they
came to carry David out, they discovered
that it was only an idol in the bed with a
cushion of goat's hair at its head.**

**[17]"Why have you betrayed me like this
and let my enemy escape?" Saul demand-
ed of Michal.**

**"I had to," Michal replied. "He threat-
ened to kill me if I didn't help him."**

19:9 Or *evil spirit.* **19:13** Hebrew *teraphim;* also in 19:16.

NOTES

19:11 ***If you don't escape tonight.*** Lit., "If you do not save your life tonight." This clause uses a participle rather than a finite verb. See GKC §159v regarding conditional sentences that utilize *'im* [TH518, ZH561] with a noun clause.

19:13 ***blankets.*** Lit., "with the blanket." See GKC §126q-s for use of the definite article in Hebrew in cases where, in English, the indefinite article is normally used.

COMMENTARY

Even though Saul had appeared to make peace with David (19:7), as soon as David again defeated the Philistines, Saul's old feelings of hatred toward him quickly returned. Once again Saul attempted to take David's life by throwing a spear at him (19:9-10). On this occasion, as before (18:10-12), the "tormenting spirit from God" had come upon Saul, and David was playing his harp in an attempt to soothe his mind.

This is the third time that we have been told that a "tormenting [evil] spirit from the LORD" came on Saul (cf. 16:14; 18:10). The expression is certainly a startling one, and perhaps even an upsetting one. As was noted above (see commentary on 16:14), it would seem that the best way to understand how an "evil spirit" could be said to come from the Lord is to conclude that God permitted this evil spirit to influence Saul after taking his own Spirit away from him. This permission was in effect God's judgment on Saul for his disobedience. We must remember that the first reference (16:14) to an "evil spirit from the LORD" comes after Saul had already disobeyed the Lord on two separate occasions (chs 13 and 15), during both of which he sought to excuse himself and justify his actions, using seemingly pious language to do so. It is only subsequent to these repeated rebellious actions by Saul that he was rejected as king, and only subsequent to that that we read of the coming of this "evil spirit from the LORD" upon him.

It would appear that what we encounter here with Saul is something similar to the case of Pharaoh in the book of Exodus, where it is repeatedly stated that the Lord "hardened Pharaoh's heart" (Exod 4:21; 7:3; 9:12; 10:1, 20, 27; 11:10; 14:4, 8, 17). If this analogy is correct, then in some way the Lord was involved with the hardening of Saul in his murderous intentions toward David, just as he was with Pharaoh's refusal to let Israel go from Egypt. This is not to suggest that Saul is a pawn in the hands of a scheming deity who deliberately provoked and manipulated him in a way that led him to a fate beyond his control and to the performance of sinful actions for which he was not really responsible (cf. Gunn 1980:123). This sort of reading of 1 Samuel is a distortion based on texts like 19:9, a reading that ignores the passages describing Saul's deliberate and repeated disobedience to the word of the prophet Samuel and his attempts to justify his actions rather than repent (chs 13 and 15).

While mystery enough remains whenever one reflects on divine sovereignty and human responsibility, it is clear that the Bible tells us that God's providence extends to everything that happens in all of time and space. Yet God is never the author of sin. When we read that God hardened Pharaoh's heart, some understand this in the passive sense of the withholding of grace. John Calvin, however, suggests that more is involved. In his view the Lord not only permitted Pharaoh to do what he pleased, but he actually executed a judgment on him that he knew to be just. Calvin says, "He [God] not only withdraws the grace of His Spirit, but delivers to Satan those whom he knows to be deserving of blindness of mind and obstinacy of heart" (Calvin 1979c:141). Calvin adds, however, that "God's judgments are not without reason called a 'great deep,' and therefore, let us regard them with admiration and not with railing" (1979c:102). It would appear that Saul's being tormented by an "evil spirit *from the LORD*" is a similar case. If this is so, then the solemn message of this chapter is that repeated disobedience of the Lord may lead to a hardening from which there is no way back. In other words, no one can continually act in deliberate disobedience to God's clearly revealed will and expect to escape serious consequences.

After escaping from Saul's attempt at murder, David fled from the court and went to his own home (19:10-11).[1] During the night, Saul sent some troops to David's house with instructions to kill him when he came out the next morning (19:11). Michal, Saul's daughter and David's wife, warned him that if he did not escape from their house during the night, he would certainly be killed the next day. So Michal helped David escape during the night hours. When the soldiers came for David the next morning, she told them that he was sick and could not see them. Saul, however, ordered that they bring David to the court to be killed, even if that required carrying him there on his bed (19:15). So the soldiers returned to apprehend David, but when they went to David's room they found that he was long gone. A household idol was in his place in his bed (cf. 19:13, 16).[2] Saul was upset that David had eluded capture, and he chided his daughter for her complicity in his escape, but Michal responded by falsely claiming that David had threatened to kill her if she wouldn't help him (19:17). The irony is that now two of Saul's own children have aligned themselves with David, whom Saul terms his "enemy" (19:17), and they have attempted to protect him from the vendetta of their father.[3]

ENDNOTES

1. The verb *malat* [TH4422, ZH4880], meaning "escape" in the Niphal and "save" or "deliver" in the Piel, dominates this section of ch 19, occurring five times in 19:10-18 (Niphal: 19:10, 12, 17, 18; Piel: 19:11).
2. It is not clear why there was a household idol (*terapim* [TH8655, ZH9572]) in David's home. Perhaps Michal had brought it with her at the time of her marriage to David.
3. Brueggemann (1990a:143) puts it this way: "The stories of verses 1-6 and 11-17 both begin with Saul's bold resolve to kill David. In verse 1, Saul's resolve is disrupted by the phrase 'But Jonathan.' In verse 11, it is disrupted by the phrase 'But Michal.' Saul's immediate problem is the powerful intervention of his own children, first his son and then his daughter, who thwart him. In verses 2-7, Jonathan had been direct with Saul and persuasive in his rhetoric. Michal, by contrast, is devious and indirect but equally effective."

◆ G. Samuel Protects David (1 Sam 19:18-24)

**18 So David escaped and went to Ramah to
see Samuel, and he told him all that Saul
had done to him. Then Samuel took David
with him to live at Naioth. 19 When the
report reached Saul that David was at
Naioth in Ramah, 20 he sent troops to cap-
ture him. But when they arrived and saw
Samuel leading a group of prophets who
were prophesying, the Spirit of God came
upon Saul's men, and they also began to
prophesy. 21 When Saul heard what had
happened, he sent other troops, but they,
too, prophesied! The same thing happened
a third time. 22 Finally, Saul himself went
to Ramah and arrived at the great well in
Secu. "Where are Samuel and David?" he
demanded.**

**"They are at Naioth in Ramah," some-
one told him.**

**23 But on the way to Naioth in Ramah
the Spirit of God came even upon Saul,
and he, too, began to prophesy all the
way to Naioth! 24 He tore off his clothes
and lay naked on the ground all day and
all night, prophesying in the presence
of Samuel. The people who were watch-
ing exclaimed, "What? Is even Saul a
prophet?"**

NOTES

19:18 ***Naioth.*** The Hebrew word (which is a Kethiv-Qere in MT) means "dwellings" or "a group of dwellings" and probably should not be understood as a place name. Klein (1983:198) comments, "This word, which only appears in this context (19:18, 19, 22, 23; 20:1), is probably not a proper noun, Naioth (RSV), since it is always associated with another place name, Ramah." It would appear that Naioth refers to a section or neighborhood in Ramah where a company of prophets lived in individual dwellings. For the sake of clarity, I will use the name Naioth (as does NLT) in the following commentary, as a designation for this neighborhood of prophets.

19:20 ***when they arrived and saw.*** The MT reads, "he saw." Medieval Hebrew mss, LXX, and other versions read, "when they saw."

COMMENTARY

After fleeing for his life, David sought refuge with Samuel at Ramah. Samuel took him to a section of Ramah where there was a company of prophets (19:18, see note). When Saul learned that David had gone to Naioth in Ramah, he sent some of his men there to capture David. But as Saul's men entered this neighborhood in Ramah and found Samuel and the company of prophets prophesying, the Spirit of God came on them, and they also began to prophesy. Exactly what is to be understood by "prophesying" in this passage is not entirely clear (cf. endnote 11 on 9:1–10:16 and endnote 2 on 18:5-30). If it was anything like the "prophesying" of the company of prophets that Saul had encountered shortly after Samuel had anointed him to be king (10:5-7, 9-13), which seems likely, then it was probably some sort of enthusiastic praising of God. In any case, Saul's men were so overpowered by the coming of God's Spirit upon them that they could not carry out their assigned task. When Saul sent a second and a third group to complete what the first group could not do, the same thing happened to them as well. So Saul decided to go to Naioth himself. While on his way, the Spirit of God also came upon him, and he prophesied (just as he had done previously near Gibeah, 10:10). When he arrived at Naioth he was no longer in control of his own actions and lay naked on the ground, prophesying for the remainder of that day and through the night. He was so incapacitated by this spontaneous working of God's Spirit that he was unable to capture David (19:24).

There are several things that seem to be going on in this very extraordinary experience for Saul. One might expect that this incident would have become a life-changing event for him and that his resistance to accepting God's revealed will for his life would have been altered because of it. But this did not happen. In spite of this remarkable experience, Saul remained determined to kill David, as subsequent narratives make very clear. Because Saul's antagonism toward David is at the same time defiance toward the Lord, this continued refusal to bow before God's will became one more important step in the ongoing process of the hardening of Saul. But there seem to be political as well as spiritual overtones to what Saul did at Naioth. Just as at the earlier occasion Saul's prophesying with a company of prophets was a confirming sign of his investiture with the role of king (10:1-13), so on this occasion, his prophesying, combined with the stripping off of his clothes, was a sign that he was divested of that same royal office.[1] Klement

(2000:136) comments, "Whereas in ch. 10 he was equipped through the prophetic spirit with the qualification for leadership, here he is now divested of it. Whereas the first meeting with the group of prophets was understood as a sign of the gift of the Spirit, the second with the scene in which he removes his clothes becomes a sign of the cancellation of the royal commission." When those who observed Saul prophesying at Gibeah had asked, "Is even Saul a prophet?" it seems to have been asked with a sort of incredulity combined with a hopeful expectancy at his surprising behavior (10:11). When the people at Naioth ask the same question, it seems now to be more in the sense of incredulity combined with the idea of preposterous absurdity rather than of surprised expectation.[2]

So at the conclusion of this chapter we find that David has survived four attempts on his life instigated by Saul. He survived one with Jonathan's help (19:1-7), one with Michal's help (19:11-13), and two by God's providential protection (19:10, 20-24). As a result, Saul became increasingly hardened in his rebellion against the Lord, and David was moved farther along the road toward the throne.[3]

ENDNOTES

1. This is the third time that garments, or a robe, have been connected in a symbolic way with royal office. When Samuel told Saul that the Lord had rejected him as king, and Saul tore Samuel's robe (15:27), Samuel used the symbolism of the torn robe to say, "The LORD has torn the kingdom of Israel from you today and has given it to someone else—one who is better than you" (15:28). When Jonathan made a solemn pact with David after David's victory over Goliath, he sealed it by "taking off his robe and giving it to David, together with his tunic, sword, bow, and belt" (18:4, cf. endnote 14 on 17:1–18:4). According to Brueggemann (1990a:145), what happens to Saul in 19:24 at Ramah is "an act of dramatic delegitimation of Saul."
2. Humphreys (1982:116, note 41) says, "The use of the proverb [*viz.* Is even Saul a prophet?] in 19:24 as well as in 10:11 sets a pair of brackets about the narrative, presenting Saul's first and last encounter with the spirit. The first comes just before he attained kingship, the last just before his full descent from kingship into madness and death."
3. This passage completes the first group of narratives within the larger section of chs 16–28 (the rise of David; the decline of Saul) that began with the anointing of David as king in ch 16. As has been pointed out above, these narratives reflect a ring structure similar to that of the so-called Appendix to 1–2 Samuel in 2 Sam 21–24 (see "Literary Style" in the Introduction).

◆ H. The Covenant between Jonathan and David (1 Sam 20:1-42)

David now fled from Naioth in Ramah and found Jonathan. "What have I done?" he exclaimed. "What is my crime? How have I offended your father that he is so determined to kill me?"

2"That's not true!" Jonathan protested. "You're not going to die. He always tells me everything he's going to do, even the little things. I know my father wouldn't hide something like this from me. It just isn't so!"

3Then David took an oath before Jonathan and said, "Your father knows perfectly well about our friendship, so he has

said to himself, 'I won't tell Jonathan—
why should I hurt him?' But I swear to you
that I am only a step away from death! I
swear it by the LORD and by your own
soul!"
4"Tell me what I can do to help you,"
Jonathan exclaimed.
5David replied, "Tomorrow we celebrate
the new moon festival. I've always eaten
with the king on this occasion, but tomor-
row I'll hide in the field and stay there un-
til the evening of the third day. 6If your
father asks where I am, tell him I asked
permission to go home to Bethlehem for an
annual family sacrifice. 7If he says, 'Fine!'
you will know all is well. But if he is angry
and loses his temper, you will know he is
determined to kill me. 8Show me this loy-
alty as my sworn friend—for we made a
solemn pact before the LORD—or kill me
yourself if I have sinned against your fa-
ther. But please don't betray me to him!"
9"Never!" Jonathan exclaimed. "You
know that if I had the slightest notion my
father was planning to kill you, I would
tell you at once."
10Then David asked, "How will I know
whether or not your father is angry?"
11"Come out to the field with me," Jona-
than replied. And they went out there to-
gether. 12Then Jonathan told David, "I
promise by the LORD, the God of Israel, that
by this time tomorrow, or the next day at
the latest, I will talk to my father and let
you know at once how he feels about you.
If he speaks favorably about you, I will let
you know. 13But if he is angry and wants
you killed, may the LORD strike me and
even kill me if I don't warn you so you can
escape and live. May the LORD be with you
as he used to be with my father. 14And may
you treat me with the faithful love of the
LORD as long as I live. But if I die, 15treat
my family with this faithful love, even
when the LORD destroys all your enemies
from the face of the earth."
16So Jonathan made a solemn pact with
David,* saying, "May the LORD destroy all
your enemies!" 17And Jonathan made Da-
vid reaffirm his vow of friendship again,
for Jonathan loved David as he loved him-
self.
18Then Jonathan said, "Tomorrow we
celebrate the new moon festival. You will
be missed when your place at the table is
empty. 19The day after tomorrow, toward
evening, go to the place where you hid be-
fore, and wait there by the stone pile.* 20I
will come out and shoot three arrows to
the side of the stone pile as though I were
shooting at a target. 21Then I will send a
boy to bring the arrows back. If you hear
me tell him, 'They're on this side,' then you
will know, as surely as the LORD lives, that
all is well, and there is no trouble. 22But if
I tell him, 'Go farther—the arrows are still
ahead of you,' then it will mean that you
must leave immediately, for the LORD is
sending you away. 23And may the LORD
make us keep our promises to each other,
for he has witnessed them."
24So David hid himself in the field, and
when the new moon festival began, the
king sat down to eat. 25He sat at his usu-
al place against the wall, with Jonathan
sitting opposite him* and Abner beside
him. But David's place was empty. 26Saul
didn't say anything about it that day, for
he said to himself, "Something must have
made David ceremonially unclean." 27But
when David's place was empty again the
next day, Saul asked Jonathan, "Why
hasn't the son of Jesse been here for the
meal either yesterday or today?"
28Jonathan replied, "David earnestly
asked me if he could go to Bethlehem.
29He said, 'Please let me go, for we are
having a family sacrifice. My brother de-
manded that I be there. So please let me
get away to see my brothers.' That's why
he isn't here at the king's table."
30Saul boiled with rage at Jonathan.
"You stupid son of a whore!"* he swore
at him. "Do you think I don't know that
you want him to be king in your place,
shaming yourself and your mother? 31As
long as that son of Jesse is alive, you'll
never be king. Now go and get him so I
can kill him!"
32"But why should he be put to death?"

Jonathan asked his father. "What has he done?" 33Then Saul hurled his spear at Jonathan, intending to kill him. So at last Jonathan realized that his father was really determined to kill David.

34Jonathan left the table in fierce anger and refused to eat on that second day of the festival, for he was crushed by his father's shameful behavior toward David.

35The next morning, as agreed, Jonathan went out into the field and took a young boy with him to gather his arrows. 36"Start running," he told the boy, "so you can find the arrows as I shoot them." So the boy ran, and Jonathan shot an arrow beyond him. 37When the boy had almost reached the arrow, Jonathan shouted, "The arrow is still ahead of you. 38Hurry, hurry, don't wait." So the boy quickly gathered up the arrows and ran back to his master. 39He, of course, suspected nothing; only Jonathan and David understood the signal. 40Then Jonathan gave his bow and arrows to the boy and told him to take them back to town.

41As soon as the boy was gone, David came out from where he had been hiding near the stone pile.* Then David bowed three times to Jonathan with his face to the ground. Both of them were in tears as they embraced each other and said goodbye, especially David.

42At last Jonathan said to David, "Go in peace, for we have sworn loyalty to each other in the LORD's name. The LORD is the witness of a bond between us and our children forever." Then David left, and Jonathan returned to the town.*

20:16 Hebrew *with the house of David.* **20:19** Hebrew *the stone Ezel.* The meaning of the Hebrew is uncertain. **20:25** As in Greek version; Hebrew reads *with Jonathan standing.* **20:30** Hebrew *You son of a perverse and rebellious woman.* **20:41** As in Greek version; Hebrew reads *near the south edge.* **20:42** This sentence is numbered 21:1 in Hebrew text.

NOTES

20:5 *third.* Some commentators (S. R. Driver 1913:161-162; Klein 1983:201, 203; McCarter 1980b:336) delete *hashelishith* [TH7992, ZH8958] (third), following the LXX, on the basis that it is a gloss anticipating 20:35.

20:6 *If your father asks where I am.* More lit., "If your father should become aware of my absence." For the grammar of the Hebrew here (an infinitive absolute that expresses doubt in a condition or a supposition that is not very likely), see Joüon and Muraoka §123g.

20:7 *But if he is angry.* The infinitive absolute here gives the idea of "on the other hand" or what is in opposition to the previous condition (20:7a; "If he says, 'Fine!' . . ."). See Joüon and Muraoka §123g.

20:8 *Show me this loyalty as my sworn friend.* Lit., "Now show kindness toward your servant." It is often suggested that *'al* [TH5921, ZH6584] (upon) should be emended to *'im* [TH5973, ZH6640] (with) as indicated by LXX (*meta* [TG4862, ZG5250], "with"). Stoebe (1973:374), however, suggests that *'al* may be a more precise, older (?) expression emphasizing the spontaneity of the demonstration of *khesed* [TH2617, ZH2876] (NLT, "loyalty").

20:9 *if I had the slightest notion.* Lit., "if I knew." See Joüon and Muraoka §123g; the Hebrew presents a "condition or supposition" as not very likely (cf. NLT).

20:10 *whether or not your father is angry.* Lit., "if your father answers you anything that is harsh." The translation of *'o mah-* [TH176/4100, ZH196/4537], which introduces this phrase, is difficult. *'O* is normally translated "or" or "or if," but that hardly fits in this context. Most commentators suggest an emendation to *'im* [TH518, ZH561] (if) on the basis of the LXX's *ean* [TG1437, ZG1569] (if). Other more complex explanations have been offered (see various commentaries). It seems preferable, however, to take *'o* here in the sense of "if perchance" (much as in Lev 26:41) even though some commentators (S. R. Driver 1913:163; Goslinga 1968:367) have disputed this suggestion.

20:12 ***I promise by the Lord, the God of Israel.*** Lit., "The LORD, the God of Israel." After this phrase, there is no need to insert *'ed* [TH5713, ZH6338] (resulting in "the LORD God of Israel *is witness*") or *khay* [TH2416A, ZH2645] (resulting in "as the LORD God of Israel *lives*"). As Stoebe (1973:374) argues, the present text is preferable as *lectio brevior.*

If he speaks favorably about you. Lit., "and if there is good toward David." Labuschagne (1973) argues that sometimes *hinneh* [TH2009, ZH2180] is to be viewed as other than a demonstrative particle, and that here, as well as elsewhere in the OT, it introduces a conditional clause.

20:13 ***if I don't warn you.*** There is no "don't" (*lo'* [TH3808, ZH4202], "do not, no") here as there is in 20:12b (lit., "will I not let you know?"). The Hebrew seems defective. Exactly how it originally read is difficult to determine. McCarter (1980b:333) translates the verse, "May God do thus to Jonathan and thus again, but if my father wishes to bring evil against you, *I will reveal it to you* and send you away." This follows the phrase in question, but leaves the maledictory oath in the first phrase of the verse hanging alone.

20:14-15a ***And may you.*** Lit., "will [you] not." This is the first of a series of five uses of *welo'-* [TH3808, ZH4202] (and not) in 20:14-15a. Translation is difficult. Some (cf. S. R. Driver 1913:164) have proposed modifying the pointing of the first two occurrences to *welu'* [TH3863, ZH4273] (and if only). The resulting literal translation would be, "And if only you, as long as I am alive—indeed, if only you would show me the kindness of the LORD, that I may not die."

20:16 ***So Jonathan made a solemn pact with David.*** Lit., "So Jonathan cut [a covenant] with the house of David." The LXX combines 20:15b and 16 and reads, "And when the Lord cuts off the enemies of David, each one from the face of the ground, *the name of Jonathan shall not be cut off from the house of David.*"

20:17 ***as he loved himself.*** For the syntax of this phrase (including the idea of comparison), see Joüon and Muraoka §125q, note 2; §125r; §174g.

20:19 ***The day after tomorrow.*** *Weshillashta* [TH8027, ZH8992] is a seldom-used verb that may be translated "do something a third time," "do something on the third day," or "do something for three days." The context here (cf. 20:26-27, 35) favors the second rendering.

toward evening. *Tered me'od* [TH3381/3966, ZH3718/4394] is literally, "You will go down exceedingly." This is an unusual use of *me'od* that could mean either "go a long way," or "go quickly." The NLT (cf. NIV), however, translates the phrase *tered me'od* as "toward evening." This may be based on Guillaume's (1954:85) suggestion that *me'od* should be revocalized as *ma'od* and considered cognate to an assumed Arabic *ma'ad* (evening), or based on the sort of explanation given by Youngblood (1992:726) that assumes that *tered me'od* has the unexpressed feminine noun *shemesh* [TH8121, ZH9087] (sun) as its subject (cf. Isa 38:8), yielding the phrase, "[the sun] goes down exceedingly" = "[the sun] had almost set."

before. Lit., "on the day of the deed." The NIV interprets the deed as "when this trouble began." The NRSV renders the phrase by "earlier" (much like NLT), and the NASB by "on that eventful day."

20:21 ***If you hear me tell him.*** One might also translate this, "If, on the one hand, I say . . ." with the "on the one hand" being derived from the use of the infinitive absolute to highlight a contrast or opposition. For use of the infinitive absolute to indicate an opposition in a conditional clause, see Joüon and Muraoka §123g.

20:23 ***for he has witnessed them.*** Lit., "The LORD is between you and me forever." The LXX reads, "The LORD *is witness* (*martus* [TG3144, ZG3459]) between you and me forever." There is no need to assume the haplography of a proposed original text containing *'ed 'ad* as does E. Finkelstein (1959). The *martus* of the LXX is likely a clarifying addition.

20:25 *with Jonathan sitting opposite him.* The Hebrew is "Jonathan arose." Many commentators (S. R. Driver 1913:169; Klein 1983:202, 204; McCarter 1980b:333, 338; Youngblood 1992:726), as well as the NLT and NIV, prefer the emendation of *wayyaqam* [TH6965, ZH7756] (he rose) to *wayyeqaddem* [TH6923, ZH7709] ("he was in front of," i.e., opposite to Saul) on the basis of the LXX *kai proephthasen ton Iōnathan* (and he [Saul] went before [i.e., was in front of] Jonathan). But the sense of LXX is not clearly equivalent and its priority is questioned by Hertzberg (1964:170) and Gordon (1986:167-168), among others.

20:29 *My brother demanded that I be there.* Klein (1983:202, 204), McCarter (1980b:334, 339), and others, following LXX and 4QSam^b, read "my brothers [plural] commanded me," but there is no necessity to abandon the singular of MT.

20:30 *You stupid son of a whore!* Lit., "You son of a perverse woman of rebelliousness!" The Hebrew expression is undoubtedly colloquial. The MT seems preferable to modification along the lines of the LXX and 4QSam^b (Klein 1983:202, 204; McCarter 1980b:334, 339) in which *na'awath* (Niphal participle of *'awah* [TH5753, ZH6390], "perverted") is changed to the improbable *na'arath* [TH5291, ZH5855] (girl of) as a designation for the mother of Jonathan.

20:41 *especially David.* The idea is apparently that David wept the most. The Hebrew is literally, "to David, he has done great." The meaning of the Hebrew is obscure. The LXX reads "for a great while," but retroversion from the Greek to the Hebrew is difficult. The precise meaning remains uncertain.

COMMENTARY

This is the first passage in a new set of five narrative units, running from 20:1–23:28, which can also be grouped in a ring structure similar to that of the narratives of chapters 16–19.[1] This set of narratives is framed by two narratives in which Saul's persistence in his determination to kill David is countered by Jonathan's faithfulness to his covenant with David (20:1-42 and 23:1-28). Just inside this frame are two narratives dealing with the relationship of David to Ahimelech and the priests of Nob, who were murdered because they assisted him (21:1-9; 22:6-23). At the center of the ring structure, David is shown to be a fugitive, moving from Gath to Adullam to Mizpeh and being instructed by the prophet Gad (21:10–22:5).[2] The resulting literary structure (as adapted and modified from Klement 2000:139) is as follows:

- 20:1-42 Saul persists in his determination to kill David; the covenant between Jonathan and David
  - 21:1-9 David and Ahimelech, the priest at Nob; Doeg, Goliath's sword
    - 21:10–22:5 David a fugitive (Gath, Adullam, Mizpeh)
  - 22:6-23 David learns from his mistakes as Ahimelech and the priests at Nob are murdered; Doeg, Goliath's sword
- 23:1-28 Saul persists in his determination to kill David; Jonathan encourages David

First Samuel 20 is a narrative that consists almost entirely of very intense dialogue between David and Jonathan.[3] David and Jonathan were each faced with momentous decisions that would chart the future course of their lives. In view of the threats that had been made on his life, the decision for David concerned whether he should leave the court of Saul for good.[4] On the one hand, he still had the obligations and responsibilities that were his as a servant of Saul, while on the other hand, he feared for his life. For Jonathan, the decision involved choosing between personal ambition and the advancement of God's Kingdom. As the narrative unfolds, David and Jonathan wrestled with these questions together, and both made decisions that demonstrated not only their commitment to each other but their commitment to live their lives to honor God.

As chapter 20 opens, we might wonder why David would even consider going back to the service of Saul.[5] In the preceding chapter, he left the court after Saul attempted to kill him. He went to Samuel in Ramah, where Saul pursued him but was prevented from capturing him because he was overcome by the Spirit of God. Certainly David had good reason for saying to Jonathan, "I swear to you that I am only a step away from death!" (20:3). But we must remember that David was still officially in the service of Saul and that he was presumably still under the obligations of the agreement between Saul and Jesse, his father, under which he had been brought to the court (cf. 16:21-22). Saul, it seems, fully expected David to return to the court, in spite of his previous treatment of him, and so asked Jonathan about him (20:27). David evidently took this responsibility very seriously. If he were to leave the court, he wanted to do so in an ethically honorable way, with a clear sense of the Lord's leading, rather than departing in a manner dictated purely by self-interest.

In the conversation between David and Jonathan, the strategy that emerged for settling this question was for David to absent himself on the next day from the meal at the court being held in celebration of the new moon (20:5). If Saul asked where David was, then Jonathan would tell him that he gave David permission to go to Bethlehem for an annual family sacrifice. If Saul accepted this explanation, then Jonathan and David would know that things were normalized, and that it would be incumbent upon David to remain in Saul's service (20:7). But if Saul became angry, then they would know that Saul still intended to kill David and that there was justifiable reason for David to leave the court.[6] In that case, Jonathan would signal David to "leave immediately, for the LORD is sending you away" (20:22b).

Saul, of course, reacted in a very negative way to David's absence. He said nothing on the first day because he thought that perhaps David was ceremonially unclean. But on the second day he asked Jonathan why David was not present at the meal. When Jonathan explained that he had given David permission to attend a family sacrifice in Bethlehem, Saul became so enraged that he excoriated Jonathan, saying, "You stupid son of a whore! . . . Do you think I don't know that you want him to be king in your place, shaming yourself and your mother? As long as that son of Jesse is alive, you'll never be king. Now go and get him so I can kill him!" (20:30-31).[7] The result was that both Jonathan and David knew that it was futile to attempt to deal further with Saul, and Jonathan not only gave David permission to leave the service of his father, but sent him away with the Lord's blessing. This confirmation from the Lord was what David was seeking as he considered leaving the service of Saul.

David's careful consideration of his responsibility to Saul takes on greater significance later on in 1 Samuel in connection with David's involvement with Nabal, the rich fool of the Old Testament (ch 25). When David asked Nabal for some remuneration for his past protection of Nabal's shepherds and flocks, Nabal implied that David was a no-good runaway (25:10). The suggestion that David had left Saul in a hasty and irresponsible manner impugned David's honor. David had held out in Saul's court for as long as possible because he understood that God was leading his life, even through the difficult circumstances at Saul's court, and he believed that God was preparing him for assuming the responsibilities of kingship in the future.

Subsequent to his anointing by Samuel, David's reaction was not, "Let me, now, quickly do all I can to assume the throne," but rather, "Now, I must place the direction of my life in God's hands more than ever before, and more than anyone else" (de Jong 1978:151). The way to the throne must be one that was prepared by the Lord. And from this perspective, as we read this chapter with all of its complicated circumstances, we find what one might term a "discerning passivity" on the part of David (de Jong 1978:151). This is not to say that David, or we, for that matter, should just sit down and passively watch as events overtake us. Certainly God's leading in the lives of his people does not mean that his people have no responsibility to take prudent actions in order to determine the direction their lives will take. But when approaching situations of this sort, there must be, as we find in this narrative, an intentional carefulness combined with a reluctance to make hasty decisions, particularly in matters of long-term significance.[8] Later in his life David said, "My eyes are always on the LORD, for he rescues me from the traps of my enemies" (Ps 25:15). This perspective is needed by God's people today every bit as much as when David wrestled with whether or not to leave the court of Saul. The eyes of God's people must constantly be on the Lord and the work of his Kingdom in the important task of charting the course of their lives.

So in seeking resolution to the conflict between a prior commitment and his own self-interest, David honored the commitment he had made in coming to the court, he submitted to hardship as part of God's providential ordering of his life, and he sought a clear confirmation of the Lord's leading before deciding that it was the Lord's will for him to leave Saul.

Jonathan also faced a crisis that arose out of the strife between Saul, his father, and David, his close friend and compatriot. In Jonathan's case the conflict was between the advancement of God's Kingdom and the advancement of his own personal ambition. Jonathan was the crown prince. He had every right to expect to succeed his father on the throne of Israel, but he was ready and willing to renounce his own interests and aspirations for the sake of submission to the Lord's choice of David to be king. Davis (1994b:70) comments that Jonathan's life was not "centered in his ambition (what I can get) but rather in God's providence (what Yahweh has given)." At the close of the chapter where we read about the final meeting between David and Jonathan, we are told that "Both of them were in tears as they embraced each other and said good-bye, especially David" (20:41). In this dramatic scene, it is Jonathan who maintained the greatest measure of self-control. And it is Jonathan who sent David off with the words, "Go in peace" (20:42).

But there is another thing to be noticed about Jonathan's actions in this time of crisis in his own life. In 20:15b Jonathan speaks of a time when the Lord will "[destroy all David's] enemies from the face of the earth"—and Jonathan no doubt knew his own father was among David's enemies. Precisely at the time when David was about to begin the life of a fugitive, it must have been reassuring for him to hear that his friend had such confidence about his future. Even more so since the immediate prospect for David was a life that would be just about as dangerous away from the court as it was at the court. In his reference to a significant reversal for David in the future, Jonathan was prophetic.

There is one more thing that Jonathan does in this narrative that calls for our attention. Jonathan appealed to David to treat him and his family with the faithful love of the Lord (20:14-15).[9] From this statement, it is quite clear that Jonathan knew that in due time David would replace his father Saul as king. According to the standard practice of that time, this would mean that Jonathan's life, and those of his children, would be very much in danger. In ancient Near Eastern culture when someone established a new dynasty, one of the first official acts was to wipe out the descendants of the king who was being replaced (this was done in Israel under Baasha, Zimri, and Jehu). Although David did not enact this practice, Jonathan was in effect asking the same thing of David as the thief on the cross asked of Jesus: "Remember me when you come into your Kingdom" (Luke 23:42). And David, like Jesus, was receptive of the request. In this feature of the dialogue between Jonathan and David, one can look far beyond David to David's greater son, Jesus. Jesus went through suffering and death in the path of obedience in a way that far surpassed David's endurance of trials. In Jesus we have a merciful king and High Priest who was tempted in every way as we are, yet without sin. And we, as Jonathan did with David, can entrust to Jesus all that we have and are, including our descendants (de Jong 1978:153).

In sum, we find in this chapter that God was faithful to both David and Jonathan. The providential direction of their lives included much adversity and trouble, but God gave encouragement for each along the way. God used the humble service of each to advance his Kingdom and bring blessing and encouragement to one another in their work for the Lord.

ENDNOTES

1. See the discussion in the Introduction.
2. Here, as in 18:5-30, Klement (2000:139) divides the central passage into two units, presumably in order to maintain the parallel with the ring structure of the Samuel Conclusion (2 Sam 21–24), which also has two parallel units at its center.
3. As Polzin (1989:191) notes, the words of David and Jonathan are characterized by a "preponderance of definitive, forceful, strident, and emotionally charged language that permeates these verses." The finite verb is strengthened or emphasized by a preceding infinitive absolute of the same stem no fewer than seven times in verses 1-21 (20:3, 5, 6 [twice], 7, 9, 21). Both David and Jonathan frequently invoke the Lord's name in solemn oath, self-imprecation, or blessing: "As the LORD lives!" (20:3, 21); "LORD God of Israel" (20:12); "May the LORD do and continue to do!" (20:13); "May the LORD be with you" (20:13); "May the LORD protect David from his enemies" (20:16); "the LORD is between you and me forever!" (20:23). The partners repeatedly protest, implore, and react in the strongest of terms: "Far from it!" (*khalilah* [TH2486, ZH2721], 20:2); "But truly (*we'ulam* [TH199, ZH219]) . . . as your soul lives!" (20:3); "Far be it from you!" (20:9); "Would I not (*welo'* [TH2050.1/3808, ZH2256/4202]) tell you?" (20:9); "Would I not then send and inform you?" (20:12); "Would you not show me the loyal love of the LORD?" (20:14); "Would you

cut off your loyalty from my house?" (20:15); and they frequently punctuate their statements with the deictic *hinneh* [TH2009, ZH2180], "behold" (20:2, 5, 12, 21, 22, 23).

4. Literary critics have traditionally said that various things described in this narrative (such as David's return to the court, Jonathan's apparent ignorance of his father's murderous intentions toward David, and Saul's expectation that David would be at his place at the table) are inconsistent with ch 19, and that this was an originally independent narrative unit that has been inserted here, out of chronological order, and then redactionally adapted to its present context (cf. Klein 1983:205).
5. If the purpose of David's return to the court was, as Klein suggests (1983:205), merely to determine whether or not Saul's intentions toward him were hostile, then the narrative does, indeed, seem to be out of place, because Saul's hostile intentions seem to be quite clear. It appears, however, that David's return was occasioned by an attempt to resolve two other questions. The first was whether or not he had done anything that merited Saul's extreme displeasure with him (20:1). On this matter, Jonathan assures him that he had not (20:2, cf. 20:32). The second question was whether or not he should permanently abandon his responsibilities at the court, and if he could do so with the Lord's blessing.
6. Polzin (1989:189) places a manipulative interpretation on David's strategy, saying that his real intention is "to provoke Saul to an angry outburst that would remove Jonathan's misconceptions, not his own."
7. Alter (1999:128) comments, "Saul concludes that David's loyalty to his clan takes precedence over his loyalty to his king, and he may even suspect that David means to use his clan as a power base to challenge the throne."
8. As de Jong (1978:148) suggests, it requires a great deal of patience and carefulness to draw conclusions concerning the will of God from someone's personal circumstances.
9. "Faithful love" is the NLT's translation of the Hebrew term *khesed* [TH2617, ZH2876]. This word, having a wide range of usage on both the human and divine planes, is a relational term that conveys the idea of "steadfast love," "faithfulness," or as the KJV translates it, "lovingkindness." In the context of this chapter it is clearly connected with the covenant relationship (NLT, "solemn pact") that existed between Jonathan and David (cf. 18:3; 20:8; 23:18). NIDOTTE 2.212, however, is correct in suggesting that it is "unwise to regard *khesed* in such a context as if it were an aspect or ingredient of covenant as such. Rather, the covenant comes in to reinforce the commitment to *khesed* in a situation where its exercise is not naturally to be expected or is likely to be put under strain by future circumstances." Brueggemann (1990a:149) rightly sees a "deliberate narrative allusion" in 20:15-16 to 2 Sam 9:1 "in which David is said to ask, 'Is there still any one left of the house of Saul, that I may show him *khesed* for Jonathan's sake?' When the pitiful, handicapped son of Jonathan is brought, David assures him, 'Do not fear; for I will show you *khesed* for the sake of your father Jonathan' (II Sam. 9:7)."

◆ I. David and Ahimelech the Priest (1 Sam 21:1-9)

**1*David went to the town of Nob to see
Ahimelech the priest. Ahimelech trembled
when he saw him. "Why are you alone?"
he asked. "Why is no one with you?"**

**2"The king has sent me on a private
matter," David said. "He told me not to tell
anyone why I am here. I have told my men
where to meet me later. 3Now, what is
there to eat? Give me five loaves of bread
or anything else you have."**

**4"We don't have any regular bread,"
the priest replied. "But there is the holy**

bread, which you can have if your young
men have not slept with any women re-
cently."
5 "Don't worry," David replied. "I never
allow my men to be with women when
they are on a campaign. And since they
stay clean even on ordinary trips, how
much more on this one!"
6 Since there was no other food available,
the priest gave him the holy bread—the
Bread of the Presence that was placed be-
fore the LORD in the Tabernacle. It had just
been replaced that day with fresh bread.
7 Now Doeg the Edomite, Saul's chief
herdsman, was there that day, having
been detained before the LORD.*
8 David asked Ahimelech, "Do you have
a spear or sword? The king's business was
so urgent that I didn't even have time to
grab a weapon!"
9 "I only have the sword of Goliath the
Philistine, whom you killed in the valley
of Elah," the priest replied. "It is wrapped
in a cloth behind the ephod. Take that if
you want it, for there is nothing else
here."
"There is nothing like it!" David replied.
"Give it to me!"

21:1 Verses 21:1-15 are numbered 21:2-16 in Hebrew text. **21:7** The meaning of the Hebrew is uncertain.

NOTES

21:2 [3] ***I have told my men where to meet me later.*** Lit., "[so] I sent [my] young men to such and such a place." "I sent" (*yoda'ti* [TH3045, ZH3359]) has been explained as a Poel from *yada'* [TH3045, ZH3359] meaning "to direct" (cf. GKC §55b, BDB 394c). Stoebe (1973:392) terms this suggestion not impossible but unlikely with verbs of the class Pe-Waw like this one. Others, on the basis of LXX, have suggested a spelling error and substituted *yo'adti,* (from *ya'ad* [TH3259, ZH3585]), meaning "to appoint" (S. R. Driver 1913:173; BDB 417a) for MT's *yoda'ti.* Thomas (1934) suggests that in some contexts *yada'* may have the meaning "to dismiss" or "send away." Of these difficult options, the MT is probably the best choice. The NLT's rendering captures this pretty well.

21:4 [5] ***women.*** This word (*'ishah* [TH802, ZH851]) is grammatically singular. See Joüon and Muraoka §136c for use of a singular noun as a noun of species or of a category that is translated as equivalent to a plural.

21:5 [6] ***I never allow my men to be with women.*** Lit., "women have been kept away from us as yesterday, three days ago." The expression "yesterday, three days ago" may be taken to mean "formerly," "customarily" (as in NLT), or "for the past few days."

And since they stay clean even on ordinary trips, how much more on this one! Lit., "The vessels of the young men are holy, even when it is an ordinary journey. How much more today will the vessels be holy." "The vessels" (*kele-* [TH3627, ZH3998]) has been understood as a reference to weapons, clothing, or euphemistically as a reference to the male sexual organ.

21:9 [10] ***a cloth.*** Lit., "the cloth." For use of the Hebrew article in cases of "imperfect determination" best translated in English by "a," see Joüon and Muraoka §137m.

COMMENTARY

This chapter opens the period of David's life in which he was a refugee or wanderer. After leaving the court, his family, and his friend Jonathan, David went to the sanctuary at Nob (21:1-9) and then on to the Philistine city, Gath (21:10–22:1). The headings of Psalms 34 and 56 attribute their origin to this time in David's life. In Psalm 56:8 [9] David says, "You keep count of my wanderings (*nodi* [TH5112, ZH5654]); put my tears into Your flask, into Your record" (NJPS). The narratives of 1 Samuel 21–31 confirm that the days of David's wandering were indeed days of tears. This was a difficult and dangerous period in his life, one in which he underwent severe testings and trials, but also one in which the Lord sustained him, in spite of his own failures and the persistence of Saul in seeking his life. Without his being shaped, purged, and refined through the hardship and struggle that he experienced during this time, it is likely that David's kingship would have been more susceptible to the sort of pride and stubbornness that were all too characteristic of Saul's reign. It was in the experiences of these difficult days that David learned much about humility and dependence on the Lord.[1]

Upon leaving the court, David sought assistance from a priest named Ahimelech[2] who officiated at a sanctuary located at Nob.[3] Just as the elders at Bethlehem trembled when Samuel arrived at their village to anoint David (16:4), so Ahimelech "trembled" when David arrived at the sanctuary in Nob (21:1). It would appear that Ahimelech, like the elders at Bethlehem, did not desire to become entangled in the well-known dispute between Saul and David. Ahimelech was probably fully aware that giving help to David was risky business. David, however, misleadingly told him that he had been sent on a secret mission by the king (21:2)[4] and that he was in need of food and a weapon.[5] Ahimelech told him that the only bread he had was the holy bread, which normally could be eaten only by descendants of Aaron at a sanctuary (cf. Lev 24:5-9). Ahimelech nevertheless agreed to give this bread to David for himself and his men, if they met the standard of ritual cleanliness concerning sexual contact (cf. Lev 15:18).[6] David assured him that this was not a problem. The only weapon Ahimelech had was the sword of Goliath, which David was pleased to receive. There is a hint of trouble to come, however, because the narrator comments in 21:7 that Doeg the Edomite, Saul's chief herdsman, was at Nob on that day.[7] The assessment of David's conduct in this incident has long been puzzling to commentators. Some have defended David's subterfuge toward Ahimelech as justified because it was intended to protect his own life as well as the lives of the few men who were allied with him (if, in fact, David really did have a contingent of his own followers with him as he alleged to Ahimelech), and also because it provided Ahimelech with the alibi that David had told him that he was on a mission for King Saul. According to this viewpoint, what David did here was little different from what the Lord instructed Samuel to do when he went to Bethlehem to anoint David (16:2). While it could be argued that these sorts of considerations exonerate David from any wrongdoing at Nob, it would seem that David himself later concluded that his visit to Nob, and his involvement of Ahimelech in his attempt to escape from Saul, was a mistake. This, of course, in no way absolves Saul from committing a reprehensible act in the slaughter of the priests of Nob.

In 22:6-23, which contains the sequel to this story, David says to Abiathar, the only person to escape Saul's slaughter of the priests of Nob, "I knew it! When I saw Doeg the Edomite there that day, I knew he was sure to tell Saul. Now I have caused the death of all your father's family" (22:22). In hindsight, it appears that David seriously regretted having ever gone to Nob, and having used the priest there for his own purposes, without informing him of what it was he was doing. Had David been honest with Ahimelech, then Ahimelech could have chosen for himself whether or not he wanted to become involved with David's plans (de Jong 1978:156).

When this incident is looked at from the long-range perspective of the ways in which David's life points forward to the life of Jesus, who acted to "fulfill all righteousness" (Matt 3:15, NLT mg), there is something in it that is discordant with David's own messianic calling. As de Jong (1978:158) points out, contrary to what David did on this occasion, when Jesus began his work in the world, he fully informed those to whom he spoke about what they were doing when they chose to align themselves with him. Jesus regularly warned those who would follow him, that they should count the cost—he didn't have a "place even to lay his head" (cf. Matt 8:20). Jesus, like David, was a wanderer, but when he called others to follow him, he told them who he was and what he was about in very clear terms. The Kingdom of God is a Kingdom of justice and integrity, not one of deception.

ENDNOTES

1. Ellsworth (1998:80) comments on this period in David's life: "So it was off to the wilderness with David. There God would break him of relying on his own wisdom and teach him to rely wholly on the word of the Lord. . . . [God] frequently brings hardship into the lives of His children in order to bring them to a higher level of maturity and usefulness."
2. Ahimelech is either an alternate name for Ahijah, or perhaps Ahijah's brother (cf. 14:3). He was the son of Ahitub (the brother of Ichabod) in the line of Eli, and the father of Abiathar (22:20).
3. Nob appears to be the primary sanctuary in Israel subsequent to the destruction of the Tabernacle at Shiloh at the time of the capture of the Ark (ch 4; Jer 7:12, 14; 26:6, 9). While the precise location of Nob is not known, Isa 10:32 suggests that it was just to the north of Jerusalem. Although the Ark remained at the house of Abinadab in Kiriath-jearim after its capture and return by the Philistines (7:1; 2 Sam 6:3), Ahimelech, the high priest at Nob, did have custody of the ephod, a means of receiving divine guidance (cf. Exod 28:6-30).
4. Is this a deliberate ambiguity, suggesting that the mission was authorized by Saul, but really meaning that it was authorized by Yahweh, the divine king?
5. In 22:10 we are told that when David visited Nob he had also asked Ahimelech to consult the Lord for him, presumably by means of the ephod. That, in fact, may have been the primary reason David went to Nob in the first place, because he probably could have acquired food and a weapon in other ways.
6. Jesus' comments on this incident in the NT make it clear that this was not a culpable act. According to Matt 12:1-8, Jesus discussed the law with the Pharisees in connection with the disciples having unlawfully picked some grain on the Sabbath. After citing this incident in ch 21 where David and his men unlawfully ate the consecrated bread, Jesus concluded, "If you had known what these words mean, 'I desire mercy, not sacrifice,' you would not have condemned the innocent. For the Son of Man is Lord of the Sabbath" (Matt 12:7-8, NIV). Jesus thus suggested that every rule has its exception, which is something difficult for legalistically minded people to accept. Recognition of what constitutes a valid exception then becomes the real problem, and this is clearly something for which great wisdom and discernment are required. Jesus, however, endorsed David and Ahimelech's decision in this particular case.
7. Alter (1999:132) comments, "This seemingly intrusive notation is a piece of ominous foreshadowing. . . . The ghastly consequences of David's visit to Nob (Chapter 22) will pivot on Doeg's fatal presence. His identity as an Edomite reflects the enlistment of foreign mercenaries in the new royal bureaucracy. It also marks him as a man who will have no inhibition in what he does to Israelites, even Israelite priests."

J. David as a Fugitive (1 Sam 21:10–22:5)

10So David escaped from Saul and went to
King Achish of Gath. 11But the officers of
Achish were unhappy about his being
there. "Isn't this David, the king of the
land?" they asked. "Isn't he the one the
people honor with dances, singing,

'Saul has killed his thousands,
and David his ten thousands'?"

12David heard these comments and was
very afraid of what King Achish of Gath
might do to him. 13So he pretended to be
insane, scratching on doors and drooling
down his beard.

14Finally, King Achish said to his men,
"Must you bring me a madman? 15We al-
ready have enough of them around here!
Why should I let someone like this be my
guest?"

CHAPTER 22

So David left Gath and escaped to the cave of Adullam. Soon his brothers and all his other relatives joined him there.
2Then
others began coming—men who were in trouble or in debt or who were just discontented—until David was the captain of about 400 men.

3Later David went to Mizpeh in Moab,
where he asked the king, "Please allow my father and mother to live here with you until I know what God is going to do for
me."
4So David's parents stayed in Moab with the king during the entire time David was living in his stronghold.

5One day the prophet Gad told David,
"Leave the stronghold and return to the land of Judah." So David went to the forest of Hereth.

NOTES

22:3 ***allow my father and mother to live here with you.*** Lit., "Let my father and my mother come out [and stay] with you." The MT has no word for "and stay." The idea must be supplied in translation. Although not without difficulty, understanding as a contracted utterance or *Breviloquenz* (cf. Stoebe 1973:404) seems better than the emendation of *yatsa'* [TH3318, ZH3655] (come out) into either *yashab* [TH3427, ZH3782] ("dwell," Klein 1983:220); *yannakh* (from *nuakh* [TH5117, ZH5663], "settle," McCarter 1980b:355); or *yutsag* [TH3322, ZH3657] ("be left behind," S. R. Driver 1913:179).

COMMENTARY

When David left Nob, he went to the land of the Philistines and sought refuge with Achish, the king of Gath (21:10). It may be puzzling to the reader why David would choose to enter enemy territory. There is nothing said in the text about what he thought could be gained by going there, though perhaps he wanted simply to place himself beyond the reach of Saul.[1] Still, silence on matters of our curiosity is often the case in Old Testament narrative. Numerous questions about the unexplained actions of major characters in biblical narratives can never be answered with certainty. Whatever David thought he could accomplish by going to Gath, in his mind it must have outweighed the consideration that the Philistines were Israel's enemies (de Jong 1978:159). It is surprising that David was able to survive this risky venture without losing his life. The Philistines did not regard David as just another Israelite. They said, "Isn't this David, the king of the land? . . . Isn't he the one the people honor with dances, singing, 'Saul has killed his thousands, and David his ten thousands'?" (21:11). This song had angered Saul (18:8) and become known to the Philistines as well. Their own observation of the internal politics and public opinion in Israel had apparently caused them to conclude that David was the de facto king.[2] The Philistines were less naive or unsuspecting than David had apparently supposed. And when David saw how they were reacting to him, he had good reason to be fearful (21:12).

When we reflect on the two events that are reported in 1 Samuel 21 (David's visits to Nob and to Gath), both of which happened at the beginning of David's life as a wanderer, it would seem reasonable to conclude with de Jong (1978:160) that God was using these experiences in David's life to show him how dangerous it was to live the life of a fugitive and wanderer. David had to learn extreme carefulness in everything that he did, and even more importantly, he had to learn to find his sense of security in this dangerous world by trusting in the Lord. It is here that Psalms 34 and 56[3] become so important for discerning the meaning of David's experiences in chapter 21.

In Psalm 56:4 and 56:11, David confesses, "I trust in God, so why should I be afraid? What can mere mortals do to me?"[4] David's time of wandering was indeed one of danger and fear, but it was also a time in which he learned to trust in God. This trust, however, did not mean that when David was arrested by the servants of Achish, he would passively wait to see what would happen. No, he took the initiative. In this case, his ingenuity led him to act like a madman, causing Achish to regard him not only as no threat to Philistia, but also as someone whom he did not want in his presence.[5]

While the specifics of David's experience in these two incidents are unique to him, the underlying principles governing how God's people are to live in a fallen world are certainly still operative today. The New Testament reminds God's people that their citizenship is not on earth but in heaven; we are pilgrims and strangers here on earth. Our task is to be engaged with the world, but never to forget that while we are in the world, we are not of the world. Our calling today, like David's in his time, is to live as aliens in a hostile environment. Because of this we should never be indifferent or oblivious to the dangers that living in a manner promoting the advancement of God's Kingdom may entail. These dangers may be more or less intense depending on the specific national and cultural environment in which we live, but they will always be present. In this connection, however, it is important to notice that David not only experienced danger and threats to his life, but he also experienced God's deliverance. God does not only put the tears of his wanderers in his bottle (or wineskin, Ps 56:8); he also helps his people. As Psalm 34:4 says, "I prayed to the LORD, and he answered me. He freed me from all my fears." Consider, on the one hand, how David must have felt when he saw Doeg at Nob and when he fell into the hands of Achish's servants, but notice, on the other hand, what he says in Psalm 34:6-7: "In my desperation I prayed, and the LORD listened; he saved me from all my troubles. For the angel of the LORD is a guard; he surrounds and defends all who fear him."

So chapter 21 provides a wake-up call to God's believing people of all times and places. It is a reminder that: (1) living as a Christian in a fallen world is inherently dangerous; (2) our own foolish behavior often heightens the dangers of this hostile environment; (3) God's mercies are new each day in spite of our failures; and (4) God's purposes for his people cannot be frustrated by the designs of the ungodly. It is important that God's people be reminded of the dangers that are endemic to their own journey through life as strangers and pilgrims on earth, and that these dangers do not just arise from without but also from within.

Subsequent to escaping Gath, David found refuge in a cave near Adullam (22:1).[6] He was joined there by family members, who probably feared that Saul would extend his vendetta against David to them as well.[7] As word spread concerning David's whereabouts, other outcasts of society joined up with him to form a small militia that eventually numbered about 400 men. While the reference to this militia might appear to suggest that David was gathering a force to seize the throne from Saul, David's consistent refusal to take Saul's life when the opportunity presented itself (chs 24 and 26) demonstrates that this was not at all his intention. Because his parents were advanced in years (cf. 17:12, "Jesse was an old man"), and were unable to cope with the danger and rigors of wilderness living, David took them to the land of Moab for safety. The king of Moab was a natural ally for David not only because he had been attacked by Saul (14:47), but also because Ruth, David's ancestor, was a Moabitess (cf. Ruth 1:22; 4:13-22).[8] After securing protection for his parents, David and his men situated themselves in an otherwise unidentified "stronghold" (22:4-5), probably located in the border region between Moab and Israel. While David was encamped in this "stronghold," the prophet Gad suddenly appeared on the scene and instructed David to return to the territory of Judah. David obediently followed his instructions, and he and his band of outcasts set up camp in the forest of Hereth.[9] David not only responded in obedience to the words of the prophet, but he also expressed his confidence in divine providence when he requested the king of Moab to permit his parents to remain in Moab until "I know what God is going to do for me" (22:3).

As was noted above (see commentary on ch 20), this narrative unit (David a fugitive; 21:10–22:5) appears at the heart of the ring structure running from 20:1 to 23:28. Its positioning calls attention to the importance of what might otherwise seem to be the divulgence of several rather inconsequential pieces of information. The sudden appearance of Gad, the prophet, telling David to return to Judah at the point in David's life when he had sought to find refuge outside the Promised Land, initially in Philistia, and subsequently in Moab, is certainly significant.[10] This is the first recorded word of a prophet to David subsequent to his anointing by Samuel. Its occurrence here serves to reinforce the contrast that is drawn between Saul and David in the remaining narratives of 1 Samuel. Saul had rejected the word of the Lord, refusing to bow before the word of the prophet, with the result that the Lord would no longer communicate with him. In contrast to this, David continued to be blessed by the Lord's guidance and protection. In the long term, the fighting force beginning to take shape in the group of men who assembled around David would become the human instrument by which the Lord, under David's leadership, liberated Israel from all of its enemies (cf. 2 Sam 8; 23:8-39).

ENDNOTES

1. Alter (1999:133) notes that going into enemy territory was "a familiar enough move on the part of political refugees. Gath was the hometown of Goliath, and so one must assume that David planned to enter the city incognito, as an anonymous Hebrew fugitive. He would clearly have had to hide the telltale sword before coming into town."

2. See de Jong (1978:259). The de facto idea may be hinted at by the designation "king of the land" rather than "king of Israel," which Fokkelman refers to as David's "essential quality" (1986:365-366). David may appear to be a refugee, but he is really a king, if only in the indefinable sense that this rather vague designation conveys.
3. Both of these psalms are linked by their headings with the time that David pretended to be insane at Gath. The name Abimelech instead of Achish in the heading of Ps 34 is probably best explained as a dynastic name or title that was used by other Philistine kings as well (cf. Gen 20; 21:22-34; 26).
4. Yancey (1986:88) notes that David's confession in Ps 56, "In God I trust," and his crediting God "with delivering his soul from death and his feet from stumbling" might sound like "God miraculously intervened and rescued David." But when we turn to ch 21 what we see is a "desperate prisoner drooling spittle and flinging himself like a madman in order to save his neck." After giving other similar examples of what might appear to be a disparity between David's Psalms and the narratives of 1–2 Samuel, he suggests that the disparity is to be seen from the perspective of David's inner and outer life. As Yancey puts it, "David believed, truly believed, that the invisible world of God, heaven, and the angels was every bit as real as his own world of swords and spears and caves and thrones. The psalms form a record of his conscious effort to subject his own daily life to the reality of that invisible world beyond him."
5. Alter (1999:134) comments, "It is noteworthy that David feigns madness in order to survive, in contrast to Saul, whose genuine madness reflects his loss of control over the kingdom."
6. Adullam was located in the Shephelah (the foothills of the central mountain range), west of Bethlehem, not far from the Philistine border.
7. That this concern was not unfounded is demonstrated by Saul's murder of the priests of Nob.
8. Davis (1994b:80) regards David's Moabite connection as evidence of God's gracious providence on behalf of David, and comments, "Yahweh plans his kindnesses long beforehand. He directed circumstances long in advance in order to bring a ray of relief in David's present distress. It was not something David set in place; it was a gift. Yahweh 'arranged' it long before."
9. The precise location of the forest of Hereth is unknown.
10. Klement (2000:99-100) points out that Gad and Nathan each appear twice in the narratives of Samuel in connection with David. In this passage Gad gives instruction, and in 2 Sam 24 he announced the punishment for David's sin in taking a census. Nathan is the prophet who gave David the promise of an everlasting dynasty (2 Sam 7) and who also confronted David with his sin in the matter of Bathsheba (2 Sam 12).

◆ K. Ahimelech and the Priests at Nob Are Murdered (1 Sam 22:6-23)

6The news of his arrival in Judah soon reached Saul. At the time, the king was sitting beneath the tamarisk tree on the hill at Gibeah, holding his spear and surrounded by his officers.

7"Listen here, you men of Benjamin!" Saul shouted to his officers when he heard the news. "Has that son of Jesse promised every one of you fields and vineyards? Has he promised to make you all generals and captains in his army?* 8Is that why you have conspired against me? For not one of you told me when my own son made a solemn pact with the son of Jesse. You're not even sorry for me. Think of it! My own son—encouraging him to kill me, as he is trying to do this very day!"

9Then Doeg the Edomite, who was

standing there with Saul's men, spoke up.
"When I was at Nob," he said, "I saw the
son of Jesse talking to the priest, Ahime-
lech son of Ahitub. 10 Ahimelech consulted
the LORD for him. Then he gave him food
and the sword of Goliath the Philistine."

11 King Saul immediately sent for
Ahimelech and all his family, who served
as priests at Nob. 12 When they arrived,
Saul shouted at him, "Listen to me, you
son of Ahitub!"

"What is it, my king?" Ahimelech asked.

13 "Why have you and the son of Jesse
conspired against me?" Saul demanded.
"Why did you give him food and a sword?
Why have you consulted God for him?
Why have you encouraged him to kill me,
as he is trying to do this very day?"

14 "But sir," Ahimelech replied, "is any-
one among all your servants as faithful as
David, your son-in-law? Why, he is the
captain of your bodyguard and a highly
honored member of your household!
15 This was certainly not the first time I
had consulted God for him! May the king
not accuse me and my family in this mat-
ter, for I knew nothing at all of any plot
against you."

16 "You will surely die, Ahimelech, along
with your entire family!" the king shout-
ed. 17 And he ordered his bodyguards, "Kill
these priests of the LORD, for they are al-
lies and conspirators with David! They
knew he was running away from me, but
they didn't tell me!" But Saul's men re-
fused to kill the LORD's priests.

18 Then the king said to Doeg, "You do
it." So Doeg the Edomite turned on them
and killed them that day, eighty-five
priests in all, still wearing their priestly
garments. 19 Then he went to Nob, the
town of the priests, and killed the priests'
families—men and women, children and
babies—and all the cattle, donkeys, sheep,
and goats.

20 Only Abiathar, one of the sons of
Ahimelech, escaped and fled to David.
21 When he told David that Saul had killed
the priests of the LORD, 22 David exclaimed,
"I knew it! When I saw Doeg the Edomite
there that day, I knew he was sure to tell
Saul. Now I have caused the death of all
your father's family. 23 Stay here with me,
and don't be afraid. I will protect you with
my own life, for the same person wants to
kill us both."

22:7 Hebrew *commanders of thousands and commanders of hundreds?*

NOTES

22:7 ***Has that son of Jesse promised every one of you.*** Lit., "Will the son of Jesse indeed (*gam*) give all of you . . . ?" For the use of *gam* [TH1571, ZH1685] to introduce intensive clauses, see GKC §153.

22:14 ***he is the captain of your bodyguard.*** Lit., "one who turns aside to your obedience." The phrase *wesar 'el-mishma'teka* [TH4928, ZH5463] is obscure (translated in KJV as "goeth at thy bidding" and in NRSV as "quick to do your bidding"). In the literal translation suggested above, *mishma'ath* (obedience) is understood in a sense similar to its use in Isa 11:14. But in 2 Sam 23:23 (// 1 Chr 11:25) *mishma'ath* seems to mean "a body of men bound to obedience," i.e., "bodyguard" (these are the only places where the term occurs in the OT). If this latter sense is adopted, then *sar 'el-* [TH5493/413, ZH6073/448] (one who turns aside to) must be emended to *sar 'al-* [TH8269A/5921, ZH6233/6584] (commander over) yielding the translation, "commander over your bodyguard." This is the translation adopted by the NIV, NASB, and NLT.

22:22 ***Now I have caused the death of all your father's family.*** Lit., "I have surrounded all the lives of your father's house." It is not necessary to emend *sabbothi* [TH5437, ZH6015] ("I have surrounded") to the unusual word *khabti* (*khub* [TH2325, ZH2549], "I am guilty," occurring only in Dan 1:10, and there in the Piel rather than the Qal suggested here) on the basis of LXX's *eimi aitios* [TG1510/156, ZG1639/162] (I am the cause or author). It seems more likely that the LXX derived its translation from the context. The word *sabbothi* here is probably to be understood in the sense of "I have surrounded to death" as suggested by de Boer (1949:43). Hertzberg (1964:186) suggests "I have endangered the life" = "I am the occasion of."

COMMENTARY

The slaughter of the priests at Nob, the central feature of this narrative and one of the more gruesome stories of the Old Testament, is one more clear manifestation of the depths to which Saul's antitheocratic kingship had fallen. As the narrative opens, Saul is informed that David has been seen in Judah (22:6). While this may not seem like very surprising news, it was sufficient to expose Saul's growing paranoid fear concerning David's supposed designs on the throne. So at a meeting with the members of his court in Gibeah, Saul charged those closest to him with complicity in an assassination plot, presumably designed by David and supported by his own son Jonathan. By means of his questions, Saul accused David of attempting to buy their allegiance: "Has that son of Jesse promised every one of you fields and vineyards? Has he promised to make you all generals and captains in his army? Is that why you have conspired against me?" (22:7-8). These questions are particularly significant because they reveal something of Saul's erroneous concept of how kingship should function in Israel. Because Saul had distributed fields and vineyards as well as prestigious positions in the military to individuals from the tribe of Benjamin who served in his court, he concluded that David must be doing the same thing.[1] But any attempt to bind officials to royal allegiance through manipulation of a desire for prestige and material gain violated the fundamental principles of the covenantal character of Israelite kingship.

When kingship was established by Samuel, it was defined in terms that distinguished it from the kingship of the surrounding nations (ch 8; 10:25; 11:14–12:25). Israel's king was not to be an autonomous, self-serving ruler, but rather an instrument of the Lord's rule over his people. The allegiance of the people to their human king was to be subservient to their allegiance to the Lord, their divine king (12:14-15). The questions that Saul put to the members of his court suggest that Saul had improperly personalized his royal position (de Jong 1978:165). A kingship that bases loyalty on personal gain and self-interest finds more affinity with the concept of kingship among the surrounding nations than it does with the covenantal idea of kingship. When Samuel had warned the elders of the land about the practices of kings among the surrounding nations (8:9-18), he said that such a king would "take away the best of your fields and vineyards and olive groves and give them to his own officials" (8:14), and he also said that some of the conscripts of the king would become "generals and captains in his army" while others would "be forced to plow in his fields and harvest his crops" (8:12). So in Saul's questions to the members of his court, we get an indirect commentary on how far Saul had strayed from an awareness of the requirements of his office as a covenantal king. He had used the land in Israel (i.e., the fields and vineyards) that really belonged to the Lord to bind his court officials to himself. He had personalized his office and then concluded that David was doing the same.[2]

Saul's personalization of his royal office had come at a high cost. In this narrative it is reflected in two prominent features of Saul's mental and emotional condition: fear and self-pity (de Jong 1978:165-166). Saul was clearly anxious and insecure in his office as king. When the loyalty of subordinates had been purchased, there was always the possibility that someone else might appear on the scene and make a higher offer. Under such conditions it is only a short step to viewing one's subordinates as conspirators or plotters, as Saul does here ("Is that why you have conspired against me? For not one of you told me when my own son made a solemn pact with the son of Jesse," 22:8). This in turn led to another harmful result, which was self-pity. Saul went on to say, "You're not even sorry for me" (22:8). By putting things in these terms, Saul attempted to place a tragic spin on the events of his life, with the purpose of arousing sympathy from his subordinates.

The reader, however, needs to be very clear about what is going on in Saul's life. Saul had made a conscious choice. Instead of confessing his guilt for attempting to hold on to his office after being told by Samuel that the Lord has rejected him (ch 15), he portrayed his situation to those around him as one that should elicit sympathy. There is, of course, a sense in which Saul's life is a tragic one. But there is a reason for this. As de Jong points out (1978:166), Saul's life is not tragic in the sense commonly understood in the ancient world—that is, that he is a victim of blind fate against which there is no escape. Instead of this, the narratives of this section of 1 Samuel demonstrate that the reason for the tragic developments in Saul's life was to be found in Saul's own wrongdoing. Saul was personally accountable and morally responsible for his evil acts. To say this is not to be unduly harsh or insensitive toward Saul, because according to biblical teaching there is a solution for sin and guilt. The solution is confession and forgiveness. It is in this distinction that we find the most important difference between Saul and David (cf. Pss 32 and 51, in which David's attitude toward his sin contrasts sharply with that of Saul). As we read further in the chapter about the murder of the priests of Nob at Saul's command, any inclination that one might have to sympathize with Saul should be quickly dispelled. This chapter tells a chilling story. Saul, the anointed king of Israel, was responsible (through Doeg) for the murder of the priests of the Lord. Saul gave the order (22:17); he exhibited no fear of God and had no scruples about exterminating the Lord's priests. His sin was conscious and deliberate. As the downward spiral of Saul's life continues in the subsequent narratives, it becomes clearer and clearer that his sin has taken him to the point of no return. So Saul's actions in this chapter present us with a terrifying possibility: the possibility that a person's persistence in sin can eventually block the way to repentance. In this narrative, then, there is a clear warning against deliberate sin that dulls the conscience and hardens the heart, and also an admonition that those whom the Lord places in positions of authority in his kingdom must always be conscious that their responsibility is to serve the Lord rather than themselves.

No one made any response to Saul's outburst except Doeg the Edomite, Saul's chief herdsman (cf. 21:7), who reported what he had observed at Nob when David had come there seeking guidance from the Lord, as well as food and a weapon (i.e., Goliath's sword; 21:1-9). Saul immediately summoned Ahimelech and his family to appear at the court, and he accused him of conspiracy and participation in an assassination plot. Although Ahimelech vehemently protested his innocence and assured Saul that he knew nothing of any plot (22:14-15),[3] Saul, in his demented irrationality, rejected his explanations and commanded his bodyguards to kill Ahimelech and his family (22:16-17). When Saul's bodyguards refused to obey his command (reminiscent of the refusal of members of his army to unjustly put Jonathan to death, cf. 14:45), Saul told Doeg to carry out the order. Doeg consented and killed 85 priests on that day, along with their wives and children, cattle, donkeys, and sheep (22:18-19).[4] Only Abiathar, one of Ahimelech's sons, was able to escape the slaughter.[5] He came to David bringing the ephod (cf. 23:6). David not only gave Abiathar assurance of protection, but also shouldered responsibility for his own unwise visit to Ahimelech (22:22; cf. commentary on 21:1-9).[6]

In spite of the horrific events of this chapter, there are nevertheless intimations of divine sovereignty and the ultimate triumph of God's Kingdom. For example, Saul's command to Doeg resulted in the slaughter of the priests at Nob, but at the same time, it accomplished the fulfillment of the judgment that had been announced on the house of Eli in 2:30-33 (Ahimelech was the great-grandson of Eli).[7] Upon reflection, one cannot fail to note the inscrutable way in which even the evil acts of men are used in the accomplishment of God's purposes.[8] And Abiathar's escape from Nob and his alignment with David at the end of the chapter is a demonstration of how the Lord frustrates attacks on his people.[9] The Lord sent a survivor of the slaughter at Nob to David to be an encouragement to him and to give him access to the word of the Lord through the Urim and Thummim. So even though the conflict between Saul and David—in reality a conflict between antimessiah and messiah[10]—is taken to a new level, God can still be seen at work through the events described in this chapter.

ENDNOTES

1. Garsiel (1990:70) comments, "The sense is clear: can the members of Saul's own tribe expect from David the lands and offices with which he himself has endowed them?"
2. Garsiel (1990:70-71) comments further, "Certainly in the course of time Saul has appointed captains of thousands and of hundreds and has given them fields and vineyards, just as Samuel predicted (8:12, 14).... Saul's speech also serves as prologue to the condemnation and murder of Ahimelech, his family and fellow citizens. The link between Saul's speech and acts and Samuel's speech consists in Saul's not merely fulfilling the fears of tyranny, but taking them to a point even beyond prediction."
3. Brueggemann (1990a:159) notes that Ahimelech's defense was actually a fourfold defense of David: "David is known to be reliable. He is the king's son-in-law. He holds high military office. He is honored at court. Are these the marks of a conspirator? No!"
4. First Samuel 22:19 is nearly identical in wording to 15:3, which contains the instructions that Samuel gave to Saul concerning the destruction of the Amalekites, instructions that Saul refused to carry out. As Brueggemann (1990a:160) points out, "It is ironic and telling that Saul refused to execute such massive destruction against the Amalekites (15:9), but now in his deterioration he will act destructively against his own people. Indeed, Doeg went beyond Saul's explicit command. The true agent who has killed is not Doeg, however, but Saul." Alter (1999:139) comments, "Now he is carrying out the ban he executed only imperfectly against Amalek (the terms used are virtually identical), but the massacre is directed at his own innocent people. Saul's madness has become sinister and lethal."

5. Davis (1994b:90) comments, "Abiathar then stands as a witness to the way Yahweh insistently preserves a remnant of his people. The priests of Yahweh may be destroyed, but not completely destroyed. The people of God may often be put down but never put out. Abiathar's escape does not mean that all God's servants are immune from the world's butchery but that the world's butchery can never wipe out all of God's servants."
6. Gunn (1980:88) points out that "whereas Agag was spared, in the one episode, to Saul's eventual discomfort, Abiathar now escapes, to David's considerable advantage (cf. 23:6)."
7. The full implementation of the judgment pronounced on the house of Eli is realized in 1 Kgs 2:27, 35 when Solomon removes Abiathar from the priesthood and replaces him with Zadok.
8. Davis (1994b:85) comments, "Doeg's butchery fulfills the word of God against the house of Eli. That word had been spoken perhaps forty, maybe fifty years before; now in the carnage at Gibeah and Nob it had come to pass. Don't berate the word of God; God is not the author of this evil. Place the blame where it belongs—on this renegade Edomite and the antichrist who commands him. . . . One can vigorously attack the 'enemy' and all the time simply be executing the enemy's will. So with Saul, with Doeg. Even in their wicked slaughter of Yahweh's priests they nevertheless fulfilled his word. God's enemies prove the truthfulness of his word. In their hostility against him they carry out his will."
9. Davis (1994b:85) points out that the "'Saul and Ahimelech' and 'David and Abiathar' sections stand in direct opposition to one another, especially the final words of Saul and David respectively: 'You shall surely die' (22:16) versus 'You will be safe with me' (22:23, NJB). David is the protector and preserver of the priests."
10. Davis (1994b:83-84) rightly points out that "in the course of history there are antichrist figures who prefigure the full embodiment of evil to come. The apostle John smelled these antichrists in their false teaching (e.g., 1 John 2:22-23). But another premier characteristic of the antichrist figure is that he opposes, enters into conflict with, and seeks to crush God's people (Dan 7:21-22). That is where King Saul comes in. In 1 Samuel 22 the veil slips away and Saul is seen for the antichrist figure he really is as he has Yahweh's priests summarily butchered. Even now, in 1 Samuel 22, many Antichrists have come."

◆ L. Saul Pursues David (1 Sam 23:1-29)

**One day news came to David that the Phi-
listines were at Keilah stealing grain from
the threshing floors. 2 David asked the
LORD, "Should I go and attack them?"**

**"Yes, go and save Keilah," the LORD told
him.**

**3 But David's men said, "We're afraid
even here in Judah. We certainly don't
want to go to Keilah to fight the whole
Philistine army!"**

**4 So David asked the LORD again, and
again the LORD replied, "Go down to Keilah,
for I will help you conquer the Philistines."**

**5 So David and his men went to Keilah.
They slaughtered the Philistines and took
all their livestock and rescued the people
of Keilah. 6 Now when Abiathar son of
Ahimelech fled to David at Keilah, he
brought the ephod with him.**

**7 Saul soon learned that David was at
Keilah. "Good!" he exclaimed. "We've got
him now! God has handed him over to me,
for he has trapped himself in a walled
town!" 8 So Saul mobilized his entire army
to march to Keilah and besiege David and
his men.**

9But David learned of Saul's plan and told Abiathar the priest to bring the ephod and ask the LORD what he should do. 10Then David prayed, "O LORD, God of Israel, I have heard that Saul is planning to come and destroy Keilah because I am here. 11Will the leaders of Keilah betray me to him?* And will Saul actually come as I have heard? O LORD, God of Israel, please tell me."

And the LORD said, "He will come."

12Again David asked, "Will the leaders of Keilah betray me and my men to Saul?"

And the LORD replied, "Yes, they will betray you."

13So David and his men—about 600 of them now—left Keilah and began roaming the countryside. Word soon reached Saul that David had escaped, so he didn't go to Keilah after all. 14David now stayed in the strongholds of the wilderness and in the hill country of Ziph. Saul hunted him day after day, but God didn't let Saul find him.

15One day near Horesh, David received the news that Saul was on the way to Ziph to search for him and kill him. 16Jonathan went to find David and encouraged him to stay strong in his faith in God. 17"Don't be afraid," Jonathan reassured him. "My father will never find you! You are going to be the king of Israel, and I will be next to you, as my father, Saul, is well aware." 18So the two of them renewed their solemn pact before the LORD. Then Jonathan returned home, while David stayed at Horesh.

19But now the men of Ziph went to Saul in Gibeah and betrayed David to him. "We know where David is hiding," they said. "He is in the strongholds of Horesh on the hill of Hakilah, which is in the southern part of Jeshimon. 20Come down whenever you're ready, O king, and we will catch him and hand him over to you!"

21"The LORD bless you," Saul said. "At last someone is concerned about me! 22Go and check again to be sure of where he is staying and who has seen him there, for I know that he is very crafty. 23Discover his hiding places, and come back when you are sure. Then I'll go with you. And if he is in the area at all, I'll track him down, even if I have to search every hiding place in Judah!" 24So the men of Ziph returned home ahead of Saul.

Meanwhile, David and his men had moved into the wilderness of Maon in the Arabah Valley south of Jeshimon. 25When David heard that Saul and his men were searching for him, he went even farther into the wilderness to the great rock, and he remained there in the wilderness of Maon. But Saul kept after him in the wilderness.

26Saul and David were now on opposite sides of a mountain. Just as Saul and his men began to close in on David and his men, 27an urgent message reached Saul that the Philistines were raiding Israel again. 28So Saul quit chasing David and returned to fight the Philistines. Ever since that time, the place where David was camped has been called the Rock of Escape.* 29*David then went to live in the strongholds of En-gedi.

23:11 Some manuscripts lack the first sentence of 23:11. **23:28** Hebrew *Sela-hammahlekoth.* **23:29** Verse 23:29 is numbered 24:1 in Hebrew text.

NOTES

23:6 The LXX contains a longer, modified version of this verse: "And it came to pass when Abiathar, the son of Ahimelech, fled to David, that he went down with David to Keilah, having an ephod in his hand." Even though the LXX rendering helps resolve the difficulty of harmonizing this verse with 22:20 (it does not seem that David was already at Keilah when Abiathar fled), and also gives help in making sense out of the puzzling syntax of the last phrase of the MT (*'epod yarad beyado* [TH646, ZH680]; "an ephod, he went down [with it] in his hand"), as Pisano (1984:208) points out, there is no explanation that satisfactorily demonstrates "how the shorter and problematic MT could have arisen." It seems clear that the MT has been garbled and that the LXX does what seems necessary to make sense of a difficult text. "This suggests that an early corruption had already taken place before LXX" (Pisano 1984:208).

23:7 ***God has handed him over to me.*** Traditionally the verb *nikkar* has been viewed as denominative and associated with the root *nakar* [TH5234A, ZH5796], carrying the idea "foreign" or "alien." This creates difficulty in understanding the meaning of the phrase that would read, lit., "God has alienated him into my hand." Because the LXX translates *nikkar* by *depraken* [TG4097, ZG4405] (has sold), many commentators (Budde 1890; de Vaux 1961b; Hertzberg 1964; Smith 1912) have emended the Hebrew text to the verb *makar* [TH4376, ZH4835] (sold). Others, including S. R. Driver (1913:184), Klein (1983:228), and McCarter (1980b:369), on the basis of similar use in Isa 19:4, have suggested *sakar* [TH5534A, ZH6127] ("shut up" = "deliver into hand of"). While this latter suggestion carries some weight, it may not be necessary. Gray (1957:190) and Barr (1968:331) argue for the existence of a verb *nakar* meaning either "to acquire" or "to sell" (depending on the stem) on the basis of a Ugaritic parallel.

23:11 The NLT follows the text of 23:11-12 found in the MT (see NLT mg). The comparison of the MT with the LXX and 4QSam[b] has given rise to complex reconstructions of the alleged "original" text (see McCarter 1980b:368, 370). But Pisano (1984:260-267), after a careful analysis of numerous proposals, concludes that the MT "seems to witness to the most original form of the text." See Pisano for a thorough discussion of the issues involved.

23:15 ***David received the news.*** Lit., "David saw" (i.e., learned). There is no need to emend *ra'ah* [TH7200, ZH8011] (he saw) to *yare'* [TH3372, ZH3707] (he feared) as S. R. Driver (1913:186), Klein (1983:227-228), and others propose. The reading of the LXX (*eiden*, as if from *oraō* [TG3708, ZG3972]; "saw, perceived") supports the MT.

23:16 ***encouraged him to stay strong in his faith in God.*** Lit., "He strengthened his hand in God." The idea is that he strengthened his "confidence" or "dependence" on God. For other occurrences of the expression, see Judg 9:24b; Isa 35:3; Jer 23:14.

23:20 ***Come down whenever you're ready.*** Lit., "Come down according to all the desire of your soul to come down."

and we will catch him and hand him over to you! Lit., "It is for us to deliver him into the hand of the king." For use of the infinitive construct as a subject of a nominal clause, see GKC §114a; Joüon and Muraoka §124b.

23:22 ***where he is staying.*** Lit., "his place where his foot is."

23:23 ***every hiding place in Judah.*** Lit., "among all the thousands of Judah." The word *'alpe* (thousands) is, perhaps, better translated here as "clans," as in 10:19.

23:28 ***Rock of Escape.*** The meaning of the Hebrew *sela' hammakhleqoth* [TH5555, ZH6154] is disputed. There are two identical roots *khalaq* [TH2505/2505A, ZH2744/2745], meaning respectively (1) divide, and (2) be smooth or slippery. Depending on which root is in view, some commentators have favored the rendering Rock of Divisions or Parting, while others have suggested Rock of Escapes. The first meaning seems to have firmer evidence from general usage. The NRSV translates this as "Rock of Escape" with a text note: "Or *Rock of Division;* meaning of Heb uncertain." The NJPS translates it as "Rock of Separation" with a text note: "Meaning of Heb. uncertain."

COMMENTARY

First Samuel 23 divides rather nicely into three sections (23:1-14, 15-18, 19-28). The first and last sections are similar in that they both tell of the betrayal of David by his own countrymen, resulting in his near capture by Saul. Sandwiched between these two sections is a description of David's encouragement by Jonathan during Jonathan's visit with him at Horesh (23:15-18). The dominant theme in each of these sections is aptly articulated by David's statement in Psalm 54:4: "But God is my helper. The Lord keeps me alive!"[1] In his status as a fugitive and wanderer, David quickly learned that there were few people whom he could trust. Nearly everyone turned against him, including those whom he might have expected to rise to his defense. But in these distressing circumstances the Lord sustained him in three different ways: at Keilah, by direct, divine guidance (23:1-14); near Horesh, by Jonathan's encouragement (23:15-18); and in the wilderness of Ziph, by a clear example of divine providence (23:19-28).

In the first section (23:1-14) we learn that even though David had been forced to flee from Saul, he was not so consumed by his own problems that he was oblivious to the needs of his countrymen (de Jong 1978:170). When he learned that the Philistines were plundering grain from the threshing floors of Keilah,[2] he immediately sought the Lord's guidance on whether or not he should go to their aid. David's reaction, reflecting the spirit of a true covenantal king, contrasts sharply with that of Saul, who, unlike his earlier response to the threats made against Jabesh-gilead by the Ammonites (ch 11), made no attempt to come to Keilah's aid. In fact, when Saul next took action it was not for the purpose of fighting the Philistines, but rather for the purpose of apprehending David.[3] And when he embarked on this disreputable mission, he clothed his deplorable act with words that were seemingly pious (23:7)—much as he had done on previous occasions (cf. 14:34, 35, 39, 41, 44; commentary on 14:24-46)—but at the same time self-deceptive.

David was able to seek direct divine guidance concerning what he should do concerning the Philistine plunder of Keilah by means of the ephod because Abiathar had brought it with him when he fled from the slaughter of the priests at Nob (23:6; cf. 22:20-23).[4] By using the ephod, David was not only assured that he should go and fight the Philistines (23:2) but also that he and his men would be successful in delivering the people of Keilah (23:4-5). This information was sufficient to overrule the objections of David's own men who were of the opinion that they had enough problems without creating a new one by engaging in a conflict with the far superior Philistine forces (23:3). As a result, David and his men attacked the Philistine raiders at Keilah, and successfully delivered its inhabitants from their oppressors (23:5).

When Saul was told that David had taken refuge at Keilah, he immediately took measures to lay siege to one of his own Israelite cities in order to capture the person whom he viewed as a threat to his throne (23:8). A king who had been anointed to rescue Israel from the Philistines (9:16) was now planning to attack a city that David had just liberated from the Philistines! David, somehow being informed of Saul's intentions, inquired of the Lord again by means of the ephod, in order to determine two things: first, whether Saul would attack Keilah, and second, whether the citizens of Keilah would betray him into Saul's hands. To his dismay he learned that both of these things would indeed happen (23:11-12).[5]

It is difficult to imagine how disappointing it must have been for David to discover that the people whom he had just delivered from Philistine oppression had so little gratitude for what he had done that they would betray him into the hands of Saul. This behavior of the inhabitants of Keilah, however, needs to be placed in context. We are informed of Saul's intent to destroy the city in 23:10. The people of Keilah were certainly well aware of Saul's massacre of the priests at Nob (22:6-23). Saul now had the reputation of being a ruthless tyrant. So even though the people of Keilah may have felt genuine gratitude toward David for what he had done for them, they were not prepared to jeopardize their own lives in order to protect him. Their behavior, then, is to be understood more as an expression of their fear of Saul than of deliberate malevolence toward David (de Jong 1978:171).[6]

Lest our assessment of the behavior of the Keilahites be too harsh, we might ask if we also have not, on occasion, acted in similar ways. We, of course, live in very different times and circumstances, and in a much later period of redemptive history. Our anointed one is not David, but, rather, David's greater son, Jesus Christ. So the question that we might ask ourselves is, how often have we, in one way or another, denied our identification with Christ out of fear of a perceived threat to our own well-being. Remember what Peter did at the time of the crucifixion of Christ (Matt 26:69-75). Is it not true that there have been occasions when we have refused to identify ourselves with Christ in situations where his name and honor were at stake? When something of this sort happens, then we, like the citizens of Keilah, have made a choice to identify with the enemies of Christ and his Kingdom, rather than with the one who has redeemed and liberated us. Fear is a powerful force. It was such a force at Keilah, and it is in our own lives as well. The Bible frequently addresses the destructive power of fear and consistently exhorts God's people in all times and places to put their trust in the Lord and, by so doing, to turn away from behavior that is motivated by fear (cf. e.g., Deut 31:8; Isa 41:10; Jer 23:4; 2 Tim 1:7-8).

In David's involvement with the town of Keilah, he was repeatedly sustained by direct divine guidance. He inquired of the Lord four times (23:2, 4, 11, 12), and four times he received precisely the information he needed in order to plan his course of action. Upon hearing that Saul's attack on Keilah was certain and that the citizens of Keilah would betray him, David and his men left the city and hid in the wilderness of Ziph.[7] There they enjoyed God's providential protection (23:14).

The second section of the chapter (23:15-18) gives a brief report of Jonathan's visit with David at Horesh[8] in the wilderness of Ziph (23:15). After his disappointing experience at Keilah, it must have been encouraging for David to receive a visit from his friend Jonathan. Jonathan had undoubtedly heard about the events at Keilah, and he responded by going into the wilderness to visit with David. The purpose for his visit was to encourage David "to stay strong in his faith in God" (23:16, see note). Jonathan accomplished this goal by putting into words what previous conversations between himself and David had already tacitly assumed (cf. 18:3-4; 20:13, 16; cf. 20:30). He said to David, "Don't be afraid. . . . My father will never find you! You are going to be the king of Israel, and I will be next to you, as my father, Saul, is well aware" (23:17). Although Jonathan's acceptance of David's becoming king had been hinted at on prior occasions, this is his first explicit statement in the narrative that he knew this would happen and that he was ready to accept a subordinate position under David in the court of the new regime. This was precisely the kind of encouragement that David needed. By assuring David of these things, Jonathan not only affirmed his own confidence that God's purposes for David's life would be accomplished, but he also strengthened David's belief that "God is my helper. The Lord keeps me alive!" (Ps 54:4).

After his meeting with Jonathan, David entered a dangerous period of time in which he moved from place to place (from Horesh in the hill country of Ziph, 23:14-15, 19; to the wilderness of Maon[9] south of Jeshimon,[10] 23:24; to En-gedi,[11] 23:29) to stay out of the reach of Saul. In 23:19-28, God appears to be distant, with no references to him at all except, ironically, in the mouth of Saul when he says to the Ziphites, "The LORD bless you. . . . At last someone is concerned about me!" (23:21, another example of Saul's misleading use of pious language [cf. 23:7], as well as his inordinate self-pity).[12] This statement was made by Saul when some Ziphites came to him and promised to show him where David was hiding. These Ziphites are depicted as willfully wicked people who are real partisans for Saul, in contrast to the citizens of Keilah who merely wanted to stay out of trouble. In Psalm 54:3, David speaks of the Ziphites as "violent people [who] are trying to kill me. They care nothing for God."

While this section of the chapter contains no mention of God's action, it is clear that God's hand of deliverance is just as much at work in what takes place in this section as it was in the events of the previous sections. In contrast to what has preceded, however, God's deliverance is now manifested in what, at least on the surface, might seem to be a mere coincidence. When Saul was led by the Ziphites to David's hiding place and was on the verge of trapping him, a messenger suddenly appeared and told Saul about a Philistine raid (23:26-28). This unexpected news caused Saul to turn away from his pursuit of David at precisely the crucial moment. The reader knows intuitively that this was not a mere coincidence. The reality is that the story of David's deliverance at Ziph is every bit as much a divine deliverance as his deliverance at Keilah. What we encounter here is a particularly striking example of the working of divine providence. In the Westminster Shorter Catechism, God's works of providence are defined as "His most holy, wise, and powerful preserving and governing all his creatures and all their actions" (Question 11). This is one of the great teachings of the Bible, and it is abundantly evident in 1–2 Samuel. The events of chapter 23 demonstrate that God was David's helper. He was the one protecting and sustaining him. And the same God who was at work to accomplish his purposes in David's life has continued to work in the lives of his people down through the centuries. He sustains those that are his today even as he did in the time of David and Saul, by special revelation (in our case, found in the Scriptures), by the encouragement of friends, and by the workings of divine providence in their lives.

ENDNOTES

1. The heading of Ps 54 links it with the betrayal of the Ziphites in 23:19-28.
2. Keilah was a small walled city located in the Shephelah (the foothills between Judah and Philistia) about eight and a half miles northwest of Hebron and three miles south of Adullam. Its location in the western part of the territory of Judah made it vulnerable to Philistine incursions.
3. Fokkelman (1986:422) calls attention to another contrast between Saul and David when he says, "One sends a town to its death [Saul in his massacre at Nob], the other restores a town to life [David in his liberation of Keilah]."
4. Reference to the ephod appears to be a shorthand designation for the breastplate of the high priest containing the Urim and Thummim that was attached to the ephod (a garment) of the high priest (Exod 28:4-14). The Urim and Thummim were a divinely ordained means for receiving divine revelation and were placed in the custody of the high priest (Exod 28:30). David's access to direct divine guidance on this occasion and later (30:7-8; 2 Sam 2:1; 5:19, 23) contrasts with Saul's lack of access; he was limited to normal, human sources of information (14:37; 28:6). Fokkelman (1986:423) speaks of the presence of the ephod with David as an "irony against Saul." He comments, "The oracular device and the priest, both having just escaped the king's savage extermination, can immediately set to work in order to avoid the next round of destruction that the king intends for David. At the level of the providential, that is an immediate countermove by God after Saul's revenge on his priests. Saul may bloody the 85 linen priestly garments called the ephod, but the one ephod which acts as a medium for the decisive word of God turns up at the place of the alternative anointed one."
5. This verse along with Matt 11:20-24 is often cited as evidence for what has been termed God's "middle knowledge," that is, "God's knowledge of what *would* have happened in situations that never actually occur (counterfactuals)" (Tiessen 2000:290). Tiessen makes use of the "middle knowledge" concept in his model for the workings of divine providence (see Tiessen 2000).
6. Alter (1999:142) comments, "The political paradox of the situation that has evolved is evident: David has achieved a victory against Israel's principal enemy; Saul now moves to destroy that victor, enlisting the aid of the people David saved."
7. Ziph was a town located about four miles southeast of Hebron, and about ten miles southeast of Keilah, in the eastern part of the hill country of Judah, and adjacent to the wilderness area leading down toward the Dead Sea.
8. This is an unidentified site in the wilderness of Ziph.
9. Maon was in southern Judah west of the Dead Sea, about seven miles south of Hebron, and three miles south of Ziph.
10. Interpreters are divided on whether Jeshimon is to be understood as a proper noun, or as a common noun meaning "wasteland." Alter (1999:144) comments, "It should be said that most translators have treated the last geographical term used by the Ziphites, 'the wasteland,' as a proper noun (*yeshimon* [TH3452/3452A, ZH3810]), but because it bears a definite article, and because yeshimon is a well-attested common noun, it is preferable not to construe it as a place-name."
11. En-gedi was an oasis in a desolate region on the western shore of the Dead Sea.
12. Fokkelman (1986:444-445) notes that Saul did "not even shrink from using his [God's] proper name, in a blessing which borders on blasphemy to those who know that God himself has reserved his blessing for the opponent." It should also be noticed that Saul was still consumed with self-pity (cf. 22:8).

◆ M. David Spares Saul's Life a First Time (1 Sam 24:1-22)

1 *After Saul returned from fighting the Philistines, he was told that David had gone into the wilderness of En-gedi. 2 So Saul chose 3,000 elite troops from all Israel and went to search for David and his men near the rocks of the wild goats.

3 At the place where the road passes some sheepfolds, Saul went into a cave to relieve himself. But as it happened, David and his men were hiding farther back in that very cave!

4 "Now's your opportunity!" David's men whispered to him. "Today the LORD is telling you, 'I will certainly put your enemy into your power, to do with as you wish.'" So David crept forward and cut off a piece of the hem of Saul's robe.

5 But then David's conscience began bothering him because he had cut Saul's robe. 6 "The LORD knows I shouldn't have done that to my lord the king," he said to his men. "The LORD forbid that I should do this to my lord the king and attack the LORD's anointed one, for the LORD himself has chosen him." 7 So David restrained his men and did not let them kill Saul.

After Saul had left the cave and gone on his way, 8 David came out and shouted after him, "My lord the king!" And when Saul looked around, David bowed low before him.

9 Then he shouted to Saul, "Why do you listen to the people who say I am trying to harm you? 10 This very day you can see with your own eyes it isn't true. For the LORD placed you at my mercy back there in the cave. Some of my men told me to kill you, but I spared you. For I said, 'I will never harm the king—he is the LORD's anointed one.' 11 Look, my father, at what I have in my hand. It is a piece of the hem of your robe! I cut it off, but I didn't kill you. This proves that I am not trying to harm you and that I have not sinned against you, even though you have been hunting for me to kill me.

12 "May the LORD judge between us. Perhaps the LORD will punish you for what you are trying to do to me, but I will never harm you. 13 As that old proverb says, 'From evil people come evil deeds.' So you can be sure I will never harm you. 14 Who is the king of Israel trying to catch anyway? Should he spend his time chasing one who is as worthless as a dead dog or a single flea? 15 May the LORD therefore judge which of us is right and punish the guilty one. He is my advocate, and he will rescue me from your power!"

16 When David had finished speaking, Saul called back, "Is that really you, my son David?" Then he began to cry. 17 And he said to David, "You are a better man than I am, for you have repaid me good for evil. 18 Yes, you have been amazingly kind to me today, for when the LORD put me in a place where you could have killed me, you didn't do it. 19 Who else would let his enemy get away when he had him in his power? May the LORD reward you well for the kindness you have shown me today. 20 And now I realize that you are surely going to be king, and that the kingdom of Israel will flourish under your rule. 21 Now swear to me by the LORD that when that happens you will not kill my family and destroy my line of descendants!"

22 So David promised this to Saul with an oath. Then Saul went home, but David and his men went back to their stronghold.

24:1 Verses 24:1-22 are numbered 24:2-23 in Hebrew text.

NOTES

24:3 [4] ***to relieve himself.*** Lit., "to cover his feet," that is, with long garments. The expression is used as a euphemism for evacuating the bowels, and it is derived from the posture assumed.

24:7 [8] ***restrained.*** *Shasa'* [TH8156, ZH9117], here translated "restrained," is literally "divide" or "cleave." The LXX has *epeisen* [TG3982, ZG4275] (persuaded), probably a guess at the meaning of the verb from the context. Stoebe (1973:435) suggests that *shasa'* is used here in a colloquial sense, meaning to take away from someone the possibility of doing something, thus the idea of restrain (cf. Klein 1983:234-235). Alter (1999:148) translates the word by the phrase "held back his men with words" and says that the meaning of *shasa'* is "disputed, but it is most plausibly linked with the noun *shesa'*, a split or cleft. The sense here would then be, he 'split off' his men from Saul, using his words to interpose a kind of barrier between them and the king" (see further Gordon 1986:180).

24:10 [11] ***Some of my men told me.*** The *we'amar* [TH559, ZH606] of the MT requires the assumption of an impersonal subject and the frequentative use of Waw consecutive with the perfect (see GKC §112rr; Stoebe 1973:433, 435). S. R. Driver (1913:194) and others advocate reading either *wayyo'mer* ("and he told me") or, on the basis of LXX (*kai ouk ēboulēthēn* [TG1014, ZG1089], "and I would not"), emending *we'amar* to *wa'ama'en* [TH3985, ZH4412] (and I refused). Klein (1983:234-235) translates, "Yet I refused."

but I spared you. The unexpected third-person feminine form of the verb *wattakhas* [TH2347, ZH2571] (look upon with compassion, pity) is probably best explained as having the unexpressed subject *'eni* [TH5869/2967.1, ZH6524/3276] (my eye), as reflected in the Vulgate (see GKC §144o). The *epheisamēn* [TG5339, ZG5767] (I spared [you]) of the LXX is alleged by some to reflect an original Qal imperfect first person form, *wa'akhus* [TH2347, ZH2571] (I spared [you]).

24:13 [14] ***As that old proverb says.*** The phrase in Hebrew, *meshal haqqadmoni* [TH6931, ZH7719] (the proverb of the ancient ones), is rendered as "the ancient proverb" by NRSV and "the old saying" by the NIV. It seems preferable to understand *haqqadmoni* as a collective (see Waltke and O'Connor 1990:115, under "gentilic nouns") and thus to use a plural in translation ("ancient ones"). This understanding is also supported by 4QSam[a], which has a plural form (cf. BHS apparatus).

COMMENTARY

The narratives of 1 Samuel 24–26 present us with three incidents in the life of David in which he refused to take vengeance on his adversaries (twice in connection with Saul [chs 24 and 26], and once in connection with Nabal [ch 25]), with the result that he received not only Saul's acknowledgment that he was "a better man"[1] than Saul was (24:17 [18]), but also Saul's admission that "you will do many heroic deeds, and you will surely succeed" (26:25).[2] Taken together, these three narratives advance David's rise to the throne in a significant way by their portrayal of David as someone who is imminently qualified to replace Saul as king.[3]

At the end of chapter 23, Saul was poised to close in on David in the wilderness of Maon but was providentially induced to give up his pursuit in order to confront a Philistine invasion of Israel. After dealing with the Philistines, Saul immediately resumed his quest for David, and there is no hint that he was aware of how close he had been to success at the end of chapter 23.[4] In his renewed attempt to apprehend David, Saul took 3,000 of his men into the wilderness of En-gedi, which is a rocky, barren area to the west of the Dead Sea in Judah, described in Psalm 63:1[5] as a "parched and weary land where there is no water." It was here that David was seeking refuge in the large caves that are common in the ravines of that area.

David is portrayed as living in conditions very different from what he might have expected after having been anointed to be king (ch 16). Instead of enjoying the life of a powerful ruler, he is isolated and vulnerable—living the life of a fugitive.

In 24:14, David speaks of himself as a "dead dog" and a "single flea," suggesting something of how powerless he must have felt. It would be unreasonable to think that in such circumstances David would feel no discouragement or fear. His trials were very real and very severe. But in this chapter, while David and his men were camped in the recesses of one of the caves in the wilderness of En-gedi, something quite remarkable happened. It was something that neither he nor his men could have either expected or planned. David and Saul's roles were suddenly reversed for a short time: David, the fugitive, is unexpectedly given an opportunity to eliminate Saul, the pursuer.[6]

As 24:3 tells us, at a certain point when Saul needed to relieve himself, he unknowingly walked into the very cave where David and his men were hiding. This turn of events was not only an enormous surprise for David and his entourage, but at the same time it was a unique test of David's leadership. Suddenly David was presented with an open opportunity to seize the throne in a premature way by taking Saul's life. This, in fact, was what David's men urged him to do. They said (24:4), "Now's your opportunity! . . . Today the LORD is telling you, 'I will certainly put your enemy into your power, to do with as you wish.'"[7] In other words, David's men interpreted the providential appearance of Saul in their cave as a directive from the Lord to take Saul's life.[8]

David, however, refused to accept their advice and continued to give honor to the royal office of Saul, even when power over Saul's life was placed squarely in his hands.[9] It might be argued that Saul's royal office had been so sullied by his abuse of it that any consideration of respect for that office had been nullified by Saul's conduct. But while it is clear that Saul was not a responsible bearer of his royal office and authority, he still remained "the LORD's anointed." Because David recognized this, he refused to lay his hand on him.[10] So David said to his men, "The LORD forbid that I should do this to my lord the king and attack the LORD's anointed one, for the LORD himself has chosen him" (24:6). Beyond this personal refusal to attack Saul, David also "restrained his men and did not let them kill Saul" (24:7). The Hebrew word translated "restrained" by NLT is a strong word, one that is difficult to fully capture in English in this context (see note on 24:7). The word suggests that David's men were so intent on exploiting Saul's vulnerability that David was forced to take strong measures in order to prevent them from taking things into their own hands.

There is much in this chain of events to ponder. David's men appealed to a surprising event as a sign that it was the Lord's will for them to do something they desired to do—a scenario familiar to most Christians. It is often difficult to argue with someone who says that in the view of certain circumstances, the Lord has led them to do such and such. But today, just as in this narrative, one must be extremely careful with an argument that uses divine providence as an equivalent for divine mandate. In the circumstances of life, what may appear on the surface to be a leading from the Lord may just as well be a temptation from Satan (de Jong 1978:178). One should always be mindful that it is never possible to infallibly interpret God's providence. For example, Saul clearly misread divine providence when, after learning that David had gone to Keilah, he concluded, "God has handed him over to me, for he has trapped himself in a walled town!" (23:7). Fokkelman (1986:454) speaks of this sort of interpretation of providence as "hitching God to our own wagon" with the simplistic idea that we "have God in our pocket" and know exactly how he relates to some particular situation. We should guard against similar sorts of speculative tendencies in our own living and focus more attention on obeying the clear commands of God (de Jong 1978:178). Deuteronomy 29:29 reminds us that "the LORD our God has secrets known to no one. We are not accountable for them, but we and our children are accountable forever for all that he has revealed to us, so that we may obey all the terms of these instructions."

Although David spared Saul's life, he did creep close enough to him in the darkness of the cave to cut off a piece of his robe. But upon reflection, even this seemingly harmless act seemed to David to border on inappropriate. In 24:5 we learn that "David's conscience began bothering him because he had cut Saul's robe." By cutting a piece from Saul's robe, David not only damaged the robe, but to some degree he also assailed Saul's office because the robe was the symbol of his office (de Jong 1978:179).[11] So to this limited extent, one might say, David's act impinged on Saul's royal office, and for this he expressed regret. David's intent, however, was something different. His intent was to appeal to Saul's conscience on the basis of his office. David used the piece of Saul's robe as proof that Saul had been within his grasp (24:11) and as a protest against the misuse that Saul had made of his royal position (24:14).

After the description of how David spared Saul's life in the cave (24:1-8), the remainder of the chapter is given over to David's attempt to convince Saul he was innocent of any designs against his life (24:9-15, which is one of the longest speeches of David in all of 1–2 Samuel), and to Saul's poignant response (24:16-21). In spite of Saul's abuse of his office, David spoke to him in language of deep respect. He addressed him as "My lord the king," and bowed to the ground before him (24:8). In his speech David made a case for his innocence (24:9-11) and asked the Lord to be the judge between Saul and himself (24:12-15). This led to Saul's confession that David was without blame (24:17; see endnote 1) and to his first explicit acknowledgment that he knew that David would become king (24:20). These words of Saul confirm Jonathan's statement to David that his father knew that David would become king (cf. 23:17b), and these words represent another decisive step forward in the narratives that describe David's rise to the throne.

David concluded his speech to Saul by placing their dispute in the Lord's hands for adjudication: "May the LORD judge between you and me. And may the LORD avenge the wrongs you have done to me, but my hand will not touch you" (24:12, NIV), and, "May the LORD be our judge and decide between us. May he consider my cause and uphold it; may he vindicate me by delivering me from your hand" (24:15, NIV). David requested that the Lord, the righteous judge, "avenge" (*naqam* [TH5358, ZH5933]) whatever wrongs Saul had committed against him and "vindicate" (*shapat* [TH8199, ZH9149]) him by deliverance from Saul's hand. A "legal case" is opened here that is not brought to a conclusion until 2 Samuel 4:8, when the head of Saul's son Ishbosheth is brought to David (note the statement there: "the LORD has given my lord the king revenge").[12] As Peels (1992:201) notes, the combination of the words *rib* [TH7378, ZH8189] (conduct a legal case; NLT, "advocate"), *din* [TH1777, ZH1906] (judge) and *shapat* (judge) in 24:12 and 15 places the reference to the "vengeance" of God in a juridical context, so that the controlling motivation for the appeal for God to avenge does not reflect a thirst for blood, but rather a thirst for justice.

These words, by which David committed both his own destiny and Saul's to the Lord, have provided much greater instruction and offered far more comfort to the readers of this narrative throughout human history than would have been the case had David acted in violence to take Saul's life (de Jong 1978:180). The central thesis of David's words is captured quite well by Paul's statement in Romans 12:19 (cf. Deut 32:35; Isa 63:4; Ezek 25:14), "Dear friends, never take revenge. Leave that to the righteous anger of God. For the Scriptures say, 'I will take revenge; I will pay them back,' says the LORD." David's words have turned out to be a much more powerful weapon than his sword could ever have been. Certainly this represents one of the high points in David's life. By placing his life and destiny in the hands of the Lord, David demonstrated in advance the spirit of the Messiah to come, who was anointed at his baptism but did not grasp for the fulfillment of God's promises prematurely. He resisted Satan's temptation to give him the kingdoms of this world (Matt 4:8-10), bowed to his Father's will, submitted to the humiliation of the Cross (Matt 26:39; Phil 2:8), and now awaits his ultimate exaltation over his enemies (Heb 10:12-13).

So David passed this test of his leadership with flying colors. The temptation that he faced was the will to power that would have denied Saul's office by killing him. The justification for doing so, as argued by his men, was the providential leading of the Lord. David's response was to let the Lord judge between him and Saul, to let the Lord vindicate him in due time. In the meantime, he respected Saul's office but also rebuked him for the violation of his trust. Both David and David's greater son have shown us to place our lives in the hands of the one who judges justly and to deny the temptation to grasp for position or power in premature and illegitimate ways.

ENDNOTES

1. "Better" is the NLT rendering of *tsaddiq* [TH6662, ZH7404] (just, righteous). Fokkelman (1986:469) suggests that because of the legal context, "The correct rendering, which is not found in the usual translations, is: 'you are in the right and I am not.'" In other words, Saul is not saying David is "more righteous" than he is (cf. e.g., NIV, NASB, NRSV), but rather that, forensically speaking, David is in the right on the basis of the evidence that he has presented in the argument that he has just made.
2. Because David is pictured in such a positive way in these narratives, particularly in his refusal to do any harm to the "LORD's anointed" (i.e., Saul), many interpreters have viewed these chapters more as pro-Davidic propaganda than as truly historical narrative. The assumption is that these stories were contrived by later writers or editors to establish that David's accession to the throne was lawful and legitimate.
3. See further the discussion at the beginning of the commentary on ch 25.
4. There is also no information provided concerning the outcome of Saul's engagement with the Philistines. The author's focus is now clearly on Saul's rebellious vendetta against David, rather than on his official duties as king.
5. The heading of Ps 63 links it with the time "when David was in the wilderness of Judah."

6. As Edelmann (1991:192) puts it, in the "cat-and-mouse game" that Saul has been playing with David, the mouse has all of a sudden become the cat.
7. The translation of 24:4a is disputed because of an ambiguity in the Hebrew text. The Hebrew can be read either as "This is the day *on which* the LORD says to you, 'I am giving your enemy into your hand'" (cf. the NLT rendering), or as "This is the day *of which* the LORD said, 'I will give your enemy into your hand.'" The latter option presupposes the existence of a previous promise by the Lord to David that he would deliver Saul into his hand, but there is no record of any such promise in any of the preceding narratives.
8. David's men were correct in viewing Saul's appearance in the cave as providential (cf. David's statement in 24:10, "The LORD placed you at my mercy back there in the cave"), but wrong in their conclusion that this was a mandate to David from the Lord to kill Saul.
9. That this is the central theme of the chapter is suggested by its repeated emphasis in the words of both David and Saul. David: 24:6, "The LORD forbid that I should . . . attack the LORD's anointed one"; 24:10, "I spared you. . . . I will never harm the king—he is the LORD's anointed one"; 24:11, "I didn't kill you. This proves I am not trying to harm you"; 24:12, "I will never harm you." And Saul: 24:18, "When the LORD put me in a place where you could have killed me, you didn't do it"; 24:19, "Who else would let his enemy get away when he had him in his power?"
10. In ancient Israel, the anointed one, whether priest or king, stood in the place of God before his people. To attack an anointed one, therefore, was equivalent to an attack on the Lord himself. R. de Vaux (1971b:163) argues that anointing was the rite by which a person was made king and established as a vassal of Yahweh. He says (1971b:166), "The king of Israel was God's representative on earth, he received his Spirit, shared in his holiness and was inviolable." Further (TDNT 9.496-509), "Saul is continually called the anointed of Yahweh by David when the issue is the inviolability of his person. Because he is in a special relation to Yahweh, the person of the *mashiakh yhwh* [TH4899/3068, ZH5431/3378] must not be touched."
11. As Edelman (1991:196) notes, this robe incident "cannot help but call to mind for both the audience and Saul the earlier robe-rending incident in 15.27-28, through which Samuel symbolized the removal of the kingdom from Saul and its transferral to 'your neighbor/companion who is better (*tob* [TH2896, ZH3202]) than you.' Thus, while on a literal level it demonstrates David's restraint and failure to kill Saul even though he had the opportunity, on another level it graphically illustrates for all concerned Samuel's earlier prediction. David now literally holds within his hand a piece of the royal cloak, a symbol for the kingdom itself."
12. Peels suggests that while David does not deny that God had delivered him and given him revenge on Saul, he does not allow that this was done in the manner assumed by Recab and Baanah (2 Sam 4:5-12). He comments (1992:202), "The fall of the dynasty of Saul is connected with the rejection of God, not with the vengeance of God." David recognized that an injustice was done by Recab and Baanah, and as Peels (1992:202) suggests, "The vengeance of God has nothing in common with injustice."

◆ N. Samuel's Death; David, Nabal, and Abigail (1 Sam 25:1-44)

Now Samuel died, and all Israel gathered for his funeral. They buried him at his house in Ramah.

Then David moved down to the wilderness of Maon.* 2There was a wealthy man from Maon who owned property near the

town of Carmel. He had 3,000 sheep and
1,000 goats, and it was sheep-shearing
time. 3This man's name was Nabal, and his
wife, Abigail, was a sensible and beautiful
woman. But Nabal, a descendant of Caleb,
was crude and mean in all his dealings.

4When David heard that Nabal was
shearing his sheep, 5he sent ten of his
young men to Carmel with this message
for Nabal: 6"Peace and prosperity to you,
your family, and everything you own! 7I
am told that it is sheep-shearing time.
While your shepherds stayed among us
near Carmel, we never harmed them, and
nothing was ever stolen from them. 8Ask
your own men, and they will tell you this
is true. So would you be kind to us, since
we have come at a time of celebration?
Please share any provisions you might
have on hand with us and with your friend
David." 9David's young men gave this
message to Nabal in David's name, and
they waited for a reply.

10"Who is this fellow David?" Nabal
sneered to the young men. "Who does this
son of Jesse think he is? There are lots of
servants these days who run away from
their masters. 11Should I take my bread
and my water and my meat that I've
slaughtered for my shearers and give it to
a band of outlaws who come from who
knows where?"

12So David's young men returned and
told him what Nabal had said. 13"Get your
swords!" was David's reply as he strapped
on his own. Then 400 men started off
with David, and 200 remained behind to
guard their equipment.

14Meanwhile, one of Nabal's servants
went to Abigail and told her, "David sent
messengers from the wilderness to greet
our master, but he screamed insults at
them. 15These men have been very good
to us, and we never suffered any harm
from them. Nothing was stolen from us
the whole time they were with us. 16In
fact, day and night they were like a wall
of protection to us and the sheep. 17You
need to know this and figure out what to
do, for there is going to be trouble for our
master and his whole family. He's so ill-
tempered that no one can even talk to
him!"

18Abigail wasted no time. She quickly
gathered 200 loaves of bread, two wine-
skins full of wine, five sheep that had
been slaughtered, nearly a bushel* of
roasted grain, 100 clusters of raisins, and
200 fig cakes. She packed them on don-
keys 19and said to her servants, "Go on
ahead. I will follow you shortly." But she
didn't tell her husband Nabal what she
was doing.

20As she was riding her donkey into a
mountain ravine, she saw David and his
men coming toward her. 21David had just
been saying, "A lot of good it did to help
this fellow. We protected his flocks in the
wilderness, and nothing he owned was
lost or stolen. But he has repaid me evil
for good. 22May God strike me and kill
me* if even one man of his household is
still alive tomorrow morning!"

23When Abigail saw David, she quickly
got off her donkey and bowed low before
him. 24She fell at his feet and said, "I ac-
cept all blame in this matter, my lord.
Please listen to what I have to say. 25I
know Nabal is a wicked and ill-tempered
man; please don't pay any attention to
him. He is a fool, just as his name sug-
gests.* But I never even saw the young
men you sent.

26"Now, my lord, as surely as the LORD
lives and you yourself live, since the LORD
has kept you from murdering and taking
vengeance into your own hands, let all
your enemies and those who try to harm
you be as cursed as Nabal is. 27And here is
a present that I, your servant, have
brought to you and your young men.
28Please forgive me if I have offended you
in any way. The LORD will surely reward
you with a lasting dynasty, for you are
fighting the LORD's battles. And you have
not done wrong throughout your entire
life.

29"Even when you are chased by those
who seek to kill you, your life is safe in the

care of the LORD your God, secure in his treasure pouch! But the lives of your enemies will disappear like stones shot from a sling! [30]When the LORD has done all he promised and has made you leader of Israel, [31]don't let this be a blemish on your record. Then your conscience won't have to bear the staggering burden of needless bloodshed and vengeance. And when the LORD has done these great things for you, please remember me, your servant!"

[32]David replied to Abigail, "Praise the LORD, the God of Israel, who has sent you to meet me today! [33]Thank God for your good sense! Bless you for keeping me from murder and from carrying out vengeance with my own hands. [34]For I swear by the LORD, the God of Israel, who has kept me from hurting you, that if you had not hurried out to meet me, not one of Nabal's men would still be alive tomorrow morning." [35]Then David accepted her present and told her, "Return home in peace. I have heard what you said. We will not kill your husband."

[36]When Abigail arrived home, she found that Nabal was throwing a big party and was celebrating like a king. He was very drunk, so she didn't tell him anything about her meeting with David until dawn the next day. [37]In the morning when Nabal was sober, his wife told him what had happened. As a result he had a stroke,* and he lay paralyzed on his bed like a stone. [38]About ten days later, the LORD struck him, and he died.

[39]When David heard that Nabal was dead, he said, "Praise the LORD, who has avenged the insult I received from Nabal and has kept me from doing it myself. Nabal has received the punishment for his sin." Then David sent messengers to Abigail to ask her to become his wife.

[40]When the messengers arrived at Carmel, they told Abigail, "David has sent us to take you back to marry him."

[41]She bowed low to the ground and responded, "I, your servant, would be happy to marry David. I would even be willing to become a slave, washing the feet of his servants!" [42]Quickly getting ready, she took along five of her servant girls as attendants, mounted her donkey, and went with David's messengers. And so she became his wife. [43]David also married Ahinoam from Jezreel, making both of them his wives. [44]Saul, meanwhile, had given his daughter Michal, David's wife, to a man from Gallim named Palti son of Laish.

25:1 As in Greek version (see also 25:2); Hebrew reads *Paran.* **25:18** Hebrew *5 seahs* [30 liters]. **25:22** As in Greek version; Hebrew reads *May God strike and kill the enemies of David.* **25:25** The name *Nabal* means "fool." **25:37** Hebrew *his heart failed him.*

NOTES

25:1 *Maon.* The MT and LXX Alexandrinus read "Paran"; LXX Vaticanus reads "Maon." Because Paran seems to be located too far to the south (cf. Gen 21:21; Num 13:3, 26) for this context (cf. 23:24-26; 25:2ff), some interpreters and translations (cf. e.g., NLT, NIV, NCV) have adopted the "Maon" reading of LXX Vaticanus. On the one hand it is tempting to accept that reading based on location and context (cf. also 22:5), but on the other hand, "Maon" may be a later "correction" to the original reading. For this reason, in my view, preference should be given to the more difficult "Paran" reading. If the MT is maintained, it would seem that 25:1 refers to a brief visit to Paran, followed by a longer sojourn in the area of Maon.

25:3 *a descendant of Caleb.* Thus according to Qere reading, "a Calebite." The Kethiv reads "like his heart"—that is, as Hertzberg (1964:199) notes, "his nature accorded with his evil deeds." Others have suggested "like a dog," but this would require emendation.

25:6 *Peace and prosperity to you.* In the Hebrew text this greeting is preceded by the words *wa'amartem koh lekhay* (lit., "And you shall say thus to the living one"). The meaning of *lekhay* [TH3807.1/2416, ZH4200/2644] (to life) in this phrase is not clear. Numerous proposals have been made to explain its significance including the following: S. R. Driver (1913:196) suggests a pausal form of *lakhay* = "to him that lives" (GKC §29v). Youngblood (1992:765) suggests that it is preferable to read *le'akhi* [TH251, ZH278] (to my brother) instead of *lekhay* (to the living one), assuming elision of the letter Aleph; the phrase would then read, "And you shall say thus to my brother," which agrees with the idea in the Vulgate. Some commentators (Keil 1956:239) suggest the word represents an elliptical exclamation of greeting, with the meaning "Good fortune to you" or "Good fortune to the living man." In a variation of this approach, G. R. Driver (1957:272-273) suggests that *lekhay* plus the two following words are similar to an Arabic expression, "every year and thou well," i.e., "many happy returns of the day!" This idea is captured in the NEB's "all good wishes for the year ahead!" The *eis hōras* [TG5610, ZG6052] (unto the time) of the LXX, as well as the "for many years" of the Old Latin (*multis annis*) and Josephus (*Antiquities* 6.297 [6.13.6]), seem to point toward a temporal significance for the expression (cf. Gen 18:10, 14; 2 Kgs 4:16 for possible use of *khay* [TH2416A, ZH2645] in the sense of "year").

25:14 ***he screamed insults at them.*** It is not certain whether the root *'yt* is to be understood as "scream" or "shriek" (on the basis of similar roots in Arabic and Syriac, as noted in BDB) or as a denominative verb from the noun *'ayit* [TH5861, ZH6514] (bird of prey) with the idea of "fly at" (cf. NEB) as in 15:19 (NLT, "rush for").

25:17 ***trouble for our master and his whole family.*** Lit., "Evil is plotted against our master and against his whole house." See Joüon and Muraoka §133b for the use of *'el . . . 'al* [TH413/5921, ZH448/6584] in sequence. Here the direction implied is hostile, so both carry the idea of "against."

so ill-tempered. Lit., "He is a son of Belial" (see note on 1:16). Other occurrences in 1–2 Samuel are 2:12; 10:27; 2 Sam 16:7; 20:1.

25:22 ***May God strike me.*** So LXX (see NLT mg). The MT reads, "May God do thus to the enemies of David." Keil (1956:242) argues for the correctness of the MT by suggesting that "David is so full of the consciousness of fighting and suffering for the cause of the kingdom of God, that he discerns in the insult heaped upon him by Nabal an act of hostility to the Lord and the cause of his kingdom." This reasoning, however, seems difficult to harmonize with the context in which David himself is the one who takes the oath and thus its malediction must be directed toward himself. Gordon (1986:167, 184) suggests that enemies here, as well as in 20:16, is a "euphemistic addition" to the original text and stands for David himself.

25:24 ***Please listen.*** Lit., "Let your handmaid speak." The Waw in the Hebrew here serves to indicate the jussive more clearly (see Joüon and Muraoka §177*l*).

25:25 ***Nabal is a wicked and ill-tempered man.*** Lit., "man of Belial" (see note on 25:17).

25:26 ***from murdering and taking vengeance.*** For the use of an infinitive absolute as the equivalent of a preceding form (in this case an infinitive construct) without repetition of the preposition, see Joüon and Muraoka §123x, §124r.

taking vengeance into your own hands. Lit., "your hand giving victory to you."

25:27 ***your young men.*** Lit., "the young men who walk at the feet of my lord" (i.e., the verb is used for retainers, who attend to someone).

25:35 ***I have heard what you said.*** Lit., "I have heard your voice and I have lifted up your face" (i.e., "I have granted your request").

25:42 ***she took along five of her servant girls as attendants.*** Lit., "her five maids who were following her." As it stands, the MT implies that these were all the maids she had, and also that all six women were riding on the donkey! It appears that a single letter He (which in this context means "who were") preceding the participle *holkoth* [TH1980, ZH2143] (following) is probably to be disregarded as the result of dittography. The NLT reflects such a decision.

COMMENTARY[1]

The narrative of David and Nabal in chapter 25 is a riveting story. It is distinguished by superb characterization and a fast-moving plot. David, the anointed but uncrowned king, was harshly insulted by an unreasonable and churlish man to whom he had given assistance and defense. David became so enraged at the unexpected and unwarranted affront of this arrogant individual (his name was "Nabal," which in Hebrew means "fool"[2]) that he resolved to kill both Nabal and his servants. When Nabal's resourceful and beautiful wife, Abigail, learned of her husband's provocation, she intervened in the dispute, and with great élan convinced David that he should not bring bloodguilt on himself by taking revenge on her foolish husband. Upon learning of what his wife had done, Nabal's heart failed, and within 10 days he was dead. David then sent for Abigail, and she became his wife.

This fascinating story is enclosed between two narratives that describe how David spared the life of the reigning king, Saul, even though Saul was seeking to take his life. The relationship between these three stories in chapters 24–26 has long intrigued interpreters of this section of 1 Samuel. The general consensus among biblical scholars has been that the two stories about David sparing Saul's life (chs 24 and 26) are variant versions of the same incident.[3] At the same time it has generally been held that there is little or no connection between chapter 25 and the two stories between which it is placed.[4] This conclusion has tended to isolate chapter 25 from the flow of its larger narrative context, with the result that it has usually been interpreted in isolation as well. For this reason the chapter has often not been viewed as contributing in any significant way to the forward movement of redemptive history in the events connected with David's rise to the throne. Because of the strong characterization in the narrative, especially of Abigail, the story has frequently been treated primarily as a character study of Abigail, in whom a role model is found for the ideal traits of the good woman.[5]

In more recent times, the relationship between the narratives in chapters 24–26 has been reassessed in light of an increasing awareness of the role of "gapping" or "narrative reticence"[6] in Hebrew narrative. For the most part, Hebrew narratives do not include any "explicit commentary" that gives the reader a clear assessment of the significance or purpose for which the narrative unit has been included in the larger composition. It is the interpreter's responsibility to fill in these narrative "gaps" in "congruity with the text's own norms."[7] This consideration, in turn, has given rise to a growing recognition of the importance of the technique of "narrative analogy" for the proper understanding of Old Testament narrative. Narrative analogy is the "oblique commentary" that may be made on a particular story when it is compared to other narratives within its larger context (Alter 1975:73). Gordon (1980) has discussed the interrelatedness of 1 Samuel 24, 25, and 26 at some length on the basis of this technique. He concludes (1980:43) that the central thesis that emerges when chapter 25 is looked at from this perspective is that "Saul does not vanish from view in 1 Samuel 25" as might seem to be the case,[8] because Saul "is Nabal's alter ego."[9] This insight provides a basis for seeing a very close connection between all three narratives. Chapter 25, then, is not to be regarded as disconnected from, or unrelated to, the two stories between which it is placed.

Gordon substantiates this thesis in a compelling way. While there is neither the need nor the space to repeat here all the specifics of his study, the following are a few examples of the sorts of things to which Gordon calls attention: In all three stories David was restrained by a "theological consideration" from seeking personal advantage through killing an antagonist (Saul or Nabal). Abigail gives elegant expression to this idea when she says to David that his conscience shouldn't be asked "to bear the staggering burden of needless bloodshed and vengeance" (25:31). Gordon also points out that "psychologically Saul and Nabal are twins. They refuse to acknowledge David for what he is, and they are alienated from those about them" (1980:44).

There are also word repetitions that link chapter 25 to chapters 24 and 26. Word repetition is an important feature of narrative analogy. Gordon comments (1980:47) that the "beauty of this device is that it enables the narrator to make his point with an absolute economy of words, whether it be to highlight parallelism, contrast, or development across the contextual divide." An example of this is found in 26:10 where David rejects Abishai's proposal to kill Saul, saying, "Surely the LORD will strike Saul down someday." When we ask why David was so certain that Saul would die as a result of divine judgment in chapter 26, we notice that in chapter 25 the narrator already told us that "the LORD struck him [Nabal], and he died" (25:38). Both "struck" in 25:38 and "strike" in 26:10 translate the Hebrew word *nagap* [TH5062, ZH5597]. The repetition of this word serves to draw a comparison between Saul and Nabal. So Gordon suggests that the "manner of Nabal's death provides the key to David's confident assertion of 26:10 and herein . . . lies also a pointer to the whole narrative thrust of 1 Samuel 24–26" (1980:49). These sorts of observations provide a basis for reading chapters 24–26 as a closely connected narrative sequence.[10]

This brings us back to chapter 25. On the surface, this chapter describes a conflict between David and the wealthy sheepherder Nabal. Below the surface it reflects the ongoing conflict between the Kingdom of God and the kingdom of Satan. Here that conflict takes the form of a surprise attack on David by the evil one, an attack that is thwarted by God's providential provision of a timely admonition to David from an unexpected source. Not only did an unnamed servant of Nabal providentially inform Abigail of impending disaster (25:14), but Abigail herself providentially intervened in the quickly developing controversy to avert a serious mistake by David (25:18-35).[11] In fact, we may say that this narrative presents us with a paradigm of temptation and divine providence.

At another level, this narrative is both parabolic and proleptic. It is parabolic in that the relationship between David and Saul is symbolized by the relationship between David and Nabal. And because of this symbolic connection, the narrative is at the same time proleptic. As was noted above, the outcome of the Nabal incident gave David reassurance about the future demise of his opponent Saul. So at this level something else is going on in the narrative. Through these events God was speaking to David about his future and telling David that he (God) would eventually take care of Saul just as he had already taken care of Nabal. All of these incidents are set in the larger context of David's rise to the throne and the series of tests through which he must pass before his eventual inauguration as the covenantal king.

As de Jong (1978:183) suggests, up to this point the evil one has been unsuccessful in tempting David to lose his patience in his relationship with Saul. David demonstrated enormous self-control when he cut just a small piece from Saul's robe in the cave in En-gedi (ch 24). But in this chapter, the evil one took a different approach. He arranged a meeting between David and Nabal for the purpose of defeating David by an attack from an unexpected direction. The common theme that links chapters 24 and 25 is the injustice that is done to David by Saul and Nabal. In both cases, David must wait for justice to come from the hand of the Lord. In the case of Saul, David understood this (24:12), but in the case of Nabal he did not, and as a result he nearly took things into his own hands.

Why is all of this significant? It is significant because redemptive-historical issues are at stake. Jesus Christ would be born from the house of David. The angel Gabriel said at the announcement of the birth of Christ, "The Lord God will give him the throne of his ancestor David" (Luke 1:32). The question, then, becomes what sort of throne would the throne of David be? In Christ we see the character of the true covenantal king revealed in all its fullness. In chapter 25, the evil one attempts to turn David away from this covenantal ideal. The evil one wants a king who takes justice into his own hands. So what the evil one had been unable to accomplish in David's relationship with Saul he now sought to accomplish in David's unexpected encounter with Nabal (de Jong 1978:184-185).

On earlier occasions David had received help from Samuel in sorting out his relationship with Saul. When David fled from Saul in chapter 19, he sought refuge with Samuel in Naioth in Ramah. On that occasion David and Samuel undoubtedly discussed David's relationship with Saul at great length ("he [David] told him [Samuel] all that Saul had done to him"; 19:18). But chapter 25 begins with an announcement of Samuel's death (25:1). This notice is not a piece of irrelevant information; it is a notice telling us that David was particularly vulnerable to the onslaughts of the evil one because he had lost his most important counselor. The evil one had coordinated his attack on David with a time in David's life when he would be particularly susceptible to defeat. Within God's providence, this occurred in order to test whether David was the sort of messianic king who would attempt to take vengeance into his own hands or choose to wait on the Lord.

When David sent some of his men to Nabal and asked him "to share any provisions" he might have with them in return for the protection of his shepherds and flocks in the past (25:7-8, 16),[12] Nabal not only refused to offer any assistance, but he did so with insulting and sarcastic language (25:10-11).[13] David's response was exactly what one might expect. He was enraged at the abusive behavior of this arrogant man. He did what most people do when they are severely provoked in a completely unwarranted manner. He responded in kind. In essence he said, "If you want to behave like a fool it will be the last time you do so." He told his men, "'Put on your swords!' So they put on their swords, and David put on his sword" (25:13, my translation). The threefold repetition of the word "sword" (*khereb* [TH2719, ZH2995]) in the Hebrew of 25:13 is significant. The Hebrew narrative uses such repetitions to draw our attention to a particular feature of the story. David also swore: "May God strike me and kill me if even one man of his household is still alive tomorrow morning!" (25:22, see note).

In this connection we encounter another expression, also highlighted by its threefold repetition, namely "delivering oneself by one's own hand," which is translated as taking or carrying out vengeance (25:26, 31, 33). This idiom can be phrased as "taking the law into one's own hands" (TDOT 6.441-447[14]). David's response to Nabal's insult was to seek revenge; he would take the law into his own hands in vindictive retaliation for Nabal's insults by killing him. Notice how sharply this contrasts with David's response to the opportunity given him in chapter 24 to take Saul's life. On that occasion he said (24:12) "May the LORD judge between us. Perhaps the LORD will punish you (*naqam* [TH5358, ZH5933], "avenge") for what you are trying to do to me, but I will never harm you."

In the midst of this temptation, however, the Lord provided David with a way of escape. That way of escape came through the counsel of Abigail, Nabal's wife.[15] Abigail did not act because of danger to herself (though she may have been in danger, cf. 25:34) but because she saw David endangering himself. Her action seems to be born of personal faith in the promises to David (cf. 25:28-31). Abigail spoke with the insight and authority of a prophetess concerning David's future (an echo of Hannah's prophetic insight in ch 2). She completely understood David's reaction to Nabal because she was Nabal's wife—she could sympathize with David's feelings. So she prepared a gift and went out to meet David in an attempt to convince him not to blemish his reputation. What she said to David amounted to this: "David, you will become king someday, and in your kingship you must act in ways that are appropriate to the true covenantal king. You, therefore, must not blemish yourself with bloodguilt." In essence she said to David what James said to Jewish believers of a much later time: "Understand this, my dear brothers and sisters: You must all be quick to listen, slow to speak, and slow to get angry. Human anger does not produce the righteousness God desires" (Jas 1:19-20). In contrast to David's initial reaction to Nabal's provocation, the true covenantal king must wait on the Lord, and he must lead God's people in doing the same.

This is not to say, however, that the true covenantal king should be a passive individual who sits around doing nothing, waiting for the Lord to act on his behalf. Notice that Abigail also said that David was one who fought "the LORD's battles" (25:28). The point is that while fighting the Lord's battles, it should also be clear that one is waiting on the Lord in the process (de Jong 1978:187). David's confrontation with Nabal was not a "battle of the LORD." It was a personal affront that provoked David to take personal revenge. Abigail became God's instrument for providing David with a way of escape from this serious temptation. Emphasis upon the providential nature of Abigail's role is found in another of the threefold verbal repetitions in the chapter. Both Abigail (25:26) and David (25:34, 39) say that the Lord "kept" David from doing wrong in his encounter with Nabal. This was because Yahweh sent Abigail (25:32).

Perhaps the most surprising aspect of this story is that David listened to Abigail. David was a powerful person who had been seriously provoked and who was livid with anger, yet he listened to Abigail's voice of reason. David, in fact, thanked Abigail profusely and praised both her and God for sending her to him (25:32, 39).

This narrative calls our attention to two primary things. First, in its redemptive-historical context, it points us forward to Christ. The standards that are here recognized for kingship in Israel foreshadow and anticipate the character of the ultimate covenantal king. Second, it calls our attention to important truths for our own walk before God. For example, Satan is at work to lead us astray from the Lord's will just as he was with David. Paul speaks of his schemes (2 Cor 2:11), and Peter describes him as a roaring lion seeking whom he may devour (1 Pet 5:8). Just as in this narrative, Satan still attempts to take God's people by surprise. He attacks at our weakest points and when we least suspect his activity. So we must always be on our guard. When we are mistreated by those around us, our response must be governed by waiting upon the Lord rather than by taking things into our own hands. As Paul said, "Never pay back evil with more evil. Do things in such a way that everyone can see you are honorable. Do all that you can to live in peace with everyone. Dear friends, never take revenge. Leave that to the righteous anger of God. For the Scriptures say, 'I will take revenge; I will pay them back,' says the LORD" (Rom 12:17-19). In his providential governance of everything that happens in our lives, God always provides a way of escape for his people when they are tempted by Satan (1 Cor 10:13). Thus this story gives us a paradigm of temptation and divine providence. The truth highlighted by the verbal repetitions in this chapter ("sword," "vengeance," "providence," and "praise") is that it is our responsibility to respond to God's gracious provision of a way to escape temptation with acceptance and thanksgiving.

ENDNOTES

1. Parts of the commentary on this chapter are adapted from Vannoy 1998.
2. Because of the improbability that anyone would be given a name such as this, Alter points out that it is likely that the name was "not originally Hebrew, and various meanings drawn from other ancient Near Eastern languages have been proposed for it, such as 'archer' and 'chosen one of the god.'"
3. Smith (1912:216) comments, "We have reason to think, therefore, that we have two versions of the same story. It is natural to suppose that one belongs with each of the two documents which make up the bulk of the narrative already considered. . . . The slight preponderance of probability seems to me to be on the side of the latter representation [ch 26] as more original." Hertzberg (1964:207), commenting on ch 26, says, "It is evident that this narrative and 22:19–24:22 make use of the same material." McCarter (1980b:386-387) comments, "The older source critics tended to regard one [story] as derived from the other . . . in a purely literary way. . . . More recent scholars, working under the impact of the insights of form criticism, have preferred to think of a traditional source common to both accounts which developed in different ways in two locations . . . the interpretation given here . . . stands closer to that of the older literary critics, who seem more persuasive." Klein (1983:236) says, "It needs to be noticed that the two chapters [24 and 26]

are probably alternate memories of one event." Koch (1969:144) notes that "literary criticism had thought that A and B [chs 24 and 26] were derived from two individual written sources," but Koch's own view (1969:143) is that these narratives "must be two versions of the same story, both of which developed in oral form quite independently of each other."

4. Koch (1969:137) says that the narrative following ch 24 that describes Nabal's folly "has nothing to do with it" [that is, with ch 24]. He also says (1969:138) that the links between ch 26 and the preceding chapter "are exceedingly loose."
5. See, e.g., Blackwood (1946:154-159), who regards the relationship of chs 24 and 26 to ch 25 as one of contrast. In his view, chs 24 and 26 display envy, wrath, and attempted murder as exhibited in the behavior of Saul. In contrast to this he finds ch 25 to be the depiction of a charming woman "courageously intervening to avert needless bloodshed" (1946:154). Blackwood accordingly organizes a sermon on this chapter around the theme "The Influence of a Woman's Charm." He develops this theme under the headings: (1) the sort of man a good woman should not marry (25:1-17); (2) the sort of woman a good man should wed (25:18-22); (3) how a good woman makes the best of a sorry mess (25:23-31); (4) how God blesses the beautiful peacemaker (25:32-42).
6. This is the recognition that the motives, causes, and purposes of the actions of individuals in Old Testament narratives are usually not explained or commented on by the author of the narrative.
7. See Sternberg 1985:188 and chapter 6, "Gaps, Ambiguity, and the Reading Process," in the same work.
8. Humphreys (1978:19), for example, alleges that "Saul vanishes from view" in ch 25.
9. A. H. van Zijl (1989:97) comments, "Whether one must completely transpose the names (Nabal is Saul) is the question, but that Nabal is a type of Saul, and therefore has been given traits of him, is clear" (my translation).
10. Edelman (1991:206) notes that Nabal is designated as *qasheh* [TH7186, ZH7997] (severe, rude) in 25:3, and David used the same term to describe Saul in 20:10. According to Edelman that "would seem to create for the audience a link between Nabal and Saul. . . . The link gains further reinforcement in the light of Samuel's use of the verb *sakal* [TH5528, ZH6118], 'to act foolishly', to describe Saul's deeds in 13.13, making Saul and Nabal fellow 'fools.'" In addition it should be noted that Saul refers to himself with the verb *sakal* (to act foolishly) in 26:21. Another link is provided by David's statement concerning Nabal that he has "repaid me evil for good" (25:21), which is a verbal echo of Saul's words concerning David and himself in 24:17.
11. Klein (1983:250-251) comments, "Abigail's actions are the proximate cause for David escaping guilt, but the real protector of the future king's integrity is Yahweh himself. . . . Abigail's journey to David is understood not as a valiant attempt to save her husband, much less an opportunistic attempt to join David's side. Rather, it was part of Yahweh's plan. . . . Abigail's bravery is immediately reinterpreted as flowing from the actions of Yahweh God of Israel."
12. A number of interpreters have placed an unwarranted, sinister spin on David's request of assistance from Nabal. As Edelman (1991:207, note 2) observes, "David's request has been characterized as a 'protection racket'" by, for example, Ackroyd (1971:195); Gunn (1980:98); Levenson (1978:19), and others. Brueggemann (1990a:176) says that David's message to Nabal was one of "intimidation and confiscation." He goes on to say that "David appears to be making a subtle but unmistakable request for protection money. . . . Now it is clear that David and his unsettled, greedy malcontents are in fact a threat to those who benefit from, value, and maintain a settled pastoral economy."

Alter (1999:153) comments, "But there is a certain ambiguity as to whether David was providing protection out of sheer good will or conducting a protection racket in order to get the necessary provisions for his guerilla band." Such assertions, however, are not at all warranted by the language of the request, and are completely contrary to the defense of David given by one of Nabal's own servants ("they were like a wall of protection to us and the sheep," 25:16) when he informs Abigail of the impending confrontation between David and Nabal (25:14-17).

13. Nabal implied that David had left Saul's service unjustly and called the men who were with him outlaws. That David did not leave Saul unjustly has been addressed in ch 20 (see commentary).
14. TDOT 6.441-447 comments, "The *locus classicus* of this usage is 1 S. 25:23-35, where the point at issue is whether David will accept Abigail's offer of reparation or 'take the law into his own hands' . . . and punish her husband by the sword."
15. Hertzberg (1964:203) comments, "She is an instrument of the Lord to keep the future king's escutcheon clean for David." He comments further (1964:204), "Through Abigail, the Lord saves David from a danger different from that in the cave with Saul, but nonetheless great. It consists, as has been said, in the possibility that David may take matters into his own hand and thus make himself master of his fate, instead of letting it be guided by the Lord."

◆ O. David Spares Saul's Life a Second Time (1 Sam 26:1-25)

Now some men from Ziph came to Saul
at Gibeah to tell him, "David is hiding on
the hill of Hakilah, which overlooks
Jeshimon."
2So Saul took 3,000 of Israel's elite
troops and went to hunt him down in the
wilderness of Ziph. 3Saul camped along
the road beside the hill of Hakilah, near
Jeshimon, where David was hiding. When
David learned that Saul had come after
him into the wilderness, 4he sent out spies
to verify the report of Saul's arrival.
5David slipped over to Saul's camp one
night to look around. Saul and Abner
son of Ner, the commander of his army,
were sleeping inside a ring formed by the
slumbering warriors. 6"Who will volunteer to go in there with me?" David asked
Ahimelech the Hittite and Abishai son of
Zeruiah, Joab's brother.
"I'll go with you," Abishai replied. 7So
David and Abishai went right into Saul's
camp and found him asleep, with his
spear stuck in the ground beside his head.
Abner and the soldiers were lying asleep
around him.
8"God has surely handed your enemy
over to you this time!" Abishai whispered
to David. "Let me pin him to the ground
with one thrust of the spear; I won't need
to strike twice!"
9"No!" David said. "Don't kill him. For
who can remain innocent after attacking
the LORD's anointed one? 10Surely the
LORD will strike Saul down someday, or he
will die of old age or in battle. 11The LORD
forbid that I should kill the one he has
anointed! But take his spear and that jug
of water beside his head, and then let's
get out of here!"
12So David took the spear and jug of water that were near Saul's head. Then he and
Abishai got away without anyone seeing
them or even waking up, because the LORD
had put Saul's men into a deep sleep.
13David climbed the hill opposite the
camp until he was at a safe distance.
14Then he shouted down to the soldiers
and to Abner son of Ner, "Wake up,
Abner!"
"Who is it?" Abner demanded.
15"Well, Abner, you're a great man,
aren't you?" David taunted. "Where in all
Israel is there anyone as mighty? So why

haven't you guarded your master the king when someone came to kill him? [16]This isn't good at all! I swear by the LORD that you and your men deserve to die, because you failed to protect your master, the LORD's anointed! Look around! Where are the king's spear and the jug of water that were beside his head?"

[17]Saul recognized David's voice and called out, "Is that you, my son David?"

And David replied, "Yes, my lord the king. [18]Why are you chasing me? What have I done? What is my crime? [19]But now let my lord the king listen to his servant. If the LORD has stirred you up against me, then let him accept my offering. But if this is simply a human scheme, then may those involved be cursed by the LORD. For they have driven me from my home, so I can no longer live among the LORD's people, and they have said, 'Go, worship pagan gods.' [20]Must I die on foreign soil, far from the presence of the LORD? Why has the king of Israel come out to search for a single flea? Why does he hunt me down like a partridge on the mountains?"

[21]Then Saul confessed, "I have sinned. Come back home, my son, and I will no longer try to harm you, for you valued my life today. I have been a fool and very, very wrong."

[22]"Here is your spear, O king," David replied. "Let one of your young men come over and get it. [23]The LORD gives his own reward for doing good and for being loyal, and I refused to kill you even when the LORD placed you in my power, for you are the LORD's anointed one. [24]Now may the LORD value my life, even as I have valued yours today. May he rescue me from all my troubles."

[25]And Saul said to David, "Blessings on you, my son David. You will do many heroic deeds, and you will surely succeed." Then David went away, and Saul returned home.

NOTES

26:1 ***Jeshimon.*** The Hebrew word may be either a place name or a general term for "wasteland" or "desert."

26:4 ***to verify the report of Saul's arrival.*** Lit., "He learned that Saul had certainly come." The Hebrew expression *'el-nakon* [TH413/3559, ZH448/3922] is unusual (cf. 23:23, there translated "when you are sure") and seems best understood as adverbial with the idea of "according to (what is) certain" thus, "certainly" or "assuredly" (Alter 1999:163; BDB 465d). NLT represents this idea with "to verify."

26:16 ***you and your men deserve to die.*** Lit., "You are sons of death."

26:19 ***let him accept my offering.*** Lit., "May he smell an offering"—that is, may he be satisfied by the odor of the offering.

26:22 ***your spear, O king.*** Kethiv reads "the spear, O king." Qere reads, "the king's spear."

26:23 ***in my power.*** Lit., "in my hand"; thus according to many Hebrew mss and the LXX. The MT has no first person suffix: "in hand."

COMMENTARY

First Samuel 26 is in many ways reminiscent of chapter 24. As we have seen, chapter 24 described Saul's inadvertent visit to the very cave in which David and his men were hiding, and how David not only refused to take Saul's life but also prevented his men from doing so. As I noted in the commentary on chapter 24, the older source critics viewed 1 Samuel 24 and 26 as variant versions of the same event. More recent literary analysis has concluded that no matter what the literary history of these two narrative units might be, chapter 26 is not to be read as a simple repetition of chapter 24, even though there are some striking similarities between the two chapters. The most prominent parallel is David's refusal to lift up his hand against the Lord's anointed on both occasions (24:6, 10, 12; 26:9-11, 23). The focus of the narrative in chapter 26, however, is different from that of chapter 24. In chapter 24, the central theme was a test of David's leadership. Would David take advantage of an unexpected opportunity to seize the throne prematurely? In chapter 26, the focus is more on Saul and his followers, and the question is whether or not they will persist in refusing to recognize David as the one whom the Lord had chosen to replace Saul as king.

Comparison of the two chapters not only reveals differences in setting and detail between the stories, but also specific "intensifications" and "narrative advances" in chapter 26. It is by the identification of these features that the difference in focus between chapters 26 and 24 is discerned. A number of features should therefore be noted before looking at the narrative in more detail. First, this is the last recorded meeting between Saul and David in 1–2 Samuel. More specifically, this is the last appearance of Saul in the narratives of 1 Samuel before the account of the events surrounding his death. So Saul's words at the end of the chapter are in effect his concession speech to David and his acknowledgment that his attempts to prevent David from acceding to the throne have failed (26:25).[1] Second, the meeting between the two contenders for the throne in this chapter is not coincidental, as their encounter in chapter 24 might be characterized. Here the encounter is the result of a deliberate initiative taken by David.[2] Third, Saul's spear is prominent in this narrative. There are six references to it (26:7, 8, 11, 12, 16, 22), and David's acquisition of it, much like his cutting of Saul's robe in chapter 24, symbolizes the transfer of power from David to Saul.[3] Fourth, the deep sleep that came over Saul and his men is a clear demonstration that the Lord was at work on behalf of David in the events that are portrayed in the chapter (26:12). Fifth, David shows a heightened confidence that the Lord will look with favor on him and displays a firm belief that Saul will die in the Lord's time and way (26:10-11). Sixth, there is a prominent new element in chapter 26, namely, the introduction of a third party, Abner, into the dialogue between David and Saul. This "narrative advance" should be viewed as a focal point of the chapter, the significance of which will be discussed below. Seventh, there is a renewed and heightened appeal for Saul to repent (26:18-20).

There are many issues that surface when 1 Samuel 26 is understood in view of the flow of narratives dealing with David's rise and Saul's demise. It is difficult to organize all these considerations into one overarching theme, but if any one feature of the chapter is to be highlighted, it can be argued that its description of Saul's last chance to repent is its primary focus. Even so, this notion is combined with other themes that also merit scrutiny. Giving attention to these emphases will demonstrate the forward movement of redemptive history in the events of the chapter.

Certainly this narrative, like the narrative of 1 Samuel 24, emphasizes David's determination not to raise his hand against Saul because he was the Lord's anointed. David regarded Saul's destiny as something that was to be left in God's hands (26:10-11; cf. 24:6, 12). So just as in chapter 24, David used the spoken word, not physical force, as his weapon against Saul. If this, however, is the only point to be gleaned from this story, one might wonder why the author would include a second narrative containing basically the same theme as chapter 24. Is the fact that David's words did not have their desired effect on Saul in chapter 24 the reason why the author has included a second, similar narrative? While Saul's seemingly contrite response to David's words in 1 Samuel 24 might seem to suggest that they were effective in changing Saul's attitude toward David (cf. 24:16-19), it is clear that whatever Saul's feelings may have been at the end of chapter 24, he quickly returned to his old ways.

When the Ziphites betrayed David to Saul a second time (26:1; cf. ch 23), Saul went out to track David down as before. This demonstrates quite clearly that David's words to Saul in chapter 24 had no enduring effect. The question is, *what will David do this time?* It is here that the scenario of chapter 26 differs from that of chapter 24 in an important way: In chapter 26 the meeting between David and Saul is the result of an initiative by David and not an unplanned encounter as before. Of course, the meeting in chapter 24 was providential as David himself recognized (cf. 24:10), but David had not arranged it. On that occasion, in a totally unexpected way, David encountered Saul in a cave and then prevented his own men from taking Saul's life. That gracious act by David ennobled David in Saul's eyes. As Saul said, "Who else would let his enemy get away when he had him in his power? May the LORD reward you well for the kindness you have shown me today" (24:19). In contrast to chapter 24, we find that in chapter 26 David plays a significant role in setting up an encounter. Why would David do this? It is usually explained as an attempt to again demonstrate that he would not lift up his hand against Saul when he had the opportunity to do so (cf. 26:23 with 24:10).

But here, a suggestion of de Jong (1978:191-193) merits serious consideration. De Jong proposes that what David did here should be viewed as something designed for the benefit of Saul and his followers rather than for the enhancement of his own stature. In this chapter, in contrast to chapter 24, Saul is constantly surrounded by his officers and troops, who are responsible for his safety. Abner, Saul's commander, is prominent; he is rebuked by David for not having protected Saul as he should have. In 26:15-16 David says to Abner, "Well, Abner, you're a great man, aren't you? . . . Where in all Israel is there anyone as mighty? So why haven't you guarded your master the king when someone came to kill him? This isn't good. . . . You and your men deserve to die, because you failed to protect your master, the LORD's anointed!" The emphasis given to this interchange with Abner must be taken into account in any evaluation of the overall focus of the chapter and how it may differ from chapter 24. De Jong suggests that the issue that David raises here, although admittedly in an oblique way, is the question of the loyalty of Abner and his men toward Saul. It appears that Abner and the men under his command did not regard David as a serious threat to Saul. They, of course, knew David well from their association with him during the time he had been at the court and served with distinction in Saul's army. Evidently, on this occasion they had not set up watches during the night because they were convinced that David would not attack Saul. But in the meantime they were still giving their allegiance to Saul, and they were still supporting him, at least in appearance, in his campaign against David. De Jong suggests that the intent of David's rebuke of Abner was to confront Abner and his men with an important choice that they needed to make. The choice was either to stay with Saul and take his agenda seriously (including seeing David as a serious threat to Saul's kingdom), or else abandon Saul altogether. David wanted them to see that they could not remain somewhere in the middle in the struggle between Saul and himself.

By his rebuke of Abner, David pointed out that it was not possible for Abner to align himself with Saul but secretly sympathize with David. David said, in effect, "If I am the most dangerous enemy that Saul has, and if you are aligned with Saul, then you must act accordingly. That is what is required of you as long as you are giving your support to Saul." David wanted Abner and his men to think seriously about what they were doing and then to ask themselves if they should really be aligned with Saul. What would they do? Would they choose the path of least resistance and remain in Saul's service, or, for the sake of a good conscience would they choose the way of reproach by aligning themselves with David? It is an important feature of this chapter that Abner and his men are confronted with an important choice.

David likewise confronted Saul with a question. In the encounter in 1 Samuel 24 the outcome of the verbal exchange with Saul was not entirely clear. That Saul's seeming contrition was not genuine is demonstrated by his renewed attempt to capture David in chapter 26. On the first occasion (ch 24) David spoke to Saul mostly about his [David's] own innocence. In this chapter his focus is more on Saul. In 26:19, David asks, in effect, "Does what you are doing come from God or from bad advisers?" Notice that David spoke in a diplomatic manner, addressing Saul's motives by attributing his behavior to either God or evil men, rather than to Saul's own initiative.[4] These were the possibilities: Either God was behind what Saul was doing, and if this were the case (which it clearly was not), perhaps he would accept an offering of appeasement; or the other possibility was that Saul's vendetta and hatred were coming from his human advisers, and if that were so, then they should be cursed. Undoubtedly, Saul felt the force of these words and perceived that in the latter alternative, David was, in fact, placing the curse on him. But David framed the alternatives for Saul as if he could choose between God and his evil advisers. This was in essence the choice of the two ways. It was the same choice David had given to Abner.

David's statement in 26:19-20 highlights some of the implications of Saul's conduct. We hear in David's words: "I too am an Israelite. As an Israelite I have a right to a place in the land that we together as the people of God have received as an inheritance. And now you are forcing me to leave it. That is not right. Because of your actions I must flee to another land where other gods are served" (de Jong 1978:194).[5] David was not suggesting that he had no responsibility to remain faithful to the Lord outside of Israel; rather, he was pointing out Saul's responsibility as king. The role of the king of Israel was to protect God's people in the land he had given them. So David warned Saul how far his regime had fallen from its divinely sanctioned purpose.

What was Saul's reaction to David's challenge? Saul responded in a more thoughtful and discerning way to David's argument than he had in chapter 24, but regrettably, on this second occasion, his response seems less generous in its confession of guilt than his first one had been (24:16-21). In short, what Saul said was "I have sinned" (26:21). Then he went on to say, "I have been a fool and very, very wrong" (26:21b).[6] In between these two statements, Saul, in a rather casual way, invited David to return to the court. While it is true that Saul's words give the appearance of the expression of remorse, as de Jong suggests (1978:195-196), they seem to be words arising more from the sphere of the admission of mistakes and sorrow for them than from the sphere of a true sense of guilt and repentance. In chapter 24 it appears that Saul was momentarily seriously shaken, even if that was primarily due to surprise. But in this chapter it appears that Saul's unbroken pride continues to shine through his remarks so David ignored his invitation to return to the court. In the final analysis, Saul's response was disappointing. It seems that David was hopeful that Saul would seize this new opportunity to mend his ways, but this was not to be. In David's final words to Saul, David placed his hope in the Lord rather than in Saul's transformation, saying, "May the LORD value my life, even as I have valued yours today. May he rescue me from all my troubles" (26:24).[7] Saul's response ("You will do many heroic deeds, and you will surely succeed"; 26:25) reflects his continued perception of the relationship between himself and David as a contest for prestige. Saul's words reveal no recognition of the fact that David was taking no initiatives to displace him from the throne. In 26:25 we learn that "David went away, and Saul returned home." They were never to see each other again.

The two ways presented in this chapter represent the choice that confronts all of God's people whenever they stand before the Messiah. There are only two ways. One may either bow in humble acceptance of the authority of God's anointed one over his or her life, or else choose to go his or her own way, which is ultimately the road that leads to destruction. This is the choice that confronted both Saul and Abner in chapter 26. This is the choice that runs through the entire Bible. As Moses said, "Today I have given you the choice between life and death, between blessings and curses. . . . Oh, that you would choose life, so that you and your descendants might live!" (Deut 30:19).

ENDNOTES

1. Brueggemann (1990a:183) comments, "In terms of narrative power and significance, chapter 26 culminates the Saul narrative. This is his last appearance. Saul's last word is a relinquishment of the future to David. Israel's storytellers will not quit until they have David fully legitimated, even in the mouth of Saul."
2. In speaking of the encounter between Saul and David in ch 24, Fokkelman (1986:540) comments, "that David encountered and stalked Saul there could still be called coincidence; fate offered him the king on a plate, as it were, in the cave, in the only circumstance which makes the absence of a bodyguard excusable. The two heroes were equally surprised. This chapter makes the difference between the two much greater. David intentionally and self-assuredly takes over the initiative and his stalking is premeditated."
3. When Abishai interpreted Saul's vulnerability as a God-given opportunity to take Saul's life, he said to David, "Let me pin him to the ground with one thrust of the spear; I won't need to strike twice!" (26:8). The latter phrase calls to mind the fact that Saul had thrown this same spear at David with lethal intent (cf. 18:11; 19:10). As Gunn (1980:102) notes, if David had given Abishai permission to use Saul's spear to kill Saul, the "irony would then be superb—that Saul should be killed by David's men

with Saul's own spear, the symbol of his authority, and in the manner in which he, for his part, had sought to kill David."

4. Alter (1999:166) comments that David's framing of this question to Saul with its two alternatives is "a kind of diplomatic maneuver. David doesn't want to put the blame squarely on Saul, so he proposes that the king either was 'incited' by God for some mysterious reason or by malicious people."
5. As Fokkelman (1986:546) notes, David's comments here anticipate "David's flight to the uncircumcised people in the west, capp. 27, 29–30."
6. Borgman (2008:89) points out that Saul does not say that "*God has abandoned me, has given me an evil spirit; rather, I myself have done wrong, I myself have been a fool, I myself have made a great mistake.* Highlighting the king's own words and underscoring prior assessments both explicit and implicit, the narrator disallows Saul (or the audience) to pin the king's problem on God. In Saul's clearheaded confession to being 'a fool,' we hear an echo of the preceding episode about Nabal, fool."
7. Fokkelman (1986:551) calls attention to how these last words of David to Saul connect with his first words to Saul in 17:37: "The Lord will deliver me from the hand of this Philistine." Fokkelman goes on to say, "The alpha and omega of David's relationship to Saul is thus distancing from and undermining of the ideology of weapons: you are not involved in my work, it is God's help I need."

◆ P. David with Achish, King of Gath (1 Sam 27:1–28:2)

But David kept thinking to himself, "Someday Saul is going to get me. The best thing I can do is escape to the Philistines. Then Saul will stop hunting for me in Israelite territory, and I will finally be safe."

2So David took his 600 men and went
over and joined Achish son of Maoch, the
king of Gath. 3David and his men and
their families settled there with Achish at
Gath. David brought his two wives along
with him—Ahinoam from Jezreel and Abigail, Nabal's widow from Carmel. 4Word
soon reached Saul that David had fled to
Gath, so he stopped hunting for him.

5One day David said to Achish, "If it is all right with you, we would rather live in one of the country towns instead of here in the royal city."

6So Achish gave him the town of Ziklag
(which still belongs to the kings of Judah to
this day), 7and they lived there among the
Philistines for a year and four months.

8David and his men spent their time
raiding the Geshurites, the Girzites, and
the Amalekites—people who had lived
near Shur, toward the land of Egypt, since
ancient times. 9David did not leave one
person alive in the villages he attacked.
He took the sheep, goats, cattle, donkeys, camels, and clothing before returning home to see King Achish.

10"Where did you make your raid today?" Achish would ask.

And David would reply, "Against the south of Judah, the Jerahmeelites, and the Kenites."

11No one was left alive to come to Gath
and tell where he had really been. This
happened again and again while he was
living among the Philistines. 12Achish be-
lieved David and thought to himself, "By
now the people of Israel must hate him
bitterly. Now he will have to stay here and
serve me forever!"

CHAPTER 28

About that time the Philistines mustered their armies for another war with Israel. King Achish told David, "You and your men will be expected to join me in battle."

2"Very well!" David agreed. "Now you will see for yourself what we can do."

Then Achish told David, "I will make you my personal bodyguard for life."

NOTES

27:10 ***Where did you make your raid today?*** S. R. Driver (1913:212) says the MT's *'al-peshattem* [TH408/6584, ZH440/7320] is untranslatable. GKC §150a (note 2) suggests that "instead of *'al-* . . . read either *'el-mi* ([or] *'al-mi* [against whom]) with the LXX, or better, *'an* [TH575, ZH625] . . . *whither?* with the Targum" (reflected in NLT's rendering).

27:11 ***This happened again and again.*** There is a question whether *wekoh mishpato* [TH4941, ZH5477] (and thus was his practice) continues to relate what the survivors of David's raids would say (cf. KJV, NASB), or is the comment of the narrator. The latter seems more likely and is reflected in the NLT rendering. S. R. Driver (1913:213) supports this view, commenting, "The athnah [a verse divider in the Hebrew text] would be better placed at *dawid* [TH1732, ZH1858], what follows . . . being obviously no part of the speech, but the remark of the narrator."

28:2 ***my personal bodyguard.*** Lit., "keeper of my head." Edelman (1991:240) suggests that this idiom "indicates a fear of decapitation, which in turn suggests that such a custom was practiced by the Philistines themselves. This minor detail plays off David's earlier decapitation of the Philistine champion, Goliath, in 17:51."

COMMENTARY

Although this is one of the shortest chapters in 1 Samuel, it is important because it lets us see a different side of David. Up to this point in the Saul/David narratives, David has been portrayed as a person who measured up quite well to the ideal of the true covenantal king. He has lived out a life of faith in the Lord and obedience to the Lord's will. He has remained faithful to the Lord in spite of severe testing and trial. Saul's life, however, has been depicted as one governed by self-interest, vindictiveness, and disobedience to the Lord. But in this chapter we see David in a different light, because here we see a breakdown or failure on the part of David (de Jong 1978:197).

The first verse of chapter 27 is in sharp contrast to the last two verses of chapter 26. At the end of chapter 26 David told Saul, "Now may the LORD value my life, even as I have valued yours today. May he rescue me from all my troubles" (26:24). Now, only two verses later (although there is certainly an unspecified time gap between the events), David says to himself, "Someday Saul is going to get me. The best thing I can do is escape to the Philistines. Then Saul will stop hunting for me in Israelite territory, and I will finally be safe" (27:1). There is a remarkable contrast between these two verses. In the statement at the end of chapter 26 David expressed confidence in the Lord and entrusted his life to God's care and provision, but in the statement at the beginning of chapter 27 there is no evidence that God is even in his thoughts.[1] In the three preceding chapters (chs 24–26), we find that David survived serious personal tests on three different occasions. The questions that these chapters raised were: (1) Would David lift up his hand against the Lord's anointed? and (2) Would David take justice into his own hands with Saul and Nabal? As I have noted, Abigail assisted David to overcome the strong temptation to kill Nabal. Then the Lord himself took care of Nabal by causing his death (25:38). In view of this, one might expect that henceforth David would be a man who had an unmovable confidence in God. David appeared to be convinced that God would deal with Saul as he had dealt with Nabal (cf. 26:10) and that he would rescue David (26:24). In fact, David's expression of confidence and trust in the Lord and his promises in 26:24 is really the high point to which the three preceding chapters lead (de Jong 1978:199).

But suddenly, with no specific provocation being mentioned, we find a surprising turn of events at the beginning of chapter 27. David has become so fearful of Saul that he flees to the land of the Philistines. The reader cannot help but wonder why David's perspective changed so dramatically and so quickly. Further, it seems curious that the narrator makes no comment on David's behavior but remains silent.

It is here that the character of Hebrew narrative is important for a proper reading of the text. Is it, in fact, valid to conclude that the narrator is completely silent about his own view of David's conduct? Or is it perhaps the case that instead of giving a direct assessment of David's actions in the text, the author has given an indirect or implied assessment by embedding his own appraisal of things in the narrative structure rather than in explicit comment? Is it not possible that the sharp juxtaposition of belief and unbelief on the part of David in chapters 26–27 may itself be the means by which the author is expressing his, as well as God's, displeasure with David? There were, after all, no chapter or verse divisions in the original text.

The author also deliberately informs us of David's private thoughts at the beginning of chapter 27. It is as if the narrator began the chapter by saying that it was not some new turn of events that suddenly required David to leave Israel. It was not some new external threat that precipitated David's action. In fact, nothing new had happened—that is, nothing new had happened except in David's mind and thoughts. David had begun to think about his precarious situation and his dire circumstances and, in so doing, left no room for God (de Jong 1978:200). Notice how strongly this contrasts with David's attitude when he went out to fight against Goliath (ch 17). There is nothing in 27:1 to suggest that God was in David's thoughts at all. However, lest we be too harsh on David, we should remember that what happened here to David is not uncommon among God's people. We may recall the case of Peter in the New Testament (Matt 14:22-33) who at one moment walked on the water, but a few moments later, began to sink when he looked at the waves rather than continuing to trust in the words of Jesus. There is no reason to conclude that the waves had suddenly become higher. The change was not in the waves but in Peter (de Jong 1978:200). This appears to be what happens with David in this chapter. The narrative suggests that suddenly David began to look with fear at the threats of Saul. In the remainder of the chapter, we see David turn into a shadow of his former self. He offered his services to the heathen ruler, Achish of Gath, in the land of the Philistines; he was given the city of Ziklag as a place where he and his men and their families might live;[2] and he became a desert raider, who could only appear before his foreign master by using guile and deception. In his raiding activities David was careful not to betray his own people, but he was forced to act as if he had betrayed them in order to preserve his status in the territory of Achish.[3] Thus because of his fear of Saul, David had become a shady and crafty sort of individual who fell far short of the dignity and integrity that might be expected of a true covenantal king.

There may be those who would question this reading of the narrative and conclude that what David did here was not a failure, but to the contrary it was an entirely appropriate and, in fact, brilliant strategy.[4] By means of his subterfuge David was able to find safety in, of all places, the territory of Israel's greatest enemy. But one must still wonder why David would go to Philistia a second time after having had such a bad experience with Achish on a previous visit (21:10-15).[5] On that occasion, when his life was clearly in jeopardy he had been forced to act like he was insane in order to escape with his life. But in that situation, in contrast to this one, he seemed to rise above his fears about what Achish might do to him; at that time he said, "I trust in God, so why should I be afraid? What can mere mortals do to me?" (Ps 56:4; written in connection with David's previous Philistine episode). In this chapter, one wonders where that confidence has gone, and why he would again seek refuge outside Israel, particularly after he was instructed by the prophet Gad to "return to the land of Judah" (22:5).

Although initially the strategy appeared to be successful because Saul did stop looking for David (27:4), in the longer term this apparent "success" had serious negative consequences. The beginnings of the unraveling of David's strategy are reported in the first two verses of chapter 28. There we are told that Achish ordered David to accompany Philistine forces in an attack against Israel. This placed David in a serious predicament. He certainly could not join the Philistines in a fight against God's own people, but neither could he refuse to do so without jeopardizing his relationship with Achish. So he attempted to buy time by replying to Achish with misleading and ambiguous words, "Very well! . . . Now you will see for yourself what we can do" (28:2). It is not until chapters 29 and 30 that we learn how the Lord providentially intervened in order to deliver David from the harmful results of his behavior in chapter 27.

It would appear that this chapter is telling us not to idealize or romanticize David and the positive ways in which he had responded in his period of persecution (de Jong 1978:203). Even though David, in general, was purified and strengthened in his faith by what he experienced on his way to the throne, this was not without ambiguity. There is a very real sense in which this chapter topples David from his pedestal. As we read it, we may wonder how David would ultimately escape the predicament into which he had placed himself, and whether or not Achish was correct in his conclusion that David's actions would force him to remain in Ziklag and serve him there forever (27:12).

When we attempt to find significance in the events of this chapter from a theocentric perspective, we may be surprised at what we find: This is a chapter that does not tell us anything about what God was doing in these events. In fact, it can be said that in a verbal sense God is totally absent from the chapter. He is never mentioned. Nevertheless, because the chapter is part of God's divine revelation to his people, there are certainly good reasons why it is included at this particular place in Holy Scripture. Among those reasons may be the following: First, God is telling us, in a rather oblique way, that David was not the seed of the woman that would crush the serpent's head (Gen 3:15). David was a messiah, an anointed one, but he was not the Messiah, who would take away the sin of the world and then rule in perfect justice and equity (de Jong 1978:200). Second, God is telling us that although David was a true representative of the ideal of the covenantal king, he was not perfect nor without fault. Even though at times in his life David gave expression to some of the greatest statements of faith in God in the entire Bible, and on many occasions he demonstrated a remarkable obedience to God's will, he was by no means perfect but shared in the fallen condition that afflicts all human beings. These things being so, we also understand an important truth for our own walk with God: Spiritual victories are never permanent realities. It is not possible for us, in this life, to reach that place of perfection where we are able not to sin. We must never forget that our life in Christ is a life in which we must die daily to ourselves and daily seek the power of the Holy Spirit to live Christ-centered lives. Our salvation is once and for all. If it is genuine, it can never be lost. But our sanctification is a process that never reaches perfection in this life. All of us will have our moments of spiritual victory, as David did, but we will also share in the kinds of failure that David also experienced. When this happens we need to remember that God has not abandoned us, even though he may seem to be absent. In this chapter, even though God is not mentioned and David has lost his sense of his presence, God has not abandoned David. As we will see in future chapters, God in his mercy and grace delivered David from this terrible predicament and overruled his foolish behavior.

ENDNOTES

1. Edelman (1991:232) comments, "Having just expressed his confidence that Yahweh will deal with the rejected king in his own time and way (26:10), David has lost sight of his own special relationship with Yahweh as the king-elect and has lost faith in Yahweh's continued protection and support. He is no longer relying upon Yahweh to guide him as his earthly vice-regent-in-training, but instead has decided on a course of action that represents a form of 'self-help'."
2. Although there is some dispute about the precise location of Ziklag, Alter (1999:169) is probably correct in saying that the "best archaeological guess is that this is a site a few miles to the northwest of Beersheba, in an area under Philistine jurisdiction but facing the border with Israel." As the narrator comments (27:6b), Ziklag remained in the possession of the kings of Judah from the time that David and his men settled there until the time of the writing of 1 and 2 Samuel.
3. David raided various enemies of Judah (cf. 27:8, including the Amalekites, whom Saul had failed to "completely destroy"), but he told Achish that he was raiding Judah and some of their allies (27:10). He killed everyone in the villages he attacked, so that there would be no witnesses to report to Achish what he was doing (27:9-11).
4. Bergen (1996:262) comments, "David's scheme was ingenious and effective. His conscious use of deceit was arguably the lesser of two evils: granted that lying is wrong and to be avoided (cf. Lev 19:11; Col 3:9), in this case David's deception saved lives and thus fulfilled the Spirit of the Torah. Not only did it enable hundreds of Israelites to avoid a deadly confrontation with Saul, but it also helped Israel fulfill military assignments left undone since the days of Moses" (i.e., destroying the Amalekites; cf. Exod 17:14-16).
5. David must have had some reason to conclude that he would be received differently by Achish on this occasion than he had been on his previous visit. Whatever the causes for the change in attitude by Achish, it appears that Achish now thought that David would be a useful accomplice in his own designs on Saul's kingdom.

◆ V. The End of Saul's Reign (1 Sam 28:3–31:13)
A. Saul and the Medium at Endor (1 Sam 28:3-25)

3 Meanwhile, Samuel had died, and all Is-
rael had mourned for him. He was buried
in Ramah, his hometown. And Saul had
banned from the land of Israel all medi-
ums and those who consult the spirits of
the dead.

4 The Philistines set up their camp at
Shunem, and Saul gathered all the army
of Israel and camped at Gilboa. 5 When
Saul saw the vast Philistine army, he be-
came frantic with fear. 6 He asked the LORD
what he should do, but the LORD refused
to answer him, either by dreams or by sa-
cred lots* or by the prophets. 7 Saul then
said to his advisers, "Find a woman who is
a medium, so I can go and ask her what
to do."

His advisers replied, "There is a medium
at Endor."

8 So Saul disguised himself by wearing
ordinary clothing instead of his royal robes.
Then he went to the woman's home at
night, accompanied by two of his men.

"I have to talk to a man who has died,"
he said. "Will you call up his spirit for
me?"

9 "Are you trying to get me killed?" the
woman demanded. "You know that Saul
has outlawed all the mediums and all who
consult the spirits of the dead. Why are
you setting a trap for me?"

10 But Saul took an oath in the name of
the LORD and promised, "As surely as the
LORD lives, nothing bad will happen to you
for doing this."

11 Finally, the woman said, "Well, whose
spirit do you want me to call up?"

"Call up Samuel," Saul replied.

12 When the woman saw Samuel, she
screamed, "You've deceived me! You are
Saul!"

13 "Don't be afraid!" the king told her.
"What do you see?"

"I see a god* coming up out of the
earth," she said.

14 "What does he look like?" Saul asked.

"He is an old man wrapped in a robe,"
she replied. Saul realized it was Samuel,
and he fell to the ground before him.

15 "Why have you disturbed me by call-
ing me back?" Samuel asked Saul.

"Because I am in deep trouble," Saul
replied. "The Philistines are at war with
me, and God has left me and won't reply
by prophets or dreams. So I have called for
you to tell me what to do."

16 But Samuel replied, "Why ask me,
since the LORD has left you and has be-
come your enemy? 17 The LORD has done
just as he said he would. He has torn the
kingdom from you and given it to your
rival, David. 18 The LORD has done this to
you today because you refused to carry
out his fierce anger against the Amale-
kites. 19 What's more, the LORD will hand
you and the army of Israel over to the Phi-
listines tomorrow, and you and your sons
will be here with me. The LORD will bring
down the entire army of Israel in de-
feat."

20 Saul fell full length on the ground,
paralyzed with fright because of Samuel's
words. He was also faint with hunger, for
he had eaten nothing all day and all
night.

21 When the woman saw how distraught
he was, she said, "Sir, I obeyed your com-
mand at the risk of my life. 22 Now do what
I say, and let me give you a little some-
thing to eat so you can regain your
strength for the trip back."

23 But Saul refused to eat anything.
Then his advisers joined the woman in
urging him to eat, so he finally yielded
and got up from the ground and sat on
the couch.

24 The woman had been fattening a calf,
so she hurried out and killed it. She took
some flour, kneaded it into dough and
baked unleavened bread. 25 She brought
the meal to Saul and his advisers, and they
ate it. Then they went out into the night.

28:6 Hebrew *by Urim.* **28:13** Or *gods.*

NOTES

28:3 *Samuel had died . . . Israel had mourned . . . Saul had banned.* See Joüon and Muraoka §118d for the Hebrew construction indicating English pluperfect or past perfect.

28:13 *I see a god coming up out of the earth.* See NLT mg for the other rendering, "gods." Alter (1999:175) comments, "When she says she sees *'elohim* [TH430, ZH466] rising up, she probably means an imposing figure like unto a god or an angel, or perhaps she is using it as a term for 'spirit.'"

28:15 *So I have called for you.* On the pointing of the cohortative, see GKC §48d. Stoebe (1973:486), following de Boer (1949:83), suggests that here the cohortative carries the idea of self-encouragement.

28:16 *your enemy.* Heb., *'areka.* S. R. Driver (1913:216-217) strongly denies the existence of a Hebrew word *'ar* [TH6145, ZH6839] meaning adversary or enemy. He suggests either a transcriptional error here for *tsareka* [TH6862A, ZH7640] (your adversary), or a reading *wayyehi 'im-re'eka* [TH5973/7453, ZH6640/8276] ("and is become on the side of thy neighbour" [i.e., David, cf. 28:17]) with LXX and Syriac. Edelman (1991:247) favors seeing MT's *'rk* as a metathesis of *r'k* ("your neighbor").

28:23 *urging.* Some mss read *patsar* [TH6484, ZH7210] (push, press) instead of *parats* [TH6555, ZH7287] (break through). It is likely that this *parats* [TH6555A, ZH7287] is a second root with the same meaning as *patsar* (cf. 2 Sam 13:25, 27; 2 Kgs 5:23), so the change is unnecessary. See further, Stoebe 1973:487 and G. R. Driver 1924:177-178.

COMMENTARY

First Samuel 28 is a mysterious and fascinating chapter. Lord Byron called it "the finest and most finished witch-scene that ever was written or conceived. . . . It beats all the ghost scenes I ever read" (quoted in Kinsley 1992:840). Unfortunately, excessive fascination with the witch scene has often diverted attention from other matters that are of greater importance for understanding the significance of the chapter in its narrative context.

In the last chapters of 1 Samuel, the author has chosen to arrange his material in a way that disrupts both narrative continuity and chronological sequence. The story in 28:3-25, which describes Saul's visit to the medium at Endor, interrupts the story of David's alliance with Achish, the Philistine ruler of Gath, at the point where David has been invited to join with the Philistine forces in a battle against Israel (28:1-2). The reader is left to wonder how David would deal with the predicament in which he found himself. Will he be forced to fight against the armies of Israel, and most particularly against Saul, whom he had repeatedly refused to attack? Chapters 29 and 30 will take us back to David's involvement with the Philistines and subsequently with the Amalekites, who plundered and burned the city of Ziklag where the families of David and his men resided. And then in chapter 31, the narrative turns again to Saul, telling of his death and that of his sons in a battle with the Philistines at Mount Gilboa.

The question that arises is why the author has presented his material in this particular way. It seems clear that chapter 28 not only interrupts the flow of the story of David and Achish, but it is also chronologically misplaced, since it occurred on the eve of the battle with the Philistines recorded in chapter 31, and subsequent to the events of chapters 29 and 30. This arrangement of the material serves to highlight a point of correspondence between the lives of Saul and David. That point of correspondence is the fact that both of their lives have been placed in serious jeopardy. Contrary to what one might expect at the end of 1 Samuel, the author does not depict David's life as one of untarnished success in contrast to Saul's defeat and failure. Instead of a black-and-white sort of contrast between these two very different individuals, the author called attention to the fact that David's reckless alliance with Achish created a situation where his own survival was at stake. This, in turn, serves to remind the reader of something quite important. At the time when God was instituting a monarchy in Israel and establishing his Kingdom in its Old Testament form, both the major players in this drama are characterized by serious failures. Saul is portrayed much like Judas Iscariot, who betrayed the Lord, while David is portrayed more like Peter, who denied his Lord (de Jong 1978:205). We find that at the end of 1 Samuel there are two anointed kings but neither of them has lived up to his God-given responsibilities. The result is that when David eventually sits on the throne in Israel, he does so only by the grace of God, who not only rescued him from his self-created predicament but also forgave him and restored him in much the same way as he did later for Peter. So as the book of 1 Samuel enters its concluding section, we encounter what might be called the humiliation of both David and Saul. Both were in a crisis. The arrangement of material calls attention to this fact. And in this way our attention is also called to an important truth: God's Kingdom, even in its Old Testament form, is founded upon God's free grace and not on the human merit or innate goodness of its first kings.

The story line of chapter 28 is a familiar one. On the eve before his final battle against the Philistines at Mount Gilboa, Saul anticipated a disastrous outcome (28:5). Because the Lord would not speak to him through his normal means of revelation (28:6), he went to a medium in Endor and asked her to communicate for him with the departed spirit of Samuel (28:7-11). Even though initially the medium did not know who Saul was because he had gone to her in disguise (28:8), she was nevertheless cautious, perhaps suspecting some sort of entrapment because Saul had "banned . . . all mediums and those who consult the spirits of the dead" from the land of Israel (28:3), and had enforced the law of Moses by making such practices a capital crime (cf. 28:9). To alleviate the woman's fear, Saul swore in the name of the Lord that no harm would come to her for complying with his request (28:10). In other words, Saul blasphemously used the name of the Lord to guarantee the woman that she could violate the law of the Lord with impunity. In the exchange between the medium and the spirit of Samuel, Samuel repeated what he had told Saul previously—namely, that the Lord had taken the kingdom away from him and given it to David (28:17; cf. 15:28). But then he went on to say that in the upcoming battle, not only would both Saul and his sons be killed, but Israel's army would also go down in defeat (28:19). In other words, Saul's kingship would end in complete failure. He would not accomplish the purpose for which he was anointed (cf. 9:16).

Many questions may be asked about exactly what went on in the séance scene that is described in these verses. Did the medium at Endor really make contact with the departed spirit of Samuel? If so, what are the implications of such an occurrence? Is it reasonable to think that God would use necromancy as a means of divine revelation? Or was this perhaps a demonic spirit by which the medium was both surprised and manipulated? But if this was a demonic spirit, how could such a spirit give a true prophecy about the death of Saul and his sons? Or was the whole procedure a deception propagated by the medium in which she simply told Saul, by means of some sort of clairvoyance or parapsychological power, what he already expected to hear? There are no clear-cut answers to these questions in the statements of the narrative, and to focus on them excessively means that attention is diverted from other important messages in the chapter[1]: First, a believer in the true God, the God of biblical revelation, should never be drawn into the realm of the occult. Consulting departed spirits was common among the Canaanites and the other heathen people of the nations surrounding Israel in the Old Testament period—and the practice still appeals to many in our day.[2] Even though such practices were strongly condemned in the Mosaic law, they continued to exert their influence in Israelite society and culture. Leviticus 20:27 says, "Men and women among you who act as mediums or who consult the spirits of the dead must be put to death by stoning. They are guilty of a capital offense." And in Deuteronomy 18:10-12 there is a list of occult phenomena about which Moses says that "anyone who does these things is detestable to the LORD" (Deut 18:12) because these things are "detestable customs" of the peoples of Canaan (Deut 18:9). These statements contain no hint that everything that happens in the realm of the occult is to be regarded as superstition or deception. It seems clear that the Bible recognizes the presence of supernatural power in many occult phenomena, and for this reason, followers of God should have no involvement with their activities. Involvement with these practices was so serious that anyone in Israel participating in them was to be put to death. At one time Saul had endorsed this policy, but now in his desperation he chose to violate his own prohibition. First Chronicles 10:13-14 gives us an assessment of the life of Saul. This assessment tells us why Saul died and why the kingdom was transferred from Saul to David. Notice what it says: "So Saul died because he was unfaithful to the LORD. He failed to obey the LORD's command, and he even consulted a medium instead of asking the LORD for guidance. So the LORD killed him and turned the kingdom over to David son of Jesse." Saul's consultation with a medium is what might be termed the last straw in Saul's persistence in disobedience to the Lord's revealed will. It led directly to his death and to the transferral of the kingdom to David.

Another important and sobering truth that surfaces in this chapter is the possibility that God may ultimately abandon those who persist in abandoning him. This is what appears to have happened in the life of Saul. The Philistines were preparing for an attack against Israel (28:1, 4). Saul was terrified about the impending battle (28:5). It is almost as if he had a premonition that this would be his last battle. In desperation he tried to obtain a word from the Lord, but the Lord would not speak to him by dreams or sacred lots or by the prophets (28:6). The silence of God signaled the end for Saul. Up to this point he had the benefit of hearing God's word, either through Samuel or Jonathan or David or even his own officials—and when that was happening there was still hope for repentance because the grace of God was still at work (van den Berg 1996b:117). But when God no longer speaks, the possibility of return to the Lord ceases to be an option.

It is notable that the remainder of the chapter takes place in the darkness of night. Saul disguises himself and goes at night to the medium (28:8), and afterwards we read "they went out into the night" (28:25). These two references bear a certain similarity to the reference to "night" in the context of the Last Supper: We are told that Satan entered into Judas; then Judas took bread from Jesus' hand and "left at once, going out into the night" (John 13:30). In situations like these, the night serves to reinforce an ominous awareness of the absence of God (van den Berg 1996b:118). The darkness of night contributes in a suggestive way to the picture of gloom and futility that is characteristic of life without God. The theme of light and darkness is one that is found in many parts of Scripture. Paul says in 1 Thessalonians 5:5-8, "For you are all children of the light and of the day; we don't belong to darkness and night. So be on your guard, not asleep like the others. Stay alert and be clearheaded. Night is the time when people sleep and drinkers get drunk. But let us who live in the light be clearheaded, protected by the armor of faith and love, and wearing as our helmet the confidence of our salvation." Isaiah rejected the consultation of mediums (Isa 8:19-22): "Should the living seek guidance from the dead? Look to God's instructions and teachings! People who contradict his word are completely in the dark. They will go from one place to another, weary and hungry. . . . They will rage and curse their king and their God. . . . Wherever they look, there will be trouble and anguish and dark despair. They will be thrown out into the darkness." This is the same sort of gloom and darkness found in 1 Samuel 28; it is the darkness of the absence of God.

So Saul set out at night with two of his servants and went in the darkness to Endor where there was a spiritist who practiced her black art. In what transpires further, we may ask a host of questions that are difficult, if not impossible, to answer with any degree of certainty. But this should not divert us from understanding the most significant thing that comes out of the dialogue between the "spirit of Samuel" and Saul. Whether the spirit was really the spirit of Samuel or a devilish spirit whom the Lord used to speak to Saul, the message was that because Saul refused to carry out the Lord's fierce anger against the Amalekites (28:18), the Lord had left him and had become his enemy (28:16). It is this message that constitutes the focal point of the chapter. This is not a message that either Saul or the reader may like to hear, but it is an important message. It tells us that it is possible that the Lord will abandon a person who persists in abandoning him.[3]

This, of course, raises some serious theological issues. Not the least of these is the question of the Bible's teaching concerning the eternal security of the believer, and closely connected with this, the question of Saul's own spiritual standing before the Lord. A related question is that of how to understand the relationship between divine sovereignty and human responsibility in human behavior. In our discussion of chapter 19, we noticed that one of its central themes was the hardening of Saul. In that chapter this theme was linked with the coming of the "evil spirit from the LORD" upon Saul as a divine judgment because of his repeated disobedience of the Lord's commands. All of this implies that Saul was never truly a child of the Lord, for elsewhere the Bible suggests quite clearly that a true child of the Lord will not persist indefinitely in turning away from the Lord and disobeying his commands

(1 John 2:1-11). The flip side of this is that God will graciously sustain the faith of a true believer, even though such an individual may experience severe testing and trial of his faith (cf. John 10:27-29; Rom 5:3-5; 8:29-38; 11:29; Phil 1:6; 2 Thess 3:4; 2 Tim 1:12; Heb 7:25; 1 Pet 1:4-5). There is in all of this a clear and relevant message that God is a holy and just God who is to be feared and obeyed. Sin has consequences. God is not mocked. Persistence in disobedience to the Lord is a serious matter and may lead to a hardening of heart from which there is no way back. This is the sobering message at the heart of this chapter. The Lord had turned away from Saul and had become his enemy (28:16).

Whenever this happens, however, as it does here, then we must be very clear about what is going on. The origin of divine abandonment did not lie in God, but rather in Saul's abandonment of the Lord. This is as true today as it was in the time of Saul. The Bible tells us that if a person persists in turning away from the Lord and refuses to mend his ways, there may come a time when the Lord will turn away from that person. In contrast to this, however, the Bible tells us that when a person finds God, the causality is reversed—then the initiative always rests with God (van den Berg 1996b:119). So when a person finds God, it is because God has first found him or her, but when one turns away from God, the initiative is always with that person.[4] God will not abandon us if we do not first abandon him.

Although it is true that the initiative is always with the human agent in turning away from God, "always" is perhaps too strong a word, because there is one exception of enormous significance: Jesus was forsaken by God even though he had not turned away from him. Certainly in this case there is great mystery, but clearly the initiative was with God the Father. And paradoxically, this single, mysterious exception guarantees that we who are in Christ will not and cannot ever experience abandonment by God (van den Berg 1996b:119).

One may remember that the abandonment of Christ by his Father was also accompanied by darkness. It was not only Saul and Judas who went out into the darkness of the absence of God; Jesus also experienced that same darkness. Mark 15:33-34 tells us, "At noon, darkness fell across the whole land until three o'clock. Then at three o'clock Jesus called out with a loud voice, '*Eloi, Eloi, lema sabachthani?*' which means, 'My God, my God, why have you abandoned me?'" Because Jesus was willing to endure the darkness of God's abandonment, we can now walk in the light of God's presence. Jesus' words on the cross remind us of Saul's words in 28:15: "God has left me and won't reply." Here, then, are two abandonments, that of Saul and that of Christ. But they are of a totally different sort. Saul's abandonment was justified and merited, while Christ's abandonment was substitutionary and redemptive. Long ago the prophet Isaiah spoke of a people walking in darkness who would see a great light (Isa 9:2). That light was radiated from the child who was to be born and who would be called "Wonderful Counselor, Mighty God, Everlasting Father, Prince of Peace. His government and its peace will never end. He will rule with fairness and justice from the throne of his ancestor David for all eternity. The passionate commitment of the LORD of Heaven's Armies will make this happen!" (Isa 9:6-7). Thanks be to God for his unspeakable gift.

ENDNOTES

1. As Alter notes (1999:174), "The narrator is discreetly silent about the actual mechanics of the conjuration procedure, perhaps out of a kind of monotheistic reticence." Youngblood (1992:779-780) says that his "own sympathies lie with the judgment of Gregory of Nazianzus, who was content to leave the text in its ambiguity: 'Samuel was raised, *or so it seems*, by the woman having a familiar spirit' (*Invective Against Julian* 1.54; emphasis mine). An element of mystery suffuses 1 Samuel 28, and it would be presumptuous to claim to have successfully plumbed its depths." Peterson (1999:127) comments, "Whatever reality there may be in the disreputable business of spiritualism, one thing seems evident: God does not reveal saving truth through such methods. What Samuel said before he says again; what Saul heard before he hears again." For more detailed discussions of different interpretations of the mechanics of the séance, see Figart 1970. Smelik (1979:164-165) places the opinions of Christian exegetes on this issue in the time prior to AD 800 in three basic categories: (1) Samuel was resuscitated by the woman (Justin Martyr, Origen, Zeno of Verona, Ambrose, Augustine, Sulpicius Severus, Dracontius, and Anastasius Sinaita); (2) either Samuel or a demon in his shape appeared at God's command (John Chrysostom, Theodoret of Cyrrhus, Pseudo-Justin, Theodore bar Koni, and Isho'dad of Merv); (3) a demon deceived Saul and gave him a forged prophecy (Tertullian, Pseudo-Hippolytus, "Pionius," Eustathius of Antioch, Ephraem, Gregory of Nyssa, Evagrius Ponticus, Pseudo-Basil, Jerome, Philastrius, Ambrosiaster, and Pseudo-Augustine).
2. In March of 1998 the number one book on the *New York Times* Best Sellers List for nonfiction was a how-to book on necromancy entitled *Talking to Heaven* by James Van Praagh. In a review (*World Magazine* March 21, 1998, p. 24), Roy Maynard says, "Much of the book is devoted to his [Van Praagh's] mysterious and inexplicable psychic gift; the remainder tells readers how to develop their own."
3. Davis (1994b:151) comments, "The text is not gentle but it is clear: If you despise God's word he will take it from you. If you persistently refuse to obey God's speech you will endure God's silence." After giving an illustration taken from the autobiography of Spurgeon of a man who was unable to repent on his deathbed after having previously mocked Spurgeon and refused Christ, Davis says, "What could be worse? To know you need to repent—and can't. It is horridly solemn. The most hopeless misery in all of life is to be abandoned by God."
4. This is the asymmetry in the nature of divine ultimacy that is discussed by, among others, Carson (1981:212), who points out that the "manner in which God stands behind evil and the manner in which he stands behind good are not precisely identical; for he is to be praised for the good, but not blamed for the evil." He goes on to say that the "negative side of divine ultimacy guarantees (1) that even my sinful deeds cannot escape God's sovereignty, and (2) that I cannot rightly shift my blame to God. The positive side of divine ultimacy is that little bit more immediate, so that I must recognize God's grace behind whatever good I may do; yet God's action remains sufficiently indirect to preserve my genuine responsibility. It is this sort of model which, however difficult it is to formulate, best conforms to the biblical data."

◆ B. David Is Delivered from Fighting against Saul (1 Sam 29:1-11)

The entire Philistine army now mobilized at Aphek, and the Israelites camped at the spring in Jezreel. [2]As the Philistine rulers were leading out their troops in groups of hundreds and thousands, David and his men marched at the rear with King Achish.

3But the Philistine commanders demanded, "What are these Hebrews doing here?"

And Achish told them, "This is David, the servant of King Saul of Israel. He's been with me for years, and I've never found a single fault in him from the day he arrived until today."

4But the Philistine commanders were angry. "Send him back to the town you've given him!" they demanded. "He can't go into the battle with us. What if he turns against us in battle and becomes our adversary? Is there any better way for him to reconcile himself with his master than by
handing our heads over to him? 5Isn't this
the same David about whom the women of Israel sing in their dances,

'Saul has killed his thousands,
and David his ten thousands'?"

6So Achish finally summoned David and said to him, "I swear by the LORD that you have been a trustworthy ally. I think you should go with me into battle, for I've never found a single flaw in you from the day you arrived until today. But the other
Philistine rulers won't hear of it. 7Please
don't upset them, but go back quietly."

8"What have I done to deserve this treatment?" David demanded. "What have you ever found in your servant, that I can't go and fight the enemies of my lord the king?"

9But Achish insisted, "As far as I'm concerned, you're as perfect as an angel of God. But the Philistine commanders are afraid to have you with them in the battle.
10Now get up early in the morning, and leave with your men as soon as it gets light."

11So David and his men headed back into the land of the Philistines, while the Philistine army went on to Jezreel.

NOTES

29:10 ***leave with your men.*** LXX Vaticanus (see *Biblia Hebraica*, ed. by R. Kittel, for a suggested Hebrew Vorlage) displays a longer text: "And go to the place I appointed for you. As for the evil report, do not take it to heart, for you have done well before me." The longer text is viewed as original by some (cf. NRSV, Klein 1983:275-276, and McCarter 1980b:425-426). Analysis is difficult. De Boer (1949:87) terms the longer text a "midrashic expatiation." See the detailed discussion by Pisano (1984:208-217) who concludes (1984:217), "The reasons both for and against the originality of the LXX plus seem so evenly balanced that a final decision is not possible, although the evidence seems to favor the originality of MT."

COMMENTARY

As this chapter opens, the outlook for Israel's future looks rather bleak. Saul, Israel's first king, has been told in 28:16 that the Lord has become his enemy. His reign is nearly over, and his death in the impending battle with the Philistines is imminent. But things are not much better with the one whom the Lord had chosen to replace the rejected Saul. David was certainly in no position to assume the throne upon Saul's demise. As we learned in 27:1–28:2, David was in a real dilemma. What would David do if he was required to join with the Philistines to fight against Israel? The seeds of David's dilemma were planted when he decided to seek refuge among the Philistines (cf. ch 27). David had been living the life of a fugitive in the Judean wilderness for a long time. Day after day, he and his men endured the difficulties of finding food and shelter while trying to elude Saul's forces. Eventually the pressures of living under these conditions became so great that David concluded that capture by Saul was inevitable (27:1). So for a second time (cf. 21:10–22:1) he decided to seek refuge with the Philistines, the enemies of God's people (27:2-12). The downside of this decision was that in the relationship he developed with Achish, he lost his freedom to act upon or speak about his true beliefs. During his fugitive days, David had developed the reputation of being a "very crafty" person.[1] This assessment is confirmed in chapter 29, where David acts in duplicitous ways with Achish.

As the chapter opens, the Philistines were assembling a large military force at Aphek,[2] in the plain of Sharon, which was located in the northernmost part of their territory. From Aphek it was their plan to go further north to Shunem and then to challenge Israel for control of the strategically important valley of Jezreel (29:1; cf. 28:4; 31:1-13). When some of the Philistine commanders noticed that David and his men were included among the troops contributed by Achish, they vociferously objected to permitting "these Hebrews" (29:3) to be part of their army. Achish, however, came to David's defense and said that he had "never found a single fault in him" in the more than a year that he had been in his service (29:3). Achish, however, was completely duped by David's cunning strategy of misinformation concerning the campaigns he launched from Ziklag (cf. 27:8-12). The Philistine commanders were not as naive as Achish. They remained unconvinced and refused to permit David and his men to be part of their army, using the argument, "What if he turns against us in battle and becomes our adversary?" (29:4).[3]

When Achish had no alternative but to tell David that he must go back to Ziklag, he did so reluctantly; in the ensuing dialogue he calls David "a trustworthy ally" (29:6), heaping up praise even to calling him "perfect as an angel of God" (29:9). It is in this interchange between Achish and David that David's duplicity becomes particularly apparent. As Fokkelman (1986:576) puts it, David played "the outraged innocent" and asked Achish, "What have I done to deserve this treatment? . . . What have you ever found in your servant, that I can't go and fight the enemies of my lord the king?" (29:8). While this was clearly a disingenuous response, it was nothing if not crafty.[4] Notice the ambiguity in the last phrase of 29:8 ("What have you ever found in your servant, that I can't go and fight the enemies of my lord the king?"). To whom was David referring with the words "my lord the king"? In context it would clearly seem to be a reference to Achish. Certainly this is the way Achish understood it, but the phrase might also apply to either Saul or to Yahweh, in which case David could be saying he would turn on Achish—in other words, he would go the very opposite of what he seemed to be saying.

In any case, it is clear that David feigned enormous distress about the decision of Achish, while the reader knows very well that inwardly David must have felt a tremendous sense of relief. He was the person who, in the words of Abigail, was "fighting the LORD's battles" (25:28). In the past David had fought those battles well, but now he found himself in a situation in which he not only could not fight the Lord's battle against the Philistines, but he might, in fact, even be forced to fight against the Lord's people. The question that looms over this narrative is this: Would David now be forced to do what he had always refused to do—that is, take up his sword against Saul? The reader remembers David's words when he and his men were in the cave into which Saul had come to relieve himself, and David's men urged David to take Saul's life, but he refused to do so because Saul was the Lord's anointed (24:6, 10, 12). On the previous occasion, however, David was in a position in which he was free to make the right choice. Now, because of his own decision to seek refuge among the Philistines and to play a deceitful game with Achish, he had lost that freedom (van den Berg 1996b:123). By his "cleverness" he had forfeited the freedom to openly follow the Lord. He had become trapped by his own duplicity.

There is a lesson here for God's people in other times and places. When a person seeks to find security by his own devices, apart from the Lord's leading, more often than not he will place himself in a position where he is no longer free to act in conformity with his deepest beliefs. But there is an additional aspect of this story that is noteworthy. That is, not only could David not act on his true beliefs, but he could not speak about them either. This becomes clear in the dialogue between Achish and David. In their conversation it becomes apparent that Achish had developed a strong trust in David during the time of their association. In 29:6 Achish summoned David and told him, "I swear by the LORD that you have been a trustworthy ally." Achish went on to express his strong confidence in David's trustworthiness (29:6-9). The reader, however, knows how misled Achish was and how treacherously David had acted behind Achish's back. It is particularly striking that Achish swore to David in the name of the Lord (i.e., in the name of Yahweh, the God of Israel). Although some commentators have suggested that this should be understood as part of the narrator's embellishment of the story and that Achish must have sworn by a Philistine deity rather than by Yahweh, the God of Israel, such suggestions are purely speculative. According to what the text says, it seems more likely that Achish's confidence in David had risen to such a level that he had also developed, at least to some degree, an interest in the God whom David served (de Jong 1978:216). And that possibility gives an even more tragic twist to what transpired in the interchange between David and Achish. Although Achish was unable to convince his Philistine colleagues of David's trustworthiness, it seems that personally he had not only developed a trust in David, but also had come to the place where he was even comfortable with using the name of David's God to swear an oath. Under normal circumstances this would have provided David with a clear opportunity to speak with Achish about the God of Israel, the creator and ruler of the universe, and the God whom David loved and served. But David was unable to do this because he was constrained by circumstances of his own making that forced him to continue to act out his hoax. David was in no position to speak the truth from his heart.

When this narrative is placed in the context of the movement of redemptive history we are reminded that when David's greater son stood before a Roman ruler, he, in contrast to David, was able to give an open and clear confession of who he was (de Jong 1978:217). Ironically, Pilate's words (Luke 23:4, 14-15; John 18:38; 19:4), "I find no fault in this Man" (NKJV), are a remarkable echo of the words of Achish about David in 29:3b ("I've never found a single fault in him"). The difference is that Jesus was truly innocent of the charges made against him, whereas David was not.[5] In Jesus we find a person who did not act with guile or craftiness, but who was always careful to position himself so that he could witness to the truth in whatever situation he found himself. Jesus thus showed himself to be greater than David.

Notice, also, how different it was for Paul, who was a prisoner before King Agrippa (Acts 25:23–26:32), than it was for David. As de Jong (1978:217) notes, Paul was in chains outwardly, but inwardly he was free and could have an honest and open conversation with Agrippa. Such an opportunity for an open and honest conversation with Achish was simply not possible for David.

One of the lessons to be learned from this chapter is that the lives of God's people should be open and transparent. God's people should be careful not to maneuver themselves into situations in which they are prevented from speaking and acting openly and clearly about their faith, situations in which they must conceal or disguise who they really are. Probably most readers of this commentary will not find themselves in situations as serious as the one that confronted David. It is usually in times of war and political oppression that circumstances of this sort arise. Because such situations can be extremely complex and difficult for those entrapped in them, it may be unwise to prejudge exactly how one should respond to them, but as a general rule the principle stated above merits serious consideration.

In spite of David's failures, the clear message of this chapter is that the Lord remained in control of all that happened in David's life, and graciously provided him with a way of escape. This is a chapter in which we see the disastrous consequences of the foolish actions of one of God's choice servants turned around by divine intervention. And it is because of this gracious intervention alone that David was delivered from his dilemma.

David had finally come to the place where his craftiness was no longer of any help. He was almost ensnared in his own web of deceit. Chapter 29, then, is not intended to be read as the story of a lucky break for David, but rather as a story of divine deliverance and providence—and a merciful divine deliverance at that. As we have previously noted, the book of Samuel is framed by poems that contain strong statements about God's providential direction of all that happens (see Introduction). The assumption of God's providential guidance of all of human history is one of the governing principles of the historiography of 1–2 Samuel. When this narrative is viewed from that perspective, it is clear that this is the intended understanding of the surprising turn of events of this chapter, though it is striking that there is no overt reference to God's mercy or deliverance.[6] Indeed, ironically, only the pagan ruler, Achish, even mentions God (he makes a reference to the Lord in 29:6 and alludes to God in 29:9) in this chapter. Nonetheless, the reader understands that it is the Lord who was at work behind the scenes to rescue David from his foolish actions.

In this light, the story takes on an almost humorous twist.[7] How did the Lord choose to deliver David? He delivered him by the insistence of the commanding officers of the Philistine army. Certainly the Philistines were improbable deliverers of David. But the Israelites would probably have had a knowing smile on their faces when they heard this story in later times. What other God is there like the God of Israel? He works in such surprising ways! He uses his enemies to bring praise to his name! And this is not the only time the Lord used the Philistines to deliver David (cf. 23:19-28).

So in 29:7 we can imagine the relief with which David watched the unfolding of this surprising turn of events. But as we have noted, he did not dare show his true feelings. It is the responsibility of the reader to connect chapter 29 with chapter 27. We have already noted in our discussion of chapter 27 that David's decision to go to the land of the Philistines was ill-advised. His decision was understandable, in certain respects, but certainly wrongheaded. Now, however, we find that the Lord's mercy pursued David even in his folly and sin. The Lord is patient with his people. He is longsuffering in his mercy. His patience is not expended when his people make foolish mistakes. So the reader can take heart from this chapter. God will not cast aside his people because of their foolish and sinful behavior. Our blunders do not nullify God's mercy. In this chapter, David's success is not due to his own craftiness or his skillful manipulation of other people; rather, it is attributable to the Lord's mercy.

Finally, we may note the contrast between the endings of chapters 28 and 29.[8] In chapter 28 Saul went off into the darkness of night to face imminent death (28:25). In chapter 29 David walked away into the light of the morning, delivered by the very Philistines who soon would be the ones to destroy Saul (29:10). In God's mercy and grace we find that his redemptive work continues to move forward in spite of human failure and sin. He is still doing so today!

ENDNOTES

1. When Saul had instructed the Ziphites to find out where David was hiding, he said to them, "I know that he is very crafty" (23:22). Although this characterization of David comes from information Saul had heard about David, and therefore may or may not be an accurate assessment of his character, it is clear that David acted very shrewdly in his dealings with Achish.
2. This is the same place that the Philistines mustered their forces some years earlier when they defeated Israel and captured the Ark (ch 4).
3. Perhaps the Philistine commanders remembered the defection of Hebrew troops from their ranks during the battle led by Jonathan against the Philistines at Micmash (cf. 14:21), and feared a recurrence in the upcoming battle at Mount Gilboa. It was not unusual, however, for soldiers in those days to function as mercenaries wherever they could find employment. In later times David employed a powerful Philistine detachment among his own troops.
4. Davis (1994b:161) appropriately comments, "David with disbelief on his face and exasperation in his voice protests the rejection he has no reason to protest. The deceived defends his deceiver, and the relieved disputes his relief!"
5. Brueggemann (1990a:200) also calls attention to the parallel between the words of Achish about David and those of Pilate in his acquittal of Jesus, but rather than emphasizing that Jesus was innocent of the charges against him, while David was not, Brueggemann suggests that Jesus, like David, was guilty of the subversion of the oppressive social order of his time. He says of Jesus, "He is indeed guilty of the charges brought against him that he subverts the establishment. As with David, however, the people around Jesus did not regard such subversiveness as a fault but as a cause for celebration and loyalty. The people were as celebrative of Jesus as they were earlier of David. Both Jesus and David provided a daring alternative to an oppressive, unresponsive social arrangement."
6. Brueggemann (1990a:199) comments, "There is no mention of God here, but we are dealing with a highly self-conscious theological literature that observes the undercurrent of divine governance without being explicit. Yahweh is with David everywhere

(18:12, 28)—surely with him among the Philistines as elsewhere, surely in chapter 29 as in those places where it is explicitly stated. The narrator is not so disbelieving as to perceive the outcome of the narrative as luck. It would be more appropriate to assert that all things work together for good with those who love God (Rom 8:28). The very same Philistines who will finally dispose of Saul (ch. 31) are the ones who unwittingly rescue David!"

7. The themes of the following three paragraphs are heavily dependent on the perceptive discussion of Davis (1994b:163-166) who organizes his analysis under the headings "God's ways are so surprising" and "God's mercy is so tenacious."
8. Attention is called to this contrast by both Davis (1994b:166) and Fokkelman (1986:578).

◆ C. David Defeats the Amalekites (1 Sam 30:1-31)

Three days later, when David and his men arrived home at their town of Ziklag, they found that the Amalekites had made a raid into the Negev and Ziklag; they had crushed Ziklag and burned it to the ground. 2They had carried off the women and children and everyone else but without killing anyone.

3When David and his men saw the ruins and realized what had happened to their families, 4they wept until they could weep no more. 5David's two wives, Ahinoam from Jezreel and Abigail, the widow of Nabal from Carmel, were among those captured. 6David was now in great danger because all his men were very bitter about losing their sons and daughters, and they began to talk of stoning him. But David found strength in the LORD his God.

7Then he said to Abiathar the priest, "Bring me the ephod!" So Abiathar brought it. 8Then David asked the LORD, "Should I chase after this band of raiders? Will I catch them?"

And the LORD told him, "Yes, go after them. You will surely recover everything that was taken from you!"

9So David and his 600 men set out, and they came to the brook Besor. 10But 200 of the men were too exhausted to cross the brook, so David continued the pursuit with 400 men.

11Along the way they found an Egyptian man in a field and brought him to David. They gave him some bread to eat and water to drink. 12They also gave him part of a fig cake and two clusters of raisins, for he hadn't had anything to eat or drink for three days and nights. Before long his strength returned.

13"To whom do you belong, and where do you come from?" David asked him.

"I am an Egyptian—the slave of an Amalekite," he replied. "My master abandoned me three days ago because I was sick. 14We were on our way back from raiding the Kerethites in the Negev, the territory of Judah, and the land of Caleb, and we had just burned Ziklag."

15"Will you lead me to this band of raiders?" David asked.

The young man replied, "If you take an oath in God's name that you will not kill me or give me back to my master, then I will guide you to them."

16So he led David to them, and they found the Amalekites spread out across the fields, eating and drinking and dancing with joy because of the vast amount of plunder they had taken from the Philistines and the land of Judah. 17David and his men rushed in among them and slaughtered them throughout that night and the entire next day until evening. None of the Amalekites escaped except 400 young men who fled on camels. 18David got back everything the Amalekites had taken, and he rescued his two wives. 19Nothing was missing: small or great, son or daughter, nor anything else that had been taken. David brought every-

thing back. 20He also recovered all the
flocks and herds, and his men drove them
ahead of the other livestock. "This plunder
belongs to David!" they said.
21Then David returned to the brook Be-
sor and met up with the 200 men who
had been left behind because they were
too exhausted to go with him. They went
out to meet David and his men, and David
greeted them joyfully. 22But some evil
troublemakers among David's men said,
"They didn't go with us, so they can't have
any of the plunder we recovered. Give
them their wives and children, and tell
them to be gone."
23But David said, "No, my brothers!
Don't be selfish with what the LORD has
given us. He has kept us safe and helped
us defeat the band of raiders that at-
tacked us. 24Who will listen when you talk
like this? We share and share alike—those
who go to battle and those who guard the
equipment." 25From then on David made
this a decree and regulation for Israel, and
it is still followed today.
26When he arrived at Ziklag, David sent
part of the plunder to the elders of Judah,
who were his friends. "Here is a present
for you, taken from the LORD's enemies,"
he said.
27The gifts were sent to the people of
the following towns David had visited:
Bethel, Ramoth-negev, Jattir, 28Aroer,
Siphmoth, Eshtemoa, 29Racal,* the towns
of the Jerahmeelites, the towns of the
Kenites, 30Hormah, Bor-ashan, Athach,
31Hebron, and all the other places David
and his men had visited.

30:29 Greek version reads *Carmel.*

NOTES

30:2 ***the women and children and everyone else.*** The MT reads "the women who were in it both small and great." The NLT follows LXX, which reads, "the women and all who were in it." The rationale for favoring this reading is found in 30:3, in which the MT speaks of their wives, their sons, and their daughters being captured (translated as "families" by the NLT).

30:8 ***Should I chase after this band of raiders?*** The clause is clearly a question, even though there is no interrogative (cf. the next phrase, "Will I catch them?" where the interrogative He is present). See Williams (1976:§542).

30:21 ***men who had been left behind.*** Lit., "[whom] they had stationed at the Wadi Besor." It seems better to vocalize the verb as a singular, retaining David as the subject (as in a few Hebrew mss; cf. BHS apparatus).

30:24 ***We share and share alike.*** Lit., "for as the share of the one who went down to the battle so shall be the share." For the use of *ke . . . ke* [TH3509.1, ZH3869] (as . . . so), see Joüon and Muraoka §174i. The idea is that the two things in reference are declared identical in some regard.

30:26 ***a present.*** Lit., "a blessing."

30:27 ***Bethel.*** Perhaps to be read as "Bethuel" in the tribal area of Simeon (Josh 19:4; 1 Chr 4:30), since Bethel seems too far north.

COMMENTARY

As will be noted in the ensuing discussion, there are a number of reasons for concluding that this chapter might appropriately be characterized as the messianic rehabilitation of David.

In the parable of the lost son in Luke 15, Jesus told the story of the younger son of a wealthy man who took his inheritance, left the security of his father's home, and then squandered his inheritance until he found himself completely trapped by his own foolish behavior. In this extremity we are told that he came to his senses (Luke 15:17) and decided to go back to his father, who then received him with open arms. There is a very real sense in which a similar thing happens with David in this chapter. After a period of foolish behavior that led to an impasse in his life, David came to his senses and returned to fellowship with and dependence on his heavenly Father.

As we have traced the threads of the lives of Saul and David in the foregoing chapters, we have found that each reached a crisis point in his life. Saul faced a battle with the Philistines fully suspecting that it would be his last battle. This was confirmed to him when he consulted the medium at Endor and was told that he would die on the next day (28:19). At the same time, because of his deceitful alliance with Achish of Gath, David found himself in the untenable position of being coerced to join the Philistines in a battle against God's people, Israel. Only a gracious divine providence rescued David from this dilemma when the Philistine commanders, other than Achish, refused to permit David to accompany them in the battle (ch 29).

But the crisis in David's life did not end with the reprieve granted at the insistence of the Philistine commanders; in fact, it had not yet reached its climax. When David and his men returned to their home city of Ziklag after a three-day journey, they found that it had been burned to the ground and that their wives, children, and cattle had disappeared. The first verse of chapter 30 tells the reader something unknown to David and his men at the time. It was their old enemy, the Amalekites, who had destroyed Ziklag, apparently in retaliation for the attacks that David and his troops had made on them in the recent past (27:8).[1] It is not difficult to envision the frame of mind of David's men on their homeward journey. After their providential deliverance from the dilemma in which they had been trapped at Aphek, they certainly would be looking forward to arriving at home, eating a meal with their wives and children, and putting the frustrations and anxieties of the previous week behind them. This must have been their expectation. But the reality proved to be quite different. Thus, it is not surprising that David's men were shocked and distressed when they discovered what had happened. The narrator tells us that they "wept until they could weep no more" (30:4). Their homes were burned to the ground and lay in smoking ruins. Their families had disappeared. In their frustration David's men became angry (NLT, "all his men were very bitter"), and their anger was aimed directly at David (30:6). It was David who had brought them to Ziklag. He was the one who had designed the strategy of duplicity in raiding the surrounding territories including the Amalekites. So David's men placed the blame for their loss squarely on David and then threatened to take his life.

This crisis in David's life closely parallels that of Saul in chapter 28. In 30:6 we read that David was "now in great danger" (NLT; NIV, "David was greatly distressed").[2] Certainly his life was in jeopardy. But unlike Saul, who sought the aid of the medium at Endor when the Lord would no longer communicate with him, David found the courage to go on by placing his trust in the Lord (30:6b). Here is the great contrast between these two men.[3]

As we reflect on this story, as well as on the other narratives of 1–2 Samuel, we are again reminded that God is at work in all the twists and turns of the daily lives of his people. In this particular narrative, God was showing David, admittedly in a very painful way, the consequences of his foolish choices. David had placed his trust in his own cleverness; now he had come face-to-face with the end result of his self-defeating self-reliance. If one were to argue that the events of this chapter are simply an example of the way things are in a fallen world, rather than an example of God's providential working in David's life, it would merely call attention to the mystery and wonder of divine providence. It is only by God's grace that the intentions and purposes of workings of divine providence in the experiences of everyday life may be discerned with any degree of clarity or certainty whether that be in David's life or our own (de Jong 1978:220). In this instance, however, it is clear that in his great distress, when everything seemed to be collapsing around him, David perceived what can be termed "God's strange providence," and as a result he again sought renewed contact with the Lord.

The expression "God's strange providence" seems appropriate because Isaiah, the prophet, uses that language in connection with God's sending discipline and judgment into the lives of his own people. When Isaiah describes the judgment coming on Israel by the hand of the Assyrians he speaks of it as God's "strange work," and his "alien task" (Isa 28:21, NIV; NLT, "strange thing," "unusual deed"). Chapter 30 provides an example of God's strange work in the life of David. Very often God's purpose for bringing hardship into the lives of his people is to break them from their natural inclination as fallen human beings to rely on their own wisdom, and to teach them to rely wholly on the Lord. So this "strange providence," that is, the providence of God's judging, disciplining action in the lives of his own people, comes every bit as much from God's love for those who are his, as does what we may describe as his "happy providence." As difficult as this "strange providence" may be for those who experience it, it is often this very thing that brings God's people to a higher level of maturity and usefulness in God's Kingdom. It was the view of C. S. Lewis that God sends severe storms into the lives of his people. In Lewis's view the winds of these storms must be strong enough to counteract the winds of his people's self-will in order to get them back on the proper course. As Burson and Walls (1998:206) put it, "The pain, anguish and suffering that we so deeply despise and desperately long to resist prove, in the long run, to be the benevolent tempest that powers us toward the ultimate safety and tranquility of the heavenly harbor."

David's turning to the Lord in this time of great distress (30:6) marks the first time in the whole series of Ziklag episodes (beginning back in ch 27) that David is portrayed as seeking the Lord's help. David's relationship with the Lord had suffered during this period because David had chosen to go his own way. But now David suddenly realized that the Lord was speaking to him through the adversity in which he found himself. So David, like the prodigal son in Luke's Gospel, finally came to his senses.

When it is recognized that it was only God's grace that enabled David to respond as he did to this crisis in his life by discerning the work of God's hand in what had happened to him and his associates and their families, it becomes apparent that God also sovereignly controls the method and severity of his disciplinary punishment (de Jong 1978:221). God would permit no more distress in David's life than was necessary for his purpose. Certainly, in this case, it is remarkable that the Amalekite raiders from the desert did not kill anyone in their attack,[4] and that David was later able to bring back his wives and children, as well as those of his men, along with all their possessions that had been carried away. So one might say that these Amalekite marauders were on God's leash. They could do nothing beyond or against God's will. Because they were an instrument of divine discipline on a wayward child, they could do no more than God permitted them to do. So we find that this very dark day in David's life became an occasion on which he was enabled to turn again to the Lord and seek strength to go forward in dependence on him.

From this low point of David's extreme distress, the story moves upward in a grand and messianic way. The messianic overtones to David's behavior that had been absent from his life ever since the beginning of chapter 27 begin to sound again in this chapter as David is rehabilitated and makes himself strong in the Lord. This change is seen in the remainder of the chapter in at least five ways (four of which are noted by de Jong 1978:221-225): First, David again sought guidance from the Lord (30:7-8); second, David showed mercy to a person in need (30:11-15); third, the Lord gave David and his men a decisive victory over their old foe, the Amalekites (30:16-19); fourth, David provided for a just distribution of the plunder taken in the battle (30:20-25); and fifth, David again identified himself with God's people and with their cause (30:26-31).

First, David again sought guidance from the Lord. David immediately requested the priest, Abiathar, to bring the ephod (30:7), and he inquired of the Lord (30:8), "Should I chase after this band of raiders? Will I catch them?" It is of interest that the answer comes back fuller than the question. God said, "Yes, go after them. You will surely recover everything that was taken from you!" It is clear that the Lord, just like the father in the parable of the prodigal son, is ready and willing to help David in his time of need. This is a useful reminder for God's people in other times and places. Whenever God's children become trapped in situations brought on by their own failures, and they humbly return to the Lord, they, too, can be certain that the Lord will take pleasure in standing by their side.

Having received God's answer, David pursued the raiders. After a three-day march from Aphek, it is not surprising that many of his men were not up to the rigor of the journey. At the Besor Ravine (30:9-10) 200 men (out of 600) were too exhausted to carry on. So David left them there to guard the supplies (cf. 30:9-10, 24). At this juncture, a rather lengthy description (30:11-16) is given of the discovery of the nearly dead Egyptian slave of an Amalekite raider (30:11). It is in this incident and its description that we find a second way in which the messianic ideal is reflected in David's conduct: David is someone who showed mercy to a person in need.

The slave was suffering from both illness and starvation. He had been abandoned by his Amalekite master because he had become sick and was left to die in the wilderness (30:13). But after he was given food and water, he quickly revived and informed David, not only that it was the Amalekites who were the ones who burned Ziklag (30:14), but most importantly that he could lead the Israelites to the Amalekite camp. What is interesting here is not just the considerable attention (six verses) given to this incident in the narrative, but also the order in which the information is arranged. The story could certainly have been told in a more abbreviated form. The writer, however, seems intent on making a particular point. He tells of the discovery of a man who is nearly dead and then tells how David and his men cared for him, *not* because of what he could offer but simply because he was a human being in need (30:11-12).[5] It is only afterwards that the man provides David with information about the Amalekites (30:14). Here again is a clear example of divine providence that is characteristic of the narratives of Samuel. But this time it is a "happy" providence rather than a "strange" one: David and his men just happen to stumble on a person who can give them inside information about the location of the Amalekites. Even more significant, however, is that when this man was found, David did not say "Leave him—we do not have time to stop! We must hurry and overtake our families' captors!" No, instead of this, David had mercy on the man and took both the time and trouble to give him the attention that he needed. This merciful act is one of the ways in which David's conduct in this chapter reflects messianic overtones. In the kingdom of the messiah, there are no unimportant people. The messianic king is a person who rescues the poor and the needy. He is a person who hears their cry for help. The narrator uses this incident to indicate to the reader that the messianic idea is alive and well again with David (de Jong 1978:222-223).

With the information that this man provided, David and his men were enabled to launch a surprise attack on the Amalekite camp, and not only rout their forces, but also recover everything that had been taken from Ziklag (30:16-20). In the aftermath of this battle, David attributed the victory to the Lord's doing, not to the military expertise of himself and his men. In 30:23 we find an explicit statement of the perspective on military success and human accomplishment that should characterize a true covenantal king. In fact, this was the perspective that characterized Saul when, prior to his inauguration as king, he led Israel to victory over the Ammonites, and said in the aftermath of that battle "today the LORD has rescued Israel" (11:13). Unfortunately, Saul did not retain this outlook. In chapter 13 he did not wait for Samuel to come and offer sacrifice before going into battle as he had been instructed (13:9-13), and in chapter 14, he did not wait for instruction from the Lord before going into battle even though he had called for the ephod to be brought to him (14:18-20). Both incidents suggest an unhealthy confidence in his own ability to achieve success in military campaigns apart from dependence on and obedience to the Lord. Instead of having acted as a true servant of the Lord, Saul's behavior increasingly appeared to be that of a person who sought to coerce the Lord into serving his own ambitions. This was confirmed when he not only set up a monument to himself in celebration of a victory over the Amalekites (15:12) but also disobeyed the Lord's explicit command concerning the taking of plunder and the sparing of Agag. So David's victory over the Amalekites, and his acknowledgment that this victory was a gift from the Lord, is placed in sharp contrast to the anticovenantal disposition of Saul that is described in the preceding chapters. It serves notice that David rather than Saul represents the ideal of the true covenantal king.[6]

David's messianic rehabilitation appears in a fourth way as well. It comes to view in the manner in which David divided the spoil that he took from the Amalekites.[7] David provided for a just distribution of the recovered possessions. When the enemy was defeated and David and his men returned to the 200 men who had stayed behind, there were some among David's men ("evil troublemakers," 30:22) who anticipated that David intended to divide the spoil in equal parts and expressed their opposition (30:22). The spirit of these men is clear. It is the spirit of the world. It is the spirit of every man for himself. But notice what David says: "No, my brothers! Don't be selfish with what the *LORD* has given us. He has kept us safe and helped us defeat the band of raiders that attacked us" (30:23; my italics). David was conscious of God's grace in his life.

It should be clear to any observer of human behavior that prosperity and success are powerful stimulants for pride and self-sufficiency. It is equally clear that a spirit of humility flourishes in the prosperous and successful person only when that individual's success is consciously placed in the context of grace. It is living by grace that encourages graciousness. The life of a person who lives by grace is no longer centered in his or her own accomplishments (de Jong 1978:224). So we are told not only that David said "We share and share alike—those who go to battle and those who guard the equipment" (30:24b), but in addition, "From then on David made this a decree and regulation for Israel, and it is still followed today" (30:25). The share of the soldier who stays with the supplies will be the same as the one who goes into battle.

Finally, David did one more thing in which the messianic character of his rule became visible. He identified himself again with God's people and with their cause (30:26-30). From the plunder that was greater than the loss from Ziklag, he sent gifts to the elders of Judah.[8] When Achish returned from the battle the Philistines had waged against Israel, he would finally learn which side David was really on. David would no longer be silent in word and deed about his true identity and beliefs, as he had been in chapter 29.

Chapter 30 thus begins at a low point in David's life and moves to a new messianic height. In a dangerous crisis David came to his senses and returned to the Lord. In this chapter the road from David to Christ is again made visible in David's renewed representation of the messianic ideal (de Jong 1978:225). He showed himself to be a person who, in the words of Micah 6:8, sought to "do what is right, to love mercy, and to walk humbly with [his] God." David's imperfect manifestation of the messianic ideal points forward to Jesus, who endured the greatest crisis of God's judgment in order to reach the ultimate messianic height, and this without any personal failure.

This chapter provides some remarkable insights into the ways in which God works in the lives of his people. The reader of these narratives learns a great deal about who God is and how he encourages, disciplines, and sustains the lives of his people. Among other things, this narrative reveals something of God's sovereign direction of matters that otherwise might be regarded as merely accidental or normal occurrences of life in a fallen world. We find an example of God's "strange" providence, designed to bring David back to dependence on the Lord rather than living on the assumption of his own invincibility and the tendency to think he could be completely self-reliant. We learn how ready God is to forgive and restore fellowship with an errant child. In addition we see how willing God is to bless and protect those who put their trust in him. Finally, we may note that all who are in Christ are called upon, like David was, to act justly, to love mercy, and to walk humbly with their God.

ENDNOTES

1. Edelman (1991:263) comments, "The use of the verb *pashat* [TH6584, ZH7320] to characterize the Amalekites' activities in the Negeb and at Ziklag, as well as David's raids that were carried out against the Gesurites, Girzites and Amalekites in 27.8, 10, highlights the retaliatory nature of the strike." In addition, the "clever use of David's absence to carry out an extensive raid" (as Fokkelman [1986:579] puts it), is not only a reminder of a similar Amalekite attack against the Israelites when they were in a vulnerable position on their way to Sinai after their Exodus from Egypt (cf. Deut 25:17-18), but also of Saul's failure to obey the Lord's commands in his battle against this same enemy.
2. Edelman (1991:264-265) notes that the use of the phrase *wattetser ledawid* [TH6887, ZH7674] (lit., "And it was too narrow for David"; NLT, "David was now in great danger") in 30:6 "seems to resonate with the other occurrences of the root *tsarar* in 13.6 and 28.15 in a similar impersonal construction. Especially apposite is 28.15 since it involves Saul's experience of distress [NLT, "I am in deep trouble"] on the eve of his final battle of Gilboa, the battle from which David has just been dismissed to his own great relief. Through the use of the same phrase, the narrator draws a link between the king and the king-elect, both of whom are experiencing the same loss of confidence in the face of an enemy attack."
3. Alter (1999:184) comments, "There is an antithetical contrast here between David, who has priest and ephod to convey to him God's oracular counsel, and Saul, who, frustrated in all his attempts to discover God's intentions, resorts to forbidden necromancy."
4. This is in sharp contrast to David's practice of leaving no one alive during his raids on the Amalekites, Gesurites, and Girzites (cf. 27:8, 11), but as Alter (1999:183) notes, "the Amalekites (who do not have David's motive of secrecy) consider the women and children to be part of the booty and have carried them off in order to exploit them as slaves."
5. Bergen (1996:277) comments, "By showing David's kind and gracious treatment of this Egyptian sojourner, the author demonstrated that even in the midst of personal tragedy David was sensitive to Torah injunctions regarding the treatment of aliens, particularly Egyptians (cf. Exod 22:21; 23:9; Lev 19:34; Deut 23:7)."
6. Gordon notes (1986:198) that it "can hardly be coincidence that Samuel's denunciation of Saul in 28:16-19 concentrates on his mishandling of the expedition against the Amalekites (cf. 15:1-33), and that so much attention is now paid to David's attack on them ('the enemies of the LORD,' 30:26)—when at this stage we might have expected the spotlight to focus on the Israelite lines in Jezreel, as they prepared for Saul's final encounter with the Philistines."
7. Brueggemann suggests that there is some sort of inconsistency or favoritism for David over Saul reflected in the contrast between Saul's not being permitted to take spoil from the Amalekites (ch 15), and his being cursed for violating this prohibition, while David is permitted to take spoil and celebrated for doing so. He comments (1990a:203), "Israel says proudly, 'This is David's spoil' (30:20). The Amalekites are resented for taking spoil; Saul is rejected for taking spoil; David is saluted and championed for doing the same! David is subject to none of the restrictions, held accountable to none of the old norms." The difference, however, between Saul's battle with the Amalekites and this battle of David's is that David's action on this occasion against the Amalekites was of a different order than was Saul's. David and his men were on a rescue-and-recovery mission, not an exercise of *kherem* under an explicit command to take no spoil.

8. It is certainly to be recognized that David's motives for sending some of the spoils of his victory over the Amalekites to his friends in Judah are not explicitly revealed in the text, and therefore may be interpreted in different ways. Alter (1999:188) says that "this act shows David the consummate political man, shoring up support among the sundry leaders of his home tribe of Judah . . . and preparing for himself a base in Hebron . . . the principal town of Judah, where he will soon be proclaimed king." In a similar vein Brueggemann (1990a:206) says, "David's power is based on calculating generosity." While political considerations may certainly have played a role in David's decision to give assistance to his fellow countrymen, the context for this act (David's renewed desire to follow the Lord's leading) suggests that one should not be overly cynical about his true motives.

◆ D. The Deaths of Saul and Jonathan (1 Sam 31:1-13)

**Now the Philistines attacked Israel, and
the men of Israel fled before them. Many
were slaughtered on the slopes of Mount
Gilboa. [2]The Philistines closed in on Saul
and his sons, and they killed three of his
sons—Jonathan, Abinadab, and Malkishua.
[3]The fighting grew very fierce around
Saul, and the Philistine archers caught up
with him and wounded him severely.
[4]Saul groaned to his armor bearer, "Take
your sword and kill me before these pa-
gan Philistines come to run me through
and taunt and torture me."
But his armor bearer was afraid and
would not do it. So Saul took his own sword
and fell on it. [5]When his armor bearer real-
ized that Saul was dead, he fell on his own
sword and died beside the king. [6]So Saul,
his three sons, his armor bearer, and his
troops all died together that same day.
[7]When the Israelites on the other side
of the Jezreel Valley and beyond the Jor-
dan saw that the Israelite army had fled
and that Saul and his sons were dead,
they abandoned their towns and fled. So
the Philistines moved in and occupied
their towns.
[8]The next day, when the Philistines
went out to strip the dead, they found the
bodies of Saul and his three sons on
Mount Gilboa. [9]So they cut off Saul's head
and stripped off his armor. Then they pro-
claimed the good news of Saul's death in
their pagan temple and to the people
throughout the land of Philistia. [10]They
placed his armor in the temple of the Ash-
toreths, and they fastened his body to the
wall of the city of Beth-shan.
[11]But when the people of Jabesh-gilead
heard what the Philistines had done to
Saul, [12]all their mighty warriors traveled
through the night to Beth-shan and took
the bodies of Saul and his sons down from
the wall. They brought them to Jabesh,
where they burned the bodies. [13]Then
they took their bones and buried them
beneath the tamarisk tree at Jabesh, and
they fasted for seven days.**

NOTES

31:1 ***the Philistines attacked Israel.*** The participial construction of the opening clause of this verse (better captured by the translation, "Meanwhile, the Philistines were fighting against Israel") suggests that Saul's battle with the Philistines was taking place at the same time as David's battle against the Amalekites reported in the preceding chapter.

31:3 ***wounded him severely.*** This phrase, however, may also be translated, "He was in great anguish (*wayyakhel me'od* [TH2342A, ZH2655]) because of the archers"—see the discussions of Alter (1999:189), Klein (1983:286), Youngblood (1992:801), as well as Fokkelman (1986:626, 739), who argues strongly against the "severely wounded" rendering.

COMMENTARY

At the same time David and his men were fighting against the Amalekites in the south (30:17), Saul and his army were drawn into battle at Mount Gilboa in the north by the Philistine forces from which David had been dismissed a few days earlier (29:11).[1] While David's battle with the Amalekites resulted in a victory for David and his men and the recovery of captured family members and possessions (30:16-20), Saul's battle with the Philistines was a disaster for Israel, resulting in the death of Saul and his three sons (Jonathan, Abinadab, and Malkishua), the complete routing of his army, and the occupation of Israelite territory by the victorious Philistines. The contrast in the outcomes of these two battles fought by Israel's two leaders could hardly be more pronounced.

While Saul had, on the occasion of his first military victory against the Ammonites at Jabesh-gilead (ch 11), declared that "the LORD has rescued Israel" (11:13), he unfortunately did not continue to hold that theocratic perspective subsequent to assuming the throne. The end result of Saul's long rebellion had now come to fruition. His refusal to embrace the responsibilities of a true covenantal king had brought calamity not only on himself and his family, but also on the nation over whom he ruled, just as Samuel had warned on the occasion of Saul's inauguration as king (12:15).

This is a poignant chapter in its description of the death of Saul and its echoes of the past, hinting to the reader at what might have been. Among Saul's sons who perished with him at Mount Gilboa was Jonathan, David's faithful friend and ally. It was Jonathan, rather than Saul, who was the one who had successfully taken the initiative to lead Israel in a battle against the Philistines at Micmash (ch 14). He was the one who "loved [David] as he loved himself" (18:1, 3), and who pledged his loyalty to him (20:16). He encouraged David "to stay strong in his faith in God" during the time that he was hiding from Saul in the desert of Ziph (23:16). And he confessed to David that he, as well as his father, knew that David rather than himself would become the next king of Israel (23:17). Part of the tragedy of Saul's demise was that his downfall brought this godly and faithful son to the grave with him.

Also among the sons who perished with Saul in the battle at Mount Gilboa was Malkishua (cf. 14:49), whose name embodies the very theocratic ideal that Saul initially embraced but had gradually come to deny. Malkishua is usually taken as a theophoric name,[2] meaning "the king [i.e., Yahweh] has delivered." By giving his son this name (perhaps in connection with his victory over the Ammonites), Saul was confessing that King Yahweh was the deliverer of his people Israel and that he recognized Yahweh as the supreme ruler of the nation. But ironically, Malkishua, whose name embodied one of Israel's core beliefs, was swept away along with his father because his father had refused to embrace the truth that his son's name proclaimed.

Contributing to the tragic overtones of this chapter is the fact that, in the end, Saul's death was self-inflicted. When Saul became convinced that death on the battlefield was inescapable, a thought probably reinforced by the prophecy of his demise received the night before the battle (28:19), he asked his armor bearer to kill him so that this distinction would not be given to the "pagan [lit., "uncircumcised"] Philistines." Upon the refusal of his armor bearer to obey his order,[3] Saul then took his own life (31:4). Here, as so often in Saul's life, there is ambiguity. In these final moments of his life, he freely chose to align himself with God's people, not only by leading Israel's forces into battle, but also by referring to the Philistines as pagans (uncircumcised). Religious distinctions and labels remained important for Saul, while the heart of religious belief, which should have demonstrated its validity and vitality in a willing submission to God's revealed will, seems to have eluded him to the very end. To Saul's credit, he did not flee from the battlefield in an attempt to avoid death, and to his credit he wished to deny the enemies of God's people (the uncircumcised Philistines) the satisfaction of killing the king of Israel. But one can wonder if suicide, even under these very dire circumstances, was justified. As Bergen (1996:282, note 163) points out, Saul's suicide was one of six suicide or assisted suicide attempts reported in the Bible (the others being: Saul's armor bearer, 31:5; Abimelech, Judg 9:54; Ahithophel, 2 Sam 17:23; Zimri, 1 Kgs 16:18; Judas, Matt 27:5; Acts 1:18).[4] While there are no direct words of approbation or condemnation connected with any of these cases, Bergen is certainly correct in noting that the "Bible seems to suggest that suicide or assisted suicide is a desperate act by a deeply troubled individual. None of the individuals who resorted to this action is portrayed as a role model for the pious." In general the Bible views life as a gift from God, and because man is made in the image of God, the unlawful taking of life is prohibited in clear terms (Gen 9:5-6; Exod 20:13), irrespective of whether this be of oneself or another person. For this reason great caution should characterize any attempt to define circumstances under which suicide or assisted suicide is deemed legitimate or justified.[5] These same principles apply not only to Saul, but also to his armor bearer who followed Saul's example and took his own life when he was certain that Saul was dead (31:5).

The Philistine rout of Saul's troops caused such panic in Israel that the inhabitants of villages in the eastern region of the valley of Jezreel, and even as far away as the eastern side of the Jordan River, fled from their homes. The Philistines quickly moved into these villages, including the important cities of Jezreel and Beth-shan, and by so doing they not only drove a wedge between the tribes of the far north and the rest of Israel, but they also gained control of the most important trade route that ran through Israel. This trade route (called by some the Great Trunk Road and by others the Via Maris) ran all the way from Egypt through the valley of Jezreel (where this battle was fought) and then on to Damascus, Aleppo, Babylon, and down the Euphrates River to the Persian Gulf. So in the aftermath of this important Philistine victory, Israel was severely weakened not only militarily but also economically.

On the day following the battle, the Philistines discovered the dead bodies of Saul and his three sons (31:8). They cut off Saul's head, displayed his armor in the temple of the Ashtoreths, and hung his decapitated body on the wall of the former Israelite city of Beth-shan[6] (31:10). In the meantime they spread the message of Saul's death and their own victory throughout their land (31:9).[7] This Philistine victory inevitably reminds the reader of the great Philistine victory over the Israelites many years before in the battle at Aphek, when to both Israel's and the Philistines' surprise, the Philistines were able to capture the Ark of the Covenant (ch 4). On that occasion the Philistine celebration was short-lived because the Ark wreaked havoc on them, causing them to break out in tumors (ch 5). So for their own safety the Philistines had to return the Ark to Israel (ch 6). On that occasion the Philistines had mistakenly concluded that because they had captured the Ark, the symbol of

Israel's deity, their god Dagon was demonstrably stronger than Israel's god, Yahweh. But Yahweh would not allow this conclusion to go unchallenged. History seems to have repeated itself. The placement of Saul's armor in the temple of the Ashtoreths (31:10) and his head in the temple of Dagon (as 1 Chr 10:10 informs us) suggests that the Philistines had again interpreted their victory, as was common in that cultural context, as a victory of their deities over the God of Israel. For the moment the reader is left to wonder how and when the Lord, the God of Israel, will disabuse them of this notion. In the course of time David would be the one who would fulfill the original mandate given to Saul (i.e., the rescue of Israel from the Philistines; 9:16; cf. 2 Sam 3:18). His eventual accomplishment of this task is reported in the statement of 2 Samuel 8:1 that David "defeated and subdued the Philistines."

A final echo of the past appears in the last three verses of the chapter (31:11-13), where it is reported that when the inhabitants of Jabesh-gilead heard about the desecration of the bodies of Saul and his sons at Beth-shan, some of their warriors quickly went to Beth-shan to recover their bodies and bring them back to Jabesh for a proper burial.[8] It was Saul's victory at Jabesh-gilead that had confirmed his qualification to be king (11:1-13) and led to his coronation (11:14–12:25). So it might be said that Saul's reign both began and ended at the same place, Jabesh-gilead. At the beginning, it was faithfulness to his calling that inspired Saul to fight fearlessly against the Ammonites at Jabesh-gilead, and at the end it was persistence in disobedience that led to his burial at the same place. Saul is thus a tragic figure, a "person who puts throne and honor before God and then spirals into a free fall of failure, jealousy, insanity, murder, foolhardiness, and self-destruction" (DBI 757).

ENDNOTES

1. Although the synchronization of these battles is not made explicit in the text, both the participial construction of the introductory phrase of 29:1 (see note) and incidental references to the movements of David and his men, as well as the Philistine troops, fit with this conclusion. Fokkelman (1986:622) comments, "The first words of the new chapter are a durative clause which makes an appreciable contribution to the great synchronism of the battles in the north and south." Fokkelman makes this statement in support of an earlier assertion (1986:595) that "the defeat of Saul and Israel on the Gilboa took place on the same day as David's victory over the Amalekites." This conclusion is based on a detailed, but in some respects questionable, reconstruction of the chronology of events reported in chs 27–30. The most important considerations for developing such a chronology are that Saul consulted the medium at Endor on the evening immediately prior to his last battle (28:19) and this occurred subsequent to the movement of the Philistine troops from Aphek (29:1-2) to the area of Jezreel (29:11) and Shunem (28:4), and after David's departure for Ziklag. The trip to Ziklag took David and his men three days (30:1).
2. A theophoric name is one that includes a title or name of God in its construction. Malkishua is a combination of the Hebrew roots *malak* [TH4427, ZH4887] (king) and *yasha'* [TH3467, ZH3828] (deliver). For the use of *malak* as a theophoric element (i.e., a reference to God) in Hebrew personal names, see Noth 1928:118-119 and Oosterhoff 1953:26-28.
3. According to the text, the armor bearer was afraid to carry out Saul's command (31:4). The reason for his fear is not given. Was this a fear to take Saul's life because he was the Lord's anointed, or was it a fear to do something that violated his responsibility and training as the armor bearer for King Saul?

4. Bergen does not include Samson in his list, even though Samson said, "Let me die with the Philistines" when he pulled down the temple of Dagon (Judg 16:30). This exclusion is justified, however, because the purpose of Samson's act was not to end his own life but rather to be obedient to his calling to begin to deliver Israel from the hands of the Philistines (Judg 13:5). Accordingly, the writer of Judges tells us that Samson "killed many more [Philistines] when he died than he had during his entire lifetime" (Judg 16:30).
5. The argument that suicide is a form of homicide included in the prohibition of the sixth commandment was defended both by Augustine and Thomas Aquinas and finds expression in the Westminster Larger Catechism, which in response to the question "What are the sins forbidden in the sixth commandment?" answers, "The sins forbidden in the sixth commandment are, all taking away the life of ourselves, or of others" (Question 136). Augustine (1950:52) says that in the sixth commandment "there are not limitations; hence, no one, not even the one who is commanded, is to be excepted." Augustine comments (1950:55) that although it might be "objected that many men have taken their lives in order not to fall into the hands of their enemies . . . neither the Patriarchs nor the Prophets nor the Apostles offer any instance of suicide. Christ the Lord Himself, who instructed them to flee from city to city if persecuted, could have bidden them to do away with themselves in order not to fall into the persecutors' hands. On the contrary, He neither bade nor counseled even those to pass out of life for whom He promised to prepare eternal mansions after their passage from earth. . . . One thing is clear: Suicide is a sin for those who worship the one true God." Augustine later says (1950:58-59), "What error, therefore, so insidious has ever stolen into men's mind as to imagine that a man may take his life because an enemy has wronged him or might wrong him."

   In more modern times Karl Barth is, if anything, even more emphatic than Augustine on the illegitimacy of suicide, although he grounds his argument in God's gracious gift of life in Jesus Christ, rather than in obedience to the moral law. Barth (1961:404-405) says that "it is not for man himself to decide whether his existence is a success or a failure, whether it is tolerable or intolerable, whether its continuation is possible or impossible, far less whether it is worthwhile or mean and worthless. The Creator, Giver and Lord of life decides all these things, and no one else. . . . Suicide cannot be extenuated, excused or justified." In discussing the case of Saul as one of "three great cases of suicide" in the Bible, he notes (1961:408-409) that the "shadow which lies over these three figures is that of the divine and not a human judgment. Properly speaking they are all sinners only against God's free grace. . . . Those who refuse God's grace and try to exist as their own lords and masters are on the way at the end of which they can only fall on their own swords like Saul or hang themselves like Ahithophel and Judas."
6. Beth-shan was located near the Jordan River about 11 miles southwest of Mount Gilboa.
7. Although Alter (1999:191) is correct in saying that there "is some grammatical ambiguity" on whether the Philistines sent "Saul's armor as a visible token of the victory" or simply sent news of Israel's defeat, the wording implies that messengers were sent to "carry the good news" (*basar* [TH1319, ZH1413]).
8. The statement in 31:12-13 that the desecrated bodies were burned, and that the remaining bones were buried raises questions about burial practices in Israel at that time. Edelman (1991:294-295) comments, "A comparative study of crematory practices suggests that such a treatment of Saul's body would have been considered an honorable form of burial, befitting a king, among surrounding non-Semitic nations. Whether the same belief was held within Israel remains to be determined. The implied honorable intentions of the Jabesh-gileadites would tend to suggest that their cremation of the retrieved royal bodies was an honorable act." See also Stone 1995.

◆ VI. David Becomes King over Judah (2 Sam 1:1–3:1)
A. The Deaths of Saul and Jonathan Reported to David (2 Sam 1:1-16)

After the death of Saul, David returned
from his victory over the Amalekites and
spent two days in Ziklag. 2On the third day
a man arrived from Saul's army camp. He
had torn his clothes and put dirt on his
head to show that he was in mourning. He
fell to the ground before David in deep
respect.

3"Where have you come from?" David
asked.

"I escaped from the Israelite camp," the
man replied.

4"What happened?" David demanded.
"Tell me how the battle went."

The man replied, "Our entire army fled
from the battle. Many of the men are
dead, and Saul and his son Jonathan are
also dead."

5"How do you know Saul and Jonathan
are dead?" David demanded of the young
man.

6The man answered, "I happened to be
on Mount Gilboa, and there was Saul
leaning on his spear with the enemy char-
iots and charioteers closing in on him.
7When he turned and saw me, he cried
out for me to come to him. 'How can I
help?' I asked him.

8"He responded, 'Who are you?'

"'I am an Amalekite,' I told him.

9"Then he begged me, 'Come over here
and put me out of my misery, for I am in
terrible pain and want to die.'

10"So I killed him," the Amalekite told
David, "for I knew he couldn't live. Then
I took his crown and his armband, and I
have brought them here to you, my
lord."

11David and his men tore their clothes
in sorrow when they heard the news.
12They mourned and wept and fasted all
day for Saul and his son Jonathan, and for
the LORD's army and the nation of Israel,
because they had died by the sword that
day.

13Then David said to the young man
who had brought the news, "Where are
you from?"

And he replied, "I am a foreigner, an
Amalekite, who lives in your land."

14"Why were you not afraid to kill the
LORD's anointed one?" David asked.

15Then David said to one of his men,
"Kill him!" So the man thrust his sword
into the Amalekite and killed him. 16"You
have condemned yourself," David said,
"for you yourself confessed that you killed
the LORD's anointed one."

NOTES

1:1 ***Amalekites.*** This follows the gentilic *ha'amaleqi* [TH1886.1/6003, ZH2021/6668] found in several Hebrew mss and the Syriac. As Smith (1912) and others have pointed out, normal Hebrew usage would require either *'amaleq* or *ha'amaleqi* rather than MT's *ha'amaleq* [TH1886.1/6002, ZH2021/6667].

1:4 ***Many.*** The word *harbeh* [TH7235D, ZH2221] (to make numerous) functions as the subject of the verb, although it is a Hiphil infinitive absolute in form (cf. BDB 915).

1:6 ***I happened to be.*** The word *niqreti,* preceded by the infinitive absolute *niqro'* [TH7122, ZH7925], appears to be the Lamedh-He/Yodh verb *qarah* [TH7136, ZH7936] but with the vowels appropriate for the Lamedh-Aleph verb *qara'* [TH7122, ZH7925]. See Joüon and Muraoka §79l and GKC §75rr. The construction of the infinitive absolute followed by the finite verb gives emphasis to the verbal idea, thus as A. Anderson (1989:4) suggests, it could mean "it was entirely by chance that I happened to be. . . ." If the verbs are read as coming from *qara',* the translation would be "I was called to. . . ."

charioteers. The expression *uba'ale happarashim* [TH1167/6571, ZH1251/7304] (lit., "owners of horses" or "owners of horsemen") is found only here in the OT. The LXX renders it as *hoi hipparchai* [TG2460, ZG2689] (the commanders of cavalry).

1:9 *terrible pain.* The word *hashabats* [TH7661, ZH8688] is a hapax legomenon. Its meaning is uncertain. NEB and NIV render it "the throes of death." A. Anderson (1989:4) suggests "the hand of death." McCarter (1984:59-60) suggests "dizziness."

and want to die. Lit., "But my life is still wholly within me."

1:12 *the LORD's army.* The LXX has "Judah's army," reading *yehudah* [TH3063, ZH3373] for *yhwh* [TH3068, ZH3378], a difference of only one letter in unpointed Hebrew text.

1:13 *a foreigner . . . who lives in your land.* The term *ger* [TH1616, ZH1731] designates a resident alien (BDB 158, "dwellers in Israel with certain conceded, not inherited rights") in distinction from a common foreigner. NIDOTTE 1.836-837 says, "The sojourner is distinguished from the foreigner in that he has settled in the land for some time and is recognized as having a special status. As individuals or a group they have abandoned their homeland for political or economic reasons and sought refuge in another community, as Abraham in Hebron (Gen 23:4), Moses in Midian (Exod 2:22), Elimelech and his family in Moab (Ruth 1:1), or the Israelites in Egypt (Exod 22:20 [22:21 in ET])." It stands to reason that a resident alien is subject to the laws of the land where he resides. Fokkelman (1986:644) views this resident alien status of the Amalekite as "the juridical basis of David's attitude and decision. David is clearly of the opinion that as a member of the Israelite community the man should be familiar with and respect such an important prohibition as the taboo concerning the king."

1:15 *one of his men.* That is, one of his attendants.

Kill him! Lit., "Come here and strike him!" See Joüon and Muraoka §177e for asyndetic connection between two imperatives.

COMMENTARY

The opening narrative of 2 Samuel sets the stage for the transition from Saul's reign to David's. The closing narrative of 1 Samuel has already reported the deaths of Saul's three sons, including Jonathan, in Israel's battle with the Philistines at Mount Gilboa (1 Sam 31:2). It has also described how a seriously wounded Saul took his own life by falling upon his sword after his armor bearer refused to put him out of his misery (1 Sam 31:3-4). In this ensuing narrative a messenger comes to David in Ziklag (cf. 1 Sam 30:26-31) and announces what the reader already knows—both Saul and Jonathan are dead. But the messenger's report about the manner of Saul's death differs in significant ways from the account of the same event in 1 Samuel 31. The messenger, who is twice identified as an Amalekite (2 Sam 1:8, 13), bowed in homage before David (1:2) and told him that he was the one who had killed Saul at Saul's own request.[1] He then presented David with Saul's crown and armband as evidence that what he said was true (1:10). So in consecutive narratives the reader is confronted with two obviously conflicting reports of how Saul died. Either the Amalekite messenger lied to David or the report of 1 Samuel 31 is erroneous in its description of how Saul died. Both of these conclusions have been drawn by interpreters of these chapters,[2] but it would seem that the narrator intends the reader to understand that his own report (1 Sam 31) is the authentic version (see Fokkelman's [1984] detailed argumentation for this conclusion based on literary analysis).[3] This means that the Amalekite's spurious story was based on his mistaken assumption that David desired to wrest the throne from Saul and that David would reward him handsomely for taking the life of his political rival.[4]

This brings the reader to the central question raised by this narrative unit. How would David respond to the Amalekite's message? Would he be taken in by his strategy and rejoice in the death of Saul and his most likely successor, Jonathan? Would he reward the Amalekite as a bearer of good tidings and the facilitator of his own ascent to royal status in Israel? Or would he rise above the enticement of personal ambition and demonstrate the same high regard for the inviolability of the royal office in Israel that he had displayed on previous occasions (cf. 1 Sam 24:6, 10; 26:16, 23)? David's response was not at all what the messenger expected. Immediately upon hearing the news, David and his associates reacted by exhibiting profound sorrow for the nation's great loss (1:11-12). David then posed further questions to the messenger and when he learned that he was a resident alien (see note on 1:13), he asked him why he had not been afraid to kill "the LORD's anointed one" (1:14).[5] As a resident alien, the Amalekite should have known and understood the inviolable nature of the royal office in Israel. Then, without waiting for a reply to the question about the killing of Saul, David commanded one of his men to put this self-condemned Amalekite to death for his offense. In this act David vindicated himself from any complicity in the death of Saul and opened the way for his own lawful and orderly accession to the throne.

In this quick and decisive action David displayed in advance something of the qualities that would subsequently surface in the exercise of his royal office. The writer of Samuel later characterizes David as doing "what was just and right for all his people" (8:15). In Psalm 101, David himself described the aspirations that he brought to his royal office: He pledged to reign in a righteous manner, to defend the cause of the faithful, and to remove the wicked from the land (van den Berg 1997:13). The vision for a just society that David describes in this remarkable psalm is one in which the godly are given generous opportunity to flourish, while the arrogant and deceitful are held accountable for their sins. Although this vision was never fully realized during David's reign, the writer of 1–2 Kings uses David's reign as a standard by which later kings are measured (cf. 1 Kgs 3:14; 6:12; 8:25; 9:4; 11:4, 6, 12-13, 33, 38; 14:8; 15:3, 5, 11; 2 Kgs 14:3; 16:2; 18:3; 22:2). In much of modern western society, David's vision has become so inverted that it is common for the deceitful and arrogant to be honored, while the godly and upright are marginalized and oppressed. As human history has run its course, it has become increasingly clear that the fullness of David's vision will be realized only when David's greater son, who is described by the apostle John as "the source of David and the heir to his throne" (Rev 22:16), assumes the throne of his father. At that time, when "the world has . . . become the Kingdom of our Lord and of his Christ" (Rev 11:15), those who are "cowards, unbelievers, the corrupt, murderers, the immoral, those who practice witchcraft, idol worshipers, and all liars" (Rev 21:8) will be excluded from the community of the new Jerusalem. Thus in David's first act as the remaining "anointed one" there is an indication of what his reign will look like. And even though David's kingdom never reached the heights that his vision for it encompassed, it did point forward in significant ways to an ultimate and complete realization of its standards in the new heavens and new earth.

ENDNOTES

1. There is irony in the fact that it is an Amalekite who announced the death of Saul to David and gave him the symbols of royal authority taken from Saul's dead body. It was Saul's disobedience to God's command to utterly destroy the Amalekites that had led to the Lord's rejection of him as king (1 Sam 15).
2. Alter (1999:197) comments, "This whole story obviously contradicts the account of Saul's death by his own hand in 1 Samuel 31. Predictably, this has led many critics to imagine two conflicting 'sources.' It is reassuring that more recent scholarly consensus has come to the sensible conclusion that the Amalekite lad is lying." Keil (1956:286) argues that the Amalekite's statement has an "air of improbability, or rather of untruth in it, particularly in the assertion that Saul was leaning upon his spear when the chariots and horsemen of the enemy came upon him, without having either an armour-bearer or any other Israelitish soldier by his side, so that he had to turn to an Amalekite who accidentally came by, and to ask him to inflict the fatal wound." For similar views see Fokkelman (1984); Goslinga (1962:12-13); Hertzberg (1964:236-238). On the other hand, Budde (1902:193-196); Smith (1912:254-255); and others have argued that the discrepancies between the two accounts are best understood as reflections of two differing and independent traditions of the manner of Saul's death. As Kennedy (1904:192) says, "On the whole, therefore, it is better with almost all recent critics to regard verses 6-10, 13-16, at least, as representing a variant tradition regarding the last moments of the unfortunate king."
3. Fokkelman (1986:639) comments, "A character cannot possibly succeed against his creator in any dispute in credibility, and the narrator has taken care to give us his own version beforehand, the authoritative one of 1 Sam 31."
4. That David understood what the Amalekite was up to is made clear by David's later comment: "Someone once told me, 'Saul is dead,' thinking he was bringing me good news. But I seized him and killed him at Ziklag. That's the reward I gave him for his news!" (4:10).
5. When Saul requested his armor bearer to take his life (1 Sam 31:4), we are informed that the armor bearer "was afraid" (*yare' me'od* [TH3372/3966, ZH3707/4394], lit., "he feared exceedingly") and would not do it.

◆ B. David's Lament for Saul and Jonathan (2 Sam 1:17-27)

17Then David composed a funeral song for
Saul and Jonathan, 18and he commanded
that it be taught to the people of Judah.
It is known as the Song of the Bow, and it is recorded in *The Book of Jashar.**

19 Your pride and joy, O Israel, lies dead on the hills!
Oh, how the mighty heroes have fallen!
20 Don't announce the news in Gath,
don't proclaim it in the streets of Ashkelon,
or the daughters of the Philistines will rejoice
and the pagans will laugh in triumph.

21 O mountains of Gilboa,
let there be no dew or rain upon you,
nor fruitful fields producing offerings of grain.*
For there the shield of the mighty heroes was defiled;
the shield of Saul will no longer be anointed with oil.
22 The bow of Jonathan was powerful,
and the sword of Saul did its mighty work.

They shed the blood of their enemies
and pierced the bodies of mighty
heroes.

23 How beloved and gracious were Saul
and Jonathan!
They were together in life and in
death.
They were swifter than eagles,
stronger than lions.
24 O women of Israel, weep for Saul,
for he dressed you in luxurious scarlet
clothing,
in garments decorated with gold.

25 Oh, how the mighty heroes have
fallen in battle!
Jonathan lies dead on the hills.
26 How I weep for you, my brother
Jonathan!
Oh, how much I loved you!
And your love for me was deep,
deeper than the love of
women!

27 Oh, how the mighty heroes have
fallen!
Stripped of their weapons, they
lie dead.

1:18 Or *The Book of the Upright.* **1:21** The meaning of the Hebrew is uncertain.

NOTES

1:17 ***funeral song.*** The word *qinah* [TH7015, ZH7806] refers to lamentation for the dead, elegy, or dirge.

1:18 ***the Song of the Bow.*** Lit., "bow." Most modern interpreters have understood *qesheth* [TH7198, ZH8008] (bow) as the title of the lament. Others (including McCarter 1984:67-68) consider it intrusive and eliminate it, following LXX Vaticanus.

1:19 ***Your pride and joy.*** The word *hatsebi* [TH6643/6643A, ZH7382/7383] is a homonym meaning either "beauty, honor" or "gazelle" (cf. BDB 840). Some (see Freedman 1972) have argued for the meaning "gazelle" in this verse as imagery for a military leader. Freedman applies the term to Jonathan. Zaph (1984:107) regards the word as deliberately ambiguous in both reference and meaning. He understands it as a reference to both Saul and Jonathan with a certain preference given to Jonathan. Zaph (1984:117) translates the phrase, "The gazelle/glory, Israel, upon your heights is slain." Although this is rather cumbersome English, it captures more of the ambiguity of the poetic language in Hebrew than does the more straightforward rendering, "your glory," or as NLT renders it, "your pride and joy." McCarter (1984:66, 68, 74) has proposed unnecessary textual emendations suggesting that the first line of the lament should be translated, "Alas, prince of Israel, slain standing erect!"

Oh, how the mighty heroes have fallen! Fokkelman (1986:653) points out that the "rule of *parallelismus membrorum,* the general effect of which (according to Kugel) is 'A, what's more B,' is turned upside-down here, because the specific clause has displaced the standard expression . . . the listener expects the order of a painful exclamation plus an explanation/development, but first he receives an alienating, specific and yet obscure, nominalizing statement, and only then a familiar, if not a worn-out, expression."

1:21 ***let there be.*** The verb is supplied on the basis of context (cf. GKC §147c).

nor fruitful fields. The meaning of this phrase (*usede therumoth* [TH8641, ZH9556], "offering") is uncertain. Although there are adequate lexical explanations for the phrase, some have needlessly attempted to address the translation problem by textual emendation (see Gevirtz 1973:85-87; Holladay 1970:170-171). The NIV renders the phrase, "nor fields that yield offerings of grain." In a similar vein, the NJPS (and NRSV) render it "Or (nor) bountiful (bounteous) fields." Others, including A. Anderson (1989:11-12) and Youngblood (1992:817), have argued that the phrase is a semantic equivalent of *merome sadeh* [TH4791/7704, ZH5294/8441] in Judg 5:18, and should be translated "mountain slopes" or "high fields" on the basis that *therumoth,* like *merome,* is derived from the root *rum* [TH7311, ZH8123] (be high, exalted). The rationale for this position is not only linguistic, however, but also stylistic. Fokkelman (1979:290-293) argues that this understanding fits better with the overall chiastic structure of 1:21. Fokkelman's suggested structure is:

O mountains of Gilboa,
  no dew
  and no rain on you,
O high fields!
For there was defiled
  the shield of the mighty,
  the shield of Saul—
no longer rubbed with oil.

While this is plausible, it is not the only possible structure, and it may at least be questioned whether chiastic structure should be determinative when there is no other example for this particular linguistic use of *therumoth.*

anointed. This follows many Hebrew mss that read *mashuakh* [TH4886, ZH5417] instead of *mashiakh* [TH4899, ZH5431] (normally used to refer to the "anointed leader" of God's people). Alter (1999:199) suggests that there is a symbolic message in the line "the shield of Saul will no longer be anointed with oil." Although it was common to rub leather shields with oil prior to battle to make their surface slippery, Saul's shield would now be "'unanointed' or 'messiah-less,' a haunting intimation that the LORD's anointed is no more. Clearly, the image of the royal shield lying befouled in the dust is a powerful metonymy for Saul himself."

1:26 *was deep.* Lit., "was wonderful." For the unusual morphology of *niple'athah* [TH6381, ZH7098], see GKC §75. It is unnecessary to emend the text to two words as suggested by F. M. Cross and D. N. Freedman (1975:26) and followed by O'Connor (1980:233) on the assumption of the loss of an Aleph by haplography. Such emendation yields the reading: *nipla' 'attah* [TH6381/859, ZH7098/911] (you are wonderful). This would then form a couplet with the following phrase, *'ahabatheka li* [TH160/3807.1/2967.1, ZH173/4200/3276] (your love was mine).

COMMENTARY

David's lament for Saul and Jonathan has long been recognized as one of the finest examples of Hebrew poetry in the Old Testament. Hertzberg (1964:238) characterizes it as "the most beautiful heroic lament of all time" and acknowledges with many others[1] that there is "no reason for doubting David's authorship." Fokkelman (1986:649) speaks of it as a "pearl of Hebrew poetry," which as "a rich and complex work of art . . . demands patience, artistic insight, and subtlety" for its proper interpretation. While there are ongoing discussions and even disagreements on many technical matters dealing with the poem's structural arrangement,[2] verse divisions, and metrical analysis, as well as with textual and lexical questions that cannot be discussed here, the fundamental purpose and theme of the poem is quite clear.

The grief that David and his men exhibited immediately upon hearing the news of the deaths of Saul and Jonathan (1:11-12) is given fuller expression by the author's inclusion of this song of lament, composed by David with the intent that it should be taught to all the people of Judah (1:18). The song was considered of such importance that it was preserved in the extrabiblical *Book of Jashar* (1:18), which appears to have been an anthology of Israelite poems (cf. Josh 10:13) that circulated in Israel during the Old Testament period.

Verse 19 functions as a heading for the composition and captures its central theme in the expression "Oh, how the mighty heroes have fallen!" This refrain is repeated three times in the course of the poem, at its beginning, middle, and end (1:19b, 25a, 27a). It is clear from the opening lines that David regarded Saul and Jonathan as national heroes and their deaths as a calamitous loss to the nation (see notes on 1:19). In 1:20 David voices his concern that the Israelite defeat at Gilboa would be the cause for celebration in the heathen cities of the Philistines, including the city of Gath where he had sought refuge during the time of his flight from Saul (1 Sam 27). Lest there be any misunderstanding among the people of Israel because of his ill-considered alliance with Achish, David expressed repugnance at the thought of Philistine women rejoicing in Israel's defeat and the pagan inhabitants of Philistia reveling in triumph over the people of Yahweh.[3] In 1:21 David gives further expression to his distress by placing a symbolic curse on the mountains of Gilboa; it was on these mountains that the disastrous defeat had occurred and the life of Saul, Israel's divinely anointed king, had been snuffed out (see notes on 1:21). From the opening three verses of the lament, we see that David was able to rise above the personal grievances of the ruptured relationship that existed between Saul and himself and give heartfelt expression of his great sorrow over the loss that the nation had sustained by her military defeat and the death of her leaders in battle.

Saul and Jonathan are eulogized in 1:22-23. Their victories in battle are celebrated and their loyalty to each other in life, as well as their companionship in death, are attested.[4] Then, after speaking of Saul and Jonathan collectively, David devoted a separate pronouncement to each of them individually (1:24, Saul; 1:25-26, Jonathan). He called upon the women of Israel to weep for Saul in recognition of the benefits he brought to the nation during his reign (cf. 1 Sam 14:47-52). (Note that the weeping women of Israel are set in sharp contrast to the joyful women of Philistia; 1:20.) Then, after a repetition of the central theme of the lament, "Oh, how the mighty heroes have fallen in battle!" (1:25a), David paid a special tribute to Jonathan (1:25b-26). The singular place that Jonathan held in David's heart is highlighted not only by the very warm and personal statement of their love for each other, but also by the noticeable change in personal pronouns from the third person, in reference to Saul (1:24), to the first and second person in connection with the relationship between himself and Jonathan (1:26). In the last verse (1:27) the central theme is again reiterated: "Oh, how the mighty heroes have fallen!"

This lament provides an unusual insight into the deepest feelings and thoughts of David at a crucial turning point in his life. Even though Saul had waged a longstanding vendetta against him, and in spite of the fact that Saul had even sought to take his life, David showed no vindictiveness toward him when he learned of his death. Instead of spiteful recriminations for the abuse he had suffered at Saul's hands, and instead of any expression of elation at his demise, David showed only respect and honor for the person whom he continued to recognize as the Lord's anointed, notwithstanding his abuse of the office with which he was entrusted. In all of this David showed himself to be a person worthy of the royal office to which he, too, had already been anointed. And in the larger context of the flow of redemptive history, David's conduct on this occasion points forward to the coming Messiah who would pray for those who crucified him (Luke 23:34), who would reconcile his chosen ones to the Father even when they were his enemies (Rom 5:8), and who would exhort his followers to love their enemies and pray for those who persecuted them (Matt 5:44; Luke 6:27-36; cf. van den Berg 1997:14-15).

ENDNOTES

1. See Gevirtz 1973:72; Holladay 1970:154; Smith 1912:258.
2. See Freedman 1972; Gevirtz 1973; Holladay 1970; O'Connor 1980.
3. Fokkelman (1986:661) notes that this is the reverse of the situation described in 1 Sam 18:6, when David along with Saul and Jonathan were acclaimed by the women of Israel after their victory over the Philistines.
4. Brueggemann (1990a:216) comments, "The poetry of grief looks past the rancors of father and son, the deception of the son and the rage of the father. Those gossip-driven tensions are now unimportant. Death has a way of permitting us to focus on the larger realities, to transcend the details of hurt and affront."

◆ C. David Becomes King over Judah (2 Sam 2:1-7)

**After this, David asked the LORD, "Should
I move back to one of the towns of
Judah?"
"Yes," the LORD replied.
Then David asked, "Which town should
I go to?"
"To Hebron," the LORD answered.
2 David's two wives were Ahinoam from
Jezreel and Abigail, the widow of Nabal
from Carmel. So David and his wives 3 and
his men and their families all moved to
Judah, and they settled in the villages
near Hebron. 4 Then the men of Judah
came to David and anointed him king over
the people of Judah.
When David heard that the men of
Jabesh-gilead had buried Saul, 5 he sent
them this message: "May the LORD bless
you for being so loyal to your master Saul
and giving him a decent burial. 6 May the
LORD be loyal to you in return and reward
you with his unfailing love! And I, too, will
reward you for what you have done. 7 Now
that Saul is dead, I ask you to be my strong
and loyal subjects like the people of Judah,
who have anointed me as their new king."**

NOTES

2:2 ***widow of.*** The literal translation of *'esheth* [TH802, ZH851] is "the wife of."

2:4 ***anointed.*** Heb., *wayyimshekhu* [TH4886, ZH5417].

David heard. Lit., "And they declared to David." The verb *wayyaggidu* [TH5046, ZH5583] (and they declared) is active and assumes "the men of Judah" of the previous sentence as its subject.

2:6 ***May the LORD be loyal to you in return and reward you with his unfailing love!*** Lit., "May the LORD do [show] lovingkindness and truth to you." There is good reason for translating *khesed we'emeth* [TH2617/571, ZH2876/622] (faithfulness and truth) as a single concept (hendiadys, see Williams 1976:§72) yielding the translation, "May the LORD show you true faithfulness."

COMMENTARY

There is no question that the death of Saul marked a major turning point in David's life and launched a new phase in the long process of his rise to the throne. Although

Saul's death meant an end to David's fugitive existence, it at the same time raised a host of questions concerning how David should proceed in dealing with the difficult political issues connected with the transition of power from one regime to another in a nation that had only recently established a monarchy and had no precedents to aid in easing such a momentous change.

Although it must have been clear to David that he and his men could no longer remain in Ziklag, the city given to them by Achish (1 Sam 27:6) and recently destroyed by the Amalekites (1 Sam 30:1), it was not so clear where they should go or what they should do next. This is the setting for David's first recorded action subsequent to learning of Saul's death. David did not want to repeat the mistake he had made when he went to Gath without first seeking the Lord's guidance (cf. 1 Sam 27:1-3), so the very first thing he did was to request the Lord's guidance.[1] When David inquired whether he should return to Judah, the Lord told him that he should; and when David asked to what town he should go, he was told to go to Hebron. This meant that David's decision to move from Ziklag to Hebron was not in the first instance a pragmatic political calculation but rather an act of obedience to an instruction he had received from the Lord (Brueggemann 1990a:219). This does not mean, however, that there were no political overtones to his course of action. Hebron was an important city in Judah. It was located about 19 miles south-southwest of Jerusalem in the Judean hill country, and at 3,000 feet above sea level, was the highest town in Palestine (A. Anderson 1989:22). There were a number of factors that made the city an ideal choice for David's initial resettlement in Israel. The city had strong ties with Israel's founding fathers;[2] it was one of the recipients of the gifts that David had recently sent to a number of cities in Judah after plundering the Amalekites (cf. 1 Sam 30:26-31); and it was a city that belonged to David's own tribe.

Therefore David and his entire entourage,[3] including the two wives with him (Ahinoam of Jezreel[4] and Abigail the widow of Nabal from Carmel) moved from Ziklag to Hebron and its surrounding area, with the result that he was there anointed king (see note on 2:4) over the people of Judah. The reader is merely told that "the men of Judah came to David and anointed him king over the people of Judah" but is given no further information about the circumstances surrounding this significant political event.[5] Perhaps the reason that this second "anointing" of David does not receive as much emphasis as one might expect is that it was more or less a recognition of David's earlier anointing by Samuel (that was accompanied by the gift of God's Spirit; 1 Sam 16:13) and not something entirely new (van den Berg 1997:17). It was the initial anointing by Samuel that was fundamental and that represented God's choice of David as the chosen ruler for his people.[6]

Subsequent to this validation of David as king by the leaders of the tribe of Judah, David again showed respect for his predecessor, Saul, by sending a commendation to the men of Jabesh-gilead for providing Saul with a proper (though headless) burial (2:4-7; cf. 1 Sam 31:11-13). Just as Saul's first act after being chosen as king was to liberate Jabesh-gilead from their Ammonite oppressors (1 Sam 11:1-13), so David's first official royal act was to pay tribute to these same people for their loyalty to Saul. Along with this compliment, David also invited the Jabesh-gileadites to join with the tribe of Judah in their recognition of his succession to Saul as the legitimate ruler over Israel (2:7). By this invitation it is clear that from the very beginning David had his sights set on consolidating his position as ruler over the entirety of God's people.

ENDNOTES

1. Although the means by which David sought guidance from the Lord is not indicated, it was most likely done through the use of the ephod that had been brought to David by Abiathar (1 Sam 23:6). David had used the ephod for seeking God's guidance on other occasions (1 Sam 23:1-4, 9-12; 30:7).
2. As Davis (1999:28) notes, Abraham and Sarah, Isaac and Rebekah, Jacob and Leah were all buried there (Gen 23:17-19; 25:9-10; 49:29-32; 50:13).
3. First Chronicles 12 suggests that the size of David's forces had grown considerably during the time he spent in the strongholds of Judah (1 Chr 12:8-18) and Ziklag (1 Chr 12:1-7, 19-22) and included representatives from the entire nation. At the heart of that chapter is a prophecy of success for David and those who joined with him because "God is the one who helps" him (1 Chr 12:18).
4. This is not the well-known northern Jezreel near the site of the Philistine victory over Israel (cf. 1 Sam 31:7), but rather a town located in the hill country of Judea (cf. Josh 15:55-56), near Carmel, the former home of Nabal and Abigail (1 Sam 25:2-3).
5. Fokkelman (1990:29) comments, "What stands out is that it is mentioned almost in passing, as something which is so self-evident . . . that it takes up little room."
6. As A. Anderson comments (1989:26), "In the light of the Saul narratives, it seems that one became the Lord's anointed once for all." Calvin (1992:55-56) recognized this as well. He notes that "a question might be raised here: How could the men of Judah dare anoint David, given that this would efface the original anointing, or declare it insufficient? And how could David allow it?" Calvin's answer to these questions is that when the men of Judah anointed David, "They were not implying that what Samuel did was ineffective, or that it was not powerful enough to accomplish anything. Rather, it is as though they were replying 'Amen', and ratifying what had been done. We should understand, therefore, that David is not elected king here by the desire of men, but that he received approbation because God authorised it, and thus men agree with it."

◆ D. War between the House of Saul and the House of David (2 Sam 2:8–3:1)

**8But Abner son of Ner, the commander of
Saul's army, had already gone to Maha-
naim with Saul's son Ishbosheth.* 9There
he proclaimed Ishbosheth king over
Gilead, Jezreel, Ephraim, Benjamin, the
land of the Ashurites, and all the rest of
Israel.**

**10Ishbosheth, Saul's son, was forty years
old when he became king, and he ruled
from Mahanaim for two years. Meanwhile,
the people of Judah remained loyal to
David. 11David made Hebron his capital,
and he ruled as king of Judah for seven
and a half years.**

**12One day Abner led Ishbosheth's troops
from Mahanaim to Gibeon. 13About the
same time, Joab son of Zeruiah led David's
troops out and met them at the pool of
Gibeon. The two groups sat down there,
facing each other from opposite sides of
the pool.**

**14Then Abner suggested to Joab, "Let's
have a few of our warriors fight hand to
hand here in front of us."**

"All right," Joab agreed. 15So twelve men were chosen to fight from each side—twelve men of Benjamin representing Ishbosheth son of Saul, and twelve representing David. 16Each one grabbed his opponent by the hair and thrust his sword into the other's side so that all of them died. So this place at Gibeon has been known ever since as the Field of Swords.*

17A fierce battle followed that day, and Abner and the men of Israel were defeated by the forces of David.

18Joab, Abishai, and Asahel—the three sons of Zeruiah—were among David's forces that day. Asahel could run like a gazelle, 19and he began chasing Abner. He pursued him relentlessly, not stopping for anything. 20When Abner looked back and saw him coming, he called out, "Is that you, Asahel?"

"Yes, it is," he replied.

21"Go fight someone else!" Abner warned. "Take on one of the younger men, and strip him of his weapons." But Asahel kept right on chasing Abner.

22Again Abner shouted to him, "Get away from here! I don't want to kill you. How could I ever face your brother Joab again?"

23But Asahel refused to turn back, so Abner thrust the butt end of his spear through Asahel's stomach, and the spear came out through his back. He stumbled to the ground and died there. And everyone who came by that spot stopped and stood still when they saw Asahel lying there.

24When Joab and Abishai found out what had happened, they set out after Abner. The sun was just going down as they arrived at the hill of Ammah near Giah, along the road to the wilderness of Gibeon. 25Abner's troops from the tribe of Benjamin regrouped there at the top of the hill to take a stand.

26Abner shouted down to Joab, "Must we always be killing each other? Don't you realize that bitterness is the only result? When will you call off your men from chasing their Israelite brothers?"

27Then Joab said, "God only knows what would have happened if you hadn't spoken, for we would have chased you all night if necessary." 28So Joab blew the ram's horn, and his men stopped chasing the troops of Israel.

29All that night Abner and his men retreated through the Jordan Valley.* They crossed the Jordan River, traveling all through the morning,* and didn't stop until they arrived at Mahanaim.

30Meanwhile, Joab and his men also returned home. When Joab counted his casualties, he discovered that only 19 men were missing in addition to Asahel. 31But 360 of Abner's men had been killed, all from the tribe of Benjamin. 32Joab and his men took Asahel's body to Bethlehem and buried him there in his father's tomb. Then they traveled all night and reached Hebron at daybreak.

CHAPTER 3

That was the beginning of a long war between those who were loyal to Saul and those loyal to David. As time passed David became stronger and stronger, while Saul's dynasty became weaker and weaker.

2:8 *Ishbosheth* is another name for Esh-baal. **2:16** Hebrew *Helkath-hazzurim.* **2:29a** Hebrew *the Arabah.* **2:29b** Or *continued on through the Bithron.* The meaning of the Hebrew is uncertain.

NOTES

2:13 ***Gibeon.*** The MT contains *yakhdaw* [TH3162B, ZH3481] (together) after Gibeon, which would be redundant if translated here.

2:14 ***Let's have a few of our warriors.*** Lit., "Let the young men arise." The verb is a jussive of *qum* [TH6965, ZH7756] (arise) strengthened by the entreating particle *na'* [TH4994, ZH5528].

fight hand to hand. Lit., "make sport." The Piel of *sakhaq* [TH7832, ZH8471] (to laugh) normally has the idea of "merrymaking" or "play." Here it seems to refer to engagement in single-handed combat (cf. NEB, "join in single combat").

2:16 ***Field of Swords.*** The Hebrew *khelqath hatsurim* [TH2521, ZH2763] is usually understood as either the "Field of the Flints" (or daggers, from *tsor* [TH6864, ZH7644]) or the "Field of the Adversaries" (from *tsar* [TH6862A, ZH7640]).

2:21 ***strip him of his weapons.*** The word *khalitsah* [TH2488/2050.2, ZH2723/2257] occurs only two times in the OT (here and in Judg 14:19). Because the root idea is "what is stripped off" (BDB 322), it may have reference to "garments" (as in Judg 14:19) and more specifically in this case to "battle gear" (as suggested by A. Anderson 1989:39-40) or "weapons" as in the NLT rendering. Gordon (1986:215) suggests the word "may refer to the belt worn by soldiers as a symbol of their military prowess." The word is rendered differently by various English translations: NRSV and NASB as "spoil"; NIV as "weapons"; NJPS as "tunic."

2:23 ***the butt end of his spear.*** Hoerth (1998:265) points out that the "butt end of a spear was sometimes fitted with two prongs so it could be stuck in the ground while not being carried. As Joab's brother learned, the prongs could be as deadly as the spearhead on the other end."

2:29 ***traveling all through the morning.*** The meaning of *habbithron* [TH1338, ZH1443], which occurs only here, is uncertain. The term is usually taken as a proper noun (BDB 144), but since the verb *bathar* [TH1334, ZH1439] means "to divide in parts" and the noun *bether* [TH1335, ZH1440] means "a divided part," *habbithron* has sometimes been taken as "division" or "cleft" and understood as the "ravine" or "gorge" that led to Mahanaim (see NLT mg, "continued on through the Bithron"). Others have understood it as an adverbial accusative of time rather than place, denoting the half of the day prior to noon time (S. R. Driver 1913:245 and NLT rendering).

2:32 ***at daybreak.*** Lit., "It was light for them in Hebron" (Joüon and Muraoka §152e).

3:1 ***David became stronger and stronger.*** For the use of a verbal adjective after the participle to express continuity, see Joüon and Muraoka §123s.

COMMENTARY

That the recognition of David as the successor to Saul by all Israel was not going to materialize quickly and without conflict[1] is made abundantly clear by the remainder of chapter 2. We are told in 2:8 that Abner,[2] the commander of Saul's army (cf. 1 Sam 14:50), took Saul's only surviving son, Ishbosheth,[3] to Mahanaim in Transjordan,[4] and there proclaimed him king not only over the territories of northern Israel but also over "all the rest of Israel" (2:9), which included Judah.[5] Although no explanation is given for the selection of Mahanaim as a provisional capital for Ishbosheth's government, it is likely that Abner sought a place for them beyond the reach of the Philistines subsequent to their victory at Mount Gilboa (A. Anderson 1989:33). In this and subsequent events, it is clear that Abner is the power behind the throne and that Ishbosheth was used by Abner to lend legitimacy to his own desire to retain military and political influence in the land.

The literary arrangement of this narrative unit (2:8–3:1) exhibits a clear chiastic structure that accentuates Abner's important role in the unfolding of the events that are described.[6] In 2:12-17 it is Abner who takes the first step toward forcing a confrontation between his own forces and those that had pledged their loyalty to David in Judah.[7] Abner's movement of troops from Mahanaim to Gibeon (about five miles northeast of Jerusalem in the territory of Benjamin) was clearly intended to let David know that his assumption of royal power in Judah would not go unchallenged.[8] In response, Joab[9] led a contingent of David's troops from Hebron to Gibeon, where they encountered Abner's forces at the "pool of Gibeon."[10] In an attempt to avoid a full-scale battle between the two forces, Abner proposed that each side select 12 men to engage in what might be called a battle by proxy (2:14).[11] When this representative battle ended in a draw, a larger conflict quickly ensued (2:15-16), and Joab's forces were victorious (2:17) while those of Abner were forced to flee for their lives.

The pursuit of Abner by Joab's brother Asahel is described in 2:18-23. When Asahel caught up with Abner, Abner urged him not to press his luck by forcing a fight between them. When Asahel refused, Abner killed him, although he was reluctant to do so because he did not want to give any unnecessary offense to Asahel's brother Joab (2:22). The reason for Abner's unwillingness to offend Joab is not mentioned. Some have suggested that he did not want to create a case of bloodguilt, although that does not seem applicable for instances of death in battle and does not seem to be the way Joab responded upon learning of his brother's death (cf. 2:27-28). Others suppose some sort of prior friendship existed between Abner and Joab. In the larger narrative context it seems more likely that Abner already harbored some doubts about the long-term success of his alliance with Ishbosheth and anticipated that a time might come when it would be prudent to cast his lot with David. If this were to happen, then a good relationship with Joab would be of great importance.

When Joab and Abishai learned what had happened to their brother Asahel, they gathered their forces and went in pursuit of Abner and his forces (2:24-25). The two armies met at "the hill of Ammah near Giah" (2:24; site identification is uncertain), where Abner appealed to Joab to abandon his pursuit in order to avoid further bloodshed (2:26). Joab blamed the entire episode on Abner (2:27) but nevertheless accepted his proposal for a truce, and the two armies retreated to their home bases. Abner's forces went back to Mahanaim and Joab's to Hebron (2:29-30). The final report of casualties in the initial battle counted 360 dead from Abner's forces, but only 19 from those of Joab. Joab took the body of Asahel and buried him at the family burial plot in Bethlehem (2:32). Although the relationship between the rival parties for the throne in Israel remained tense, it became increasingly clear that David was likely to prevail (3:1).

ENDNOTES

1. Fokkelman (1990:38, 40) finds in this passage "the seeds of conflict between a regime created by a high-handed general and a monarchy announced long ago by a prophet and currently recognized by a community. . . . The fact of two kings in one country is quite explosive and quickly leads to strife."
2. Abner was a cousin of Saul. They were both grandsons of Abiel. Kish the father of Saul and Ner the father of Abner were brothers, the sons of Abiel (cf. 1 Sam 9:1; 14:50-51).
3. This is shown by comparison of 1 Sam 31:2 with 1 Chr 8:33; 9:39, where a fourth son of Saul (named Esh-baal [man of Baal] instead of Ishbosheth ["man of shame"]) is listed. It is usually assumed that even though "Baal" (meaning "lord," or "master") may

originally have been used in reference to Yahweh, its more common association with the heathen Canaanite deity led later scribes to substitute *bosheth* (shame) for the original "Baal" (master or lord). It appears that the son of Saul named Ishvi (perhaps a shortened form of Ishiah [man of Yahweh]) in 1 Sam 14:49 is the same individual as Ishbosheth / Esh-baal (so NLT mg).

4. The precise location of Mahanaim is uncertain, but it is usually considered to be near the border between Gad and Manasseh on the northern side of the Jabbok River in Transjordan.
5. There is insufficient information in the text to completely resolve the question of how to harmonize the statements that Ishbosheth reigned for two years in Mahanaim (2:10) and that David reigned for seven and a half years in Hebron (2:11). Because it appears that David became king over all Israel shortly after the death of Saul (5:1-5), it would seem best to link the two years of Ishbosheth's reign with the last years of David's reign in Hebron. Perhaps it took Abner and Ishbosheth a number of years to gain recognition of the legitimacy of Ishbosheth's rule over the areas mentioned in 2:9.
6. This structure has been aptly framed by Youngblood (1992:822) in the following manner:

   A. Ishbosheth is king in Mahanaim; David is king in Hebron (2:8-11).
      B. Abner suggests that hostilities begin (2:12-17).
         C. Abner kills Asahel (2:18-23).
      B'. Abner suggests that hostilities cease (2:24-28).
   A'. Ishbosheth's men return to Mahanaim; David's men return to Hebron (2:29-32).

7. Abner's support of Ishbosheth involved a conscious decision to refuse to accept the Lord's choice of David as king in place of Saul. David had challenged Abner to make that choice on a previous occasion (see commentary on 1 Sam 26:15-16), and Abner had chosen to remain aligned with Saul. Abner was aware of David's legitimate claim to the throne (see 3:9, 17-18).
8. Davis (1999:35) comments, "It is Abner's deliberate attempt to impose northern might on David's Judean kingdom. Abner is on the attack."
9. Joab (previously mentioned in 1 Sam 26:6) was a nephew of David who later became the commander of David's armies and showed himself to be a ruthless and powerful leader (his mother, Zeruiah, was a sister or half sister of David, cf. 17:25; 1 Chr 2:16; his father is never mentioned).
10. Walled cities often had pools or reservoirs fed by springs to ensure water supply during a time of siege (cf. the pool of Siloam in Jerusalem, Neh 3:15; John 9:7, 11). Excavations at Gibeon have revealed a tunnel leading to a spring outside the city wall (Pritchard 1962:35ff).
11. The encounter of David and Goliath (1 Sam 17) is another example of representative combat. Fensham (1970:357-358), citing parallels in Hittite literature, suggests that such encounters may be understood as an ordeal by battle in which the deity is viewed as an arbiter who gives the verdict by an ordeal on the guilty party. Although Fensham admits that "nowhere in the narrative of 2 Sam. ii 12ff. the Lord is *expressis verbis* called in as Judge to decide the ordeal by battle, the role of the Lord who has chosen David and rejected Saul is clearly discernable in the background." It might also be argued, however, that if, in fact, Abner and Joab understood the representative combat to be battle by ordeal, the fact that the battle ended in a draw demonstrates that on this occasion the Lord refused to be manipulated in this way.

◆ VII. David's Reign (2 Sam 3:2–20:26)
A. David's Sons Born in Hebron (2 Sam 3:2-5)

2These are the sons who were born to David in Hebron:

The oldest was Amnon, whose mother
was Ahinoam from Jezreel.
3 The second was Daniel,* whose mother
was Abigail, the widow of Nabal
from Carmel.
The third was Absalom, whose mother
was Maacah, the daughter of
Talmai, king of Geshur.
4 The fourth was Adonijah, whose
mother was Haggith.
The fifth was Shephatiah, whose
mother was Abital.
5 The sixth was Ithream, whose mother
was Eglah, David's wife.

These sons were all born to David in Hebron.

3:3 As in parallel text at 1 Chr 3:1 (see also Greek version, which reads *Daluia*, and Dead Sea Scrolls, which read *Dan[iel]*); Hebrew reads *Kileab*.

NOTES

3:3 *Daniel.* See NLT mg. The reading is uncertain. The LXX has *Dalouia,* while 1 Chr 3:1 has *daniyye'l* [TH1840, ZH1975] (Daniel). The text of 4QSam[a], although fragmented here, in fact begins with the equivalent of *dal-*, and was likely in agreement with the LXX. Aquila, Symmachus, and Theodotian read *Abia.* It is possible that Daniel and Kileab (or "Chileab," KJV) were alternate names, but there is a strong suspicion that Kileab (found in MT) is the result of dittography since *l'b* in *kil'ab* [TH3609, ZH3976] are the same letters as the first three letters of the next word *la'abigel* [TH3807.1/26, ZH4200/28] (to Abigail).

COMMENTARY

It has been the general consensus of mainstream biblical scholars that two major blocks of tradition centering on the life of David (the Narrative of the Rise of David in 1 Sam 16:14–2 Sam 5, and the Court History of David [sometimes designated the Succession Narrative], chs 9–20; 1 Kgs 1–2)[1] have been combined to form the description of David's life and reign in 1–2 Samuel.[2] However, it is my view that considerations of narrative structure suggest that 2 Samuel 3:2–20:6 should be regarded as a literary unity. This conclusion is based on the detailed analysis of the literary structure of 1–2 Samuel by Klement (2000), who calls attention to the presence of the characteristic features of the literary structure of the so-called Samuel Appendix (chs 21–24) in earlier sections of the book.[3] Of significance for marking the beginning of the author's description of the reign of David is the structuring function of a series of "lists" that appear in three of the four ring structures[4] that together constitute the remainder of 2 Samuel.[5] The first of these four ring structures (*a-b-c-c-b-a*) is found in 3:2–5:16. It consists of six parts and is opened and closed by a list of David's sons. The first list is of the sons who were born while David was in Hebron (3:2-5), and the second list is of the sons who were born while David was in Jerusalem (5:13-16). Four narrative units make up the core of this literary grouping. The two "*b*" units concern David's becoming king over all Israel, first by means of a covenant made with Abner (3:6-21) and later by means of a covenant made with the elders of all Israel (5:1-12). The two central units (*c-c*) describe the murder of Abner (3:22-39) and the murder of Ishbosheth (4:1-12).

During the seven and a half years that David resided in Hebron, he married four women in addition to the two wives (Ahinoam and Abigail)[6] he had acquired before he left Ziklag to settle in Hebron (cf. 2:2). His new wives were: Maacah, the daughter of Talmai, king of Geshur, a small kingdom in northern Transjordan; and Haggith, Abital, and Eglah, of whom nothing further is known. Although no information is given about the particulars surrounding any of these marriages, it is possible, particularly with Maacah, that political alliances may have played a role. But no matter what justification David may have given for his multiple marriages, this action was a violation of Moses's statement that the king in Israel "must not take many wives for himself" (Deut 17:17). So this surprising announcement, standing as it does at the very beginning of the description of the reign of David, sounds an ominous note. And sure enough, as the reign of David unfolds, three of the sons born during David's stay in Hebron (Amnon, Absalom, Adonijah) later become the source of great heartache for both him and his family.[7]

ENDNOTES

1. Second Samuel 6 is usually viewed as part of an originally separate Ark Narrative that is now divided between 1 and 2 Samuel (1 Sam 4:1–7:1 and 2 Sam 6).
2. See the fuller discussion of these issues in the Introduction under the heading "Date and Occasion of Writing."
3. See the fuller discussion in the Introduction under the heading "Literary Style."
4. (1) 3:2–5:16; (2) 5:17–8:14; (3) 8:15–20:26; (4) 21:1–24:25.
5. See the diagram in the Introduction under the heading "Literary Style." There are three sets of double lists that serve a structuring function in the remainder of the book. These lists are of David's sons (3:2-5; 5:13-16), his officials (8:15-18; 20:23-26), and his warriors (21:15-22; 23:8-39).
6. This does not include Michal whom Saul had given to another man after David fled from his court. She is returned to David in 3:14 where he calls her "my wife."
7. Amnon, who raped his half sister Tamar, with the result that he was murdered by her brother Absalom (3:2; cf. chs 13–14); Absalom, who conspired against his father and forced him to flee Jerusalem (3:3; cf. chs 15–19); Adonijah, who attempted to displace Solomon from succession to the throne (3:4; cf. 1 Kgs 1–2).

◆ B. Abner Defects to David's Kingship (2 Sam 3:6–21)

6As the war between the house of Saul
and the house of David went on, Abner
became a powerful leader among those
loyal to Saul. 7One day Ishbosheth,* Saul's
son, accused Abner of sleeping with one
of his father's concubines, a woman
named Rizpah, daughter of Aiah.

8Abner was furious. "Am I some Judean
dog to be kicked around like this?" he
shouted. "After all I have done for your father, Saul, and his family and friends by
not handing you over to David, is this my
reward—that you find fault with me about
this woman? 9May God strike me and even
kill me if I don't do everything I can to help
David get what the LORD has promised him!
10I'm going to take Saul's kingdom and
give it to David. I will establish the throne
of David over Israel as well as Judah, all the
way from Dan in the north to Beersheba in
the south." 11Ishbosheth didn't dare say
another word because he was afraid of
what Abner might do.

12Then Abner sent messengers to David,

saying, "Doesn't the entire land belong to
you? Make a solemn pact with me, and I
will help turn over all of Israel to you."
13"All right," David replied, "but I will
not negotiate with you unless you bring
back my wife Michal, Saul's daughter,
when you come."
14David then sent this message to Ish-
bosheth, Saul's son: "Give me back my
wife Michal, for I bought her with the
lives* of 100 Philistines."
15So Ishbosheth took Michal away from
her husband, Palti* son of Laish. 16Palti
followed along behind her as far as Bahu-
rim, weeping as he went. Then Abner told
him, "Go back home!" So Palti returned.
17Meanwhile, Abner had consulted with
the elders of Israel. "For some time now,"
he told them, "you have wanted to make
David your king. 18Now is the time! For the
LORD has said, 'I have chosen David to save
my people Israel from the hands of the Phi-
listines and from all their other enemies.'"
19Abner also spoke with the men of Benja-
min. Then he went to Hebron to tell David
that all the people of Israel and Benjamin
had agreed to support him.
20When Abner and twenty of his men
came to Hebron, David entertained them
with a great feast. 21Then Abner said to
David, "Let me go and call an assembly of
all Israel to support my lord the king. They
will make a covenant with you to make
you their king, and you will rule over
everything your heart desires." So David
sent Abner safely on his way.

3:7 *Ishbosheth* is another name for Esh-baal. 3:14 Hebrew *the foreskins.* 3:15 As in 1 Sam 25:44; Hebrew reads *Paltiel,* a variant spelling of Palti.

NOTES

3:6 *Abner became a powerful leader.* Lit., "He was making himself strong." On the use of a participle in reference to the past with *hayah* [TH1961, ZH2118] (to be), see Joüon and Muraoka §1121f.

3:7 *Ishbosheth.* The MT has no explicit subject, although a few Hebrew mss have *'ish-bosheth* [TH378, ZH410] (Ishbosheth). The LXX uncials Alexandrinus, Coislinianis, and Basilio-Vaticanus have "Ishbosheth son of Saul," while LXX Vaticanus and Lucianic mss have "Mephibosheth son of Saul."

3:12 *and I will help turn over all of Israel to you.* In the Hebrew text, this clause is introduced by *wehinneh* [TH2050.1/2009, ZH2256/2180] (and behold), which in this instance is used to introduce a purpose clause (see McCarthy 1980:339).

3:13 *unless you bring.* The MT is, lit., "unless before your bringing." S. R. Driver (1913:248) points out that *ki 'im* [TH3588/518, ZH3954/561] (unless) and *lipne* [TH3807.1/6440, ZH4200/7156] (before) exclude one another. It should read either *lipne hebi'aka* [TH935, ZH995] (before your bringing) or *ki 'im hebe'tha* [TH935, ZH995] (except you bring).

3:16 *weeping as he went.* See GKC §113s regarding the coordination of two infinitive absolutes, here, "to weep" and "to go."

3:18 *David to save.* Many mss and most versions have the first-person singular *'oshia'* [TH3467, ZH3828], "I [the Lord] will save," rather than the infinitive construct/Hiphil perfect third-person masc. sg., (*hoshia'* [TH3467, ZH3828]) of the MT. A. Anderson (1989:53) suggests that the original reading may have had the infinitive absolute before the imperfect, intensifying the meaning: "I will indeed save."

COMMENTARY

In this fascinating account of intrigue and treachery within the royal court of Ishbosheth, the reader is given further insight into the ambition and duplicity of Abner, the kingmaker in the north. When Abner was accused by Ishbosheth of sleeping with Rizpah, one of Saul's concubines, Abner became so infuriated that he threatened to defect to David and deliver the support of the northern tribes to David as well (3:8-10). The background for the importance that Ishbosheth seems to have attached to Abner's relationship with Rizpah is the ancient Near Eastern idea that a sexual relationship with a concubine of the former ruler constituted a claim to the royal office.[1] Abner understood very well what Ishbosheth was suggesting by his reprimand, and responded by saying in effect, "If this is all the respect I get for what I have done for you, see what good your claim to the throne is without me." Then in a sudden reversal of allegiance Abner told Ishbosheth that he would deliver his kingdom over to David.[2] Included in his remarks is the revealing statement that he would do all he could to "help David get what the LORD has promised him" (3:9). From this assertion it is clear that Abner knew from the beginning that the Lord intended for David to rule in Israel. In spite of this knowledge, he had so far been unwilling to relinquish the position of power he had enjoyed in the court of Saul. To show that he was making no idle threat, Abner sent representatives to David in Hebron with the message that if David would make a pact with him, then he would help bring all Israel to David's side (3:12). Besides the treachery involved in this defection from Ishbosheth, it is clear that Abner was now devising a strategy designed to curry favor with David, with whom he envisioned a more promising future.

Given the background of political intrigue and duplicity connected with Abner's strategy, it is surprising for the reader to learn that David quickly agreed to accept his proposals, although only on the condition that Michal, Saul's daughter and rightfully his wife (cf. 1 Sam 18:20-28; 25:44), be returned to him (3:13). It is not clear whether this demand by David was motivated by personal devotion to Michal or by the desire to gain political capital for acceptance of the legitimacy of his kingship by virtue of marriage to the daughter of the former king. Michal had in the meantime been given in marriage to another man, Palti, after David had left the court (cf. 1 Sam 25:44). Surprisingly, Ishbosheth acquiesced to David's demand, and Abner delivered Michal to David in Hebron. The narrative tells the reader nothing about Michal's reception by David upon her arrival in Hebron, and her significance now seems to be merely that of a political pawn in the chess game being played by Abner and David. Ishbosheth's compliance in the arrangement is most likely explained by the statement in 3:11 that he was fearful of what Abner might do if he resisted his agenda. In the meantime Abner lobbied the leadership of the northern tribes, including Benjamin, the tribe of Saul, to throw their support behind David. In these consultations Abner made the intriguing comment that "For some time now . . . you have wanted to make David your king" (3:17). It appears that Abner realized that his alliance with Ishbosheth was doomed to failure, and that support for David had been growing in the north.[3] After laying the groundwork for the acceptance of David as king over all Israel, Abner took 20 of his men and went to Hebron where he was received by David with open arms. At a festive banquet, Abner promised David that the northern territories were prepared to accept him as their king and was sent away with the understanding that his mission was accomplished (3:20-21).[4]

Many questions can be raised about the dealings of both Abner and David in this passage. Was David beginning to play the political game by seeking legitimacy for his claim to the throne through reinstating his marriage to the daughter of the former king? Where is the patience that David had displayed for such a long time in waiting for the Lord to place him on the throne in his own time and way? Did David really need the assistance of a rogue like Abner to bring him to power in Israel? Should David have agreed to make a pact with him? In this situation, why is there no reference to David's desire to seek the Lord's will as with his move from Ziklag to Hebron (cf. 2:1)? In fact, one might even ask where God is in all the intrigues of this chapter. The narrator does not address any of these questions, and the reader is left to ponder them in the larger context of the flow of events in this section of the book of Samuel. One thing is abundantly clear: Events were quickly moving toward the realization of God's promise that David would be king over all Israel (cf. 1 Sam 13:14; 15:28; 16:1-13; 24:20; 25:28-31; 26:25). Here we see that God was working not just in spite of human plots and schemes but even by means of them (van den Berg 1997:24). This, of course, gives no sanction to the behavior of either Abner or David. Both remain completely responsible before God for their decisions and actions. But, as Scripture makes clear on numerous occasions, even the wicked actions of sinful human beings may be used by God to bring about the advance of his redemptive purposes (cf. Gen 50:20). It is this perspective that must be kept in mind when reading about these fascinating but disturbing episodes in the rise of David to the throne.

ENDNOTES

1. Brueggemann (1990a:226) comments, "We should not misunderstand Abner's move. It was not simply a sexual act. It was a defiant public, political challenge that could not be ignored." Fokkelman (1990:70) notes that "reaching for the harem means reaching for power and at least giving rise to the impression of being a pretender to the throne." For other examples of this practice in the OT, see 12:8; 16:21; 1 Kgs 2:22.
2. Fokkelman (1990:72) suggests that Abner may have begun his relationship with Ishbosheth out of "a genuine desire to continue Saulide rule" but after experiencing serious disappointments with him, Ishbosheth's accusation became the straw that broke the camel's back.
3. Fokkelman (1990:88) points out that if what Abner said was untrue it would have "provoked protest and irritation in his audience." But at the same time, this means that now "it becomes clearly visible that Abner's own project, the truncated Saulide state, was a forced and high-handed construction which was really doomed to an inglorious collapse."
4. Although there is no explicit statement in the narrative that David and Abner sealed their alliance with a treaty or covenant, there are hints in the text that lend support to this conclusion (Gordon 1990a:29-32). A "great feast" is mentioned in 3:20. As Gordon (1990a:20) notes, "The sharing of a meal as a feature of covenant-making in the ancient Near East is too well-known to require much comment here." A second hint that David and Abner concluded a covenant is the "thrice repeated statement in verses 21-23 that Abner left 'in peace.'" In many contexts the term "peace" carries a covenantal connotation, and may do so here as well (Gordon 1990a:29). Finally, the fivefold curse that David places upon Joab (3:29) may reflect the transfer to Joab of the covenant curse that properly would fall upon David for violation of his covenant with Abner (Gordon 1990a:31). Gordon argues that "the oath of 29b . . . is in narrative apologetic terms the reflex of the covenant or pact of verses 12-21. It draws attention to the fact. . . . that David and Abner were covenant partners, and it thus reinforces the narrator's point that David was so bound by his covenant undertaking as to be incapable of plotting Abner's death."

◆ C. The Murder of Abner; David's Lament (2 Sam 3:22-39)

22 But just after David had sent Abner
away in safety, Joab and some of David's
troops returned from a raid, bringing
much plunder with them. 23 When Joab
arrived, he was told that Abner had just
been there visiting the king and had been
sent away in safety.

24 Joab rushed to the king and demanded,
"What have you done? What do you mean
by letting Abner get away? 25 You know per-
fectly well that he came to spy on you and
find out everything you're doing!"

26 Joab then left David and sent mes-
sengers to catch up with Abner, asking
him to return. They found him at the well
of Sirah and brought him back, though
David knew nothing about it. 27 When Ab-
ner arrived back at Hebron, Joab took him
aside at the gateway as if to speak with
him privately. But then he stabbed Abner
in the stomach and killed him in revenge
for killing his brother Asahel.

28 When David heard about it, he de-
clared, "I vow by the LORD that I and
my kingdom are forever innocent of this
crime against Abner son of Ner. 29 Joab
and his family are the guilty ones. May
the family of Joab be cursed in every gen-
eration with a man who has open sores or
leprosy* or who walks on crutches* or dies
by the sword or begs for food!"

30 So Joab and his brother Abishai killed
Abner because Abner had killed their
brother Asahel at the battle of Gibeon.

31 Then David said to Joab and all those
who were with him, "Tear your clothes
and put on burlap. Mourn for Abner." And
King David himself walked behind the
procession to the grave. 32 They buried
Abner in Hebron, and the king and all the
people wept at his graveside. 33 Then the
king sang this funeral song for Abner:

"Should Abner have died as fools die?
34 Your hands were not bound;
your feet were not chained.
No, you were murdered—
the victim of a wicked plot."

All the people wept again for Abner.
35 David had refused to eat anything on
the day of the funeral, and now everyone
begged him to eat. But David had made a
vow, saying, "May God strike me and even
kill me if I eat anything before sun-
down."

36 This pleased the people very much. In
fact, everything the king did pleased
them! 37 So everyone in Judah and all Is-
rael understood that David was not re-
sponsible for Abner's murder.

38 Then King David said to his officials,
"Don't you realize that a great command-
er has fallen today in Israel? 39 And even
though I am the anointed king, these two
sons of Zeruiah—Joab and Abishai—are
too strong for me to control. So may the
LORD repay these evil men for their evil
deeds."

3:29a Or *or a contagious skin disease*. The Hebrew word used here can describe various skin diseases.
3:29b Or *who is effeminate;* Hebrew reads *who handles a spindle*.

NOTES

3:22 ***But just after.*** For the use of *hinneh* [TH2009, ZH2180] in the sense of immediacy, see Lambdin (1971:168-169).

3:24 ***What do you mean by letting Abner get away?*** Lit., "Why did you send him away? Now he is gone!" The infinitive absolute after the verb (*wayyelek halok* [TH1980, ZH2143]) may intensify the idea of the verb or indicate continuance. Here the former seems preferable. See GKC §113r, u.

3:28 ***I vow by the LORD.*** Lit., "Before the LORD." The word *me'im* [TH4480/5973, ZH4946/6640] (before) is used with the idea of the exoneration regarded as coming from the Lord—i.e., the Lord is the author or source of the acquittal (see BDB 579).

3:29 *who walks on crutches.* Whether to translate *umakhaziq bappelek* [TH2388/6418, ZH2616/7134] as "walk on a staff/crutch" or "handle a spindle" is debated. McCarter (1984:118) cites evidence from the Karatepe inscription that Phoenician *plkm* means "crutches" and concludes "this sense seems better to me here." It is clear, however, that the noun *pelek* is used in Prov 31:19 for "spindle" (cf. KJV). As Layton (1989:84-85) points out, in the ancient Near East there was a clear "nexus between the spindle and female beings. The association between these two is strong, and we are justified in describing the spindle as the feminine implement par excellence." Layton says that "for one of Joab's male descendants . . . to grasp a spindle was to strike a note of discord in the mind of the reader. Instead of being mighty men of war like their forefather, Joab's descendants would by the curse be relegated to menial women's work."

3:31 *Mourn for Abner.* Lit., "mourn before (*lipne* [TH3807.1/6440, ZH4200/7156]) Abner." Some interpreters understand this statement to mean that Joab was to walk "before" or in front of Abner in the funeral procession—that is, David compelled Joab to lead the funeral procession. In the next phrase David is said to have walked behind the procession.

King David. Brueggemann (1990a:230) calls the reader's attention to the fact that this is the first time that the narrator links David's personal name with the royal office. He comments, "It is when the threat of the north has been decisively eliminated in the death of Abner that the throne is secure enough to warrant this powerful phrase. No one doubts David's governance in this moment of grief, honor, and rebuke."

3:33 *Should Abner have died.* The imperfect is used here with the modal nuance of "must." See Joüon and Muraoka §113m.

3:38 *a great commander.* This is often translated "a prince and a great man" (cf. NIV). But because *sar* [TH8269, ZH8569] may mean either "prince" or "commander," the expression *sar wegadol* [TH1419, ZH1524] (great) is probably best taken as hendiadys, i.e., "a great commander," as NLT (see Youngblood 1992:841-842).

COMMENTARY

Upon the successful conclusion of the negotiations between David and Abner, things appeared to be moving toward an outcome with significant benefits for both individuals. David would finally become king over all Israel, and Abner would have positioned himself to play an important role in David's court. But neither David nor Abner anticipated Joab's reaction to the agreement that they had made. During the time of Abner's visit to Hebron, Joab had been away from the city on a military expedition.[1] Joab was furious when he returned to the city and learned that during his absence Abner had consulted with David. After accusing David of naiveté for not having discerned Abner's allegedly sinister intentions, he quickly sent messengers after him with the request that he return to Hebron. Joab, and perhaps Abishai, met Abner at the city gate, and leading him to believe that he wanted to continue discussions with him, he suddenly drew his sword and killed him.

Ostensibly the justification for Joab's action was revenge for Abner's killing of Joab's brother Asahel (2:22-23). But the reader suspects that there is more going on than is explicit in the text. Certainly there was not room in David's court for two strongmen of the likes of Joab and Abner. It is clear from this and other passages that Joab was someone who brooked no rivals (cf. especially 20:8-10 where Joab is depicted as the murderer of Amasa who had been appointed commander of David's armies in place of himself). In the aftermath of Joab's murder of Abner, even David admitted that Joab was too strong for him (3:39). Future events will show that while Joab was an important contributor to David's military success, he was a complex personality who sometimes chose to go his own way, even defying David's explicit commands.

But to return to the intrigues of David's court at Hebron, we find that David's immediate reaction upon learning of Abner's murder was to emphatically distance himself from any complicity with it. The narrator places David's statement of innocence ("I vow by the LORD that I and my kingdom are forever innocent of this crime against Abner son of Ner") in the verse (3:28) that immediately follows the description of Joab's murder of Abner (3:27). David then took a number of additional actions to accentuate his strong disapproval of Joab's behavior: He placed a curse on Joab and his descendants (3:29); he ordered Joab and his warriors to publicly mourn for Abner (3:31; see note); he participated in the funeral procession and openly wept at Abner's grave (3:31-32); he composed a lament for Abner as he had done for Saul and Jonathan (3:33-34); he publicly fasted until the end of the day of the funeral (3:35), and later he eulogized Abner with the statement that "a great commander" had fallen in Israel (3:38; see note). The result was that "everyone in Judah (lit., "all the people") and all Israel understood that David was not responsible for Abner's murder" (3:37).[2]

While the text is clear in its assertions that David was innocent of any involvement in Abner's murder,[3] questions may still be asked about the wisdom of David's negotiations with him. It could be argued that David should have been more careful about entrusting his rise to the throne over all Israel to the schemes of a person who had shown himself untrustworthy in his relationship with Ishbosheth. As the events of this chapter unfold, another question arises concerning David's ongoing relationship with Joab the commander of his army. In the aftermath of the murder of Abner, David seemed to be unwilling or unable to bring Joab to justice. It is not until David was on his deathbed that he instructed Solomon to put Joab to death because of his murders of Abner and Amasa (cf. 1 Kgs 2:5-6, 31-33). For the present, however, David merely forced Joab to participate in the funeral procession for Abner, and then placed a curse on him and his family. He took no overt disciplinary action against him. In this instance one wonders if justice has really been served, and at the same time one wonders what David's actions on this occasion augur for the future.

ENDNOTES

1. He was probably continuing the sorts of raids that he and David had conducted from Ziklag (1 Sam 27:8-9).
2. The narrator uses the expression "all the people" seven times and "all Israel" once in 3:31-37 to emphasize the universal recognition that David had no part in Abner's murder, and that he genuinely grieved over what had happened to him.
3. This, however, does not mean that interpreters have always taken the text at face value. There is, in fact, a long tradition of those who have concluded that the narrative is a propagandistic document designed by its author or editor to hide David's complicity in Abner's murder (see the discussion above on "The Narrative of the Rise

of David" [1 Sam 16–2 Sam 5] prefaced to the commentary on 1 Sam 16). Accordingly McKenzie (2000:121) says that it "is logical to assume that Joab acted on orders from David, who was the chief beneficiary of Abner's death." Proposing a somewhat less overt scenario, J. VanderKam concludes that David cynically calculated that Joab would kill Abner, and that the purpose of his pact with Abner was to cause this very thing to happen (1980:533). Cryer (1985:392) takes a much more negative view of the text and claims that there "are reasons for supposing that the various texts providing Joab with a motive for murdering Abner are secondary, and that they are in reality fictions designed to camouflage the fact that David himself had pronounced judgment upon Abner." Halpern (2001:73-103) goes so far as to label David "a serial killer," and links him with the deaths of Nabal, Saul and his sons at Gilboa, Ishbaal (Ishbosheth), Abner, other descendants of Saul, Amnon, Absalom, Amasa, and Uriah. It suffices to say that the conclusions to which these interpreters come require the assumption that the present text deliberately distorts what really took place and is to be regarded as an example of early Israelite political propaganda.

◆ D. The Murder of Ishbosheth (2 Sam 4:1-12)

When Ishbosheth,* Saul's son, heard about Abner's death at Hebron, he lost all courage, and all Israel became paralyzed with fear. 2Now there were two brothers, Baanah and Recab, who were captains of Ishbosheth's raiding parties. They were sons of Rimmon, a member of the tribe of Benjamin who lived in Beeroth. The town of Beeroth is now part of Benjamin's territory 3because the original people of Beeroth fled to Gittaim, where they still live as foreigners.

4(Saul's son Jonathan had a son named Mephibosheth,* who was crippled as a child. He was five years old when the report came from Jezreel that Saul and Jonathan had been killed in battle. When the child's nurse heard the news, she picked him up and fled. But as she hurried away, she dropped him, and he became crippled.)

5One day Recab and Baanah, the sons of Rimmon from Beeroth, went to Ishbosheth's house around noon as he was taking his midday rest. 6The doorkeeper, who had been sifting wheat, became drowsy and fell asleep. So Recab and Baanah slipped past her.* 7They went into the house and found Ishbosheth sleeping on his bed. They struck and killed him and cut off his head. Then, taking his head with them, they fled across the Jordan Valley* through the night. 8When they arrived at Hebron, they presented Ishbosheth's head to David. "Look!" they exclaimed to the king. "Here is the head of Ishbosheth, the son of your enemy Saul who tried to kill you. Today the LORD has given my lord the king revenge on Saul and his entire family!"

9But David said to Recab and Baanah, "The LORD, who saves me from all my enemies, is my witness. 10Someone once told me, 'Saul is dead,' thinking he was bringing me good news. But I seized him and killed him at Ziklag. That's the reward I gave him for his news! 11How much more should I reward evil men who have killed an innocent man in his own house and on his own bed? Shouldn't I hold you responsible for his blood and rid the earth of you?"

12So David ordered his young men to kill them, and they did. They cut off their hands and feet and hung their bodies beside the pool in Hebron. Then they took Ishbosheth's head and buried it in Abner's tomb in Hebron.

4:1 *Ishbosheth* is another name for Esh-baal. 4:4 *Mephibosheth* is another name for Merib-baal. 4:6 As in Greek version; Hebrew reads *So they went into the house pretending to fetch wheat, but they stabbed him in the stomach. Then Recab and Baanah escaped.* 4:7 Hebrew *the Arabah.*

NOTES

4:1 ***he lost all courage.*** Lit., "his hands weakened" (cf. Isa 13:7; Jer 6:24). Alter (1999:217) comments, "The force of the idiom is a little like the colloquial English 'lost his grip.'"

4:6 ***The doorkeeper, who had been sifting wheat, became drowsy and fell asleep. So Recab and Baanah slipped past her.*** This follows the LXX; see NLT mg for Hebrew. In the MT, the unusual use of the participle for "fetching wheat" has raised some uncertainty about the text. The NLT along with S. R. Driver (1913:255), Gordon (1986:222-223), McCarter (1984:125-126), Smith (1912:285), Wellhausen (1871:161-162), and RSV prefer the LXX over the MT. S. R. Driver (1913:255), following Wellhausen (1871:161-162), suggests a Vorlage of *wehinneh sho'ereth* [TH7778A, ZH8788] *habbayith soqlah* [TH5619, ZH6232] *khittim wattanam* [TH2050.1/5123, ZH2256/5670] *wattishan* [TH2050.1/3462, ZH2256/3822]. NRSV, NIV, NJPS, and A. Anderson (1989:65-66) retain MT's reading.

4:8 ***the LORD has given . . . the king revenge.*** For the plural *neqamoth* [TH5360, ZH5935] (vengeances), see Joüon and Muraoka's (§136j) discussion of the "plural of generalisation."

4:10 ***That's the reward I gave him for his news!*** The use of *'asher* [TH834, ZH889] (which) in this statement is grammatically difficult, and can be interpreted differently. McCarter (1984:124) suggests, "a man to whom it would have been suitable for me to give a reward."

COMMENTARY

After demonstrating that David had no part in the murder of Abner in chapter 3, the narrator now absolves him of any complicity in the murder of Saul's son, Ishbosheth.[1] Chapter 4 opens with a description of the panic that was created in the north by the report of Abner's death. Upon hearing this unsettling news, Ishbosheth abandoned any remaining hope of retaining his throne, and those who had given him their allegiance feared an imminent military attack by David (4:1). In this time of uncertainty and political instability, two of Ishbosheth's military officers saw an opportunity for personal advancement. These two men assumed that if they killed Ishbosheth they would gain a high standing with David, whom they now fully expected to reign as king over the entire nation. The narrator, however, is careful to report that these men, Recab and Baanah, were both from Ishbosheth's own tribe (Benjamin) and that they had no connection with either David or the tribe of Judah (4:2-3). At the same time, the narrator informs the reader that the only other surviving male in the house of Saul was a young lad named Mephibosheth, who was too young to rule and physically incapable of assuming the throne (4:4). So the way was clear for the house of David to replace the house of Saul on the throne in Israel.

After this introductory material (4:1-4), the narrator proceeds to describe the assassination of Ishbosheth, and David's response to this nefarious deed. Gaining entrance into Ishbosheth's residence, Recab and Baanah murdered him while he was asleep in his own bed during an afternoon nap. They cut off his head and carried it to David's court in Hebron (4:5-7). As they entered David's presence and presented him with Ishbosheth's head, they said, "Today the LORD has given my lord the king revenge on Saul and his entire family!" (4:8b). Although this is a shrewdly designed statement, it betrays two serious errors of judgment. The first error is the presumption that their wicked deed was a divinely sanctioned act, and the second is the assumption that David desired to avenge himself against the house of Saul by the murder of Ishbosheth for the mistreatment he had experienced from Saul's hand in the past.

The first error is similar to the one made by David's associates when Saul entered the cave in which they were hiding and they interpreted his vulnerability to assault as a divine imperative to kill him (1 Sam 24:4). As in that instance it was improper for David's men to interpret divine providence as a divine mandate (see commentary on 1 Sam 24), so in this instance it was equally improper for Recab and Baanah to equate the accomplishment of their wicked deed as evidence that the Lord sanctioned what they had done. These men were in the service of Ishbosheth. Ishbosheth had every reason to expect their loyalty and devotion. Their heinous act was one of betrayal and treachery performed not out of desire for justice, or even the conviction that it was the will of God for David to rule over Israel, but rather out of the desire for personal advancement and pragmatic self-interest. As Calvin (1992:155) notes, "These men had no reason to kill their king. They did it out of spite. They were traitors and perverse." Their statement to David not only misused the name of the Lord, in violation of the third commandment (Exod 20:7), but also attempted to give divine sanction to the violation of the sixth commandment ("You must not murder," Exod 20:13). To claim that the Lord had given David revenge on Saul by means of their act was a hypocritical attempt to cover their wickedness by cloaking it under the guise of doing God's will.

All of this, however, is not to deny that there is a sense in which David finally did come to the throne over all Israel as a result of God's providential ordering of a series of events that even included the murder of Ishbosheth.[2] This must be so because God's providential governance of the universe encompasses everything that happens. But this understanding of providence is not what is being claimed by Recab and Baanah. To recognize that David's advancement came through their misdeeds is not to say that God endorsed their behavior.[3] Calvin (1992:163) points out that when the sons of Eli were killed, this happened because it was God's purpose that they be put to death (1 Sam 2:25; see commentary). But this does not mean that the Philistines were guiltless before God for the deaths of Hophni and Phinehas (1 Sam 4:11), nor for their attack on Israel. They certainty were not. Their intent was to wipe out God's people and take their land for themselves. The same can later be said of Assyria, which was a "rod of [God's] anger" (Isa 10:5) to bring judgment on the northern kingdom, but which, in turn, was judged by God for its pride (Isa 10:12). It is for this reason that Calvin (1992:163) says that "we must always consider the intention of him who does every deed." It was not the intention of Recab and Baanah to bring honor to the Lord by the murder of Ishbosheth. Their statement to David was a self-serving attempt to justify an evil act.

The second error of Recab and Baanah was the assumption that David regarded Ishbosheth as an enemy upon whom he sought revenge. Ever since being anointed by Samuel (1 Sam 16), David had consistently refused to seek the life of either Saul or his son Ishbosheth. It was David's stated conviction that vengeance belonged to the Lord (1 Sam 24:12; 26:10-11), and on this occasion he reaffirmed that it was the Lord who had delivered him from all his enemies (4:9). So David was not swayed by Recab and Baanah's argument, and as he had done with the Amalekite who claimed to have killed Saul, he let them stand condemned by their own words (4:9-12). At David's order they were both put to death, and Ishbosheth's head was given a proper burial in Abner's tomb in Hebron.

ENDNOTES

1. As with the murder of Abner in the previous chapter, there are those scholars who suspect that David also played a role in the elimination of Ishbosheth, the last viable successor to Saul from his own family. VanderKam (1980:534) comments, "Here, too, one may suspect that the ambitious drives of David lurk somewhere in the background, but the brief narrative that has survived does not permit the conclusion that he arranged Eshbaal's [Ishbosheth's] assassination, although it certainly proved convenient for him." This, however, does not prevent Halpern (2001:81-82) from saying, "If David commissioned the killing, or even solicited tenders on a contract, his killing the assassins is standard mob-style procedure. . . . the punishment of the killers . . . indicates that he understood the danger that he would indeed be accused. What is more, the killers are Gibeonites, who, we shall see, were David's allies. *Chances are David commissioned the hit*" (my italics).
2. As Brueggemann (1990a:235-236) points out, "David knows, beyond a hint of public doubt, that it is Yahweh, only Yahweh, who redeems his life (4:9). That strange, welcome redemption, however, takes place in and through the ambitious, miscalculating, bloody deeds of less discerning, less cunning people. . . . David's destiny advances precisely through their misdeeds."
3. Calvin (1992:141) notes that God "has a secret method which is incomprehensible to us, to bring all his works to completion. In this, he uses the wicked and employs them in whatever way pleases him—not that they are to be excused."

◆ E. David Becomes King of All Israel and Captures Jerusalem (2 Sam 5:1-12)

Then all the tribes of Israel went to David at Hebron and told him, "We are your own flesh and blood. [2]In the past,* when Saul was our king, you were the one who really led the forces of Israel. And the LORD told you, 'You will be the shepherd of my people Israel. You will be Israel's leader.'"

[3]So there at Hebron, King David made a covenant before the LORD with all the elders of Israel. And they anointed him king of Israel.

[4]David was thirty years old when he began to reign, and he reigned forty years in all. [5]He had reigned over Judah from Hebron for seven years and six months, and from Jerusalem he reigned over all Israel and Judah for thirty-three years.

[6]David then led his men to Jerusalem to fight against the Jebusites, the original inhabitants of the land who were living there. The Jebusites taunted David, saying, "You'll never get in here! Even the blind and lame could keep you out!" For the Jebusites thought they were safe. [7]But David captured the fortress of Zion, which is now called the City of David.

[8]On the day of the attack, David said to his troops, "I hate those 'lame' and 'blind' Jebusites.* Whoever attacks them should strike by going into the city through the water tunnel.*" That is the origin of the saying, "The blind and the lame may not enter the house."*

[9]So David made the fortress his home, and he called it the City of David. He ex-

**tended the city, starting at the support-
ing terraces* and working inward. 10And
David became more and more powerful,
because the LORD God of Heaven's Armies
was with him.
11Then King Hiram of Tyre sent mes-
sengers to David, along with cedar timber
and carpenters and stonemasons, and
they built David a palace. 12And David re-
alized that the LORD had confirmed him as
king over Israel and had blessed his king-
dom for the sake of his people Israel.**

5:2 Or *For some time.* 5:8a Or *Those 'lame' and 'blind' Jebusites hate me.* 5:8b Or *with scaling hooks.* The meaning of the Hebrew is uncertain. 5:8c The meaning of this saying is uncertain. 5:9 Hebrew *the millo.* The meaning of the Hebrew is uncertain.

NOTES

5:6 ***Jebusites.*** The singular gentilic noun *hayebusi* [TH2983, ZH3294] is taken as a collective here.

could keep you out. Lit., "will turn you back." Regarding the singular verb with a plural subject here, see GKC §145o.

For the Jebusites thought they were safe. Lit., "saying, 'David cannot enter here,'" a line intended to clarify the meaning of the preceding statement. The NLT renders according to the general sense.

5:8 ***"I hate those 'lame' and 'blind' Jebusites."*** From the Hebrew wording it is not clear whether the lame and blind hate David (see NLT mg) or David hates the lame and the blind. The idea that David hates the Jebusites is supported by the Qere, *senu'e nepesh dawid* is "hated of/by David's soul," and by the reading of 1QSam[a], *sn'h npsh dwyd,* yielding the translation "David's soul hates." The Kethiv, however, would read *sane'u nepesh dawid* (they hate David's soul), and, as Youngblood (1992:858, note 8) points out, the Qere could also be vocalized as *sone'e nepesh dawid* (haters of David's soul). Some have argued that 5:8b gives preference to this second reading, but the argument is not strong.

through the water tunnel. The meaning of the Hebrew word *tsinnor* [TH6794, ZH7562] is uncertain (so NLT mg). It occurs only here and in Ps 42:7 [8] where it is usually translated "waterfall." Most interpreters have concluded that the term is a reference to the water supply for the stronghold and that David's men made use of a tunnel that connected the fortress of Zion with the spring of Gihon outside the city walls in order to either enter the city itself, or to cut off its water supply.

5:10 ***became more and more powerful.*** On the infinitive absolute *halok* [TH1980, ZH2143] (to walk) used to express (figuratively) continuity, see Joüon and Muraoka §123s.

COMMENTARY

Second Samuel 5 is a pivotal chapter in 1–2 Samuel. It brings to a climax much of what has preceded it and also introduces much of what is to follow.[1] Retrospectively, the chapter concludes the long series of narratives dealing with David's rise to the throne in Israel,[2] for it is in this chapter that David finally begins his reign over the entire nation (5:3). Prospectively, the chapter launches the reader into another series of narratives that will portray the reign of David in all of its splendor, intrigue, and complexity (chs 5–24).

In the aftermath of the deaths of Abner (3:22-39) and Ishbosheth (ch 4), the elders of the tribes formerly allied with the abortive reign of Saul's son Ishbosheth journeyed to David at Hebron and joined with Judah in recognizing David as their king. In their discussions with David, they cited three reasons for their decision to accept David as the legitimate ruler over the entire nation. First, they were united with David by kinship ("We are your own flesh and blood," 5:1). This qualification fulfilled the requirement of the "law of the king" (Deut 17:14-20) that mandated the appointment of "a fellow Israelite; he may not be a foreigner" (Deut 17:15b). Second, in retrospect, they were forced to admit that even during the reign of Saul, David was the most successful military leader in the land (5:2a; cf. David's victory over Goliath [1 Sam 17], the song of the women of Israel [1 Sam 18:7], and David's repeated military successes [1 Sam 18:12-16]).[3] Third, and most importantly, David was the one whom the Lord had chosen to rule over his people (5:2b; cf. 1 Sam 13:14; 16:12-13). This qualification was also a requirement of the law of the king (Deut 17:15).

The terminology used and the procedures followed in the brief description of David's installation as king (5:1-5) reflect something of the duality of the divine and human dimensions involved in the transactions that took place. The term that is used in 5:2 to designate the position David will occupy is "leader." This is the same term found in 1 Samuel 9:16 and 10:1 (cf. "ruler," NLT) with regard to Saul's position over Israel (see also 6:21 and the note on 1 Sam 9:16). In 5:3, another term, "king," is used to designate David's position. Usage in 1–2 Samuel suggests that the term "leader" is a term of divine designation carrying a religious implication, while the term "king" is a word more closely associated with the human political dimensions of the office. As van den Berg (1997:34) suggests, the interfacing of divine and human actions is something that is generally characteristic of biblical narrative, and in this instance one can say that God has made David "leader" over Israel. But with equal legitimacy one can say the people have made David "king." Notice that from the human point of view David was made "king" by anointing[4] and by the establishment of a covenant between David and the elders of the various tribes (5:3). From the divine perspective, God had providentially guided events over a long period of time so that his promise to David finally came to fruition.

It is of interest that the narrator makes reference to the establishment of a covenant between David and "all the elders of Israel" (5:3). It seems clear that this covenant was an agreement negotiated between David and the representatives of the various tribes. It also seems clear that the agreement was ratified in a religious ceremony because David is said to have made the covenant "before the LORD." Here again we see the kingship and covenant theme in 1–2 Samuel (see "Theological Concerns" in the Introduction). The covenant in view on this occasion is not the covenant that established the nation of Israel as the covenant people of Yahweh (Exod 19), which had been renewed at the inauguration of Saul's reign (1 Sam 11:14–12:25). According to the terms of that covenant, Israel was a theocratic state and Yahweh was her Great King. An important function of the covenant renewal assembly connected to Saul's inauguration was the incorporation of human kingship into the structure of the theocracy in a way that would not jeopardize the ongoing covenant relationship between Yahweh and his people (see commentary on 1 Sam 11:14–12:25). But in 2 Samuel 5, the covenant in view is between David and the leaders of the nation. Presumably this covenant described the responsibilities and duties that the people would assume toward their ruler, on the one hand, and the responsibilities and duties that David would assume toward his subjects on the other. So this covenant was one of a political nature, as well as one that was established in a religious ceremony, presumably with an oath taken in the name of the Lord by both parties. In chapter 7, yet another covenant comes into view, in which the Lord promises David that he will give him a dynasty that will endure forever.

After some brief notations about the length of David's reign (5:4), the narrative goes on to mention several of its highlights, including David's capture of the stronghold of Zion for a national capital (5:6-10), his arrangement with Hiram of Tyre for the building of a palace (5:11-12), his additional marriages and the birth of more children in Jerusalem (5:13-16), and the description of two resounding victories over the Philistines (5:17-25). These events are probably not presented in a strict chronological order. It is likely, for example, that the building of David's palace (5:11-12) took place later in his reign than did his victories over the Philistines (5:17-25). The first thing that the narrator chooses to mention after describing the beginning of David's reign over all Israel is his capture of the stronghold of Zion. At the time this was a small but heavily fortified city inhabited by Jebusites.[5] It was located on the southeastern ridge of what would later become the Temple Mount of Jerusalem. From a political standpoint, Zion was ideally situated for a new seat of government. It was centrally located, positioned on the border between Judah (David's tribe) and Benjamin (Saul's tribe) and belonging to neither. In addition, because the site was surrounded on three sides by deep valleys and was strongly fortified, it provided Israel with a nearly impregnable national capital.

Even though this accomplishment of David is described in only a few verses (5:6-10),[6] its importance cannot be overstated. This is an event of far-reaching significance because as David's capital city, Zion was not only to become the religious and political center of Israel, but it would also come to occupy a very important place in the history of both Judaism and Christianity, and indeed world history in general.[7] After David brought the Ark of God to Zion (ch 6), this city was recognized as the place where the Lord had chosen "to cause his name to dwell there" (cf. Deut 12:5, 11, KJV). From this point forward, numerous texts in the Old Testament speak of Zion not only as David's royal city and the capital of the nation of Israel, but also as the place from which Israel's divine king, Yahweh, reigns over the whole earth (see Pss 9:11; 76:2; 99:2; 132:13; Isa 8:18; Jer 8:19). According to biblical teaching, Zion (Jerusalem), the dwelling place of Yahweh, Israel's divine king, will continue to be a focal point of human history until the creation of a new heaven and new earth (Isa 2:1-4; 24:23; 60:14; 65:17-25; Joel 3:17, 21; Mic 4:2, 7; Zech 8:1-3).

ENDNOTES

1. As was noted earlier in the discussion introducing 1 Sam 16:1–28:2 (David's Rise and Saul's Decline), this commentary does not accept the theory of the existence of an originally independent "History of David's Rise" (1 Sam 16:14–2 Sam 5). One of the problems with the theory is disagreement among its advocates over where it begins and ends. Although most scholars place its end at ch 5, Stoebe (1973:296ff) places it at ch 1, while Mildenberger (1962:x), Nübel (1959:81-82), and Weiser (1966:342ff) place it at ch 7. As is argued in this commentary, ch 5 is better viewed as a transition chapter in a continuous narrative flow rather than the beginning or ending of an originally independent block of material.
2. The narratives concerning David's rise and Saul's demise begin with the rejection of Saul in 1 Sam 13 and 15, and the Lord's choice of David to replace him in 1 Sam 16.

3. In 5:2 the pronoun "you" referring to David is emphatic in the Hebrew text.
4. This is the third time that David was anointed. He was first anointed by Samuel at the Lord's command (1 Sam 16:13). He was subsequently anointed by the leaders of the tribe of Judah after Saul's death (2:4, see commentary), and then he is in this passage anointed by the elders of Israel. Solomon was also anointed more than once. He was anointed by Nathan and Zadok at Gihon as commanded by David (1 Kgs 1:32-39), and he was later anointed at a public assembly held in Jerusalem (1 Chr 29:22). As Calvin noted in connection with the anointing of David by the leaders of Judah, this was not intended to denigrate the original anointing by Samuel. Calvin (1992:181) makes the same point here, saying, "The elders of Israel did not want to efface this mark which had been given by Samuel, but they testified their consent to it, as if they had responded 'amen' to what God had already declared."
5. During the time of the conquest, both Benjamin and Judah had attacked the city, but it had remained inhabited by the Jebusites (Judg 1:8, 21).
6. There are two difficult interpretive problems in 5:6-8. The first concerns the meaning of the saying in 5:8, "The blind and the lame may not enter the house." Here it is not clear what "house" is in view, or why "the blind and the lame" are excluded from it. The two previous references to the blind and the lame in 5:6 seem to suggest that Zion was so impregnable that even "the blind and the lame" could defend it against attack. The second interpretive problem concerns the meaning of the term translated "water tunnel" in NLT. See note on 5:8.
7. For a collection of informative studies on Zion, see Hess and Wenham 1999.

◆ F. David's Sons Born in Jerusalem (2 Sam 5:13-16)

13After moving from Hebron to Jerusalem, David married more concubines and wives, and they had more sons and daughters. 14These are the names of David's sons who were born in Jerusalem: Shammua, Shobab, Nathan, Solomon, 15Ibhar, Elishua, Nepheg, Japhia, 16Elishama, Eliada, and Eliphelet.

NOTES

5:13 ***After moving from Hebron to Jerusalem, David married more concubines and wives.*** Lit., "After he came from Hebron, David took more concubines and wives *from Jerusalem*" (my italics). Because of the Hebrew preposition "from" (*mi-* [TH4480, ZH4946]), some interpreters have suggested that the wives were Jebusite women. That this is an unnecessary conclusion is demonstrated by Sarna (1959:310-316). The parallel in 1 Chr 14:3 reads "in (*bi-* [TH871.2, ZH928]) Jerusalem."

COMMENTARY

The narratives that describe the reign of David in 2 Samuel are set in a series of four ring structures, three of which are framed by "lists."[1] The first of these ring structures is found in 3:2–5:16 and opens and closes with lists of David's sons. The first list names the sons born to David in Hebron (3:2-5), while the second list names the sons born to David in Jerusalem (5:13-16). Six sons are mentioned in the first list along with the names of their mothers. Eleven sons are mentioned in the second list, but the mother's names are not included.[2] First Chronicles 3:5 tells us that Bathsheba was the mother of four of David's sons: Shammua, Shobab, Nathan, and Solomon. In the narratives describing David's reign in Jerusalem, Bathsheba is the only wife that David took during this time who is mentioned by name (ch 11). Klement (2000:72) suggests that the three double lists included in the description of the reign of David (those of sons, officials, and warriors) call attention to the "groups of people who must be regarded as the principal beneficiaries of the new order of society." In Klement's view, the double list of sons born in Hebron and Jerusalem calls attention to "the appearance of a royal family with all its arrogation of power, its intrigues, and its scandals." The birth of these many sons can be viewed in both a positive and a negative way. There is a sense in which numerous offspring can be viewed as a blessing of God (cf. 5:12; Ps 127:3-5) and evidence of the increasing strength of David's royal household. But at the same time, the reader cannot help but be disturbed by David's apparent violation of the Deuteronomic "law of the king" that prohibited the king from taking "many wives for himself" (Deut 17:17).[3] Subsequent narratives describe the heartache that came to David in the aftermath of his marriage to Bathsheba in connection with the behavior of his sons Amnon, Absalom, and Adonijah (chs 13–19; 1 Kgs 1–2).

ENDNOTES

1. The four ring structures are: (1) 3:2–5:16; (2) 5:17–8:14; (3) 8:15–20:26; (4) 21:1–24:25. Structures 1, 3, and 4 are framed by lists.
2. A more comprehensive list of David's sons is found in 1 Chr 3:1-9, which is nearly paralleled in 1 Chr 14:3-7.
3. Calvin (1992:203) comments, "Here one sees how his [David's] virtues were mixed with his vices—which should certainly be condemned—and above all, that this taking many wives is a corruption of marriage, which God has chosen to consecrate in his name."

◆ G. David Defeats the Philistines (2 Sam 5:17-25)

**17 When the Philistines heard that David
had been anointed king of Israel, they
mobilized all their forces to capture him.
But David was told they were coming, so
he went into the stronghold. 18 The Philis-
tines arrived and spread out across the
valley of Rephaim. 19 So David asked the
LORD, "Should I go out to fight the Philis-
tines? Will you hand them over to me?"**

**The LORD replied to David, "Yes, go ahead.
I will certainly hand them over to you."**

**20 So David went to Baal-perazim and
defeated the Philistines there. "The LORD
did it!" David exclaimed. "He burst through
my enemies like a raging flood!" So he
named that place Baal-perazim (which
means "the Lord who bursts through").
21 The Philistines had abandoned their
idols there, so David and his men confis-
cated them.**

**22 But after a while the Philistines re-
turned and again spread out across the
valley of Rephaim. 23 And again David asked
the LORD what to do. "Do not attack them
straight on," the LORD replied. "Instead,
circle around behind and attack them near
the poplar* trees. 24 When you hear a sound
like marching feet in the tops of the poplar
trees, be on the alert! That will be the sig-
nal that the LORD is moving ahead of you
to strike down the Philistine army." 25 So
David did what the LORD commanded, and
he struck down the Philistines all the way
from Gibeon* to Gezer.**

5:23 Or *aspen*, or *balsam;* also in 5:24. The exact identification of this tree is uncertain. **5:25** As in Greek version (see also 1 Chr 14:16); Hebrew reads *Geba*.

NOTES

5:18 ***spread out.*** First Chronicles 14:9, a parallel passage, substitutes "made a raid" (*wayyipshetu* [TH6584, ZH7320]) for "spread out" (*wayyinnateshu* [TH5203, ZH5759]).

COMMENTARY

As the résumé of David's accomplishments in chapter 5 is completed, the reader is informed that David not only removed the internal opposition to his reign by negotiating a covenant with the leaders of the northern tribes—former allies of the house of Saul—he also defeated the Philistines, Israel's formidable long-term enemy. As soon as the Philistines learned of the unification of Israel under David's rule, they mobilized their forces for an attack in the hope of preventing David from consolidating his power.[1] When the Philistine troops assembled in the valley of Rephaim,[2] David asked the Lord what he should do in response. The Lord told him that he should go out and fight the Philistines and that he would be victorious in the battle. David's reliance on the Lord for this battle is evident: He seeks the Lord's guidance beforehand and attributes the victory to the Lord (5:20). Thus, with the Lord's help, David did something that Saul had never been able to accomplish. Because David captured some idols abandoned by the Philistines (5:21),[3] the victory not only confirmed the Lord's presence with David in his new role as national leader but also demonstrated the superiority of Yahweh over the heathen deities of the Philistines.[4] The reference to the capture of the Philistine idols reminds the reader of the time when the Philistines had captured the Ark of the Covenant and placed it in the temple of Dagon, only to be coerced to return it when it brought disease to all the cities to which it was taken (1 Sam 4–6).

Realizing that David's leadership of Israel was a serious threat to their own existence as an independent nation, the Philistines returned for a repeat engagement (5:22-25).[5] When David once again asked the Lord how to respond to their challenge, the Lord told him that this time he should use a different tactic and attack the Philistine troops from the rear. The Lord promised to give David a signal to attack by causing a sound in the tops of the balsam trees (5:23, NLT mg). This time the result was a rout of the Philistine forces, which were pursued all the way to Gezer, located northwest of Jerusalem on the border of Philistine territory. There is no indication of a continuing Philistine threat to Israel in the remainder of 2 Samuel (cf. 8:1).

In the ring structure that makes up 5:17–8:18, the report of David's victories over the Philistines (5:17-25) parallels the report of victories over all of Israel's external enemies in 8:1-14 (see the diagram in the section on Literary Style in the Introduction). These two reports frame two of the most important narratives in all of 1–2 Samuel: 2 Samuel 6, which tells of David's bringing of the Ark of God to Jerusalem, and chapter 7, which describes the covenant the Lord made with the house of David.

ENDNOTES

1. Chronologically this attack is to be placed immediately after the anointing of David in 5:3 and prior to the capture of Zion in 5:6-9. This means that the "stronghold" (5:17) in which David took refuge was not the "fortress of Zion" (5:7), but probably the stronghold of Adullam (see 23:13-14 and perhaps 1 Sam 22:4-5). Adullam is located

in Judah about 16.5 miles west-southwest of Jerusalem in the Shephelah (the foothills of the central mountain range).

2. The valley of Rephaim is usually identified with a location west-southwest of Jerusalem on the border between Benjamin and Judah (Josh 15:8; 18:16).
3. The Philistines evidently had taken some idols of their deities into battle, much like the Israelites had taken the Ark of the Covenant into battle against the Philistines many years earlier (1 Sam 4).
4. According to 1 Chr 14:12, David and his men burned the captured Philistine idols.
5. The text gives no indication of how long a time elapsed between the two battles.

◆ H. David Brings the Ark to Jerusalem (2 Sam 6:1-23)

Then David again gathered all the elite troops in Israel, 30,000 in all. 2He led them to Baalah of Judah* to bring back the Ark of God, which bears the name of the LORD of Heaven's Armies,* who is enthroned between the cherubim. 3They placed the Ark of God on a new cart and brought it from Abinadab's house, which was on a hill. Uzzah and Ahio, Abinadab's sons, were guiding the cart as it left the house, 4carrying the Ark of God. Ahio walked in front of the Ark. 5David and all the people of Israel were celebrating before the LORD, singing songs* and playing all kinds of musical instruments—lyres, harps, tambourines, castanets, and cymbals.

6But when they arrived at the threshing floor of Nacon, the oxen stumbled, and Uzzah reached out his hand and steadied the Ark of God. 7Then the LORD's anger was aroused against Uzzah, and God struck him dead because of this.* So Uzzah died right there beside the Ark of God.

8David was angry because the LORD's anger had burst out against Uzzah. He named that place Perez-uzzah (which means "to burst out against Uzzah"), as it is still called today.

9David was now afraid of the LORD, and he asked, "How can I ever bring the Ark of the LORD back into my care?" 10So David decided not to move the Ark of the LORD into the City of David. Instead, he took it to the house of Obed-edom of Gath. 11The Ark of the LORD remained there in Obed-edom's house for three months, and the LORD blessed Obed-edom and his entire household.

12Then King David was told, "The LORD has blessed Obed-edom's household and everything he has because of the Ark of God." So David went there and brought the Ark of God from the house of Obed-edom to the City of David with a great celebration. 13After the men who were carrying the Ark of the LORD had gone six steps, David sacrificed a bull and a fattened calf. 14And David danced before the LORD with all his might, wearing a priestly garment.* 15So David and all the people of Israel brought up the Ark of the LORD with shouts of joy and the blowing of rams' horns.

16But as the Ark of the LORD entered the City of David, Michal, the daughter of Saul, looked down from her window. When she saw King David leaping and dancing before the LORD, she was filled with contempt for him.

17They brought the Ark of the LORD and set it in its place inside the special tent David had prepared for it. And David sacrificed burnt offerings and peace offerings to the LORD. 18When he had finished his sacrifices, David blessed the people in the name of the LORD of Heaven's Armies. 19Then he gave to every Israelite man and woman in the crowd a loaf of bread, a cake of dates,* and a cake of raisins. Then all the people returned to their homes.

20When David returned home to bless his own family, Michal, the daughter of Saul, came out to meet him. She said in disgust, "How distinguished the king of

Israel looked today, shamelessly exposing
himself to the servant girls like any vulgar
person might do!"
[21]David retorted to Michal, "I was danc-
ing before the LORD, who chose me above
your father and all his family! He appointed
me as the leader of Israel, the people of the
LORD, so I celebrate before the LORD. [22]Yes,
and I am willing to look even more foolish
than this, even to be humiliated in my own
eyes! But those servant girls you mentioned
will indeed think I am distinguished!" [23]So
Michal, the daughter of Saul, remained
childless throughout her entire life.

6:2a *Baalah of Judah* is another name for Kiriath-jearim; compare 1 Chr 13:6. **6:2b** Or *the Ark of God where the Name is proclaimed—the name of the LORD of Heaven's Armies.* **6:5** As in Dead Sea Scrolls and Greek version (see also 1 Chr 13:8); Masoretic Text reads *before the LORD with all manner of cypress wood.* **6:7** As in Dead Sea Scrolls; Masoretic Text reads *because of his irreverence.* **6:14** Hebrew *a linen ephod.* **6:19** Or *a portion of meat.* The meaning of the Hebrew is uncertain.

NOTES

6:1 *gathered.* The verb is *'asap* [TH622, ZH665] (gather) not *yasap* [TH3254, ZH3578] (add), as is clear from the context and from the parallel *wayyaqhel* [TH6950, ZH7735] (assembled, summoned) in 1 Chr 13:5. For the elision of Aleph in verbs where it is the first radical, see GKC §68h and Stek 1986:293.

6:2 *to Baalah of Judah.* This is another name for Kiriath-jearim (cf. NLT mg; Josh 15:9; 1 Chr 13:6). The MT, apparently erroneously, reads *miba'ale yehudah* [TH1167/3063, ZH1251/3373]. This could be translated "[some] from the citizens of Judah" (as LXX, Targum, Syriac, Vulgate) or "from Baale/Baal of Judah." It is clear, however, that David and his men are going to Kiriath-jearim, not coming from it. It is preferable then to translate the phrase, as do A. Anderson (1989:97) and NLT, in agreement with 4QSam[a] (and 1 Chr 13:6), which reads *b'lh hy' qry[th y'rym]* (to Baalah, which is Kira[th-jearim]). See further, Alter (1999:225); Gordon (1984:32-33).

the name of the LORD. See NLT mg. The repetition of *shem* [TH8034, ZH9005] (name) in the MT (cf. "the Name, the name of the LORD," NIV) may be due to dittography. "Name" occurs only once in the LXX and in 1 Chr 13:6, a parallel verse. For this reason the NLT (cf. RSV, ESV) translates "name" only once here.

6:3-4 *guiding the cart as it left the house, carrying the Ark of God.* In comparison to other textual witnesses, the MT's description of the bringing of the Ark from the house of Abinadab has a longer, repetitive text. Nearly all commentators and translations have seen dittography in the MT. A phrase found in the middle of 6:3 is repeated verbatim beginning with the last word of 6:3 and going into 6:4. The six repeated words follow the repeated word for "cart" in the MT, lit., "guiding the *new cart, and they brought it out of the house of Abinadab, which was on the hill*" (repeated words in italics; Heb., *'agalah khadashah wayyissa'uhu mibbeth 'abinadab 'asher baggib'ah*). Pisano (1984:273) comments, "The conclusive grammatical proof of the erroneous MT is the lack of article with *khadashah* [TH2319, ZH2543; "new"] while it is supposed to be modifying *ha'agalah* [TH5699, ZH6322; "cart"]. A comparison of MT with LXX, 4QSam[a] and with the parallel text at 1 Chr 13:7 confirms the textual accident in MT here."

Some commentators (A. Anderson 1989:96, 98; McCarter 1984:161, 163) suggest a further correction of the text by the insertion of "Uzzah walked alongside the Ark" after "with the Ark of God on it." While this may make sense in light of 6:6-7, it is not necessary for understanding the text. Pisano (1984:276-277) concludes, "As Schulz has pointed out, the absence of Uzzah in OG [LXX] here makes it unlikely that he was part of the Hebrew text here. As a result of this examination, therefore, we may consider MT to have been disturbed by a dittography in 6:3b-4, but otherwise the text of MT is preferable to any other form."

6:5 *singing songs.* See NLT mg. The MT reads, lit., "with all kinds of woods of cypresses" (*bekol 'atse beroshim* [TH6086/1265, ZH6770/1360]). Some have understood this to mean, "with all kinds of wooden instruments made of cypress." This, however, seems to be a strange way to say this in Hebrew. Comparison with a parallel verse, 1 Chr 13:8 (*bekol-'oz ubeshirim* [TH5797/7892, ZH6437/8877], "with all [their] might and with songs"), as well as 4QSam[a] (cf. Ulrich 1978:195) suggests a scribal error has obscured the original wording in the MT of 2 Samuel.

6:6 *his hand.* These two words are not in the MT. But the versions, 1 Chr 13:9 (a parallel verse), and 4QSam[a] add them: *'eth-yado* [TH853/2050.2, ZH906/2257] (his hand).

6:7 *because of this.* As the NLT mg indicates, the MT is usually read as, "because of his irreverence." The meaning of the Hebrew words (*'al-hashal* [TH5921/7944, ZH6584/8915]) in question, however, is obscure. Keil (1956:332) suggests "on account of the offence." He regards *shal* (which occurs only here in the OT) as derived from *shalah* [TH7951, ZH8922] in the sense of "erring or committing a fault." KBL (972) suggests "irreverence" on the basis of an Akkadian term for sin. The parallel verse, 1 Chr 13:10, reads, "because he had laid his hand on the Ark" (*'al 'asher-shalakh* [TH7971, ZH8938] *yado 'al-ha'aron*). Ulrich (1978:195) shows that even though part of 4QSam[a] is missing, there is enough space for reading a parallel with 1 Chr 13:10. He then concludes that the MT originally contained the extra words and agreed with 4QSam[a]. Pisano (1984:106) concludes, "The reading in MT here is either irretrievably corrupt or else the meaning of the word has become unintelligible. Because of the difficulty in seeing how it could be a corruption of the longer text of 1 Chr and 4Q, which appears rather to be an expansion, MT seems to witness here to the older form of the text."

6:20 *like any vulgar person might do!* Lit., "as one of the riffraff might uncover himself." In the Hebrew wording the exact significance of the infinitive absolute (*nigloth* [TH1540, ZH1655]) emphasizing an infinitive construct (*higgaloth* [TH1540, ZH1655]) is not clear. GKC (§75y) suggests it is probably a "subsequent correction of an erroneous repetition of *higgaloth*."

COMMENTARY

Second Samuel 6 and 7 deal with matters that lie at the heart of the entire book of Samuel. As noted in previous discussions, kingship and covenant are the two most important themes in 1–2 Samuel. When the elders of Israel asked for a king like the nations around them (1 Sam 8), they denied the covenant and rejected the Lord who was their king. But when Samuel was instructed by the Lord to give the people a king, he did so in a covenant renewal ceremony. This ceremony both established Israel's monarchy in the context of a renewal of their allegiance to Yahweh, and integrated human kingship into the structure of the theocracy; there would be a human king, but Yahweh would continue to be recognized as Israel's divine king (1 Sam 11:14–12:25). The human king in Israel was to be an agent of Yahweh's rule over his people. He was not an autonomous king, like kings of the surrounding nations. He was obligated to obey the requirements of the Mosaic law and the instructions of the prophets. Saul, Israel's first king, had proved to be a disappointment, however. He did not function in his royal office in a way that demonstrated the continued recognition of Yahweh as Israel's true sovereign. He repeatedly disobeyed the word of the Lord and when confronted about his disobedience attempted to justify his actions rather than acknowledge his sin. The

Lord therefore rejected Saul, and David was anointed to replace him. Once David became the ruler of all Israel, he made an extremely significant decision to bring the Ark of the Covenant to Zion/Jerusalem (ch 6), his newly acquired capital city. Implicit in bringing the Ark to Jerusalem was David's recognition that Yahweh was Israel's divine sovereign.[1] In fact, by this act David and the people were publicly acknowledging that Yahweh was their Great King.[2] So in chapter 6 David honors the Lord by affirming his kingly rule over the nation, and in chapter 7, the Lord honors David by promising him a dynasty that will endure forever.

Second Samuel 6 describes two attempts to bring the Ark to Zion. The first attempt ended in tragedy and failure (6:1-10), but the second attempt was successful and was accomplished with great joy and celebration (6:12-19). During the entire duration of Saul's reign, the Ark had remained in obscurity at the house of Abinadab in Kiriath-jearim, where it had been placed shortly after being returned to Israel after its capture by the Philistines (1 Sam 4–6). Saul's subsequent failure to provide the Ark with a visible and prominent place in Gibeah, his capital city, was symptomatic of his failure to fully recognize the sovereignty of Yahweh as Israel's divine king. Now we learn that David was determined to place his reign on a different footing than Saul had chosen. From the arrangement of the narratives in 2 Samuel, it seems clear that the narrator desired to call attention to this remarkable contrast between Saul and David. The placement of the story of the bringing of the Ark to Jerusalem immediately after the accounts of David's capture of Jerusalem and his defeat of the Philistines is certainly significant.[3] The close connection between David's exaltation of Yahweh's kingship and Yahweh's exaltation of David's kingship is emphasized in a structural way not only by the placement of chapters 6 and 7 at the center of the first ring structure, after the inauguration of David's rule as king, but also by the correspondence between these two chapters and David's Song in Praise of God's Reign (2 Sam 22:1-51) and David's Last Words about His Reign (2 Sam 23:1-7), which are placed at the center of the last ring structure in the book.[4] In fact, it is the emphasis on the relationship between the kingship of Yahweh and the kingship of David that not only accounts for the difference between the reign of David and the reign of Saul, but also accounts for the significant attention that is given to the dark side of David's reign when he failed to take the responsibility of covenant faithfulness seriously.

David's desire to bring the Ark to Jerusalem was certainly commendable, but on his first attempt to do so he failed to ascertain the proper means for its transport. As a symbol of the public significance of bringing the Ark to Zion, David sent a large military force to the house of Abinadab in Baalah of Judah (another name for Kiriath-jearim, see note on 6:2) to accompany the Ark on its journey and to escort it in a stately procession into the City of David. The Ark itself was placed on a new cart, pulled by oxen, and accompanied by Abinadab's two sons, Uzzah and Ahio. But this method of transport, which was the same that had been used by the Philistines when they returned the Ark to Israel (1 Sam 6), was a violation of the instructions the Lord had given to Moses requiring that the Ark be carried by Kohathites from the tribe of Levi (Num 4:4-6, 15, 17-20). When the oxen stumbled and Uzzah reached out to keep the Ark from falling, the Lord struck him dead, just as the Mosaic regulations had warned. This calamity brought the celebratory procession to an abrupt halt, and David responded to it with anger (6:8) and fear (6:9). David's first reaction seems to have been strong resentment that both his and Uzzah's good intentions could be repudiated in such a shocking manner by the God whom they were seeking to honor (6:8). But his anger quickly turned to fear (6:9). In this instance, the fear did not appear to be the wholesome fear of a proper awe and respect for God that promotes worship and adoration, but rather a guilt-induced fear that fosters disaffection and alienation. The name that David gave to the place where Uzzah was killed (cf. 6:8, Perez-uzzah, meaning "to burst out against Uzzah") suggests that David saw a connection between the Lord's anger on this occasion and his anger against the Philistines (cf. 5:20, where David called the place where the Philistines were defeated Baal-perazim, meaning "the Lord who bursts through"). The implication is that David seemed to have concluded that the Lord had become his enemy. In this frame of mind he decided to abandon his attempt to bring the Ark to Jerusalem, and he placed it in the home of Obed-edom.[5]

After three months in which David must have reflected on what went wrong in his first attempt to bring the Ark to Zion, and after learning that the Lord had blessed the household of Obed-edom where the Ark was being kept (6:12), David decided to make a new attempt to bring the Ark to the nation's capital city. This time the Ark was carried by the Levites (cf. 6:13; 1 Chr 15:2, 13-15). And this time the Ark was successfully brought to the City of David, accompanied by great rejoicing and celebration. The Ark was placed in a special tent David had prepared for it,[6] and burnt offerings and peace offerings were offered up to the Lord, indicating that fellowship had been restored between the Lord and his people (6:17). It is significant that peace offerings, involving a communal meal, were part of the covenant renewal ceremony at Gilgal on the occasion of the establishment of kingship in Israel (see commentary on 1 Sam 11:14-15, especially endnote 4). Now on the occasion of a renewed recognition of Yahweh's kingship over his people, these offerings were again appropriate.[7]

The final section of the chapter (6:20-23) describes the reaction of Michal to David's behavior during the processional in which the Ark was brought to Zion. In Michal's eyes, David disgracefully humiliated himself before the people of Israel by his enthusiastic dancing in a simple linen tunic that she viewed as something inappropriate for his royal status (6:16, 20). But Michal completely misunderstood David's actions. David responded vigorously to her critique by asserting that it was the Lord who had chosen him above her father to be the ruler over his people, and that he (David) was willing to look even more foolish than he had on this occasion in order to celebrate the kingship of Yahweh (6:21-22).[8] As van den Berg (1997:41) suggests, David was here displaying something of his messianic status by identifying with slaves much as later Jesus, David's greater son, would humiliate himself and take on the form of a slave (Phil 2:7). The narrator concludes the chapter with the comment that Michal remained childless for the rest of her days (6:23). The statement implies that the Lord closed her womb because she, as her father before her, was unwilling to bow before the kingship of Yahweh. The end result was the termination of the royal line of Saul (1 Sam 13:14).

ENDNOTES

1. When God gave Moses instructions for building the Tabernacle (Exod 25–27), the Ark of the Covenant was the very first component to be described. The Ark was a rectangular box made of wood and covered with gold that measured about 4 x 2½ x 2½ feet. It was to be placed behind a curtain in the Most Holy Place, into which the high priest could enter only once a year on the Day of Atonement (Lev 16). The space above the Ark between the cherubs on either end of its cover was the focal point of God's dwelling among his people. (In Exod 25:22 God told Moses "I will meet with you there and talk to you from above the atonement cover between the gold cherubim that hover over the Ark of the Covenant. From there I will give you my commands for the people of Israel." Second Samuel 6:2 and 1 Sam 4:4 speak of the Lord as "seated" or "enthroned" above or between the cherubim (cf. Ps 132:7, 8, 13, 14). Using a similar metaphor, 1 Chr 28:2 and Ps 132:7 refer to the Ark as the "footstool" of the throne of Yahweh. Moses was instructed to deposit a copy of the Ten Commandments inside the Ark (Exod 25:16, 21; 40:20; Deut 10:5). So among the symbolic functions of the Ark, two of the most prominent are those of container and throne. Because the Ark was a box containing a copy of the law of the God who was invisibly enthroned above it (cf. de Vaux 1961a:297-302; 1971a; Durham 1987:357-360), it was a visible symbol of Yahweh's divine kingship over his people Israel. In a number of psalms it is affirmed that Yahweh reigns from the Holy City of Zion where he sits enthroned (Pss 48, 78, 132). For a detailed study of Jerusalem as the Holy City and its significance as the place from which Yahweh exercised his royal dominion, see Schreiner 1963.
2. This understanding of the significance of the events of this chapter differs from what is usually encountered in the mainstream of contemporary biblical studies. Most scholars have regarded ch 6 as the reflection of a hypothetical annual festival in ancient Israel that included a reenactment of the entry of the Ark into Jerusalem among its observances. The precise nature and features of this annual festival are disputed. Mowinckel (1967:1.128-130, 175-176), for example, viewed it as a festival of "Yahweh's enthronement," while Kraus (1951:27-35; 1966:183-185) regarded it as a "royal Zion festival" intended to commemorate the choice of Zion and the election of David. The assumption behind these views is that the author "had no contemporary reports about the festival from the time of David, so he described it on the model of the celebration of his own day" (Mowinckel 1967:1.175, 237-239). One of the results of this sort of approach is that the historicity of ch 6 is opened to serious question. Miller and Roberts (1977:16), however, challenged "the widespread tendency to regard 2 Samuel 6 as the reflex of a regular temple liturgy" by calling attention to Mesopotamian analogies for this chapter such as Asshurbanipal's return of Marduk's image to its shrine in Babylon after a generation of captivity. Miller and Roberts (1977:23) comment: "2 Sam 6 may be compared to the historical chronicles that record the return of despoiled images by victorious monarchs." McCarter (1983), however, has challenged Miller and Roberts's "return" theory because in his view Yahweh is not really returning to Zion but rather is entering Jerusalem for the first time. McCarter (1983:274) argues that the account "is concerned with the inauguration, not reestablishment, of his cult there." In McCarter's approach (1983:275) it is David, not Yahweh, who is "the center of interest in the account. The introduction of Yahweh's Ark represents the sanction of the national deity for David's kingship and his new capital." In other words, McCarter sees the central purpose of the events described in ch 6 as legitimization of David, not the recognition of Yahweh. In a similar manner, McKenzie (2000:135) says, "The presence of the Ark in Jerusalem strongly suggested that the God whom the northerners worshiped and who was represented by the Ark supported

David's reign." There is much that is speculative about these theories concerning the background for the narrative of ch 6. In my view the chapter should be taken as an authentic account of the bringing of the Ark to Zion/Jerusalem by David in order to celebrate the kingship of Yahweh over his covenant people. The central focus of the chapter is on the kingship of Yahweh, not on the legitimation of David's royal office. If David's kingship is sanctioned in this chapter at all, it is only in the secondary sense of presenting himself as a ruler who conforms to the ideal of a true covenantal king by his acknowledgment of the kingship of Yahweh.

3. It appears that the purpose of the placement of these narrative units is to emphasize the covenantal issues about which they speak, rather than to provide data for a chronology of David's reign. Klement (2000:93-97) calls attention to what he terms "aspectival perception" (as contrasted with "perspectival perception"), which is characteristic of chiastic literature that "places more value on the typical, and places alongside each other in cumulative and dual form those aspects which are important to the context. In this way there emerges a total picture which is a collage of aspects, but unable to be confined in an all-embracing conclusion or formula." This, of course, has implications for chronology. As Klement notes (2000:93), "If these ring-structures with their binary correspondences have determined the arrangement of the texts, then this may be the reason for the fact that on a linear-perspectival reading there are often chronological tensions to be noted." He goes on to say (2000:94) that the "opening sentences of both the central chapters, concerning Yahweh's taking-up of residence in Jerusalem and the promise of an everlasting dynasty, thus have as their starting-point the already accomplished end of all fighting, even though this is not described until later." This helps explain the difficulties of establishing a chronology for David's reign from the data included in 1–2 Samuel. Merrill (1987:238-248) has also suggested that David did not bring the Ark to Jerusalem until the last years of his reign.
4. Although this last ring structure (chs 21–24) has often been called the "Samuel Appendix" and considered an intrusion into the Succession Narrative that allegedly flows on into 1 Kgs 1–2, it is more appropriate to regard chs 21–24 not as an appendix but rather as a conclusion for the book of Samuel that has been designed to call attention to the same covenantal issues that have been addressed throughout the book (cf. Klement 2000 and "Literary Style" in the Introduction).
5. Perhaps the same Obed-edom mentioned in 1 Chr 15:18, 21, 24. If this is the case, Obed-edom was a Levite.
6. It is not clear why David did not bring the Tabernacle to Zion at the same time that he brought the Ark. Chronicles indicates that the Tabernacle was at Gibeon during the reigns of David and Solomon (1 Chr 16:39; 21:29; 2 Chr 1:3) until Solomon finally brought it to Jerusalem (2 Chr 5:5).
7. This understanding of the purpose of the peace offering in this context differs from that suggested by Klement (2000:64), who follows the view of Flanagan (1983), who attempted to adapt the views of van Gennep on "rites of passage" to chs 6 and 7. According to van Gennep, rites of passage involve three phases. Flanagan thus speaks of a "separation phase," where an old order is abandoned, a "liminality phase" of insecurity and transition, and a "reaggregation phase" where a new order is adopted. Flanagan and Klement find the "liminality phase" reflected in chs 6 and 7, and Flanagan suggests two other episodes in which a *shelamim* offering is mentioned in connection with a scene of inauguration: 1 Sam 11:14 and 1 Kgs 8:63-64. Klement (2000:65) summarizes Flanagan's conclusions on ch 6 by finding in it "a transition from a 'segmental tribal organization of the Yahwistic community' to a 'centralized territorial governance',

and simultaneously as a change of rule from the 'northern leadership of the house of Saul' to the Judaic family of Jesse and the house of David. The former is executed through the transfer of the Ark as the symbol of the tradition of the tribal community, the latter through the role of Michal. Her childlessness is not only seen as reflecting her own personal tragedy, but must also be understood as the definitive destiny of the family of Saul, for which there can be no possibility of a return to the throne." While some of these concerns may well be involved in the events described in ch 6, it is this writer's conclusion that the central issue in the chapter is not the legitimation of David's kingship, but rather David's public recognition of the kingship of Yahweh. The function of the *shelamim* offering (6:17) is then not a "ritual to legitimate David's authority" (Klement 2000:64) but rather a means of expressing the renewal of covenant fellowship between Yahweh and his people after a period of time in which Yahweh's kingship had been eclipsed by that of the human ruler, Saul.

8. The inclusion of this episode at the conclusion of the narrative describing the transfer of the Ark to Jerusalem confirms that the focus of the entire narrative is intended to exalt the kingship of Yahweh rather than legitimize the kingship of David (see endnote 2).

◆ I. The Lord Makes a Covenant with David (2 Sam 7:1-29)

When King David was settled in his palace and the LORD had given him rest from all the surrounding enemies, [2]the king summoned Nathan the prophet. "Look," David said, "I am living in a beautiful cedar palace,* but the Ark of God is out there in a tent!"

[3]Nathan replied to the king, "Go ahead and do whatever you have in mind, for the LORD is with you."

[4]But that same night the LORD said to Nathan,

> **[5]"Go and tell my servant David, 'This is what the LORD has declared: Are you the one to build a house for me to live in? [6]I have never lived in a house, from the day I brought the Israelites out of Egypt until this very day. I have always moved from one place to another with a tent and a Tabernacle as my dwelling. [7]Yet no matter where I have gone with the Israelites, I have never once complained to Israel's tribal leaders, the shepherds of my people Israel. I have never asked them, "Why haven't you built me a beautiful cedar house?"'**
>
> **[8]"Now go and say to my servant David, 'This is what the LORD of Heaven's Armies has declared: I took you from tending sheep in the pasture and selected you to be the leader of my people Israel. [9]I have been with you wherever you have gone, and I have destroyed all your enemies before your eyes. Now I will make your name as famous as anyone who has ever lived on the earth! [10]And I will provide a homeland for my people Israel, planting them in a secure place where they will never be disturbed. Evil nations won't oppress them as they've done in the past, [11]starting from the time I appointed judges to rule my people Israel. And I will give you rest from all your enemies.**
>
> **"'Furthermore, the LORD declares that he will make a house for you—a dynasty of kings! [12]For when you die and are buried with your ancestors, I will raise up one of your descendants, your own offspring, and I will make his kingdom strong. [13]He is the one who will build a house—a temple—for my name. And I will secure his royal throne forever. [14]I will be his father, and he will be my son. If he sins, I will correct**

and discipline him with the rod, like
any father would do. [15]But my favor
will not be taken from him as I took it
from Saul, whom I removed from your
sight. [16]Your house and your kingdom
will continue before me* for all time,
and your throne will be secure forever.'"

[17]So Nathan went back to David and told
him everything the LORD had said in this
vision.

[18]Then King David went in and sat be-
fore the LORD and prayed,

"Who am I, O Sovereign LORD, and what
is my family, that you have brought me
this far? [19]And now, Sovereign LORD,
in addition to everything else, you
speak of giving your servant a lasting
dynasty! Do you deal with everyone this
way, O Sovereign LORD?*

[20]"What more can I say to you? You
know what your servant is really like,
Sovereign LORD. [21]Because of your
promise and according to your will,
you have done all these great things
and have made them known to your
servant.

[22]"How great you are, O Sovereign
LORD! There is no one like you. We have
never even heard of another God like
you! [23]What other nation on earth is
like your people Israel? What other
nation, O God, have you redeemed from
slavery to be your own people? You
made a great name for yourself when
you redeemed your people from Egypt.
You performed awesome miracles and
drove out the nations and gods that
stood in their way.* [24]You made Israel
your very own people forever, and you,
O LORD, became their God.

[25]"And now, O LORD God, I am your
servant; do as you have promised
concerning me and my family. Confirm
it as a promise that will last forever.
[26]And may your name be honored
forever so that everyone will say, 'The
LORD of Heaven's Armies is God over
Israel!' And may the house of your
servant David continue before you
forever.

[27]"O LORD of Heaven's Armies, God
of Israel, I have been bold enough to
pray this prayer to you because you
have revealed all this to your servant,
saying, 'I will build a house for you—a
dynasty of kings!' [28]For you are God,
O Sovereign LORD. Your words are truth,
and you have promised these good
things to your servant. [29]And now, may
it please you to bless the house of your
servant, so that it may continue forever
before you. For you have spoken, and
when you grant a blessing to your
servant, O Sovereign LORD, it is an
eternal blessing!"

7:2 Hebrew *a house of cedar.* **7:16** As in Greek version and some Hebrew manuscripts; Masoretic Text reads *before you.* **7:19** Or *This is your instruction for all humanity, O Sovereign LORD.* **7:23** As in Greek version (see also 1 Chr 17:21); Hebrew reads *You made a great name for yourself and performed awesome miracles for your land. You did this in the sight of your people, whom you redeemed from Egypt, from nations and their gods.*

NOTES

7:7 *tribal leaders.* Context suggests that *shebet* [TH7626, ZH8657] (rod, staff, tribe) may mean not only "tribe" but also "tribal leader" (A. Anderson 1989:75, 110-111; Fokkelman 1990:218, 381). A NJPS mg note suggests "scepters of" as a metonym for tribal leaders. There is, therefore, no need to emend to *shopte* [TH8199, ZH9149] (judge) as in 1 Chr 17:6. McCarter (1984:192) takes *shibte* as a plural participial form: "the staff bearers of [Israel]."

7:19 *Do you deal with everyone this way, O Sovereign LORD?* See NLT mg for the alternative rendering: "This is your instruction for all humanity, O Sovereign LORD." Both the translation and the meaning of this phrase have long been debated. A basic question is whether it is an interrogative or an exclamation. The parallel in 1 Chr 17:17, although worded differently and more fully, does not suggest an interrogative. Another key point in the discussion is the meaning of *torath* [TH8451, ZH9368] (instruction, rule, manner). Various other translations include, "Is this your usual way of dealing with man, O Sovereign LORD?" (NIV) and "May this be instruction for the people, O Lord GOD!" (NRSV). Kaiser (1974:315) argues convincingly for the translation, "And this [new addition to the promise doctrine] is the Charter (*torath*) for all mankind, O Lord God!"

7:22 ***There is no one like you.*** Regarding the "asseverative" use of *ki* [TH3509.1, ZH3869] ("truly" or "indeed" there is no one like you) in this phrase, see Williams 1976:§449.

7:23 ***and drove out.*** This emends the MT's *le'artseka* [TH776, ZH824] (for your land) to *legaresh* [TH1644, ZH1763] (drive out) in agreement with the parallel in 1 Chr 17:21 and the *tou ekbalein* [TG1544, ZG1675] of LXX.

7:27 ***I have been bold enough.*** Lit., "your servant has found his heart."

COMMENTARY

The Lord's words to Eli in 1 Samuel 2:30, "I will honor those who honor me," capture something of the relationship between 2 Samuel 6 and 7. While chapter 6 speaks of David's desire to honor the Lord by bringing the Ark of God to Zion, chapter 7 speaks of the Lord's desire to honor David by giving him the promise of a dynasty that will endure forever.

Chapter 7 opens with a description of David's consultation with the prophet Nathan[1] concerning the advisability of building a permanent structure to house the Ark of God.[2] David had come to the conclusion that the contrast between the beauty and permanence of his own residence and the simplicity and temporary character of the tent he had provided for the Ark of God (cf. 6:17) was unsuitable (7:1-2). If the Ark was the throne of the divine king (cf. endnote 2 on 1 Sam 4:1b-22; ch 6; Ps 132; and endnote 1 in the commentary on ch 6), did it not deserve a more fitting resting place? Nathan agreed with David's assessment and told him to do whatever he thought appropriate, assuring him that the Lord would be with him in his endeavor (7:3). It seems that neither David nor Nathan imagined that there could be any objection to their desire to build a Temple for the Lord. But we must remember what the Lord said to Isaiah: "My thoughts are nothing like your thoughts. . . . And my ways are far beyond anything you could imagine" (Isa 55:8). That night the Lord spoke to Nathan and told him to go and tell David that he was not to build a "house" (*bayith* [TH1004, ZH1074]) for the Lord, but rather that the Lord would build a "house" (*bayith*) for David—a dynasty (7:11, 16).[3] It would be left for David's son to build a "house" (*bayith*) for the Lord (7:12-13; cf. 1 Kgs 5–6; 1 Chr 22:2-5; 28:2-3, 6). In this beautiful wordplay on the term "house," the Lord gave David one of the most significant promises in the entire Bible. It is this promise that stands at the heart of chapter 7, and in fact, at the heart of the entire book of Samuel. It is a promise that lays the groundwork for messianic expectation in Israel and is often referred to as the Davidic covenant.[4]

Second Samuel 7 may be divided into three distinct sections: an introduction by the narrator (7:1-4); a description of the instructions and the promise that the Lord gave to David through the prophet Nathan (7:5-16); and a description of David's prayer of praise to the Lord in response to the divine oracle he had received (7:18-29).

Although the Lord sent Nathan to David to correct his earlier word of approval for David's desire to build a Temple to house the Ark, the Lord couched his veto in gracious and friendly terms. In the initial section of Nathan's oracle to David (7:5-7), God addressed David as "my servant"[5] (7:5) and explained to him that he (God) had never asked for a "cedar house," and that for the present, he was content to continue "to dwell" in a tent as he had done ever since the Ark was constructed. In contrast to the heathen deities of surrounding nations, Yahweh, the God of Israel, exhibited his splendor in the works he performed on behalf of his people, rather than in the grandeur of a building (van den Berg 1997:44). The deliverance of Israel from Egypt (7:6) said much more about the glory of Yahweh than a structure of wood and stone ever could. Although David's desire to honor Yahweh by building a Temple was a legitimate desire,[6] and in the Lord's time, this task would be accomplished by David's son, Solomon, a Temple building would introduce the danger of placing confidence in the external appearance of the site of the Lord's habitation among his people rather than in the majesty of the Lord's person.

The second part of Nathan's oracle to David (7:8-16) concerns the house (dynasty) that the Lord promised to build for David and his descendants. The Lord introduced this dynastic promise by placing it in the larger context of the Lord's purposes for both David and the nation over which he had been set as ruler (7:8-11). The Lord reminded David that He had chosen him to be the leader of the nation at a time when he was no more than an obscure young shepherd tending the flocks of his father (7:8). In the intervening years the Lord had guided and protected David, not only during the time of his presence in the court of Saul when his life was repeatedly threatened by Saul's jealousy of his successes, but also during the years of his fugitive existence in the wilderness of Judea and the time of his questionable alliance with the Philistine ruler, Achish of Gath (7:9). It was now the Lord's purpose to use David to provide Israel with secure borders and to deliver her from the enemies that threatened her continued existence as a nation (7:10-11a). This is the context in which the Lord said that it was his purpose to build a house (dynasty) for David (7:11b).

This dynastic promise to David in 7:11b is expanded in a threefold manner in 7:12-16. First, David will be succeeded on the throne of Israel by his own son, who, unlike Saul and Ishbosheth, will rule over an established and powerful kingdom (7:12). Second, this son of David will be the person who will build a Temple to house the Ark (7:13a). The Lord's purpose was for his own work to precede and make possible the work of David's son. The Lord would first build a house for David (a dynasty) through which Israel would become secure. When this was accomplished, David's son would build a house (Temple) for the Lord so that the Lord might dwell among his people in conditions of security and peace.[7] Third, the throne of David's son will endure forever (7:13b) because God will establish a father-son relationship with him (7:14a)—and even though he would be disciplined if he went astray from his covenantal obligations (7:14b), the Lord would never remove his unfailing love from him as he had done with Saul (7:15b). The Lord then repeated the promise that David's royal line would endure forever (7:16).[8] This startling and far-reaching promise, appropriately termed the "matrix of biblical messianism" by Gordon (1986:236), provides the basis for the subsequent development of the messianic hope in the writings of the prophets and psalmists and finds its ultimate fulfillment in "Jesus the Messiah, a descendant of David and of Abraham" (Matt 1:1).[9]

David was deeply moved by the promise he had received, and 7:18-29 records David's prayerful response to it. David went to the tent where the Ark of God had been placed ("David went in and sat before the LORD," 7:18) and lifted up his voice to God, expressing his amazement at what the Lord had already done for him and his family by bringing him to the throne in Israel (7:18). He praised God[10] for the astonishing scope of the promise, in spite of his own unworthiness as a recipient of it (7:18-21). He then celebrated the Lord's greatness for the mighty works he had performed on behalf of the people he had redeemed from slavery and brought to himself (7:22-24). Finally, David pleaded for the fulfillment of that which the Lord had promised (7:25-29).

David's understanding that the promise that he had received carried universal and messianic implications is expressed in 7:19b.[11] David's declaration, in fact, also expresses his surprise at the astounding implication that was wrapped up in God's promise to him and his descendants: "This is your instruction for all humanity, O Sovereign LORD" (7:19, NLT mg; see note on 7:19). David thus gave expression to his awareness that the long-standing promise of Genesis 3:15 (the offspring of the woman will strike the head of the serpent), that was carried forward in the promises to Abraham ("all the families of the earth will be blessed through you and your descendants" [Gen 28:14b]), and subsequently narrowed to the tribe of Judah (Gen 49:10), was now to be fulfilled through one of his own descendants. Given David's consciousness of his own unworthiness for the honor bestowed on him, he confessed that its explanation could lie only in the Lord's sovereign purpose and plan (7:21).

In his prayer, David extolled the greatness and the uniqueness of Yahweh and denied the existence of any other deities—and he did so in language reminiscent of Moses's confession on the plains of Moab (7:22; cf. Deut 4:35-39). This uniqueness of Yahweh translates into the uniqueness of Israel because Israel is the one nation that God had chosen to redeem to himself out of all the nations of the earth (7:23-24).

ENDNOTES

1. Nathan appears in this chapter for the first time in 1–2 Samuel and in the Bible. As a prophet, he is the bearer of the Lord's word to David. He is the same prophet who later confronted David about his sin with Bathsheba (ch 12), and subsequently he played a significant role in securing the succession of the throne from David to Solomon when this was challenged by Adonijah (1 Kgs 1). He is referred to by the Chronicler as the author of written accounts of the reigns of David and Solomon (1 Chr 29:29; 2 Chr 9:29).
2. There is a long and complex history of literary analysis of ch 7. For good summaries of the issues involved, see A. Anderson 1989:112-116; McCarter 1984:210-231; Gakuru 2000.

3. This is one of a number of passages in the OT in which it is clear that a distinction may be made between a prophet speaking his "own words" and speaking the "word of the Lord." In speaking of Nathan's initial response to David's inquiry, Schelhaas (1974:291) comments, "The prophet should first have waited for God's revelation. A good intention does not always mean that we are allowed to execute it. That Nathan too desired a temple for the God of Israel was not wrong in itself. The mistake made here was that he spoke as *man* and not as *prophet*, while his opinion as a prophet had been specifically asked for."
4. Although the word "covenant" does not occur in ch 7 as a designation for the Lord's promise to David, this term is used by David in 23:5, and it occurs with reference to this promise in numerous other OT passages as well (1 Kgs 8:23; 2 Chr 13:5; Pss 89:3, 28, 34, 39; 132:12; Isa 55:3; Jer 33:21).
5. Fokkelman (1990:214) notes that prior to this time this title had been conferred by God on only two individuals, namely Abraham (Gen 26:24) and Moses (Num 12:7-8; Josh 1:2-7; 2 Kgs 21:8; Mal 4:4). The designation suggests a close relationship between the Lord and David, and says something of the Lord's confidence in David's loyalty and devotion. In the following verses David picks up on this title and refers to himself 10 times as "your servant" in his prayer of praise to the Lord (7:19, 20, 21, 25, 26, 27 [two times in Hebrew], 28, 29 [two times]).
6. See 1 Kgs 8:18-19: "You wanted to build the Temple to honor my name. Your intention is good, but you are not the one to do it."
7. See 1 Kgs 5:3. Dumbrell (1984:149) posits a connection between certain features of the Abrahamic covenant and their counterparts in the Davidic covenant in ch 7. He suggests that the appeal to "the underlying theology of the Abrahamic covenant and the understanding of it by the writer of 2 Samuel is clear. Certainly 2 Sam 7:9b-11a has in mind the establishment of Israel's ideal Abrahamic borders (note the 'place' of 7:10—the Abrahamic borders of Gen 15:18ff are defined in Deut 11:24ff as Israel's 'place'). This would bring David a 'great name' (cf. 2 Sam 7:9 with Gen 12:2), and this conjunction of a great people, ideally governed, living in predetermined geographical dimensions will result finally in the experience by Israel of the tantalizing but biblically fundamental promise of rest. The logic of the chapter recognizes that only when this ideal result has been achieved should a sanctuary be built. This will then mark out the promised land as 'holy space' and will point to the kingship of God which undergirds the whole Davidic programme." In addition it should be noted that the Chronicler not only emphasizes that David's son Solomon would be "a man of peace" and therefore a more appropriate person to build a Temple than David (1 Chr 22:9-10), but also that it was because David "shed so much blood" that he would not be permitted to build a Temple to honor the Lord's name (1 Chr 22:8). Why "shedding blood" should disqualify David from building the Temple is not explained. Murray (2002:475) suggests that "David's unusual degree of ritual defilement is in irresolvable tension with the demand for a unique degree of ritual purity in the temple-builder."
8. The enduring character of David's dynasty is mentioned seven times in ch 7 (7:13b, 16a, 16b, 24, 25, 29a, 29b).
9. Brueggemann (1990a:253-254) suggests that the initiative for the claim of an enduring dynasty lies with David rather than with Yahweh's sovereign disposition, and that David is here attempting to secure an ability for his dynasty that is immune from the normal vacillations of political fortunes. He terms the promise (1990a:256-257), "royal propaganda or ideology designed to enhance and legitimate the new state. Nathan is a prophet of God, but one schooled to package God's truth in ways useful

to the regime. . . . Thus the high statement of theology lives very close to self-serving ideology and may be heard as an act of royal propaganda." This cynical reading of the text not only challenges the authenticity of the prophetic function of Nathan, but poses serious questions about the integrity of both Nathan and David. Surprisingly, however, Brueggemann is still able to say that he regards the Lord's promise to David as "the most crucial theological statement in the Old Testament," because he sees it as a "vehicle for the Bible's best theology of grace and messianism" (1990a:258). Is there not something problematic with finding the Bible's "best theology of grace and messianism" in a propagandistic fabrication?

10. The reverence with which David addresses God in his prayer is notable. He uses the expression "Sovereign LORD" (lit., "Lord Yahweh"; *'adonay yhwh*) seven times (7:18, 19 [two times], 20, 22, 28, 29); "the LORD of Heaven's Armies" (*yhwh tseba'oth*) two times (7:26, 27); "God of Israel" (*'elohe yisra'el*) two times (7:26, 27); and "LORD God" (*yhwh 'elohim*) once (7:25).
11. This understanding of an admittedly difficult text is ably developed and defended by Kaiser (1974).

◆ J. All David's Enemies Defeated with the Lord's Help (2 Sam 8:1-14)

After this, David defeated and subdued the
Philistines by conquering Gath, their larg-
est town.* 2David also conquered the land
of Moab. He made the people lie down on
the ground in a row, and he measured
them off in groups with a length of rope.
He measured off two groups to be execut-
ed for every one group to be spared. The
Moabites who were spared became David's
subjects and paid him tribute money.

3David also destroyed the forces of Ha-
dadezer son of Rehob, king of Zobah,
when Hadadezer marched out to strength-
en his control along the Euphrates River.
4David captured 1,000 chariots, 7,000
charioteers,* and 20,000 foot soldiers. He
crippled all the chariot horses except
enough for 100 chariots.

5When Arameans from Damascus arrived
to help King Hadadezer, David killed 22,000
of them. 6Then he placed several army gar-
risons in Damascus, the Aramean capital,
and the Arameans became David's subjects
and paid him tribute money. So the LORD
made David victorious wherever he went.

7David brought the gold shields of
Hadadezer's officers to Jerusalem, 8along
with a large amount of bronze from Ha-
dadezer's towns of Tebah* and Berothai.

9When King Toi of Hamath heard that
David had destroyed the entire army of
Hadadezer, 10he sent his son Joram to
congratulate King David for his successful
campaign. Hadadezer and Toi had been
enemies and were often at war. Joram
presented David with many gifts of silver,
gold, and bronze.

11King David dedicated all these gifts to
the LORD, as he did with the silver and
gold from the other nations he had de-
feated—12from Edom,* Moab, Ammon,
Philistia, and Amalek—and from Hada-
dezer son of Rehob, king of Zobah.

13So David became even more famous
when he returned from destroying 18,000
Edomites* in the Valley of Salt. 14He placed
army garrisons throughout Edom, and all
the Edomites became David's subjects. In
fact, the LORD made David victorious
wherever he went.

8:1 Hebrew *by conquering Metheg-ammah,* a name that means "the bridle," possibly referring to the size of the town or the tribute money taken from it. Compare 1 Chr 18:1. **8:4** As in Dead Sea Scrolls and Greek version (see also 1 Chr 18:4); Masoretic Text reads *captured 1,700 charioteers.* **8:8** As in some Greek manuscripts (see also 1 Chr 18:8); Hebrew reads *Betah.* **8:12** As in a few Hebrew manuscripts and Greek and Syriac versions (see also 8:14; 1 Chr 18:11); most Hebrew manuscripts read *Aram.* **8:13** As in a few Hebrew manuscripts and Greek and Syriac versions (see also 8:14; 1 Chr 18:12); most Hebrew manuscripts read *Arameans.*

NOTES

8:1 *by conquering Gath, their largest town.* See NLT mg. The Hebrew (*metheg 'ammah* [TH4965, ZH5497]) is an otherwise unknown place, but if the Hebrew is not taken as a proper name (Metheg Ammah), its meaning is uncertain. BDB (607) suggests "authority of the mother-city," assuming *metheg* [TH4964, ZH5496] (bridle) to be figurative for authority or control and *'ammah* [TH517, ZH562] (mother) figurative for the greatest of the Philistine cities. The parallel in 1 Chr 18:1 suggests "Gath and its surrounding towns," which is the understanding represented in the NLT translation. A. Anderson (1989:129), following Hertzberg (1964:288), suggests "wresting supremacy," based on understanding the Hebrew as meaning literally "the reins [*metheg*] of the forearm [*ha'ammah*]."

8:3 *to strengthen his control.* Some translate this phrase as "to restore his monument," taking *yado* [TH3027/2050.2, ZH3338/2257] as "his monument" (rather than "his hand," i.e., NLT's "control") on the basis of similar usage in 18:18 and 1 Sam 15:12.

Euphrates River. The Kethiv of MT is "by a river." The NLT follows the Qere, "by the Euphrates River," in agreement with LXX and 1 Chr 18:3.

8:4 *1,000 chariots, 7,000 charioteers.* MT reads "1,700 charioteers." Ulrich (1978:56-57) argues that 4QSam[a] probably supports the LXX reading, "1,000 chariots and 7,000 charioteers" (so NLT). There is little on which to base a preferred reading.

8:7 *gold shields.* It has been effectively argued that *shilte hazzahab* [TH7982/2091, ZH8949/2298] is better rendered as "gold quivers" or "golden bow cases"; see McCarter's (1984:250) summarization of the evidence presented by Borger (1972).

COMMENTARY

Chapter 8 contains lists of David's military conquests (8:1-14) and governmental officials (8:15-18), a feature appropriately suited to the narrative at this point. As Halpern (1996:54) has pointed out, "David has become king of Judah, then king of Israel, then king in Jerusalem, and has brought the ark into his capital and received a dynastic oracle. In the narrative logic, the stage is set for a summary of David's positive achievements."[1] Not only does this chapter present the reader with a positive assessment of David's career as king, but it also discloses some important things about the Lord's faithfulness to his covenantal promises. So chapter 8 provides an appropriate conclusion to the mostly affirmative description of David's reign found in chapters 1–8. A set of narratives depicting some of the darker side of David's reign follows in chapters 9–20.

In the preceding chapter it is clear that David understood that security from external enemies and conditions of peace in the land of Israel were a prerequisite for building a temple.[2] For this reason David devoted a significant part of his reign to the establishment of the peaceful conditions necessary for this endeavor.[3] Part of this process was the extension of Israel's political jurisdiction to the boundaries that had been promised to Abraham (Gen 15:18-21) and then confirmed to Moses (Num 34:1-15; Deut 1:7; 11:24) and Joshua (Josh 1:4), but not realized at the time of the conquest of Canaan (Josh 11:16-17). In addition, the Lord had promised David that he would make the kingdom of his son a strong kingdom (7:12), and that David's name would be "as famous as anyone who has ever lived on the earth" (7:9). Second Samuel 8 describes how these promises were fulfilled.[4] The expression "the LORD made David victorious wherever he went" occurs twice in the chapter

(8:6, 14), strongly emphasizing that David's success was because of the Lord's blessing on his military campaigns. As a result of these victories, David "became even more famous" (8:13; cf. 7:9), and Israel became a major player in the international politics of the time. This chapter, therefore, proclaims an important message to Israel as well as to every reader from that time to this: *The Lord is faithful to his promises.*[5] Viewed from this perspective, David's conquests are not in the first instance to be viewed as demonstrations of his military skill, although he was clearly a capable military leader, but rather as evidence of God's faithfulness to his promises.

From a structural standpoint it is striking that the list of peoples whom David conquered is divided into two parts (8:1-6 and 8:13-14). The first part tells of David's victories over the Philistines (8:1) and the Moabites (8:2), the conquest of the territory of Hadadezer near the Euphrates River (8:3-4), and of the Arameans of Damascus (8:6). The second part of the list tells of the subjection of Edom (8:13-14). These victories gave David control over a large territory stretching from the Euphrates River in the north to the border of Egypt in the south, including the three major trade routes running from Egypt to Mesopotamia. The division of the list of defeated peoples into two parts provides a frame for 8:7-12, and by so doing sets these verses off as what Fokkelman (1990:255) terms the "center of gravity" of the chapter. It is in these verses that David's covenantal faithfulness is highlighted. This central section of the narrative unit tells how David "dedicated . . . to the LORD" (8:11) all the booty and spoil of battle (8:7-8, 11-12) as well as the tribute that was given to him as a conquering king (8:9-10). The defeated nations had become "David's servants" (8:6, 14; NLT, "David's subjects"), and therefore they brought him tribute and gifts. David in turn demonstrated that he was a servant of the Lord (cf. 7:5, 8, 20-29) by turning these gifts over to the treasury of the Lord (Polzin 1993:92). The Lord blessed David with victories (8:6, 14), and David responded by dedicating the spoils of battle to the Lord.

These positive aspects of David's behavior as a covenantal king are qualified, however, by an action that may suggest a tendency in his reign toward policies inconsistent with the behavior of a true covenantal king. In connection with David's defeat of Hadadezer, we are told that David "crippled all the chariot horses except enough for 100 chariots" (8:4). During the time of the conquest when Joshua faced a northern coalition of kings led by Jabin of Hazor, who also had large numbers of chariots and horses (Josh 11:4), the Lord told Joshua to "cripple their horses and burn their chariots" (Josh 11:6). It seems that the reason for this command was that the Lord did not want his people to trust military might as the basis for national security. If Israel built an army of equal or greater strength than the armies of their enemies, this could easily become a serious temptation. Because the Lord was concerned for the spiritual well-being of his people, he wanted them to put their trust exclusively in himself. As David confesses in Psalm 20, Israel was not to look for national security in "chariots and horses," like other nations (Ps 20:7), but rather to place her confidence in the Lord and in his promises to protect her from her enemies (Exod 23:22; Deut 20:1-4). It was only as Israel was different from other nations with respect to her military capabilities that she could remain in a relationship of complete trust in the Lord. So the bottom line was that the Lord did not want Israel to create a military establishment. This was one of the provisions of the "law of the king" in Deuteronomy that prohibited the king in Israel from building up "a large stable of horses for himself" (Deut 17:16). So when Joshua was victorious over Jabin and his army, we are told that he "crippled the horses and burned all the chariots, as the LORD had instructed" (Josh 11:9). Because David adopted a similar policy in the aftermath of his victory over Hadadezer, it seems likely that David was familiar with what Joshua had done at the time of the conquest. But contrary to Joshua's action, David made an exception for 100 horses that he kept for his own use. While this was a small number in comparison with the numbers of horses and chariots of the surrounding nations, and therefore may not have violated the prohibition of Deuteronomy 17:16, it nevertheless suggests a subtle move in David's military policy toward that of surrounding nations. Saul had no chariots or horses. David had only a few. However, his son Solomon built cities to house his numerous chariots and horses (1 Kgs 9:19), and he even engaged in a lucrative trading business in chariots and horses (1 Kgs 10:28-29). Solomon's policy established a pattern in Israel that continued to plague the nation throughout its history (Isa 2:7-8), a pattern that ultimately will be broken by the messianic king of the future who will "remove the battle chariots from Israel and the warhorses from Jerusalem" (Zech 9:9-10). So in the seemingly insignificant comment in 8:4 that David "crippled all the chariot horses *except enough for 100 chariots,*" we encounter something that might represent the first step in a process that culminated in David's sin of counting the fighting men of Israel (ch 24) and led to even more serious trouble among succeeding kings. So while this chapter provides us with a portrait of David in which his positive accomplishments as a true representative of the ideal of the covenantal king are emphasized, a hint of the imperfection of his reign is included as well.

ENDNOTES

1. Good (2001:129) argues that "2 Samuel 8 may reflect an inscription or text contemporary with the reign of King David. It has a number of features that could be explained if an inscription lay behind the biblical text, the most striking of which is its repetitive naming of the monarch, paralleling Darius' Behistun Inscription."
2. David made his proposal to build the Temple after "the LORD had given him rest from all the surrounding enemies" (7:1). It appears that David waited for these conditions to materialize before making his proposal to build the Temple because of his awareness that the Lord had told Moses that it was not until Israel had been given "rest" from all their enemies, that they were to bring their offerings to a central sanctuary (Deut 12:10-11).
3. But when David was ready to begin construction, the Lord told him that his involvement in bloodshed and warfare disqualified him from temple-building because the builder of the Temple should be a man of peace (1 Chr 22:8-10; 28:3). This is not to say that David's military activities were improper, nor that they were not blessed by the Lord—it was the Lord who gave him his victories (7:9; 8:6, 14)—but it was the Lord's purpose for the Temple to be built by a peaceful ruler. See further, endnote 7 in the commentary on 2 Sam 7:1-29 and Braun 1976.
4. David's victories over Moab and Edom are also fulfillments of the prediction of the Balaam oracle of Num 24:17-19.

5. Brueggemann (1990a:262-263) suggests a much more negative and suspicious reading of the narrative's linkage of David's success with the Lord's blessing. He characterizes this as coming close to "state ideology" in which "David or his ideologues are very close to identifying the rule of God and the rule of David." He finds a "mismatch" between "the old notion of being 'God's holy people' and the ambitious state of David and Solomon." He then gives a contemporary application to what he observes in this narrative when present-day claims of "being God's people" becomes a "rationale for political and military adventurism." He says that "word-mongers then and now . . . are capable of hiding the mismatch and recruiting religionists to support the new ambition," and concludes his discussion by saying that this chapter "can be read as an example of the ways in which large ideological claims cover over politics that are in fact betrayals of old convictions." There are, of course, a host of implications of such an interpretation. Not the least of these is the characterization of the narrator as a "word-monger" rather than a divinely inspired historian who presents a trustworthy description of these events in Israel's history from a covenantal perspective.

◆ K. List of David's Officials (2 Sam 8:15-18)

**15So David reigned over all Israel and did
what was just and right for all his people.
16Joab son of Zeruiah was commander of
the army. Jehoshaphat son of Ahilud was
the royal historian. 17Zadok son of Ahitub
and Ahimelech son of Abiathar were the
priests. Seraiah was the court secretary.
18Benaiah son of Jehoiada was captain of
the king's bodyguard.* And David's sons
served as priestly leaders.***

8:18a Hebrew *of the Kerethites and Pelethites.* **8:18b** Hebrew *David's sons were priests;* compare parallel text at 1 Chr 18:17.

NOTES

8:16 *royal historian.* The precise duties of the "royal historian" are disputed. Because the term itself (*mazkir* [TH2142C, ZH4654]) means "one causing to remember," it is usually concluded that Jehoshaphat's duties involved the keeping of public records (2 Kgs 18:18, 37; 2 Chr 34:8). On analogy with the Egyptian office of "speaker" (*whmh*), some view Jehoshaphat as a "royal herald," while others suggest a function like that of "secretary of state" (A. Anderson 1989:136; McCarter 1984:255; and the additional literature there cited).

8:17 *Zadok.* This descendant of Aaron through Eleazar and Ahitub (1 Chr 6:4-8, 50-52; 24:1-3) shared the duties of high priest with Abiathar during the time of David. He supported Solomon as David's successor rather than Adonijah, who was supported by Abiathar (1 Kgs 1:7-8). The line of Zadok held the office of high priest until the destruction of the Temple in 587 BC.

Ahimelech son of Abiathar. Also in 1 Chr 24:3, 6, 31. It seems likely that the order of the names has been transposed because elsewhere Abiathar is consistently said to be the colleague of Zadok (15:29, 35; 17:15; 19:11; 20:25; 1 Kgs 1:7-8, 19; 2:27, 35; 4:4). Abiathar was a descendant of Aaron through Ithamar (1 Chr 24:3), in the line of Eli, which was replaced by the Zadokite line in the time of Solomon (cf. 1 Sam 2:31-33; 1 Kgs 2:26-27).

court secretary. Various suggestions have been made concerning the nature of the function of the "court secretary." It appears that *soper* [TH5608A, ZH6221] (the normal Hebrew word for "scribe") is used here as a title for an official in David's court. Some regard the position as similar to a secretary of state; others see the position as that of an assistant to Jehoshaphat, the "royal historian." Whether the positions in David's court are reflections of Egyptian or Canaanite models has been a topic of much discussion (Walton, Matthews, and Chavalas 2000:335).

8:18 *Benaiah.* He was from Kabzeel and was the son of Jehoiada (a priest, 23:20; 1 Chr 27:5) who not only commanded the "king's bodyguard" but was also considered the most outstanding of David's 30 mightiest warriors (23:20-23). Benaiah also served as the commander of one of the divisions of the army that were activated on a monthly basis (1 Chr 27:5). He later replaced Joab, whom he killed at Solomon's command, as the commander-in-chief of Israel's army (1 Kgs 2:34-35).

was captain. This is not in the MT, which simply lists Benaiah's name followed by the groups called Kerethites and Pelethites. Most translations (e.g., NLT, KJV, NASB, NIV) follow the parallels in 20:23b and 1 Chr 18:17, which read "was over (*'al* [TH5921, ZH6584]) the Kerethites and Pelethites."

king's bodyguard. See NLT mg. The Kerethites and Pelethites are generally viewed as mercenary soldiers (of Cretan and Philistine origin) in the personal service of David. They remained loyal to David during the revolts of Absalom (15:18) and Sheba (20:7) and supported the anointing of Solomon instead of Adonijah as David's successor on the throne (1 Kgs 1:38, 44-45). See further, Bierling 1992:173-176.

priestly leaders. The LXX reads "chiefs of the court" (*aularchai*) in place of MT's "priests" (*kohanim* [TH3548, ZH3913]). While some have seen the LXX reading as evidence of textual corruption in MT (Wenham 1975) others regard the LXX and Chronicles rendering as "interpretive paraphrases" of MT (McCarter 1984:254-255).

COMMENTARY

This evaluative summary of David's reign (8:15) along with the list of his court officials (8:16-18) plays a transitional role in the larger narrative flow of 2 Samuel by drawing to a close the brief, preliminary, and mostly positive summary of David's reign (chs 3–8), while also introducing a fuller description of his reign, including some of his failures (chs 9–20). The list of the foremost officials in David's court (8:16-18) initiates a new ring structure that is closed by 20:23-26, where a similar list of officials is found. At the same time this list of court officials mirrors the list of warriors (23:8-39) in chapters 21–24, the "Samuel Conclusion" (often termed the "Appendix" to 2 Samuel; see "Literary Style" in the Introduction).

In 8:15 the whole course of David's reign is characterized in a single sentence. In this statement the narrator tells us that (1) David was ruling over the entire nation, not just a segment of it ("all Israel"), and (2) he "did what was just and right for all his people," regardless of their social, political, or tribal affiliations. This statement characterizes David not only as a person who exhibited the qualities that the Lord desired in all his people (Ezek 18:5, 19, 21, 27), but more particularly as a person who possessed the qualities essential for someone with royal authority (Deut 17:18-19; Jer 22:3). To "do what was just and right" was to be obedient to the requirements of the Mosaic covenant (Ezek 18:5-9). In speaking of the great messianic king of the future, Isaiah said the "shoot" that will come out of "the stump of David's family" (Isa 11:1) will judge the needy with "righteousness" and the "poor" with "justice" (Isa 11:4, NIV; NLT reads, "He will give *justice* to the poor and *make fair decisions* for the exploited"), and Jeremiah says the "righteous descendant" (lit., "righteous branch") who will sit on the throne of David will be a king who does what is "just and right" (Jer 23:5; 33:15). These are, in fact, the very qualities that characterize God's own governance of all his creatures (cf. Pss 33:5; 45:6; 72:1;

Isa 33:5; Jer 9:24). Psalms 89:14 and 97:2 even go so far as to speak of "righteousness and justice" as the foundation of the throne of God. So this brief but sweeping statement in 8:15 is telling us that in spite of the flaws and failures associated with David's life, his kingship exhibited something of the character of God's own reign. In contrast to Saul, David was a true, albeit imperfect, representative of the ideal of the covenantal king.[1]

The names of David's court officials are given in 8:16-18. Six individuals are included in the list and placed in a concentric pattern (*a-b-c-c-b-a*) according to their function. In the outer ring are two military leaders (Joab,[2] the commander of the army [8:16a], and Benaiah, captain of the king's bodyguard [8:18a]). In the secondary ring are two administrative officials (Jehoshaphat, the royal historian [8:16b], and Seraiah, the court secretary [8:17b]). And at the center are two religious leaders (Zadok and Ahimelech the priests [8:17a]). This leaves the reference to the unnamed sons of David who served as "priestly leaders" (8:18b, NLT; Hebrew is "priests") as an appendage to the concentric pattern. Exactly what is to be made of the last statement is not clear. The parallel text in 1 Chronicles 18:17 does not use the term "priest" but designates David's sons as the "king's chief assistants." Certainly David's sons did not meet the qualifications for priesthood, because they were neither Levites nor descendants of Aaron (Lev 8–9; Num 3:1-10, 16-20). Could the narrator be conveying his own reservations about the legitimacy of this function of David's sons by excluding them from the concentric pattern? If so, is this another indication that everything was not as it should be in the court of David? Perhaps.[3] On the other hand, a priestly function of David's sons does not seem to have had permanency. In the parallel passage in 20:23b, nothing is said about David's sons being priests, and 20:26 tells us that Ira the Jairite (from the tribe of Manasseh, cf. Num 32:41) was "David's personal priest" in contrast to Zadok and Abiathar, who were the conventional priests (20:25b). In 1 Kings 4:5, Zabud, the son of Nathan (again, not of the tribe of Levi, nor a descendant of Aaron), is named as a priest and an adviser to King Solomon. Do these references to non-Levitical priests suggest that in the early days of David's court some distinction was made between priests who performed the duties prescribed in the Mosaic ritual legislation and some sort of "unofficial" priestly duties performed in personal attendance on David and Solomon? Perhaps.[4] Again, there is insufficient information in the text to answer all our questions including why Ira, the Jairite, replaced David's sons as priests (8:18; 20:26) and why the Chronicler did not use the term "priest" in his reference to the function of David's sons (1 Chr 18:17).

ENDNOTES

1. As Keys (1996:201) notes, there are numerous references to David in 1–2 Kings that speak of his righteous behavior: "He is said to have done what was right in the eyes of Yahweh (1 Kgs 11:33, 38; 14:8; 15:5, 11; 2 Kgs 14:3; 16:2; 18:3; 22:2); to have kept his statutes and commandments (1 Kgs 3:14; 11:33, 34, 38); to have been upright in heart (1 Kgs 11:33); righteous (1 Kgs 3:6; 9:4); faithful (1 Kgs 3:6) and wholly true to Yahweh (1 Kgs 11:4; 15:3); to have followed Yahweh with all his heart (1 Kgs 14:8); to have walked in integrity of heart (1 Kgs 9:4) and in the ways of Yahweh (1 Kgs 3:14)."
2. See endnote 9 at the commentary on 2:8–3:1.

3. Fokkelman (1990:263) comments, "The concentric organisation of the lines in 8:16-18a gives 18b an air of being an outsider. These priests do not occur next to *the* priests, a fact which, in itself, might suggest that the office does not go with the sons of David."
4. Armerding (1975:85) argues that both David and Solomon held a "priestly investiture that was different from that of the Levitical order" and that it was linked with the royal priesthood of Melchizedek (cf. Ps 110). He suggests (1975:83) that David's sons partook "of the royal order connected with the Jerusalem shrine, which David himself served as monarch under Yahweh in his country." This view is shared by Merrill (1987:265-266) and rests to a large degree on the observation that a number of texts that speak of David or Solomon offering sacrifices have no concomitant reference to an officiating priest. It should be noted, however, that this conclusion rests on an argument from silence and a number of other inferences that are not completely persuasive.

◆ L. David Befriends Mephibosheth (2 Sam 9:1–13)

One day David asked, "Is anyone in Saul's family still alive—anyone to whom I can show kindness for Jonathan's sake?" [2]He summoned a man named Ziba, who had been one of Saul's servants. "Are you Ziba?" the king asked.

"Yes sir, I am," Ziba replied.

[3]The king then asked him, "Is anyone still alive from Saul's family? If so, I want to show God's kindness to them."

Ziba replied, "Yes, one of Jonathan's sons is still alive. He is crippled in both feet."

[4]"Where is he?" the king asked.

"In Lo-debar," Ziba told him, "at the home of Makir son of Ammiel."

[5]So David sent for him and brought him from Makir's home. [6]His name was Mephibosheth*; he was Jonathan's son and Saul's grandson. When he came to David, he bowed low to the ground in deep respect. David said, "Greetings, Mephibosheth."

Mephibosheth replied, "I am your servant."

[7]"Don't be afraid!" David said. "I intend to show kindness to you because of my promise to your father, Jonathan. I will give you all the property that once belonged to your grandfather Saul, and you will eat here with me at the king's table!"

[8]Mephibosheth bowed respectfully and exclaimed, "Who is your servant, that you should show such kindness to a dead dog like me?"

[9]Then the king summoned Saul's servant Ziba and said, "I have given your master's grandson everything that belonged to Saul and his family. [10]You and your sons and servants are to farm the land for him to produce food for your master's household.* But Mephibosheth, your master's grandson, will eat here at my table." (Ziba had fifteen sons and twenty servants.)

[11]Ziba replied, "Yes, my lord the king; I am your servant, and I will do all that you have commanded." And from that time on, Mephibosheth ate regularly at David's table,* like one of the king's own sons.

[12]Mephibosheth had a young son named Mica. From then on, all the members of Ziba's household were Mephibosheth's servants. [13]And Mephibosheth, who was crippled in both feet, lived in Jerusalem and ate regularly at the king's table.

9:6 *Mephibosheth* is another name for Merib-baal. 9:10 As in Greek version; Hebrew reads *your master's grandson.* 9:11 As in Greek version; Hebrew reads *my table.*

COMMENTARY

This is the first of two narratives about David's relationship with members of the tribe of Benjamin (Mephibosheth and Sheba) who were potential rivals for his throne. These two narratives are the second and fifth units (9:1-13 and 20:1-22) of the ring structure introduced by the preceding narrative unit (8:15-18) and encompassing 8:15–20:26 (see "Literary Style" in the Introduction). The ring structure in which this narrative is set is the third such structure in chapters 3–20. The two central units in each of these ring structures call attention to what are arguably the most important issues of David's reign. In the first structure (3:2–5:16) the two central narrative units call attention to David's innocence in the murders of Abner (3:22-39) and Ishbosheth (4:1-12). Consistent with David's behavior during the lifetime of Saul (1 Sam 24, 26; and especially 1 Sam 26:10-11), he refused to take the initiative in displacing Saul or his sons from the throne; rather, he waited for the Lord to establish the conditions necessary for his own assumption of the royal office in Israel. Thus, David came to power in Israel not by means of a coup d'état, but by patiently waiting for the Lord's timing and public recognition of his qualifications for the office (5:1-2). The two central units in the second ring structure (5:17–8:14) call attention to David's recognition of the kingship of Yahweh by bringing the Ark of the Covenant (i.e., the throne seat of Yahweh), into his capital city (ch 6), and to the Lord's promise to David that his dynasty would endure forever (ch 7). These two chapters address two of the most important themes of the books of Samuel: the kingship of Yahweh (ch 6) and the establishment of the Davidic covenant (ch 7). It is the Davidic covenant that undergirds the development of messianic expectation associated with the royal line of David in the remainder of the Old Testament. The two central units in the third ring structure depict David's involvement in the double crime of adultery and murder (10:1–12:31) and the ensuing tragic events that develop in his own household, including the murder of Amnon and the rebellion of Absalom (13:1–19:43). This third ring structure comprises narrative material that traditionally has been viewed as an originally independent and self-contained literary entity (encompassing chs 9–20 and 1 Kgs 1–2),[1] designated either as the "Court History of David" or more commonly as the "Succession Document" (Flanagan 1972). As was noted in the Introduction, even though this theory of composition has dominated discussions of this section of 2 Samuel ever since Rost (1926) suggested the "Succession Narrative" hypothesis, in recent years serious questions have arisen not only over the "unit's extent, genre, theme, message and dating" (Frolov 2002:81—Frolov documents the relevant discussions), but also over the question of whether or not there ever was such a thing as an independent "Succession Narrative" (see the Introduction, "Date and Occasion of Writing" and "Literary Style"). As early as 1964, Carlson suggested that the whole description of David's reign in chapters 2–24 should be seen as a depiction of "David under blessing" (chs 2–7) and "David under curse" (chs 9–24). "David under blessing" centers on aspects of David's life that demonstrate obedience to the requirements of the covenant; "David under curse" centers on examples of David's disobedience and their consequences. This approach anticipates the analysis of Keys (1996), who regards 2 Samuel 10–20 as descriptive of the "sin and punishment" of David,[2] rather than part of an alleged "Succession Narrative" (see also Keys 1988). In view of the narrative structures outlined above, it seems warranted to conclude that the author or editor of 1–2 Samuel intended to depict David's reign as a true, although imperfect, representation of the ideal of the covenantal king. In the first two ring structures (3:2–5:16; 5:17–8:14) the emphasis is, for the most part, on the positive aspects of his reign, while in this third ring structure (8:15–20:26), even though chapters 8 and 9 continue to be positive in their portrayal of David, the overriding emphasis lies on his failures to measure up to the covenantal ideal.[3]

With this as background, we find that chapter 9 opens with a question posed by David concerning the continued existence of any survivors of the house of Saul (9:3). The reason for David's interest in this information was that he wanted to fulfill the promises he had made to his friend Jonathan, as well as to Jonathan's father, Saul, to spare their children should he ever come to the throne in Israel (1 Sam 18:3; 20:14-17, 42; 23:18; 24:21-22). To David's credit he did not forget these promises when he became king, although it appears that it was many years after the beginning of his reign before he took any action to fulfill his pledge.

It is unclear just where to place this event chronologically in David's reign (cf. comments on chronology in the commentary on 2 Sam 6:1-23, endnote 3). Some have argued that David's question (9:1, 3) presupposes that his execution of seven of Saul's descendants (21:1-14) in atonement for Saul's violation of a covenant with the Gibeonites[4] had already taken place. This suggestion, however, founders on the comment in 21:7 that David "spared Jonathan's son Mephibosheth" at that time, thereby indicating that he knew about Mephibosheth when that execution took place.[5] At the same time, it is clear that David's search for any living descendants of Saul and Jonathan did not happen at the beginning of his reign because Mephibosheth was a young lad of five years of age when his father and grandfather were killed in the battle against the Philistines at Mount Gilboa (4:4). But at the time David began his search in this chapter (9:1), Mephibosheth was a grown man with a son of his own, named Mica (9:12). All things considered, it seems best to place David's search for descendants of Saul and Jonathan sometime in the middle period of his reign, prior to the rebellion of Absalom.[6] It is for this reason that Calvin, while commending David for his "magnanimity to Mephibosheth," at the same time reproaches him for the long delay in carrying out his pledge.[7]

In spite of David's procrastination, chapter 9 calls attention to David's faithfulness to his covenant with Jonathan. The term *khesed* [TH2617, ZH2876] (here translated "kindness") occurs three times (9:1, 3, 7) in the description of David's desire to demonstrate his benevolence toward Jonathan's descendants. Many attempts have been made to define the term *khesed*.[8] Generally, the term expresses "magnanimity" and "a sacrificial, humane willingness to be there for the other. . . . It is a given that *khesed* always has to do in some way with the life of the other, and that one expects and hopes from the recipient of such *khesed* a similar willingness that in turn surpasses the obligatory" (TLOT 2.456). Either "kindness" or "loving-kindness" are good one-word renderings in English, but the semantic range of the word is difficult to capture in a single English word. This "kindness" is termed "*God's* kindness" in 9:3, corresponding with the expression the "kindness of the

LORD" (translated "faithful love of the LORD" in NLT) in 1 Samuel 20:14. It is not clear whether the linkage of *khesed* with a designation of deity in these two places is intended to express the idea that God is the witness and guarantor of the pledge between David and Jonathan,[9] or that the kindness in view is intended to be understood in a superlative sense (NIDOTTE 2.212).[10] Either understanding is possible. But the "kindness" in view is clearly a "kindness" that is undergirded by the commitment of a covenant (1 Sam 23:18) that was sworn to by an oath before the Lord (1 Sam 20:42; 24:21-22).[11]

David sought out a former servant of Saul named Ziba, of whom he inquired regarding the whereabouts of any of Saul's descendants. Ziba told him that a son of Jonathan named Mephibosheth was living[12] in Lo-debar[13] at the home of Makir, son of Ammiel (9:3-4).[14] David sent for Mephibosheth. It is probable that Mephibosheth thought his life was in jeopardy because he was a descendant of Saul, and it was common for the founders of new dynasties to murder all potential successors to the throne from the royal house they displaced (cf. 1 Kgs 15:29; 16:11; 2 Kgs 10:7; 11:1). This fear, however, was unfounded because David was a king who "did what was just and right for all his people" (8:15).[15] David had sworn an oath, and he was determined to carry out his promises to Jonathan and Saul. So to Mephibosheth's great surprise (9:8), David told him that he would be given all the property that had belonged to his grandfather Saul, and that in addition he would be given a place at the king's table in David's own court (9:10). David placed Ziba, along with his sons and servants, as managers over Mephibosheth's properties (9:10), and he brought Mephibosheth to Jerusalem where he lived as one of David's own sons (9:11).

There are readers of this narrative who take a rather cynical view of David's behavior in this chapter and draw the conclusion that the bringing of Mephibosheth to Jerusalem was more an attempt by David to keep Mephibosheth under surveillance than it was a desire to honor his pledge to Saul and Jonathan.[16] This reading, however, finds little support in the narrative itself, where the emphasis is consistently on David's sincerity and generosity.[17] In addition to the emphasis in the chapter on David's "kindness" toward Jonathan's descendants (9:1, 3, 7), attention is also drawn to the favor that David granted to Mephibosheth by inviting him to "eat at the king's table." This expression occurs four times in the space of a few verses (9:7, 10-11, 13). Sitting together at a table carries strong connotations of friendship and fellowship between the participants at the meal. Shared meals were a common means of covenant ratification (Gen 26:26-30; Exod 24:9-11) and of the expression of covenant solidarity (the "peace offering," for example, involved a shared meal—see commentary on 6:17 and on 1 Sam 11:15, endnote 4). David's kindness toward Mephibosheth may anticipate something of the invitation of David's greater son to his followers to sit at his table—they are considered as members of his own household (Matt 8:11; 22:1-14; Luke 22:15-30; and van den Berg 1997:60). The New Testament institution of the Lord's Supper was intended to give expression to the bond of fellowship that exists between Christ and his followers, who even though they were unworthy servants (Luke 17:10) and justly deserving of punishment and even death, are, nevertheless, invited to share in a meal as children in the household of God.

ENDNOTES

1. This construal assumes that the so-called Samuel Appendix (chs 21–24) disrupts the flow and original unity of this allegedly once independent narrative unit.
2. Keys (1996:179) argues that chs 10–20 are "structured around three separate, yet closely interlocking units or sections, namely chs 10–12, 13–14 and 15–20." It is her view that chs 10–12 are the "pivotal section of the work, containing both its statement of themes and its main interest." For her, the "chief concern of chs 10–12 is theological: The Sin and Punishment of David. It is the story of David's double crime of adultery and murder and Yahweh's response in sentencing and punishing the guilty party." She views chs 13–20 as the "outworking of this punishment." She goes on to suggest (1996:180) that the purpose of this section of Samuel is theological and that "2 Samuel 10–20 appears to be a demonstration of the inevitable consequences of transgression. The work serves to show that even despite repentance and forgiveness (for David begged and attained Yahweh's forgiveness in 12:13 and the sentence was reduced), punishment invariably follows sin." Keys's analysis is similar to that of Davis (1999:99-100, note 2) who rejects the "Succession Narrative" hypothesis and views chs 9–20 as descriptive of "A Servant Under God's Rod" divided into four parts: (1) the fidelity of David's relationships, chs 9–10; (2) the morass of David's guilt, chs 11–12; (3) the trouble from David's house, 13:1–19:8a; (4) the turmoil in David's kingdom, 19:8b–20:26.
3. The presence of the positive evaluative summary of David's reign (David "did what was just and right for all his people" [8:15]) in the third (8:15–20:26), rather than in the first or second of these ring structures, has the effect of compensating for the generally opprobrious content of the third ring structure. The result is that even though David is portrayed in these narratives as someone who did not measure up to the ideal of the true covenantal king, his reign, could, nevertheless, still be characterized in a generally positive manner.
4. See Cartledge 2001:478; Hertzberg 1964:381; McCarter 1984:260-263. Cartledge comments, "Obviously the narrative would make better sense if chapter 21 preceded chapter 9, for the sons of Saul's concubines appear to be out of the picture when David begins his search for Saul's survivors."
5. Cartledge (2001:479) views the reference to Mephibosheth in 21:7 as an editorial insertion intended to harmonize the material in ch 21 with what has already been presented in ch 9.
6. Second Samuel 16:7-8 seems to be a reference to the executions of Saul's descendants mentioned in 21:1-4.
7. Calvin (1992:431) comments that David "should have remembered the house of Jonathan immediately after he was given possession of the kingdom, or at the very least after the death of Ishbosheth, but he did not do so. Now this is why he is to be blamed. However, it is better late than never. This, therefore, is said in his praise—that he asked, without anyone urging him, to do good to those who might be survivors of the house of Saul."
8. For good summaries of discussions surrounding the use of this term in the OT see NIDOTTE 2.211; TWOT 1.305-307; and TLOT 2.449-464.
9. Fokkelman (1981:26) understands the expression as indicating *khesed* [TH2617, ZH2876] "which is pleasing to God and for which he sets the standard."
10. Alter (1999:240) argues that "God here has the force of an intensifier." In addition, Alter points out that the "tight link" of this narrative with the covenant between Jonathan and David described in 1 Sam 20:42 is an argument against the commonly held idea that ch 9 marks "the beginning of a wholly independent Succession Narrative

which continues till 1 Kings 2." This is, perhaps, strengthened by Fokkelman's (1981:29) observation that not only does the keyword *khesed* [TH2617, ZH2876] occur three times in both ch 9 and 1 Sam 20, but also the word "table" occurs four times in ch 9 and two times in 1 Sam 20, and these are nearly the only occurrences of the word "table" in all of 1–2 Samuel (cf. 19:28 [29]), thus implying some verbal and thematic connections between the two narratives.

11. There is disagreement among those who have studied usage of the term *khesed* [TH2617, ZH2876] on whether or not it is always to be understood as "covenantal faithfulness" and regarded as a "covenantal term." Part of this debate is on whether or not the term describes something that is "freely given" or something that is the fulfillment of an "obligation." As TLOT 2.454 points out, 1 Kgs 20:31 provides an example of a case where *khesed* is "unexpected." Ben-hadad had been defeated and had no claim to any "obligation" from Ahab, but rather hoped for an expression of "mercy" or "kindness" from him as a defeated enemy. In this and other cases, *khesed* seems to transcend the confines of covenant relationships, although it is often used in the context of covenant relationships.
12. Ziba apparently tells David nothing about some other members of Saul's household that were still living (21:8).
13. Possibly to be identified with Umm ed-Dabar, located 10 miles south-southeast of the Sea of Galilee, east of the Jordan River in Gilead (Rasmussen 1989:119).
14. Apparently this was a well-to-do person who was friendly toward the house of Saul, but who later was helpful to David during the time of Absalom's rebellion (17:27).
15. This characterization of David's reign is a proper one, in spite of his failure in the matter of Bathsheba and Uriah, because it reflects the general character of his governance rather than a suggestion that his reign was without any blemish.
16. Halpern (2001:342) argues that Mephibosheth "was at best a hostage at the court, and sufficiently impaired to prevent his being a rallying-point for Israelites disaffected from David." He argues further (2001:343) that the seeming generosity to Mephibosheth "conceals a policy of graft and kickbacks" in connection with Ziba's installment as "tenant manager," and he views the entire incident as part of "a complex political deal." Alter (1999:243) speaks of David's arrangement for Mephibosheth as "a kind of luxurious house arrest." Suspicions of a less radical but similar nature are expressed in Hertzberg 1964:300-301; McCarter 1984:265; Sternberg 1985:255; and Youngblood 1992:918.
17. Baldwin (1988:227, note 1) comments that the "suggestion that David acted out of 'calculated prudence' and aimed to bring people who could be a potential threat to him under watchful supervision (Mauchline, p. 241) seems to me unjustified. In my judgment it would have been more prudent to have left the situation alone, but David was not afraid to take risks, and went out of his way to be unusually generous."

◆ M. The Ammonite War; David, Bathsheba, Uriah, and Nathan (2 Sam 10:1–12:31)

1. The Ammonites defeated (2 Sam 10:1–11:1; 12:26–31)

[N.B. 2 Sam 11:2–12:25 is presented in the next section of the commentary]

Some time after this, King Nahash* of the Ammonites died, and his son Hanun became king. ²David said, "I am going to show loyalty to Hanun just as his father, Nahash, was always loyal to me." So David sent ambassadors to express sympathy to Hanun about his father's death.

But when David's ambassadors arrived

in the land of Ammon, 3the Ammonite commanders said to Hanun, their master, "Do you really think these men are coming here to honor your father? No! David has sent them to spy out the city so they can come in and conquer it!" 4So Hanun seized David's ambassadors and shaved off half of each man's beard, cut off their robes at the buttocks, and sent them back to David in shame.

5When David heard what had happened, he sent messengers to tell the men, "Stay at Jericho until your beards grow out, and then come back." For they felt deep shame because of their appearance.

6When the people of Ammon realized how seriously they had angered David, they sent and hired 20,000 Aramean foot soldiers from the lands of Beth-rehob and Zobah, 1,000 from the king of Maacah, and 12,000 from the land of Tob. 7When David heard about this, he sent Joab and all his warriors to fight them. 8The Ammonite troops came out and drew up their battle lines at the entrance of the city gate, while the Arameans from Zobah and Rehob and the men from Tob and Maacah positioned themselves to fight in the open fields.

9When Joab saw that he would have to fight on both the front and the rear, he chose some of Israel's elite troops and placed them under his personal command to fight the Arameans in the fields. 10He left the rest of the army under the command of his brother Abishai, who was to attack the Ammonites. 11"If the Arameans are too strong for me, then come over and help me," Joab told his brother. "And if the Ammonites are too strong for you, I will come and help you. 12Be courageous! Let us fight bravely for our people and the cities of our God. May the LORD's will be done."

13When Joab and his troops attacked, the Arameans began to run away. 14And when the Ammonites saw the Arameans running, they ran from Abishai and retreated into the city. After the battle was over, Joab returned to Jerusalem.

15The Arameans now realized that they were no match for Israel. So when they regrouped, 16they were joined by additional Aramean troops summoned by Hadadezer from the other side of the Euphrates River.* These troops arrived at Helam under the command of Shobach, the commander of Hadadezer's forces.

17When David heard what was happening, he mobilized all Israel, crossed the Jordan River, and led the army to Helam. The Arameans positioned themselves in battle formation and fought against David. 18But again the Arameans fled from the Israelites. This time David's forces killed 700 charioteers and 40,000 foot soldiers,* including Shobach, the commander of their army. 19When all the kings allied with Hadadezer saw that they had been defeated by Israel, they surrendered to Israel and became their subjects. After that, the Arameans were afraid to help the Ammonites.

CHAPTER 11

In the spring of the year,* when kings normally go out to war, David sent Joab and the Israelite army to fight the Ammonites. They destroyed the Ammonite army and laid siege to the city of Rabbah. However, David stayed behind in Jerusalem.

◆ 12:26Meanwhile, Joab was fighting against Rabbah, the capital of Ammon, and he captured the royal fortifications.* 27Joab sent messengers to tell David, "I have fought against Rabbah and captured its water supply.* 28Now bring the rest of the army and capture the city. Otherwise, I will capture it and get credit for the victory."

29So David gathered the rest of the army and went to Rabbah, and he fought against it and captured it. 30David removed the crown from the king's head,* and it was placed on his own head. The crown was made of gold and set with gems, and it weighed seventy-five pounds.* David took a vast amount of plunder from the city. 31He also made

slaves of the people of Rabbah and forced them to labor with* saws, iron picks, and iron axes, and to work in the brick kilns.* That is how he dealt with the people of all the Ammonite towns. Then David and all the army returned to Jerusalem.

10:1 As in parallel text at 1 Chr 19:1; Hebrew reads *the king.* **10:16** Hebrew *the river.* **10:18** As in some Greek manuscripts (see also 1 Chr 19:18); Hebrew reads *charioteers.* **11:1** Hebrew *At the turn of the year.* The first day of the year in the ancient Hebrew lunar calendar occurred in March or April. **12:26** Or *the royal city.* **12:27** Or *captured the city of water.* **12:30a** Or *from the head of Milcom* (as in Greek version). Milcom, also called Molech, was the god of the Ammonites. **12:30b** Hebrew *1 talent* [34 kilograms]. **12:31a** Or *He also brought out the people of Rabbah and put them under.* **12:31b** Or *and he made them pass through the brick kilns.*

NOTES

10:3 ***No!*** This word is not in the MT, but the rhetorical question ("Do you really think these men . . . ?") serves as a forcible denial. See GKC §148c.

10:7 ***all his warriors.*** Lit., "all the army, the mighty men." Waltke and O'Connor (1990:230 [§12.3b.4]) suggest that when the lead word is a common noun, the appositive may provide information about a subclass to which the lead word belongs, thus, "the entire army of fighting men."

10:9 ***some of Israel's elite troops.*** Lit., "from all the choice men of Israel." There is no need to omit the Beth after a construct participle with the Qere and a few Hebrew mss. See Waltke and O'Connor (1990:147 [§9.5.2f]).

11:1 ***In the spring of the year.*** Lit., "At the return of the year."

kings. This concurs with 1 Chr 20:1, many Hebrew mss, LXX, Old Latin, Targum, Vulgate. The MT reads, "the messengers," or "the angels," a difference of only one letter. Although the context strongly favors the reading "kings," GKC §23g regards "the messengers" as the preferred reading.

12:30 ***crown.*** Horn (1973:170-180) notes that this is the only place in the OT that records the capture of a crown. He suggests that the crown may have resembled the crowns on eight bearded Ammonite stone sculptures that have been found near Amman, Jordan, dating from the first half of the first millennium BC.

king's head. See NLT mg. The Hebrew word rendered "king" can be vocalized either as *malkam* [TH4428/3963.1, ZH4889/4392] ("their king"; so MT) or as *milkom* [TH4445B, ZH4904] ("Milcom," the name of the chief Ammonite deity).

and set. This follows the reading *ubah* [TH871.2/1886.3, ZH928/2023] (on it) with 1 Chr 20:2 and the Targum; it is lacking in the MT.

gems. The Hebrew noun is singular. Here it is translated as plural on the assumption that the singular form is a collective noun.

12:31 ***and forced them to labor with saws.*** Lit., "He set [them to work] with saws." A. Anderson (1989:167) suggests the reading "and put them at tearing her down" by repointing the MT's *megerah* [TH4050, ZH4490] (saw) as a Piel, from *magar* [TH4048, ZH4489] (to drag down), an infinitive construct with a third-person fem. sg. pronominal suffix. In this case, "her" would refer to the city of 12:30.

and to work in the brick kilns. Lit., "He caused them to cross over to the brick mold" (reading *bammalben* [TH4404, ZH4861] with the Qere rather than the anomalous *bammalken* [TH4404A, ZH4905] of the Kethiv). Considering the context, it seems best to amend *he'ebir* [TH5674, ZH6296] (to cross over) to *he'ebid* [TH5647, ZH6268] (to make serve, to enslave); "he set them to work (or employed them) at the brick mold."

COMMENTARY

David's involvement in a series of wars with the Ammonites is described in 10:1–11:1 and 12:26-31.[1] The story of David's double sin of adultery and murder (11:2–12:25) is set within the framework of these wars. Nahash, the king of the Ammonites, had died. Presumably this is the same Nahash who had been defeated by Saul (1 Sam 11) shortly after Saul was chosen by lot to be king (1 Sam 10:17-24) and just prior to the inauguration of his reign (1 Sam 11:14–12:25). Upon hearing of Nahash's death, David decided to show "kindness" (10:2; *khesed* [TH2617, ZH2876]; "loyalty," NLT) to his son and successor Hanun, just as Nahash had previously shown "kindness" (*khesed;* NLT, "was always loyal") to David. The use of the term *khesed* here provides a link with the preceding chapter and David's kindness toward Mephibosheth, a descendant of Saul and Jonathan. The way in which *khesed* is used in 10:2 suggests the existence of some sort of a formal relationship, perhaps even a treaty, between Nahash and David, although there is no biblical reference to any prior contact between the two rulers. If such a formal relationship existed, it is likely that it was established during the time that David was a fugitive from the court of Saul. At the time of the death of a treaty partner it was customary for the living partner to send emissaries to the successor of the deceased ruler to reaffirm the treaty relationship and to express continued solidarity with the new regime. This seems to have been David's reason for sending his delegation to Hanun.

Hanun's military advisers, however, suspected David's representatives were coming under false pretenses with the intent to spy out the city (probably the capital, Rabbah [present-day Amman, the capital of Jordan], cf. 11:1) in preparation for an attack. David's growing power in the region and his defeat of the Moabites (8:2) may have lent credibility to their misgivings. So when the Israelite envoys arrived in Rabbah, they were taken hostage, shamefully treated (half of each man's beard was shaved off and their robes were cut off at the buttocks, exposing their genitals), and sent home in humiliation (10:4). The beard was a sign of manhood and a source of pride to men in the ancient Near East, and it was, therefore, a serious insult to degrade someone's beard (DBI 80). This nefarious insult extended to David and the entire nation he and his envoys represented. Out of concern for their embarrassment, David made arrangements for them to stay in Jericho until their beards had regrown (10:5).

The Ammonites were fully cognizant of the implications of their actions and clearly expected David to respond with military force. To prepare for this eventuality they secured mercenary troops from several small Aramean kingdoms including Beth-rehob, Zobah, Maacah, and Tob[2] (10:6). When David learned that the Ammonites had assembled their forces, he sent Joab and the Israelite army against them. Upon arriving in the area of Rabbah, Joab found that the Aramean mercenaries were arrayed in the fields of the surrounding region, while the Ammonite forces were positioned to defend the city. This meant that the Israelites would have to fight on two fronts. So Joab divided his army and sent some of his men under the leadership of his brother Abishai to attack the Ammonites, while he took the remaining forces to engage the Arameans, who constituted the more significant threat. It is at this juncture in the narrative that the only reference to Yahweh in the entire chapter is found, and it occurs in a statement uttered by Joab when he charged the troops to be courageous and to fight bravely, concluding his challenge with the words, "May the LORD's will be done" (10:12).[3]

Joab is a willful and inscrutable personality in the narratives of Samuel and the early chapters of 1 Kings, who at times shows great loyalty and affection for David but at other times either refuses to obey David's commands (18:14-33) or takes actions clearly contrary to David's wishes (2 Sam 3:27-30; 19:1-3; 20:3-23). During the last days of David's life, Joab aligned himself with Adonijah in defiance of David's designation of Solomon as his successor. For this and other misdeeds, he was put to death after Solomon replaced his father on the throne (1 Kgs 2:5-6, 34). Whatever one may think of Joab's piety (or lack of it) on this occasion and on the occasion of David's sin in connection with taking a census of Israel's fighting men (24:3), Joab made statements reflecting a recognition of the Lord's providential guidance of historical events.[4] As Calvin (1992:464) notes, Joab "understood that no matter how bravely he behaved, all his forces could still do nothing unless God gave the victory." In Calvin's view there are many circumstances in life in which God wants us "to remain in suspense . . . and to leave it all to his secret counsel and his providence" (1992:465). We can be assured that God will never abandon his people, but even so,

> *we must remain in suspense about many things. For instance, when we ask God for our daily bread, it is not that we are assured that he will send us a good harvest or a great vintage. We should leave that in his hands and patiently await what pleases him. When we have any illness, we must rest well assured that he has not forgotten us, and that we have such access to him, and that in the end, we will feel that he has looked on us in pity. The promise of God should be fully sufficient in regard to that. However, when we would like to have the word that today or tomorrow he will restore our health, we do not know—we are even in doubt of living or dying. (Calvin 1992:464-465)*

On this occasion, however, it pleased the Lord to give Israel a victory under the leadership of Joab and Abishai. The Arameans fled to the north and the Ammonites retreated into the security of Rabbah. But this victory was not the end of the matter because the Arameans retreated only to regroup and gather additional forces from as far away as the northern side of the Euphrates River. This time, David himself led the Israelite army out to meet the Arameans in battle. The forces engaged at Helam,[5] and again the Arameans were routed and their commander Shobach was killed (10:18). This removed any continuing threat of Aramean assistance for the Ammonites, and it created the context in which David could now deal more decisively with Hanun's show of contempt for the diplomatic delegation that David had sent to Rabbah. In the spring of the following year, David sent Joab out to complete the job, while David remained in Jerusalem (11:1). Joab quickly routed the Ammonite forces and laid siege to Rabbah. As the siege continued,[6] the story of David's sin with Bathsheba and Uriah unfolded back in Jerusalem (11:2–12:25). But when Joab was able to gain control of the water supply to the city (12:27), he called for David to come with additional troops so that the honor of the capture of the city would accrue to David rather than to himself (12:28). So David went to Rabbah, and when the city surrendered, the crown of Hanun, king of the Ammonites, was placed on David's head. David's sovereignty now extended over the territory of the Ammonites, and many of the Ammonite people were placed in forced labor (12:31).

ENDNOTES

1. These wars appear to have occurred prior to the decisive defeat of Hadadezer recorded in 8:3-12. The chronological relationship between 10:1–11:1, 12:26-31, and 8:3-12 appears to be the same as the chronological relationship between 1 Chr 19:1–20:3 and 1 Chr 18:3-8, in which the events of 1 Chr 18:3-8 (which parallels 8:3-12) are to be placed after those described in 1 Chr 19:1–20:3 (Selman 1994:191-192).
2. Beth-rehob was located west of Damascus in the area of the source of the Jordan River. Zobah was in the area north of Damascus and south of Hamath. Hadadezer was king of Zobah (8:3; 10:16). Maacah was located southwest of Mt. Hermon and northeast of Hazor in Transjordan; and Tob was located north of Gilead in Transjordan.
3. This statement may also be translated as an affirmation: "The LORD will do what is good in his sight."
4. This, in fact, is one of the major themes of 1–2 Samuel. It is voiced by nearly every major player in the events that the book describes. In 1 Sam 3:18, Eli says, "It is the LORD's will. . . . Let him do what he thinks best." In 1 Sam 11:13, Saul says, "No one will be executed today, for today the LORD has rescued Israel." In 1 Sam 14:6, Jonathan says, "Perhaps the LORD will help us, for nothing can hinder the LORD. He can win a battle whether he has many warriors or only a few!" In 1 Sam 30:23, David says, "Don't be selfish with what the LORD has given us. He has kept us safe and helped us defeat the band of raiders that attacked us." In 8:14, the narrator says, "The LORD made David victorious wherever he went."
5. The location of Helam is uncertain, but it is usually placed about 35 miles east of the Sea of Galilee in Transjordan.
6. This must have lasted for more than a year because all the events of 11:2-25 are placed within the time frame of this siege.

◆ 2. David, Bathsheba, Uriah, and Nathan (2 Sam 11:2–12:25)

**[2]Late one afternoon, after his midday rest,
David got out of bed and was walking on
the roof of the palace. As he looked out
over the city, he noticed a woman of un-
usual beauty taking a bath. [3]He sent
someone to find out who she was, and he
was told, "She is Bathsheba, the daughter
of Eliam and the wife of Uriah the Hit-
tite." [4]Then David sent messengers to get
her; and when she came to the palace, he
slept with her. She had just completed the
purification rites after having her men-
strual period. Then she returned home.
[5]Later, when Bathsheba discovered that
she was pregnant, she sent David a mes-
sage, saying, "I'm pregnant."**

**[6]Then David sent word to Joab: "Send
me Uriah the Hittite." So Joab sent him to
David. [7]When Uriah arrived, David asked
him how Joab and the army were getting
along and how the war was progressing.
[8]Then he told Uriah, "Go on home and re-
lax.*" David even sent a gift to Uriah after
he had left the palace. [9]But Uriah didn't
go home. He slept that night at the palace
entrance with the king's palace guard.**

**[10]When David heard that Uriah had not
gone home, he summoned him and asked,
"What's the matter? Why didn't you go
home last night after being away for so
long?"**

[11]Uriah replied, "The Ark and the armies

of Israel and Judah are living in tents,* and Joab and my master's men are camping in the open fields. How could I go home to wine and dine and sleep with my wife? I swear that I would never do such a thing."

12"Well, stay here today," David told him, "and tomorrow you may return to the army." So Uriah stayed in Jerusalem that day and the next. 13Then David invited him to dinner and got him drunk. But even then he couldn't get Uriah to go home to his wife. Again he slept at the palace entrance with the king's palace guard.

14So the next morning David wrote a letter to Joab and gave it to Uriah to deliver. 15The letter instructed Joab, "Station Uriah on the front lines where the battle is fiercest. Then pull back so that he will be killed." 16So Joab assigned Uriah to a spot close to the city wall where he knew the enemy's strongest men were fighting. 17And when the enemy soldiers came out of the city to fight, Uriah the Hittite was killed along with several other Israelite soldiers.

18Then Joab sent a battle report to David. 19He told his messenger, "Report all the news of the battle to the king. 20But he might get angry and ask, 'Why did the troops go so close to the city? Didn't they know there would be shooting from the walls? 21Wasn't Abimelech son of Gideon* killed at Thebez by a woman who threw a millstone down on him from the wall? Why would you get so close to the wall?' Then tell him, 'Uriah the Hittite was killed, too.'"

22So the messenger went to Jerusalem and gave a complete report to David. 23"The enemy came out against us in the open fields," he said. "And as we chased them back to the city gate, 24the archers on the wall shot arrows at us. Some of the king's men were killed, including Uriah the Hittite."

25"Well, tell Joab not to be discouraged," David said. "The sword devours this one today and that one tomorrow! Fight harder next time, and conquer the city!"

26When Uriah's wife heard that her husband was dead, she mourned for him. 27When the period of mourning was over, David sent for her and brought her to the palace, and she became one of his wives. Then she gave birth to a son. But the LORD was displeased with what David had done.

CHAPTER **12**

So the LORD sent Nathan the prophet to tell David this story: "There were two men in a certain town. One was rich, and one was poor. 2The rich man owned a great many sheep and cattle. 3The poor man owned nothing but one little lamb he had bought. He raised that little lamb, and it grew up with his children. It ate from the man's own plate and drank from his cup. He cuddled it in his arms like a baby daughter. 4One day a guest arrived at the home of the rich man. But instead of killing an animal from his own flock or herd, he took the poor man's lamb and killed it and prepared it for his guest."

5David was furious. "As surely as the LORD lives," he vowed, "any man who would do such a thing deserves to die! 6He must repay four lambs to the poor man for the one he stole and for having no pity."

7Then Nathan said to David, "You are that man! The LORD, the God of Israel, says: I anointed you king of Israel and saved you from the power of Saul. 8I gave you your master's house and his wives and the kingdoms of Israel and Judah. And if that had not been enough, I would have given you much, much more. 9Why, then, have you despised the word of the LORD and done this horrible deed? For you have murdered Uriah the Hittite with the sword of the Ammonites and stolen his wife. 10From this time on, your family will live by the sword because you have despised me by taking Uriah's wife to be your own.

11"This is what the LORD says: Because of what you have done, I will cause your own household to rebel against you. I will give your wives to another man before

your very eyes, and he will go to bed with
them in public view. 12 You did it secretly,
but I will make this happen to you openly
in the sight of all Israel."

13 Then David confessed to Nathan, "I
have sinned against the LORD."

Nathan replied, "Yes, but the LORD has
forgiven you, and you won't die for this
sin. 14 Nevertheless, because you have
shown utter contempt for the LORD* by
doing this, your child will die."

15 After Nathan returned to his home,
the LORD sent a deadly illness to the child
of David and Uriah's wife. 16 David begged
God to spare the child. He went without
food and lay all night on the bare ground.
17 The elders of his household pleaded
with him to get up and eat with them, but
he refused.

18 Then on the seventh day the child
died. David's advisers were afraid to tell
him. "He wouldn't listen to reason while
the child was ill," they said. "What drastic
thing will he do when we tell him the
child is dead?"

19 When David saw them whispering, he
realized what had happened. "Is the child
dead?" he asked.

"Yes," they replied, "he is dead."

20 Then David got up from the ground,
washed himself, put on lotions,* and
changed his clothes. He went to the Tab-
ernacle and worshiped the LORD. After
that, he returned to the palace and was
served food and ate.

21 His advisers were amazed. "We don't
understand you," they told him. "While
the child was still living, you wept and
refused to eat. But now that the child is
dead, you have stopped your mourning
and are eating again."

22 David replied, "I fasted and wept
while the child was alive, for I said, 'Per-
haps the LORD will be gracious to me and
let the child live.' 23 But why should I fast
when he is dead? Can I bring him back
again? I will go to him one day, but he
cannot return to me."

24 Then David comforted Bathsheba,
his wife, and slept with her. She became
pregnant and gave birth to a son, and Da-
vid* named him Solomon. The LORD loved
the child 25 and sent word through Nathan
the prophet that they should name him
Jedidiah (which means "beloved of the
LORD"), as the LORD had commanded.*

11:8 Hebrew *and wash your feet,* an expression that may also have a connotation of ritualistic washing. **11:11** Or *at Succoth.* **11:21** Hebrew *son of Jerub-besheth.* Jerub-besheth is a variation on the name Jerub-baal, which is another name for Gideon; see Judg 6:32. **12:14** As in Dead Sea Scrolls; Masoretic Text reads *the Lord's enemies.* **12:20** Hebrew *anointed himself.* **12:24** Hebrew *he;* an alternate Hebrew reading and some Hebrew manuscripts read *she.* **12:25** As in Greek version; Hebrew reads *because of the LORD.*

NOTES

11:3 *She is Bathsheba, the daughter of Eliam and the wife of Uriah the Hittite.* The report to David is to be understood as an assertion rather than a question, even though in the Hebrew it is introduced by interrogative He (lit., "Is this not Bathsheba . . ."). GKC §150e notes that "a surprising communication is introduced in this way (by *halo'* [TH1886.2/3808, ZH2022/4202]) in order to show it to be absolutely true."

11:15 *Station.* A. Anderson (1989:151-152) suggests reading the Hiphil imperative *habe'* (from *bo'* [TH935, ZH995], "send") with the LXX (*eisagage* [TG1521, ZG1652]) in place of MT's plural *habu* [TH3051, ZH2035] (from *yahab,* "set" or "station").

11:25 *The sword devours this one today and that one tomorrow!* Lit., "The sword consumes thus and thus."

12:3 *It ate.* For the frequentative use of the imperfect, see GKC §107e; Williams 1976§168.

12:5 *As surely as the LORD lives.* Or, "'As the LORD lives,' he vowed, 'surely any man who would do such a thing deserves to die.'" For this use of *ki* [TH3588, ZH3954] (surely) see Waltke and O'Connor 1990:679.

12:8 ***I would have given you much, much more.*** Lit., "I would have added as they and as they."

12:12 ***You did it secretly.*** NLT leaves the first word in the Hebrew text (*ki* [TH3588, ZH3954]) untranslated. For the use of *ki* as "although" ("Although you did it secretly"), see Williams 1976:§448.

12:14 ***contempt for the Lord.*** See NLT mg. The MT reads "the enemies of the LORD." This appears to be a euphemistic expression intended to avoid saying "you have shown utter contempt for the LORD" and has led to translations such as the NASB's "you have given occasion to the enemies of the LORD to blaspheme." See Kitchen (1966:166), who cites a similar euphemism in an Egyptian text.

12:17 ***but he refused.*** Lit., "but he would not eat." See GKC §75rr for *bara'* [TH1262A, ZH1356] instead of the expected *barah* [TH1262, ZH1356].

12:22 ***Perhaps.*** For *mi yodea'* [TH4310/3045, ZH4769/3359] used to convey doubt, see Waltke and O'Connor 1990:321.

COMMENTARY

The story of David, Bathsheba, and Uriah is not only one of the most celebrated narratives in the Old Testament, it is also widely recognized as one of the greatest literary masterpieces ever written. The narrative presents such a compelling and dramatic depiction of events connected with the religious and moral failure of the king who was "a man after [God's] own heart" (1 Sam 13:14) that any commentary on it is certain to be overshadowed by the grandeur of the story itself. The story is written in a compact and sparse literary style that leaves the reader with clarity on the serious nature of David's sin as expressed in the last phrase ("But the LORD was displeased with what David had done," [11:27b]), but at the same time provides little insight into the thoughts, motivations, and feelings of the various personalities involved in the plotline of the story. While it is the psychological motivations for the behaviors of the various individuals described in this narrative that are often of most interest to modern readers, the narrative itself places the emphasis on what David and others did, not on what they might have felt or thought.

Over the centuries both Jewish and Christian scholars have sought creative ways to harmonize the story of David's moral failure with his image as Israel's greatest and most revered monarch. In the Christian tradition, David's typal significance, pointing forward to the messianic ruler of the future, has compounded this difficulty. In an effort to minimize David's moral failure, some Jewish scholars have suggested that it was customary for Israelite soldiers to divorce their wives before going to war so that they might escape levirate marriage should their husbands die in battle. If the husband returned, then they would remarry. If it is assumed that this was done by Uriah and Bathsheba, in spite of strong contextual arguments to the contrary, then David is absolved of the sin of adultery. By the same token, some rabbis have justified Uriah's death by arguing that his disobedience of David's order to go to his house was a treasonous act (McCarter 1984:228). Among early Christian interpreters, St. Eucherius "treats 'The Adultery of David' as a complex allegory of the Messiah (David), the Law (Bathsheba), and the Jewish people (Uriah). St. Isidore of Seville chooses . . . to follow St. Augustine . . . in interpreting Bathsheba as the

Church, Uriah as Lucifer, and David as the beloved Redeemer 'who has liberated us from the Devil through his mercy'" (Huttar and Frontain 1992:183).

More recent analysis of the narrative among both Jewish and Christian scholars has called attention to the artful use of the literary strategies of ambiguity and irony in the narration of the story. Many of these studies call attention to the author's reticence to deal with the motivations and feelings of the main players in the story while providing lucid descriptions of their actions. Why, for example, does David remain in Jerusalem while his troops go out to war (11:1)? The narrative itself gives no explanation. Is this opening line of the story already intended by the author to be a veiled ironical attack on David for remaining at home, preparing the way for numerous other ironies that follow in the remainder of the narrative? Did Bathsheba deliberately bathe in a place where she knew that David would see her? Did she willingly come when David summoned her? Did Uriah know that David had slept with his wife when he refused to sleep with her himself? How much did Joab know or suspect about David's scheme to have Uriah killed in battle? The answers to all of these questions and many more are left to the reader's imagination.[1] It is the view of many advocates of this sort of literary analysis that ambiguity is part of a literary strategy that draws the reader into an imaginative personal involvement with the story in a way that enhances the effectiveness of its moral purpose (Yee 1988:251). While there may be some validity to this idea, caution is certainly in order, lest the historical grounding of the story is sacrificed to theoretical constructions of the artistic intentions of the author.

The last phrase of 11:1 tells us that David remained in Jerusalem when the Israelite army went out to lay siege to the Ammonite capital, Rabbah. This statement sets up the transition from the story of David's Ammonite wars to the story of his adulterous involvement with Bathsheba. There is a long history of faulting David for remaining in the safety of Jerusalem while Israel's army was enduring the discomforts and dangers of battle. In fact, some have found the seeds of David's sin of adultery and murder in this unfortunate, if not "sinful," decision to remain at home.[3] One should be careful, however, of placing too much emphasis on the moral dimension of David's decision not to accompany the troops in their engagement with the Ammonites. The text itself makes no comment on the matter, and there could be many legitimate reasons for David's decision to remain at home. Sternberg (1985:193-195), who views 11:1 as an ironical attack on David who remained at home, supports his view by saying, among other things, that "the monarchy owes its very rise . . . to the Israelite determination to have a king 'go out before us and fight our battles' (1 Sam 8:19)," and in addition it "leaps to the eye that this is the first war in which David fails to lead the army in person" (1985:194). Both of these statements, however, are of questionable validity since Israel's request for a king to "go out before us and fight our battles" (NIV) was included in the request for a "king . . . like all the other nations have" that both the Lord and Samuel described as sinful (1 Sam 8:5, 7; 10:19; 12:17-20). And this was not the "first war" in which David failed to lead Israel's army into battle. At the beginning of his reign David sent Joab on important missions while he remained at home (2:12-32; 3:20-23). In addition there is also no indication that David fought in all the battles against

Edom (1 Kgs 11:14-16; 1 Chr 18:12-13; Ps 60:TITLE), and in the immediate context David had sent Joab and Abishai to engage the Arameans and Ammonites while he remained in Jerusalem (10:7-14). It was not until the development of a more serious threat by a larger Aramean coalition that David himself accompanied his troops against them (10:17-19). But the military operation in view in this particular passage was not a continuation of normal combat, but rather the siege of a city (Rabbah), which would likely last for a long time, and not something for which David's presence was necessary.[4] So while it is clear that David's remaining in Jerusalem provided the occasion for his sinful behavior that ensued, it does not seem warranted to conclude that this, in itself, should be regarded as a culpable act.[5]

David's adulterous relationship with Bathsheba is described in clear and concise language in 11:2-5. One evening while David was walking on the roof of his palace his eyes fell on a woman bathing herself in either a courtyard or on the roof of her own nearby house. The flat roofs of the houses of that time provided cool and comfortable places for evening relaxation (1 Sam 9:25; Dan 4:29). The Hebrew text says that the woman was "a woman of unusual beauty" (11:2). David immediately wanted to know who she was, so he sent someone to inquire for him. He was informed that her name was Bathsheba, and that she was "the daughter of Eliam and the wife of Uriah the Hittite" (11:3).[6] This identification meant that both her father and her husband were members of an elite group of David's soldiers (23:34, 39) and that her grandfather, Ahithophel (23:34), was David's most important adviser (16:23).[7] So Bathsheba was a woman who moved in the highest circles of David's courtiers. But neither this knowledge of her identity, with all of its potential for imbroglio,[8] nor David's own religious and moral beliefs proved strong enough to deter David from his desire to have a sexual liaison with her. The irrational power of David's lust overwhelmed all other considerations, and David took the fateful step of having Bathsheba brought to him at the royal palace. Suddenly, David began to function like the kings of "all the other nations" who took from their people in order to satisfy their own desires (1 Sam 8:11-20). Suddenly he saw himself as above the law and became a law unto himself, rather than being a king who was submissive to the law of the Lord and the words of the prophets. Suddenly David acted in ways inconsistent with the behavior of a true covenantal king. The Hebrew text speaks here with amazing brevity and clarity. Brueggemann eloquently summarizes its flow:

> *The action is quick. The verbs rush as the passion of David rushed. He sent; he took; he lay (11:4). The royal deed of self-indulgence does not take very long. There is no adornment to the action. The woman then gets some verbs: she returned, she conceived. The action is so stark. There is nothing but action. There is no conversation. There is no hint of caring, of affection, of love—only lust. David does not call her by name, does not even speak to her. At the end of the encounter she is only "the woman" (11:5). [The name "Bathsheba" does not appear in the Hebrew of 11:5, although it is used in the NLT.] The verb that finally counts is "conceived." But the telling verb is "he took her." (1990a:117)*

In the midst of this quick-flowing description of the course of events, 11:4 contains a parenthetical explanatory remark ("She had just completed the purification rites after having her menstrual period"[9]) that carries enormous significance for Bathsheba's pregnancy. Intercourse was forbidden for Israelites during the time of a woman's menstruation (Lev 18:19). Since Bathsheba had recently completed her menstrual cycle,[10] she could not have been made pregnant by her own husband who was away from home with the army at Rabbah. In the only two words that Bathsheba speaks in the entire narrative (*harah 'anoki* [TH2030/595, ZH2226/644]; "I'm pregnant," 11:5), she informs David of the calamitous results of their liaison.[11]

David immediately recognized the implications of Bathsheba's statement and quickly devised a cover-up for his involvement in her pregnancy. He sent a message to Joab requesting that Uriah be sent back to Jerusalem. When Uriah arrived, David asked him some perfunctory questions about how the war was going (11:7)[12] and then told him to "go on home and relax" (11:8).[13] Uriah, however, refused to follow David's instructions and instead of going home, spent the night at the quarters of the palace guard (11:9). When David was told that he had not spent the night with his wife, he called him in and asked why he had refused to visit with his wife. Uriah responded that he could not go home to sleep with his wife with a good conscience when his comrades in arms were sleeping in the open fields.[14] After another day elapsed, David dined with Uriah and caused him to become intoxicated in the hope that in an inebriated condition his conscience would be dulled and that he would then take the opportunity to go and sleep with his wife. But to David's dismay Uriah again spent the night at the quarters of the palace guard (11:13).

Realizing that his initial cover-up plan would not work, David devised a new strategy to deal with his complicity in Bathsheba's pregnancy. He wrote a letter to Joab and instructed him to place Uriah in the front lines of the battle and then to suddenly withdraw the other troops so that Uriah would be killed (11:15). Uriah carried this letter containing his own death warrant to Joab at the front lines. After Joab complied with David's request and Uriah was indeed killed (11:16-17), he sent a messenger back to David with a report of the battle. He told the messenger that if David asked why troops had been placed so close to the wall of the city, he was to respond that Uriah the Hittite had been among those who were killed (11:21). When the messenger reported this news to David, David told him to tell Joab not to be discouraged because death was an inevitable part of warfare, but rather to be reenergized in his effort to take the city (11:25). So David's concern to cover up his sin with Bathsheba produced a callous disregard for the life of Uriah, a faithful and dedicated warrior in his army. In this incident David clearly failed to act as a true shepherd of his people. Meanwhile the reader is informed that after a period of mourning,[15] David brought Bathsheba to his palace to be one of his wives and that in due course she gave birth to a son. As far as outward appearances were concerned, David had been successful in concealing his adulterous relationship with Bathsheba. Uriah was dead, Bathsheba had become his wife, and the son that was born to them had the appearance of legitimacy. But the last sentence of chapter 11 reveals a different and ultimately far more important fact: "The LORD was displeased with what David had done" (11:27b).[16]

David may have been relieved that up to this point there had been no public exposure of his nefarious acts. But if he thought that this was the end of the matter, he was sorely mistaken. Nothing was hidden from the Lord, nor, as he would quickly learn, was he free from the guilt of his own violated conscience (Ps 32:3-4).

The last phrase of chapter 11 ("The LORD was displeased with what David had done") leads directly into the opening line of chapter 12 ("So the LORD sent Nathan the prophet to tell David this story"[17]). The juxtaposition of these two clauses (chapter divisions being a later contrivance) is the hinge on which the narrative moves from a description of David's sins (11:2-27) to a description of the Lord's calling David to account (12:1-25).

Nathan was the same prophet who had told David that his dynasty would endure forever (ch 7). Now, however, he brought a radically different message. It was Nathan's duty to confront David with the enormity of his sins and to announce to him the severe consequences that they would spawn in the life of his family and his court. He gained David's attention by telling him a story (12:2-4) about a rich man and a poor man.[18] The rich man, who possessed an abundance of flocks and herds, took a much-loved "pet" lamb from the poor man in order to provide a meal for a guest. Nathan conveyed this story to David in such a convincing manner that David swore (note the oath formula: "As surely as the LORD lives," [12:5a]) that "any man who would do such a thing deserves to die!" (12:5b). Then, apparently realizing that a death penalty was excessive, because theft was not legally punishable by death, David modified it to the fourfold restitution required in the Mosaic law (12:6; cf. Exod 22:1).[19] Up to this point, David was completely unaware that his response was at the same time his own indictment. All of this changed, however, with Nathan's next words: "You are that man!" (12:7). With this statement, Nathan introduced the judicial case that the Lord was bringing against David. Lest there be any misunderstanding, Nathan said explicitly that he was not merely giving his own opinion on the matter, but was speaking in the name of the Lord (cf. 7:3-5, 12-13 where Nathan was compelled by the Lord to alter his previously expressed opinion).

Nathan's words in 12:7-12 reflect features common to what has sometimes been called the "prophetic lawsuit" in which a messenger from the Lord, the Great King, brings charges against an unfaithful vassal.[20] These features include an introduction using the "messenger formula" (12:7a); a recital of previous beneficent acts performed by the Great King for the well-being of the vassal (12:7b-8); an accusation in the form of a question answered by the messenger himself (12:9); and the verdict introduced by the expression "From this time on. . . . This is what the LORD says" (12:10-12).[21] At the heart of this deposition is the contrast between the Lord's gracious acts toward David (12:7-8), and David's failure to live up to his covenantal responsibilities (12:9a). David's sins are designated as murder and as the stealing of the wife of another man (12:9b). Because of these sins, David will suffer a threefold punishment: (1) the sword will afflict his family, as he had inflicted it upon Uriah (12:9-10); (2) insurrection will arise from within his own household (12:11a); and (3) his wives will be publicly—not privately—humiliated by another man (12:11b-12). The ensuing narratives in 2 Samuel and the early chapters of 1 Kings describe the fulfillment of these punishments. David's sons, Amnon (13:28-29), Absalom (18:14), and Adonijah (1 Kgs 2:25) were put to death by the sword. David was driven out of Jerusalem by his own son Absalom when he attempted to seize his father's throne (15:1-15). And Absalom lay with David's concubines in public view after he captured Jerusalem (16:21-22).

Upon hearing Nathan's indictment, David immediately responded with words of repentance and contrition: "I have sinned against the LORD" (12:13).[22] David's confession was complete, unqualified, and unequivocal. In contrast with Saul, who attempted to shift responsibility and justify his sinful behavior when he was confronted by Samuel (cf. 1 Sam 13:11-12; 15:15, 20-21), David assumed full responsibility for his sinful acts. From Psalm 32:3-4, it appears that David's unconfessed sins weighed heavily on his spirit. He was ready to repent. His acknowledgment that his sin was "against the LORD" (cf. Ps 51:4) was not intended to deny any offense against Uriah and Bathsheba, and by extension against the entire nation of Israel, but was rather a recognition that all sin is in the first instance a breaking of God's law.[23] At its root, David's sin was exactly as Nathan had described it. It was a despising of the word of the Lord (12:9). In this instance the "word of the LORD" was the Mosaic law that the king in Israel was commanded to read all the days of his life so that he might learn to fear the Lord his God by keeping all the words of these "instructions and decrees" (Deut 17:19). The true covenantal king was not above the law or a law unto himself. He was obligated to honor the law of the Lord in the same way as every other Israelite. In the fuller description of David's confession found in Psalm 51, David asks the Lord to have mercy on him and to "blot out the stain of [his] sins," cleanse him "from [his] guilt," and "purify [him] from [his] sin" (Ps 51:1-2). He pleaded with the Lord not to banish him from his presence nor take his Holy Spirit from him (Ps 51:11). The phrasing of this request seems to reflect David's acute awareness that these things were exactly what the Lord had done to Saul (7:15; 1 Sam 16:1, 14). His petition, therefore, was a direct appeal to God's promise that, unlike the house of Saul, his own dynasty would not be cast aside, but would endure forever (ch 7). Even though this petition is not included in the narrative of 2 Samuel 12, the Lord's forgiveness of David ("Nathan replied, 'Yes, but the LORD has forgiven you, and you won't die for this sin,'" 12:13b) seems to be rooted as much in this gracious covenantal promise as it is in David's repentant spirit.[24]

Although Nathan assured David that the Lord had forgiven him, this did not annul the previously announced punishments. The forgiveness consisted in David's exemption (12:13) from the legally prescribed death penalty for adultery and murder (Lev 20:10; 24:17) that would enable his royal line to survive in conformity with God's previously announced promise. But it also came combined with another punishment: the death of the son that was born out of his illicit relationship with Bathsheba (12:18; cf. 11:27). Although David would live, there would still be a death in his house. Davis (1999:129) comments that "it is as if the child is David's substitute." He goes on to say, "I do not intend to read New Testament meanings back into an Old Testament text, I only want readers to note the pattern here, for there are some of us who know this paradox of forgiveness that is both free and costly, because a son of David has been our substitute."

When the Lord sent an illness upon the child,[25] David fasted (12:16b-18) and pleaded with the Lord to spare his child's life because he thought, "Perhaps the LORD will be gracious to me and let the child live" (12:22). But when, after seven days, the child died (12:18), David accepted the outcome as the fulfillment of Nathan's word and went to the Tabernacle to worship (12:20). David responded to his punishment in a way that demonstrated an acceptance of the Lord's will, even though he recognized that this was only the beginning of the serious consequences that his sin would generate in the life of his family.

David then sought to bring comfort to Bathsheba in her sorrow over the loss of her child. He slept with her and she became pregnant with another son whom they named Solomon, a name that sounds like (and is perhaps derived from) the Hebrew word for peace. That this was a child on whom the Lord's special favor rested is made clear by the statement of the narrator that "the LORD loved the child" (12:24) and sent Nathan to tell David and Bathsheba that they should name him "Jedidiah (which means 'beloved of the LORD')" (12:25).[26] It does not appear that the purpose of this secondary name was to supplant the name Solomon (the name by which the child was publicly known throughout his life), but rather that it was given as a reminder to David and Bathsheba of the special place that this child would hold in the eyes of the Lord.[27] This is the son who would become David's successor on the throne of Israel,[28] who would build the Temple as the Lord had promised, and who would establish conditions of peace and security for the nation (cf. 1 Chr 22:9).

There is something both disturbing and reassuring about this narrative. On the personal level it provides one of the Scripture's most vivid reminders that all human beings, no matter how elevated their status in the eyes of those around them, no matter what special calling they may have received from the Lord, are still fallen creatures and capable of the most unimaginable iniquities. It is for this reason that the Bible encourages us to place our trust in the Lord rather than in other people (Pss 118:8; 146:3). Human beings will always disappoint, but the Lord will never fail those who are his. With few exceptions (no sin is mentioned in the life of Daniel; and some argue the same with Joseph), the heroes of the Bible are not portrayed as sinless saints, including the most godly of Israel's rulers in the Old Testament period.

Over against human sinfulness, however, this narrative also portrays a God who not only graciously intervened in David's life to confront him with his sin,[29] but who also graciously spared his life and then gave him another son who would carry the line of promise forward.[30] Thus, the narrative is marked by the reassurance of grace. Just as in the Garden of Eden the Lord confronted Adam and Eve after they disobeyed the probationary commandment, so on this occasion the Lord did not allow David to think that his evil acts were hidden from divine scrutiny. Just as in the Garden of Eden God's pursuit of Adam and Eve was not conditioned on their prior repentance, so in David's case the Lord took the initiative to bring him to repentance. Although God's forgiveness of David did not exempt him from suffering the consequences of his sin,[31] God was faithful to his promise to David to preserve his house, and as David later declared, the Lord continued to be his "hiding place" (Ps 32:7) and the one whose "unfailing love" surrounded him no matter how difficult the experiences of life might become (Ps 32:10).

Regarding David's place in the unfolding drama of redemptive history, we find that while he embodied the ideal of the true covenantal king in a way that neither Saul nor any other Israelite king after him ever did, his kingship was, nevertheless, a flawed kingship. At its best it adumbrated the kingship of the great future messianic ruler who will establish a kingdom in which justice and peace are full and complete.

As David's failures were multiplied and expanded by those who followed him on the throne, the prophets began to point forward to a king from David's line who would be known as a "righteous Branch" (Jer 23:5; NLT, "righteous descendant"). This king would be a person who would not only reign "with wisdom" and do "what is just and right" (Jer 23:5), but he would also be a person known by the remarkable title: "The LORD Is Our Righteousness" (Jer 23:6). What Jeremiah's message anticipated, but did not fully explain, was that David's greater son would be a king who was not only sinless himself but would extend his righteousness to those over whom he ruled by making atonement for their sins. His name would be called Jesus, "for he will save his people from their sins" (Matt 1:21). He will sit on the throne of his father David, and his Kingdom will have no end (Isa 9:7; Luke 1:33).

ENDNOTES

1. An example of the extent to which questions such as these are asked and analyzed in current discussions on this narrative can be seen from Sternberg's comments (1985:528, note 25) on what David thinks Uriah thinks: "At this stage, then, the two hypotheses about David generate four alternative plots: (1) Uriah does not know, and David believes that Uriah does not know; (2) Uriah knows, and David believes that Uriah does not know; (3) Uriah does not know, and David believes that Uriah knows; (4) Uriah knows, and David believes that Uriah knows."
2. Sternberg (1985:228-229), for example, speaks of a difference between "multiple systems of gap-filling in real life" and the same in a "literary work." In real life, Sternberg says that "a person torn between two conflicting hypotheses knows only too well that only one hypothesis 'fits' the case, that only one can be right, and it is only for lack of sufficient wit or knowledge that he (or she) remains powerless to decide. One can only continue to hope for additional information to turn up in due course and resolve the issue." But in contrast to this, in a literary work "two contradictory hypotheses may both be valid, since their coexistence may be motivated and legitimated in terms of *artistic intentions* [my italics]. Hence the Bible and its reader can luxuriate on the Gordian knot that David must cut." Here, contrary to Sternberg's general affirmation of approaching biblical narrative from the multiple perspectives of historiography, aesthetics, and ideology, it seems that the literary perspective has trumped the historical.
3. Calvin (1992:479-480) comments, "This circumstance was put here in order to show that David did not carry out his duty. By thus sparing himself and staying in his house in order to be at his ease, he threw himself into the net of Satan, and one evil fed on another. . . . He did not carry out the charge which was committed to him, thus giving an opening to the devil. The temptation which came to him, then, was like a payment for his moral laxness." Baldwin (1988:231) says, "While others spent themselves and risked their lives, he was 'killing time,' acting like one of the kings of the nations round about, and exercising a kind of *droit de seigneur*." Youngblood (1992:928) speaks of David's remaining at home as not only "reprehensible in itself" but also the thing that "opens the way for royal behavior that is more despicable still."
4. See Garsiel 1993:249-250 for a similar argument, arrived at independently.
5. McCarter (1984:285) comments, "David's decision not to accompany the army is not disgraceful in itself: It may have been made in the spirit of 21:15-17 or for other reasons. It was the author of 11:2ff who saw the ironic potential in the decision and exploited it. After all, it is not for his failure to accompany the army to war that the king is going to be condemned; it is for what he does at home while the troops are in the field."

6. Because Uriah is a good Hebrew name (meaning "Yahweh is my light"), it seems unlikely that he was a foreign mercenary. Youngblood (1992:930) quotes Beal (1983:81): "Although Uriah may have been a free-lance soldier from one of the numerous north-Syrian Syro-Hittite states, he more likely was a descendant of those Hittite refugees who more than a century earlier had settled in the land of Palestine, in flight from the collapsing Hittite Empire."
7. This assumes that Bathsheba's father is the same Eliam who is referred to in 23:34.
8. Ahithophel's subsequent involvement in Absalom's conspiracy against David may have been related to David's ruthless treatment of his granddaughter and her husband.
9. The NLT rendering of this circumstantial clause is more explicit than the Hebrew, which reads, "She had just purified herself from her uncleanness." The nature of the "uncleanness" is not defined in the original text. Context, however, strongly suggests that it was the ritual uncleanness of the menstrual period that was in view. As S. R. Driver (1913:289) notes, this is a "circumstantial clause, defining the state of Bath-sheba at the time" that David slept with her. This clause is, therefore, not telling us that Bathsheba purified herself from the uncleanness of her sexual relationship with David subsequent to their illicit intercourse, as advocated, for example, by Calvin (1992:487-488) and Keil (1956:383-384). As S. R. Driver (1913:289) also notes, "the *athnach* is thus in its right place," grouping the circumstantial clause with the beginning of the sentence rather than with "she returned home."
10. This assumes that Bathsheba has just completed the seven-day period of ritual uncleanness described in Lev 15:19, and that she was now in the time frame in which ovulation normally occurred and conception was most likely to happen. There is no indication, however, that David was aware of this timing.
11. Alter (1999:251) comments, "Astonishingly, these are the only words Bathsheba speaks in this story. In keeping with the stringent efficiency of biblical narrative, the story leaps forward from the sexual act to the discovery of pregnancy."
12. That David's primary interest was not in how the war was going, but rather in how he could cover up his adultery with Bathsheba is conveyed by the author's exclusion from the narrative of any response from Uriah. There is a certain irony in David's asking about the welfare (*shalom* [TH7965, ZH8934]) of Joab, of the army, and of the battle (*shalom* is used three times), when he has just destroyed the *shalom* of Uriah's marriage, of his own marriages, and of many personal relationships within the court.
13. This is the NLT's rendering of the expression "Go home and wash your feet." Some commentators have understood "wash your feet" as a euphemism for sexual intercourse. Yee (1988:245), for example, says, "David's encouraging words to Uriah to go 'wash your feet' are themselves double entendres. They imply not only refreshment from travel, but given the euphemistic understanding of 'feet' as 'penis' (Gen 18:4; 19:2; 24:32; 43:24; Jdg 19:21; 1 Sam 25:41), David also insinuates that Uriah enjoy his wife sexually. If Uriah indeed 'washes his feet,' he will relieve David of his paternity." Garsiel (1993:257), however, challenges this reading, saying that this "cannot be a euphemism for sexual intercourse, as David cannot bring suspicion on himself by a direct order, although it is what he is hoping for." Gordon (1986:254) notes that "wash your feet" could "refer to a ritual ablution releasing a soldier from the vow of sexual abstinence during a military campaign (cf. 1 Sam 21:5)," but on the other hand "if feet is euphemistic for genitalia, the expression refers more overtly to sexual relations." Bergen (1996:365) understands the expression "wash your feet" as a reference to receiving "gracious domestic hospitality (cf. Gen 18:4; 19:2; 24:32; 43:24) from his wife; implicitly it was an order to spend a night of marital intimacy with Bathsheba." All things considered, this sort of indirect double entendre, rep-

resented in the NLT by the expression "go home and relax," seems to be the best understanding.

14. Uriah's words are clearly an ironic rebuke to David, who had no such scruples.
15. The length of the period of mourning is not indicated, but a period of between seven and thirty days seems reasonable. Joseph observed a seven-day period of mourning at the time of the burial of his father Jacob (Gen 50:10), and the men of Jabesh-gilead "fasted" for a period of seven days after the deaths of Saul and his sons at Mount Gilboa (1 Sam 31:13). Israel observed 30-day periods of mourning in connection with the deaths of Moses and Aaron (Num 20:29; Deut 34:8). It seems likely, then, that Bathsheba became David's wife before her pregnancy was outwardly noticeable.
16. There is an ironic repetition of the expression *yera' be'ene* [TH7489/5869, ZH8317/6524] ("be evil in the eyes of") in 11:25 and 11:27 that is obscured in English translation. In 11:25 David told the messenger to tell Joab that he was "not to be discouraged" by the death of his warriors (lit., "Do not let this thing be evil in your eyes"); in 11:27b the narrator tells the reader that "the LORD was displeased" with David's behavior in this entire episode (lit., it "was evil in the eyes of the LORD").
17. This "divine sending" that opens ch 12 contrasts with ch 11 where "human sendings" are center stage. Simon (1967:209) notes that the "root *shalakh* [TH7971, ZH8938] (send) occurs 12 times in the 27 verses of chapter 11 in 2 Sam." For example: David "sent" Joab to war (11:1), he "sent" messengers to Bathsheba (11:3-4), he "sent" messengers to Joab (11:6, 14), and he "sent" for Bathsheba to become his wife (11:27). Bathsheba "sent" David the message that she was pregnant (11:5). Joab "sent" Uriah to David (11:6) and later "sent" him the message of Uriah's death (11:18).
18. Simon (1967) has characterized Nathan's story as a "juridical parable." Simon (1967:220-221) defines a "juridical parable" as "a realistic story about a violation of the law, related to someone who had committed a similar offence with the purpose of leading the unsuspecting hearer to pass judgment on himself. The offender will only be caught in the trap set for him if he truly believes that the story told him actually happened, and only if he does not detect prematurely the similarity between the offence in the story and the one he himself has committed. . . . The juridical parable is a disguised parable designed to overcome man's own closeness to himself, enabling him to judge himself by the same yardstick that he applies to others." Simon finds five examples of such parables in the OT (Nathan's story: 12:1-14; the story of the wise woman of Tekoa: 14:1-20; the story of a "son of a prophet" to Ahab: 1 Kgs 20:35-43; the "Song of the Vineyard": Isa 5:1-7; Israel as an unfaithful wife: Jer 3:1-5).
19. Cartledge (2001:515) reads the Hebrew expression *ben-maweth* [TH1121/4194, ZH1201/4638] (lit., "son of death," translated in NLT as a person who "deserves to die") as a negative invective much like the modern expression "son of a bitch." He argues that this enables us to "avoid the difficult problem of David's passing two dissimilar sentences: one of death and the other of a relatively small financial penalty." Although he claims that there are no "good parallels" for translating the expression as someone who "deserves to die," 1 Sam 26:16 seems to controvert this claim.
20. This literary form finds its roots in the treaty/covenant analogy (cf. endnote 11 in the commentary on 1 Sam 11:14–12:25). For detailed discussions of the "covenant lawsuit," see Blenkinsopp 1971; Huffmon 1959; Wright 1962.
21. *We'attah* [TH2050.1/6258, ZH2256/6964] (and now) is the first word of 12:10 in the Hebrew text, and *koh 'amar yhwh* [TH3541/559/3068, ZH3907/606/3378] (Thus says the LORD) are the first words of 12:11 in the Hebrew text.
22. In the Hebrew text, Nathan utters the indictment of David ("You are that man!"; 12:7) with only two words. Similarly, David speaks only two words when he confesses his guilt. These two very brief statements embody the heart of the dynamics of this entire narrative

unit. As Simon (1967:232) notes, "Nathan's 'Thou art the man' and David's response: 'I have sinned against the LORD' derive their force from their quintessential brevity."

23. Ridderbos (1973:173) comments that this insight is worthy of attention in a time when there is a strong inclination to let the first commandment ("Love the Lord with all your heart, soul, and mind") be swallowed up by the second commandment ("Love your neighbor as yourself").
24. Here, as on other occasions in the life of both Abraham and David, is an example of behavior that is the fruit of the grace of God at work in David's life. This suggests that while David's repentance was a necessary condition for God's forgiveness, it was not the meritorious grounds for that forgiveness.
25. The text describes the child as the one "Uriah's wife bore to David," and not as "the son of David and Bathsheba" (12:15).
26. Second Samuel 12:25 contains the only occurrence of the name in the entire Bible.
27. The name was a message that would have had particular significance to Bathsheba, who had lost her husband, as well as the first child she had conceived in her relationship with David, and who undoubtedly was concerned about what would become of this second child. Here was a message of comfort to a woman who had been caught up in a maelstrom of misery and distress that was not of her own choosing. Here was a message that Bathsheba could often think about and quietly treasure in her heart as Mary would do at a later stage in redemptive history (Luke 2:19).
28. First Kings 1:13, 17, 30 make reference to an oath that David had sworn to Bathsheba that Solomon would succeed him as king. There is no reference to this oath in 2 Samuel, but it is reasonable to assume that it was sworn at the time of Solomon's birth. There is no need to assume, as some have suggested, that when David was on his deathbed, Nathan and Bathsheba conspired to deceive a "senile king" by concocting a nonexistent oath (Brueggemann 2000b:14-15; Fretheim 1999:24; Nelson 1987:20). Nelson (1987:20) comments that "we are not quite taken in by Nathan, his memory of a vow called out of thin air, his half-truths and unsubstantiated allegations, his deferential speech, or his contrived confirmation of Bathsheba's words. But David is, and the throne passes to Solomon by a trick." To the contrary, the Chronicler tells us that the Lord had told David that Solomon would be the anonymous "seed" of the covenantal promise of 1 Chr 17:11, and that it would be Solomon who would build the Temple (1 Chr 22:9).
29. Davis (1999:122) speaks of a grace that "pursues and exposes the sinner in his sin. . . . Not that God's pursuing grace is enjoyable. But what if grace did not pursue? What if Yahweh abandoned us when we succeeded at sin?"
30. Van den Berg (1997:71) comments (my translation), "Not Amnon or Absalom but Solomon will be the link in the outworking of God's messianic promise. In this way David's sinful relationship with Bathsheba ultimately assumes a role in God's redemptive work and Bathsheba acquires a place in the genealogy of Jesus. God is so great that he uses our sins, no matter how villainous they may be, as building blocks for his salvation. 'Oh the depth of the riches of the wisdom and knowledge of God, how unsearchable are his judgments and his ways past finding out!'"
31. As Davis (1999:128-129) notes, "Yahweh forgives the guilt of sin but inflicts the consequences of sin. He cleanses sin's defilement but may continue its discipline." Calvin (1992:614-615) notes that God had "put away" David's sin, so that his punishment is not to be viewed as a "type of satisfaction" but rather as something that has reference to the future. The punishment, therefore, serves the purpose of subduing David and making him feel the gravity of his offences as well as providing instruction for others. David later acknowledged, "My suffering was good for me, for it taught me to pay attention to your decrees" (Ps 119:71).

N. Civil War; Tamar, Amnon, Absalom, and Ahithophel (2 Sam 13:1–19:43)

1. Amnon's sin against Tamar (2 Sam 13:1-22)

[NB: Notes and commentary on 2 Sam 12:26-31 may be found on pp. 323–327.]

Now David's son Absalom had a beautiful
sister named Tamar. And Amnon, her half
brother, fell desperately in love with her.
2Amnon became so obsessed with Tamar
that he became ill. She was a virgin, and
Amnon thought he could never have her.
3But Amnon had a very crafty friend—
his cousin Jonadab. He was the son of
David's brother Shimea.* 4One day Jona-
dab said to Amnon, "What's the trouble?
Why should the son of a king look so de-
jected morning after morning?"
So Amnon told him, "I am in love with
Tamar, my brother Absalom's sister."
5"Well," Jonadab said, "I'll tell you what
to do. Go back to bed and pretend you are
ill. When your father comes to see you,
ask him to let Tamar come and prepare
some food for you. Tell him you'll feel bet-
ter if she prepares it as you watch and
feeds you with her own hands."
6So Amnon lay down and pretended to
be sick. And when the king came to see
him, Amnon asked him, "Please let my sis-
ter Tamar come and cook my favorite dish*
as I watch. Then I can eat it from her own
hands." 7So David agreed and sent Tamar
to Amnon's house to prepare some food
for him.
8When Tamar arrived at Amnon's house,
she went to the place where he was lying
down so he could watch her mix some
dough. Then she baked his favorite dish
for him. 9But when she set the serving
tray before him, he refused to eat. "Every-
one get out of here," Amnon told his ser-
vants. So they all left.
10Then he said to Tamar, "Now bring the
food into my bedroom and feed it to me
here." So Tamar took his favorite dish to
him. 11But as she was feeding him, he
grabbed her and demanded, "Come to bed
with me, my darling sister."
12"No, my brother!" she cried. "Don't be
foolish! Don't do this to me! Such wicked
things aren't done in Israel. 13Where could
I go in my shame? And you would be
called one of the greatest fools in Israel.
Please, just speak to the king about it, and
he will let you marry me."
14But Amnon wouldn't listen to her, and
since he was stronger than she was, he
raped her. 15Then suddenly Amnon's love
turned to hate, and he hated her even
more than he had loved her. "Get out of
here!" he snarled at her.
16"No, no!" Tamar cried. "Sending me
away now is worse than what you've al-
ready done to me."
But Amnon wouldn't listen to her. 17He
shouted for his servant and demanded,
"Throw this woman out, and lock the door
behind her!"
18So the servant put her out and locked
the door behind her. She was wearing a
long, beautiful robe,* as was the custom
in those days for the king's virgin daugh-
ters. 19But now Tamar tore her robe and
put ashes on her head. And then, with her
face in her hands, she went away crying.
20Her brother Absalom saw her and
asked, "Is it true that Amnon has been
with you? Well, my sister, keep quiet for
now, since he's your brother. Don't you
worry about it." So Tamar lived as a deso-
late woman in her brother Absalom's
house.
21When King David heard what had
happened, he was very angry.* 22And
though Absalom never spoke to Amnon
about this, he hated Amnon deeply be-
cause of what he had done to his sister.

13:3 Hebrew *Shimeah* (also in 13:32), a variant spelling of Shimea; compare 1 Chr 2:13. **13:6** Or *a couple of cakes;* also in 13:8, 10. **13:18** Or *a robe with sleeves,* or *an ornamented robe.* The meaning of the Hebrew is uncertain. **13:21** Dead Sea Scrolls and Greek version add *But he did not punish his son Amnon, because he loved him, for he was his firstborn.*

NOTES

13:6 *my favorite dish.* Exactly what type of food is represented by the verb *labab* [TH3823A, ZH4221] and the plural noun *lebiboth* [TH3834, ZH4223] is not clear. A. Anderson (1989) and McCarter (1984) suggest "dumplings," which fits with the terms *bashal* [TH1310, ZH1418] (boil, cook) in 13:8 and *yatsaq* [TH3332, ZH3668] (pour out) in 13:9.

13:9 *she set the serving tray before him.* Lit., "she took the pan and poured out its contents before him."

13:15 *and he hated her.* For the translation of *ki* [TH3588, ZH3954] as "indeed he hated her" see R. J. Williams 1976:§449.

13:18 *in those days.* This translation reflects the emendation of *me'ilim* [TH4598, ZH5077] (robes) to *me'olam* [TH4480/5769, ZH4946/6409] (from ancient time) as suggested by Wellhausen and others, with support from Josephus (*Antiquities* 7.171). McCarter (1984:318-319), however, (followed by A. Anderson 1989:171) prefers the rendering "from puberty" on the assumption that the text was originally *me'alom* (derived from *'alam*, "be sexually mature").

13:21 See NLT mg for the additional phrase found in the LXX and 4QSam[a]. On the basis of LXX, Wellhausen (1871) had argued in favor of the additional words, while S. R. Driver (1913:301) remained undecided, commenting, "The words, if a gloss, are at any rate an instructive one." The many commentators who have adopted the addition usually explain its loss as haplographic (a skipping from the *welo'* [TH2050.1/3808, ZH2256/4202] at the beginning of the lost section to the *welo'* at the beginning of 13:22). Ulrich (1978:84) has shown that the fragmentary evidence of 4QSam[a] agrees with LXX. Pisano (1984:223) notes that the "presence of the plus in 4Q indicates that it most likely was found in LXX's Hebrew *Vorlage* as well, but I suggest that it is not possible here to determine, on the merits of the plus alone, whether it should be considered original to the narrative or not."

COMMENTARY

The story of Amnon's incestuous rape of Tamar (13:1-22)[1] leading to Absalom's murder of Amnon (13:23-39) is the first in a series of interconnected narratives (chs 13–19) depicting the outworking of Nathan's description of David's punishment recorded in 12:10-11. This climaxed in Absalom's attempt to seize the throne from his father (chs 15–18). Amnon was the eldest son of David (3:2). His mother was Ahinoam, David's first wife (not including Michal, whom Saul had given to Paltiel; cf. 2:2; 1 Sam 25:43; 27:3). Tamar was a full sister of Absalom, but a half sister of Amnon (cf. 13:1).[2] Just as David had lusted after Bathsheba in ch 11, so, in this chapter, Amnon lusted after his half sister Tamar.[3] Having become obsessed with his unfulfilled sexual desire for her, but finding no way to satisfy it, he took the advice of his cousin Jonadab[4] to feign an illness (13:5) and then request his father, David, to allow Tamar to come to his living quarters to prepare a meal for him (13:6).[5] Unaware of Amnon's illicit designs, David granted the request, and ordered Tamar to go to Amnon's house to prepare the meal (13:7). Amnon dismissed all his personnel, so that he and Tamar could be left alone in his bedroom (13:9). When Tamar approached his bed with the food, Amnon attempted to coerce her to have sex with him. Tamar, however, refused his advances and attempted to reason with him, by designating his act a "wicked thing" (13:12) and by saying that it would bring her to shame and cause him to be viewed as a foolish person (13:13). She then urged him to appeal to their father David, who, she alleged, would give approval to their marriage. Amnon, however, did not listen to her arguments, and he overpowered her and raped her (13:14).[6] Amnon's lust having been satisfied, his feelings turned from "love" to "hate" (13:15),[7] and he ordered one of his servants to remove her from his house, and not to permit her to return (13:17). Tamar was, of course, devastated by Amnon's brutal violation of her dignity and virginity. When her full brother, Absalom, learned about what had happened, he attempted to console her, took her into his own house, and counseled her to keep the matter quiet rather than make it into a public scandal (13:20).[8] But when David was informed about what had happened, all we are told is that "he was very angry" (13:21). He took no initiative to hold Amnon responsible for his criminal behavior (see note on 13:21).[9] This failure to act,[10] however, came back to haunt him, because it was David's inaction that set the stage for Absalom's taking matters into his own hands, which in turn led to alienation from his father and the attempt to seize the throne for himself.

The final verse of this section of chapter 13 tells us that although Absalom did not immediately confront Amnon about his sinful act, he bided his time, nurturing a deep hatred toward him in his heart (13:22). This is an ominous note that links this narrative unit with the one that immediately follows.

ENDNOTES

1. Ridout (1974:75) remarks that this brief narrative unit contains no less than eleven repetitions of the word "brother" (*'akh*) and eight of the word "sister" (*'akhoth*) highlighting the family relationships of the individuals involved in the narrative. As he notes, "This is a story of David's family, and how it came about that this royal family started on a tragic course of self-destruction." Ridout (1974:81) also suggests that the narrative has been set in the following chiastic structure:

   A. Amnon is in love with Tamar (13:1-4).
      B. Tamar comes to Amnon's house and bakes bread for him (13:5-9a).
         C. Amnon orders his servants out, that he might be alone with Tamar (13:9b-10).
            D. Amnon commands Tamar to come lie with him; she pleads with him but to no avail (13:11-14a).
               E. Amnon rapes Tamar, and his love for her turns to hate (13:14b-15a).
            D'. Amnon commands Tamar to get out; she pleads with him but to no avail (13:15b-16).
         C'. Amnon calls a servant back and orders him to lock Tamar out (13:17).
      B'. Tamar leaves Amnon's house, mourning her fate (13:18-19).
   A'. Absalom hates Amnon for having raped Tamar (13:20-22).

2. The mother of Absalom and Tamar was Maacah, the daughter of Talmai, king of Geshur. David married Maacah during the time he reigned over Judah from Hebron (cf. 3:3). The marriage was undoubtedly politically motivated since Geshur was located on Ishbosheth's northern border.
3. Alter (1999:265) comments, "The catastrophic turn in David's fortune began when he saw a beautiful woman and lusted after her. Now, the curse pronounced by Nathan on the house of David begins to unfold through the very same mechanism: a sexual transgression within the royal quarter resulting in an act of murder elsewhere." Fokkelman (1981:106) speaks of Amnon becoming "a prey of sexual lust" just as his

father David had. Hertzberg (1964:322) says that "the son is dominated by the same sensuality as his father."

4. Hill (1987) views Jonadab as a court sage who had aligned himself with Absalom in a long-term conspiracy to get rid of Amnon (David's eldest son, and thus the crown prince) by "taking advantage of a basic weakness in Amnon's character" (1987:389) as means of eventually securing the throne for Absalom. He designates him (1987:390) as a "co-conspirator in the Absalom coup." While this suggestion may have some merit, it rests on a number of assumptions that can neither be proved nor disproved, and it seems to place too much emphasis on the "succession" idea as the overriding concern of chs 13–19. As Conroy (1983:121) notes, "There is no indication that Absalom hated Amnon as a rival for the throne; his hatred and the subsequent fratricide were clearly motivated by a desire to avenge the wrong done to Tamar (13:22, 32)." In fact, as Brueggemann (1974:176) notes, the central issue that runs through the Absalom narratives "is not who will succeed David, but whether David will be sustained on the throne. Or put in terms of the countertheme, the issue is whether Yahweh will honor his royal promise and whether David will trust in it."
5. The motif of feigning an illness to lure an unsuspecting woman to a sexual encounter is found in Egyptian literature, and Hill (1987:389), along with others, has suggested that familiarity with such stories is the source for Jonadab's proposal to Amnon. An example, quoted by Hill from W. K. Simpson (1973:300), is the following: "Now I'll lie down inside and act as if I'm sick. My neighbors will come in to visit, and with them my girl. She'll put the doctors out, for she's the one to know my hurt."
6. According to the regulations of Deut 22:28-29, a man who rapes an unengaged virgin is required to pay the girl's father 50 shekels of silver (this appears to be the combination of an average bride-price plus some punitive damages, cf. Tigay 1996:208), and the girl shall become his wife. In such cases the man will then have no right of divorce. In this instance, however, the law does not apply because sexual relations and marriages between brothers and sisters were not permitted (cf. Lev 18:9-11; 20:17; Deut 27:22). Tigay (1996:256) in commenting on Deut 27:22 says that "this . . . makes it clear that one may not marry (or have sexual relations with) even a half sister." It is not necessary to argue that the laws of Deuteronomy and Leviticus must not have been in effect at this time since Tamar suggested to Amnon that David would approve of a marriage between them (much like the marriage of Abraham and Sarah). It would seem better to assume that Tamar's argument was simply a desperate attempt to buy some time and find a possible way out of the very threatening situation that she faced, or that although aware of the inappropriateness of what she proposed, she was more concerned with appearances than with legalities.
7. The intensity of Amnon's hatred is indicated by the occurrence of the Hebrew root *sane'* [TH8130, ZH8533] (hate) four times in 13:15, accompanied by the modifiers "great" (*gadol* [TH1419, ZH1524]) and "exceedingly" (*me'od* [TH3966, ZH4394]). As Ridout (1974:83) points out, the contrast of "love" and "hate" appears "strikingly at the extremes (A and A') and the center (E) of the chiasm" (see endnote 1 above).
8. Propp (1993:45) understands Absalom's command to Tamar to "keep quiet for now" as meaning that Tamar should "refrain from demanding marriage" because "such a union would be incestuous" (see 13:13).
9. Although David is rightly faulted by many commentators for abdicating his royal as well as parental duty to punish Amnon in some way for his reprehensible conduct, it

should be kept in mind that the case law of the Mosaic code provided no clear legal basis for dealing with this specific type of misdeed (see endnote 6 above). Calvin (1992:641) speaks of David as "lax" and "not as severe or stringent as he should have been" and categorizes his inaction as "sin." Although there was no legal basis for the death penalty (which Calvin suggests would have been appropriate), certainly some sort of fitting punishment was in order.

10. The Masoretic Text gives us no explanation as to why David failed to take any action against Amnon. On the basis of the LXX reading of 13:21, some have concluded that the reason for David's inaction was the special place that Amnon held in David's heart as his firstborn son. This is a possible explanation, but it is valid only to the extent that one considers LXX the preferable reading (see note at 13:21). Others have suggested that David lost the moral authority to discipline Amnon because of his own compromised behavior in the area of sexual ethics. Whatever the reason might be, the conclusion that David was negligent in disciplining his sons is reinforced by his granting permission to Absalom to return from his self-imposed exile without suffering the legal consequences for his murder of Amnon (ch 14).

◆ 2. Absalom murders Amnon (2 Sam 13:23-39)

[23]Two years later, when Absalom's sheep were being sheared at Baal-hazor near Ephraim, Absalom invited all the king's sons to come to a feast. [24]He went to the king and said, "My sheep-shearers are now at work. Would the king and his servants please come to celebrate the occasion with me?"

[25]The king replied, "No, my son. If we all came, we would be too much of a burden on you." Absalom pressed him, but the king would not come, though he gave Absalom his blessing.

[26]"Well, then," Absalom said, "if you can't come, how about sending my brother Amnon with us?"

"Why Amnon?" the king asked. [27]But Absalom kept on pressing the king until he finally agreed to let all his sons attend, including Amnon. So Absalom prepared a feast fit for a king.*

[28]Absalom told his men, "Wait until Amnon gets drunk; then at my signal, kill him! Don't be afraid. I'm the one who has given the command. Take courage and do it!" [29]So at Absalom's signal they murdered Amnon. Then the other sons of the king jumped on their mules and fled.

[30]As they were on the way back to Jerusalem, this report reached David: "Absalom has killed all the king's sons; not one is left alive!" [31]The king got up, tore his robe, and threw himself on the ground. His advisers also tore their clothes in horror and sorrow.

[32]But just then Jonadab, the son of David's brother Shimea, arrived and said, "No, don't believe that all the king's sons have been killed! It was only Amnon! Absalom has been plotting this ever since Amnon raped his sister Tamar. [33]No, my lord the king, your sons aren't all dead! It was only Amnon." [34]Meanwhile Absalom escaped.

Then the watchman on the Jerusalem wall saw a great crowd coming down the hill on the road from the west. He ran to tell the king, "I see a crowd of people coming from the Horonaim road along the side of the hill."*

[35]"Look!" Jonadab told the king. "There they are now! The king's sons are coming, just as I said."

[36]They soon arrived, weeping and sobbing, and the king and all his servants wept bitterly with them. [37]And David mourned many days for his son Amnon.

Absalom fled to his grandfather, Talmai
son of Ammihud, the king of Geshur. 38He
stayed there in Geshur for three years.
39And King David,* now reconciled to Am-
non's death, longed to be reunited with
his son Absalom.*

13:27 As in Greek and Latin versions (compare also Dead Sea Scrolls); the Hebrew text lacks this sentence. **13:34** As in Greek version; Hebrew lacks this sentence. **13:39a** Dead Sea Scrolls and Greek version read *And the spirit of the king.* **13:39b** Or *no longer felt a need to go out after Absalom.*

NOTES

13:27 ***So Absalom prepared a feast fit for a king.*** This follows LXX and Latin versions. The Hebrew does not include this sentence (cf. NLT mg). In 4QSam[a], Ulrich (1978:85) notes that "there is a gap of ½ line . . . which is perfectly filled with the plus as reconstructed from [LXX]." Many commentators, including McCarter (1984:329-330) and A. Anderson (1989:178-179), as well as translations (e.g., JB, NAB, NEB, NRSV), have accepted the additional wording as original, usually on the assumption that MT lost the sentence due to homoeoteleuton at the repeated word *hammelek* [TH4428, ZH4889] (the king). Pisano (1984:224-225) notes the similarity of the additional sentence with 1 Sam 25:36 and suggests it "is possible that LXX found it illogical that Amnon's heart was merry with wine if no meal was referred to in the account, and it could have supplied the missing element based on the story of Nabal." But then, noting that haplography is possible, he concludes, "It does not seem possible to determine which form, MT or LXX, contains the original reading here."

13:34 ***coming from the Horonaim road.*** The MT's *midderek 'akharayw* [TH1870/310, ZH2006/339] (from the road behind him) is often emended (in general agreement with LXX) to *midderek khoronayim* [TH2773, ZH2589] ("from the Horonaim road"; cf. NLT mg). This is based on a larger LXX addition that contains the watchman's report to David ("He came and reported to the king, 'I see men coming down the hill from Horonaim.'"). Regarding this, Pisano (1984:231-232) concludes, "It is not necessary for the narrative that the watchman actually express his message to David. 1 Sam 14:16f shows that in the narrative style of Sam[uel], it is sufficient that the watchman see something, while the report to the interested party is understood from the context. LXX or its *Vorlage* may not have been satisfied with this technique here at 2 Sam 13:34, and filled in what it considered to be a lacuna in the text. If this is the case here, then the text has been augmented in such a way that the longer LXX appears to be 'haplogenic' because of the repetition of the place name which the LXX text used in order to make its insertion here."

13:39 ***And King David.*** Some LXX mss and 4QSam[a] read "And the spirit of King David." The feminine form of the verb seems to require *ruakh* [TH7307, ZH8120] (spirit) as either the implied or explicit subject.

longed to be reunited. Commentators are divided over the best way to translate this phrase (for an alternative translation, see the NLT mg). A. Anderson (1989:182, 184, 187) and McCarter (1984:335, 338), for example, support translations similar to that found in the NLT mg. The translation issue turns on the meaning of the verb *kalah* [TH3615, ZH3983]. Does it mean David "longed" for Absalom, or does it mean that David "was spent" in the sense that he no longer "felt a need" to pursue Absalom? Although either rendering is possible, McCarter's suggestion (1984:344) that the meaning is "that David is no longer openly hostile to Abishalom and, therefore, ready to be prodded step by step towards a reconciliation" is probably more agreeable with the broader context. The way in which this phrase is translated will inevitably affect the way in which the first phrase of 14:1 is translated (NLT, "Joab realized how much the king longed to see Absalom."). Literally, 14:1 reads, "Now Joab, son of Zeruiah, perceived that the king's mind was on Absalom." The literal wording of

14:1 gives no indication of whether the king's attitude toward Absalom was affirmative or hostile. The NLT assumes the affirmative interpretation, which is consistent with its rendering of 13:39b. Others, such as A. Anderson (1989:182), translate 14:1a in a hostile sense: "Joab, son of Zeruiah, perceived that the king's heart was still set against Absalom." Some have argued that if David "longed to see" Absalom (14:1), then there would be no need for Joab's elaborate scheme to secure Absalom's return to Jerusalem as reported in 14:1-20 (Davis 1999:143-144). This, however, is not as clear as it might seem. There appears to have been a deep ambivalence in David's heart concerning how to deal with Absalom's murder of Amnon and his self-imposed exile. It is possible that Joab perceived this ambivalence and decided that the best course of action was to push David toward reconciliation.

COMMENTARY

Absalom bided his time for two years before he found an appropriate occasion for dealing with Amnon's crime (13:23). Sheepshearing was a festive enterprise usually performed in the early summer. During the time of sheepshearing, shepherds were rewarded for the number of sheep they presented, and the arduous work of the shearing itself was interspersed with celebrations and feasting. Absalom saw in this event an opportunity to take Amnon by surprise. So he invited his father David and his court officials, as well as all of his brothers, to join him for the annual sheepshearing festivities (13:24). David, however, declined the invitation because of Absalom's having to bear the costs of hosting such a large group of people (13:25). Absalom then requested that at a minimum his brother Amnon be sent to join the gathering. David's response, "Why Amnon?" (13:26), appears to reflect some suspicion concerning why Amnon should be singled out for an invitation. But his suspicion seems to have been dismissed when Absalom persisted in his request—David agreed to send not only Amnon but all of his brothers as well (13:27).[1]

When the visitors had arrived at Baal-hazor and a great feast was prepared (13:27, see note), Absalom instructed his men to wait until Amnon was drunk, and then to kill him when he gave them a signal to do so.[2] He told them to have no fear for the consequences of their deed because they were acting at his command. So the men complied with Absalom's instructions and murdered Amnon, causing the remaining brothers to flee in fear for their lives (13:29). Baal-hazor is usually identified with a site located about six miles north-northeast of Bethel. After killing Amnon, Absalom was in a good position for his flight to the kingdom of Geshur, further north in the Transjordanian area of Golan, to the east of the Sea of Galilee.

David and his advisers were stunned when a rumor reached the palace in Jerusalem that all of David's sons had been murdered by Absalom (13:30-31). Jonadab, however, aware of Absalom's longstanding intent to take revenge on Amnon for his rape of Tamar, reassured David and his advisers that only Amnon had been murdered. It was not long before the entire entourage of the surviving sons was seen approaching Jerusalem, confirming Jonadab's assertion. The escapees arrived in anguish over the tragic death of Amnon, and David quickly joined them in grief. In the meantime, we are told that Absalom had escaped (13:34) and sought asylum in Geshur where his grandfather was king (13:37). He remained in Geshur for three years (13:38). The narrative unit concludes with the statement that David "longed to be reunited with his son Absalom" (see note on 13:39).

The tragic events of Amnon's rape of Tamar (13:1-22) and Absalom's murder of Amnon (13:23-39) were not only reminders of David's adultery with Bathsheba and his arrangement for the murder of Bathsheba's husband, Uriah,[3] but also of the pronouncement of Nathan to David that because of his sins, "from this time on" his "family will live by the sword" (12:10). But this was only the beginning of the realization of the fulfillment of this foreboding oracle. The chain of events set in motion by David's adultery and murder (which were mirrored in the behavior of Amnon and Absalom in chapter 13) was far from over. The house of David would suffer even more serious challenges as time moved on, and it would become increasingly clear that David's kingdom fell far short of the ideal of the messianic kingdom.

ENDNOTES

1. Fokkleman (1981:115-116) sees in the dialogue between Absalom and David a very carefully contrived strategy on the part of Absalom that was designed to manipulate David into unwitting support for his plan to kill Amnon. He says that Absalom's "intention is psychologically fairly simple: he poses two questions, having calculated beforehand that David will or must refuse them, and, in so doing, he drives his father into the uncomfortable corner of having to say no. He deliberately asks for too much at first." When David refuses, Absalom then "counters with a question that is far too specific, i.e., whether or not Amnon will come. But this is the other extreme! . . . Absalom dares to use the very name which must not become obvious. This appears to have a paradoxical effect, just as though Absalom has nothing up his sleeve. . . . David puts himself at ease by giving Amnon the company of his brothers. For Absalom they are no hindrance, however, but a good cover needed to receive Amnon fittingly at his country-seat."
2. There is no need to link Absalom's murder of Amnon (David's firstborn, 3:2) with a scheme by Absalom to clear the way for his own succession to the throne (as in e.g., Brueggemann 1990a:290). This sort of reading is too heavily influenced by the theory that this section of 2 Samuel is a "Succession Narrative" rather than simply the story of David's "sin and its punishment" (see the commentary on ch 9 and the Introduction, "Date and Occasion of Writing" and "Literary Style"). Further, this reading ignores the fact that Solomon has already been designated as David's successor (see endnote 28 on 11:2–12:25). Surely, this was not unknown to Absalom.
3. As Youngblood (1992:969) puts it, "David's adultery with Bathsheba is mirrored in his son Amnon's rape of Tamar, and David's murder of Uriah is reprised in Absalom's execution of Amnon." Fokkelman (1981:124-125) speaks of the parallel between the two sexual crimes and the two arranged murders and concludes that Amnon and Absalom "are chips off the old block."

◆ 3. The wise woman of Tekoa (2 Sam 14:1-24)

Joab realized how much the king longed
to see Absalom. 2So he sent for a woman
from Tekoa who had a reputation for great
wisdom. He said to her, "Pretend you are
in mourning; wear mourning clothes and
don't put on lotions.* Act like a woman
who has been mourning for the dead for
a long time. 3Then go to the king and tell
him the story I am about to tell you." Then
Joab told her what to say.

4When the woman from Tekoa ap-
proached the king, she bowed with her
face to the ground in deep respect and
cried out, "O king! Help me!"

5"What's the trouble?" the king asked.
"Alas, I am a widow!" she replied. "My
husband is dead. 6My two sons had a fight
out in the field. And since no one was
there to stop it, one of them was killed.
7Now the rest of the family is demanding,
'Let us have your son. We will execute him
for murdering his brother. He doesn't de-
serve to inherit his family's property.' They
want to extinguish the only coal I have
left, and my husband's name and family
will disappear from the face of the
earth."
8"Leave it to me," the king told her.
"Go home, and I'll see to it that no one
touches him."
9"Oh, thank you, my lord the king," the
woman from Tekoa replied. "If you are
criticized for helping me, let the blame
fall on me and on my father's house, and
let the king and his throne be innocent."
10"If anyone objects," the king said,
"bring him to me. I can assure you he will
never complain again!"
11Then she said, "Please swear to me by
the LORD your God that you won't let any-
one take vengeance against my son. I
want no more bloodshed."
"As surely as the LORD lives," he replied,
"not a hair on your son's head will be dis-
turbed!"
12"Please allow me to ask one more
thing of my lord the king," she said.
"Go ahead and speak," he responded.
13She replied, "Why don't you do as
much for the people of God as you have
promised to do for me? You have con-
victed yourself in making this decision,
because you have refused to bring home
your own banished son. 14All of us must
die eventually. Our lives are like water
spilled out on the ground, which cannot
be gathered up again. But God does not
just sweep life away; instead, he devises
ways to bring us back when we have been
separated from him.
15"I have come to plead with my lord
the king because people have threatened
me. I said to myself, 'Perhaps the king will
listen to me 16and rescue us from those
who would cut us off from the inheri-
tance* God has given us. 17Yes, my lord the
king will give us peace of mind again.' I
know that you are like an angel of God in
discerning good from evil. May the LORD
your God be with you."
18"I must know one thing," the king re-
plied, "and tell me the truth."
"Yes, my lord the king," she responded.
19"Did Joab put you up to this?"
And the woman replied, "My lord the
king, how can I deny it? Nobody can hide
anything from you. Yes, Joab sent me and
told me what to say. 20He did it to place
the matter before you in a different light.
But you are as wise as an angel of God,
and you understand everything that hap-
pens among us!"
21So the king sent for Joab and told
him, "All right, go and bring back the
young man Absalom."
22Joab bowed with his face to the
ground in deep respect and said, "At last
I know that I have gained your approval,
my lord the king, for you have granted me
this request!"
23Then Joab went to Geshur and brought
Absalom back to Jerusalem. 24But the king
gave this order: "Absalom may go to his
own house, but he must never come into
my presence." So Absalom did not see the
king.

14:2 Hebrew *don't anoint yourself with oil.* **14:16** Or *the property;* or *the people.*

NOTES

14:3 ***Then Joab told her what to say.*** Lit., "And Joab put words in her mouth."

14:4 ***approached.*** This follows the reading *wattabo'* [TH935, ZH995] (came) with many Hebrew mss and LXX. The MT has *watto'mer* [TH559, ZH606] (said).

14:7 ***Now.*** Regarding this use of *wehinneh* [TH2009, ZH2180] (behold), see Waltke and O'Connor 1990:678.

14:10 ***If anyone objects.*** Lit., "If anyone speaks to you." For the conditional use of a participle followed by Waw consecutive with the perfect, see Waltke and O'Connor 1990:535-536.

14:13 ***in making this decision.*** Lit., "in speaking this word."

14:14 ***But God does not just sweep life away; instead, he devises ways to bring us back.*** S. R. Driver (1913:308) and A. Anderson (1989:183-184), following Ewald, translate this sentence, "But God will not take away the life of him that deviseth plans to not banish from him one that is banished." This is then understood as an encouragement to David to recall Absalom. The difference between the two translations turns on Ewald's suggestion to emend *wekhashab* [TH2803, ZH3108] (but he [God] devises) to *khosheb* (him that devises).

14:16 ***the inheritance God has given us.*** This translates *nakhalath 'elohim* [TH5159/430, ZH5709/466], an expression that occurs only here in the Hebrew Bible (see NLT mg for alternate translation suggestions). After a detailed discussion of the translation issues involved, including biblical and extrabiblical parallels to the wording, Lewis (1991:608) constructs a good case for concluding that *nakhalath 'elohim* "refers to the ancestral estate." This is the view represented by the NLT rendering.

14:19 ***Nobody can hide anything from you.*** Lit., "There is no (*'im-'ish* [TH518/786, ZH561/838]) turning to the right or the left from anything which my lord the king has spoken."

Yes. Regarding the asseverative use of *ki* [TH3588, ZH3954], see Williams 1976:§449.

14:22 ***for.*** See Williams (1976:§468) for this use of *'asher* [TH834, ZH889] (that, which).

granted me. Lit., "granted his servant." Qere and 4QSam[c] read, "granted your servant."

COMMENTARY

After three years had passed (13:38), Joab, the powerful and enigmatic commander of David's armies, took the initiative to arrange for Absalom's safe return to Jerusalem from his self-imposed exile (14:23-24). Ironically, this is the same Joab who would later assassinate Absalom in violation of David's explicit command to spare his life (18:5, 14). Joab's reasons for attempting to facilitate Absalom's reconciliation with David are not stated. If one accepts the NLT translation of 13:39 and 14:1 (see note on 13:39), it would seem that Joab perceived that David longed for a restored relationship with his son but remained ambivalent concerning his responsibility as king to maintain justice on the one hand and his personal affection for his son on the other. Even so, it is clear that there is much more to this story than is being told to the reader.

It is possible that Joab's motives for the attempt to rehabilitate Absalom were more patriotic than personal (see 10:12 for an expression of Joab's loyalty to the nation) and that he regarded Absalom as someone who could deal with a growing dissatisfaction with David's reign among various segments of Israelite society.[1] It is also probable that Joab would not have regarded Absalom's murder of Amnon as a disqualification for rehabilitation because he also was a murderer—and he had retained his position as commander of the armies. (Joab had killed Abner after Abner killed Joab's half brother; see commentary on 2:18-23; 3:22-39.) In this connection it is worthy of note that the words spoken by the "wise woman" from Tekoa on blood revenge, which were intended to move David toward reconciliation with Absalom, had been placed in her mouth by Joab (see note on 14:3). That Joab did not align himself with Absalom's rebellion may have been due to unanticipated developments subsequent to Absalom's return. Two years after returning to Jerusalem, Absalom took action against his benefactor, Joab, by setting his field on fire as a means of coercing him to convince David to grant him full acceptance into the court (14:30-33). And later, when Absalom began to gather accomplices for his revolt against his father, he appointed Amasa (a nephew of David, and a cousin of both Absalom and Joab) rather than Joab as the commander of his army (17:25).[2] But perhaps even more significant in the estrangement that developed between Absalom and Joab was the friendship that Absalom established with Ahithophel, an important counselor in David's court (15:12). Ahithophel was the father of Eliam (one of David's 30 elite warriors) and the grandfather of Bathsheba (11:3; 23:34). Because Joab had played such a significant role in the death of Uriah (Eliam's son-in-law; cf. 11:14-25), he would have had every reason to be on his guard against blood revenge from members of this influential family. Ahithophel was to become the power behind the scenes in Absalom's revolution, and revenge born out of a long-smoldering resentment toward David and Joab for their crime against Uriah may have been a motivating factor in Ahithophel's alliance with Absalom. So even though the complex relationships in David's court eventually generated distrust, intrigue, and even conspiracies, it seems that at this particular point in time, Joab had concluded that it was in the best interest of both David and the nation to attempt to heal the rift that existed between David and Absalom.

In order to accomplish this objective, Joab secured the services of a wise woman from Tekoa (14:2). He instructed her to go to David as a woman in mourning, and to tell him a fictitious story (see endnote 18 in the commentary on 11:2–12:25 regarding the "juridical parable") in order to trick him into giving the desired verdict.[3] The woman, performing her task with great skill, told David that she was a widow with two sons. During a fight, one of the sons killed his brother, and now other members of the family were seeking blood revenge on the remaining son. Should this happen, then the widow's family line would be extinguished, and her husband's property would be taken by those seeking her son's death (14:6-7). When David assured her that he would take measures to protect her living son (14:8-10), she elicited an even stronger commitment from him; she requested him to place his pledge under oath by swearing to it in the name of the Lord (14:11). When David did this as well, the woman told him that she had just one more request. She proceeded to ask David why he didn't do the same thing for Israel that he had just sworn to do for her (14:13), namely, bring home his own banished son with the assurance that he need not fear for his life. She attempted to support her case by reminding David that all human beings are mortal, and that when someone dies nothing can be done to bring that person back to life (14:14). The implication is that Amnon is dead, but Absalom still lives; therefore, Absalom's life should be protected, just as David had guaranteed the safety of her own guilty son. She then argued that God is merciful and finds ways to restore those who have been estranged from himself (see note on 14:14). The woman thus appealed to David's parental inclinations toward reconciliation with his son by suggesting that justice should be tempered by mercy (14:14).[4]

Having made her case, the woman turned the conversation back to her own situation and then flattered David by asserting that he was "like an angel of God in discerning good from evil" (14:15-17). Surely he would do the right thing in this situation. It is at this point in the conversation that David realized he had just been manipulated into permitting the safe return of Absalom, and he immediately suspected that Joab must have put the woman up to this task. When he asked her if Joab had sent her, she confessed that he had and said that Joab had done it in order to enable David to look at his relationship with Absalom from a new and different perspective (14:18-20).

When David then sent for Joab and told him to arrange for Absalom's return, it appeared that Joab's strategy had been successful (14:21). Joab was much relieved by David's decision. His statement in 14:22 ("At last I know that I have gained your approval") suggests that he had been uncertain and fearful about how David might react to his unrequested—and perhaps even undesired—intervention in a distressing and sensitive family dispute. So Absalom was brought back to Jerusalem in safety. It quickly became apparent, however, that there was still uncertainty in David's mind about Joab's desire for Absalom's complete acquittal, because even though Absalom was brought home, David still refused to see him (14:23-24). Return had been accomplished, but reconciliation between father and son did not happen. The ambivalence in David's heart between his love for his son and his responsibility to hold him accountable for his crime seems to have continued unresolved.

ENDNOTES

1. The fact that Absalom later instigated an initially successful rebellion against his father suggests that David's popularity was not as strong as it once had been. Bright (1981:209) speaks of "a mass of indefinable grievances" that had given rise to discontent among the general populace.
2. When David appointed Amasa to be commander of his own armies in the aftermath of Absalom's revolt, Joab murdered Amasa as well (19:13; 20:8-13).
3. Although comparisons are often drawn between Nathan's parable in 12:1-7 and the parable of the wise woman of Tekoa, it is generally recognized that in spite of broad similarities there are also significant differences. For example, the clarity and purpose of Nathan's parable is much more apparent than is the parable of the wise woman of Tekoa. The reason for this is that David's situation in chs 11–12 has a much clearer link with Nathan's parable than David's situation in chs 13–14 does with the parable of the wise woman of Tekoa. Although both the woman and David were dealing with cases of fratricide, the extenuating circumstances of the woman's case were quite different from those of David and Absalom. Contrary to the example in the woman's parable, David's house would not be extinguished if Absalom were to die, because David had numerous other living sons. In addition, Nathan's direct application of the parable in ch 12 with the statement "You are that man!" (12:7) has no clear parallel in ch 14, although something approaching it is found in 14:13, to which the wise woman of Tekoa feels compelled to add a word of explanation in 14:14. Simon (1967:225) notes that this parable (ch 14) is different from other examples of the "juridical parable" in that "it requires bolstering by an extensive outside argument." Nevertheless, the story does serve its purpose to the extent that it induces David to take the action necessary to permit Absalom to safely return to Jerusalem. Perhaps

the most significant difference, however, is in the contrast between the two authority figures behind the stories and the two quite different purposes that the stories were intended to serve. Nathan is sent to David by Yahweh. The wise woman of Tekoa is sent to David by Joab. And as Davis (1999:147, quoting Blaikie), comments: "'Nathan's parable was designed to rouse the king's conscience as against his feelings; the woman of Tekoah's was prompted by Joab, to rouse his feeling as against his conscience.' . . . To appeal to God's mercy (14:14) in a case that requires his justice is not wisdom but sentimentality."

4. This argument would carry particular force with David because God had been merciful to him by sparing his own life after he had committed adultery with Bathsheba and murdered Uriah (12:13). Fokkelman (1981:133) suggests that by means of the woman's story a "conflict between two legal principles is formulated, one negative and the other positive. Should the family's claim be honoured so that the blood revenge can be carried out? Or will the king allow the survival of a *beth 'ab* ('the father's house') to prevail over the old tribal law? The dilemma can more broadly be seen as 'justice or mercy.'"

4. Absalom's reconciliation with David (2 Sam 14:25-33)

25Now Absalom was praised as the most
handsome man in all Israel. He was flawless from head to foot. 26He cut his hair
only once a year, and then only because it
was so heavy. When he weighed it out, it
came to five pounds!* 27He had three sons
and one daughter. His daughter's name
was Tamar, and she was very beautiful.

28Absalom lived in Jerusalem for two
years, but he never got to see the king.
29Then Absalom sent for Joab to ask him
to intercede for him, but Joab refused to
come. Absalom sent for him a second
time, but again Joab refused to come. 30So
Absalom said to his servants, "Go and set
fire to Joab's barley field, the field next to
mine." So they set his field on fire, as
Absalom had commanded.

31Then Joab came to Absalom at his
house and demanded, "Why did your servants set my field on fire?"

32And Absalom replied, "Because I
wanted you to ask the king why he
brought me back from Geshur if he didn't
intend to see me. I might as well have
stayed there. Let me see the king; if he
finds me guilty of anything, then let him
kill me."

33So Joab told the king what Absalom
had said. Then at last David summoned
Absalom, who came and bowed low before
the king, and the king kissed him.

14:26 Hebrew *200 shekels* [2.3 kilograms] *by the royal standard.*

NOTES

14:30 ***set fire.*** This reading follows the Qere and 4QSam[c] in place of the Kethiv, "and I shall bring it out." See Smith 1912:339 and A. Anderson 1989:185.

they set his field on fire. LXX, 4QSam[c], and Old Latin contain a lengthy addition that both A. Anderson (1989:184-185) and McCarter (1984:337, 343) restore. The addition reads, "And the servants of Joab, having rent their garments, came to him and said, 'The servants of Absalom have set the field on fire.'" After a detailed discussion of this reading, Pisano (1984:236) concludes, "Summing up this case, therefore, we see that LXX or its *Vorlage* has inserted a plus designed to show the reaction of Joab's servants to the burning of his field, and to make the report of the event to Joab, while MT's shorter text left this up to the reader. The plus has been inserted in such a way that it has created a text in which the repetition of one word at the beginning and end of the insertion has led some to blame its absence from MT on a textual accident due to homoeoteleuton, whereas it is the shorter text of the MT which is the more original here."

14:31 ***your servants.*** This follows reading the noun as a plural, as found in many mss. The MT and 4QSam^c have "your servant."

COMMENTARY

One might wonder why the narrator moves so abruptly from a description of David's refusal to see Absalom (14:24) to such a flattering description of Absalom's personal appearance[1] and beautiful family (14:25-27).[2] What does this portrayal of Absalom's physical appearance have to do with the plotline of the story? With some reflection the reader will certainly sense that this is not a random or arbitrary intrusion of extraneous information, but rather an important strategic move by the narrator that serves a larger purpose. The depiction he gives of Absalom is one of royal proportions. As such, it subtly prepares the reader for Absalom's long-term ambitions. The reader is reminded of the depiction of Saul as a person who stood "head and shoulders taller than anyone else in the land" (1 Sam 9:2; 10:23) and was "the most handsome man in Israel" (1 Sam 9:2). In spite of his impressive appearance, Saul had turned out to be an antitheocratic king. After Saul was rejected by the Lord and Samuel was commissioned to anoint a successor from among the sons of Jesse of Bethlehem, Samuel was initially very much taken by Eliab who also had an imposing appearance (1 Sam 16:6). But the Lord told Samuel "Don't judge by his appearance or height, for I have rejected him" (1 Sam 16:7). In the stories of 1–2 Samuel men of imposing stature and appearance are not always what they might seem. Ironically, the depiction of Absalom's attractive appearance does not carry positive overtones for the future but instead places the reader on notice that a new phase of the narrative is about to begin in which Absalom will take center stage and in which he will play a negative and destructive role.

Absalom's dissatisfaction with the stigma of being permitted to reside in Jerusalem but not being permitted access to his father simmered over a two-year period (14:28). After two unsuccessful attempts to meet with Joab in order to secure his assistance in resolving the standoff between himself and his father, Absalom finally got Joab's attention by burning his barley field (14:28-30). When this action produced the desired meeting with Joab, Absalom laid out two alternatives. David should either receive him or carry out the death sentence against him. When Joab relayed Absalom's ultimatum to David, David finally agreed to meet with Absalom face-to-face. The narrator, however, gives the reader no account of any conversation between father and son, but only says that Absalom "bowed low before the king" and that David "kissed him" (14:33). This sparse description of a highly emotional and significant meeting between father and son five years after Absalom had murdered his brother Amnon leaves many questions unanswered. It is certainly possible that the encounter was brief and that few or no words were spoken. But without spoken words the reader is left wondering about the significance of Absalom's bow and of David's kiss. Was this a genuine reconciliation, or merely a formal truce in which outstanding issues were covered over and left unresolved? As events unfold, the disingenuousness of Absalom's obeisance becomes increasingly clear.

ENDNOTES

1. Particular attention is called to Absalom's luxuriant hair, suggesting both the vanity and glamorous appearance that Absalom will use to gain popular support for his revolt against his father. R. Alter (1999:280) suggests that the reference to Absalom's hair not only foreshadows the circumstances of his death (cf. 18:9-15) but also invokes a comparison with Samson, who also had luxuriant hair and burned the fields of the Philistines, much like Absalom's burning the field of Joab. Alter concludes, "Perhaps the parallel with Samson is meant to foreshadow Absalom's fate as a powerful leader whose imprudence brings him to an early death."
2. Although we are here told that Absalom had three sons and one daughter, 18:18 tells us that Absalom built a monument to himself because he did not have a son to carry on his name. Some regard this incongruity as a reflection of conflicting traditions (e.g., Smith 1912:338, 359), while others (e.g., A. Anderson 1989:190; Gordon 1986:269) suggest that the sons must have died in their youth and are thus unnamed. H. W. Hertzberg (1964:360) conjectures that Absalom may have built the monument to himself out of sorrow over the death of his sons.

◆ 5. Absalom conspires against David (2 Sam 15:1-12)

After this, Absalom bought a chariot and horses, and he hired fifty bodyguards to run ahead of him. 2He got up early every morning and went out to the gate of the city. When people brought a case to the king for judgment, Absalom would ask where in Israel they were from, and they would tell him their tribe. 3Then Absalom would say, "You've really got a strong case here! It's too bad the king doesn't have anyone to hear it. 4I wish I were the judge. Then everyone could bring their cases to me for judgment, and I would give them justice!"

5When people tried to bow before him, Absalom wouldn't let them. Instead, he took them by the hand and kissed them. 6Absalom did this with everyone who came to the king for judgment, and so he stole the hearts of all the people of Israel.

7After four years,* Absalom said to the king, "Let me go to Hebron to offer a sacrifice to the LORD and fulfill a vow I made to him. 8For while your servant was at Geshur in Aram, I promised to sacrifice to the LORD in Hebron* if he would bring me back to Jerusalem."

9"All right," the king told him. "Go and fulfill your vow."

So Absalom went to Hebron. 10But while he was there, he sent secret messengers to all the tribes of Israel to stir up a rebellion against the king. "As soon as you hear the ram's horn," his message read, "you are to say, 'Absalom has been crowned king in Hebron.'" 11He took 200 men from Jerusalem with him as guests, but they knew nothing of his intentions. 12While Absalom was offering the sacrifices, he sent for Ahithophel, one of David's counselors who lived in Giloh. Soon many others also joined Absalom, and the conspiracy gained momentum.

15:7 As in Greek and Syriac versions; Hebrew reads *forty years.* **15:8** As in some Greek manuscripts; Hebrew lacks *in Hebron.*

NOTES

15:2 *He got up early every morning.* Heb., *wehishkim* [TH7925, ZH8899]. On the frequentative use of the *weqatalti* aspect of the verb, see Joüon and Muraoka §119v.

would ask. Lit., "he would call . . . and would say"; (*wayyiqra'* . . . *wayyo'mer* [TH7122/559, ZH7925/606]). On the frequentative use of the *wayyiqtol* pattern, see Joüon and Muraoka §118n.

15:4 ***I wish I were the judge.*** Lit., "Who will appoint me as judge in the land?" but with the meaning, "Would that someone would make me judge!" Regarding wishes expressed by exclamatory questions, see Joüon and Muraoka §163d.

cases. The Hebrew text has two words connected by a conjunction (*rib umishpat* [TH7379/4941, ZH8190/5477]); literally, "a suit and a case for judgment." Conroy (1978:148) suggests that the word pair may be taken as a "legal pleonasm" so that "one need not feel obliged on stylistic grounds to differentiate between *rib* and *mishpat.*" McCarter (1984:354) adds the possibility of reading the word pair as hendiadys for a "just suit."

15:7 ***After four years.*** The NLT's "four" agrees with Lucianic mss of the LXX, Syriac, Vulgate, and Josephus (*Antiquities* 7.196). The MT (followed by LXX Vaticanus) has "forty." In the context forty years seems highly unlikely; according to McCarter (1984:355), it is "impossible."

15:8 ***if he would bring me back.*** The Hebrew here is unusual in that two different roots are used in the sequence of the infinitive absolute and the finite verb. Youngblood (1992:991) points out a similar phenomenon in Zeph 1:2.

COMMENTARY

Having been restored to good standing in Jerusalem, Absalom began to carry out a deliberate plan to undermine the political authority of his father and to secure a following among the people for his own royal ambitions. As the scheme unfolds, the reader is reminded of the message Nathan had given to David after his sin with Bathsheba: "I will cause your own household to rebel against you" (12:11).[1] The events of chapters 15–19, including Absalom's rebellion (15:1-12), David's flight from Jerusalem (15:13-37), David's defeat of Absalom, and Absalom's death (16:15–18:18) are all to be seen as the outworking of this prophetic pronouncement of punishment.

The ways in which Absalom sought to gain the admiration of the common people in Israel and to discredit his father are described in 15:1-6. The first thing mentioned by the narrator is the securing of horses and a chariot along with the employment of a corps of 50 troopers to accompany him wherever he went (15:1). Absalom understood something about image making. He knew that, in general, people are impressed with the symbols of power and the ceremonial trappings of office. In Israel chariots and horses were not common (see commentary on 8:4). This was not because Israel was a backward nation; rather, it was because Israel had been taught that her national security was to be found in the Lord's promise to protect her from her enemies instead of in the acquisition of the modern weapons systems of her day (cf. Exod 23:22; Deut 20:1-4; Ps 20:7-8). Moses had warned Israel that when kingship was established her king "must not build up a large stable of horses for himself" (Deut 17:16). Kingship in Israel was not to mimic the kingship of the surrounding nations. Samuel had clearly warned Israel about kings of this sort (1 Sam 8). Among other things, he said, such a king will "draft your sons and assign them to his chariots and his charioteers, making them run before his chariots" (1 Sam 8:11). Samuel's warning sounds almost like an exact description of what Absalom did. Absalom was giving a signal to the people that in his view the way forward for Israel was to abandon the antiquated traditions of the past and to begin to live in the "modern" world.

Not only did Absalom challenge the royal military tradition with which his father David was linked, but he also sought to undermine the confidence of the people in David's competence as the chief legal officer in the land. He did this by working the crowds at the city gate of Jerusalem, schmoozing with everyone who came across his path. He told those who had come to the city for a hearing on a judicial matter that the king had no one available to serve their needs, and then he sent them on their way saying that, if he were in charge, their cases would be heard promptly and treated justly (15:2-5). Four years of this sort of cynical and hypocritical behavior enabled Absalom to sow seeds of doubt in the minds of the people about the effectiveness of David's royal administration and to win the hearts of the people for himself (15:6-7).[2]

When Absalom concluded that conditions were favorable for an uprising against his father, he asked him for permission to go to Hebron[3] in order to offer a sacrifice in the fulfillment of a vow that he had made while he was in exile in Geshur. Even though Absalom had been back in Jerusalem for six years, David apparently had no suspicions[4] about either his plot or the implausibility of his request.[5] Absalom's use of an act of religious worship to camouflage the skillful manipulation of his father speaks volumes about his devious and irreverent character. Upon arriving in Hebron, Absalom launched his carefully planned revolution. When a prearranged signal was given, messengers were sent throughout the land to announce the rebellion. The large entourage of 200 men that had accompanied Absalom to Hebron was not privy to his plans in advance, but they were brought along as a supporting cast when his intentions became clear. At the last minute, Ahithophel, a trusted adviser of David, was invited to join Absalom in Hebron in order to give the conspiracy[6] added credibility.[7]

ENDNOTES

1. Davis (1999:154-155) notes that in Nathan's pronouncement and Absalom's rebellion we see both "the truthfulness of God's word (12:11) and the wickedness of Absalom's acts. And the latter fulfills the former." This is one of the many places where one might raise the question of how to understand the interworking of divine sovereignty and human responsibility in connection with the evil acts of human beings. As Davis notes, Peter addresses both sides of this issue in his Pentecost sermon: "'This Jesus, delivered up according to the definite plan and foreknowledge of God, you crucified and killed by the hands of lawless men' (Acts 2:23). God ordained it and you are guilty for doing it. It is mystery, but a mystery is not irrational, only insoluble." For further discussion of this issue, see the commentary on 1 Sam 2:25b; 19:8-17; 28:16; and "A Lofty Concept of God That Acclaims Divine Sovereignty" in the Introduction, under "Theological Concerns."
2. It is not clear how much of Absalom's success in stirring up opposition to his father was based on genuine grievances toward David's administration of the justice system. As Cartledge (2001:559) points out, "If the king cared nothing for justice, it is surprising that Joab's ruse of 14:5-11 was so successful, for it depended on an unwashed widow from tiny Tekoa successfully gaining access to the king himself and obtaining a favorable judgment." This certainly contradicts Absalom's claim that it was no longer possible to get a royal hearing for a case (15:3). Yet it is also possible that public awareness of David's sin with Bathsheba had eroded his moral authority and provided this opening for Absalom to exploit.

3. Hebron was a city with strong credentials for launching a claim to the throne. It was in Hebron that David had reigned over the tribe of Judah for seven and a half years prior to assuming kingship over the entire nation (2:11; 5:1-3), and it was in Hebron that Absalom had been born (3:2-3). However, choosing Hebron as the place to hatch his revolution was not without danger. Hebron was located in the heart of the tribe of Judah, about 18 miles south of Jerusalem. Judah was David's own tribe, and it was the tribe in which he found his strongest supporters (cf. 19:14-15). So it appears that Absalom took a calculated risk in his choice of Hebron. If he could succeed in gaining support for his cause in Hebron, then he would have neutralized his strongest opposition at the very beginning of his revolt.
4. Although there is no hint in the text that David had any knowledge of Absalom's plot, some commentators have concluded that he must have been aware of what was going on but unwisely chose to ignore it (Cartledge 2001:565).
5. Since Absalom's traitorous activities were carried out in the public square over a four-year period of time, it is surprising that David seems to have been unaware of them. Was David losing touch with what was going on in his kingdom? Were his political advisers afraid to speak negatively to him about the conduct of his son? Or, as seems to have been the case with Ahithophel, were some of his advisers actually in sympathy with Absalom's designs? Because questions such as these are not addressed in the text, answers to them must remain speculative. What is clear, however, is that God was providentially at work to bring about the fulfillment of Nathan's prophecy ("I [the Lord] will cause your own household to rebel against you," 12:11). David's blindness to his son's activities (or his decision to ignore them, if he actually was aware of them) seems to have been one of the means by which God enabled Absalom to succeed with his devious plans. Elsewhere the narrator speaks specifically of the divine hand in the events connected with Absalom's rebellion (15:25-26; 16:11-12; 17:14). In such instances the inspired sacred historian provides insights that are not discernable to ordinary human perception. While Scripture clearly teaches that God sovereignly controls all that comes to pass, the precise ways in which God acts in history are in most instances not open to human discernment. As "the Teacher" says, "In my search for wisdom . . . I realized that no one can discover everything God is doing under the sun" (Eccl 8:16-17).
6. The narrator's use of the term "conspiracy" (*qesher* [TH7195, ZH8004], 15:12) indicates that he did not view Absalom's revolution as a popular uprising growing out of widespread dissatisfaction with David's rule.
7. For a discussion of what might have motivated Ahithophel to align himself with Absalom's revolution, see the commentary on 14:1-24.

◆ 6. David flees Jerusalem and sends the Ark back (2 Sam 15:13-37)

**[13]A messenger soon arrived in Jerusalem
to tell David, "All Israel has joined Absa-
lom in a conspiracy against you!"
[14]"Then we must flee at once, or it will
be too late!" David urged his men. "Hurry!
If we get out of the city before Absalom
arrives, both we and the city of Jerusalem
will be spared from disaster."
[15]"We are with you," his advisers re-
plied. "Do what you think is best."
[16]So the king and all his household set
out at once. He left no one behind except
ten of his concubines to look after the
palace. [17]The king and all his people set
out on foot, pausing at the last house [18]to
let all the king's men move past to lead**

the way. There were 600 men from Gath who had come with David, along with the king's bodyguard.*

19 Then the king turned and said to Ittai, a leader of the men from Gath, "Why are you coming with us? Go on back to King Absalom, for you are a guest in Israel, a foreigner in exile. 20 You arrived only recently, and should I force you today to wander with us? I don't even know where we will go. Go on back and take your kinsmen with you, and may the LORD show you his unfailing love and faithfulness.*"

21 But Ittai said to the king, "I vow by the LORD and by your own life that I will go wherever my lord the king goes, no matter what happens—whether it means life or death."

22 David replied, "All right, come with us." So Ittai and all his men and their families went along.

23 Everyone cried loudly as the king and his followers passed by. They crossed the Kidron Valley and then went out toward the wilderness.

24 Zadok and all the Levites also came along, carrying the Ark of the Covenant of God. They set down the Ark of God, and Abiathar offered sacrifices* until everyone had passed out of the city.

25 Then the king instructed Zadok to take the Ark of God back into the city. "If the LORD sees fit," David said, "he will bring me back to see the Ark and the Tabernacle* again. 26 But if he is through with me, then let him do what seems best to him."

27 The king also told Zadok the priest, "Look,* here is my plan. You and Abiathar* should return quietly to the city with your son Ahimaaz and Abiathar's son Jonathan. 28 I will stop at the shallows of the Jordan River* and wait there for a report from you." 29 So Zadok and Abiathar took the Ark of God back to the city and stayed there.

30 David walked up the road to the Mount of Olives, weeping as he went. His head was covered and his feet were bare as a sign of mourning. And the people who were with him covered their heads and wept as they climbed the hill. 31 When someone told David that his adviser Ahithophel was now backing Absalom, David prayed, "O LORD, let Ahithophel give Absalom foolish advice!"

32 When David reached the summit of the Mount of Olives where people worshiped God, Hushai the Arkite was waiting there for him. Hushai had torn his clothing and put dirt on his head as a sign of mourning. 33 But David told him, "If you go with me, you will only be a burden. 34 Return to Jerusalem and tell Absalom, 'I will now be your adviser, O king, just as I was your father's adviser in the past.' Then you can frustrate and counter Ahithophel's advice. 35 Zadok and Abiathar, the priests, will be there. Tell them about the plans being made in the king's palace, 36 and they will send their sons Ahimaaz and Jonathan to tell me what is going on."

37 So David's friend Hushai returned to Jerusalem, getting there just as Absalom arrived.

15:18 Hebrew *the Kerethites and Pelethites.* **15:20** As in Greek version; Hebrew reads *and may unfailing love and faithfulness go with you.* **15:24** Or *Abiathar went up.* **15:25** Hebrew *and his dwelling place.* **15:27a** As in Greek version; Hebrew reads *Are you a seer?* or *Do you see?* **15:27b** Hebrew lacks *and Abiathar;* compare 15:29. **15:28** Hebrew *at the crossing points of the wilderness.*

NOTES

15:17 ***the last house.*** Possibly a place name, "Beth-merkhaq." The literal meaning of the Hebrew words is "house of the distant place."

15:19 ***Why are you coming with us?*** The pronoun "you" is emphatic in Hebrew.

a foreigner in exile. As Carlson (1964:170) notes, when translating the phrase *goleh* [TH1540, ZH1655] *'attah limeqomeka* (lit., "an exile from your place"), it is not necessary to emend the preposition *l-* [TH3807.1, ZH4200] to *mi-* [TH4480, ZH4946] because "*l-* in Hebrew often means 'from'; a similar change of aspect is common in e.g. Ugaritic and Akkadian." For other examples of *l-* in the sense of "from," see Dahood 1966:406.

15:20 *I don't even know where we will go.* Lit., "while I go wherever I will go?" See Joüon and Muraoka (§158o) regarding the use of an identical word (in this case, *halak* [TH1980, ZH2143]) in the main clause and the relative clause to express indeterminateness.

and may the LORD show you his unfailing love and faithfulness. This rendering follows the LXX as indicated in the NLT mg. The shorter MT reads, "Return and take your brothers, [and] may unfailing love and faithfulness go with you." The omission in MT appears to be the result of homoeoteleuton connected to the word *'immak* [TH5973/3509.2, ZH6640/3870] (with you). Pisano (1984:238) comments, "Since the plus consists of only three words, and not a long passage such as is found in many of the other LXX pluses, the chances of its having been accidentally omitted from MT are greatly increased." (Cf. the similar expression in 2:6.)

15:23 *toward the wilderness.* S. R. Driver (1913:314-315) and A. Anderson (1989:198, 200) assume that *'eth-* [TH854, ZH907] (a grammatical sign of the object) is a scribal error for *zayith* [TH2132, ZH2339] (olive) and translate the expression (on the basis of the Lucianic LXX mss), "the way of the wild olive tree." Emendation is unnecessary if the MT is read *'el-* [TH413, ZH448] (unto) with two mss, or omitted (many mss).

15:24 *offered sacrifices.* See NLT mg. The word *wayya'al* [TH5927, ZH6590] may mean "went up" (Qal) or "offer [sacrifices]" (Hiphil). On the elliptical use of *wayya'al* (Hiphil) with the omission of the object (sacrifices), see Fokkelman 1981:455. To translate, "Abiathar came up" seems awkward in the context.

15:27 *Look.* See NLT mg. The MT reads, "Are you a seer?" (*ro'eh* [TH7200A, ZH8014]). The LXX reads, "Look—go back to the city in peace"; "look" (*idete* [TG3708/B, ZG3972/1625]) represents Heb., *ra'ah* [TH7200, ZH8011] rather than *ro'eh*, essentially a difference of vowel pointing. Because it is unusual for "seer" to refer to a priest, Hoftijzer (1971) suggests, "Pay good attention!" which is adopted by Fokkelman (1981:455) and Youngblood (1992:996). NJPS has "Do you understand?"

15:30 *was covered.* Gordon (1986:275) cites Gordis and Driver for evidence of a second root *khapah* [TH2645, ZH2902] (cover) meaning "to uncover." (See also Ezek 24:17, 23 for the uncovering of the head and the removal of footwear as a sign of mourning.)

15:31 *told David.* This follows the reading *ledawid* [TH3807.1/1732, ZH4200/1858] with 4QSam[a], a few Hebrew mss, and the Versions (in place of the MT's *wedawid* [TH2050.1/1732, ZH2256/1858]), and perhaps *hugad* (Hophal) in place of *higgid* (Hiphil) as well, with a Hebrew ms (although see Williams 1976:§160 for the possibility of *higgid* as a passive construction). The MT could be translated "But David announced that his adviser Ahithophel . . ."

15:32 *where people worshiped God.* Lit., "where one would prostate himself to God." See GKC §107g for use of the imperfect as a customary repeated action.

15:34 *and tell Absalom.* Lucianic mss of the LXX have additional wording: "Your brothers departed and the king, your father, after me departed." LXX Vaticanus reads slightly differently (cf. McCarter 1984:367). Pisano (1984:141) concludes, "LXX's form . . . with its wordy repetition of the news of the departure of Absalom's brothers and father, seems meaningless in the context here. If it was the original OG [Old Greek, i.e., LXX], it attests to a corruption which already took place in the *Vorlage.*"

I will now . . . just as I was. The double use of the conjunction Waw with *'ani* [TH589, ZH638] (I) is unusual. Pisano (1984:140-141) comments, "A number of commentators simply omit the Waw in each case, without explaining how they might have arisen. The fact, however, that they occur as apparent correlatives may be an indication that, if they are original, they are intended to provide some kind of emphasis to Hushai's plea to be accepted as Absalom's servant ('even I who was once your father's servant, so now I myself will be your servant')."

15:35 ***Zadok and Abiathar, the priests, will be there.*** Lit., "Are not Zadok and Abiathar the priests with you there?" This is a case where the interrogative serves to "express the conviction that the contents of the statement are well known to the hearer, and are unconditionally admitted by him" (GKC §150e).

15:37 ***just as Absalom arrived.*** See Joüon and Muraoka §113ga on the use of the *yiqtol* conjugation with the idea of a "concomitant notion of simultaneity or contemporaneity."

COMMENTARY

Upon learning that "all Israel" had joined Absalom's conspiracy (15:13), David decided that he and his followers should immediately leave the city of Jerusalem. Abandoning Jerusalem would protect the city and its inhabitants from the ravages of war and prevent a premature military clash with Absalom's forces (15:14). The result was a massive exodus from the city by David and his loyal courtiers, with the exception of the concubines who were left to tend the palace (15:15-16).[1] This quick and decisive response by David to the crisis that suddenly confronted him reveals something of both his military acumen and his respect for the lives of the innocent civilian inhabitants of the city.

Near the outskirts of Jerusalem David allowed the entire procession to pass him by so he could determine exactly who had joined with his cause. Among those in the throng were "the king's bodyguard," (cf. NLT mg; see note on 8:18) as well as 600 Philistine soldiers from the city of Gath (plus their wives and children) who were under the command of Ittai (15:17-18). David singled out Ittai, the commander of the Philistine soldiers, and suggested that he and his men with their families should go back to Jerusalem because they were foreigners who had only recently found asylum in Israel as exiles from their own land. There was no need for them to become involved in the uncertainties of the conflict between himself and his son, Absalom (15:19-20). This rather surprising proposal tells us at least two things about David (van den Berg 1997:88-89). First, it shows that David honored both the spirit and letter of the law in Leviticus 19:33-34 concerning the fair treatment of foreigners. David knew firsthand what it was like to be a political exile in a foreign land. He was the "foreigner" when he fled from Saul and resided in the Philistine city of Ziklag (1 Sam 27). Israel's obligation to treat foreigners with love and respect cuts against the natural human inclination to consider foreigners as second-class citizens, if not something worse. In this instance, David's action reflects something of the love that God's people were instructed to have for the foreigners who resided in their midst.

Second, David's action shows that he placed the interests and safety of Ittai and his people above his own self-interest. Under the circumstances, 600 Philistine soldiers allied with his forces would seem to be a godsend. It might be expected that David would say to Ittai, "Look, I gave you and your people asylum in Jerusalem, now I want you and your men to join me in my fight to retain my throne." But to the contrary, David put no pressure on Ittai to lend his support; instead, he even urged him to stay out of the fight and go back to Jerusalem. If Ittai and his people were to do this, David assured them that he would not hold it against them, but he would send them on their way with his blessing (15:20). Ittai, however, refused to accept David's gracious offer and swore to go with David regardless of the consequences (15:21).[2] In David's dealings with Ittai we find a different person than the David of the Bathsheba-Uriah episode; we see David at his best, reflecting the generosity and humility of the true covenantal king.

Two priests, Abiathar and Zadok, as well as the "Ark of the Covenant of God" (carried by the Levites), were also in the procession that went out of Jerusalem. After crossing the Kidron Valley, the Ark was set down, and Abiathar offered sacrifices while the remainder of David's followers exited the city (15:23-25). Then David did another surprising thing. He told Zadok and Abiathar to take the Ark of God back into the city of Jerusalem. This action also tells us something important about David and his beliefs. Contrary to the idea that taking the Ark into battle would ensure a victory, as was thought in the time of Eli (1 Sam 4), David understood that it was not possible to manipulate God by means of the symbol of his presence (see commentary on 1 Sam 4–7). In addition to acknowledging that his own destiny was in the hands of God (15:25-26)[3] by sending the Ark back to Jerusalem, David also confessed that Yahweh was the ultimate sovereign over the entire nation. David recognized the Ark for what it was, the throne seat of Yahweh (1 Sam 4:4; 6:2), and that being so, it was his conviction that the nation's capital was the only proper location for this important symbol of God's presence and sovereignty.[4]

Acknowledgment that God was sovereignly in control of all that was happening (15:25-26) did not preclude David's implementation of carefully planned measures designed to defeat Absalom's rebellion.[5] He commissioned the two priests, Zadok and Abiathar, to return to Jerusalem with the Ark and then to gather as much information as they could about Absalom's plans (15:27-29). Their two sons, Ahimaaz and Jonathan, were to go with them and act as couriers for any information that might be useful to David (15:35-36).

As David and his followers continued along the road leading to the Mount of Olives, weeping as they went, David received some more bad news: He was informed that Ahithophel had cast his lot with Absalom (15:30-31; cf. 15:12). Immediately grasping the significance of this development for Absalom's rebellion, David prayed that the Lord would cause Ahithophel to give Absalom "foolish advice" (15:31). Upon reaching the summit of the Mount of Olives, David received an answer to his prayer. There he encountered Hushai, another one of his advisers. He told Hushai to also return to Jerusalem and to offer his services to Absalom, just as Ahithophel had done, but in his case with the purpose of thwarting Ahithophel's advice. Hushai agreed to do this and arrived in Jerusalem to carry out his undercover work just as Absalom also entered the city (15:37).[6]

ENDNOTES

1. This, of course, would eventually result in the last of Nathan's predictions being carried out: "I will give your wives to another man before your very eyes, and he will go to bed with them in public view. You did it secretly, but I will make this happen to you openly in the sight of all Israel" (12:11-12; 16:21-22).

2. Ittai's response to David echoes the response of Ruth to Naomi when Naomi urged her to return to her native Moab (Ruth 1:16-17).
3. Implicit in David's humble attitude toward the Lord is an ongoing recognition of his sin and an acute awareness that it may be the Lord's purpose to remove him from his position of leadership of the nation. He was ready to accept this outcome if it was God's will. His confession, "Let him do what seems best to him" (15:26) expresses a confidence that God does all things well, and that, at the end of the day, the outcome of this crisis was in God's hands. This is the same sentiment expressed so well in the hymn of Samuel Rodigast (1675): "What-e'er my God ordains is right: Holy his will abideth; I will be still what-e'er he doth, and follow where he guideth: He is my God; though dark my road, He holds me that I shall not fall: Wherefore to him I leave it all."
4. If this was indeed David's motivation in returning the Ark to Jerusalem, then this chapter is closely related to the kingship and covenant theme that is central to all of 1-2 Samuel. For a discussion of how the Ark of the Covenant is connected with this theme, see the commentary on ch 6.
5. As van den Berg (1997:92) notes, David's recognition that his fate is in God's hands (15:26) does not mean that he will sit back, do nothing, and just passively await the predetermined outcome, even though this is sometimes said to be the unavoidable consequence of belief in divine sovereignty. David was anything but apathetic; he took the initiative to thwart Absalom's revolt.
6. Just as David saw no contradiction between recognition of God's sovereignty and his responsibility to take the initiative to do what he could to thwart Absalom's rebellion (see endnote 5), neither did David see any contradiction between praying for God to cause Ahithophel to give Absalom foolish advice and taking his own initiative to send Hushai back to Jerusalem to counter Ahithophel's advice. David understood that prayer and action are not inconsistent but work in tandem.

◆ 7. David's kindness to Ziba (2 Sam 16:1-4)

When David had gone a little beyond the summit of the Mount of Olives, Ziba, the servant of Mephibosheth,* was waiting there for him. He had two donkeys loaded with 200 loaves of bread, 100 clusters of raisins, 100 bunches of summer fruit, and a wineskin full of wine.

2"What are these for?" the king asked Ziba.

Ziba replied, "The donkeys are for the king's people to ride on, and the bread and summer fruit are for the young men to eat. The wine is for those who become exhausted in the wilderness."

3"And where is Mephibosheth, Saul's grandson?" the king asked him.

"He stayed in Jerusalem," Ziba replied. "He said, 'Today I will get back the kingdom of my grandfather Saul.'"

4"In that case," the king told Ziba, "I give you everything Mephibosheth owns."

"I bow before you," Ziba replied. "May I always be pleasing to you, my lord the king."

16:1 *Mephibosheth* is another name for Merib-baal.

COMMENTARY

When David had gone just beyond the summit of the Mount of Olives, he encountered Ziba, a former servant of Saul whom David had appointed as manager of the assets of Mephibosheth, the crippled son of Jonathan and the grandson of Saul. David had not only given Mephibosheth the holdings of his grandfather Saul, but he had also provided him with living quarters at the court in Jerusalem in fulfillment of his promise to Jonathan and Saul that he would spare their children should he ever come to the throne in Israel (ch 9). As David and Ziba met, David noticed that Ziba was in possession of two donkeys loaded with provisions. When David asked him what the provisions were for, Ziba told him that they were to help sustain him and his followers in the wilderness (16:2). David then asked Ziba where Mephibosheth was, and Ziba told him that Mephibosheth had remained in Jerusalem. The reason for this, according to Ziba, was that Mephibosheth thought that by so doing he would "get back the kingdom of [his] grandfather Saul" (16:3). Ziba's statement implied that Mephibosheth still had designs on David's throne and that he hoped that when all the dust had settled from the confusion surrounding Absalom's rebellion, the royal office would be returned to the house of Saul. Accepting Ziba's statement at face value, David told him that he would give him all of Mephibosheth's property. Although one cannot be certain on the basis of the information provided in the text, it would seem that Ziba was attempting to ingratiate himself with David for his own advantage by making false allegations against Mephibosheth.[1] Later, when David returned to Jerusalem after Absalom's defeat, Mephibosheth strongly denied Ziba's charges (cf. 19:24-28). At that time, still being unable to determine who was telling the truth, David partially revoked the transfer of Mephibosheth's properties to Ziba (19:29). Whatever the real facts may have been, Ziba's allegations added one more name to the list of adversaries with whom David had to contend. The opening lines of Psalm 3 ("O LORD, I have so many enemies; so many are against me. So many are saying, 'God will never rescue him!'") tell us something about how David felt during this time of severe hardship.[2]

ENDNOTES

1. Gordon (1986:276-277) says, "David should never have fallen for Ziba's preposterous claim." Other commentators are less certain about who is telling the truth. Conroy admits (1983:123), "It is not easy to decide whether it is [Mephibosheth] or Ziba who is telling the truth." In the final analysis the narrator seems to leave this as an open question, but Conroy (1978:106) suggests that "perhaps a way out of the difficulty can be found by suggesting that the narrator's apparent refusal or inability to come to a clear decision is really a subtle way of showing that both Merib-baal [Mephibosheth] and Ziba deserve the reader's contempt. The narrator wants the whole House of Saul to be seen in an unfavorable light, and the concluding Sheba episode would tend to confirm that interpretation."
2. This assumes that the historical titles (a category distinct from the authorship titles) of the psalms (there are 14 such titles) provide reliable information about the circumstances of their composition. For discussion of this question, see Longman 1988:40-42.

◆ 8. Shimei curses David (2 Sam 16:5-14)

**5As King David came to Bahurim, a man
came out of the village cursing them. It
was Shimei son of Gera, from the same
clan as Saul's family. 6He threw stones at
the king and the king's officers and all
the mighty warriors who surrounded
him. 7"Get out of here, you murderer, you
scoundrel!" he shouted at David. 8"The
LORD is paying you back for all the blood-
shed in Saul's clan. You stole his throne,**

and now the LORD has given it to your
son Absalom. At last you will taste some
of your own medicine, for you are a
murderer!"
[9]"Why should this dead dog curse my
lord the king?" Abishai son of Zeruiah
demanded. "Let me go over and cut off
his head!"
[10]"No!" the king said. "Who asked your
opinion, you sons of Zeruiah! If the LORD
has told him to curse me, who are you to
stop him?"
[11]Then David said to Abishai and to all
his servants, "My own son is trying to kill
me. Doesn't this relative of Saul* have
even more reason to do so? Leave him
alone and let him curse, for the LORD has
told him to do it. [12]And perhaps the LORD
will see that I am being wronged and will
bless me because of these curses today."
[13]So David and his men continued down
the road, and Shimei kept pace with them
on a nearby hillside, cursing as he went
and throwing stones at David and tossing
dust into the air.
[14]The king and all who were with him
grew weary along the way, so they rested
when they reached the Jordan River.*

16:11 Hebrew *this Benjaminite.* 16:14 As in Greek version (see also 17:16); Hebrew reads *when they reached their destination.*

NOTES

16:5 ***came out of the village cursing them.*** See Joüon and Muraoka (§123m) for an infinitive absolute used to express the "simultaneousness or quasi-simultaneousness of a second action," although here, as Joüon and Muraoka note (§123n), a participle is found instead of a second infinitive absolute.

16:9 ***curse.*** The verbal form may suggest the cursing was continuing as Abishai spoke: "Why is this dead dog cursing my lord the king?" On the use of *yiqtol* forms for durative actions, see Joüon and Muraoka §113d.

16:12 ***that I am being wronged.*** The translation of this phrase is difficult. There are several possibilities depending on whether one opts for the Qere (my eye/eyes; Targum reads "tears of my eyes") or the Kethiv (my iniquity, guilt). Further, a few Hebrew mss, LXX, Syriac, and Vulgate give another reading, rendered in the NIV ("my distress") and the NLT. This text is listed among the *tiqqune sopherim* ("the emendations of the Scribes," i.e., 18 passages in the OT that were emended for theological reasons). If so, this probably means that both the Qere and the Kethiv are emendations from "with his [i.e., the Lord's] own eyes." Given the complexity of the manuscript evidence, it is difficult to choose which reading to follow.

Davis (1999:165-168) argues for "perhaps the Lord will look *on my iniquity*" as the preferred reading. While he admits that this rendering does not fit as well as "on my affliction" (cf. NIV, NLT) in the immediate context, he suggests that it fits very well when one looks at the larger context. If 12:10-12 (Nathan's pronouncement of David's punishment) controls all of chs 13–20 (and that is a reasonable conclusion), then "iniquity" is perfectly appropriate. Davis says, "David then recognizes that the cursing is what he deserves, not, as Shimei holds, for bleeding Saul's house, but for his sin of chapters 11–12." From this statement Davis concludes that "David has a deep-seated confidence in a God of unguessable grace, who has a tendency to replace cursing with goodness! . . . Should this word not come as special hope to Christians who believe they've made a royal curse-job of their lives. . . . What if they can get a glimpse of David's God?" Brueggemann (1974:181) also prefers the "on my iniquity" reading in 16:12, and concludes that this text "affirms graciousness as the substance of Yahweh's retribution," though he views this not as the view of the historical David, but of the creators of the so-called Succession Narrative.

COMMENTARY

As David approached Bahurim, a village on the eastern slope of the Mount of Olives, he was accosted by an angry man named Shimei. Shimei threw stones and launched a tirade of abusive language against David for his alleged involvement in the murder of various members of Saul's family. Shimei was a member of Saul's clan, and evidently harbored bitter resentment over the house of David having replaced the house of Saul on the throne in Israel. He accused David of having "stolen" the throne from the house of Saul, and interpreted Absalom's revolution against David as divine retribution for David's crimes (16:8).

Shimei's accusations, of course, were unreasonable distortions of the facts.[1] David had nothing to do with the death of Saul or of his sons. Saul's sons, Jonathan, Abinadab, and Malkishua were killed by the Philistines in a battle on Mount Gilboa (1 Sam 31:1-2). In that same battle Saul was seriously wounded; and when his armor bearer refused to honor Saul's request to kill him, he fell on his own sword (1 Sam 31:4-5). David's expression of profound sorrow over their deaths is found in 1:17-27. In the aftermath of Saul's death, David was anointed king over the tribe of Judah in Hebron (2:1-7), while Saul's son Ishbosheth reigned over the northern tribes from Mahanaim (2:8-10). During the preceding years, David had consistently refused to take any initiative toward the removal of Saul from his royal office (1 Sam 24, 26), even though the Lord had rejected the kingship of Saul and chosen David as his successor (1 Sam 15, 16). When war broke out between the house of David and the house of Saul, and Ishbosheth was murdered by two of his own officers (ch 4), David had no connection with the plot, and he put to death the two men who carried it out (ch 4). So Shimei was living in an imaginary world of his own creation that had little connection with reality. But in spite of this he had no hesitancy to claim that David's present predicament was the Lord's retribution on him for his murderous actions against the house of Saul. The reality was, Absalom's revolution had nothing to do with David's dealings with the house of Saul; it had everything to do with his dealings with Bathsheba and Uriah.

Abishai, the brother of Joab, angered by Shimei's disrespectful treatment of David, requested David's permission to silence him by cutting off his head (16:9). David, however, took a much more tolerant view of Shimei's abuse and denied the requested permission. David was reluctant to take vengeance on Shimei because he was acutely aware of his own sin, and he hypothesized that this verbal abuse might be a part of the punishment that the Lord was bringing his way (16:10). So David left the matter in the Lord's hands, with the comment that "perhaps the LORD will see that I am being wronged and will bless me because of these curses today" (16:12). David's behavior is striking because it goes against the natural human inclination to retaliate against unjustified harassment. It reflects something of the behavior of Jesus, many years later, who told Peter, "Put your sword back into its sheath," after he had cut off the ear of Malchus, the servant of the high priest (John 18:10-11), and it corresponds with Peter's description of Jesus as someone who "did not retaliate when he was insulted, nor threaten revenge when he suffered. He left his case in the hands of God, who always judges fairly" (1 Pet 2:23). Peter explained that Jesus is an example of the patient enduring of unjust suffering, and we are to "follow in his steps" (1 Pet 2:21).

So David and his followers continued on their way toward the Jordan River, accompanied by the cursing and stone throwing of Shimei as they went (16:13). When they finally arrived at the Jordan, they stopped for rest (16:14).

ENDNOTE

1. Because Shimei associates David's alleged crimes against Saul's family with the "stealing of his throne" (16:8), it seems unlikely that his reference is to the killing of Saul's descendants who David handed over to the Gibeonites (2 Sam 21) even though the chronology of that occasion is obscure (see endnote 1 in the commentary on 2 Sam 21:1-14). That incident had nothing to do with the transfer of the royal office from Saul to David. As was previously noted, however, there are many commentators who suggest, much as Shimei does, that David had a hand in the murder of Abner, Ishbosheth's military commander (3:22-29), as well as the murder of Ishbosheth himself (2 Sam 4:1-12). See the commentary on those passages. In Brueggemann's (1990a:307) discussion of Shimei's accusations against David, he leaves open the possibility of their legitimacy and says that the narrator's earlier efforts to exonerate David of such charges in chs 2–4 can be taken as an indication of "the vitality of the charge" and concludes that we must be "content without any easy certitude of David's innocence."

◆ 9. Ahithophel's advice to Absalom (2 Sam 16:15–17:29)

15 Meanwhile, Absalom and all the army of Israel arrived at Jerusalem, accompanied by Ahithophel. 16 When David's friend Hushai the Arkite arrived, he went immediately to see Absalom. "Long live the king!" he exclaimed. "Long live the king!"

17 "Is this the way you treat your friend David?" Absalom asked him. "Why aren't you with him?"

18 "I'm here because I belong to the man who is chosen by the LORD and by all the men of Israel," Hushai replied. 19 "And anyway, why shouldn't I serve you? Just as I was your father's adviser, now I will be your adviser!"

20 Then Absalom turned to Ahithophel and asked him, "What should I do next?"

21 Ahithophel told him, "Go and sleep with your father's concubines, for he has left them here to look after the palace. Then all Israel will know that you have insulted your father beyond hope of reconciliation, and they will throw their support to you." 22 So they set up a tent on the palace roof where everyone could see it, and Absalom went in and had sex with his father's concubines.

23 Absalom followed Ahithophel's advice, just as David had done. For every word Ahithophel spoke seemed as wise as though it had come directly from the mouth of God.

CHAPTER 17

Now Ahithophel urged Absalom, "Let me choose 12,000 men to start out after David tonight. 2 I will catch up with him while he is weary and discouraged. He and his troops will panic, and everyone will run away. Then I will kill only the king, 3 and I will bring all the people back to you as a bride returns to her husband. After all, it is only one man's life that you seek.* Then you will be at peace with all the people." 4 This plan seemed good to Absalom and to all the elders of Israel.

5 But then Absalom said, "Bring in Hushai the Arkite. Let's see what he thinks about this." 6 When Hushai arrived, Absalom told him what Ahithophel had said. Then he asked, "What is your opinion? Should we follow Ahithophel's advice? If not, what do you suggest?"

7 "Well," Hushai replied to Absalom,

"this time Ahithophel has made a mistake. 8You know your father and his men; they are mighty warriors. Right now they are as enraged as a mother bear who has been robbed of her cubs. And remember that your father is an experienced man of war. He won't be spending the night among the troops. 9He has probably already hidden in some pit or cave. And when he comes out and attacks and a few of your men fall, there will be panic among your troops, and the word will spread that Absalom's men are being slaughtered. 10Then even the bravest soldiers, though they have the heart of a lion, will be paralyzed with fear. For all Israel knows what a mighty warrior your father is and how courageous his men are.

11"I recommend that you mobilize the entire army of Israel, bringing them from as far away as Dan in the north and Beersheba in the south. That way you will have an army as numerous as the sand on the seashore. And I advise that you personally lead the troops. 12When we find David, we'll fall on him like dew that falls on the ground. Then neither he nor any of his men will be left alive. 13And if David were to escape into some town, you will have all Israel there at your command. Then we can take ropes and drag the walls of the town into the nearest valley until every stone is torn down."

14Then Absalom and all the men of Israel said, "Hushai's advice is better than Ahithophel's." For the LORD had determined to defeat the counsel of Ahithophel, which really was the better plan, so that he could bring disaster on Absalom!

15Hushai told Zadok and Abiathar, the priests, what Ahithophel had said to Absalom and the elders of Israel and what he himself had advised instead. 16"Quick!" he told them. "Find David and urge him not to stay at the shallows of the Jordan River* tonight. He must go across at once into the wilderness beyond. Otherwise he will die and his entire army with him."

17Jonathan and Ahimaaz had been staying at En-rogel so as not to be seen entering and leaving the city. Arrangements had been made for a servant girl to bring them the message they were to take to King David. 18But a boy spotted them at En-rogel, and he told Absalom about it. So they quickly escaped to Bahurim, where a man hid them down inside a well in his courtyard. 19The man's wife put a cloth over the top of the well and scattered grain on it to dry in the sun; so no one suspected they were there.

20When Absalom's men arrived, they asked her, "Have you seen Ahimaaz and Jonathan?"

The woman replied, "They were here, but they crossed over the brook." Absalom's men looked for them without success and returned to Jerusalem.

21Then the two men crawled out of the well and hurried on to King David. "Quick!" they told him, "cross the Jordan tonight!" And they told him how Ahithophel had advised that he be captured and killed. 22So David and all the people with him went across the Jordan River during the night, and they were all on the other bank before dawn.

23When Ahithophel realized that his advice had not been followed, he saddled his donkey, went to his hometown, set his affairs in order, and hanged himself. He died there and was buried in the family tomb.

24David soon arrived at Mahanaim. By now, Absalom had mobilized the entire army of Israel and was leading his troops across the Jordan River. 25Absalom had appointed Amasa as commander of his army, replacing Joab, who had been commander under David. (Amasa was Joab's cousin. His father was Jether,* an Ishmaelite.* His mother, Abigail daughter of Nahash, was the sister of Joab's mother, Zeruiah.) 26Absalom and the Israelite army set up camp in the land of Gilead.

27When David arrived at Mahanaim, he was warmly greeted by Shobi son of Nahash, who came from Rabbah of the Ammonites, and by Makir son of Ammiel from Lo-debar, and by Barzillai of Gilead from Rogelim. [28]They brought sleeping mats, cooking pots, serving bowls, wheat and barley, flour and roasted grain, beans, lentils, [29]honey, butter, sheep, goats, and cheese for David and those who were with him. For they said, "You must all be very hungry and tired and thirsty after your long march through the wilderness."

17:3 As in Greek version; Hebrew reads *like the return of all is the man whom you seek.* **17:16** Hebrew *at the crossing points of the wilderness.* **17:25a** Hebrew *Ithra,* a variant spelling of Jether. **17:25b** As in some Greek manuscripts (see also 1 Chr 2:17); Hebrew reads *an Israelite.*

NOTES

17:9 ***and attacks and a few of your men fall.*** There is an ambiguity in the Hebrew phrase *kinpol bahem battekhillah* related to the meaning of *napal* [TH5307, ZH5877] as either "fall in battle" (i.e., "die") or "fall upon" (i.e., "attack"). The phrase could thus be translated either "if he should attack your troops first" or "when some of the men fall at the first [attack]." The NLT has combined these two alternatives.

17:11 ***you personally lead the troops.*** Lit., "your presence going to battle." The LXX reads "among them" instead of "to battle."

17:12 ***like dew that falls on the ground.*** A simile for a stealthy and sweeping attack on David. Fokkelman (1981:218) comments, "Dew is heavy and yet light. It falls silently, gradually, and inimitably."

17:15 ***what Ahithophel had said . . . and what he himself had advised instead.*** Lit., "'such and such' Ahithophel had said and 'such and such' he had advised instead."

17:17 ***so as not to be seen.*** On the use of the *yiqtol* form in a circumstantial clause with the idea of simultaneity or contemporaneity, see Joüon and Muraoka §113ga.

17:25 ***Ishmaelite.*** See NLT mg; cf. Youngblood (1992:1015) who prefers "Jezreelite," which is the reading of LXX Coislinianus, and which in his view provides the best explanation for the other two readings (i.e., Israelite, Ishmaelite).

COMMENTARY

At 16:15 the scene shifts from a description of David's departure from Jerusalem to a description of Absalom's arrival. The reader is immediately informed that both Ahithophel and Hushai were in Absalom's attendance (16:15-16). These two individuals are particularly important because, in the final analysis, the outcome of Absalom's rebellion will turn on how he responds to the conflicting counsel that they will give. Ahithophel had accompanied Absalom from Hebron to Jerusalem (16:15). Hushai arrived back in the city, in compliance with David's instructions, at the same time that Absalom and his followers arrived (16:16; cf. 15:37). When Hushai presented himself to Absalom and hailed him with the words "Long live the king!" he was already playing a duplicitous language game. The implication of his statement was that he was endorsing Absalom's revolution, and that is certainly the way Absalom understood it. But it should be noted that Hushai did not say, "Long live Absalom!" He said, "Long live the king!" David was the only legitimate king. By the ambiguous wording Hushai could have been endorsing David's reign just as well as Absalom's. Perhaps surprised by Hushai's presumed switch of allegiance, Absalom asked him how he could treat his father in such a disloyal manner, and why he had not remained with David and his other followers. Again Hushai responded ambiguously by using words seeming to suggest loyalty to

Absalom but which, in fact, could only truly apply to David. He said, "I belong to the man who is chosen by the LORD and by all the men of Israel" (16:18). David, not Absalom, was the king who had been chosen by the Lord and all the men of Israel. Absalom, however, understood Hushai to be saying that he viewed the initial success of his own revolution as the Lord's endorsement of his rise to the throne. This was certainly what Absalom wanted to believe and what he was ready to hear. Hushai went on to say that he would be Absalom's adviser just as he had previously been an adviser to Absalom's father David (16:19). This statement was true enough. But what Absalom did not understand, and what Hushai did not say, was that his advice would not necessarily serve Absalom's best interests.

After entering Jerusalem, Absalom asked Ahithophel what he should do next (16:20). That Absalom sought this advice from Ahithophel rather than Hushai seems to reflect his higher comfort level with Ahithophel. In any event, Ahithophel did not hesitate to suggest a radical action that would accentuate the seriousness of the insurrection and proclaim in a clear and unambiguous way that there could be no future accommodation between Absalom and his father.[1] Ahithophel told Absalom to sleep with the concubines that his father had left in the city, and to do this within public view.[2] It was Ahithophel's opinion that this clear signal of the seriousness of Absalom's determination to persevere to the end would result in increased public support for his cause. Absalom considered Ahithophel's advice as wise as if it had been an oracle from God (16:23), and he did exactly what Ahithophel had recommended. Probably unknown to either Ahithophel or Absalom was that by this action the word that Nathan had spoken to David (12:11-12; "I will give your wives to another man . . . and he will go to bed with them in public view") was now fulfilled.[3]

Ahithophel then gave Absalom some additional, apparently unsolicited, advice (17:1-4). He proposed that Absalom authorize him to select some troops and immediately pursue David with the intent of finding him and killing him so that the revolution would not result in a large-scale civil war with the death toll this would inevitably bring. It was Ahithophel's argument that this strategy would insure the success of his revolt in a way that would gain the loyalty of the people. Although Absalom and his counselors initially concluded that Ahithophel's advice was sound (17:4), for some reason Absalom decided to seek a second opinion from Hushai (17:5). It is difficult to discern all the dynamics involved in this decision. Some of Absalom's hesitation to implicitly follow Ahithophel's advice may have been connected with his concern about who would gain the honor for the actual defeat and death of David if Ahithophel's plan were carried out. Ahithophel's advice contains five first-person verbs in the Hebrew text.[4] The scenario he proposed placed himself in the position of leadership for the important political act of terminating David's life.[5] When Hushai was consulted and informed about Ahithophel's plan, he immediately countered with a radically different proposal (17:7-13).

Hushai intuitively sensed that stroking Absalom's ego could be a means of defeating his strategy and buying David precious time. He began his response to Absalom by reminding him of the vast military experience of his father and his father's troops and of their reputation as courageous men (17:10). He questioned whether it would be as easy to find David as Ahithophel thought it would be; and even if he were found, he suggested that Absalom's inexperienced soldiers would be no match for those of David. To avoid a hasty and ill-conceived attack, Hushai recommended that Absalom recruit an army "as numerous as the sand on the seashore" (17:11) from the whole of the nation (from Dan to Beersheba) so that they would have sufficient strength to annihilate both David and his army. But most importantly, Hushai said that he thought that Absalom should "personally lead the troops" (17:11). It was the role of the king to lead his troops in battle (cf. 1 Sam 8:20). David had done this with great success. And Saul had been marginalized during his reign because it was David rather than himself who led Israel's forces to victory in battle (cf. 1 Sam 18:16). Hushai thus played to Absalom's hubris with the result that he and his counselors concluded that his advice was "better than Ahithophel's" (17:14a), and the plans for an immediate attack on David were dropped. So David's prayer that Ahithophel would give Absalom "foolish advice" (15:31), as well as his commissioning of Hushai to "frustrate and counter Ahithophel's advice" (15:34), were remarkably productive. The advice was not foolish from the perspective that it entailed a quick attack, because this was precisely what should have been done; it was foolish because Ahithophel's desire for personal revenge caused him to place himself in the position of honor that should have been Absalom's.

But underneath all the scheming and strategizing of both sides of the struggle between Absalom and David there was something else far more significant going on. The hand of the Lord was at work in defense of David.[6] The narrator informs the reader of this in 17:14b ("For the LORD had determined to defeat the counsel of Ahithophel, which really was the better plan, so that he could bring disaster on Absalom!"[7]). This is one of those rare places in the books of Samuel that the narrator provides the reader with theological commentary on the events that have been portrayed.[8] Typically the reader is forced to work out theological significance by means of inference from the narrative itself without any direct help from the narrator. As von Rad (1944:200) has pointed out, "This was the turning-point in the rebellion, and the change in the situation was the work of God himself, who had heard the prayer of the King in his profound humiliation." In spite of appearances to the contrary, God was still at work in hidden ways[9] to preserve David's throne and to insure that Solomon rather than Absalom would be his successor.

In the meantime, Hushai informed the priests Zadok and Abiathar, who had complied with David's instructions to return to Jerusalem (15:24-29), about what both he and Ahithophel had advised Absalom. He urged the priests to send word to David through their sons Jonathan and Ahimaaz that he should cross the Jordan River immediately in order to avoid capture, in case Ahithophel's advice should be followed rather than his own. In the cloak-and-dagger episode that followed, Jonathan and Ahimaaz were hidden in a well in Bahurim[10] by a man and his wife after their whereabouts had been reported to Absalom's agents.[11] Escaping capture, they reached David with the urgent message, and David and those accompanying him were able to cross the Jordan that same night.

Upon learning that his advice was not followed, and being convinced that the conspiracy would fail as a result, Ahithophel returned to his home in Giloh (see 15:12) and there took his own life (17:23).[12] It should be noted, however, that Ahithophel's role in this story is not merely that of someone who chose the wrong side in a political struggle.[13] The issues go much deeper. Ahithophel was someone who conspired to bring about the death of the Lord's anointed one. In the end, this resulted in his own death. In a much later period of redemptive history, another traitor, Judas, conspired to bring about the death of the Lord's Anointed, Jesus. Judas, like Ahithophel before him, also went out and hanged himself after having aligned himself with the opponents of the Messiah (Matt 27:5).[14]

The two concluding paragraphs of chapter 17 (17:24-29) not only provide background information for understanding the narratives of the next three chapters (chs 18–20),[15] they also inform us of support for David that came from some surprising sources. As David arrives in Mahanaim, we read that Absalom had gathered his troops, crossed the Jordan River, and set up camp in the same general area. He had also appointed a commander for his army: Amasa. Amasa's genealogy is given, revealing that he was a nephew of David and a cousin of both Joab and Absalom (Zeruiah, David's half sister, was also the sister of Amasa's mother Abigail; 1 Chr 2:16).[16] With this information in hand, the reader is prepared for the battle that will ensue between David and his rebellious son.

After David arrived safely at the Transjordanian city of Mahanaim, the former capital of Ishbosheth,[17] he was greeted by three individuals who provided him and his troops with much needed supplies (17:27-29). These individuals were the Ammonite Shobi (apparently the brother of Hanun; see 10:2-4) of Rabbah, an Ammonite center that David had conquered earlier in his reign (12:26-31); Makir, a former supporter of Mephibosheth (cf. 9:4-5); and Barzillai, an elderly and wealthy individual from the Gileadite city Rogelim (its precise location is unknown). To come to David's aid before the outcome of the struggle between Absalom and David was determined involved a great deal of risk and courage on the part of these three individuals (cf. Judg 8:6, where, in a similar situation, assistance was refused until the outcome of a battle was clear). At a time when numerous Israelites had aligned themselves with Absalom, the usurper of David's throne, we find that a conquered foreigner, Shobi (someone who might be expected to resent David's power), along with Makir, a former supporter of the house of Saul, came to the assistance of David. One is reminded of John the Baptist's statement (Matt 3:9; Luke 3:8): "Don't just say to each other, 'We're safe, for we are descendants of Abraham.' That means nothing, for I tell you, God can create children of Abraham from these very stones." In this instance, the Lord provided assistance and encouragement to David from very unexpected and unlikely sources.

ENDNOTES

1. The conclusion that having sexual relations with the concubines of the former ruler is a way of making a claim for royal office is a common interpretation of this passage as well as 3:6-11 and 1 Kgs 2:13-25. See, for example, Alter (1999:295), who comments, "Cohabiting with the sexual consorts of a ruler is an assertion of having taken over all his prerogatives of dominion" and de Vaux (1961a:116), who says that "possession of the harem was a title to the throne." Stone (1995), however, argues that this rather common conclusion is a "reading hypothesis" that is adopted to provide a plausible

interpretation for these texts. In Stone's view, the significance of such behavior is more likely not so much political as anthropological, and his own conclusion is that it is a means of attacking the masculinity of the ruler so that his prestige in the eyes of other men is diminished. Stone contends that the practice (1995:568) is something that is not "a 'custom' about monarchical legitimacy. It is rather a complex bundle of premises about masculinity, sexual practice, and prestige which the anthropological literature helps to clarify." But as Stone admits (1995:568), his reading "is not entirely at odds with a reading which links the wives and concubines of a previous king to monarchical succession and legitimacy."

2. It is ironic, as Alter (1999:295) and others have noted, that Absalom's sexual relations with David's concubines "takes place on the very palace roof from which his father first looked lustfully at Bathsheba."
3. The events of this chapter provide interesting examples of the evil acts of human beings becoming the means of the accomplishment of God's previously announced purposes. As Brueggemann (1990a:310) comments, "Ahithophel's advice unwittingly fulfills the threat of Nathan. Absalom's defiance and challenge to David may be an act of raw, daring politics; it is at the same time, however, as the narrative makes clear, an implementation of Yahweh's decree given long before Absalom and Ahithophel are present in the narrative. The coup of Absalom, informed by the wisdom of Ahithophel, implements Yahweh's awesome judgment voiced by Nathan." While there is mystery in the way in which divine sovereignty and human responsibility interface in situations such as these, it is clear that divine providence extends to all that comes to pass, including the evil acts of human beings. (For further discussion see the commentary on 1 Sam 2:25 and 16:14 and the Introduction, "A Lofty Concept of God That Acclaims Divine Sovereignty," under "Theological Concerns.")
4. "Let *me* choose 12,000 men" (17:1); "*I* will catch up with him" (17:2); "*I* will terrify him, and he and all the people with him will flee" (a literal translation; NLT, "He and his troops will panic," 17:2); "*I* will kill only the king" (17:2); "and *I* will bring all the people back to you" (17:3).
5. Some interpreters have regarded Ahithophel's unsolicited advice as an expression of his intense personal desire to take revenge on David because of David's mistreatment of his granddaughter, Bathsheba (cf. 11:3 and 23:34 and the commentary on 11:2-5, including endnotes 7 and 8). It was this intense personal desire for revenge that served to elevate his own role in the plan while excluding any role for Absalom. And it is this exclusion that, in turn, caused Absalom to seek a second opinion from Hushai.
6. Although in human terms it was Hushai's advice that convinced Absalom to defer an attack on David, as Fokkelman (1981:205) says, "Once again divine providence and human action flow together in one undivided event."
7. Note how the narrator's statement contradicts the mistaken idea of Shimei (16:8) who told David that the Lord had given his throne to Absalom.
8. Rosenberg (1987:138) points out that "this is one of only two points in the story (see 11:27b) where YHWH's intentions toward David are indicated by the narrator rather than by dialogue or ellipsis. . . . Here, as in 1 Samuel 25 [cf. vv. 32-34], David's fate is conspicuously beyond his control; it is divine intervention (through human agents) that saves him. However astutely David has handled his two exiles, [caused by Saul and Absalom] the two critical turning points are not his doing but YHWH's."
9. Davis (1999:175-176) comments, "More often than not that is the manner of God's work. His sceptre is unseen, his sovereignty hidden behind the conversations and decisions and activities and crises of our lives. . . . He is not absent but neither is he obvious. Sometimes we must be told that lest we become too enamored with our Hushais."

10. Located in the territory of Benjamin, east of Jerusalem, on the road to Jericho.
11. The woman's protection of Jonathan and Ahimaaz on this occasion and her deception of Absalom's agents are parallel to the action of Rahab with the spies that Joshua had sent into Jericho (Josh 2). Although the ethics of the action of this woman and of Rahab is not the point of either story, only a truncated view of truth would conclude that the behavior of either woman was misguided. For a fuller discussion of this issue, see endnote 10 in the commentary on 1 Sam 16:1-13.
12. Fokkelman (1981:229) considers 17:23 as "one of the most impressive jewels of biblical narrative art." He comments, "With iron logic Ahithophel foresees that he will in due course fall into David's hands, and he now decides to escape this and a humiliating execution for high treason, by taking his own life. Without hesitation he goes and hangs himself." Although this is a reasonable interpretation, it is also possible that Ahithophel was so severely depressed by Absalom's rejection of his advice that he took his own life.
13. Carver (1992:27) notes that in English literature Ahithophel "became a conventional tag for traitor, wicked politician, and suicide." He notes that in Dryden's satire *Absalom and Achitophel*, "Ahithophel is a synonym for political machination and rebellion. A verb was even coined out of his name, one poet writing of a group of plotters being 'out-Achitophel'd' by another."
14. This parallel between Ahithophel's betrayal of David and his flight from Jerusalem and Judas's betrayal of Jesus and his via dolorosa is only one of several that have been noticed by commentators. When leaving Jerusalem both David and Jesus crossed the Kidron Valley (15:23; John 18:1) and went up the road toward the Mount of Olives (15:30-32; Matt 26:30). Just as David voluntarily submitted himself to whatever the Lord's will was for his future (15:25-26), so also Jesus prayed to his Father that not his own will but his Father's will should be done (Matt 26:39, 42).
15. This includes the accounts of the death of Absalom in a battle with David's troops (ch 18), David's subsequent appointment of Amasa as the commander of his forces in place of Joab (ch 19), and Joab's ensuing murder of Amasa (ch 20).
16. Because the father of Abigail and Zeruiah is said to be Nahash instead of Jesse, it would appear that their mother had married Jesse after the death of Nahash.
17. Mahanaim was a walled city located on the border of Gad and Gileadite Manasseh along the Jabbok River.

◆ 10. Absalom's death (2 Sam 18:1-18)

**David now mustered the men who were
with him and appointed generals and
captains* to lead them. 2He sent the
troops out in three groups, placing one
group under Joab, one under Joab's brother Abishai son of Zeruiah, and one under
Ittai, the man from Gath. The king told his
troops, "I am going out with you."**

**3But his men objected strongly. "You
must not go," they urged. "If we have to
turn and run—and even if half of us die—
it will make no difference to Absalom's
troops; they will be looking only for you.
You are worth 10,000 of us,* and it is better that you stay here in the town and
send help if we need it."**

**4"If you think that's the best plan, I'll do
it," the king answered. So he stood alongside the gate of the town as all the troops
marched out in groups of hundreds and of
thousands.**

**5And the king gave this command to
Joab, Abishai, and Ittai: "For my sake, deal
gently with young Absalom." And all the
troops heard the king give this order to
his commanders.**

[6]So the battle began in the forest of Ephraim, [7]and the Israelite troops were beaten back by David's men. There was a great slaughter that day, and 20,000 men laid down their lives. [8]The battle raged all across the countryside, and more men died because of the forest than were killed by the sword.

[9]During the battle, Absalom happened to come upon some of David's men. He tried to escape on his mule, but as he rode beneath the thick branches of a great tree, his hair* got caught in the tree. His mule kept going and left him dangling in the air. [10]One of David's men saw what had happened and told Joab, "I saw Absalom dangling from a great tree."

[11]"What?" Joab demanded. "You saw him there and didn't kill him? I would have rewarded you with ten pieces of silver* and a hero's belt!"

[12]"I would not kill the king's son for even a thousand pieces of silver,*" the man replied to Joab. "We all heard the king say to you and Abishai and Ittai, 'For my sake, please spare young Absalom.' [13]And if I had betrayed the king by killing his son—and the king would certainly find out who did it—you yourself would be the first to abandon me."

[14]"Enough of this nonsense," Joab said. Then he took three daggers and plunged them into Absalom's heart as he dangled, still alive, in the great tree. [15]Ten of Joab's young armor bearers then surrounded Absalom and killed him.

[16]Then Joab blew the ram's horn, and his men returned from chasing the army of Israel. [17]They threw Absalom's body into a deep pit in the forest and piled a great heap of stones over it. And all Israel fled to their homes.

[18]During his lifetime, Absalom had built a monument to himself in the King's Valley, for he said, "I have no son to carry on my name." He named the monument after himself, and it is known as Absalom's Monument to this day.

18:1 Hebrew *appointed commanders of thousands and commanders of hundreds.* **18:3** As in two Hebrew manuscripts and some Greek and Latin manuscripts; most Hebrew manuscripts read *Now there are 10,000 like us.* **18:9** Hebrew *his head.* **18:11** Hebrew *10 shekels of silver,* about 4 ounces or 114 grams in weight. **18:12** Hebrew *1,000 shekels,* about 25 pounds or 11.4 kilograms in weight.

NOTES

18:6 *forest of Ephraim.* One might wonder why a forest in Transjordan would be called the "forest of Ephraim." The most likely explanation is that migrants from Ephraim had settled in this area (Judg 12:4; McCarter 1984:405).

18:9 *left him dangling in the air.* Lit., "and he was put (*wayyuttan* [TH5414, ZH5989]) between heaven and earth." 4QSam[a] reads, "and he was left hanging (*wayyital* [TH8518, ZH9434]) between heaven and earth." Brueggemann (1990a:319) and Fokkelman (1981:242), among others, suggest that this language is more than merely descriptive of Absalom's physical position and that it carries a symbolical meaning as well. Fokkelman comments: "'Between heaven and earth' means that he has become a nowhere man. His pride, his ambition and his rebelliousness—in short, his ego—have brought him to a point where he is no longer in control. His bid for power has removed the ground from beneath his feet and led to complete impotence."

18:10 *dangling from a great tree.* The Hebrew word here translated "dangling" (or "hanged," KJV) is *taluy* [TH8518, ZH9434]. As Polzin (1993:186) points out, this word is used twice in Deut 21:22-23 where "being hung on a tree" is equivalent to being "cursed in the sight of God." In the historical narratives of the OT, it is kings who usually suffer this fate (Josh 8:29, the king of Ai; Josh 10:26, five Amorite kings). In this narrative, both the language used and the unlikely entrapment of Absalom by the limbs of a tree suggest that Absalom's fate was a judgment coming from God's own hand. Davis (1999:186) suggests that Absalom's death "as a man under the curse is typical of what will be the lot of all who at any time set themselves against God's kingdom, his chosen King, and/or his people. This is a somber truth, but Yahweh's true subjects have no hope unless it *is* true."

18:11 *I would have.* The Hebrew *we'alay* [TH5921, ZH6584] (and upon me) expresses something that is upon someone and weighs him down, or is a burden to him. Joüon and Muraoka (§133f) suggest the translation "it would have been incumbent on me."

rewarded you. Lit., "to give" (*latheth* [TH5414, ZH5989]). Regarding the infinitive construct as subject of a nominal clause, as in the Hebrew of this verse, see Joüon and Muraoka §124b.

18:17 *into a deep pit.* As Alter (1999:306) notes, "To be flung into a hole in the field and covered with a heap of stones is a shameful burial."

COMMENTARY

During the time it had taken Absalom to recruit an army from all of Israel, David was able to establish himself in Mahanaim, secure additional forces for his own cause, and organize them into an effective fighting force. Second Samuel 18 opens (18:1-2a) with a brief description of the deployment of David's troops in three battle groups under the command of Joab, Abishai (Joab's brother), and Ittai (the Philistine who had aligned himself with David at the time of his flight from Jerusalem, 15:19-22). When David announced that he intended to accompany his forces on the battlefield (18:2b-4), his followers objected so strongly that he agreed to remain in the town and to join the battle only if things went so badly that his help was needed. It was clear to all that the death of either Absalom or David would determine the victory. Remaining off the battlefield would preclude the loss of David's life. Ironically, Absalom had chosen not to follow the advice of Ahithophel to remain behind the scenes (17:1-3); he followed Hushai's advice and personally led Israel's troops in battle (17:11). The result would be death for Absalom and victory for David.

When David's troops marched out of the city gates of Mahanaim, he told them (cf. 18:12) and their commanders, "For my sake, deal gently with young Absalom" (18:5). Although David's language was not explicit, it was clear to all that he wanted them to spare Absalom's life (this was certainly the understanding of the soldier who discovered Absalom hung up in the tree and who told Joab that David had asked them to "please spare young Absalom," 18:12b).[1] The remainder of the chapter is centered around this remarkable command, with very few details given about the battle itself. All that is said is that the battle was fought in the forest of Ephraim, that David's men were victorious over Israel's army, and that 20,000 soldiers lost their lives (18:6-8). The remainder of this section of chapter 18 (18:9-18) is focused on what is central to the narrator's concern, namely, Absalom's death.

During the course of the battle, Absalom encountered a contingent of David's forces from which he attempted to escape. Riding through the forest, he was swept off his mule when his head was caught in the low hanging branches of an oak tree[2] and he was left "dangling in the air" (18:9; cf. NLT mg). His predicament was seen by one of David's men who reported it to Joab (18:10). Joab reprimanded him for not having killed Absalom, but the soldier defended himself by reminding Joab of David's command, and suggested that if he had killed Absalom, Joab would most certainly have scolded him for that as well (18:11-13). Rather than prolong the discussion, Joab went to the scene and, contrary to David's command, plunged three knives into Absalom's body as he hung helplessly from the tree (18:14). Absalom's execution was completed by some of Joab's armor bearers, and Joab then signaled the remainder of the troops that the battle was over (18:15-16). Absalom's body was thrown in a hole in the ground in the forest, and a heap of stones was placed over it. Recognizing that the revolution had failed, Absalom's military forces returned in terror to their homes (18:17).

The question of Joab's motivation for disobeying David's order and taking the life of Absalom is something that has long intrigued readers of this narrative. Because the narrative itself does not address the issue, it is difficult, if not impossible, to discern all that prompted Joab's action. What is clear from the larger narrative context is that Joab was a complex personality. Although he was crafty, unmanageable, willful, and impetuous, he could also be loyal and dependable. With respect to this particular occasion, some commentators regard Joab's disobedience as an example of political realism and, therefore, as a commendable thing, because it was Joab's intent to protect David from what is viewed as a foolish sort of fatherly sentimentality[3] that erroneously thought that his kingdom could be secured even if Absalom were not killed.[4] Others take a more cynical view of Joab's action and suggest that it was rooted in personal antagonism toward Absalom born out of past affronts.[5] Whatever the real reasons may have been, by defying David's order, Joab plunged David into a deep and inconsolable sorrow.

One final vignette on Absalom's life is found in 18:18 where the reader is informed that Absalom had erected and named a monument after himself because "[he had] no son to carry on [his] name."[6] Although this may seem like a trivial piece of information, it speaks volumes about Absalom's mind-set. It was customary in the ancient world for rulers to make monuments to themselves and to celebrate their accomplishments by means of stone inscriptions, but this was something rare in Israel. We are told of only two individuals in the Old Testament who made monuments to themselves. These were Absalom (in this text) and Saul (1 Sam 15:12, see commentary). Making a monument to oneself, or attempting to create a "name" for oneself, was not fitting behavior for someone whose self-understanding had been formed by biblical understanding. In the early chapters of Genesis, "making a name" for oneself is first connected with the line of Cain. It was Cain who named a city after his son Enoch (Gen 4:17). A few chapters later, the offspring of the sinful relationship between the "sons of God" and the "daughters of men" (see NLT mg on Gen 6:2) are designated as "men of the name" (a literal translation; NLT, "famous warriors"; Gen 6:4). We are told that one of the purposes for the building of the tower of Babel was so that the builders could "make a name for themselves" (NLT, "make us famous," Gen 11:4). These references to human attempts "to make a name for oneself" stand in contrast to the promise that God gave to Abraham: "I will make your name great" (NLT, "I will . . . make you famous," Gen 12:2). This promise was repeated to David when the Lord said to him through Nathan, "I will make your name as famous as anyone who has ever lived on the earth" (7:9). So in Israel, if a person's name is to be made great, it is the Lord who will do this for the person, rather than something that the person attempts to do for himself. Isaiah says that the Lord will bestow "a new name" on his people (Isa 62:2; 65:15), and this theme is echoed in the words of the Lord to the church at Pergamum (Rev 2:17). In biblical categories, then, it is not the name a person makes for himself, but rather the name one receives from the Lord that counts, and it is this name that will remain for eternity. Exalting the name of the Lord rather than "making a name for oneself" is what should characterize the people of God.

ENDNOTES

1. The reader is given no explanation for why David wanted Absalom's life spared. Was it merely paternal love for a wayward son? Certainly David knew that if Absalom had the opportunity to take his life, he would not hesitate to do so. Van den Berg (1997:109) suggests that David's motivation lay in his own experience of God's forgiveness, and that in Absalom's case he simply wanted to be an imitator of God. For this reason, he also wanted his forgiveness of Absalom to be open and public, even though Absalom neither asked for it nor deserved it.
2. Understanding exactly how Absalom became "hung up" in a tree is puzzling. Josephus placed the blame on Absalom's luxuriant growth of hair (Josephus *Antiquities* 7.239). As McCarter notes (1984:406), the Talmud takes a similar view but adds a moralizing element by suggesting that because Absalom "gloried in his hair he was hanged by it." Modern commentators disagree on whether it was his head or his hair that was caught (see NLT mg at 18:9). Hertzberg (1964:359) argues that even though it "is not said that his vast head of hair is a contributory factor in his entanglement . . . it is clear that he cannot get free without assistance." This suggests that the hair must have played a role.
3. As noted above (endnote 1), van den Berg (1997) suggests a more principled basis for David's merciful attitude toward Absalom than simply fatherly sentimentality. It is his view that David wanted to publicly extend to Absalom the same sort of forgiveness that he himself had received from God. This view has much to commend it.
4. Fokkelman (1981:246) comments, "He liquidates Absalom because it is politically necessary and there is no alternative for the arch-rebel. . . . To return Absalom to Jerusalem in custody would be equivalent to taking half-measures. . . . His political assessment is that the Davidic State can be sound only by radically cutting out the growth."
5. Joab had facilitated Absalom's return from exile in the aftermath of the murder of Amnon (14:1-24). But for two years David refused to see Absalom and to resolve the breach between them. Absalom eventually resorted to burning Joab's fields (14:28-30) in an attempt to get his attention and enlist his support for a complete reconciliation with his father. When Absalom later chose key associates for his rebellion, he appointed Amasa rather than Joab as the commander of his military forces (17:25). How Joab viewed this appointment is not clear. He may have felt insulted that Amasa was chosen rather than himself. It is at least possible that Joab had earlier thought that Absalom might be a good replacement for David as an effective ruler (see commentary on 14:1-24). Although at times Joab showed loyal support for David, he was eventually persuaded to break with him and join the attempt by Adonijah to wrest the succession to the throne from Solomon to Adonijah (1 Kgs 1:7).
6. Regarding how this statement may be harmonized with 14:27, which speaks of Absalom's having three sons and a daughter, see endnote 2 in the commentary on 14:25-33.

◆ 11. David mourns for Absalom (2 Sam 18:19–19:8)

19 Then Zadok's son Ahimaaz said, "Let
me run to the king with the good news
that the LORD has rescued him from his
enemies."
20 "No," Joab told him, "it wouldn't be
good news to the king that his son is
dead. You can be my messenger another
time, but not today."
21 Then Joab said to a man from Ethio-
pia,* "Go tell the king what you have
seen." The man bowed and ran off.
22 But Ahimaaz continued to plead with
Joab, "Whatever happens, please let me
go, too."
"Why should you go, my son?" Joab re-
plied. "There will be no reward for your
news."
23 "Yes, but let me go anyway," he
begged.
Joab finally said, "All right, go ahead."
So Ahimaaz took the less demanding
route by way of the plain and ran to Ma-
hanaim ahead of the Ethiopian.
24 While David was sitting between the
inner and outer gates of the town, the
watchman climbed to the roof of the gate-
way by the wall. As he looked, he saw a
lone man running toward them. 25 He
shouted the news down to David, and the
king replied, "If he is alone, he has news."
As the messenger came closer, 26 the
watchman saw another man running to-
ward them. He shouted down, "Here comes
another one!"
The king replied, "He also will have
news."
27 "The first man runs like Ahimaaz son
of Zadok," the watchman said.
"He is a good man and comes with good
news," the king replied.
28 Then Ahimaaz cried out to the king,
"Everything is all right!" He bowed before
the king with his face to the ground and
said, "Praise to the LORD your God, who
has handed over the rebels who dared to
stand against my lord the king."
29 "What about young Absalom?" the
king demanded. "Is he all right?"
Ahimaaz replied, "When Joab told me to
come, there was a lot of commotion. But
I didn't know what was happening."
30 "Wait here," the king told him. So
Ahimaaz stepped aside.
31 Then the man from Ethiopia arrived
and said, "I have good news for my lord
the king. Today the LORD has rescued you
from all those who rebelled against you."
32 "What about young Absalom?" the
king demanded. "Is he all right?"
And the Ethiopian replied, "May all of
your enemies, my lord the king, both now
and in the future, share the fate of that
young man!"
33 *The king was overcome with emo-
tion. He went up to the room over the
gateway and burst into tears. And as he
went, he cried, "O my son Absalom! My
son, my son Absalom! If only I had died
instead of you! O Absalom, my son,
my son."

CHAPTER 19

1 *Word soon reached Joab that the king
was weeping and mourning for Absalom.
2 As all the people heard of the king's deep
grief for his son, the joy of that day's vic-
tory was turned into deep sadness. 3 They
crept back into the town that day as though
they were ashamed and had deserted in
battle. 4 The king covered his face with his
hands and kept on crying, "O my son Ab-
salom! O Absalom, my son, my son!"
5 Then Joab went to the king's room and
said to him, "We saved your life today and
the lives of your sons, your daughters,
and your wives and concubines. Yet you
act like this, making us feel ashamed of
ourselves. 6 You seem to love those who
hate you and hate those who love you.
You have made it clear today that your
commanders and troops mean nothing to
you. It seems that if Absalom had lived
and all of us had died, you would be
pleased. 7 Now go out there and congratu-
late your troops, for I swear by the LORD
that if you don't go out, not a single one

of them will remain here tonight. Then
you will be worse off than ever before."
8So the king went out and took his seat
at the town gate, and as the news spread
throughout the town that he was there,
everyone went to him.

Meanwhile, the Israelites who had supported Absalom fled to their homes.

18:21 Hebrew *from Cush;* similarly in 18:23, 31, 32. **18:33** Verse 18:33 is numbered 19:1 in Hebrew text. **19:1** Verses 19:1-43 are numbered 19:2-44 in Hebrew text.

NOTES

18:19-31 *good news.* The root *bsr* [TH1319/1309, ZH1413/1415] occurs in various forms nine times in 18:19-31 (used one time by Ahimaaz, 18:19; four times by Joab, 18:20, 22; three times by David, 18:25, 26, 27; one time by the Ethiopian, 18:31). Its forms in the context are *bissar, mebasser, besorah.* In 18:27 *tobah* [TH2896, ZH3202], "good," occurs as a modifier.

TDOT 2.315-316 points out that in the majority of its uses, *bsr* [TH1319, ZH1413] in both its noun and verbal forms denotes "a good message or good news." In various cognate Semitic languages *bsr* "always mean[s] 'to bring good news.'" On the basis of the use of *mebasser* in 1 Sam 4:17 to designate the messenger who brings the "bad news" to Eli of the death of his sons and Israel's defeat, some scholars have argued that *bsr* is a neutral word in Hebrew, and that it must be modified by some other adjective, or placed in the context of its usage, to indicate whether the news is good or bad. TDOT 2.314-315 disagrees with this, asserting that the basic meaning of *bsr* in Hebrew usage is "good news" and that 1 Sam 4:17 should be regarded as a departure from this norm that "does not compel us to postulate that the original meaning in Hebrew was neutral." *Bsr* in its verbal and substantive forms is translated in the LXX by *euangelizomai* [TG2097A, ZG2294] (bring good news) and *euangelion* [TG2098, ZG2295] (the good news), which are the same words used in the NT for proclaiming the Good News of the gospel.

18:33 [19:1] *If only I had died.* The literal translation of the Hebrew phrase is "who will give (*mi-yitten* [TH4310/5414, ZH4769/5989]) the dying of me—I in the place of you?" For the exclamatory use of *mi-yitten* in the sense of "may God grant," see Joüon and Muraoka §163d and 146d.

COMMENTARY

Overjoyed by the death of Absalom and the defeat of his army, Ahimaaz (one of the two couriers of information between Hushai and David's forces, cf. 15:36) petitioned Joab for permission to bring the "good news" of the victory to David (18:19). Joab, however, knew all too well that David would not consider the death of his son as good news, and in anticipation of the impassioned manner in which David would react to the death of his son, he refused Ahimaaz's request, and drafted a man from Ethiopia to report the day's events to the king instead. But when Ahimaaz refused to take no for an answer and persisted in his request, Joab eventually relented. After warning him that he would not receive any reward for his effort, he gave him permission to also carry the news of the day to David (18:22-23). By choosing a longer but easier route, Ahimaaz was able to reach Mahanaim ahead of the Ethiopian (18:23).

In a switch of the scene of action, the narrator describes the approach of the two runners to the city where David anxiously awaited news of the day's battle (18:24-27). When David was told by the watchman on the wall that a single runner was approaching, David concluded that this must mean that his army had not been defeated, and that the news was good. When the watchman saw a second runner and told David that the first one looked like Ahimaaz, David said, "He is a good man and comes with good news" (18:27).[1] Upon reaching David, Ahimaaz told him that the rebels had been defeated, and that all was well (18:28). David, however, immediately asked him about what concerned him most, namely, what had happened to Absalom (18:29). Ahimaaz avoided a direct answer by describing the confusion on the battlefield and pleading ignorance about Absalom's fate.[2] When the Ethiopian arrived and also told David that he had "good news" and that the rebellion had been defeated, David put the same question to him that he had put to Ahimaaz, "What about young Absalom? . . . Is he all right?" (18:32). The Ethiopian couched his response in clear but diplomatic language by saying, "May all of your enemies, my lord the king, both now and in the future, share the fate of that young man!"

In the opening verses of this section the narrator repeatedly uses the expression "(good) news" (see note on 18:19-31). If repetition has any importance for discerning what is significant in biblical narrative, then surely this is a case where the phrase "(good) news" takes center stage. The story, however, is full of irony because what was good news for the messengers was the defeat and death of Absalom. And certainly God's granting of victory to David over his enemies was good news in the broadest sense of the words. But for David "good news" had a very different meaning. What he longed to hear, but did not, was the good news that Absalom was still alive.

Upon learning that Absalom was dead, David was devastated. He withdrew from his associates to a room above the gate where he wept bitterly, and cried over and over again "O my son Absalom! My son, my son Absalom!" (18:33; 19:4).[3] His inconsolable grief caused the returning troops to feel disgraced rather than triumphant. When Joab perceived that his behavior was so destructive that it risked alienating David's followers and subverting the kingdom itself, he went to David and after strongly rebuking him, told him to go out and congratulate the troops. David listened to Joab and made an appearance before his supporters (19:8). The text, however, is silent on what David said to them.

In this poignant scene that contrasts David's overwhelming grief with what is usually regarded as Joab's clearheaded political realism, it is usually concluded that Joab was justified for taking Absalom's life and for scolding David for what is perceived to be his inappropriate if not irrational behavior after learning of Absalom's death. After all, should foolish parental sentimentality trump justice, particularly when the future of David's kingdom was at stake? Because the reader has already been informed by the narrator that it was the Lord's purpose to "bring disaster on Absalom" (17:14b), it is clear that Absalom's death was in agreement with God's will.[4] As Davis (1999:192) puts it, "If the kingdom of God under God's chosen king is to be saved then the enemy who assaults that kingdom must be destroyed." From this perspective, David's command to his troops to "deal gently with young Absalom" (18:5) was mistaken from the outset. But this is not the only way to evaluate David's desire to spare Absalom, nor to assess his grief when he learned of his death. The reader of biblical narrative, however, must tread cautiously in such matters. As a general rule the motives and psychology of the players in biblical narrative remain hidden and any conclusions that are drawn must therefore be held loosely. As was noted above (endnote 1 on 18:1-18), van den Berg (1997) argues that David's desire to spare Absalom was not the expression of parental sentimentality but rather was the expression of a forgiving spirit rooted in David's own experience of having been forgiven by God. If this is so, then David's grief also carries a very different significance than is normally suggested. When David exclaims, "If only I had died instead of you!" (18:33), could it not be viewed as something that warrants admiration instead of critique?[5] Van den Berg (1997:115) argues that even though David was fully aware that Absalom would not have spared his father's life had the roles been reversed, he still did not disown Absalom as a son. Should this not be commended? Even though under the circumstances David's willingness to give his own life for that of his son might not be viewed as normal human behavior, could it be, as van den Berg suggests, "nothing less than messianic"? Does David here anticipate the self-giving love of his greater son?[6] In Romans 5:7-8 Paul says, "Now, most people would not be willing to die for an upright person, though someone might perhaps be willing to die for a person who is especially good. But God showed his great love for us by sending Christ to die for us while we were still sinners." This is exactly what David wished he could have done for Absalom. Even though Absalom deserved nothing but his condemnation, David was ready to forgive him and, if necessary, even to trade his own life for that of his son.[7]

If one accepts this reading of the narrative, it is clear that Joab understood nothing of what was going on in David's mind and heart and that he assessed matters in a completely different way. It was Joab's view that David's behavior was unworthy of his office and was political suicide. Because Joab realized that the security of David's throne was still precarious (ch 20), he took it upon himself to confront David and attempt to convince him to rise above his grief by assuming his responsibilities as the leader of the nation. This is probably the reading of the narrative that has the most to be said for it. Even so, an unresolved issue remains: How does one harmonize the pragmatic considerations of political success with God's command to love one's neighbor as oneself (Lev 19:18)? In Joab's appeal to David he says, "You seem to love those who hate you and hate those who love you" (19:6). Joab's construal of things appears valid. But at the same time "loving those who hate you" is exactly how Jesus characterizes the obligation that rests on all of God's people (Matt 5:44; cf. Luke 6:27). And when this obligation is placed in a political context, it becomes particularly difficult to know exactly how it is to be applied.[8] Even if this standard is regarded as the motivation for David's behavior on this occasion (as in the view of van den Berg), it would appear that his observance of it was highly selective.

ENDNOTES

1. It is clearly a non sequitur to say that because Ahimaaz was a "good man" he must be the bearer of "good news." David's statement tells us much more about his mind-set and about what he so desperately wanted to hear than it does about reality.
2. This was certainly a disingenuous reply because it is clear that Ahimaaz knew that Absalom was dead (18:20).
3. The expression "my son" occurs eight times in two verses (18:33 and 19:4).

4. This, however, does not necessarily vindicate Joab's killing of Absalom. Jesus' death was also according to God's will, but it was the acts of "lawless" men that accomplished it (Acts 2:23).
5. Fokkelman (1981:262-263) regards David's statement in the final phrase of 18:33 [19:1] (NLT, "If only I had died instead of you! O Absalom, my son, my son") in a very different way. He sees it as "a virtually inextricable mixture of unreal pathological longing, nay, it must be said, masochism on the one hand, and deep upright fatherly love on the other hand. From a father who suddenly loses a son due to an accident, war or for whatever cause, the exclamation "had *I* but died in your place!" is moving, understandable, and sound, but in the mouth of this father who has not the courage required for drastic remedies in connection with such an incorrigible spoiled son, the same exclamation is quite different, a sign of pure self-torment." He goes on to say that David's expressed desire to trade places with his son "reveals a huge and terrible hole in that part of David's soul where there should be self-confidence and where a sound feeling of self-esteem belongs." The question is: Who has understood what is going on with David correctly? Is it van den Berg, who credits David with honestly expressing the highest form of self-giving love? Or is it Fokkelman, who charges David with pathological self-torment? Or does the truth lie somewhere in between?
6. Again, it should be realized that analyzing the reasons for David's grief and the motivations that drove his response to Absalom's death is uncertain at best. Davis (1999:193) suggests that it was David's guilt that inflamed his grief, and that his response to Absalom's death should be interpreted in light of Nathan's pronouncement that "from this time on, your family will live by the sword" (12:10). On this basis Davis suggests that David wished that he had died in place of Absalom "because he knew he deserved to die. Guilt has aggravated grief."
7. Both Moses before him (Exod 32:32-33) and Paul after him (Rom 9:3-4) expressed similar sentiments towards God's rebellious people.
8. While this narrative certainly exhibits a tension between David's "political role" and his "paternal role" as Alter (1999:309), among others, maintains, the tension between political pragmatism and the ethical demands of the covenantal law is even more pronounced.

◆ 12. David's return to Jerusalem (2 Sam 19:9-43)

[9]And throughout all the tribes of Israel there was much discussion and argument going on. The people were saying, "The king rescued us from our enemies and saved us from the Philistines, but Absalom chased him out of the country. [10]Now Absalom, whom we anointed to rule over us, is dead. Why not ask David to come back and be our king again?"

[11]Then King David sent Zadok and Abiathar, the priests, to say to the elders of Judah, "Why are you the last ones to welcome back the king into his palace? For I have heard that all Israel is ready. [12]You are my relatives, my own tribe, my own flesh and blood! So why are you the last ones to welcome back the king?" [13]And David told them to tell Amasa, "Since you are my own flesh and blood, like Joab, may God strike me and even kill me if I do not appoint you as commander of my army in his place."

[14]Then Amasa* convinced all the men of Judah, and they responded unanimously. They sent word to the king, "Return to us, and bring back all who are with you."

[15]So the king started back to Jerusalem. And when he arrived at the Jordan River, the people of Judah came to Gilgal to

meet him and escort him across the river.
16Shimei son of Gera, the man from Bahu-
rim in Benjamin, hurried across with the
men of Judah to welcome King David. 17A
thousand other men from the tribe of
Benjamin were with him, including Ziba,
the chief servant of the house of Saul, and
Ziba's fifteen sons and twenty servants.
They rushed down to the Jordan to meet
the king. 18They crossed the shallows of
the Jordan to bring the king's household
across the river, helping him in every way
they could.

As the king was about to cross the river,
Shimei fell down before him. 19"My lord
the king, please forgive me," he pleaded.
"Forget the terrible thing your servant did
when you left Jerusalem. May the king
put it out of his mind. 20I know how much
I sinned. That is why I have come here
today, the very first person in all Israel* to
greet my lord the king."
21Then Abishai son of Zeruiah said,
"Shimei should die, for he cursed the
LORD's anointed king!"
22"Who asked your opinion, you sons of
Zeruiah!" David exclaimed. "Why have you
become my adversary* today? This is not
a day for execution but for celebration!
Today I am once again the king of Israel!"
23Then, turning to Shimei, David vowed,
"Your life will be spared."

24Now Mephibosheth,* Saul's grandson,
came down from Jerusalem to meet the
king. He had not cared for his feet,
trimmed his beard, or washed his clothes
since the day the king left Jerusalem.
25"Why didn't you come with me, Mephi-
bosheth?" the king asked him.
26Mephibosheth replied, "My lord the
king, my servant Ziba deceived me. I told
him, 'Saddle my donkey* so I can go with
the king.' For as you know I am crippled.
27Ziba has slandered me by saying that I
refused to come. But I know that my lord
the king is like an angel of God, so do
what you think is best. 28All my relatives
and I could expect only death from you,
my lord, but instead you have honored me
by allowing me to eat at your own table!
What more can I ask?"
29"You've said enough," David replied.
"I've decided that you and Ziba will divide
your land equally between you."
30"Give him all of it," Mephibosheth
said. "I am content just to have you safe-
ly back again, my lord the king!"

31Barzillai of Gilead had come down
from Rogelim to escort the king across
the Jordan. 32He was very old, about
eighty, and very wealthy. He was the one
who had provided food for the king dur-
ing his stay in Mahanaim. 33"Come across
with me and live in Jerusalem," the king
said to Barzillai. "I will take care of you
there."
34"No," he replied, "I am far too old to
go with the king to Jerusalem. 35I am
eighty years old today, and I can no longer
enjoy anything. Food and wine are no lon-
ger tasty, and I cannot hear the singers as
they sing. I would only be a burden to my
lord the king. 36Just to go across the Jor-
dan River with the king is all the honor I
need! 37Then let me return again to die in
my own town, where my father and moth-
er are buried. But here is your servant, my
son Kimham. Let him go with my lord the
king and receive whatever you want to
give him."
38"Good," the king agreed. "Kimham
will go with me, and I will help him in any
way you would like. And I will do for you
anything you want." 39So all the people
crossed the Jordan with the king. After
David had blessed Barzillai and kissed
him, Barzillai returned to his own home.
40The king then crossed over to Gilgal,
taking Kimham with him. All the troops of
Judah and half the troops of Israel es-
corted the king on his way.

41But all the men of Israel complained
to the king, "The men of Judah stole the
king and didn't give us the honor of help-
ing take you, your household, and all your
men across the Jordan."
42The men of Judah replied, "The king is
one of our own kinsmen. Why should this

make you angry? We haven't eaten any of the king's food or received any special favors!"
43"But there are ten tribes in Israel," the others replied. "So we have ten times as much right to the king as you do. What right do you have to treat us with such contempt? Weren't we the first to speak of bringing him back to be our king again?" The argument continued back and forth, and the men of Judah spoke even more harshly than the men of Israel.

19:14 Or *David;* Hebrew reads *he.* 19:20 Hebrew *in the house of Joseph.* 19:22 Or *my prosecutor.* 19:24 *Mephibosheth* is another name for Merib-baal. 19:26 As in Greek, Syriac, and Latin versions; Hebrew reads *I will saddle a donkey for myself.*

NOTES

19:19 [20] ***May the king put it out of his mind.*** Lit., "Let the king not take it to heart."

19:22 [23] ***Who asked your opinion . . . ?*** Lit., "What have I and you?" (cf. 16:10 for the same expression). The Hebrew may also be translated, "What has this to do with you?" (NJPS).

19:24 [25] ***grandson.*** Lit., "son." In Semitic languages, "son" is often used in the sense of "descendant."

19:31 [32] ***to escort the king across the Jordan.*** The Hebrew construction combining the sign of the object with *bayyarden* [TH871.2/3383, ZH928/3720] is garbled. As Youngblood (1992:1041) suggests, "The best solution is perhaps to omit *'eth-* (as a few Heb. mss do; cf. BHS) and to translate 'from the Jordan' (= NIV 'from there') with the Lucianic recension of the LXX."

19:32 [33] ***wealthy.*** Lit., "great."

19:34 [35] ***I am far too old.*** Lit., "How many are the days of the years of my life?"

19:38 [39] ***in any way you would like.*** Lit., "all that you choose (to lay) upon me."

19:42 [43] ***or received any special favors!*** The word *nisse'th* [TH5375, ZH5951] (Niphal participle) is problematic. If the participle is translated as a substantive (an option S. R. Driver [1913:339] terms "precarious"), the phrase would read, "Or has anything been carried away by us as a portion?" An alternative is to read *mas'eth* [TH4864A, ZH5368] ("portion, gift"; translated as "or has a gift been given to us?"), while others have suggested *nisso'* (Niphal infinitive absolute), rendered literally "or has anything been taken for us?" an option followed in the NLT.

COMMENTARY

The death of Absalom was a defining moment for Israel; it instantly changed the political landscape. Old political conflicts had to be reassessed, and new alliances needed to be formed. Recognizing that Absalom's rebellion had failed and remembering David's past successes as a military leader, the people of the northern tribes were quickly prepared to invite David to return as their king (19:9-10). Judah, however, was slower to deal with the new political realities. It was in the heart of Judah, at Hebron, that Absalom's rebellion had been given birth. So David commissioned the trusted priests Zadok and Abiathar to seek support for his return to Jerusalem by the tribe of Judah (19:11-14). Carrying out David's instructions, Zadok and Abiathar solicited Judah's allegiance by appealing to their tribal solidarity with David, and by announcing the replacement of Joab as the commander of David's army with Amasa, who was the former commander of

Absalom's forces (cf. 17:25). After accepting this appointment, Amasa was able to aid Zadok and Abiathar in persuading the people of Judah to invite David to return. While these arrangements were an important step in preparing the way for Judah's reconciliation with David, at the same time they provoked charges by the northern tribes of favoritism on the part of David toward Judah (19:41-42).

Here, as in the preceding narratives, it is difficult to know exactly what prompted David's appointment of Amasa in Joab's place. Was this simply a political ploy to garner the support of those who had allied themselves with Absalom? Was it an attempt to assuage their fear by signaling that he had no intention of enacting reprisals for their insurrection? Was it a retaliation against Joab for insubordination in connection with the death of Absalom? Perhaps all these considerations were at work. In weighing the options, it must be admitted that it is unclear how much David knew of Joab's involvement in Absalom's death. It would appear that in this series of narratives that describe God's punishment of David for his sin (cf. 12:10-12), the overriding concern is not an explanation of the motivations of all the players in the story but a depiction of God's providential securing of David's kingdom in fulfillment of the promise of 7:16.[1] This providential guidance of the historical process is hidden behind the maneuverings and machinations of political scheming and counterscheming; nevertheless, it moves inexorably forward in accordance with God's purposes for David's life and dynasty.

On his journey back to Jerusalem, David encountered Shimei (19:16-23), Mephibosheth (19:24-30), and Barzillai (19:31-39) along the way.[2] Shimei brought 1,000 men from the tribe of Benjamin as evidence of his political clout, and he joined with the people of Judah to escort David across the Jordan River (19:15-18). Shimei was the same man who had accosted David when he was fleeing from Jerusalem and called him a "murderer" and a "scoundrel" who had stolen Saul's throne (16:5-8). Now, however, recognizing the new political reality, he bowed before David and begged for forgiveness, confessing that he had sinned against him (19:18-20). Abishai, Joab's brother, was loath to hear any words of repentance and instead called for his death (19:21),[3] but David rebuked Abishai and asked why the "sons of Zeruiah" had become his adversary on that day (19:22). David's use of the plural "sons" would suggest that Joab (Abishai's brother) was included in the rebuke (cf. David's comments in 3:29-30, 39). David told Shimei that his life would be spared (19:23). When David spoke of the sons of Zeruiah as his "adversary" (Heb., *satan* [TH7854, ZH8477]), it seems he meant that Joab and Abishai were a hindrance to the proper exercise of his messianic kingship. From David's perspective, the day that his kingship was restored was to be a day of celebration rather than a day on which political scores were settled. David's statement is similar to Saul's on the day of his inauguration as Israel's first king, when some of his supporters called for the execution of those who had opposed him. Saul had said, "No one will be executed today, for today the LORD has rescued Israel!" (1 Sam 11:13). This does not mean, however, that Shimei's offense was completely forgotten; it only meant that he would enjoy amnesty during David's lifetime. On David's deathbed he gave instructions to Solomon to see that justice was done to Shimei (1 Kgs 2:8-9).[4]

The next person David encountered was Mephibosheth, the son of Jonathan and the grandson of Saul. David had befriended Mephibosheth in fulfillment of his covenant with Jonathan and Saul (ch 9; 1 Sam 20:14-17; 24:21-22), but later had disenfranchised him based on the report of Ziba, Mephibosheth's servant, who said that Mephibosheth hoped to regain his grandfather's throne (16:1-4). Now a disheveled Mephibosheth, who had not groomed himself since David left Jerusalem,[5] came to the king and claimed that Ziba had betrayed him at the time of David's escape from the city as a means of ingratiating himself with David. Although the narrator does not give any indication of who was telling the truth, he does report that upon hearing Mephibosheth's story, David rescinded the grant of all of Mephibosheth's property to Ziba (16:4), and ordered that the property should henceforth be divided between the two of them (19:29).

David's third reported encounter is with Barzillai, the wealthy individual from the area of Gilead, who had provided David and his followers with food during their time at Mahanaim (17:27-29). David invited him to join his entourage in its journey back to Jerusalem where he promised to reward him for his kindness by giving him an honored place in the court. Barzillai declined the offer because of his age and because of his desire to die in his own town; however, he asked David to accept his son Kimham in his place (19:32-37). David agreed to this arrangement (cf. 1 Kgs 2:7). Then he and his followers crossed the Jordan to make their way back to Jerusalem, but not before first stopping at Gilgal (19:38-40). Gilgal was a place of enormous significance for the monarchy in Israel. It was here that Saul's reign had been both inaugurated (1 Sam 11:14–12:25) and terminated (1 Sam 15; cf. 1 Sam 13). Certainly there was no more appropriate place for David's kingship to be renewed.[6]

In spite of the invitations from both Israel and Judah to David to return to Jerusalem as king, suspicion and jealousy between the northern tribes and the tribe of Judah continued unabated (19:41-43). The northern tribes suspected David of favoritism toward Judah because representatives of Judah accompanied David across the Jordan, when it was the northern tribes that had first agreed to welcome David back to the throne. The northern tribes represented a much greater proportion of the population of the nation, and in their view this in itself merited much more attention from David than they had received. Judah denied having received any special favors from David but nevertheless pointed out that they had a special relationship with David by virtue of their common tribal origin. These tensions remained unsettled and did not bode well for the future.

ENDNOTES

1. This combination of punishment and protection reflects the dual emphases of the Davidic covenant on both law and promise. These dual emphases are reflected in the Lord's words to David through Nathan the prophet that his son (i.e., Solomon, cf. endnote 28 in the commentary on 11:2–12:25) would build the Temple and that his throne would be established forever (7:13). But Nathan then went on to say (2 Sam 7:14-15), "I will be his father, and he will be my son. If he sins, I will correct and discipline him with the rod, like any father would do. But my favor will not be taken from him as I took it from Saul, whom I removed from your sight."

2. With one exception, these are three of the same individuals David had met on his flight from Jerusalem (Ziba, 16:1-4; Shimei, 16:5-13; Barzillai 17:27). The exception is that on his return David met Mephibosheth himself, rather than meeting only Ziba, Mephibosheth's servant.
3. Abishai had already asked David for permission to "cut off [Shimei's] head" at the time of their first encounter, but David had refused to allow him to do so (16:9-12). Abishai's aggressive nature can also be seen in his request for permission to take Saul's life while he was sleeping (1 Sam 26:8). David refused him on that occasion as well (1 Sam 26:9-11).
4. David's instructions to Solomon to take action against Shimei should not be viewed as an act of personal revenge but rather as something necessary to honor Solomon's office and ensure the consolidation of Solomon's reign.
5. Mephibosheth's disheveled condition reflects his distress over David's plight and lends credibility to the claim that he had been deceived by Ziba.
6. Mettinger (1976:118-119) goes so far as to suggest that a second "coronation" of David took place at Gilgal, probably including both a new "anointing" and an official "acclamation" of David as king even though no description of such a ceremony is provided by the narrator. Any account of exactly what took place at Gilgal, however, must remain speculative.

◆ O. Sheba's Rebellion against David; the Murder of Amasa (2 Sam 20:1-22)

There happened to be a troublemaker there named Sheba son of Bicri, a man from the tribe of Benjamin. Sheba blew a ram's horn and began to chant:

"Down with the dynasty of David!
We have no interest in the son of Jesse.
Come on, you men of Israel,
back to your homes!"

2So all the men of Israel deserted David and followed Sheba son of Bicri. But the men of Judah stayed with their king and escorted him from the Jordan River to Jerusalem.

3When David came to his palace in Jerusalem, he took the ten concubines he had left to look after the palace and placed them in seclusion. Their needs were provided for, but he no longer slept with them. So each of them lived like a widow until she died.

4Then the king told Amasa, "Mobilize the army of Judah within three days, and report back at that time." 5So Amasa went out to notify Judah, but it took him longer than the time he had been given.

6Then David said to Abishai, "Sheba son of Bicri is going to hurt us more than Absalom did. Quick, take my troops and chase after him before he gets into a fortified town where we can't reach him."

7So Abishai and Joab,* together with the king's bodyguard* and all the mighty warriors, set out from Jerusalem to go after Sheba. 8As they arrived at the great stone in Gibeon, Amasa met them. Joab was wearing his military tunic with a dagger strapped to his belt. As he stepped forward to greet Amasa, he slipped the dagger from its sheath.*

9"How are you, my cousin?" Joab said and took him by the beard with his right hand as though to kiss him. 10Amasa didn't notice the dagger in his left hand, and Joab stabbed him in the stomach with it so that his insides gushed out onto the ground. Joab did not need to strike again, and Amasa soon died. Joab and his brother Abishai left him lying there and continued after Sheba.

[11]One of Joab's young men shouted to Amasa's troops, "If you are for Joab and David, come and follow Joab." [12]But Amasa lay in his blood in the middle of the road, and Joab's man saw that everyone was stopping to stare at him. So he pulled him off the road into a field and threw a cloak over him. [13]With Amasa's body out of the way, everyone went on with Joab to capture Sheba son of Bicri.

[14]Meanwhile, Sheba traveled through all the tribes of Israel and eventually came to the town of Abel-beth-maacah. All the members of his own clan, the Bicrites,* assembled for battle and followed him into the town. [15]When Joab's forces arrived, they attacked Abel-beth-maacah. They built a siege ramp against the town's fortifications and began battering down the wall. [16]But a wise woman in the town called out to Joab, "Listen to me, Joab. Come over here so I can talk to you." [17]As he approached, the woman asked, "Are you Joab?"

"I am," he replied.

So she said, "Listen carefully to your servant."

"I'm listening," he said.

[18]Then she continued, "There used to be a saying, 'If you want to settle an argument, ask advice at the town of Abel.' [19]I am one who is peace loving and faithful in Israel. But you are destroying an important town in Israel.* Why do you want to devour what belongs to the LORD?"

[20]And Joab replied, "Believe me, I don't want to devour or destroy your town! [21]That's not my purpose. All I want is a man named Sheba son of Bicri from the hill country of Ephraim, who has revolted against King David. If you hand over this one man to me, I will leave the town in peace."

"All right," the woman replied, "we will throw his head over the wall to you." [22]Then the woman went to all the people with her wise advice, and they cut off Sheba's head and threw it out to Joab. So he blew the ram's horn and called his troops back from the attack. They all returned to their homes, and Joab returned to the king at Jerusalem.

20:7a Hebrew *So Joab's men.* **20:7b** Hebrew *the Kerethites and Pelethites;* also in 20:23. **20:8** Hebrew *As he stepped forward, it fell out.* **20:14** As in Greek and Latin versions; Hebrew reads *All the Berites.* **20:19** Hebrew *a town that is a mother in Israel.*

NOTES

20:1 *troublemaker.* Lit., "son of Belial." See note on 1 Sam 1:16.

20:6 *where we can't reach him.* Lit., "and takes away our eye"; the meaning of the Hebrew is uncertain. It could be an idiom for "elude our sight" (close to the idea of the NLT rendering), or it could mean "to cause injury."

20:8 *was wearing his military tunic.* Lit., "and Joab was girded in his tunic, his clothing." There seems to be some confusion in the MT with the double use of the root *khagar* [TH2296/2290, ZH2520/2512] and the double words for clothing (*mad* [TH4055, ZH4496], *lebush* [TH3830, ZH4230]).

20:12 *everyone was stopping.* This idea is expressed twice in the Hebrew text, once here and again at the end of the verse (cf. KJV). The second instance reads, lit., "when he saw everyone who came by him, and stopped." S. R. Driver (1913:344) suggests that *we'amad* [TH5975, ZH6641] (stop) is the perfect with Waw conversive, carrying on the participle *kal-habba'* [TH3605/935, ZH3972/995] (all who came) as a frequentative in past time (GKC §116x), just as it does in present time. He goes on to cite Jer 21:9 *wehayyotse' wenapal* [TH3318/5307, ZH3655/5877] "whoever goes out and falls." Fokkelman (1981:460) takes *we'amad* as the iterative continuation of the participle *ba'* [TH935, ZH995] (coming).

20:14 *Abel-beth-maacah.* The MT reads "Abel and Beth-maacah."

Bicrites. This follows the Greek and Latin versions (cf. NLT mg). The MT reads "all the Berites." "Berite" is unattested elsewhere, and Sheba is described as the son of Bicri (20:1).

followed him into the town. The Hebrew *bo' 'akhar* [TH935/310, ZH995/339] means "to enter after someone into a place," as e.g., in Exod 14:17; 1 Sam 26:3; 2 Kgs 11:15 (S. R. Driver 1913:345). On the unusual use of *'ap* [TH637, ZH677] (also, even) in the phrase in this verse, see Conroy (1978:118, note 15).

20:15 *built.* Lit., "poured"—that is, poured earth from baskets.

20:18 *ask advice.* Lit., "asking let them ask" or "they surely asked." For the infinitive absolute differing in stem from the main verb, see GKC §113w; Joüon and Muraoka §123p; S. R. Driver 1913:347.

20:19 *I am one who is peace loving and faithful in Israel.* According to the LXX the end of 20:18 flows into the beginning of 20:19: "Ask advice in the town of Abel and Dan whether that which the trusted ones of Israel ordained has been carried out." McCarter (1984:429-430) concludes that LXX reflects the original text and says that Abel and Dan were "adjacent cities at the northern extreme of Israel proper. . . . The woman defends Abel as a model city. Here and in Dan, she says one could expect to find the intentions of the founding fathers of Israel cherished and faithfully performed. Why, then, would Joab harm Abel?" Gordon (1993:216), however, prefers the MT, but reads the first-person pronoun (*'anoki* [TH595, ZH644]) as a case of "a city speaking in the first-person singular, much as does Ekron in 1 Sam 5:10." On this basis he suggests that the woman is saying "that her city is at peace with the faithful of Israel, as distinct from being in league with rebel types like Sheba" (1993:226). Though the textual and translational problems here make for a difficult choice, in context it probably makes more sense to understand the first person pronoun "I" as a personification of the city rather than as a reference to the "wise woman" herself.

you are destroying an important town in Israel. Lit., "You are seeking to destroy a town and a mother in Israel" (see NLT mg). Brueggemann (1990a:331) understands this statement as a way of saying that Abel-beth-maacah is "an old and venerable city. Indeed, this old city is a 'mother in Israel,' a place to which people have looked for guidance, well-being, and life." Alter (1999:326) explains the expression as "a hendiadys that clearly means something like 'principal town.'" This is the understanding represented in NLT.

COMMENTARY

By taking advantage of the harsh words that had passed between the representatives of the northern tribes and the tribe of Judah, a man named Sheba,[1] from the tribe of Benjamin,[2] was able to convince the northern troops to break their alignment with David and to return to their northern territories, leaving only Judah, and perhaps Simeon, loyal to David (20:1-2). The words Sheba used ("Down with the dynasty of David! We have no interest in the son of Jesse.") were a harbinger of the division in the kingdom after the death of Solomon (note the wording of 1 Kgs 12:16). Although there is no indication that Sheba's revolt rested on the sort of careful planning that had characterized Absalom's revolt, the fact that Sheba could convince the northern troops to abandon David at such a crucial moment demonstrates the vulnerability of David's status as ruler over a united kingdom including both Judah and the northern tribes. After the death of Saul, it had been Judah that first welcomed David as their king (cf. 2:4). The northern tribes did not come to embrace him until seven and a half years later (2:11; 5:1-3). The underlying weakness of northern support for David had apparently never been fully overcome, and Sheba was able to exploit a long-simmering discontent and undermine the unity and stability of the kingdom. David recognized this as something that was a serious threat to the viability of his kingdom and something that needed to be addressed quickly (20:6). As McCarter (1984:431) points out, Sheba's was a different sort of threat than Absalom's. Absalom's revolt threatened the king, but Sheba's revolt threatened the kingdom itself.

Before continuing with a description of how David handled this challenge, the narrator explains how David dealt with the 10 concubines who had remained in Jerusalem when he was forced to flee by Absalom's revolt (20:3). While making provision for the concubines' sustenance for as long as they lived, David could no longer seek their intimacy because of Absalom's unlawful sexual liaison with them in public view (16:22).[3] This announcement serves as another reminder to the reader that David's punishment for his sin with Bathsheba would continue throughout the remainder of his reign (12:11-12).

When Amasa, the newly appointed commander of David's troops (19:13), failed to gather an army and to report to David within a set three-day time limit, David authorized Abishai, Joab's brother, to take David's own troops[4] and pursue after Sheba (20:4-6). Although Joab was given no command responsibilities by David, he accompanied his brother on the chase after Sheba (20:7). When Amasa's forces and Abishai's forces happened to meet at Gibeon, Joab approached Amasa under the guise of a friendly greeting and stabbed him with a dagger that was concealed in his left hand. Amasa was left to die on the road; Joab and Abishai continued in their pursuit of Sheba (20:8-10). That Joab was now the de facto commander of the troops is made clear by the statement of one of the followers of Joab to Amasa's troops: "If you are for Joab and David, come and follow Joab" (20:11). Here loyalty to David is linked with loyalty to Joab. So the irrepressible Joab has again taken matters into his own hands and reemerged as Israel's supreme military commander (20:23).

When the sight of Amasa's dead body lying in the roadway became a hindrance to the movement of the troops, it was placed in a nearby field and covered with a cloak, so the pursuit of Sheba could be continued without delay. In the meantime, Sheba had gone through "all the tribes of Israel" (20:14), apparently in an effort to convince them to renounce their allegiance to David as king. Eventually, he, along with other members of his own clan, took refuge in the fortified city of Abel-beth-maacah. When Joab and his forces arrived at the town, they laid siege to it and began the attempt to break down its walls (20:15). Their effort to take the city was interrupted by an appeal made to Joab by a "wise woman" to spare the destruction of "an important town in Israel" (20:16-19; see note on 20:19). Joab responded that it was not his desire to destroy the city but only to capture Sheba because of his revolt against David. The "wise woman" was able to convince the people of Abel-beth-maacah to agree to Joab's demand, and they cut off the head of Sheba and threw it over the wall to Joab (20:20-21). In response, Joab lifted the siege on the city and returned to Jerusalem (20:22).

It is not clear whether the designation "wise woman" is to be understood as a title for some sort of official function (Goitein 1988:10) performed by this woman, or merely a characterization of her reputation as someone who had a special gift for settling disputes (Fokkelman 1986:141; Hoftijzer 1970:429). It does appear that Abel-beth-maacah was known as a place where people came to find help for solving intractable arguments (20:18). In this instance the "wise woman" maneuvered Joab into a defensive position by contrasting his attempt to destroy the city with its peace-loving ways (see note on 20:19) and by arguing that what he was seeking to destroy was something that "belongs to the LORD." Joab recognized the force of her argument and agreed to a solution that not only saved the town of Abel-beth-maacah from being identified with Sheba's northern secession movement but also enabled him to return to David, having averted a civil war and eliminated a threat to his kingdom.

ENDNOTES

1. Sheba is characterized as a "troublemaker" (20:1). See note on 20:1 and note on 1 Sam 1:16.
2. In the ring structure that begins with "K. List of David's Officials (2 Sam 8:15-18)" and ends with "P. List of David's Officials (2 Sam 20:23-26)" in our outline of 1–2 Samuel, this pericope ("O. Sheba's Rebellion against David; the Murder of Amasa [2 Sam 20:1-22]") is the fifth element and corresponds with "L. David Befriends Mephibosheth (2 Sam 9:1-13)" (see discussions under "Literary Style" and "Outline" in the Introduction). In these two pericopes we see that: (1) David was faithful to his promise to Saul and Jonathan to provide protection for their descendants (Mephibosheth), and (2) there was still resentment among some members of the tribe of Benjamin over David's succession to the throne (Sheba).
3. David's policy on this matter is perhaps based on the prohibition of Lev 18:15.
4. This included the Kerethites and Pelethites (see NLT mg and note on 8:18), as well as David's mighty warriors (23:8-39).

◆ P. List of David's Officials (2 Sam 20:23-26)

23Now Joab was the commander of the army of Israel. Benaiah son of Jehoiada was captain of the king's bodyguard. 24Adoniram* was in charge of the labor force. Jehoshaphat son of Ahilud was the royal historian. 25Sheva was the court secretary. Zadok and Abiathar were the priests. 26And Ira, a descendant of Jair, was David's personal priest.

20:24 As in Greek version (see also 1 Kgs 4:6; 5:14); Hebrew reads *Adoram.*

COMMENTARY

It seems clear that this second list of David's officials serves as a literary structuring device that, along with the corresponding list of officials in 8:15-18, frames the "sin and punishment" narratives of 2 Samuel 9–20, setting them apart from both the generally positive presentation of David's reign in chapters 5–8 and the so-called Appendix or Conclusion that follows in chapters 21–24 (see the comments on literary structure in the Introduction under "Literary Style," where it is noted that the architecture of 2 Samuel employs three double lists: lists of sons, officials, and warriors). This list of officials differs in several respects from the list in 8:15-18. The two most striking differences are the reference to Ira as David's personal priest in place of the reference to David's sons serving in a priestly capacity (cf. discussion at 8:18) and more importantly, the naming of Adoniram as the administrator of the "labor force" (20:24). It was dissatisfaction with the "forced labor" system that was introduced in David's reign and intensified in Solomon's reign that became one of the principal causes of the division of the kingdom subsequent to Solomon's death (cf. 1 Kgs 12). So this seemingly innocuous statement portends future trouble, and it suggests that even though David's kingship had survived some serious challenges, it was at best a flawed example of what true covenantal kingship was intended to be. Full realization of the messianic kingdom would await the coming of David's greater son who would embody the ideal of the covenantal king in a full and complete manner.

◆VIII. The Samuel Conclusion (2 Sam 21:1–24:25)

Until recently, the widespread acceptance of Rost's "Succession Narrative" hypothesis (for more detail, see "Date and Occasion of Writing" and "Literary Style" in the Introduction) has prompted most mainstream biblical scholars to conclude that 2 Samuel 21–24 is a collection of miscellaneous prose and poetic literary units that disrupts the storyline of the narratives beginning in chapter 9 and concluding in 1 Kings 1–2 with the accession of Solomon to the throne of Israel.[1] In general, chapters 21–24 have been regarded as having little substantive connection with the preceding narratives of David's reign, and have been viewed as a collection of additions to the so-called Deuteronomistic History that was gradually assembled through a complex redactional process after the Deuteronomistic History had been divided into separate books.[2] Rost's "Succession Narrative" hypothesis is normally linked with the assumption that the "David Story" of 1–2 Samuel is for the most part the result of the combination of two major blocks of material: "The History of David's Rise" (1 Sam 16:14–2 Sam 5)[3] and "The Succession Narrative" (2 Sam 9—1 Kgs 2). This assumption means that the chapters from 5 or 6 through 8 as well as chapters 21–24, are narratives standing outside of the two major blocks of tradition that make up the "David Story." As was noted in the Introduction, some serious questions have been raised in recent studies on the legitimacy of this way of grouping the narratives of 1–2 Samuel. As more attention has been given to the sophisticated structural arrangement of the narratives of 2 Samuel, the idea that chapters 21–24 stand in a loose connection with the preceding narratives has come to be questioned. Although it has long been recognized that the literary units making up these chapters have a clear chiastic structure,[4] it was not until recently that connections have been drawn between the structure of chapters 21–24 and the structure of the preceding narratives (see the Introduction, "Literary Style"). These connections suggest that chapters 21–24 should be regarded as a carefully designed conclusion for the book of Samuel rather than as an intrusive body of miscellaneous additions that has severed 1 Kings 1–2 from its original connection with chapters 9–20.[5]

Although various scholars have begun to recognize that chapters 21–24 are more than a disruptive "Appendix" to the David narratives, there is as yet no agreement on how these narratives are to be connected with the preceding narratives in 2 Samuel with respect to their function or meaning. Brueggemann (1988; 1990b; 1990c) has argued that the six elements of chs 21–24 are intended to deconstruct the triumphalistic view of David that he finds enshrined in the six elements of chapters 5–8, where there is a corresponding chiastic structure of six elements.[6] While there is certainly good reason to applaud Brueggemann's acceptance of a linkage between chapters 5–8 and chapters 21–24, his reading of both these sections of 2 Samuel may be questioned. As Firth (2001) has pointed out, chapters 5–8 are not nearly as triumphalistic as Brueggemann suggests, nor are chapters 21–24 as critical of David as Brueggemann contends. I contend that there is a clear and significant structural correspondence between chapters 5–8 and chapters 21–24, and that in the final analysis chapters 21–24 are intended to provide the reader with a generally positive final assessment of David's reign in which David is pictured as a true although flawed example of what a covenantal king was intended to be. It should be noticed that the writer arranges the material of this final section of the book in a manner that sets David's reign in contrast with that of Saul, who failed to live up to the covenantal ideal.[7] These chapters draw together the major themes of 1–2 Samuel. It was God's purpose for Israel to have a king, but kingship in Israel was to function in a manner consistent with Israel's covenant relationship with Yahweh. When Saul's kingship failed to live up to the covenantal ideal, the Lord rejected him as king and replaced him with David, "a man after his own heart" (1 Sam 13:14). This means that in spite of the descriptions of the sin and punishment of David that have been the focus of the narratives in chapters 10–20, David remained a person who recognized Yahweh as the sovereign ruler over himself and the nation, the one to whom all worship and honor was due. It was the Lord who had protected David and promised him and his descendants an enduring throne. It is these issues that are addressed in the Samuel Conclusion (chs 21–24).[8]

ENDNOTES

1. It has been commonplace to label these chapters the "Samuel Appendix." This designation goes back as far as Budde (1902).
2. This was the view of Noth (1981:124-125) who said: "2 Sam 21–24 is full of additions, which gradually accumulated after Dtr.'s [the Deuteronomist's] history had been divided into separate books. 2 Sam 21:1-14 and 24:1-25 were the first passages to be added, as we can tell from the thematic connection between 24:1a and 21:1-14. This connection was later broken by the interposition of the anecdotes and lists of David's 'mighty men' (2 Sam 21:15-22 and 23:8-39). This latter complex of traditional material, held together by its subject matter, was then split in two when the poetic passages (ch 22 and 23:1-7) were inserted." Brueggemann (2003:142) nicely summarizes the standard assessment of these chapters with the comment, "In 2 Samuel 21–24 we are offered a collection of random tribal memories that clearly interrupt the flow of the narrative that leaps from 2 Samuel 20 to 1 Kings 1 and that purports to reflect earlier moments in David's life. It is characteristic in scholarship to read these materials as random and of little moment for the whole."
3. See the commentary on 5:1-12, endnote 1, for comments on the disagreement among scholars over where "The History of David's Rise" terminates.
4. This idea also goes as far back as Budde (1902:304), who called attention to the chiastic structure of the "Anhänge" (Appendix) that included two narratives, two lists, and at its center, two poems. The clear chiastic arrangement of these narratives can be seen from the following outline:

A. The Lord's anger against Israel; Saul's offense (21:1-14)
  B. List of warriors (21:15-22)
    C. David's song in praise of the Lord's kingship (22:1-51)
    C'. David's last words concerning his own kingship (23:1-7)
  B'. List of warriors (23:8-39)
A'. The Lord's anger against Israel; David's offense (24:1-25)

Although as Firth (2001:212) notes, "Chiasm, like beauty, is frequently in the eyes of the beholder," in this instance it seems beyond dispute that we have what Gordon (1986:45) terms a "purposeful symmetry."

5. As Firth (2001) has argued, it is by no means clear that chs 9–10 are properly categorized as a "Succession Narrative," and at the same time he has argued that chs 21–24 are more "tightly integrated" with the previous material in 2 Samuel than has normally been recognized. Firth finds "important structural reasons in terms of the architecture of 2 Samuel 5–24" to suggest that chs 5–24 display a literary unity. In his view, chs 21–24 give us "a closing summary on David's reign so that 1 Kings 1–2 can introduce us to that of Solomon." Thus chs 21–24 provide a fitting conclusion for the book of Samuel.
6. Second Samuel 5–8 may be outlined as follows:

A. List of David's sons born in Jerusalem (5:13-16)
  B. The Philistines defeated (5:17-25)
    C. David brings the Ark to Jerusalem (6:1-23)
    C'. The Lord makes a covenant with David (7:1-29)
  B'. All David's enemies defeated (8:1-14)
A'. List of David's officials (8:15-18)

It should be noted that the correspondence in literary structure between the Samuel Appendix and the six elements of chs 5–8 suggests that the entirety of chs 5–24 has more literary coherence than has been generally recognized by mainstream biblical scholars during most of the twentieth century.

7. Klement (2000:165-166) argues that the three main accusations that are brought against Saul in the narratives of 1–2 Samuel surface again in the first three rings of the six-ring chiasm that comprises the Samuel Conclusion. In 21:1-14 (The Lord's anger against Israel; Saul's offense) Saul appears as an unrepentant covenant breaker who leaves a legacy of famine for the nation over which he ruled. In 21:15-22 (List of warriors), the references to David's battles with the Philistines, including a reference to Goliath, are a reminder of Saul's failure to live up to his responsibility to deliver Israel from Philistine oppression. David's Song in Praise of the Reign of God (2 Sam 22:1-51) begins with a reminder that the Lord had delivered David from the hand of Saul, who had sought to kill him, demonstrating not only his hatred toward David but also his disdain for the Lord who had chosen David as his replacement. Klement (2000:166) concludes his discussion by saying, "The comparison between Saul and David thus not only determines the two main divisions of the book, but is also reflected in the theme which brings the concluding and summarizing note to the book in the six sections. The things which are stated in the texts about Saul entirely justify his rejection as king and the commissioning of another king, David."
8. As Firth (2001:220) has said, the narratives that make up chs 21–24 provide the reader with "a sophisticated reflection on the whole of David's reign, a reflection that wants to assert that the whole of David's reign is to be assessed positively." Because the "Conclusion" contains two allusions to events described in chs 9–20 (the narratives describing David's punishment for his sin), it is clear at the same time that the final

narrator does not intend to ignore David's failures. With this caveat, Firth maintains that "one can affirm the generally positive nature of David's reign in full awareness of all that had taken place" (i.e., in chs 9–20). This seems to be a valid conclusion.

◆ A. The Lord's Anger against Israel, Saul's Offense (2 Sam 21:1-14)

There was a famine during David's reign that lasted for three years, so David asked the LORD about it. And the LORD said, "The famine has come because Saul and his family are guilty of murdering the Gibeonites."

2So the king summoned the Gibeonites. They were not part of Israel but were all that was left of the nation of the Amorites. The people of Israel had sworn not to kill them, but Saul, in his zeal for Israel and Judah, had tried to wipe them out. 3David asked them, "What can I do for you? How can I make amends so that you will bless the LORD's people again?"

4"Well, money can't settle this matter between us and the family of Saul," the Gibeonites replied. "Neither can we demand the life of anyone in Israel."

"What can I do then?" David asked. "Just tell me and I will do it for you."

5Then they replied, "It was Saul who planned to destroy us, to keep us from having any place at all in the territory of Israel. 6So let seven of Saul's sons be handed over to us, and we will execute them before the LORD at Gibeon, on the mountain of the LORD.*"

"All right," the king said, "I will do it." 7The king spared Jonathan's son Mephibosheth,* who was Saul's grandson, because of the oath David and Jonathan had sworn before the LORD. 8But he gave them Saul's two sons Armoni and Mephibosheth, whose mother was Rizpah daughter of Aiah. He also gave them the five sons of Saul's daughter Merab,* the wife of Adriel son of Barzillai from Meholah. 9The men of Gibeon executed them on the mountain before the LORD. So all seven of them died together at the beginning of the barley harvest.

10Then Rizpah daughter of Aiah, the mother of two of the men, spread burlap on a rock and stayed there the entire harvest season. She prevented the scavenger birds from tearing at their bodies during the day and stopped wild animals from eating them at night. 11When David learned what Rizpah, Saul's concubine, had done, 12he went to the people of Jabesh-gilead and retrieved the bones of Saul and his son Jonathan. (When the Philistines had killed Saul and Jonathan on Mount Gilboa, the people of Jabesh-gilead stole their bodies from the public square of Beth-shan, where the Philistines had hung them.) 13So David obtained the bones of Saul and Jonathan, as well as the bones of the men the Gibeonites had executed.

14Then the king ordered that they bury the bones in the tomb of Kish, Saul's father, at the town of Zela in the land of Benjamin. After that, God ended the famine in the land.

21:6 As in Greek version (see also 21:9); Hebrew reads *at Gibeah of Saul, the chosen of the Lord.*
21:7 *Mephibosheth* is another name for Merib-baal. **21:8** As in a few Hebrew and Greek manuscripts and Syriac version (see also 1 Sam 18:19); most Hebrew manuscripts read *Michal.*

NOTES

21:1 ***David asked the LORD about it.*** Lit., "David sought the face of the LORD."

21:2 ***The people of Israel had sworn not to kill them.*** Lit., "The sons of Israel had sworn to them."

21:3 ***How can I make amends.*** "Make amends" is the translation of the Piel form of the verb *kapar* [TH3722, ZH4105], which is often translated as "atone."

so that you will bless. Lit., "And you shall bless." On the use of the imperative following Waw to indicate purpose in the apodosis an interrogative sentence, see Joüon and Muraoka §162m.

21:6 *we will execute them.* The precise meaning of the Hiphil form of the verb *yaqa'* [TH3363, ZH3697] (NLT, "execute") here and in 21:9 is not clear (BDB 429, "some solemn form of execution, but meaning uncertain"). *Yaqa'* occurs in the Hiphil stem in only one other place in the OT (Num 25:4). Alter (1999:331) translates the word as "impale" and comments, "There is no scholarly consensus on the exact form of execution, except that it obviously involves exhibiting the corpses. Some understand it as a kind of crucifixion."

at Gibeon, on the mountain of the LORD. The NLT follows the LXX in reading "Gibeon" in place of MT's Gibeah (see NLT mg and 21:9, MT). The NLT (cf. NJPS, NRSV) also follows the suggested emendation of A. Anderson (1989:246-247) and McCarter (1984:438) in reading "on the mountain of the LORD" in place of MT's "the chosen one of the LORD."

21:10 *stayed there the entire harvest season.* Lit., "from the beginning of harvest until water was poured on them from the heavens." Alter (1999:331) comments, "This would be in April. The bereaved Rizpah then watches over the corpses throughout the hot months of the summer, until the rains return—heralding the end of the long famine—in the fall."

COMMENTARY

At some point, presumably early in David's reign, Israel experienced a severe famine that lasted for three years.[1] When David asked the Lord why Israel was plagued with famine, he was told that it was because Saul had violated the provisions of a treaty between Israel and the Gibeonites that was made during the time of Joshua (Josh 9). Contrary to the provisions of this treaty, which had been sworn in the name of Yahweh, the God of Israel (Josh 9:15, 19), Saul had taken the lives of many Gibeonites in an attempt to eradicate them from the land.[2] The result was that Israel now stood under the Lord's curse rather than his blessing. Saul's murder of Gibeonites had not only polluted the land (cf. Num 35:30-34) but had also invited whatever curses may have been attached to the treaty with the Gibeonites as well as those of Leviticus 26:20 and Deuteronomy 28:18 for taking the name of Yahweh in vain.

After learning why Israel was plagued with famine, David summoned the Gibeonites to ask them what he might do to make amends (see note on 21:3) for their abuse at the hands of Saul. The Gibeonites told him that monetary reparations would not rectify the injustice done to them and that they had no authority to impose the death penalty on an Israelite (21:4). When David inquired further about what he could do to change their attitude toward Israel, they said they wanted him to turn over to them seven of Saul's sons for execution (21:6, see note).[3] Since this request was consistent with the provisions of the Mosaic law for dealing with the unlawful taking of human life (Lev 24:21-22; Num 35:30-34),[4] David agreed to their proposal, and seven of Saul's sons were executed by the Gibeonites in Saul's ancestral city, Gibeon.[5]

For a proper understanding of what some today might consider a barbaric remedy for the famine, this narrative needs to be understood in its Old Testament context.[6] Israel was the nation Yahweh had chosen to be his own people. Two of the most important features of Yahweh's relationship with Israel were that he had given them a land in which to dwell, and he had come to live among them in this land (Exod 40:34-38 and 1 Kgs 8:10-13 make a clear link between the visible manifestation of God's presence among his people and the Tabernacle and Temple). This meant that the land of Israel must not be defiled[7]—it had become "holy ground" (Exod 3:5; Zech 2:10-12). The Old Testament mentions three things that would pollute or corrupt the land. These were idolatry (Jer 3:9; Ezek 36:17-18), sexual immorality (Lev 18; Jer 3:1), and murder (Num 35:30-34; Ps 106:38; Ezek 36:18). In this particular narrative, we find that bloodguilt rested on Saul and his house because Saul had unlawfully killed an unspecified number of Gibeonites (21:1). According to Numbers 35:33, only "the execution of the murderer" could "purify the land from murder." As Davis (1999:223) points out, "Atonement is never nice, but always gruesome." Sin, whatever its form, is ugly and atonement for sin is costly. This is true whether looked at from the context of Old Testament procedures for securing atonement for sin and the propitiation of divine wrath,[8] or from the New Testament description of the atoning death of Jesus by means of crucifixion, to which all the Old Testament sacrifices ultimately pointed.

The narrative concludes with a description of the subsequent actions of Rizpah (21:10) and David (21:11-14). Rizpah was a concubine of Saul, and the mother of two of the men who were executed. She protected the bodies of the slain men from mutilation by wild animals or birds during the extended time that they were left exposed to the elements (see note on 21:10).[9] David was moved by her example, and provided an honorable burial not only for the seven executed men, but also for Saul and Jonathan, whose bones he retrieved from Jabesh-gilead.[10]

As was mentioned above, one of the purposes of the Samuel Conclusion is to remind the readers of 1–2 Samuel of the contrast that has been drawn between the reigns of Saul and David in the preceding narratives of 1–2 Samuel. While Saul was rejected as king over Israel because of his persistence in disobedience to the word of the Lord and his refusal to repent in a genuine and unqualified manner, David found favor with the Lord because he sought to reign in a manner consistent with the covenant; when he failed to do so, he sought the Lord's forgiveness in true repentance. It is this sort of contrast that is highlighted by the first (21:1-14) and sixth narratives (24:1-25) of the ring structure in the Samuel Conclusion. These two narratives describe offenses by Saul and David, respectively, which provoked the Lord's anger to burn against Israel. In the narrative about Saul's unlawful killing of the Gibeonites (21:1-14), atonement was eventually achieved. But this atonement was accomplished by the payment of life for life with no reference to any remorse or repentance for the misdeed by Saul himself. In the parallel member of the ring structure (ch 24) the Lord's anger also burned against Israel, but this time it was because of David's improper census of Israel's fighting men. David, however, was conscience stricken. He confessed his sin (24:10, 17), prayed for the resulting plague to be lifted, and offered a sacrifice to the Lord (24:25). The Lord responded to David's repentance by removing the plague. So the difference between Saul and David that is highlighted in these two narratives is not the difference between a sinful ruler (Saul) and a sinless ruler (David) but that of heart attitude. Saul was a ruler who arrogantly went his own way. David was a ruler who willingly bowed before the Lord, confessed his sin, and sought to exercise his authority as king in a manner consistent with the covenant. So in the initial narrative of the Samuel Conclusion we find a reminder of Saul's failure to live up to the responsibilities of the covenantal king with the result that the legacy he left for David was a nation of starving people.[11]

Beyond this fundamental contrast between Saul and David, there are at least two other subsidiary ways in which 21:1-14 places David in a more favorable light than it does Saul. While Saul violated the covenant Israel had made with the Gibeonites (21:1), David honored the covenant he had made with Jonathan (21:7). When David delivered seven of Saul's descendants to the Gibeonites, he spared Jonathan's son Mephibosheth because of his oath with Jonathan. So Saul is depicted as a covenant breaker, while David is portrayed as a covenant keeper.

A second subsidiary way in which Saul and David are contrasted in 21:1-14 is found in the dishonor and decimation that comes to the house of Saul[12] compared with the honor and permanence associated with the house of David. The execution of seven of Saul's descendants, excluding only Mephibosheth, seems to have nearly extinguished the line of Saul. The genealogies of 1 Chronicles 8:29-39 and 9:35-44 contain no descendants of Saul other than those from the line of Jonathan through Mephibosheth (also known as Merib-baal). In contrast to Saul, David remained on the throne in Israel, and his line endured not only throughout the Old Testament period but reached its zenith in the New Testament account of the birth of David's greater son, Jesus Christ (Matt 1:1).

The following comments of Klement (2000:174) on 21:1-14 provide an appropriate conclusion for our own assessment of this narrative:[13]

> *With Saul's reign thus finally summed up as a sinful one which dragged him and his family to their deaths, David appears in contrast as an upright king who is prepared at Yahweh's behest to uphold the law, even with regard to Amorites. At the same time David remains, again in contrast to Saul, bound to the covenant obligations entered into by him with respect to Jonathan, and shows himself, measured against the opportunities for the despotic exercise of power, remarkably magnanimous to the family of Saul.*

ENDNOTES

1. The materials in the ring structure of chs 21–24 stand in a nonchronological order, just like the material in the parallel ring structure of chs 5–8 (for further discussion, see endnote 3 in the commentary on ch 6). This means that no direct indication of when the famine occurred is included in the narrative. It seems likely, however, that it occurred sometime after David had brought Mephibosheth to his court (ch 9 and 21:7 both speak of the sparing of Mephibosheth), and prior to the time of Absalom's rebellion (ch 15). Some have argued that this incident, among others, was behind Shimei's cursing of David during his flight from Jerusalem when he said that the Lord was paying him back for "all the bloodshed in Saul's clan" (see 16:8 and further discussion in the commentary on ch 9).
2. Because there is no reference to this action by Saul in the narratives of 1 Samuel, it is not known exactly what prompted it. The statement in 21:2 that he acted in "zeal for Israel and Judah" suggests that the action was an expression of some sort

of extreme nationalism. The fact that the Gibeonites lived near Saul's hometown of Gibeah and in the tribal territory of Benjamin may have exacerbated his disdain for them.

3. The number seven represents a full number (seven symbolizing completeness) even though many more Gibeonites had been slain by Saul, since we are told he "had tried to wipe them out" (v. 2).
4. Numbers 35:33 says that "no sacrifice except the execution of the murderer can purify the land from murder." This seems to be the fundamental principle that is being addressed by the execution of seven of Saul's sons. In this instance the murderer (Saul) could not be executed himself because he was already dead. But on the basis of Deut 24:16 ("Parents must not be put to death for the sins of their children, nor children for the sins of their parents"), it might be questioned whether the execution of seven of Saul's sons really was consistent with the Mosaic law. Davis (1999:222) suggests that the transgenerational punishment prohibition of Deut 24:16 "regulated individual criminal cases." Saul's offense against the Gibeonites was not "individual" but rather "national." The oath sworn to the Gibeonites during the time of Joshua represented the entire nation and entailed a corporate responsibility. Tigay (1996:227) points out that the "few instances where punishment of children was legally sanctioned were not criminal cases but those involving offenses against God, such as violations of the *kherem* [TH2764, ZH3051] and national oaths." This would appear to be such a case. That the procedure adopted was acceptable to the Lord is indicated by the statement of 21:14: "After that, God ended the famine in the land."
5. Saul's great-grandfather was known as the "father of Gibeon" (1 Chr 8:29-33; 9:35-39).
6. Although it is more appropriate to regard the execution of Saul's sons and grandsons as a form of capital punishment (Gen 9:5-6) rather than a form of human sacrifice, there is, nevertheless, a fine line between these categories. As Num 35:33 says, "No sacrifice except the execution of the murderer can purify the land from murder." In a discussion of God's command to Abraham to sacrifice his son Isaac, Vos (1975:92) says, "The statement that God commands Abraham to offer up Isaac distinctly implies that in the abstract, the sacrifice of a human being cannot be condemned on principle. It is well to be cautious in committing one's self to that critical opinion, for it strikes at the very root of the atonement. The rejection of the 'blood theology' as a remnant of a very barbaric type of primitive religion rests on such a basis."
7. The Lord commanded Israel to "not defile the land where you live, for I live there myself. I am the LORD, who lives among the people of Israel" (Num 35:34). As Milgrom (1989:296) notes, "Land and tabernacle are but two sides of the same coin. The land of Israel is also God's residence and is therefore equivalent in holiness to His sanctuary."
8. Leviticus 17:11 tells us that "the life of the body is in its blood. I have given you the blood on the altar to purify you, making you right with the LORD."
9. De Graaf (1978:182) suggests that the reason why the corpses of the slain men were allowed to remain unburied for so long was in order to let "all Israel see that something was being done about Saul's sin" that had caused the three-year famine, and it is for this reason that they "were not removed until the first drops of rain showed that the curse had been lifted (2 Sam 21:1)."
10. Why David permitted the long exposure of the dead bodies of the executed men to the elements without proper burial is not explained. Some (contra de Graaf in endnote 9)

have argued that the fact that this happened does not speak well of David and diminishes his stature as a true covenantal king.

11. Klement (2000:167-168) speaks of famine as being a "legacy" of Saul's guilt in the Gibeonite matter.
12. As Klement (2000:169) notes, "Just as the beheaded corpse of Saul and the dead bodies of his three fallen sons had been hanged up in the open air on the city wall of Bethshan, so now it was the case with seven more of his sons. The shameful demise of Saul and his sons who were hanged, ten in all, sets the final seal on Yahweh's verdict on Saul's kingdom."
13. Like Klement's, my evaluation of both the Samuel Conclusion as a whole, and 21:1-14 in particular, contrasts radically with the assessment of Brueggemann that is mentioned above in the introduction to the Samuel Conclusion (2 Sam 21–24). Brueggemann supports what he calls a "suspicious" reading of the narrative of 21:1-14 as opposed to what he terms a "conventional" reading of the narrative with its stated sequence of bloodguilt—famine—expiation. According to Brueggemann's "suspicious" reading of the narrative (1988:386), "It presents David as a political killer who hides his actions in religious justification." The religious justification of which Brueggemann speaks is the divine oracle in 21:1 in which the Lord told David that the three-year famine was caused by Saul's violation of the treaty with the Gibeonites. It is Brueggemann's claim (1990a:337) that this divine oracle is a "piece of Davidic fabrication" intended to provide "royal justification for David's elimination of Saul's sons who continue to threaten" the security and stability of his regime (1990c:91). But as Gordon (1986:300-301) notes, "There is nothing in the text to suggest that he [David] engineered the situation so as to be rid of potential rivals from the house of Saul. That he could have benefited from the Gibeonites' revenge is no proof of Machiavellian plotting on his part."

◆ B. List of Warriors (2 Sam 21:15-22)

15 Once again the Philistines were at war with Israel. And when David and his men were in the thick of battle, David became weak and exhausted. 16 Ishbi-benob was a descendant of the giants*; his bronze spearhead weighed more than seven pounds,* and he was armed with a new sword. He had cornered David and was about to kill him. 17 But Abishai son of Zeruiah came to David's rescue and killed the Philistine. Then David's men declared, "You are not going out to battle with us again! Why risk snuffing out the light of Israel?"

18 After this, there was another battle against the Philistin loosenes at Gob. As they fought, Sibbecai from Hushah killed Saph, another descendant of the giants.

19 During another battle at Gob, Elhanan son of Jair* from Bethlehem killed the brother of Goliath of Gath.* The handle of his spear was as thick as a weaver's beam!

20 In another battle with the Philistines at Gath, they encountered a huge man with six fingers on each hand and six toes on each foot, twenty-four in all, who was also a descendant of the giants. 21 But when he defied and taunted Israel, he was killed by Jonathan, the son of David's brother Shimea.*

22 These four Philistines were descendants of the giants of Gath, but David and his warriors killed them.

21:16a Or *a descendant of the Rapha;* also in 21:18, 20, 22. **21:16b** Hebrew *300 shekels* [3.4 kilograms]. **21:19a** As in parallel text at 1 Chr 20:5; Hebrew reads *son of Jaare-oregim.* **21:19b** As in parallel text at 1 Chr 20:5; Hebrew reads *killed Goliath of Gath.* **21:21** As in parallel text at 1 Chr 20:7; Hebrew reads *Shimei,* a variant spelling of Shimea.

NOTES

21:16 *Ishbi-benob was a descendant of the giants.* This agrees with some Greek mss. The word in MT may be understood differently (see NLT mg). There is, however, good reason to conclude that the MT's *harapah* [TH7497B, ZH8335] (21:16, 18, 20, 22 and spelled *harapa'* [TH7498, ZH8325] in the parallel texts in 1 Chr 20:6, 8) is a term associated with a race of giants. Deuteronomy 2:10-11, 20 tells us that the *repa'im* [TH7497, ZH8328] were "tall" and called the "Emim" by the Moabites and the "Zamzummim" by the Ammonites. Og, the king of Basha defeated by Joshua, is identified with the *repa'im* [TH7497, ZH8328], and possessed an iron bedstead 13 feet long (Deut 3:11; Josh 12:4; 13:12). See further Waltke 1975:64-66; NIDOTTE 4.676-678.

he was armed with a new sword. Lit., "He was belted anew."

21:19 *Elhanan son of Jair from Bethlehem killed the brother of Goliath of Gath.* The MT reads, "Elhanan the son of Jaare-oregim, the Bethlehemite, killed Goliath, the Gittite" (cf. NLT mg). "Gittite" is the gentilic adjective for Gath. There has been much ink spilt over how best to reconcile the MT of 21:19 that says Elhanan killed Goliath, with the statements in 1 Sam 17:4, 51, 57; 21:9 and 1 Chr 20:5 that say David killed Goliath. Some scholars have attempted to explain the discrepancy by suggesting that an older tradition of a heroic act by an obscure individual named Elhanan was later transferred to David as means of enhancing David's reputation as a great warrior (e.g., Kennedy 1904:122). Although this explanation assumes that 1 Chr 20:5 has modified the wording of 21:19 in order to harmonize it with the David/Goliath tradition of 1 Sam 17, the nature of the differences in the Hebrew of the texts is much more readily explained by assuming that 1 Chr 20:5 contains the original tradition and that 2 Sam 21:19 is the result of the occurrence of several copyist errors. For the linguistic details supporting this conclusion, see the fuller discussions by Archer (1982:178), Fouts (2000), D. Payne (1970:318-319), and Youngblood (1992:1060-1061). Suggestions by some that there is no real conflict between the two traditions because there were two Philistines named Goliath, or because David (a throne name) was also known as Elhanan (a personal name), are not convincing.

COMMENTARY

The two poems standing at the center of the Samuel Conclusion (David's Song in Praise of God's Reign, 22:1-51, and David's Last Words about His Reign, 23:1-7) are framed by two lists of warriors who contributed in significant ways to David's military victories over Israel's enemies.[1] The first of these lists names four of David's warriors (Abishai, Sibbecai, Elhanan, and Jonathan) who killed four Philistine giants (see note on 21:16; two of these giants are named: Ishbi-benob and Saph, one is identified as "the brother of Goliath" and the fourth is unnamed). One of the reasons the Lord had placed Saul on the throne in Israel many years earlier was to deliver Israel from Philistine oppression (1 Sam 9:16). But Saul failed to take the initiative in this important cause (see commentary on 1 Sam 10:5-7 and 1 Sam 13–14), and at his death the Philistines were a more serious threat to the nation than they were when he had begun his reign. In contrast to Saul, David was successful against the Philistines, not only as evidenced by his killing of their hero Goliath in hand-to-hand combat (1 Sam 17) when Saul was afraid to take up Goliath's challenge, but also by his defeat of the Philistine armies on numerous occasions (5:17-25; 8:1; 1 Sam 23:1-6). As Klement (2000:166) notes, the reference to the four Philistine giants in this passage "is a reminder that it was not possible for Saul to overcome even one of them." So even though Saul is not mentioned by name in this narrative, the enumeration of the defeat of four Philistine giants by David's warriors serves as a "reminder of Saul's failure" (Klement 2000:166).

From the few statements in the list that are not concerned with information about the names of the combatants, the locations of battles, or the might of the Philistine opponents, we gain further understanding about David. David is described as "weak and exhausted" (21:15). He had been cornered by Ishbi-benob, a Philistine giant who wielded a bronze spearhead weighing more than seven pounds, and was on the verge of being killed when Abishai suddenly came to his rescue (21:17). The implication of this scenario is that David was not invincible in himself; he needed the help of his fellow warriors, and moreover was dependent on God's providential protection. This is not a picture of a self-sufficient, all-powerful Near Eastern potentate but rather of someone whose frailty and vulnerability is readily apparent. The heroic acts that are enumerated are not those of David himself; rather, they are those of his subordinates.

However, David's importance is not minimized, because in the aftermath of this incident we are told that David's men decided that he should no longer accompany them in battle because of the risk that the "light of Israel" would be "snuff[ed] out" (21:17). In Hebrew idiom, snuffing out one's light is an expression for dying (Job 18:5-6; 21:17; Prov 13:9; 20:20; 24:20). As Gordon (1986:303) puts it, "David's death would be tantamount to the extinction of the life of the community (cf. Lam 4:20)." So this statement by David's warriors speaks of their perception of the importance of David's life for the nation. David had come to embody the "light" and "life" of Israel, and his men understood that God's chosen people could ill afford to lose his leadership. The same idiom is later applied to David's descendants whom the Lord raised up to succeed him on the throne in Israel (1 Kgs 11:36; 15:4; 2 Kgs 8:19; 2 Chr 21:7; and Ps 132:17).

The picture of David that emerges from this list of his warriors is that of a ruler who, in contrast with Saul, was able to subdue Philistine oppression, a ruler highly valued by his subordinates, but at the same time a ruler who was vulnerable and dependent on them for their loyalty and support. Most importantly, David was a ruler who needed the protection and guidance of the one who had promised that his dynasty would endure forever.[2]

ENDNOTES

1. This literary structure parallels the ring structure of chs 5–8, where the two central narratives ("David Brings the Ark to Jerusalem" [ch 6] and "The Lord Makes a Covenant with David" [ch 7]) are framed by two lists of David's victories ("David Defeats the Philistines" [5:17-25] and "All David's Enemies Defeated with the Lord's Help" [8:1-14]).
2. This reading of 21:15-24 contrasts sharply with that of Brueggemann who, as mentioned above, reads the whole of the "Samuel Appendix" as a "deconstruction" of the royal pretensions of the Davidic court. Brueggemann (1988:387) labels the reference to David as the "light of Israel" in 21:17 as "a massive assertion of royal ideology." But he then suggests (1990c:92) that this "statement of royal ideology"

is made so that it can be "assaulted." It is placed between the statements of David being "weak and exhausted" (21:15), and the statement of the MT that Elhanan killed Goliath (21:19). In his view (1990c:92) it is "plausible" that Elhanan had in fact killed Goliath and that "in the great narrative of 1 Samuel 17 that victory is reassigned by the tradition to David." But this then means that 21:19 is intended "to debunk David by taking the victory away from David and reassigning it to Elhanan" (1990c:92-93). Brueggemann's bottom line is that "the ideological claim of 2 Samuel 21:17 is made empty and ludicrous by being placed between the note on David's weariness and the claim of Elhanan" (1990c:93). It should be noted that Brueggemann's reading of this passage rests heavily on the assumption that David did not kill Goliath, just as his "suspicious" reading of 21:1-14 rests heavily on the assumption that the divine oracle of 21:1 is a Davidic fiction (see endnote 12 in the commentary on 21:1-14).

◆ C. David's Song in Praise of God's Reign (2 Sam 22:1-51)

David sang this song to the LORD on the day the LORD rescued him from all his enemies and from Saul. 2He sang:

"The LORD is my rock, my fortress, and my savior;
3 my God is my rock, in whom I find protection.
He is my shield, the power that saves me,
and my place of safety.
He is my refuge, my savior,
the one who saves me from violence.
4 I called on the LORD, who is worthy of praise,
and he saved me from my enemies.

5 "The waves of death overwhelmed me;
floods of destruction swept over me.
6 The grave* wrapped its ropes around me;
death laid a trap in my path.
7 But in my distress I cried out to the LORD;
yes, I cried to my God for help.
He heard me from his sanctuary;
my cry reached his ears.

8 "Then the earth quaked and trembled.
The foundations of the heavens shook;
they quaked because of his anger.
9 Smoke poured from his nostrils;
fierce flames leaped from his mouth.
Glowing coals blazed forth from him.
10 He opened the heavens and came down;
dark storm clouds were beneath his feet.
11 Mounted on a mighty angelic being,* he flew,
soaring* on the wings of the wind.
12 He shrouded himself in darkness,
veiling his approach with dense rain clouds.
13 A great brightness shone around him,
and burning coals* blazed forth.
14 The LORD thundered from heaven;
the voice of the Most High resounded.
15 He shot arrows and scattered his enemies;
his lightning flashed, and they were confused.
16 Then at the command of the LORD,
at the blast of his breath,
the bottom of the sea could be seen,
and the foundations of the earth were laid bare.

17 "He reached down from heaven and rescued me;
he drew me out of deep waters.
18 He rescued me from my powerful enemies,

from those who hated me and were
too strong for me.
19 They attacked me at a moment when
I was in distress,
but the LORD supported me.
20 He led me to a place of safety;
he rescued me because he delights
in me.
21 The LORD rewarded me for doing right;
he restored me because of my
innocence.
22 For I have kept the ways of the LORD;
I have not turned from my God to
follow evil.
23 I have followed all his regulations;
I have never abandoned his decrees.
24 I am blameless before God;
I have kept myself from sin.
25 The LORD rewarded me for doing right.
He has seen my innocence.

26 "To the faithful you show yourself
faithful;
to those with integrity you show
integrity.
27 To the pure you show yourself pure,
but to the wicked you show
yourself hostile.
28 You rescue the humble,
but your eyes watch the proud and
humiliate them.
29 O LORD, you are my lamp.
The LORD lights up my darkness.
30 In your strength I can crush an army;
with my God I can scale any wall.

31 "God's way is perfect.
All the LORD's promises prove true.
He is a shield for all who look to
him for protection.
32 For who is God except the LORD?
Who but our God is a solid rock?
33 God is my strong fortress,
and he makes my way perfect.
34 He makes me as surefooted as
a deer,
enabling me to stand on mountain
heights.
35 He trains my hands for battle;
he strengthens my arm to draw
a bronze bow.
36 You have given me your shield
of victory;
your help* has made me great.
37 You have made a wide path for
my feet
to keep them from slipping.

38 "I chased my enemies and destroyed
them;
I did not stop until they were
conquered.
39 I consumed them;
I struck them down so they did
not get up;
they fell beneath my feet.
40 You have armed me with strength
for the battle;
you have subdued my enemies
under my feet.
41 You placed my foot on their necks.
I have destroyed all who hated me.
42 They looked for help, but no one came
to their rescue.
They even cried to the LORD, but he
refused to answer.
43 I ground them as fine as the dust
of the earth;
I trampled them* in the gutter
like dirt.

44 "You gave me victory over my
accusers.
You preserved me as the ruler over
nations;
people I don't even know now
serve me.
45 Foreign nations cringe before me;
as soon as they hear of me, they
submit.
46 They all lose their courage
and come trembling* from their
strongholds.

47 "The LORD lives! Praise to my Rock!
May God, the Rock of my salvation,
be exalted!
48 He is the God who pays back those
who harm me;
he brings down the nations
under me
49 and delivers me from my enemies.

You hold me safe beyond the reach
of my enemies;
you save me from violent
opponents.
50 For this, O LORD, I will praise you
among the nations;
I will sing praises to your name.
51 You give great victories to your king;
you show unfailing love to your
anointed,
to David and all his descendants
forever."

22:6 Hebrew *Sheol.* **22:11a** Hebrew *a cherub.* **22:11b** As in some Hebrew manuscripts (see also Ps 18:10); other Hebrew manuscripts read *appearing.* **22:13** Or *and lightning bolts.* **22:36** As in Dead Sea Scrolls (see also Ps 18:35); Masoretic Text reads *your answering.* **22:43** As in Dead Sea Scrolls (see also Ps 18:42); Masoretic Text reads *I crushed and trampled them.* **22:46** As in parallel text at Ps 18:45; Hebrew reads *come girding themselves.*

NOTES

22:3 ***my God.*** This reflects the vocalization *'elohay* [TH430/2967.1, ZH466/3276] (my God), which matches the understanding of the LXX, rather than the vocalization *'elohe* (the God of) found in MT.

22:11 ***soaring.*** This follows the reading *wayyede'* (from *da'ah* [TH1675, ZH1797], "soar, swoop down") with Ps 18:10 [11] instead of *wayyera'* ("he appeared"; Niphal imperfect of *ra'ah* [TH7200, ZH8011]) with the MT (see NLT mg).

22:24 ***sin.*** The *-y* suffix on *'awon* [TH5771, ZH6411] (sin) is likely an "old genitive case ending" (Youngblood 1992:1079).

22:26 ***those with integrity.*** Lit., "with the blameless mighty man" (*gibbor tamim* [TH1368A/8549, ZH1475/9459]), while the parallel text in Ps 18:26 has "with the blameless man" (*gebar tamim* [TH1397/8549, ZH1505/9459]; cf. NLT, "the pure").

22:33 ***God is my strong fortress.*** An alternate translation following 4QSam[a] is "He is the God who girded me with strength." 4QSam[a] reads *me'azzereni* [TH247/5204.1, ZH273/5761] (who girded me) for *ma'uzzi* [TH4581/2967.1, ZH5057/3276] (my fortress).

he makes my way perfect. This follows the reading *wayyitten* [TH5414, ZH5989] ("he makes"; cf. Ps 18:33) rather than *wayyatter* [TH5425A, ZH6001] (he sets free), and follows MT's Qere, *darki* [TH1870/2967.1, ZH2006/3276] (my way), rather than the Kethiv *darko* [TH1870/2050.2, ZH2006/2257] (his way). The consonantal text of the MT reads, "He sets the blameless free in his way."

22:34 ***mountain heights.*** The MT reads, "my heights."

22:37 ***You have made a wide path for my feet.*** Lit., "You enlarge my steps under me."

22:41 ***You placed my foot on their necks.*** Lit., "You have made my enemies to me a back of the neck." An alternate understanding of the expression is, "You caused all my enemies to flee" (that is, they show the back of their necks—hence, they flee).

22:51 ***You give great victories to your king.*** This follows the Kethiv (*magdil* [TH1431, ZH1540], i.e., to the one who magnifies the victories of his king; cf. Ps 18:50 [51]) rather than the Qere (*migdol* [TH4024, ZH4460], "tower"), which gives the reading, "He is a tower of deliverance for his king" (A. Anderson 1989:259, 261).

COMMENTARY

This remarkable song of 51 verses[1] closely resembles Psalm 18 and was composed by David,[2] presumably toward the end of his reign. It places some of the central themes of 1–2 Samuel in theological perspective.[3] As was noted in the introduction to the Samuel Conclusion (see pp. 393-396), 22:1-51 is one of the two texts (along with 23:1-7) that stand at the center of its ring structure. This literary arrangement suggests that the writer of 1–2 Samuel considered these two texts to be of particular importance for a proper understanding of the book.[4] Reflection on their content, as well as on the larger issues that surrounded the establishment of kingship in Israel, confirms this conclusion. The incorporation of human kingship into the structure of Israel's theocracy created the potential for the monarchy to eclipse Israel's continued recognition of Yahweh as her divine king. For this reason when Samuel presented Israel with their newly chosen king, he did so in the setting of a covenant renewal ceremony in which Israel reaffirmed her allegiance to Yahweh as her divine king—a ceremony that simultaneously inaugurated Saul's reign (see commentary on 1 Sam 11:14–12:25). Second Samuel 22 is a strong affirmation by David, as Israel's anointed king (22:51), that he continued to recognize Yahweh as his and Israel's ultimate sovereign. When David says in 22:29 that the Lord is the "lamp" that lights up his darkness, the reader is reminded that in the previous chapter David was referred to by his own warriors as being the "light of Israel" (21:17). A comparison of these two statements suggests that David understood that whatever "light" his life may project is merely a reflected light. He had no "light" to give in and of himself and was "Israel's light" only to the extent that his own life and reign reflected something of the "light of Yahweh." Although Yahweh is not referred to in the Song by the designation "king," his universal divine sovereignty—and David's wholehearted affirmation of it and praise to God for it—is the dominant theme of the chapter.[5] It is striking that this is the same theme that is emphasized in the first text at the heart of the ring structure of 5:17–8:14, which is structurally parallel with the ring structure of the Samuel Conclusion. In 5:13–8:14, the two central texts are 6:1-23 (David Brings the Ark to Jerusalem) and 7:1-29 (The Lord Makes a Covenant with David). The theme of 6:1-23 is David's recognition of the kingship of Yahweh. There David demonstrated his affirmation of Yahweh's sovereignty over the nation by bringing the Ark of the Covenant (the throne seat of Yahweh) to Jerusalem (see commentary on ch 6). The understanding that every human king who sat on the throne in Israel was not autonomous in his authority but acted in the role of a vice-regent of Yahweh was foundational to the way in which the monarchy was intended to function in Israel (see 1 Sam 10:25 and commentary on "the rights and duties of the king").[6] The acceptance or denial of this principle was the clearest distinguishing feature between the reigns of David and Saul.

A question that has drawn much attention in the study of the books of 1–2 Samuel is why the Lord removed Saul from the throne for disobeying the word of the prophet Samuel (1 Sam 13 and 15), when David, who also sinned grievously in the matter of Uriah and Bathsheba, was forgiven for his sin (ch 12) and given a promise that his dynasty would endure forever (ch 7). This thorny question is responded to in a very clear way in this chapter. In 22:21-27 David says two times that the Lord rewarded him for "doing right" (22:21, 25). He claims that he followed all the Lord's "regulations" and never abandoned his "decrees" (22:23), and therefore he was "blameless before God" (22:24). He goes on to say that the Lord shows himself faithful to those who are faithful, and pure to those who are pure, but to the wicked he shows himself hostile (22:26-27). In addition, he says the

Lord rescues the humble, but he humiliates the proud (22:28). These statements occur immediately after David had described in the vivid language of theophany (22:8-16) how the Lord had rescued him from the throes of death (22:5-7, 17-20). The reason why the Lord rescued him is stated in 22:20. It was because the Lord delighted in him. And the reason the Lord delighted in him was because he did right (22:21, 25), he was faithful (22:26), and he was pure (22:27) and humble (22:28) rather than proud (22:28) or wicked (22:27). In the context it seems that David used these categories as a means of drawing a distinction between himself and Saul. The Lord rescued the "humble" (himself), but he "humiliated" the "proud" (Saul). It will be argued below that the rescue of which David speaks is his rescue from the hand of Saul, who had attempted to kill him on numerous occasions (1 Sam 18:11, 25; 19:1, 10, 15; 20:31; 23:7). It will also be argued that David was not claiming anything approaching sinless perfection, nor was he making prideful self-righteous pronouncements; rather, he was humbly saying that, unlike Saul, the general pattern of his life demonstrated that his heart's desire was to walk in the way of covenant faithfulness. So why did the Lord forgive David for his sin, but remove Saul from the throne for his? It was because David repented and sought the Lord's forgiveness when he sinned (12:13; 24:10, 17). In contrast, when Saul sinned he attempted to justify his behavior and did not bow before the Lord and Samuel in true humility and repentance (1 Sam 13 and 15).

The Song in chapter 22 may be divided into four parts: introduction (22:1-4), David's deliverance and the reasons for it (22:5-30), David's victories in battle (22:31-46),[7] and a conclusion (22:47-51). The two major sections within the body of the Song may be further divided as follows: the story of David's deliverance (22:5-19), the reasons for David's deliverance (22:20-30), the equipping and empowering of the king (22:31-37), the victories of the king (22:38-43), and the dominion of the king (22:44-46).[8] It seems likely that the various divisions within the Song reflect something of the chronology of David's life (Ridderbos 1962:189). As was mentioned above, 22:5-19 speaks of David's crying out to the Lord in the face of mortal danger (22:7) and then receiving the Lord's help. This seems to refer to the time when David's life was threatened by Saul. In what follows, David explains why the Lord was pleased to deliver him from Saul (22:20-30). The remainder of the Song refers to David's successes in battle during the course of his reign (22:31-46). In this section, David was careful not to take personal credit for military achievements, but rather to attribute his success to the Lord who equipped him for battle (22:34-37, 40-41) and who gave him the victories (22:44).

There are a number of indicators in the Song that support this understanding of its various parts (Ridderbos 1962:189). First, the language of 22:38-46 clearly reflects situations in which David was king and led Israel into battle. Second, the situation described in 22:20-30, in which David draws a contrast between the humble and the proud and between the righteous and the wicked, appears to reflect an internal Israelite comparison rather than a more universal one (more about this below). Third, there are significant differences in language between the first major section of the Song (22:5-30) and the second major section (22:31-46). In the first major section the enemies are "scattered" and "confused" (22:15), and David is "rescued" from those who hate him (22:18). In the second major section (22:31-46) the enemies are "destroyed" and "conquered" (22:38); they are "subdued" under David's feet (22:40) and "ground . . . as fine as the dust of the earth" (22:43). In the first major section David is in mortal danger and delivered from it, but in the second major section David is active and in control. He is the one before whom "foreign nations cringe" (22:45) and "lose their courage" (22:46). He is the one who became a "ruler over nations" (22:44). Taken together these indicators suggest that the first major section has reference to the time of David's flight from Saul, and the second major section to the time of David's reign.

The first verse of the introduction (22:1) not only identifies David as the author of the Song, it also says that the Song was occasioned by the Lord's deliverance of David from Saul as well as from other enemies. The reference to Saul by name gives good reason to anticipate that David's deliverance from Saul will have a prominent place in what follows. The remainder of the Introduction refers to God with numerous powerful metaphors: rock (22:2-3), fortress (22:2), savior (22:2-3), shield (22:3), power (22:3), place of safety (22:3), and refuge (22:3); it concludes with David's ascription of praise to the Lord for responding to his prayer and delivering him from his enemies (22:4).

In the next section of the Song (22:5-19), David speaks of his deliverances from danger in the dramatic language of rescue from the clutches of death itself (22:5-6). In fear for his life, David cried out to the Lord for help. The Lord heard his prayer and responded to his request (22:7). In 22:8-16, David borrows from the language of theophany to depict the Lord's intervention on his behalf (see Exod 19; Deut 33:2; Judg 5:4-5 for similar language).[9] Although the picture that he draws is surely to be understood figuratively rather than literally, it is nevertheless a majestic portrayal of an awesome and powerful God who has come in anger (22:8) to take up the cause of his anointed one (David refers to himself as the Lord's anointed in 22:51 and the one in whom the Lord delights in 22:20). David used the imagery of earthquake and storm, thunder and lightning, dark clouds and powerful winds, and perhaps even a volcanic eruption (22:13) to convey the overwhelming power of the God who came to his rescue.

In 22:20-30 David proceeds to explain why the Lord delivered him. It is here (especially in 22:21-25) that David makes the surprising statements mentioned above. He argues that he was delivered because he did "right" (22:21a, 25a),[10] because the Lord had seen his "innocence" (22:21b, 25b),[11] because he followed the Lord's "regulations" and never abandoned his "decrees" (22:23), and because he was "blameless before God" and "kept [himself] from sin" (22:24). On its face, these would seem to be preposterous statements from a person who had committed both adultery and murder (ch 11). The reader may wonder how David could possibly make such assertions.[12] For a correct understanding of what David was saying, one must place his statements in the context of what is meant elsewhere in the Old Testament, and particularly in the Psalms and the Wisdom Literature, by the terms "the righteous" and "the wicked." Righteous behavior as grounds for deliverance is a theme that appears not only in this Song of David but also elsewhere in the Old Testament, as, for example, in Psalms 7, 17, and 44 (Kwakkel 2002). The books of Psalms and Proverbs frequently use the categories of "the righteous" and "the wicked" as descriptive of two classes of people.[13] Examination of the way in which these categories are used suggests that all people, and most importantly God's own people, the Israelites, may be divided into these two groups: those who have a way of life characterized by loyalty to Yahweh and those who have "an attitude and behaviour in which Israel's God and his will are ignored" (Kwakkel 2002:298-299). This use of the term "righteous," however, does not mean that the "righteous" are people of moral perfection. They are not sinless, but, as Ridderbos (1962:47) says, they are "people who, whenever they fall into sin, confess their sins, and seek the LORD's forgiveness." Given this background it would appear that what David was claiming in 22:21-25 is that "he has been faithful to Yahweh by respecting his commandments, so that his way of life agreed with what Yahweh could expect from him" (Kwakkel 2002:250). In essence, David was claiming that because his life had been characterized by covenant loyalty and covenant faithfulness, the Lord had been his rescuer and defender. David had these same two categories of people in view in 22:26-28 in which he set those who are the "faithful," the "pure," and the "humble" over against the "wicked" and the "proud." The Lord is hostile to the wicked and humiliates the proud, but he shows himself faithful to those who are faithful to him (22:26), and he rescues the humble (22:28).[14]

It is important to see how this significant section of David's Song connects with what precedes in 1–2 Samuel. Situated in this larger context, it seems clear that the author of the book has placed this psalm of David at this particular point in the Samuel Conclusion in order to call attention to the clear contrast that is to be found between Saul and David. It is from Saul that the Lord had rescued David from mortal danger. Saul had rejected the Lord, and for this reason the Lord had rejected him (1 Sam 15:23, 26). In contrast to Saul, serious sins notwithstanding, David could still legitimately claim to have remained loyal to Yahweh. This is what David means by his statements about "doing right" (22:21, 25) and keeping "the ways of the LORD" (22:22). David's way of life was characterized by a significant degree of faithfulness to the covenant, and this all-important fact set his reign and manner of life apart from that of Saul in clearly discernable ways.[15] When David, for example, says that he is "blameless before God" (22:24), this is not to be understood as a claim of moral perfection, but rather as a claim of covenant faithfulness.[16] Kwakkel (2002:247) calls attention to the statement by Moses in Deuteronomy 18:13 that the Israelites are to "be blameless before the LORD [their] God" (the expression in the Hebrew text is the same as in 22:24) and points out that in its context "it implies that one does not engage in divination, sorcery, witchcraft and the like (see Deut 18:10-12, 14), but, on the contrary, that one gives evidence of loyalty to Yahweh by listening to what he will reveal about the future through the word of his prophets (see Deut 18:15-19)." The nuances of this expression in Deuteronomy 18:13 have particular relevance to the contrast between David and Saul because Saul did engage in witchcraft and he did not listen to the words of Samuel the prophet, while the Old Testament contains no record of David ever engaging in false worship and provides numerous examples of his responding obediently to the instructions and corrections of the prophets whom the Lord sent his way. Even if one might justifiably question whether the nuances of being "blameless" in 22:24 are exactly the same as those in Deuteronomy 18:13, given their different contexts, it would still seem legitimate to conclude, as does Kwakkel (2002:147), that being blameless "was evidently related to the acceptance of [Yahweh's] commandments as the decisive directive for his life (cf. 22:23)."[17] David could legitimately make this claim; Saul could not.

A secondary issue that surfaces in connection with David's obedience as contrasted with Saul's disobedience is that of whether or not David's obedience merited divine favor in the same way that Saul's disobedience merited God's judgment. Here it is clear that there is a difference. Although Saul's disobedience certainly merited the judgment he received, David's obedience was far from perfect and therefore incapable of meriting God's favor.[18] But recognizing this does not mean that David's obedience was unimportant or of no significance. There are a number of texts pertaining to both the Abrahamic and Davidic covenants that suggest God took Abraham's and David's obedience up into the promulgation of the promises he gave to them, not in the sense of efficient cause or meritorious reward, but in the sense of a divinely ordained means of the administration of promise. It was God who was at work in both Abraham and David to will and to do his good pleasure, so their obedience was the fruit of the grace of God operative in their lives.[19] Their obedience, therefore, although not meriting the reward of the promise, was nevertheless integrally bound up with the administration of the promise. God's choice of Abraham and David as instruments of his redemptive purposes did not preclude their response of faith and obedience in the sense of obviating their importance, but rather included them as an inevitable accompaniment of the working of divine grace in their lives. This means, of course, that ultimately David's favor with Yahweh rested in Yahweh's sovereign choice of David to be "a man after his own heart" (1 Sam 13:14). As Long puts it (1993a:170), "The distinction between Saul and David, between a rejected king and an accepted one, is not that one is a sinner and the other is not, for both are sinners. Rather, the distinction lies in the very different attitudes to faith and repentance displayed by the two and, at a deeper level still, in the sovereign election of the one, the 'man of God's own choosing' (1 Sam 13:14), over the other."[20]

The final major section of the Song (22:32-46) celebrates David's victories over enemy nations. David begins this section by posing a rhetorical question: "For who is God except the LORD?" (22:32). The expected answer, of course, is "No one." Yahweh is the one and only true God, and Yahweh is the God in whom both David and Israel have put their trust. Because the gods of the heathen nations are nonexistent, they are useless. This leads into David's use of two metaphors for the protection and safety that he found by putting his trust in Yahweh whom he describes as a "solid rock" and a "strong fortress" (22:32b-33a). In the following verses David attributes all of his military successes to the Lord, who had given him the qualities and skills necessary to defeat his and Israel's enemies (22:33b-44). It was the Lord who trained his hands for battle (22:35a), who strengthened his arm "to draw a bronze bow" (22:35b), whose help had made him great (22:36b), and who armed him with "strength for the battle" (22:40a). By these statements David claimed no glory for himself for the military successes of his reign, but instead praised the Lord, who had subdued his enemies under his feet (22:40b) and who alone was worthy of praise.[21] In the final analysis it was the Lord alone who had preserved him as the ruler over nations so that people he did not know now served him (22:44).

This leads to the rousing exclamation of praise that introduces the conclusion (22:47-51) to the Song: "The LORD lives! Praise to my Rock! May God, the Rock of my salvation, be exalted!" (22:47). In the remaining four verses, David summarizes the central theme of the entire Song by repeating that it was the Lord who had brought down the nations under him (22:48b) and who had given him "great victories" (22:51). For this David says he will praise the Lord among the nations and sing praises to the name of the Lord (22:50). The Song ends with David's acknowledgment that he is a vice-regent of Yahweh (he refers to himself as "your [Yahweh's] king"), and the one who is "your [Yahweh's] anointed." Because of this the Lord will show him and his descendants his "unfailing love" forever (22:51). With this final statement David shifts the focus from how the Lord had sustained him during the course of his own reign to the long-term implications of the Lord's promise to him that his dynasty would endure forever. This statement serves as a transition to "David's last words" that immediately follow in 23:1-7, and it anticipates the rise of messianic expectation in Israel that was linked with his royal line.

As a final comment on this Song and its significance for the entirety of 1–2 Samuel, it should be noted that David's Song in Praise of God's Reign (22:1-51), along with David's Last Words about His Reign (23:1-7), and Hannah's Song (1 Sam 2:1-10) at the beginning of the book, give expression to the theological themes that govern all of 1–2 Samuel (see "Literary Style" in the Introduction). While many of the narrative units in the body of the book leave the reader with no explicit theological or ethical evaluation of the episodes of this period of Israel's history, here in these songs the reader is told that "Yahweh is behind all events, both successes and failures; Yahweh supports and rewards the faithful; Yahweh supports the Davidic king" (Watts 1992a:38). While Hannah's Song anticipates the establishment of kingship in Israel (1 Sam 2:10), David's Song celebrates both its realization and the remarkable promise associated with his own reign as the Lord's anointed one. It is these broad theological perspectives that provide the reader with the lens through which the narrative material of 1–2 Samuel is to be read.

ENDNOTES

1. Usually identified as a "royal song of thanksgiving."
2. Although David's authorship of this psalm, and its slightly different but parallel text in Ps 18, is generally accepted by scholars in the conservative tradition of biblical scholarship, this is the exception rather than the rule among scholars in the mainstream of biblical studies. Among nonevangelical scholars, both Weiser (1962) and Hertzberg (1964) are open to Davidic authorship. Weiser (1962:186) comments that the Song "does not contain anything which would exclude the possibility that it was composed at the time of David." After considering various possible objections to this statement, he draws the following conclusion: "We shall therefore have to reckon with the possibility that the psalm was composed by David or, as the stereotyped forms of the liturgical 'court-style' suggest . . . by a poet of his court." Hertzberg

(1964:392-393) says, "In view of the parallels from the Babylonian and Egyptian environments there is nothing against the assumption that the custom of using such a psalm belonged to the earliest period of the monarchy, i.e. to the time of David himself. It is beyond dispute that David was a poet. It is hard to deny that he wrote psalms; had he not done so, the attribution of so many psalms to him would be incomprehensible. This particular psalm belongs to the narrower circle of those which might possibly be of Davidic authorship." Alter (1999:336) is less sanguine about Davidic authorship, and says that "the idea that he actually composed this poem, though unlikely, cannot be categorically dismissed." Both A. Anderson (1989:261-262) and McCarter (1984:474-475) challenge Davidic authorship and opt for later dates. A. Anderson thinks that a Deuteronomist editor combined two earlier poems (now found as 22:2-20 and 29-51ab) and added connecting material (22:21-28) so that "the psalm in its present form cannot be earlier than the seventh century B.C." McCarter draws a similar conclusion. On the basis of the identification of "archaic elements of language, theme, and prosody throughout the poem" by Cross and Freedman (1953), he is open to the possibility that the two "major parts of the psalm may have been composed as early as the time of David," but he regards the psalm in its present form as "a product of the seventh century or later."

Although the points of difference between ch 22 and Ps 18 are of minor importance, the historical and textual relationship between the two texts has provoked much discussion. See Keil (1956:468-469) for a summary of the most significant differences between the two texts and for his own assessment of the reasons for them. It is Keil's opinion that "the text of the Psalms bears the stamp of poetical originality more than the text before us [ch 22], and the latter indicates a desire to give greater clearness and simplicity to the poetical style. Consequently neither of the two texts that have come down to us contains the original text of the psalm of David unaltered; but the two recensions have been made quite independently of each other, one for the insertion of the psalm in the Psalter intended for liturgical use, and the other when it was incorporated into the history of David's reign, which formed the groundwork of our books of Samuel. The first revision may have been made by David himself when he arranged his Psalms for liturgical purposes; but the second was effected by the prophetic historian, whose object it was, when inserting David's psalm of praise in the history of his reign, not so much to give it with diplomatic literality, as to introduce it in a form that should be easily intelligible and true to the sense." For further discussion of the relationship between Ps 18 and ch 22, see Berry 1993; Chisholm 1983; Cross and Freedman 1953; and Watts 1992b.

3. As Watts (1992b:108-109) notes, this psalm "serves as a theological commentary on David's life" and in doing so it characterizes David "as Yahweh's favorite and Israel's ideal king."
4. Klement (2000:198) argues that the "two poetic pieces in 2 Sam 22 and 23:1-7 which are placed by the ring-structure into the centre appear to be of prime importance in determining both the theological tendency of the chiastically structured unit of the concluding chapters and also the intention of the literary structure of the whole book. Both texts have as their central theme the relationship of the Davidic kingdom to Yahweh, or the attitude of Yahweh towards the Davidic dynasty."
5. Watts (1992b:104) comments that "the psalm makes explicit the divine causality behind all of David's successes and focuses attention on Yahweh as the primary subject of the Samuel narratives." Brueggemann (1990a:344) comments that the Song "gladly celebrates David as the great warrior and deliverer. But David is celebrated only penultimately. Israel knows that not David but Yahweh is the deliverer and

rescuer who wins battles. The psalm, which seems to assert the significance of the king, in the end qualifies the significance of the king and refuses to give the king excessive credit or stature. . . . It is Yahweh, only Yahweh, who is sovereign in Israel, among the nations, and in all creation." While Brueggemann is certainly correct in his assessment that the Song asserts that only Yahweh is sovereign, this is quite different from his claim that the purpose of the Song is to subvert the royal ideology of David's court. Here Brueggemann mistakenly assumes that the royal ideology of David's court excluded recognition of the supremacy of Yahweh over the king and the nation.

6. Eaton (1976:135) argues that the connection between divine kingship and human kingship is of "all-pervading importance" in the "royal psalms." He comments, "The Davidic king is considered to serve within the sphere of God's own kingship. God remains the active king of all, not least of the community centered at Jerusalem; Davidic rule is his instrument. This view of a single kingdom, which is God's, dominates the psalms relating to the king's ordination, 2 and 110. The imagined rebellion is against a dominion exercised jointly by 'Yahweh and his anointed' (2:2). The king is to take the throne beside Yahweh, who will crush opposition to this joint sovereignty (110:1, 5; 2:12)."
7. Weiser (1962:187) says, "Like the two spires of a cathedral the two parts of the mighty hymn soar to heaven, a hymn of praise to the glory of God." Contrary to some interpreters, Weiser sees the Song as an original unity and says, "Though each of the psalm's two parts has a character of its own appropriate to its special subject-matter, yet it is only when they are viewed as a unity that they produce the full effect of a perfect testimony to the majestic power of the Living God and to the unimpaired trust of the royal singer, who is sure of his blessings and rejoices in them."
8. Because the various sections of the psalm flow together smoothly, it is difficult to draw hard and fast lines between the various sections.
9. For a thorough and useful study of theophanies in the OT, as well as the similarities and differences between Egyptian, Hittite, Mesopotamian, and Canaanite theophanies and the biblical tradition, see Niehaus 1995.
10. A literal translation of this line is "The Lord rewarded me according to my righteousness."
11. A literal translation is "According to the cleanness of my hands he recompensed me."
12. Eerdmans (1947:160) questions the Davidic origin of the psalm on this basis. He comments, "The conclusion of the scribes, who assigned the psalm to David, therefore appears to be unjustified. . . . The protestation of righteousness and innocence in 22:21-25 is contradictory with David's confession of sin in 2 Sam. xii." More recently some scholars have suggested that these statements are not original to David but were inserted by an editor reflecting the Deuteronomistic theology of the seventh century or later (A. Anderson 1989:261-262; McCarter 1984:475). Others have attempted to alleviate the alleged problem by suggesting that the statements speak of David's life prior to the Uriah/Bathsheba incident (see Kirkpatrick 1901:85-86, which reads, "The free and joyous tone of the psalm, and its bold assertions of integrity, point to a time before his sin with Bath-sheba and Absalom's rebellion"). But placing the Song prior to the time of the Uriah/Bathsheba incident does not fit with David's statement introducing the Song that says it celebrates his deliverance from "all his enemies" (22:1), because at the time of the Uriah/Bathsheba incident he was still fighting the Ammonites (11:1) and 22:44-46 goes on to speak of David's victories over numerous other foreign nations. Still others have suggested that the Song provides an "idealized picture" of David, such as that found in 1 and 2 Chronicles, which contrasts with the David of real life (Carlson 1964:253, 257; Watts 1992b:108-109). It is, then, this "idealized" David that is used in the narratives of 1 and 2 Kings to critique the

reigns of David's successors. This idea, however, founders on the reality that whoever was responsible for the final form of 1–2 Samuel did not eliminate ch 11 (the David/Bathsheba/Uriah incident) and its aftermath, as well as other unflattering incidents in David's life from the picture of David that is drawn in the whole of 1–2 Samuel as one might expect if the author/editor's purpose was to portray David as the ideal king.

13. Kwakkel (2002:298) lists Pss 1; 11:2-3, 5-6; 31:17-18 [18-19]; 32:10-11; 34:15-22 [16-23]; 37:12, 16-17, 21, 28-32, 34-40; 58:9-10 [10-11]; 68:2-3 [3-4]; 75:10 [11]; 92:7 [8], 12 [13]; 97:10-12; 112:6, 10; 140:4 [5], 8 [9], 12 [13]; 141:5, 10; 146:8-9 and Prov 2:20-22; 3:33; 4:18-19; 9:7-9; 10:3, 6-7, 11; 11:8, 23; 12:5, 7, 21; 13:5, 9, 25; 14:19, 32; 15:6, 8, 28-29; 24:15-16; 28:1, 12, 28; 29:2, 7, 16, 27.
14. This is a general principle expressed elsewhere in Scripture (Ps 28; Prov 3:34; Ezek 18:23ff; Jas 4:6; 1 Pet 5:5).
15. Watts (1992b:105-106) notes the verbal links between David's claim of "doing right" (lit., "my righteousness") in 22:21 and 25 and David's statement to Saul in 1 Sam 26:23 that "the LORD gives his own reward for *doing good*" (NLT; lit., "The LORD repays each man for his *righteousness*"), as well as Saul's acknowledgment in 1 Sam 24:17 that David is "a better man than I am, for you have repaid me good for evil" (NLT; lit., "You are more *righteous* than I because you have treated me well even though I have treated you wrongly"). Watts then concludes, "The psalm's language thus combines with the reference to Saul in the superscription to evoke the period of David's flight from Saul as the experience reflected in the first part of the psalm. The effect of the psalm is to transform the literal language of the narratives into metaphors of Yahweh's protection of David and to make explicitly clear that it was not the accidents of geography and war but rather God's relationship with David which brought him to the throne of Israel." One might also note Jonathan's positive statements about David to his father, Saul, in 1 Sam 19:4 and Abigail's statement to David in 1 Sam 25:28 that he had "not done wrong throughout [his] entire life." In addition, the Lord himself characterizes David's life as one that was marked by obedience to his commands in 1 Kgs 3:14; 9:4; 11:33-34, 38; 14:8.
16. When David says in 22:24b that he has "kept [himself] from sin," Calvin (1979a:283) comments that the "verb he uses does not denote one fall only, but a defection which utterly removes and alienates a man from God. David, it is true, sometimes fell into sin through the weakness of the flesh, but he never desisted from following after godliness, nor deserted the service to which God had called him." Brueggemann reads the statements in 22:21-28 quite differently, however, and claims that the assertions of these verses are clearly in conflict with David's life. In this connection it should be noted that Brueggemann does not accept the Davidic authorship of the Song but instead views it as words that are placed in David's mouth. He says (1990a:339), "The shapers of Samuel have taken a well-known liturgical piece and placed it here as a concluding theological reflection on the life and faith of David." So Brueggemann (1990c:96) contends that David's life (particularly the David/Bathsheba incident) makes it clear that "David is not marked by *tsedaqah* [TH6666, ZH7407] (righteousness) and is not *tamim* [TH8549, ZH9459] (perfect)." This in turn means for Bruegemann that 22:21-28 must be read "ironically" (1990c:97) with the result that the Song "debunks the very royal claims of David it seems to celebrate" (2000a:344). So Brueggemann (1988:389) says that "the middle section [of the Song] does not celebrate this king, but in fact indicts him and shows how the life-realities of David require a God who hears and acts freely." While Brueggemann is certainly correct in concluding that David's sin required the free, gracious response of God's forgiveness, it is not so clear

that 22:21-28 "indict" David rather than vindicate him when they are placed in the context of the broader contours of David's life of faithfulness to the covenant.

17. Borgman (2008:216) comments that some regard "David's claim of blamelessness so incongruous in light of the whole story as to suggest an obvious and quite awkward gloss by a writer supporting royal ideology with an eye blind to David's abuses of royal prerogative, to his wrongdoing. But David's claim is a *tamim* that is defined as being completely tuned to, and dependent on, God. This state of *tamim*, of being without fault, is not only the condition of having had his sin put away by God, but an orientation of David to God that is completely loyal. Proper response to wrongdoing—penitence and steadfast loyalty—moves God to put away the penitent's wrongdoing, together with the incurred guilt. That is, all is in order between David and God."
18. For further discussion see NIDOTTE 4.1140-1149 on the "Theology of Retribution" in the OT.
19. Calvin (1979a:280-281) says, "When the Scripture uses the word *reward* or *recompense*, it is not to show that God owes us anything, and it is therefore a groundless and false conclusion to infer from this that there is any merit or worth in works. God, as a just judge, rewards every man according to his works, but he does it in such a manner as to show that all men are indebted to him, while he himself is under obligation to no one. The reason is not only that which St. Augustine has assigned, namely, that God finds no righteousness in us to recompense, except what he himself has freely given us, but also because, forgiving the blemishes and imperfections which cleave to our works, he imputes to us for righteousness that which he might justly reject. If, therefore, none of our works please God, unless the sin which mingles with them is pardoned, it follows, that the recompense which he bestows on account of them proceeds not from our merit, but from his free and undeserved grace."
20. See further endnote 4 in the commentary on 1 Sam 13:1-15.
21. Eaton (1976:138), in a discussion of psalms that glorify the king, says that even in such psalms the king "is not often pictured as himself active in conquering his enemies, and when he is so depicted the point is that God empowers him. The most vivid example is [Ps] 18:29-51, where the king appears as a marvelously skilled and potent warrior, fighting on foot with wonderful agility, a deadly archer, routing and pursuing his foes single-handed; clearly the passage testifies to God who has 'lit his lamp,' dressed him in might, guided his feet, trained his hands, shielded and upheld him (and similarly 144:1f)."

◆ D. David's Last Words about His Reign (2 Sam 23:1-7)

These are the last words of David:

"David, the son of Jesse, speaks—
David, the man who was raised up so high,
David, the man anointed by the God of Jacob,
David, the sweet psalmist of Israel.*

2 "The Spirit of the LORD speaks through me;
his words are upon my tongue.
3 The God of Israel spoke.
The Rock of Israel said to me:
'The one who rules righteously,
who rules in the fear of God,
4 is like the light of morning at sunrise,
like a morning without clouds,
like the gleaming of the sun
on new grass after rain.'

5 "Is it not my family God has chosen?
Yes, he has made an everlasting covenant with me.

His agreement is arranged and
guaranteed in every detail.
He will ensure my safety and
success.
6 But the godless are like thorns
to be thrown away,
for they tear the hand that
touches them.
7 One must use iron tools to chop
them down;
they will be totally consumed
by fire."

23:1 Or *the favorite subject of the songs of Israel;* or *the favorite of the Strong One of Israel.*

NOTES

23:1 *who was raised up so high.* This follows the reading of the MT, *huqam 'al* [TH6965/5920, ZH7756/6583] (*'al* taken as a substantive for "height"). 4QSam[a] reads *heqim 'el* [TH6965/410, ZH7756/446] (the man whom God raised up) with *'el* read as "God." It should be noted, however, that some have argued that *'al* (the MT reading) may also be used as a divine name cognate to *'elyon* [TH5945B, ZH6610] and also meaning "Most High" in several OT poetic passages as well as elsewhere in the ancient Near East with the resulting translation, "the oracle of the man exalted by the Most High" (Youngblood 1992:1080-1081). While it is difficult to choose which of these readings is preferable (i.e., original), they all speak of David's elevation to the throne.

David, the sweet psalmist of Israel. See NLT mg for alternate translations. The translation of this phrase is difficult and uncertain. The "sweet psalmist of Israel" is the traditional rendering, and is based on *ne'im* [TH5273A, ZH5834] (NLT, "sweet") having a musical connotation. Others have suggested that the following word *zemiroth* [TH2158, ZH2369] is derived from a root *zamar* meaning "be strong," and translate the phrase as "the favorite of the Strong One of Israel" (cf. A. Anderson 1989:266-268; McCarter 1984:476; NRSV).

23:4 *without.* On the use of *lo'* [TH3808, ZH4202] (no, not) in the sense of "without," see Joüon and Muraoka §160o.

23:5 *Is it not my family God has chosen? . . . He will ensure my safety and success.* The NLT takes *ki-lo'* [TH3588/3808, ZH3954/4202] as having an asseverative force and translates its two occurrences in the verse in a positive rather than in an interrogative sense (A. Anderson 1989:266-269, and others he cites). Some translations take *ki-lo'* as introducing a negative rhetorical question (NIV, "Is not my house right with God? . . . Will he not bring to fruition my salvation . . . ?").

23:6 *godless.* The Hebrew word translated "godless" is *beliya'al* [TH1100, ZH1175] (see note on 1 Sam 1:16).

23:7 *One must use.* Lit., "be filled"; the idea is to be armed or filled in the sense of having a weapon in one's hand.

they will be totally consumed by fire. The MT adds "on the spot" (lit., "in the sitting," i.e., in the same place).

COMMENTARY

In this short poem of seven verses that has come to be known as "David's Last Words" (taken from the superscription, 23:1a),[1] David acknowledges the honor and responsibility of the unique position in which the Lord has placed him and his family by virtue of choosing him as the anointed king (23:1) and giving him the astounding promise that his dynasty would endure forever (23:5). While in the preceding Song (ch 22) the focus was on David's acknowledgment of Yahweh as both his and Israel's ultimate sovereign, in this poem the focus is on the responsibilities of David and his descendants as rulers over God's chosen people. As was mentioned in the Introduction (see "Literary Style"), 23:1-7 is the second of the two poetic units placed at the center of the ring structure of the Samuel Conclusion that draw together the themes of the entirety of 1–2 Samuel. As was also pointed out in the Introduction (as well as in the commentary on ch 22), there is a parallel between the ring structure of 5:13–8:14 and the ring structure of the Samuel Conclusion (chs 21–24). The two units at the heart of these two ring structures display a remarkable correlation in emphasis. By bringing the Ark of the Covenant to Jerusalem (6:1-23), David publicly acknowledged Yahweh as the ultimate ruler over himself and the nation. This emphasis is mirrored in chapter 22, the first of the two poems placed at the heart of the ring structure of the Samuel Conclusion. The second unit at the heart of the ring structure of 5:13–8:14 is a description of the promise Yahweh gave to David that his dynasty would endure forever (7:1-29). This emphasis on the role of David and his descendants as the divinely appointed rulers of God's people is mirrored in David's last words (23:1-7). So here at the heart of the Samuel Conclusion, David addresses the question of how both human kingship and divine kingship may be affirmed and celebrated without inherent compromise or contradiction.

David began the poem with a fourfold self-description (23:1b; he is "the son of Jesse," he was "raised up so high," he was "anointed by . . . God," and he was "the sweet psalmist of Israel"). The first three of these designations are similar in their basic thrust to the overall theme of David's Song in the previous chapter. David was nothing in himself. Although he was the youngest son of an obscure individual from Bethlehem (Jesse),[2] he had been chosen by God to be lifted up and anointed as king.[3] David's prominence and success are attributable only to God's sovereign decision to place him on the throne in Israel, and then to equip and sustain him in the responsibilities of his office. The fourth designation ("the sweet psalmist of Israel") provides a transition to the important statement David makes in 23:2b that the Lord not only had anointed him to be king but had also endowed him with the function of a prophet. David was the "sweet psalmist of Israel" because the Spirit of the Lord spoke through him. Although David did not use the term "prophet," the assertion of 23:2 is one of the classic statements on the essence of the prophetic function to be found in the Old Testament (cf. Acts 2:30). It closely parallels the idea found in Deuteronomy 18:18 and Jeremiah 1:5, 9 regarding God's placing his words in his prophet's mouth. Although David's psalms give us glimpses into a wide range of his own personal spiritual experiences, their formulation was so guided by God's Spirit that they have also become an "enduring articulation of the piety of the community which experiences God's merciful judgment and judging mercy, which experiences, in short, growth in repentance, forgiveness, regeneration" (Willis-Watkins 1989:120).

In 23:3-4, David gives the reader God's own definition of a true covenantal king. This is a king who "rules righteously" and a king who "rules in the fear of God." On the horizontal plane of the relationship between the king and the people, it was the king's responsibility to guarantee the administration of justice throughout his domain. On the vertical plane of the relationship between the king and God, his rule was to be carried out "in the fear of God." As Klement says (2000:220), "Fear of God and justice are understood as related and mutually dependent: it is only the one who fears God who can be a just ruler, and it is impossible for someone who is not prepared to fear God to be a just ruler."[4] Kings whose reigns conform to these two essential requirements are then described in 23:4 with two similes that compare the blessings of the reign of the true covenantal king with the magnificence of the rising sun and the vitalizing effect of rain. This is contrasted in 23:6-7 with "godless" rulers who are compared to "thorns" that are good for nothing but to "be totally consumed by fire." While in the preceding Song David argued that the righteous pattern of his personal life (22:21, 25; NLT, "doing right") was the reason the Lord had delivered him from Saul (see commentary there), here in 23:3-4 it seems that the specific focus of God's statement is on the righteous character of the king's royal administration. In this public role, just as in his private life, David lived up to the requirements of the ideal of the covenantal king in a true, albeit imperfect, manner.[5] Earlier in the book the writer has given the reader a concise evaluative summary of David's reign (8:15; see commentary) by saying that he "reigned over all Israel and did what was just and right for all his people." Contrary to the positions taken today by many American politicians and political pundits on ethical standards for public officials, the divinely given requirements for the true covenantal king allowed for no separation between personal ethics and public ethics—the true covenantal king was expected to display righteous behavior in both his private and his public life.

The divinely given description of the contrast between rulers who govern "righteously" in the "fear of God" (23:3-4) and godless rulers who are depicted as "thorns" that will be "consumed by fire" (23:6-7) is broken at its midpoint where David responds in amazement with a description of the promise God had given him and his descendants (23:5, see note). It is clear that David discerned a connection between the characteristics of the ideal king described in 23:3-4 and God's promise to him and his family. David makes no claim to have in any way merited God's favor, but he aligns himself with those "who rule righteously" rather than with the "godless." He then expresses his incredulity at the enormousness of the implications of the promise he and his family had received. David was clearly humbled by God's gracious condescension to honor him in such a remarkable way. His response here is similar to his response at the time Nathan had originally conveyed the promise to him (see 7:18-19; 1 Chr 17:16-17). But here David uses a new descriptor, calling the promise an "everlasting covenant" that is "arranged and guaranteed in every detail" (the term "covenant" was not used in ch 7 to designate the Lord's promise, but it does appear in Ps 89:3, 28, 34, 39, while Ps 132:11 speaks of it as an "oath" that the Lord "will never take back"). There is no possibility that the promise to David would fail to be fulfilled. And David understood that the realization of the promise carried far-reaching implications for the future of the nation as well as for the future of his house. The Davidic dynasty was the human instrument through which God would exercise his rule over his people. God remains the ultimate sovereign over his people (ch 22), but from this point forward the house of David would be at center stage in the administration of the divine rule. This promise, of course, has messianic implications.[6] In the end, it would be the ruler from the line of David (Luke 1:31-33; Rom 1:3) who would remove the tension between the reign of God and the reign of the Davidic king, because this great ruler would be both God and man in one person.[7]

ENDNOTES

1. The designation "the last words of David" does not mean that David spoke these words on his deathbed. In context it is more reasonable to say, as does Van Groningen (1990:305), that these are David's "last words as an inspired poet" (23:1b-2a)—that is, this was the last of the inspired songs composed by David. In this connection it should be noted that 1 Kgs 2:2-9 contains David's deathbed charge to Solomon. Scholars differ on the authorship and date of the poem in 23:1-7. Many have accepted its claim to Davidic authorship in 23:1 as authentic (cf. Hertzberg 1964:400). According to Cross (1973:234), "Archaic elements suggest a tenth century date. Whether it is to be assigned to David himself or to a later poet setting forth the covenant ideology attributed to David is difficult to decide." McCarter (1984:484) asserts that "its traditional assignment to David is by no means impossible." He then responds in a detailed way to arguments of scholars such as Budde, Mettinger, Mowinckel, Nowack, and H. P. Smith, who have argued for a later date running from the "time of Solomon" to the "late years of the monarchy."
2. When Samuel was sent to the home of Jesse in Bethlehem to anoint one of his sons as the person whom the Lord had chosen to replace Saul on the throne, even David's father, Jesse, did not think David merited presentation to Samuel. Jesse sent for David only after Samuel inquired if he had any other sons (1 Sam 16:11-12).
3. This coincides with one of the primary themes of Hannah's Song at the beginning of 1–2 Samuel, namely that God often sovereignly brings about a reversal of status in the affairs of individuals and nations.
4. Fokkelman's (1990:359) translation of 23:3b is "He who governs the people righteously, governs in awe of God," but he suggests that the phrases may also be translated jussively as "he who wishes to be a ruler of integrity must ever proceed in the fear of God" or "he who wishes to govern with integrity can succeed in this only if . . ." In other words, in order to rule "righteously" one must rule "in the fear of God."
5. It is here again that Brueggemann's (1988; 1990a; 1990b) attempt to read the entirety of the Samuel Conclusion as a "deconstruction" of "the high royal theology" of chs 5–8 fails to convince. He says (1990a:98-99) that the "role of the king . . . is premised on *tsaddiq*" [TH6662, ZH7404] (ruling righteously) and that this means that the covenant is not everlasting, but rather "for as long as the rule of the king is just and power is administered covenantally." But surely Brueggemann has not given sufficient attention to the messianic implications of these statements; David and his successors could only fulfill the requirements in an imperfect manner at best, and this inherent weakness points to a messianic fulfillment in the future when there will be a descendant of David who rules in a manner that perfectly fulfills the demands of the true covenantal king. While this may "deconstruct" the "high royal theology" to the extent that it recognizes that the picture that is drawn of David in the Samuel narratives is not a picture of someone who perfectly fulfilled the ideal of the true covenantal king, it is, nevertheless, a picture of someone who measured up to this ideal in a way that no other king of Israel ever did prior to the Messiah.
6. As Van Groningen (1990:308) notes, the "one who rules righteously" and "in the fear of God" (23:3b) proclaims the "ideal for which each representative [of the house of David] must strive, but will be achieved only by the promised royal eternal Ruler."
7. It is certainly understandable that the Targum of Jonathan (an Aramaic paraphrase of the Hebrew text that reflects ancient Jewish exegesis) interprets "David's Last Words" as a messianic prophecy. See Kirkpatrick (1919:237) for a translation of the Targum's rendering of 23:1-7, which, for example, speaks of "the Messiah, who shall arise and rule in the fear of Jehovah" (23:3).

E. List of Warriors (2 Sam 23:8-39)

8 These are the names of David's mightiest warriors. The first was Jashobeam the Hacmonite,* who was leader of the Three*—the three mightiest warriors among David's men. He once used his spear to kill 800 enemy warriors in a single battle.*

9 Next in rank among the Three was Eleazar son of Dodai, a descendant of Ahoah. Once Eleazar and David stood together against the Philistines when the entire Israelite army had fled. 10 He killed Philistines until his hand was too tired to lift his sword, and the LORD gave him a great victory that day. The rest of the army did not return until it was time to collect the plunder!

11 Next in rank was Shammah son of Agee from Harar. One time the Philistines gathered at Lehi and attacked the Israelites in a field full of lentils. The Israelite army fled, 12 but Shammah* held his ground in the middle of the field and beat back the Philistines. So the LORD brought about a great victory.

13 Once during the harvest, when David was at the cave of Adullam, the Philistine army was camped in the valley of Rephaim. The Three (who were among the Thirty—an elite group among David's fighting men) went down to meet him there. 14 David was staying in the stronghold at the time, and a Philistine detachment had occupied the town of Bethlehem.

15 David remarked longingly to his men, "Oh, how I would love some of that good water from the well by the gate in Bethlehem." 16 So the Three broke through the Philistine lines, drew some water from the well by the gate in Bethlehem, and brought it back to David. But he refused to drink it. Instead, he poured it out as an offering to the LORD. 17 "The LORD forbid that I should drink this!" he exclaimed. "This water is as precious as the blood of these men* who risked their lives to bring it to me." So David did not drink it. These are examples of the exploits of the Three.

18 Abishai son of Zeruiah, the brother of Joab, was the leader of the Thirty.* He once used his spear to kill 300 enemy warriors in a single battle. It was by such feats that he became as famous as the Three. 19 Abishai was the most famous of the Thirty* and was their commander, though he was not one of the Three.

20 There was also Benaiah son of Jehoiada, a valiant warrior* from Kabzeel. He did many heroic deeds, which included killing two champions* of Moab. Another time, on a snowy day, he chased a lion down into a pit and killed it. 21 Once, armed only with a club, he killed a great Egyptian warrior who was armed with a spear. Benaiah wrenched the spear from the Egyptian's hand and killed him with it. 22 Deeds like these made Benaiah as famous as the Three mightiest warriors. 23 He was more honored than the other members of the Thirty, though he was not one of the Three. And David made him captain of his bodyguard.

24 Other members of the Thirty included:

Asahel, Joab's brother;
Elhanan son of Dodo from Bethlehem;
25 Shammah from Harod;
Elika from Harod;
26 Helez from Pelon*;
Ira son of Ikkesh from Tekoa;
27 Abiezer from Anathoth;
Sibbecai* from Hushah;
28 Zalmon from Ahoah;
Maharai from Netophah;
29 Heled* son of Baanah from Netophah;
Ithai* son of Ribai from Gibeah (in the land of Benjamin);
30 Benaiah from Pirathon;
Hurai* from Nahale-gaash*;
31 Abi-albon from Arabah;
Azmaveth from Bahurim;
32 Eliahba from Shaalbon;
the sons of Jashen;
Jonathan 33 son of Shagee* from Harar;
Ahiam son of Sharar from Harar;

[34] Eliphelet son of Ahasbai from Maacah;
Eliam son of Ahithophel from Giloh;
[35] Hezro from Carmel;
Paarai from Arba;
[36] Igal son of Nathan from Zobah;
Bani from Gad;
[37] Zelek from Ammon;
Naharai from Beeroth, Joab's
armor bearer;
[38] Ira from Jattir;
Gareb from Jattir;
[39] Uriah the Hittite.

There were thirty-seven in all.

23:8a As in parallel text at 1 Chr 11:11; Hebrew reads *Josheb-basshebeth the Tahkemonite.* **23:8b** As in Greek and Latin versions (see also 1 Chr 11:11); the meaning of the Hebrew is uncertain. **23:8c** As in some Greek manuscripts (see also 1 Chr 11:11); the meaning of the Hebrew is uncertain, though it might be rendered *the Three. It was Adino the Eznite who killed 800 men at one time.* **23:12** Hebrew *he.* **23:17** Hebrew *Shall I drink the blood of these men?* **23:18** As in a few Hebrew manuscripts and Syriac version; most Hebrew manuscripts read *the Three.* **23:19** As in Syriac version; Hebrew reads *the Three.* **23:20a** Or *son of Jehoiada, son of Ish-hai.* **23:20b** Hebrew *two of Ariel.* **23:26** As in parallel text at 1 Chr 11:27 (see also 1 Chr 27:10); Hebrew reads *from Palti.* **23:27** As in some Greek manuscripts (see also 1 Chr 11:29); Hebrew reads *Mebunnai.* **23:29a** As in some Hebrew manuscripts (see also 1 Chr 11:30); most Hebrew manuscripts read *Heleb.* **23:29b** As in parallel text at 1 Chr 11:31; Hebrew reads *Ittai.* **23:30a** As in some Greek manuscripts (see also 1 Chr 11:32); Hebrew reads *Hiddai.* **23:30b** Or *from the ravines of Gaash.* **23:33** As in parallel text at 1 Chr 11:34; Hebrew reads *Jonathan, Shammah;* some Greek manuscripts read *Jonathan son of Shammah.*

NOTES

23:8 *Three.* The MT's *hashalishi* is anomalous (see NLT mg). The reading "three" (*shalosh* [TH7969, ZH8993]) with Lucianic mss of the LXX seems likely because of similar references in 23:9 and 23:23 (but cf. 1 Chr 11:11). Another possible translation is "the chief officer" (taking the preceding *ro'sh* [TH7218, ZH8031] as "chief" instead of as "leader" and the *hashalishi* as *shalish*). Gordon (1986:312) notes correctly that the form in MT hovers between "third" (*shelishi* [TH7992, ZH8958]) and "captain" (*shalish* [TH7991B, ZH8957]).

23:11 *at Lehi.* The NLT follows numerous interpreters (A. Anderson 1989:271; S. R. Driver 1913:365; cf. NRSV with NJPS) in revocalizing *lakhayyah* [TH3807.1/2416D, ZH4200/2653] (into a community, band, or company) to *lekhyah* [TH3896/1886.5, ZH4306/2025] ("to Lehi," cf. Judg 15:9 and Lucianic mss of the LXX). Without revocalization the MT reads, "The Philistines were gathered together into a band." Youngblood (1992:1093) views revocalization as "unnecessary," particularly since the same term (*khayyah* [TH2416D, ZH2653]) appears in 23:13 where it is not possible to read it as a proper name.

23:15 *Oh, how I would love some of that good water.* For the expression of a wish by an exclamatory question as found in the MT, see Joüon and Muraoka §163d.

23:17 *This water is as precious as the blood.* The MT reads, "Is it the blood of the men who went?" As A. Anderson (1989:273) notes, "The rhetorical question seems to be equivalent to a strong negative assertion." In other words, "It is the blood of the men who went at the risk of their lives, so I am not willing to drink it."

23:19 *was the most famous.* Lit., "Was he honored?" The Hebrew interrogative particle (*hakhi* [TH1886.2/3588, ZH2022/3954]) requires an affirmative answer.

COMMENTARY

The double list of warriors found in 23:8-39 and 21:15-22 form the intermediate ring of the Samuel Conclusion's ring structure, framing its two central texts (22:1-51 and 23:1-7). Because the two lists are set in this clear literary pattern, Klement (2000:185) is certainly correct when he says that they "are not to be regarded as a clumsy insertion of book-keeping data," even though an initial reading might give this impression. Given their content and placement, two questions arise. First, why has the writer included these two lists in the Samuel Conclusion? And second, why are they placed on either side of the Samuel Conclusion's central texts? The literary pattern would suggest that the lists should be understood in connection with the purpose of the central texts. Klement (2000:185) argues that since the central texts have as their primary focus the praise of the Lord for granting David victory over his enemies (ch 22) and honoring him with the promise of a dynasty that would endure forever (23:1-7), then "in the lists, clear recognition is given to the names of those without whom the victories would not have been achieved." In other words, these lists are saying to the reader that David was not the sort of ruler who demanded personal credit for all the successes of his armies, nor was he the sort of person who feared giving honor and recognition to those who fought under his command. David was a ruler who exercised his royal authority as a vice-regent of Yahweh. He did so with a humble spirit, fully conscious that much of his success depended upon the loyal support of those who had aligned themselves with his cause.

Second Samuel 23:8-39 may be divided into three distinct parts. The exploits of David's three most prominent warriors, who were known as "the Three" (see note on 23:8) are described in 23:8-12. A longer list of other prominent warriors is given in 23:18-39; these men were less notable than "the Three" but still outstanding in their military prowess. These warriors were known as "the Thirty." Between the two lists of warriors is a narrative (23:13-17) describing an inadvertent remark of David's that resulted in his warriors risking their lives to fulfill his longing for a drink of water from the well of his hometown.

The first section (23:8-12) describes the remarkable military feats of Jashobeam the Hacmonite (23:8), Eleazar son of Dodai (23:9-10), and Shammah son of Agee (23:11-12). Each of these men was instrumental in defeating vastly superior forces, either single-handedly, or in the case of Eleazar, in partnership with David (23:9). But more important than the military prowess of either these men or David, the compiler of the list tells us in 23:10 and 23:12 that it was the Lord who brought about the victories. So while recognizing the important contribution that David's warriors made to his military triumphs, here, as in the two central texts of the Samuel Conclusion, it is in the Lord's gracious intervention that one finds the ultimate reason for David's success.

The second section (23:13-17) tells of an incidental and, in retrospect, perhaps foolish remark made by David when he and his men were hiding in the cave of Adullam, surrounded by the Philistine army (perhaps the same situation described in 1 Sam 22). In these dire circumstances David expressed to his comrades in arms how much he would enjoy a drink of water from the well by the entrance to his hometown of Bethlehem (23:15). Little did he expect that his wish would be their command. In a time when drinking water came from wells, springs, or cisterns rather than from centralized public water authorities, not all water had the same taste. For David, the taste of the water from the well of the town where he had grown up was a special treat. Upon hearing David's remark, the three warriors mentioned in the preceding verses[1] broke through the Philistine lines, made their way to Bethlehem, and brought back some water from the well of David's childhood at the risk of their own lives (23:16). Realizing how unseemly it was for the lives of his men to have been put at risk simply in order to satisfy his longing for a drink of his favorite water, David refused to drink it, but instead poured it out on the ground as an offering to the Lord (23:17). In this way David was able to validate the loyalty and sacrifice of his associates and affirm his solidarity with them in a way that turned his inadvertent remark into something good.[2]

The chapter concludes with a second list of outstanding warriors (23:18-39) who were known as "the Thirty," even though 23:39 indicates that there were 37 warriors in total.[3] Abishai, the brother of Joab, was the commander of "the Thirty" and was their most famous member (23:19). He and Benaiah, who stood out above all the other members of "the Thirty," are singled out for special comment. Benaiah served as captain of David's bodyguard (23:23). Just prior to David's death, he refused to join with those who were plotting to place Adonijah on David's throne in place of Solomon. Solomon subsequently appointed Benaiah as commander of Israel's army in place of Joab (1 Kgs 2:35). The remaining members of this group are simply identified by their name, the place from which they came, and in some cases by a brief indication of lineage. There are two names that merit additional comment. The first, Joab, stands out by virtue of not appearing on the list, even though he was the most dominant military commander of the Davidic era (it is interesting that the name of Joab's armor bearer does appear on the list in 23:37).[4] Joab's exclusion from the list may be due to his not infrequent insubordination to David, as well as to his involvement in the murders of Abner (3:27), Absalom (18:14), and Amasa (20:9-10).[5] Just prior to David's death, Joab again defied David's wishes and joined the conspiracy to place Adonijah on the throne (1 Kgs 1:5-53). The second name that merits comment is the last name on the list, Uriah the Hittite. The inclusion of Uriah's name, and its placement at the end, serves to remind the reader of David's sin with Uriah's wife, Bathsheba. Once again attention is called to the fact that David did not live up to the ideal of the true covenantal king. As Klement (2000:197) points out, there is a certain tension between David's behavior in the cave of Adullam (23:13-17) and the reference to Uriah (23:39) "whose name represents the other, blameworthy side of David's character. This hint at a balancing of the picture with the reference through the mention of Uriah to David's guilt does not, however, cancel out the positive aspect, but discourages any heroic over-idealizing of the king. . . . David's failure is not concealed, it qualifies—without negating—the positive evaluation of his character as a whole." So the picture of David that emerges in the various components of the Samuel Conclusion is that of a king who could legitimately be characterized as someone who "did what was just and right" (8:15) but at the same time was not a perfect representation of the covenantal king.

ENDNOTES

1. Because these three warriors are identified as being "among the Thirty" (23:13), some interpreters understand them to be anonymous warriors and not the same as "the Three" mentioned in the preceding verses.
2. Firth comments (2001:218), "David thus demonstrated that he would not pull rank—the lives of his men were of equal importance to his own." Brueggemann (1990a:349) regards this story as serving "a propagandistic function" designed to enhance David's

image in a way that protests "against the David of selfish arrogance and absolute ideology" that is found in chs 5–8. Certainly Brueggemann is correct in concluding that David's behavior on this occasion does not project the image of a king who abuses his power in a despotic manner, but that begs the question of whether it is proper to characterize the picture of David drawn in chs 5–8 as that of "a brutal despot," as Brueggemann does (1990c:109).

3. The designation "the Thirty" is probably best understood as the name of a recognized military contingent whose membership varied from time to time depending on deaths and new additions, rather than as a reference to thirty specific individuals. This is consistent with the statement in 23:39b that there were "thirty-seven" warriors who were members of "the Thirty."
4. In addition, Abishai (23:18) and Asahel (23:24) are listed as the brothers of Joab.
5. In commenting on the absence of Joab's name among "the Thirty," Cartledge has a less suspicious view of the absence (2001:681), suggesting that since Joab was such a well-known figure the reader "should understand it as a given that Joab was chief of the armed forces" even though his name is not included in the lists of "the Three" and "the Thirty."

◆ F. The Lord's Anger against Israel for David's Sin (2 Sam 24:1–25)

Once again the anger of the LORD burned against Israel, and he caused David to harm them by taking a census. "Go and count the people of Israel and Judah," the LORD told him.

2So the king said to Joab and the commanders* of the army, "Take a census of all the tribes of Israel—from Dan in the north to Beersheba in the south—so I may know how many people there are."

3But Joab replied to the king, "May the LORD your God let you live to see a hundred times as many people as there are now! But why, my lord the king, do you want to do this?"

4But the king insisted that they take the census, so Joab and the commanders of the army went out to count the people of Israel. 5First they crossed the Jordan and camped at Aroer, south of the town in the valley, in the direction of Gad. Then they went on to Jazer, 6then to Gilead in the land of Tahtim-hodshi* and to Dan-jaan and around to Sidon. 7Then they came to the fortress of Tyre, and all the towns of the Hivites and Canaanites. Finally, they went south to Judah* as far as Beersheba.

8Having gone through the entire land for nine months and twenty days, they returned to Jerusalem. 9Joab reported the number of people to the king. There were 800,000 capable warriors in Israel who could handle a sword, and 500,000 in Judah.

10But after he had taken the census, David's conscience began to bother him. And he said to the LORD, "I have sinned greatly by taking this census. Please forgive my guilt, LORD, for doing this foolish thing."

11The next morning the word of the LORD came to the prophet Gad, who was David's seer. This was the message: 12"Go and say to David, 'This is what the LORD says: I will give you three choices. Choose one of these punishments, and I will inflict it on you.'"

13So Gad came to David and asked him, "Will you choose three* years of famine throughout your land, three months of fleeing from your enemies, or three days of severe plague throughout your land? Think this over and decide what answer I should give the LORD who sent me."

14"I'm in a desperate situation!" David replied to Gad. "But let us fall into the hands of the LORD, for his mercy is great. Do not let me fall into human hands."

[15]So the LORD sent a plague upon Israel that morning, and it lasted for three days.* A total of 70,000 people died throughout the nation, from Dan in the north to Beersheba in the south. [16]But as the angel was preparing to destroy Jerusalem, the LORD relented and said to the death angel, "Stop! That is enough!" At that moment the angel of the LORD was by the threshing floor of Araunah the Jebusite.

[17]When David saw the angel, he said to the LORD, "I am the one who has sinned and done wrong! But these people are as innocent as sheep—what have they done? Let your anger fall against me and my family."

[18]That day Gad came to David and said to him, "Go up and build an altar to the LORD on the threshing floor of Araunah the Jebusite."

[19]So David went up to do what the LORD had commanded him. [20]When Araunah saw the king and his men coming toward him, he came and bowed before the king with his face to the ground. [21]"Why have you come, my lord the king?" Araunah asked.

David replied, "I have come to buy your threshing floor and to build an altar to the LORD there, so that he will stop the plague."

[22]"Take it, my lord the king, and use it as you wish," Araunah said to David. "Here are oxen for the burnt offering, and you can use the threshing boards and ox yokes for wood to build a fire on the altar. [23]I will give it all to you, Your Majesty, and may the LORD your God accept your sacrifice."

[24]But the king replied to Araunah, "No, I insist on buying it, for I will not present burnt offerings to the LORD my God that have cost me nothing." So David paid him fifty pieces of silver* for the threshing floor and the oxen.

[25]David built an altar there to the LORD and sacrificed burnt offerings and peace offerings. And the LORD answered his prayer for the land, and the plague on Israel was stopped.

24:2 As in Greek version (see also 24:4 and 1 Chr 21:2); Hebrew reads *Joab the commander.* **24:6** Greek version reads *to Gilead and to Kadesh in the land of the Hittites.* **24:7** Or *they went to the Negev of Judah.* **24:13** As in Greek version (see also 1 Chr 21:12); Hebrew reads *seven.* **24:15** Hebrew *for the designated time.* **24:24** Hebrew *50 shekels of silver,* about 20 ounces or 570 grams in weight.

NOTES

24:2 ***and the commanders of.*** The NLT follows the reading *we'el-sare* [TH2050.1/413/8269, ZH2256/448/8569] with LXX and 1 Chr 21:2 (so also in 24:4). The MT reads, "the commander of" (*sar* [TH8269, ZH8569]).

tribes of Israel. Lit., "the people of Israel." Perhaps both occurrences of *ha'am* [TH1886.1/5971A, ZH2021/6639] (people) in this verse and also 24:9-10 are better understood as troops (cf. 24:9, where the numbers given are the numbers of fighting men as well as the statement in 1 Chr 27:23 that David "did not count those who were younger than twenty years of age").

24:5 ***and camped.*** Lucianic mss of the LXX read *kai ērxanto* [TG2532/756, ZG2779/806] (and they began) suggesting a *Vorlage* that read *wayyakhellu* [TH3176, ZH3498] instead of *wayyakhanu* [TH2583, ZH2837].

south of. The MT reads "on the right side of" (*yemin* [TH3225, ZH3545], perhaps here intended to mean "south" because when facing east, the right is south; for similar usage, cf. 1 Sam 23:19, 24; Ezek 16:46). Although the Lucianic mss of the LXX read "and from," presupposing *wemin* [TH2050.1/4480, ZH2256/4946] instead of *yemin,* there is no compelling reason to abandon MT.

24:9 ***people.*** Or "troops" (see note on 24:2, "tribes of Israel").

24:25 ***answered . . . prayer.*** The narrative in 21:1-14 ends with the same Hebrew verb as this one (rendered by NLT as "ended the famine" in 21:14). In both verses, the Lord *wayye'ather* [TH6279, ZH6983] (answered prayer, was entreated), and the result was the lifting of the judgment after atonement had been made.

COMMENTARY

The narratives of chapter 24 and 21:1-14 constitute the outer ring of the Samuel Conclusion's ring structure. There are striking similarities between these two narratives. Both describe a sin (the taking of a census in ch 24 and the violation of an oath in ch 21) that leads to a divine judgment (a plague in ch 24 and a famine in ch 21) that requires a proper atonement (the burnt and peace offerings in ch 24 and the executions in ch 21), after which the Lord responds to prayer and brings an end to the judgment (see note on 24:25). Although the narratives display similarities in their overall plotline, they also portray a sharp contrast between the way in which Saul and David carried out the responsibilities of their office as kings. As was noted in the commentary on 21:1-14, Saul's legacy in Israel was a starving people because of his failure to live up to the responsibilities of a covenantal king and his murder of the Gibeonites in particular. It then became David's responsibility to make atonement for Saul's failure. In chapter 24, David's offense against the Lord (taking a census) brought a judgment, but unlike Saul, David owned up to his failure, sought the Lord's forgiveness, and relied on the Lord's mercy. Here, as throughout the Samuel Conclusion, it seems that one of the purposes of the author or editor was to highlight the contrast between the reigns of Saul and David. Saul was a ruler who not only failed to live up to his covenantal responsibilities as king, but he also failed to respond in true repentance and confession of sin after turning aside from walking in the ways of the Lord. It is in these responses that the most significant difference between Saul and David is found. Like Saul, David did not always walk in the ways of the Lord, but in contrast to Saul, when David failed to do so he repented for his sin and sought the Lord's forgiveness by casting himself on divine mercy and by making proper atonement through sacrifice.

The first sentence of chapter 24 raises some difficult exegetical and theological questions. Why was the Lord angry with Israel? Why should taking a census bring "harm" on Israel? How could God hold David accountable for doing something that he had "caused" David to do? Although the text itself provides no answers to these questions, it is possible to find reasonable responses to them when this chapter is placed in the context of the preceding narratives of 2 Samuel, its parallel passage in 1 Chronicles 21, and Old Testament revelation in general.

As Goslinga (1962) and Keil (1956:501) have argued, it seems likely that the events of 2 Samuel 24 are to be placed in the closing years of David's reign, and that the "anger of the LORD" that "burned against Israel" was an anger provoked by the rebellions of Absalom and Sheba (chs 15–20), who had attempted to remove the "Lord's anointed" from the throne in Jerusalem.[1] The Lord did not take lightly the rebellion against those he had placed in positions of leadership (see, e.g., Num 16:1-35; 1 Sam 24:6, 10; 26:9, 11, 16, 23). It is therefore reasonable (although not indisputable) to understand "the anger of the LORD burned against Israel" in 24:1 as a reference to the Lord's response to the events of the preceding chapters (chs 15–20), and therefore a clear signal to the reader that rebellion against divinely appointed leadership carries serious consequences with it. The second half of 24:1 describes how the Lord's anger was expressed: "He caused David to harm them by taking a census." That is, the Lord caused David to do something that, at least initially, would have detrimental consequences for both David and the nation. But here more questions arise. Was taking a census inherently sinful, and if so, is this text telling us that, on this occasion, God is the initiator of a sinful action? How can this be consistent with the teaching of James 1:13-15 that God "never tempts anyone"? In response to this question interpreters have often pointed to the different wording of the parallel text in 1 Chronicles 21:1—"*Satan* rose up against Israel and caused David to take a census" (my italics)—and then have concluded that it was Satan rather than God who "caused" David to take the census. Sometimes advocates of this method of resolving the difference between 24:1 and 1 Chronicles 21:1 assume that the reason for the difference between the texts is that Samuel's rendering (God caused David to take the census) reflects an older theology and a less developed concept of God than does the Chronicler's rendering (Satan caused David to take the census). The purpose of the change in wording is then viewed as an attempt by the Chronicler to protect his more sophisticated understanding of the holiness of God.[2] Advocates of this view argue that the two texts reflect an advance in Israel's concept of God during the time between the writing of Samuel and Chronicles. But as Goslinga notes (1962:453), this sort of explanation suggests that Samuel and Chronicles express fallible human opinions rather than statements bearing the weight and accuracy of assertions clothed with divine authority. In other words, if both of these statements are viewed as carrying divine authority, this means there can be no final conflict between them. For this reason, it seems that the best solution for resolving the difference between the two texts is to regard the Samuel statement as speaking from the standpoint of God's general providential governance of everything that comes to pass, while the Chronicler's statement speaks more specifically of Satan as the immediate cause of David's action.[3]

What is surprising to the reader, however, is that when David told Joab and his other commanders to go out and take a census of his entire realm, Joab, of all people, objected (24:2-3). Although as the chapter proceeds it becomes clear that the decision to take a census was a sinful act (24:10, 15), exactly how or why it was sinful is never specifically addressed. It is clear that at the time of the Exodus the Lord had instructed Moses to take a census on three separate occasions. On the first occasion the census and its associated per capita atonement money, or census tax, provided resources for the construction of the Tabernacle (Exod 30:11-16; 38:24-28). On the other two occasions, the census had military objectives (Num 1:2-3, prior to Israel's conquest of the Transjordan; and Num 26:2, prior to Israel's conquest of the land of Canaan); their purpose was to count "the men twenty years old or older who are able to go to war" (Num 1:2-3; 26:2). David's census was similarly designed to list the "capable warriors . . . who could handle a sword" (24:9) and not those "younger than twenty years of age" (1 Chr 27:23). If, then, a census for military purposes was appropriate in the time of Moses, one might wonder why it should be inappropriate in the time of David. For this reason some say that it was not the census itself that was sinful but rather the manner in which it was conducted. Because no reference is made in either Samuel or Chronicles to the payment by David of the per capita atonement money, or census tax, which is specified in the Mosaic regulations for the census taken prior to the construction of the Tabernacle (Exod 30:12-14), some have concluded that it was this negligence that was David's mistake. The validity of this conclusion, however, is undermined by David's statement that he had "sinned greatly by taking this census" (24:10). David did not say he sinned by not collecting the proper tax, but rather that he sinned by taking the census itself, which he said was both foolish and wrong (24:10, 17). In addition, it is not clear whether the "census tax" of Exodus 30:12-14 was intended to be binding for every census or was just a "one time imposition for the building of the Tabernacle" (Sarna 1991:195). Given these considerations, it has usually been concluded that David's sin was not just that he took a census or that he did it in a wrong manner, but rather that he did it for the wrong reasons. Joab did not make any explicit statement of why he objected to David's proposal, but he did say he hoped the Lord would grant David a hundred times more people in his kingdom than he currently had (24:3). The implication of Joab's statement is that David's mind was set in some improper way on the importance of numbers and that he was more concerned with how many fighting men he could muster than he was with trust in the Lord's promise to make the nation great and to protect his people from their enemies.[4] This seems to be the best of the available interpretive options and would indicate that David's motivation for taking the census was not only a denial of his own previously expressed convictions[5] but also a serious abrogation of his responsibility to rule over Israel as a true covenantal king.

In spite of their objections to David's proposal, Joab and his associates began to take the census because David insisted that they do so (24:4). After spending nine months and twenty days (24:8), they reported to David on their progress (24:9). The parallel passage in 1 Chronicles informs us that when the report was given, the census had not been completed because the tribes of Levi and Benjamin had not yet been surveyed (1 Chr 21:6). But the census was stopped before it was completed because David had a change of heart. As David reflected on the implications of what he was doing, his conscience began to bother him. The result was he confessed to the Lord that he had sinned by taking the census and asked the Lord for forgiveness, saying he had done a "foolish thing" (24:10). The very next day the prophet Gad told David that the Lord would give him three options for punishment (three years of famine, three months of fleeing from his enemies, or three days of severe plague [24:13]), presenting him with the dismal task of making a very difficult choice. Because each of the punishments would involve not only David but also the entire nation, it seems clear that the Lord's purpose was to simultaneously punish both David and the nation for their sins (cf. 24:1). David did not know how to choose between the famine and the plague, both of which were acts of God. But because he knew Yahweh to be a merciful and gracious God, he preferred placing himself and the nation in God's hands rather than in the hands of their enemies. So the Lord sent a plague on the land that lasted for three days and killed 70,000 people. As the "death angel" approached Jerusalem and stood by the threshing floor of Araunah the Jebusite (whether this appearance was visionary or actual is not clear), David prayed for the Lord's mercy, confessing his sin, and asking for judgment to fall on himself and his family rather than on his subjects (24:17).[6] David's petition reflects something of the true covenantal king who was more concerned with the welfare of his people than he was with himself. After David had prayed, he was instructed by the prophet Gad to build an altar on Araunah's threshing floor that was located just outside the city of Jerusalem. When David explained to Araunah that he wanted to purchase his threshing floor in order to build an altar to the Lord, Araunah offered to give him the ground along with materials for a sacrifice. But David refused his offer, saying that he could not offer burnt offerings to the Lord that had cost him nothing. So David purchased the threshing floor as well as some oxen from Araunah for 50 shekels of silver. He then built an altar on the threshing floor and sacrificed burnt offerings and peace offerings upon it, with the result that the Lord answered his prayer and stopped the plague (24:16, 25).

As this narrative moves from David's sin and its punishment to his prayer for mercy, and finally to the offering of a sacrifice on the threshing floor of Araunah, several important theological issues come into view. The first concerns the character of God. David knew the God whom he served. Yahweh was a God who had described his own attributes to Moses: "Yahweh! The LORD! The God of compassion and mercy! I am slow to anger and filled with unfailing love and faithfulness. I lavish unfailing love to a thousand generations. I forgive iniquity, rebellion, and sin. But I do not excuse the guilty" (Exod 34:6-7). David had already experienced the Lord's mercy and forgiveness in the matter of Uriah and Bathsheba (12:13). While mercy and forgiveness did not eliminate punishment for sin, David knew that the Lord was a God who remembered mercy in judgment. Accordingly, he knew he could place his and the nation's destiny in Yahweh's hands with the confidence that he would deal with them in a manner consistent with his character as a compassionate and merciful God. David's conviction that the Lord was a compassionate and merciful God also comes into focus by the statement of the narrator that after David had prayed and offered sacrifices and the plague was about to enter Jerusalem, "The LORD relented and said to the death angel, 'Stop! That is enough!'" (24:16; 1 Chr 21:15). Here is an example of God's "relenting" (or "repenting") that brings an end to a divine judgment already in progress (cf. Exod 32:14; Hos 11:8-9; Amos 7:3, 6). This "relenting" speaks of something intrinsic to God's relationship with his people. The God of Israel is a God who responds to the ways in which his people either embrace or reject their covenantal obligations (Jer 18:1-10). The God of Moses, David, and Israel is not an "unmoved mover" but rather a personal God who interacts with his people and responds to their prayers in ways consistent with his character as a compassionate and merciful God. David's understanding of the character of Yahweh provided him with a strong motivation to intercede for God's mercy and grace.

The Lord's instruction to David to build an altar on the threshing floor of Araunah the Jebusite was important theologically. It not only provided the means for resolving the crisis of the moment, but also eventuated in something long anticipated in Old Testament revelation, something that would become central to Israel's worship for the remainder of her history as a nation. The Lord had told Moses that when Israel would find rest from her enemies and live safely in the land of Canaan, she was to bring her sacrifices to "the designated place of worship, the place the LORD your God chooses for his name to be honored" (Deut 12:11). As 1 Chronicles 22:1 makes clear, the threshing floor of Araunah became the site for the Temple, the central sanctuary of ancient Israel, and the altar that David built there became the central altar of Israel. So the Lord's designation of Araunah's threshing floor as the place where David was to build an altar is the fulfillment of the Lord's word to Moses that when Israel was settled in the land of Canaan, there would be a place that the Lord would "choose from among all the tribes—the place where his name will be honored" (Deut 12:5).[7] The irony of this narrative is that the Lord used David's and Israel's sin as the occasion for designating the place that from that time forward would be the place where his name is honored and the place where Israel would find atonement for her sins. Here one finds a remarkable example of a situation in which sin and guilt do not prevent the realization of God's redemptive purposes but rather are incorporated into their actualization (van den Berg 1997:134). This does not mean that David's and Israel's sins were overlooked; in fact, they were severely punished (70,000 people died, 24:15). But it does mean that as a result of David's confession of his sin and his prayer for divine mercy, the Lord designated a place where atonement for sin could be found. The altar on the threshing floor of Araunah pointed forward to another place of atonement near the city of Jerusalem that was far more significant. It was at Golgotha (Matt 27:33) that Jesus reconciled the world unto himself (2 Cor 5:19) because there "God made Christ, who never sinned, to be the offering for our sin, so that we could be made right with God through Christ" (2 Cor 5:21). While David's kingship was superior to Saul's, it remained flawed, requiring a place of atonement for the sins of David himself and of the people. At the same time, David's kingship foreshadowed the reign of his descendant, who would be the true and ultimate covenant king. Thus, in addition to demonstrating again that David fell short of the ideal of the true covenantal king, the concluding episode in 1–2 Samuel opens a grand vista of God's redemptive purpose that has its climax in the kingship of the one who is "both the source of David and the heir to his throne" (Rev 22:16), the Lord of all lords and King of all kings, Jesus Christ (Rev 17:14; 19:16).

ENDNOTES

1. Both Absalom's and Sheba's rebellions found support from all of Israel (cf. 15:2, 10; 20:2).
2. Smith (1912:390), for example, says that "the Chronicler could not conceive of Yahweh's inciting David to sin," so he began the account by saying that Satan did this rather than Yahweh.
3. For different perspectives on the issues raised by the different wording of 2 Sam 24:1 and 1 Chr 21:1, see standard commentaries on Samuel and Chronicles as well as the more detailed discussions of these issues in Adler 1996; Dillard 1985; and Sailhamer 1989. De Graaf (n.d.:220) argues that there was nothing inherently wrong with taking a census. What was sinful was David's attempt to find security for the nation based on the size of his military force rather than by putting his trust in the Lord. The statement in 24:1 that the Lord "caused David to harm them by taking a census" is therefore to be understood in the sense that the Lord "caused" the sin that was already present in David's heart to be translated into action. So in this instance the Lord was punishing David by giving him over to an already-existing sinful desire of his own heart. This suggestion allows the interpreter to attribute an active role to God in "causing" David to take the census, instead of limiting his role to the passive function of his permissive

will, as has often been done, in which case Satan rather than God is viewed as the real instigator of David's action. While de Graaf's suggestion provides a reasonable explanation for the Samuel text in which God is the "cause" for David's taking the census, it is less successful in accommodating both the Samuel text and the Chronicles text where Satan is said to be the one who "caused" David to take the census. It would seem that the only way to do justice to both the Samuel and the Chronicles statements is to adopt a solution that folds Satan's action into God's overall providential governance of everything that comes to pass. For further discussion of how to understand divine sovereignty and human responsibility in connection with the evil actions of human beings see the commentary on 1 Sam 2:25. See also 16:10; 17:14; Exod 4:21; Deut 2:30; Josh 11:20; 1 Kgs 12:15, 24; Ps 105:25; Isa 6:10; 10:5-19; 54:16; Acts 4:27-28; Eph 1:11.

4. Dillard (1985:105) argues that the Chronicler's statements (1 Chr 27:23-24)—that when David took the census he did not count those younger than twenty years of age "because the LORD had promised to make the Israelites as numerous as the stars in heaven" and that Joab "began the census but never finished it because the anger of God fell on Israel"—suggest that God's promise to the patriarchs (cf. Gen 12:2; 13:16; 15:5; 22:17) was in some way associated with Joab's objections to the census. Dillard concludes that "the arena of David's transgression appears to be that taking a census impugns the faithfulness of God in the keeping of His promises—a kind of walking by sight instead of by faith." According to Dillard this inappropriate attitude on the part of David toward God's faithfulness was combined with an inappropriate desire to expand his territorial domain beyond that of the boundaries delineated in the specifications of the land promise given to the patriarchs and repeated to Moses and Joshua (Gen 15:12-21; Deut 1:7-8; Josh 1:3-4). Since David already had jurisdiction over all of this territory, Dillard argues (1985:106) that any mobilization of forces for additional conquest "beyond the divine land grant to Israel" would be a "transgression of the fixed boundaries allotted to Israel by her suzerain." It is this combination of errors that constituted David's sin in taking the census.
5. When David challenged Goliath to battle, he did not put his trust in superior military armament but rather in the Lord's protection. He told Goliath, "You come to me with sword, spear, and javelin, but I come to you in the name of the LORD of Heaven's Armies—the God of the armies of Israel, whom you have defied. Today the LORD will conquer you, and I will kill you and cut off your head" (1 Sam 17:45-46). In 22:34-37, 40-41, David is careful to attribute full credit to the Lord for all his successes in military endeavors, rather than credit his own military acumen, armaments, or forces. Psalm 20:7 (a psalm ascribed to David) says, "Some nations boast of their chariots and horses, but we boast in the name of the LORD our God." This outlook is consistent with Jonathan's statement (1 Sam 14:6) that "nothing can hinder the LORD. He can win a battle whether he has many warriors or only a few!" This outlook is also consistent with the Lord's statement through a prophet to Amaziah, king of Judah, who at a later time in Israel's history had taken a census (2 Chr 25:5) in preparation for a war with Edom. At that time he was told not to go into battle with troops he had hired from the northern kingdom, because if he were to do so he would "be defeated by the enemy no matter how well you fight. God will overthrow you, for he has the power to help you or to trip you up" (2 Chr 25:8).
6. It appears that the prayer of David that is described in 24:17 was made prior to the Lord's "relenting," described in 24:16 (cf. also 24:25).
7. Klement (2000:184) comments that in this last narrative of 1–2 Samuel, "Jerusalem is implicitly portrayed as the city which Yahweh has chosen." When this honor for

Jerusalem is combined with the status that the city already possessed by virtue of its being the location for the Ark of the Covenant, the city's "high cultic significance" is thus "doubly authenticated." Given these considerations it would seem that what has come to be known as the "Zion tradition" finds its origin in the time of David. This, of course, challenges the widely held view that the "Zion tradition" developed at a much later date. As Dekker (2004:277) rightly points out, "It would be difficult to underestimate the importance the transfer of the Ark to Jerusalem by King David had for the development of the Zion tradition." He goes on to say that the heart of the Zion tradition "rests in the conviction that Yahweh has chosen Zion as his abode and that Zion therefore is the city of the great king."

BIBLIOGRAPHY

Abraham, W.
1982 *Divine Revelation and the Limits of Historical Criticism.* Oxford: Oxford University Press.

Ackroyd, P.
1971 *The First Book of Samuel.* Cambridge Bible Commentary 9. Cambridge: Cambridge University Press.

Adler, J. J.
1996 David's Census: Additional Reflection. *Jewish Biblical Quarterly* 24:255-257.

Aharoni, Y., and M. Avi-Yonah
1993 *The Macmillan Bible Atlas.* 3rd ed. New York: Macmillan.

Ahlström, G. W.
1979 1 Samuel 1,15. *Biblica* 60:254.

Albright, W. F.
1951 The Old Testament and the Archaeology of Palestine. Pp. 1-26 in *The Old Testament and Modern Study.* Editor, H. H. Rowley. Oxford: Clarendon.

1968 *Yahweh and the Gods of Canaan.* Garden City, NY: Doubleday.

Alter, R.
1975 A Literary Approach to the Bible. *Commentary* 60:70-78.

1981 *The Art of Biblical Narrative.* New York: Basic.

1999 *The David Story: A Translation with Commentary of 1 and 2 Samuel.* New York: W. W. Norton & Company.

Althann, R.
1981 1 Sam 13:1; A Poetic Couplet. *Biblica* 62:241-246.

Anderson, A. A.
1989 *2 Samuel.* Word Biblical Commentary 11. Waco: Word.

Anderson, G. W.
1951 Hebrew Religion. Pp. 283-310 in *The Old Testament and Modern Study.* Editor, H. H. Rowley. Oxford: Clarendon.

Archer, G. L.
1981 A Reassessment of the Value of the Septuagint of 1 Samuel for Textual Emendation, in the Light of Qumran Fragments. Pp. 223-240 in *Tradition and Testament: Essays in Honor of Charles L. Feinberg.* Editors, J. S. Feinberg and P. D. Feinberg. Chicago: Moody.

1982 *Encyclopedia of Bible Difficulties.* Grand Rapids: Zondervan.

Armerding, C. E.
1975 Were David's Sons Really Priests? Pp. 75-86 in *Current Issues in Biblical and Patristic Interpretation. Studies in Honor of Merrill C. Tenney Presented by his Former Students.* Editor, G. Hawthorne. Grand Rapids: Eerdmans.

Augustine
1950 *The City of God. Books I-VII.* Translators, D. B. Zema and G. G. Walsh. New York: Fathers of the Church.

Auld, A. G.
1999 The Deuteronomists and the Former Prophets, or What Makes the Former Prophets Deuteronomistic? Pp. 116-126 in *Those Elusive Deuteronomists: The Phenomenon of Pan-Deuteronomism.* Editors, L. S. Schearing and S. L. McKenzie. Journal for the Study of the Old Testament Supplement 268. Sheffield: Sheffield Academic.

Baldwin, J.
1988 *1 and 2 Samuel: An Introduction and Commentary.* Tyndale Old Testament Commentaries. Downers Grove, IL: InterVarsity.

Baltzer, K.
1971 *The Covenant Formulary in Old Testament, Jewish, and Early Christian Writings.* Translator, D. E. Green (Das Bundesformular, 1964). Philadelphia: Fortress.

Barr, J.
1968 *Comparative Philology and the Text of the Old Testament.* Oxford: Clarendon.

Barth, K.
1961 *Church Dogmatics III/4.* Editors, G. W. Bromiley and T. F. Torrance. Edinburgh: T&T Clark.

Barthélemy, D., et al.
1979 *Preliminary and Interim Report on the Hebrew Old Testament Text Project,* vol. 2. New York: United Bible Societies.

1982 *Critique Textuelle de l'Ancien Testament. Rapport final du comité pour l'analyse textuelle de l'A.T. hébreu.* Göttingen: Vandenhoeck & Ruprecht.

Barthélemy, D., D. W. Gooding, J. Lust, and E. Tov
1986 *The Story of David and Goliath: Textual and Literary Criticism.* Orbis Biblicus et Orientalis 73. Göttingen: Vandenhoeck & Ruprecht.

Barton, J.
1996 *Reading the Old Testament.* Louisville: Westminster John Knox.

Beal, R.
1983 The Hittites after the Empire's Fall. *Biblical Illustrator* 10/1:81.

Beamer, L.
1992 Philistine. Pp. 610-611 in *A Dictionary of Biblical Tradition in English Literature.* Editor, D. L. Jeffrey. Grand Rapids: Eerdmans.

Ben-Barak, Z.
1972 The Manner of the King and the Manner of the Kingdom: Basic Factors in the Establishment of the Israelite Monarchy in the Light of Canaanite Kingship [Hebrew]. PhD diss., Hebrew University of Jerusalem.

Berg, M. R. van den
1996a *Het eerste boek Samuël. Opkomst en fiasco van een messiaans koningschap. Deel 1: hoofdstuk 1–15.* Amsterdam: Buijten & Schipperheijn.

1996b *Het eerste boek Samuël. Van koeienjongen tot voortvluchtige messias. Deel 2: hoofdstuk 16–31.* Amsterdam: Buijten & Schipperheijn.

1997 *Het tweede boek Samuël. Balans van een messiaans koningschap.* Amsterdam: Buijten & Schipperheijn.

Bergen, R. D.
1996 *1, 2 Samuel.* New American Commentary. Nashville: Broadman & Holman.

Berry, D. K.
1993 *The Psalms and their Readers: Interpretive Strategies for Psalm 18.* Sheffield: Journal for the Study of the Old Testament Press.

Bierling, N.
1992 *Giving Goliath His Due: New Archaeological Light on the Philistines.* Grand Rapids: Baker.

Birch, B. C.
1976 *The Rise of the Israelite Monarchy: The Growth and Development of 1 Sam 7–15.* Society of Biblical Literature Dissertation Series 27. Missoula, MT: Scholars Press.

Blackwood, A.
1946 *Preaching from Samuel.* Nashville: Abingdon-Cokesbury.

Blenkinsopp, J.
1971 The Prophetic Reproach. *Journal of Biblical Literature* 90 (3):267-278.

1983 *A History of Prophecy in Israel.* Philadelphia: Westminster.

Blocher, H.
1988 Biblical Narrative and Historical Reference. Pp. 102-122 in *Issues in Faith and History.* Editor, N. M. des Cameron. Scottish Bulletin of Evangelical Theology Special Study 3. Edinburgh: Rutherford House.

Boecker, H. J.
1969 *Die Beurteilung der Anfänge des Königtums in den deuteronomistischen Abschnitten des 1. Samuelbuches.* Wissenschaftliche Monographien zum Alten und Neuen Testament 31. Neukirchen-Vluyn: Neukirchener Verlag.

Boer, P. A. H. de
1949 Research into the Text of 1 Samuel xviii-xxxi. Pp. 1-100 in *Oudtestamentische Studiën,* vol. 6. Leiden: Brill.

Borger, R.
1972 Die Waffenträger des Königs Darius. *Vetus Testamentum* 22 (4):385-398.

Borgman, P.
2008 *David, Saul, and God: Rediscovering an Ancient Story.* New York: Oxford University Press.

Braun, R. L.
1976 Solomon, the Chosen Temple Builder: The Significance of I Chronicles 22, 28, 29 for the Theology of Chronicles. *Journal of Biblical Literature* 95:582-584.

Bright, J.
1981 *A History of Israel.* 3rd ed. Philadelphia: Westminster.

Brueggemann, W.
1974 On Coping with Curse: A Study of 2 Sam 16:5-14. *Catholic Biblical Quarterly* 36:175-192.

1988 2 Sam 21–24: An Appendix of Deconstruction. *Catholic Biblical Quarterly* 50:383-397.

1990a *First and Second Samuel.* Interpretation. Louisville: John Knox.

1990b I Samuel 1: A Sense of Beginning. *Zeitschrift für die alttestamentliche Wissenschaft* 102:33-48.

1990c Pretensions to Royal Absolutism: An Alternative. Pp. 86-115 in *Power, Providence, and Personality: Biblical Insights into Life and Ministry.* Louisville: Westminster John Knox.

1997 *Theology of the Old Testament: Testimony, Dispute, Advocacy.* Minneapolis: Fortress.

2000a *David's Truth.* Minneapolis: Augsburg / Fortress.

2000b *1 & 2 Kings.* Smyth & Helwys Bible Commentary. Macon, GA: Smyth & Helwys.

2003 *An Introduction to the Old Testament.* Louisville: Westminster John Knox.

Budde, K.
1890 *Die Bücher Richter und Samuel. Ihre Quellen und ihr Aufbau.* Giessen: Ricker.

1902 *Die Bücher Samuel. Kurzer Hand-Commentar zum Alten Testament.* Tübingen: J. C. B. Mohr (Siebeck).

Burson, S. R., and J. L. Walls
1998 *C. S. Lewis and Francis Schaeffer.* Downers Grove, IL: InterVarsity.

Caird, G. B.
1953 *The First and Second Books of Samuel.* The Interpreter's Bible 2. Nashville: Abingdon.

Calderone, P. J.
1961 HDL-II in Poetic Texts. *Catholic Biblical Quarterly* 23:451-460.

1962 HDL-II in Poetic Texts. *Catholic Biblical Quarterly* 24:412-419.

Calvin, J.
1979a *Commentaries on the Book of Psalms,* vol. 1. Grand Rapids: Baker.

1979b *Commentaries on the First Book of Moses Called Genesis.* Grand Rapids: Baker.

1979c *Commentaries on the Four Last Books of Moses Arranged in the Form of a Harmony,* vol. 2. Grand Rapids: Baker.

1992 *Sermons on 2 Samuel. Chapters 1-13.* Carlisle, PA: Banner of Truth.

Campbell, A.
1975 *The Ark Narrative (1 Sam 4–6; 2 Sam 6): A Form-critical and Traditio-historical Study.* Society of Biblical Literature Dissertation Series 16. Missoula, MT: Society of Biblical Literature and Scholars Press.

2003 *1 Samuel.* The Forms of Old Testament Literature, vol. VII. Grand Rapids: Eerdmans.

Campbell, E. F.
1967 Sovereign God. *McCormick Quarterly* 20:173-186.

Carlson, R. A.
1964 *David the Chosen King: A Traditio-historical Approach to the Second Book of Samuel.* Stockholm: Almqvist & Wiksell.

Carson, D. A.
1981 *Divine Sovereignty and Human Responsibility: Biblical Perspectives in Tension.* Grand Rapids: Baker.

Cartledge, T. W.
2001 *1 & 2 Samuel.* Smyth & Helwys Bible Commentary. Macon, GA: Smyth & Helwys.

Carver, L.
1992 Ahithophel. Pp. 27-28 in *A Dictionary of Biblical Tradition in English Literature.* Editor, D. L. Jeffrey. Grand Rapids: Eerdmans.

Childs, B. S.

1979 *Introduction to the Old Testament as Scripture.* Philadelphia: Fortress.

Chisholm, R. B.

1983 An Exegetical and Theological Study of Psalm 18/2 Samuel 22. ThD diss., Dallas Theological Seminary.

1996 Divine Hardening in the Old Testament. *Bibliotheca Sacra* 153:410-434.

Clements, R. E.

1974 The Deuteronomistic Interpretation of the Founding of the Monarchy in I Sam. VIII. *Vetus Testamentum* 24:398-410.

Coggins, R.

1999 What Does "Deuteronomistic" Mean? Pp. 22-35 in *Those Elusive Deuteronomists: The Phenomenon of Pan-Deuteronomism.* Editors, L. S. Schearing and S. L. McKenzie. Journal for the Study of the Old Testament Supplement Series 268. Sheffield: Sheffield Academic.

Conrad, L. I.

1984 The Biblical Tradition for the Plague of the Philistines. *Journal of the American Oriental Society* 104/2:281-287.

Conroy, C.

1978 *Absalom Absalom! Narrative and Language in 2 Sam 13-20.* Analecta Biblica 81. Rome: Biblical Institute.

1983 *1–2 Samuel, 1–2 Kings with an Excursus on Davidic Dynasty and Holy City Zion.* Wilmington, DE: Michael Glazier.

Cross, F. M.

1966 The Contribution of the Qumran Discoveries to the Study of the Biblical Text. *Israel Exploration Journal* 16:81-95.

1973 *Canaanite Myth and Hebrew Epic.* Cambridge, MA: Harvard University Press.

1975 The Evolution of the Theory of Local Texts. Pp. 306-320 in *Qumran and the History of the Biblical Text.* Editors, F. M. Cross and S. Talmon. Cambridge, MA: Harvard University Press.

1985 The Text behind the Text of the Hebrew Bible. *Bible Review* 1:12-25.

2005 *Qumran Cave 4.XII: 1–2 Samuel.* DJD XVII. Oxford: Clarendon.

Cross, F. M., and D. N. Freedman

1953 A Royal Song of Thanksgiving: II Samuel 22 = Psalm 18. *Journal of Biblical Literature* 72:15-34.

1975 *Studies in Yahwistic Poetry.* Missoula, MT: Scholars Press.

Cryer, F. H.

1985 David's Rise to Power and the Death of Abner. *Vetus Testamentum* 35 (4):385-394.

Dahl, G.

1928 The Case for the Currently Accepted Date of Deuteronomy. *Journal of Biblical Literature* 47:358-379.

Dahood, M.

1966 Hebrew-Ugaritic Lexicography IV. *Biblica* 47/3:403-419.

Davies, P. R.

1992 *In Search of Ancient Israel.* Journal for the Study of the Old Testament Supplement Series 148. Sheffield: Sheffield Academic.

1995 Method and Madness: Some Remarks on Doing History with the Bible. *Journal of Biblical Literature* 114:699-705.

Davis, D. R.

1994a *Looking on the Heart: Expositions of 1 Samuel 1–14,* vol. 1. Grand Rapids: Baker.

1994b *Looking on the Heart: Expositions of 1 Samuel 15–31,* vol. 2. Grand Rapids: Baker.

1999 *Expositions of the Book of 2 Samuel: Out of Every Adversity.* Ross-shire: Christian Focus.

Day, J., editor

1998 *King and Messiah in Israel and the Ancient Near East.* Journal for the Study of the Old Testament Supplement Series 270. Sheffield: Sheffield Academic.

Deist, F. E.

1978 *Towards the Text of the Old Testament.* Pretoria: N. G. Kerkboekhandel Transvaal.

Dekker, J.

2004 *De rotsvaste fundering van Sion. Een exegetisch onderzoek naar het Sionswoord van Jesaja 28,16.* Zoetermeer: Uitgeverij Boekencenturm.

Dever, W. G.

1998 Archaeology, Ideology, and the Quest for an Ancient or Biblical Israel. *Near Eastern Archaeology* 61:39-52.

2000 Save Us from Postmodern Malarkey. *Biblical Archaeology Review* 26/2:28-68.

Dillard, R. B.

1985 David's Census: Perspectives on II Samuel 24 and I Chronicles 21. Pp. 94-107 in *Through Christ's Word.* Editors, W. R. Godfrey and J. L. Boyd III. Phillipsburg, NJ: Presbyterian & Reformed.

Dorsey, D. A.

1999 *The Literary Structure of the Old Testament: A Commentary on Genesis—Malachi.* Grand Rapids: Baker.

Driver, G. R.

1924 The Root p-r-ts in Hebrew. *Journal of Theological Studies* 25:177-178.

1957 A Lost Colloquialism in the Old Testament [I Samuel xxv.6]. *Journal of Theological Studies* 8:272-273.

Driver, S. R.

1913 *Notes on the Hebrew Text and the Topography of the Books of Samuel.* Oxford: Clarendon.

1956 *An Introduction to the Literature of the Old Testament.* New York: Meridian. (Orig. pub. 1897.)

Dumbrell, W. J.

1984 *Covenant and Creation.* Nashville: Thomas Nelson.

1988 The Prospect of Unconditionality in the Sinaitic Covenant. Pp. 141-155 in *Israel's Apostasy and Restoration. Essays in Honor of Roland K. Harrison.* Editor, A. Gileadi. Grand Rapids: Baker.

Durham, J. I.

1987 *Exodus.* Word Biblical Commentary 3. Waco: Word.

Eaton, J. H.

1976 *Kingship and the Psalms.* Studies in Biblical Theology Second Series 32. London: SCM.

Edelman, D.

1984 Saul's Rescue of Jabesh-gilead (1 Sam 11:1-11): Sorting Story from History. *Zeitschrift für die alttestamentliche Wissenschaft* 96:195-209.

1991 *King Saul in the Historiography of Judah.* Journal for the Study of the Old Testament Supplement 121. Sheffield: Sheffield Academic.

Eerdmans, B. D.

1947 *The Hebrew Book of Psalms.* Leiden: Brill.

Eichrodt, W.

1961 *Theology of the Old Testament,* vol. 1. London: SCM.

Eissfeldt, O.

1965 *The Old Testament: An Introduction.* New York: Harper & Row.

Ellsworth, R.

1998 When God's Arrows Fall Beyond Us: God's Strange Providence. *Southern Baptist Journal of Theology* 2/3:78-83.

Eslinger, L. M.

1985 *Kingship of God in Crisis: A Close Reading of 1 Samuel 1–12.* Sheffield: Almond.

Eybers, I. H.

1960 Notes on the Texts of Samuel Found in Qumran Cave 4. Pp. 1-17 in *Studies on the Books of Samuel.* Potchefstroom: Pro Rege Pers Beperk.

Fensham, F. C.

1970 The Battle between the Men of Joab and Abner as a Possible Ordeal by Battle? *Vetus Testamentum* 20:357-358.

Figart, T.

1970 Saul, the Spiritist, and Samuel. *Grace Theological Journal* 11:13-29.

Fincke, A.

2001 *The Samuel Scroll from Qumran: 4QSam^a Restored and Compared to the Septuagint and 4QSam^c.* Leiden: Brill.

Finkelstein, E.

1959 An Ignored Haplography in Samuel. *Journal of Semitic Studies* 4:356-357.

Finkelstein, I.

1996 The Archaeology of the United Monarchy: An Alternative View. *Levant* 28:177-187.

1998 Bible Archaeology or Archaeology of Palestine in the Iron Age? A Rejoinder. *Levant* 30:167-173.

2001 *The Bible Unearthed: Archaeology's New Vision of Ancient Israel and the Origin of Its Sacred Texts.* New York: Free Press.

Firth, D. G.

2001 Shining the Lamp: The Rhetoric of 2 Samuel 5-24. *Tyndale Bulletin* 52/2:203-224.

Fishbane, M.

1982 I Samuel 3: Historical Narrative and Narrative Poetics. Pp. 191-203 in *Literary Interpretations of Biblical Narratives,* vol. 2. Editors, K. R. R. Gros Louis and J. S. Ackerman. Nashville: Abingdon.

Flanagan, J. W.

1972 Court History or Succession Document. *Journal of Biblical Literature* 91:172-191.

1983 Social Transformation and Ritual in 2 Samuel 6. Pp. 361-371 in *The Word of God Shall Go Forth: Essays in Honor of David Noel Freedman in Celebration of His Sixtieth Birthday.* Editors, C. L. Meyers and M. O'Connor. Winona Lake, IN: Eisenbrauns.

Fokkelman, J. P.

1979 שׂדי תרומת in II Sam 1:21a—A Non-existent Crux. *Zeitschrift für die alttestamentliche Wissenschaft* 91/2:290-293.

1981 *King David: Narrative Art and Poetry in the Books of Samuel,* vol. 1. Assen: Van Gorcum.

1984 A Lie Born of Truth, Too Weak to Contain It. A Structural Reading of 2 Sam 1:1-16. *Old Testament Studies* 23:39-55.

1986 *The Crossing Fates: Narrative Art and Poetry in the Books of Samuel,* vol. 2. Assen: Van Gorcum.

1990 *Throne and City: Narrative Art and Poetry in the Books of Samuel,* vol. 3. Assen: Van Gorcum.

1993 *Vow and Desire: Narrative Art and Poetry in the Books of Samuel,* vol. 4. Assen: Van Gorcum.

Fouts, D. M.

2000 Who Really Killed Goliath? 2 Samuel 21:19 Versus 1 Chronicles 20:5. *Journal of Translation and Textlinguistics* 13:14-24.

Fox, E.

1999 *Give Us a King! Samuel, Saul and David: A New Translation of Samuel I and II.* New York: Schocken.

Freedman, D. N.

1972 The Refrain in David's Lament over Saul and Jonathan. Pp. 119-120 in *Ex Orbe Religionum: Studia Geo Widengren.* Studies in the History of Religions/Supplements to Numen 21. Leiden: Brill.

Fretheim, T.

1985 Divine Foreknowledge, Divine Constancy, and the Rejection of Saul's Kingship. *Catholic Biblical Quarterly* 47:595-602.

1999 *First and Second Kings.* Louisville: Westminster John Knox.

Frisch, A.

1996 "For I Feared the People, and I Yielded to Them" (1 Sam 15,24)—Is Saul's Guilt Attenuated or Intensified? *Zeitschrift für die alttestamentliche Wissenschaft* 108 (1):98-104.

Frolov, S.

2002 Succession Narrative: A Document or a Phantom? *Journal of Biblical Literature* 121 (1):81-104.

Fuller, D.

1980 *Gospel and Law: Contrast or Continuum?* Grand Rapids: Eerdmans.

Gakuru, G.

2000 *An Inner-biblical Exegetical Study of the Davidic Covenant and the Dynastic Oracle.* Mellon Biblical Press Series 59. Lewiston, NY: Mellen.

Garsiel, M.

1990 *The First Book of Samuel: A Literary Study of Comparative Structures, Analogies and Parallels.* Jerusalem: Rubin Mass.

1993 The Story of David and Bathsheba: A Different Approach. *Catholic Biblical Quarterly* 55:244-262.

Gennep, A. van

1960 *The Rites of Passage.* London: Routledge / Kegan Paul. (Orig. pub. 1909.)

Gerstenberger, E. S.

1995 Hat O'Brien das DtrG gerettet? Ich habe Zweifel daran. *Biblische Zeitschrift* 39:114-115.

Gevirtz, S.

1973 *Patterns in the Early Poetry of Israel.* 2nd ed. Chicago: University of Chicago Press.

Gnuse, R.
1982 A Reconsideration of the Form-critical Structure in I Samuel 3: An Ancient Near Eastern Dream Theophany. *Zeitschrift für die alttestamentliche Wissenschaft* 3:379-390.
1984 *The Dream Theophany of Samuel: Its Structure in Relation to Ancient Near Eastern Dreams and Its Theological Significance.* Lanham, MD: University Press of America.

Goitein, S. D.
1988 Women as Creators of Biblical Genres. *Prooftexts* 8:1-34.

Goldman, S.
1962 *Samuel.* London: Soncino.

Good, R. M.
2001 2 Samuel 8. *Tyndale Bulletin* 52 (1):128-138.

Gooding, D. W.
1975 A Recent Popularisation of Professor F. M. Cross' Theories on the Text of the Old Testament. *Tyndale Bulletin* 26:113-132.

Gordon, R. P.
1980 David's Rise and Saul's Demise. *Tyndale Bulletin* 31:37-64.
1984 *1 & 2 Samuel.* Sheffield: Journal for the Study of the Old Testament Press.
1985 Review: K. Gnuse. *The Dream Theophany of Samuel. Vetus Testamentum* 35:125.
1986 *1 & 2 Samuel: A Commentary.* Exeter: Paternoster.
1987 Review: S. Pisano. Additions or Omissions in the Books of Samuel. The Significant Pluses and Minuses in the Massoretic, LXX and Qumran Texts. *Vetus Testamentum* 37/2:383-384.
1988 Simplicity of the Highest Cunning: Narrative Art in the Old Testament. *Scottish Bulletin of Evangelical Theology* 6/2:69-80.
1990a Covenant and Apology in 2 Samuel 3. *Proceedings of the Irish Biblical Association* 13:24-34.
1990b Word-play and Verse-order in 1 Samuel XXIV 5-8. *Vetus Testamentum* 40:139-144.
1993 The Variable Wisdom of Abel: The MT and Versions at 2 Samuel XX 18-19. *Vetus Testamentum* 43/2:215-226.

Goslinga, C. J.
1948 *I Samuël.* Kampen, Kok.
1962 *Het Tweede Boek Samuel.* Kampen: Kok.
1968 *Het Eerste Boek Samuel.* Kampen: Kok.

Graaf, S. G. de
n.d. *Het Eerste en Tweede Boek van Samuël.* Kampen: Kok.
1978 *Promise and Deliverance: The Failure of Israel's Theocracy.* St. Catharines, ON: Paideia.

Gray, J.
1957 *The Legacy of Canaan.* Leiden: Brill.

Greidanus, S.
1999 *Preaching Christ from the Old Testament.* Grand Rapids: Eerdmans.

Grønbaek, J. H.
1971 *Die Geschichte vom Aufstieg Davids (1. Sam. 15–2. Sam. 5): Tradition und Komposition.* Acta Theologica Danica 10. Copenhagen: Munksgaard.

Guillaume, A.
1954 מְאֹד in I. Samuel xx,19. *Palestine Exploration Quarterly* 86:83-86.

Gundry, S. N., editor
2003 *Show Them No Mercy: Four Views on God and Canaanite Genocide.* Grand Rapids: Zondervan.

Gunkel, H.
1964 *The Legends of Genesis.* Translator, W. H. Carruth. New York: Schocken.

Gunn, D. M.
1975 David and the Gift of the Kingdom (2 Sam 2–4, 9–20; 1 Kgs 1–2). *Semeia* 3:14-45.
1980 *The Fate of King Saul: An Interpretation of a Biblical Story.* Journal for the Study of the Old Testament Supplement 14. Reprinted with minor corrections and bibliographic additions, 1989. Sheffield: Journal for the Study of the Old Testament Press.

Gutbrod, K.
1956 *Das Buch vom König: Das erste Buch Samuel. Die Botschaft des alten Testaments XI/1.* Stuttgart: Calwer.

Habel, N.
1965 The Form and Significance of the Call Narratives. *Zeitschrift für die alttestamentliche Wissenschaft* 77:297-323.

Halpern, B.
1981a *The Constitution of the Monarchy in Israel.* Harvard Semitic Monographs 25. Chico, CA: Scholars Press.

1981b The Uneasy Compromise: Israel between League and Monarchy. In *Traditions in Transformation: Turning Points in Biblical Faith.* Festschrift for F. M. Cross. Editors, B. Halpern and J. D. Levenson. Winona Lake, IN: Eisenbrauns.

1996 The Construction of the Davidic State: An Exercise in Historiography. Pp. 44-76 in *The Origins of the Ancient Israelite States.* Editors, V. Fritz and P. R. Davies. Journal for the Study of the Old Testament Supplement Series 228. Sheffield: Sheffield Academic.

2001 *David's Secret Demons: Messiah, Murderer, Traitor, King.* Grand Rapids: Eerdmans.

Haran, M.
1969 Zebah hayyamim. *Vetus Testamentum* 19:11-22.

Harris, R. L.
1971 Continuity in the Old Testament Historical Literature. *Journal of the Evangelical Theological Society* 14 (3):173-178.

Harrison, R. K.
1969 *Introduction to the Old Testament.* Grand Rapids: Eerdmans.

Hays, J. D.
2005 Reconsidering the Height of Goliath. *Journal of the Evangelical Theological Society* 48:701-714.

Hertzberg, H. W.
1964 *I & II Samuel.* Old Testament Library. Philadelphia: Westminster.

Hess, R. S., and G. J. Wenham
1999 *Zion, City of Our God.* Grand Rapids: Eerdmans.

Hill, A.
1987 A Jonadab Connection in the Absalom Conspiracy? *Journal of the Evangelical Theological Society* 30 (4):387-390.

Hodge, C. H.
1952 *Systematic Theology,* vol. 3. Grand Rapids: Eerdmans.

Hoerth, A. J.
1998 *Archaeology and the Old Testament.* Grand Rapids: Baker.

Hoffmeier, J. K.
1991a The Aftermath of David's Triumph over Goliath. *Archaeology in the Biblical World,* vol. 1 (1):18-23.

1991b The Sling in Ancient Warfare. *Archaeology in the Biblical World,* vol. 1 (1):20.

Hoffner, H. A.
1975 Propaganda and Political Justification in Hittite Historiography. Pp. 49-62 in *Unity and Diversity: Essays in the History, Literature, and Religion of the Ancient Near East.* Editors, H. Goedicke and J. J. M. Roberts. Baltimore: Johns Hopkins University Press.

Hoftijzer, J.
1970 David and the Tekoite Woman. *Vetus Testamentum* 20:419-444.

1971 A Peculiar Question: A Note on 2 Sam. xv 27. *Vetus Testamentum* 21/5:606-609.

1995 Some Remarks on the Semantics of the Root *b't* in Classical Hebrew. Pp. 777-783 in *Pomegranates and Golden Bells.* Editor, D. P. Wright. Winona Lake, IN: Eisenbrauns.

Holladay, W. L.
1970 Form and Word-play in David's Lament over Saul and Jonathan. *Vetus Testamentum* 20:170-171.

Holter, K.
1989 Was Philistine Dagon a Fish-god? Some New Questions and an Old Answer. *Scandinavian Journal of the Old Testament* 1:142-147.

Horn, S.
1973 The Crown of the King of the Ammonites. *Andrews University Seminary Studies* 11:170-180.

House, P. R.
1995 *1, 2 Kings.* New American Commentary 8. Nashville: Broadman & Holman.

Howard, D.
1989 The Transfer of Power from Saul to David in 1 Sam 16:13-14. *Journal of the Evangelical Theological Society* 32 (4):473-483.

1993 *An Introduction to the Old Testament Historical Books.* Chicago: Moody.

1998 *Joshua.* Nashville: Broadman & Holman.

Huffmon, H.
1959 The Covenant Lawsuit in the Prophets. *Journal of Biblical Literature* 78:285-295.

Hughes, P. E.
1962 *Paul's Second Epistle to the Corinthians.* Grand Rapids: Eerdmans.

Humphreys, W. L.
1978 The Tragedy of King Saul. *Journal for the Study of the Old Testament* 6:18-27.

1980 The Rise and Fall of King Saul. *Journal for the Study of the Old Testament* 18:74-90.

1982 From Tragic Hero to Villain. *Journal for the Study of the Old Testament* 22:95-117.

Huttar, C. A., and R.-J. Frontain
1992 David. Pp. 180-185 in *A Dictionary of Biblical Tradition in English Literature.* Editor, D. L. Jeffrey. Grand Rapids: Eerdmans.

Hylander, I.
1932 *Der Literarische Samuel-Saul Komplex (I Sam 1–15) Traditionsgeschichtlich untersucht.* Uppsala: Almqvist & Wiksell.

Jobling, D.
1976 Saul's Fall and Jonathan's Rise: Tradition and Redaction in 1 Sam 14:1-46. *Journal of Biblical Literature* 95:367-376.

Johnson, P. E.
1991 *Darwin on Trial.* Downers Grove, IL: InterVarsity.

1995 *Reason in the Balance.* Downers Grove, IL: InterVarsity.

Jong, H. de
1978 *De Twee Messiassen.* Kampen: Kok.

Joüon, P., and T. Muraoka
1991 *A Grammar of Biblical Hebrew.* 2 vols. Rome: Pontifical Biblical Institute.

Kaiser, W.
1974 The Blessing of David: Humanity's Charter. Pp. 298-318 in *The Law and the Prophets.* Editor, J. H. Skilton. Philadelphia: Presbyterian & Reformed.

1975 The Present State of Old Testament Studies. *Journal of the Evangelical Theological Society* 18:69-79.

1978 *Toward an Old Testament Theology.* Grand Rapids: Zondervan.

1983 *Toward Old Testament Ethics.* Grand Rapids: Zondervan.

1992 *More Hard Sayings of the Old Testament.* Downers Grove, IL: InterVarsity.

1995 *The Messiah in the Old Testament.* Grand Rapids: Zondervan.

1999 Review of Satterthwaite, Hess and Wenham (1995). *Journal of the Evangelical Theological Society* 42:99-102.

Karlberg, M. W.
1980a Reformed Interpretation of the Mosaic Covenant. *Westminster Theological Journal* 43 (1):1-57.

1980b Justification in Redemptive History. *Westminster Theological Journal* 43 (2):213-246.

Keil, C. F.
1956 *Biblical Commentary on the Books of Samuel.* Grand Rapids: Eerdmans. (Orig. pub. 1864.)

Kennedy, A. R. S.
1904 *Samuel.* The Century Bible. Edinburgh: T. C. & E. C. Jack.

Keys, G.
1988 The So-called Succession Narrative: A Reappraisal of Rost's Approach to Theme in II Samuel 9–20 and I Kings 1–2. *Irish Biblical Studies* 10:140-155.

1996 *The Wages of Sin: A Reappraisal of the Succession Narrative.* Journal for the Study of the Old Testament Supplement 221. Sheffield: Sheffield Academic.

Kinsley, W.
1992 Witch of Endor. Pp. 840-841 in *A Dictionary of Biblical Tradition in English Literature.* Editor, D. L. Jeffrey. Grand Rapids: Eerdmans.

Kio, S. H.
1996 What Did Saul Ask For: Ark or Ephod? *Bible Translator* 47/2:240-246.

Kirkpatrick, A. F.
1901 *The Book of Psalms: With Introduction and Notes.* Cambridge: Cambridge University Press.
1918 *The First Book of Samuel: With Notes and Introduction.* Cambridge: Cambridge University Press.
1919 *The Second Book of Samuel: With Notes and Introduction.* Cambridge: Cambridge University Press.

Kitchen, K. A.
1966 *Ancient Orient and Old Testament.* London: Tyndale.
1970 Ancient Orient, Deuteronomism, and the Old Testament. Pp. 1-24 in *New Perspectives on the Old Testament.* Editor, J. B. Payne. Waco: Word.
1989 The Fall and Rise of Covenant, Law, and Treaty. *Tyndale Bulletin* 40:118-135.
2003 *On the Reliability of the Old Testament.* Grand Rapids: Eerdmans.

Klein, R. W.
1970 The Song of Hannah. *Concordia Theological Monthly* 41:674-684.
1974 *Textual Criticism of the Old Testament.* Philadelphia: Fortress.
1983 *1 Samuel.* Word Biblical Commentary 10. Waco: Word.

Klement, H. H.
2000 *2 Samuel 21–24: Structure, Context and Meaning in the Samuel Conclusion.* European University Studies. Series 23, Theology. Vol. 682. Frankfurt am Main: Peter Lang.

Kline, M.
1963 *Treaty of the Great King.* Grand Rapids: Eerdmans.
1968 *By Oath Consigned.* Grand Rapids: Eerdmans.
1972 *The Structure of Biblical Authority.* Grand Rapids: Eerdmans.
1983 Of Works and Grace. *Presbyterion* 9:85-92.

Koch, K.
1969 *The Growth of Biblical Tradition.* New York: Charles Scribner's Sons.

Koolhaas, A. A.
1957 *Theocratie en Monarchie in Israël.* Wageningen: H. Veenman en Zonen.

Koorevaar, J. J.
1997 De Macrostructuur van het Boek Samuël en de Theologische Implicaties Daarvan. *Acta theologica* 2:56-86.

Kraus, H.-J.
1951 *Die Königherrschaft Gottes im Alten Testament.* Beiträge zur Historischen Theologie 13. Tübingen: J. C. B. Mohr.
1966 *Worship in Israel: A Cultic History of the Old Testament.* Translator, G. Buswell. Richmond: John Knox.

Kruger, P. A.
1988 The Symbolic Significance of the Hem (*K N F*) in 1 Samuel 15.27. Pp. 105-116 in *Text and Context: Old Testament and Semitic Studies for F. C. Fensham.* Editor, W. Claassen. Journal for the Study of the Old Testament Supplement Series 48. Sheffield: Journal for the Study of the Old Testament Press.

Kwakkel, G.
2002 *According to My Righteousness: Upright Behaviour as Grounds for Deliverance in Psalms 7, 17, 18, 26 and 44.* Oud Testamentische Studiën Vol. XLVI. Leiden: Brill.

Labuschagne, C. J.
1973 The Particles Hen and Hinneh. *Oudtestamentische Studien* 18:1-14.

Lambdin, T. O.
1971 *Introduction to Biblical Hebrew.* New York: Charles Scribner's Sons.

Layton, S. C.
1989 A Chain Gang in 2 Samuel iii 29? A Rejoinder. *Vetus Testamentum* 39:81-86.

Lee, H. Y.
1996 From Historical Criticism to Narrative Hermeneutics in Old Testament Studies. PhD diss., Potchefstrommse Universiteit.

Lemche, N. P.
1978 David's Rise. *Journal of the Study of the Old Testament* 10:2-25.
1998 *The Israelites in History and Tradition.* Louisville: Westminster John Knox.

Levenson, J.
1978 1 Samuel 25 as Literature and History. *Catholic Biblical Quarterly* 40:11-28.
1979 The Davidic Covenant and Its Modern Interpreters. *Catholic Biblical Quarterly* 41:205-219.

Levenson, J., and B. Halpern
1980 The Political Import of David's Marriages. *Journal of Biblical Literature* 99:507-518.

Lewis, T. J.
1991 The Ancestral Estate (נַחֲלַת אֱלֹהִים) in 2 Samuel 14:16. *Journal of Biblical Literature* 110 (4):597-612.

Linnemann, E.
1990 *Historical Criticism of the Bible: Methodology or Ideology?* Grand Rapids: Baker.

Long, V. P.
1985 Review of K. Gnuse, *The Dream Theophany of Samuel. Journal of the Evangelical Theological Society* 28 (2):230-231.
1989 *The Reign and Rejection of King Saul: A Case for Literary and Theological Coherence.* Atlanta: Scholars Press.
1993a First and Second Samuel. Pp. 165-181 in *A Complete Literary Guide to the Bible.* Editors, L. Ryken and T. Longman III. Grand Rapids: Zondervan.
1993b Interpolation or Characterization: How Are We to Understand Saul's Two Confessions? *Presbyterion* 19 (1):49-53.
1994 *The Art of Biblical History.* Grand Rapids: Zondervan.
1999 Historiography and the Old Testament. Pp. 145-175 in *The Face of Old Testament Studies: A Survey of Contemporary Approaches.* Editors, D. W. Baker and B. T. Arnold. Grand Rapids: Baker.

Longman, T., III
1983 1 Sam 12:16-19: Divine Omnipotence or Covenant Curse? *Westminster Theological Journal* 45:168-171.
1987 *Literary Approaches to Biblical Interpretation.* Grand Rapids: Zondervan.
1988 *How to Read the Psalms.* Downers Grove, IL: InterVarsity.
2006 *Proverbs.* Baker Commentary on the Old Testament Wisdom and Psalms. Grand Rapids: Baker.

Longman, T., III, and R. B. Dillard
2006 *An Introduction to the Old Testament.* Grand Rapids: Zondervan.

Longman, T., III, and D. G. Reid
1995 *God Is a Warrior.* Grand Rapids: Zondervan.

MacDonald, G.
1983 *The Baronet's Song.* Editor, M. Phillips. Minneapolis: Bethany.

MacRae, A. A.
1975 Prophets and Prophecy. Pp. 875-903 in *The Zondervan Pictorial Encyclopedia of the Bible,* vol. 4. Editor, M. C. Tenney. Grand Rapids: Zondervan.

Maier, G.
1974 *The End of the Historical-critical Method.* Translators, E. W. Leverenz and R. F. Norden. St. Louis: Concordia.

Manley, G. T.
1957 *The Book of the Law: Studies in the Date of Deuteronomy.* London: Tyndale.

Martin, J. A.
1984 The Text of 1 and 2 Samuel. *Biblica Sacra* 141:209-222.

Mauchline, J.
1971 *I and II Samuel.* London: Oliphants.

Maynard, R.
1998 Review of *Talking to Heaven* by James Van Praagh. *World Magazine* 13 (11):24.

Mazar, A.
1997 Iron Age Chronology: A Reply to I. Finkelstein. *Levant* 29:157-167.

Mazar, A., and J. Camp
2000 Will Tel Rehov Save the United Monarchy? *Biblical Archaeology Review* 26 (2):38-51, 75.

Mazar, B.
1954 Gath, Gittaim. *Israel Exploration Journal* 4:227-235.

McCarter, P. K., Jr.
1980a The Apology of David. *Journal of Biblical Literature* 99 (4):498-504.

1980b *I Samuel*. The Anchor Bible 8. New York: Doubleday.

1983 The Ritual Dedication of David in 2 Samuel 6. Pp. 273-278 in *The Word of the Lord Shall Go Forth: Essays in Honor of David Noel Freedman in Celebration of His Sixtieth Birthday*. Editors, C. L. Meyers and M. O'Connor. Winona Lake, IN: Eisenbrauns.

1984 *II Samuel*. The Anchor Bible 9. New York: Doubleday & Company.

1986 The Historical David. *Interpretation* 40 (2):117-129.

McCarthy, D. J.
1972 *Old Testament Covenant: A Survey of Current Opinions*. Richmond: John Knox.

1978 *Treaty and Covenant: A Study in Form in the Ancient Oriental Documents and in the Old Testament*. Analecta Biblica 21A. Rome: Biblical Institute Press.

1980 The Uses of והנה in Biblical Hebrew. *Biblica* 61:330-342.

McComiskey, T.
1985 *The Covenants of Promise: A Theology of the Old Testament Covenants*. Grand Rapids: Baker.

McConville, J. G.
1984 *Law and Theology in Deuteronomy*. Journal for the Study of the Old Testament Supplement 33. Sheffield: Journal for the Study of the Old Testament Press.

1993 *Grace in the End: A Study in Deuteronomic Theology*. Grand Rapids: Zondervan.

1994 Deuteronomy. Pp. 198-232 in *The New Bible Commentary*. Editors, D. A. Carson, R. T. France, J. A. Motyer, and G. J. Wenham. Downers Grove, IL: InterVarsity.

1995 Messianic Interpretation of the Old Testament in Modern Context. Pp. 1-17 in *The Lord's Anointed: Interpretation of Old Testament Messianic Texts*. Editor, Philip E. Satterthwaite. Carlisle: Paternoster.

1997 The Old Testament Historical Books in Modern Scholarship. *Themelios* 22 (3):3-13.

2002 *Deuteronomy*. Apollos Old Testament Commentary 5. Downers Grove, IL: InterVarsity.

McKenzie, S. L.
2000 *King David: A Biography*. New York: Oxford University Press.

Mendelsohn, J.
1956 Samuel's Denunciation of Kingship in the Light of the Akkadian Document from Ugarit. *Bulletin of the American Schools of Oriental Research* 143:17-22.

Merrill, E. H.
1987 *Kingdom of Priests: A History of Old Testament Israel*. Grand Rapids: Baker.

1994 *Deuteronomy*. New American Commentary 4. Nashville: Broadman & Holman.

Mettinger, T. N. D.
1976 *King and Messiah*. Coniectanea Biblica. Old Testament Series 8. Lund: C. W. K. Gleerup.

Mildenberger, F.
1962 Die vordeuteronomistische Saul-David-überlieferung. PhD diss., Universität Tübingen.

Milgrom, J.
1989 *Numbers*. New York: Jewish Publication Society.

Miller, J. M.
1975 Geba/Gibeah of Benjamin. *Vetus Testamentum* 25:145-166.

Miller, P. D., and J. J. M. Roberts
1977 *The Hand of the Lord: A Reassessment of the Ark Narrative of 1 Samuel*. Baltimore: Johns Hopkins University Press.

Moberly, R. W. L.
1998 "God is Not a Human That He Should Repent" (Numbers 23:19 and 1 Samuel 15:29). Pp. 112-123 in *God in the Fray: A Tribute to Walter Brueggemann*. Editors, R. Linafelt and T. K. Beal. Minneapolis: Fortress.

Moran, W. L.

1963 The Ancient Near Eastern Background of the Love of God in Deuteronomy. *Catholic Biblical Quarterly* 25:77-87.

Mowinckel, S.

1967 *The Psalms in Israel's Worship.* 2 vols. New York: Abingdon.

Murray, D. F.

2002 Under YHWH's Veto: David as Shedder of Blood in Chronicles. *Biblica* 82 (4):457-476.

Nelson, R. D.

1981 *The Double Redaction of the Deuteronomistic History.* Journal for the Study of the Old Testament Supplement 18. Sheffield: Journal for the Study of the Old Testament Press.

1987 *First and Second Kings.* Interpretation. Louisville: John Knox.

Nicholson, E. W.

1967 *Deuteronomy and Tradition.* Oxford: Basil Blackwell.

Niehaus, J. J.

1988 Joshua and Ancient Near Eastern Warfare. *Journal of the Evangelical Theological Society* 31 (1):37-50.

1995 *God at Sinai: Covenant and Theophany in the Bible and the Ancient Near East.* Grand Rapids: Zondervan.

Noth, M.

1928 *Die israelitischen Personennamen im Rahmen der gemeinsemitischen Namengebung.* Beiträge zur Wissenschaft vom Alten und Neuen Testament 10. Stuttgart: Kohlhammer.

1981 *The Deuteronomistic History.* Journal for the Study of the Old Testament Supplement 15. Sheffield: Journal for the Study of the Old Testament Press. (Orig. pub. 1943.)

Nübel, H.-U.

1959 *Davids Aufstieg in der frühe israelitischer Geschichtsschreibung.* Bonn: Rheinische Friedrich-Wilhelms Universität.

O'Brien, M.

1989 *The Deuteronomist History Hypothesis: A Reassessment.* Freiburg: Universitätsverlage.

O'Connor, M.

1980 *Hebrew Verse Structure.* Winona Lake, IN: Eisenbrauns.

Oehler, G. F.

1891 *Theology of the Old Testament.* Reprinted, Grand Rapids: Zondervan, n.d.

Oosterhoff, B. J.

1953 *Israëlietische Persoonsnamen.* Exegetica I/4. The Hague: Uitgeverij van Keulen.

Oss, D.

1988 Canon as Context: The Function of Sensus Plenior in Evangelical Hermeneutics. *Grace Theological Journal* 9.1:105-127.

Oswalt, J. N.

1986 *The Book of Isaiah: Chapters 1–39.* Grand Rapids: Eerdmans.

Paul, M. J.

1988 *Het Archimedische Punt van de Pentateuchkritiek.* The Hague: Uitgeverij Boekencentrum.

Payne, D. F.

1970 1 and 2 Samuel. Pp. 284-319 in *The New Bible Commentary.* Rev. ed. Editors, D. Guthrie and J. A. Motyer. Grand Rapids: Eerdmans.

Payne, J. B.

1973 *Encyclopedia of Biblical Prophecy.* New York: Harper & Row.

Peels, H. G. L.

1992 *De Wraak van God.* Zoetermeer: Uitgeverij Boekencentrum B.V.

1996 *Wie is als Gij? Schaduwzijden aan de Godsopenbaring in het Oude Testament.* Zoetermeer: Uitgeverij Boekencentrum.

Peterson, E. H.

1999 *First and Second Samuel.* Louisville: Westminster John Knox.

Pisano, S.

1984 *Additions or Omissions in the Books of Samuel: The Significant Pluses and Minuses in the Massoretic, LXX and Qumran Texts.* Orbis biblicus et orientalis 57. Göttingen: Vandenhoeck & Ruprecht.

Polzin, R.

1989 *Samuel and the Deuteronomist.* San Francisco: Harper & Row.

1993 *David and the Deuteronomist: A Literary Study of the Deuteronomic History. Part Three: 2 Samuel.* Bloomington: Indiana University Press.

Porter, S. E.

2007 *The Messiah in the Old and New Testaments.* Grand Rapids: Eerdmans.

Pratt, R. L.

1990 *He Gave Us Stories: The Bible Student's Guide to Interpreting Old Testament Narrative.* Phillipsburg, NJ: P & R.

Preuss, H. D.

1993 Zum deuteronomistischen Geschichtswerk. *Theologische Rundschen* 58:229-264, 341-395.

Pritchard, J. B.

1962 *Gibeon: Where the Sun Stood Still.* Princeton: Princeton University Press.

Propp, W. H.

1993 Kinship in 2 Samuel 13. *Catholic Biblical Quarterly* 55:39-53.

Provan, I.

1995a Ideologies, Literary and Critical: Reflections on Recent Writing on the History of Israel. *Journal of Biblical Literature* 114:585-606.

1995b The Messiah in the Book of Kings. Pp. 67-86 in *The Lord's Anointed: Interpretation of Old Testament Texts.* Editors, P. E. Satterthwaite, R. S. Hess, and G. J. Wenham. Grand Rapids: Baker.

1997 The End of Israel's History? A Review Article on K. W. Whitelam's *The Invention of Ancient Israel. Journal of Semitic Studies* 42:283-300.

Provan, I., V. P. Long, and T. Longman III

2003 *A Biblical History of Israel.* Louisville: Westminster John Knox.

Rad, G. von

1931 The Tent and the Ark. Repr. pp. 103-124 in *The Problem of the Hexateuch and Other Essays.* Edinburgh: Oliver & Boyd, 1966.

1944 The Beginnings of Historical Writing in Ancient Israel. Repr. pp. 166-204 in *The Problem of the Hexateuch and Other Essays.* Edinburgh: Oliver & Boyd, 1966.

1947 The Deuteronomic Theology of History in I and II Kings. Repr. pp. 205-221 in *The Problem of the Hexateuch and Other Essays.* Edinburgh: Oliver & Boyd, 1966.

1965 *Old Testament Theology,* vol. 1. New York: Harper & Row.

Radday, Y. T.

1974 Chiasm in Samuel. *Linguistica Biblica* 9/10:21-31.

Rasmussen, C. G.

1989 *Zondervan NIV Atlas of the Bible.* Grand Rapids: Zondervan.

Ratner, R.

1987 Three Bulls or One? A Reappraisal of 1 Samuel 1,24. *Biblica* 68:98-102.

Rayburn, R. S.

1998 Finding God's Will. *Covenant* 13 (2):4-7, 16.

Reimer, S.

1991 The Sling in Modern Warfare. *Archaeology in the Biblical World* 1:21.

Rendtorff, R.

1998 *The Covenant Formula: An Exegetical and Theological Investigation.* Translator, M. Kohl. Edinburgh: T&T Clark.

Ridderbos, N. H.

1939 *De "Werkers der Ongerechtigheid" in de Individueele Psalmen.* Kampen: Kok.

1962 *De Psalmen. Eerste Deel: Psalm 1–41.* Kampen: Kok.

1973 *De Psalmen. Tweede Deel: Psalm 42–60.* Kampen: Kok.

Ridout, G.

1974 The Rape of Tamar: A Rhetorical Analysis of 2 Sam 13:1-22. Pp. 75-84 in *Rhetorical Criticism: Essays in Honor of James Muilenburg.* Editors, J. J. Jackson and M. Kessler. Pittsburgh: Pickwick.

Römer, T.

2003 The Form-critical Problem of the So-called Deuteronomistic History. Pp. 240-252 in *The Changing Face of Form Criticism for the Twenty-first Century.* Editors, M. A. Sweeney and E. B. Zvi. Grand Rapids: Eerdmans.

Rosenberg, J.

1987 1 and 2 Samuel. Pp. 122-145 in *The Literary Guide to the Bible.* Editors, R. Alter and F. Kermode. Cambridge: Belknap.

Rost, L.

1926 *Die Überlieferung von der Thronnachfolge Davids.* Beiträge zur Wissenschaft vom Alten und Neuen Testament 42. Stuttgart: Kohlhammer.

1982 *The Succession to the Throne of David.* Sheffield: Almond. [N.B. This is a translation of his 1926 work listed above.]

Rowley, H. H.

1967 *Worship in Ancient Israel: Its Forms and Meaning.* London: SPCK.

Rummel, S.

1976 Clothes Maketh the Man—an Insight from Ancient Ugarit. *Biblical Archaeological Review* 2 (2):6-8.

Sailhamer, J. H.

1989 1 Chronicles 21:1—A Study in Inter-biblical Interpretation. *Trinity Journal* 10:33-48.

Sarna, N. M.

1959 The Interchange of the Prepositions Beth and Min in Biblical Hebrew. *Journal of Biblical Literature* 78:310-316.

1991 *Exodus.* JPS Torah Commentary. New York: Jewish Publication Society.

Satterthwaite, P. E.

1995 David in the Books of Samuel: A Messianic Expectation? Pp. 41-66 in *The Lord's Anointed: Interpretation of Old Testament Texts.* Editors, P. E. Satterthwaite, R. S. Hess, and G. J. Wenham. Grand Rapids: Baker.

Satterthwaite, P. E., R. S. Hess, and G. J. Wenham, editors

1995 *The Lord's Anointed: Interpretation of Old Testament Texts.* Grand Rapids: Baker.

Schaeffer, F.

1974 *No Little People.* Downers Grove, IL: InterVarsity.

Schelhaas, J.

1974 II Samuel 7:1-5. Pp. 283-297 in *The Law and the Prophets.* Editor, J. Skilton. Philadelphia: Presbyterian & Reformed.

Schicklberger, F.

1973 *Die Ladeerzählungen des ersten Samuel-Buches, Eine literaturwissenschaftliche und theologiegeschichtliche Untersuchung.* Forschung zur Bibel 7. Würzburg: Echter Verlag.

Schmid, R.

1964 *Das Bundesopfer in Israel.* Studien zum Alten und Neuen Testaments 9. Munich: Neukirchener Verlag.

Schreiner, J.

1963 *Sion-Jerusalem. Jahwes Königssitz. Theologie der Heiligen Stadt im Alten Testament.* Studien zum Alten und Neuen Testaments 7. Munich: Neukirchener Verlag.

Schultz, R. L.

2004 How Many Isaiahs Were There and What Does It Matter? Pp. 150-170 in *Evangelicals & Scripture: Tradition, Authority and Hermeneutics.* Editors, V. Bacote, L. C. Miguelez, and D. L. Okholm. Downers Grove, IL: InterVarsity.

Sellin, E., and G. Fohrer

1965 *Introduction to the Old Testament.* Nashville: Abingdon.

Selman, M. J.

1994 *1 Chronicles: An Introduction and Commentary.* Tyndale Old Testament Commentaries. Downers Grove, IL: InterVarsity.

Simon, U.

1967 The Poor Man's Ewe-lamb: An Example of a Juridical Parable. *Biblica* 48:207-242.

Simpson, W. K.

1973 *The Literature of Ancient Egypt.* Editor, W. K. Simpson. New Haven, CT: Yale University.

Smelik, K. A. D.
1977 *Saul, de voorstelling van Israels eerste Konig in the Masoretische tekst van het Oude Testament.* Amsterdam: Drukkerij en Uitgeverij P. E. T.

1979 The Witch of Endor, I Samuel 28 in Rabbinic and Christian Exegesis till 800 A. D. *Vigiliae Christianae* 33:160-179.

1989 The Ark Narrative Reconsidered. Pp. 128-144 in *New Avenues in the Study of the Old Testament.* Editor, A. Van der Woude. Leiden: Brill.

Smith, H. P.
1912 *The Books of Samuel.* Edinburgh: T&T Clark.

Speiser, E.
1940 Of Shoes and Shekels. *Bulletin of the American Schools of Oriental Research* 77:15-20.

Stek, J.
1986 What Happened to the Chariot Wheels of Exod 14:25? *Journal of Biblical Literature* 105 (2):293-294.

Sternberg, M.
1985 *The Poetics of Biblical Narrative.* Bloomington: Indiana University Press.

Stoebe, H. J.
1973 *Das erste Buch Samuelis.* Kommentar zum Alten Testament VIII/1. Gütersloh: Verlagshaus Gerd Mohn.

Stone, G. O.
1995 Burial and Cremation. Pp. 207-208 in *New Dictionary of Christian Ethics and Pastoral Theology.* Editors, D. J. Atkinson and D. H. Field. Downers Grove, IL: InterVarsity.

Strauss, D. F.
1973 *Life of Jesus Critically Examined.* New York: Fortress.

Talmon, S.
1970 The Old Testament Text. Pp. 159-199 in *The Cambridge History of the Bible,* vol. 1. Editors, P. R. Ackroyd and C. F. Evans. Cambridge: Cambridge University Press.

1986 "The Rule of the King." 1 Samuel 8:4-22. Pp. 53-67 in *King, Cult and Calendar in Ancient Israel.* Jerusalem: Magnes.

Thenius, O.
1864 *Die Bücher Samuels.* Leipzig: S. Hirzel.

Thomas, D. W.
1934 The root yd' in Hebrew. *Journal of Theological Studies* 35:298-306.

1953 A Consideration of Some Unusual Ways of Expressing the Superlative in Hebrew. *Vetus Testamentum* 3:209-224.

1957 *Some Observations on the Root* hdl. Vetus Testamentum Supplement 4. Leiden: Brill.

Thompson, J. A.
1974 The Significance of the Verb "Love" in the David-Jonathan Narratives in 1 Samuel. *Vetus Testamentum* 24:334-338.

Thompson, T. L.
1974 The Historicity of the Patriarchal Narratives. *Zeitschrift für die alttestamentliche Wissenschaft* 133. Berlin: de Gruyter.

1992 *Early History of the Israelite People from the Written and Archaeological Sources.* Studies in the History of the Ancient Near East 4. Leiden: Brill.

1999 *The Mythic Past: Biblical Archaeology and the Myth of Israel.* New York: Basic.

Thornton, T. C. G.
1967 Studies in Samuel. *Church Quarterly Review* 168:413-423.

Tiessen, T.
2000 *Prayer and Providence.* Downers Grove, IL: InterVarsity.

Tigay, J. H.
1996 *Deuteronomy.* Philadelphia: Jewish Publication Society.

Toorn, K. van der, and C. Houtman
1994 David and the Ark. *Journal of Biblical Literature* 113 (2):209-231.

Tov, E.
1986 The David and Goliath Saga: How a Biblical Editor Combined Two Versions. *Bible Review* 11 (4):34-41.

Tsevat, M.

1987 Die Namengebung Samuels und die Substitutionstheorie. *Zeitschrift für die alttestamentliche Wissenschaft* 99 (2):250-254.

Tsumura, D. T.

1992 Hamor Lehem (1 Samuel XVI 20). *Vetus Testamentum* 42 (3):412-413.

Tucker, G. M.

1973 *Form Criticism of the Old Testament.* Philadelphia: Fortress.

Ulrich, E. C., Jr.

1978 *The Qumran Text of Samuel and Josephus.* Harvard Semitic Monographs 19. Missoula, MT: Scholars Press.

Van Groningen, G.

1990 *Messianic Revelation in the Old Testament.* Grand Rapids: Baker.

VanderKam, J.

1980 Davidic Complicity in the Deaths of Abner and Eshbaal: A Historical and Redactional Study. *Journal of Biblical Literature* 99/4:521-539.

Vannoy, J. R.

1978 *Covenant Renewal at Gilgal: A Study of 1 Samuel 11:14–12:25.* Cherry Hill: Mack. Repr., Eugene, OR: Wipf & Stock, 2008.

1996 Samuel, First and Second, Theology of. Pp. 703-708 in *Evangelical Dictionary of Biblical Theology.* Editor, W. A. Elwell. Grand Rapids: Baker.

1997a Joshua, Theology of. Pp. 810-819 in *New International Dictionary of Old Testament Theology and Exegesis,* vol. 4. Editor, W. A. VanGemeren. Grand Rapids: Zondervan.

1997b Retribution, Theology of. Pp. 1140-1149 in *New International Dictionary of Old Testament Theology and Exegesis,* vol. 4. Editor, W. A. VanGemeren. Grand Rapids: Zondervan.

1998 David and Nabal: A Paradigm of Temptation and Divine Providence. Pp. 79-90 in *Reading and Hearing the Word: From Text to Sermon. Essays in Honor of John H. Stek.* Editor, A. C. Leder. Grand Rapids: CRC Publications.

Vaux, R. de

1961a *Ancient Israel: Its Life and Institutions.* New York: McGraw-Hill.

1961b *Les Livres de Samuel.* Paris: Les Editions du Cerf.

1971a The Ark of the Covenant and Tent of Reunion. Pp. 136-151 in *The Bible and the Ancient Near East.* Garden City, NY: Doubleday.

1971b The King of Israel, Vassal of Yahweh. Pp. 152-166 in *The Bible and the Ancient Near East.* Garden City, NY: Doubleday.

1971c Single Combat in the Old Testament. Pp. 122-135 in *The Bible and the Ancient Near East.* Garden City, NY: Doubleday.

Vos, G.

1975 *Biblical Theology.* Grand Rapids: Eerdmans. (Orig. pub. 1948.)

Vriezen, Th. C.

1961 *De Literatuur van Oud-Israël.* The Hague: Servire.

1962 *An Outline of Old Testament Theology.* Oxford: Basil Blackwell.

Walters, S. D.

1988 Hanna and Anna: The Greek and Hebrew Texts of 1 Samuel 1. *Journal of Biblical Literature* 107:385-412.

2002 Reading Samuel to Hear God. *Calvin Theological Journal* 37:62-81.

Waltke, B.

1975 Rephaim. Pp. 64-66 in *Zondervan Pictorial Encyclopedia of the Bible,* vol. 5. Editor, M. C. Tenney. Grand Rapids: Zondervan.

1988 The Phenomenon of Conditionality within Unconditional Covenants. Pp. 123-139 in *Israel's Apostasy and Restoration. Essays in Honor of Roland K. Harrison.* Editor, Avraham Gileadi. Grand Rapids: Baker.

1989 Aims of OT Textual Criticism. *Westminster Theological Journal* 51 (1):93-108.

2007 *An Old Testament Theology.* Grand Rapids: Zondervan.

Waltke, B. K., and M. O'Connor

1990 *An Introduction to Biblical Hebrew Syntax.* Winona Lake, IN: Eisenbrauns.

Walton, J. H., V. H. Matthews, and M. W. Chavalas

2000 *The IVP Bible Background Commentary: Old Testament.* Downers Grove, IL: InterVarsity.

Ware, B. A.

2000 *God's Lesser Glory: The Diminished God of Open Theism.* Wheaton, IL: Crossway.

Watts, J. W.

1992a Hannah's Song (1 Samuel 2.1-10). Pp. 19-40 in *Psalm and Story: Inset Hymns in Hebrew Narrative.* Journal for the Study of the Old Testament Supplement 139. Sheffield: Journal for the Study of the Old Testament Press.

1992b David's Thanksgiving (2 Samuel 22). Pp. 99-117 in *Psalm and Story: Inset Hymns in Hebrew Narrative.* Journal for the Study of the Old Testament Supplement 139. Sheffield: Journal for the Study of the Old Testament Press.

Webb, B. G.

1987 *The Book of Judges: An Integrated Reading.* Journal for the Study of the Old Testament Supplement 46. Sheffield: Journal for the Study of the Old Testament Press.

Weinfeld, M.

1996 Deuteronomy's Theological Revolution. *Bible Review* 12 (1):38-41, 44-45.

Weiser, A.

1962 *The Psalms.* Old Testament Library. London: SCM.

1966 Die Legitimation des Königs David: zur Eigenart und Entstehung der sogen. Geschichte von Davids Aufsteig. *Vetus Testamentum* 16:325-354.

Wellhausen, J.

1871 *Der Text der Bücher Samuelis.* Göttingen: Vandenhoeck & Ruprecht.

1899 *Die Composition des Hexateuch und der historischen Bücher des Alten Testaments.* Berlin.

1957 *Prolegomena to the History of Ancient Israel.* New York: World.

Wenham, G.

1975 Were David's Sons Priests? *Zeitschrift für die alttestamentliche Wissenschaft* 87:79-82.

1979 *The Book of Leviticus.* Grand Rapids: Eerdmans.

1985 The Date of Deuteronomy: Linch-pin of Old Testament Criticism. *Themelios* 10 (3):15-20; 11 (1):15-18.

Westermann, C.

1994 *Die Geschichtsbücher des Alten Testaments: Gab es ein deuteronomistisches Geschichtswerk?* Theologische Bucherei 87. Gütersloh: Chr. Kaiser Verlag.

Whitelam, K. W.

1996 *The Invention of Ancient Israel: The Silencing of Palestinian History.* London: Routledge.

Whybray, R. N.

1968 *The Succession Narrative.* Studies in Biblical Theology Second Series 9. London: SCM.

Wilkinson, J.

1976–1977 The Philistine Epidemic of I Samuel 5 and 6. *Expository Times* 88:137-140.

Williams, R. J.

1976 *Hebrew Syntax: An Outline.* 2nd ed. Toronto: University of Toronto Press.

Willis, J. T.

1972 Cultic Elements in the Story of Samuel's Birth and Dedication. *Studia theologica* 26/1:33-61.

1973 The Song of Hannah and Psalm 113. *Catholic Biblical Quarterly* 35:139-154.

Willis-Watkins, D.

1989 Calvin's Prophetic Reinterpretation of Kingship. Pp. 116-134 in *Probing the Reformed Tradition.* Editors, E. McKee and B. Armstrong. Philadelphia: Westminster/John Knox.

Wilson, R. R.

1999 Who Was the Deuteronomist? (Who Was Not the Deuteronomist?): Reflections on Pan-Deuteronomism. Pp. 67-82 in *Those Elusive Deuteronomists: The Phenomenon of Pan-Deuteronomism.* Editors, L. S. Schearing and S. L. McKenzie. Journal for the Study of the Old Testament Supplement Series 268. Sheffield: Sheffield Academic.

Windschuttle, K.

1997 *The Killing of History: How Literary Critics and Social Theorists Are Murdering Our Past.* New York: Free Press.

Wolf, H.
1992 Judges. Pp. 373-506 in *The Expositor's Bible Commentary*, vol. 3. Editor, F. E. Gaebelein. Grand Rapids: Zondervan.

Wood, L.
1976 *The Holy Spirit in the Old Testament.* Grand Rapids: Zondervan.

Woudstra, M.
1965 *The Ark of the Covenant from Conquest to Kingship.* Philadelphia: Presbyterian & Reformed.

Wright, C. J. H.
1962 The Lawsuit of God. Pp. 26-67 in *Israel's Prophetic Heritage. Essays in Honor of James Muilenburg.* Editors, B. W. Anderson and W. Harrelson. New York: Harper & Row.

1983 *An Eye for an Eye: The Place of Old Testament Ethics Today.* Downers Grove, IL: InterVarsity.

Würthwein, E.
1979 *The Text of the Old Testament.* Grand Rapids: Eerdmans.

Yamauchi, E.
1994 The Current State of Old Testament Historiography. Pp. 1-36 in *Faith, Tradition and History: Old Testament Historiography in its Near Eastern Context.* Editors, A. R. Millard, J. K. Hoffmeier, and D. W. Baker. Winona Lake, IN: Eisenbrauns.

Yancey, P.
1986 Inside King David's Diary. *Christianity Today* 30 (2):88.

Yee, G. A.
1988 Fraught with Background: Literary Ambiguity in II Samuel 11. *Interpretation* 42:240-253.

Young, E. J.
1964 *An Introduction to the Old Testament.* Grand Rapids: Eerdmans.

Youngblood, R. F.
1983 The Abrahamic Covenant: Conditional or Unconditional? Pp. 31-46 in *The Living and Active Word of God: Studies in Honor of Samuel J. Schultz.* Editors, M. Inch and R. Youngblood. Winona Lake, IN: Eisenbrauns.

1992 1, 2 Samuel. Pp. 551-1104 in *The Expositor's Bible Commentary*, vol. 3. Editor, F. E. Gaebelein. Grand Rapids: Zondervan.

Zaph, D. L.
1984 How Are the Mighty Fallen! A Study of 2 Samuel 1:17-27. *Grace Theological Journal* 5/1:95-126.

Zevit, Z.
2002 Three Debates about Bible and Archaeology. *Biblica* 83 (1):1-27.

Zijl, A. H. van
1969 The meaning of the name Samuel. Pp. 122-129 in *Biblical Essays.* Potchefstroom: Pro Rege Pers Beperk.

1989 *I Samuël.* Prediking van het Oude Testament. Nijkerk: Callenbach.

Zwickel, W.
1994 Dagons Abgeschlagener Kopf (1 Samuel V 3-4). *Vetus Testamentum* 44 (2):239-249.